Gypsy and Travell

Gypsy and Traveller Law

SECOND EDITION

Edited by Chris Johnson and Marc Willers

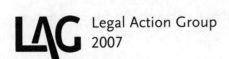 Legal Action Group
2007

This edition published in Great Britain 2007
by LAG Education and Service Trust Limited
242 Pentonville Road, London N1 9UN
www.lag.org.uk

© Chris Johnson, Marc Willers and Legal Action Group 2007

First published 2004

British Library Cataloguing in Publication Data
a CIP catalogue record for this book is available from the British Library.

Crown copyright material is produced with the permission of the Controller of HMSO and the Queen's Printer for Scotland.

ISBN   978 1 903307 52 6

Typeset and Printed by Hobbs the Printers, Totton, Hampshire

Foreword

by Lord Avebury

It was a real pleasure to be asked to contribute a foreword to this Handbook on *Gypsy and Traveller Law*, and thus to have the chance to congratulate the authors on their comprehensive coverage of this increasingly important subject. This second edition will be an essential reference not only for legal practitioners, but for local authority officials, Citizens' Advice Bureaux, Gypsy and Traveller activists, councillors and Members of both Houses of Parliament. Journalists, who bear the heavy responsibility of reporting fairly on the relationships between Gypsies and Travellers and the rest of society, ought to make an effort to study the legal background.

Throughout the forty years that have elapsed since the Caravan Sites Act 1968 was introduced, progress towards eliminating the inequality and deprivation that afflict the Gypsy and Traveller communities has been lethargic and spasmodic. The 1968 Act was not brought into force until several years after it had been enacted, because of the supposed financial difficulties of local authorities at the time. Then, Ministers refrained from using the powers of direction in the Act until the late 1980s, in spite of the buck-passing between Districts, and arguments between Districts and Counties about where new sites were to be developed. When the process finally began to operate as it should have done from the start, given the political will, well over 6,000 pitches were provided on council sites. If the same rate of progress had been maintained, the shortage of sites would have been largely eliminated by now; but there was a serious backward step in 1994. The duty of local authorities to provide sites was abolished, and the substitute was an ineffectual Circular that was supposed to encourage planning permissions for private sites. As many predicted at the time, the private sector was incapable of making up the site deficit, and ending public site development without providing any other means of ensuring that Gypsies and Travellers had somewhere to live was the framework legacy within which many of the legal issues dealt with here must be seen.

Homelessness is an everyday fact of existence for Gypsies and Travellers, with over one in five living on unauthorised encampments or sites without planning permission, and the proportion has remained stubbornly at this level for the last six years, after dipping briefly under 20% at the end of the last century with the last remnants of council sites coming on stream. Where a Gypsy or Traveller family becomes homeless, the local authority must do its best to find them a lawful site if that is what the family wants, and it is pointed out that as the current planning revolution approaches completion in 2011, it will become easier to offer the choice.

The new planning framework is succinctly described in this book. Local authorities have to produce Gypsy and Traveller accommodation needs assessments (GTAAs), which are used to determine the numbers of pitches for which land is to be provided in each authority by the regional spatial strategy. Though some GTAAs have not been as well conducted as others, there is a mechanism for correcting estimates that are manifestly ill prepared, and there is every likelihood that at the end of the process, the allocations to each authority will be generally accepted. Though some may not be delighted to have land in their neighbourhood identified as suitable for Gypsies, they will have to acknowledge that here at last is a carefully worked out mechanism designed to ensure that every local authority makes an appropriate and proportionate response to meeting a national need, as with housing.

In the meanwhile, authorities that drag their feet are advised by Circular 1/2006 (reinforced by a letter to chief planning officers from the Planning Inspectorate of July 2006) that specified good quality information is expected from them at appeals. In the absence of robust information, inspectors will accept evidence submitted by appellants on the shortage of sites, and accordingly those appeals are more like to succeed, as indeed has already begun to happen. The authors underline the growing importance of the Human Rights Act in planning appeals by Gypsies and Travellers, a story that is still evolving.

Since it is widely recognised that Gypsies and Travellers suffer greater discrimination than any other ethnic group, it might be expected that the Race Relations Acts, and particularly the Act of 2000, which created a positive duty on all public authorities to promote racial equality, would have had a positive impact. However, the authors are able to cite only one case where an authority was taken to court for a breach of the statutory duty to consider the race equality effects before taking the action in question. The new Commission for Equality and

Human Rights has power to issue a notice requiring a public authority to provide information on which to base an assessment of compliance, and where they conclude that a breach has occurred, to apply for a High Court order requiring the authority to comply. But as this book concludes, race equality legislation has made relatively little difference to the lives of Gypsies and Travellers so far, and the latest powers are as yet untested.

Neither the Human Rights Act nor the Race Relations Acts have been effective tools for delivering better education and healthcare to Gypsies and Travellers. Reference is made to the finding that 10,000–12,000 Gypsy and Traveller children of secondary age were not registered and did not attend school, and to the Government's proposals for spreading good practice to raise the achievement of Gypsy and Traveller pupils. There is a right to education in law, but the first condition for its implementation is that children should have access to a school near their home, and regular proximity to services is also high on the list of factors influencing the health of the Gypsy and Traveller population. Recent research cited demonstrates quantitatively for the first time that these communities have significantly worse health than the settled population, raising questions as to whether Primary Care Trusts should be taking steps to improve access to and uptake of health care by Gypsies and Travellers.

The law cannot by itself ensure that everybody has an equal chance in life, or that everybody enjoys some minimum standard of accommodation and the use of public services. Gypsies and Travellers will only get off the bottom rung of the ladder when society as a whole gets the message that permanent deprivation of these communities, passed down from one generation to the next, is extremely bad for us all, Gypsies and Gorgios alike. But it is the law that provides the toolbox for the solutions, and here they are before us.

Eric Avebury
August 2006

Preface and acknowledgements

For several years now the Legal Action Group (LAG) has organised an annual training day on the law relating to Gypsies and Travellers. At one such event in September 2002 a Romani Gypsy called out from the back of the room and asked us to write a book on the subject so that she and other Gypsies and Travellers could learn more about their rights.

We decided to take up the challenge and approached LAG with a rough plan for a book. The staff at LAG were very interested in the idea and agreed that there was a real need for a book that could highlight the law and issues that had an impact on the lives of Gypsies and Travellers

We sent our initial draft of the first edition of this book to Legal Action in May 2004. By the time of its publication in August 2004 there had already been several dramatic changes in the legal landscape that led us to insert a hastily compiled 'Recent Developments' section at the front of the first edition. Little did we realise then just how many more fundamental changes would take place over the following 3 years and how important it would be for us to produce a second edition of this book.

We would like to thank our co-authors in this endeavour who are: Sasha Barton, Sharon Baxter, Stephen Cottle, Murray Hunt, Tim Jones, Angus Murdoch and David Watkinson. We would also like to thank all the staff at LAG and, particularly, Esther Pilger for her enthusiasm and encouragement. Special thanks are also due from Marc to his wife Zoe for her support and patience whilst he worked on editing the book.

We are grateful to a number of people for providing us with information and comments on various parts of the book: Arthur Ivatts for comments on education, Michael McIlvaney for comments on the homelessness chapter, Brenda Parkes for comments on the race discrimination chapter; Siobhan Spencer for her assistance on the organisations list and Ian Taggart for information on the policing situation in Scotland.

We must also pay tribute to the other lawyers and advisers who have specialised in the representation of Gypsies and Travellers and have, through their case work, helped bring about many of the developments that we discuss in the book. In this regard, we would like to acknowledge: the other members of the Travellers' Advice Team at the Community Law Partnership (CLP) – Roberta Kellie, Parminder Sanghera, and the Team's administrator, Emma Westwood; the other members of the Gypsy and Traveller team at Garden Court Chambers, namely Val Easty, Stephen Knafler, Michael Paget, Stephen Simblet and the rest. We must also acknowledge Jan Luba QC, Richard Drabble QC, Charles George QC and Alex Offer who have been involved in some of the leading cases in this area that you will be reading about in the book.

There is an enormous list of other academics, lawyers, planning consultants, researchers, support workers and campaigners who have inspired, encouraged and assisted us in our work over the years. Many of those people work with the organisations and bodies listed in appendix C. Special mention must also be made of the Traveller Law Research Unit at Cardiff Law School (now unfortunately 'in mothballs') and the inspirational work of Luke Clements and Rachel Morris.

It is also important to make mention of the general support given by: the partners (Mike McIlvaney and Rosaleen Kilbane) and other staff at CLP; and the administrative teams at Garden Court Chambers (in particular, Amanda Boylan, Caroline Mitchell and Lauren Barber). We thank them all for their enthusiastic backing for the work that is done in this area and make the point that none of the cases that have been taken by CLP and Garden Court Chambers would have ever got off the ground without their devastating efficiency.

Above all, our thanks must go to our Gypsy and Traveller clients who, by their courage, tenacity, enthusiasm and humour, have kept us going even after the worst setbacks.

Finally, we would like to dedicate this book to Johnny Delaney whose tragic death is reported in chapter 1. Hopefully, this book will help draw attention to the difficulties that Gypsies and Travellers face in our society and help them in their struggle to achieve equality.

The law as it relates to Gypsies and Travellers in England and Wales is correct as at 1 August 2007.

Marc Willers and Chris Johnson
1 August 2007

Contributors

Sasha Barton worked at the Commission for Racial Equality (CRE) from 2002-2007, most recently in the Legal Department. Sasha developed a three-year strategy on Gypsies and Travellers for the CRE and led a research project to examine local authority compliance with the race equality duty in relation to Gypsy sites across England and Wales. She worked closely with central and local government, Gypsies and Irish Travellers and other key stakeholders on these projects.

Sharon Baxter is a solicitor working in the Travellers' Advice Team at Community Law Partnership in Birmingham. Having practised housing law, representing tenants and homeless people for seven years, Sharon has specialised in advising Gypsies and Travellers since 2001. She formulated the argument which was ultimately successful in the homelessness case of *R on the application of Price v Carmarthenshire County Council* and she has won many planning appeals and court cases on behalf of her clients.

Stephen Cottle is a barrister practising at Garden Court Chambers in London, specialising in housing law, judicial review, planning law as it affects Gypsies and Travellers, the law relating to mobile homes and low impact developments. His many reported cases include *South Buckinghamshire District Council v Porter (No 1)* and *Wrexham County Borough Council v Berry*. Stephen is the co-author of *Housing Act 2004: a practical guide* (Jordans, 2005). He is also a member of the Housing Law Practitioners Association.

Murray Hunt is legal adviser to the Parliamentary Joint Committee on Human Rights. One of the founding members of Matrix chambers, Murray specialises in human rights law and public law. He is author of *Using Human Rights Law in English Courts* (Hart Publishing, 1997) and contributing editor to a number of other works. He has written articles for *European Human Rights Law Review* and *Journal of Law and Society*.

Chris Johnson is a solicitor and one of the founding partners of Community Law Partnership in Birmingham, and Team Leader of the Travellers' Advice Team (TAT) within the firm. TAT was first set up in 1995 and advises and acts for Gypsies and Travellers throughout England and Wales. TAT have, since 2002, had a dedicated advice line for Gypsies and Travellers funded by Community Legal Services Direct. Chris has acted on some of the leading cases involving Gypsies and Travellers . He travels the country representing Gypsies and Travellers as well as lecturing, training, writing and campaigning on issues affecting Gypsy and Traveller rights. He writes regularly for *Legal Action*. Chris represented the first Gypsies and Travellers in Great Britain to negotiate a new clause in their council site licence agreement introducing security of tenure. Chris drafted, at the request of the Gypsy and Traveller Law Reform Coalition, the Caravan Sites (Security of Tenure) Bill 2006 which was introduced as a Ten Minute Rule Bill.

Tim Jones is a barrister at No 5 Chambers, Birmingham, London and Bristol, specialising in planning and local government law. He has appeared in numerous Gypsy and Traveller cases, including *Buckley v UK, Chapman v UK, R v Hereford and Worcester County Council ex p Smith and Butler v Bath and North East Somerset District Council*. His writing includes articles published in *European Human Rights Law Review, European Advocate, Justice Review* (Slovakia) and the *Law Society's Gazette*. He has spoken at numerous seminars including ones organised the Legal Action Group, European Roma Rights Center, National Association of Gypsy and Traveller Officers, Irish Traveller Movement and Council of Europe. He is a member of the Bar Human Rights Committee. He is also a member of the Bars of Ireland and of Northern Ireland, and a Fellow of the Chartered Institute of Arbitrators.

Dr Angus Murdoch is an adviser at the Community Law Partnership in Birmingham and a member of their Travellers Advice Team (TAT) since 1998. TAT provide specialist legal advice and representation to the Gypsy and Traveller community throughout England and Wales. He is an experienced trainer, lecturer and writer on Gypsy and Traveller issues. Angus has acted in some of the leading Gypsy and Traveller cases and has one of the most outstanding success rates in public inquiry work for Gypsies and Travellers of anyone in England and Wales. He is a member of the Institute of Town Planning and is qualified as a planning consultant.

David Watkinson is a barrister practising at Garden Court Chambers in London, specialising in housing law, judicial review and planning law as it affects Gypsies and Travellers. His many reported cases include *South Hams District Council v Gibb, R v Lincolnshire County Council ex p Atkinson, South Bucks District Council v Porter (No 1) and Chichester District Council v First Secretary of State and Doe, Yates and Eames* and in June 2006 he appeared at the Olympics Public Inquiry for the residents of the affected Gypsy and Traveller sites. David is a contributor to *Law in a Housing Crisis* (1975); co-author of *Squatting, Trespass and Civil Liberties* (1976); *Civil Rights Guide* (1978); contributor to *Squatting: The Real Story* (1980) and *Critical Lawyers Handbook* (1992). He has also contributed reviews, articles and case notes to *Legal Action, All England Legal Opinion, Solicitors Journal, Roof* (Shelter's Housing Magazine) and *From the Lawyer's Collective* (Mumbai, India). David has lectured on courses organised by Legal Action Group, Housing Law Practitioners' Association, South Bank Polytechnic, Warwick University, Central Law Training, Administrative Law Bar Association and Legal Services Commission. He is Executive member of the Housing Law Practitioners' Association, former member of the Civil Justice Council and current deputy chair of its housing and land sub-committee. He is also a member of the Legal Action Group and Haldane Society. In 2005 David received the Barrister of the Year award at the Legal Aid Lawyer of the Year awards.

Marc Willers is a barrister practising at Garden Court Chambers in London. He specialises in public law, human rights and planning law, with a particular emphasis on the representation of Gypsies and Travellers. Marc has appeared in a number of the key cases in the field, including, *Coster v UK, Clarke v Tunbridge Wells Borough Council, Smith v First Secretary of State and Mid-Bedfordshire District Council, R on the application of Wilson v First Secretary of State, R on the application of O'Brien v Basildon District Council* and *Lisa Smith v Secretary of State for Trade and Industry and the London Development Agency*. Marc has presented numerous seminars on human rights, both in this country and abroad for organisations such as the Council of Europe and the United Nations High Commissioner for Refugees. Marc is a contributor to *Your Rights* (Liberty, 2005) and writes regularly for *Legal Action*. He is a member of the Irish Bar and is also a trustee of Friends, Families and Travellers.

Contents

Foreword   v
Preface and acknowledgements   ix
Contributors   xi
Table of cases   xix
Table of statutes   xxxiv
Table of statutory instruments   xli
Table of circulars and guidance   xliv
Table of European legislation   l
Abbreviations   liii

1   **Introduction   1**
     by Angus Murdoch and Chris Johnson
     Introduction   2
     Who are the Gypsies and Travellers?   3
     Historical context   4
     Racialising Gypsy people   8
     Irish Travellers   10
     The end of the road for nomadism?   12
     Defining Gypsies in law   13
     Accommodation for Gypsies and Travellers   13
     New Travellers   15
     Culture   18
     Outline of the book   18

2   **How the Human Rights Act 1998 affects Gypsies and
     Travellers   21**
     by Murray Hunt and Marc Willers
     The duties on public authorities under the Human Rights
          Act 1998   23
     The most relevant Convention rights   25
     Article 8 decision making   24
     The European Court of Human Rights' appproach to
          proportionality – general principles derived from *Buckley*
          and *Chapman*   30
     Article 8 and relevant domestic decisions post-Human Rights
          Act 1998   34

Article 14: general principles 47
Commission for Equality and Human Rights 58
Conclusion 59

3   **Rented Gypsy/Traveller sites   61**
     *by David Watkinson, Chris Johnson, Sharon Baxter and
         Stephen Cottle*
     Introduction 62
     Provision of sites 63
     The legal regime 65
     Non-local authority sites 85
     Conclusion 87

4   **Planning law   89**
     by Tim Jones, Marc Willers and Angus Murdoch
     Introduction 91
     Structure of the planning system 92
     Making an application for planning permission 127
     Appealing against a refusal of planning permission 129
     An application to the High Court 131
     Enforcement 133
     Funding for planning inquiries 147
     Conclusion 149

5   **Evictions from unauthorised encampments   151**
     by Chris Johnson and David Watkinson
     Introduction 153
     Methods of eviction and substantive defences 156
     Public law challenges 192
     Other matters 207
     Conclusion 210

6   **Homelessness as it relates to Gypsies and Travellers   213**
     by Chris Johnson, Marc Willers and David Watkinson
     Homelessness legislation 173
     Effect of the homelessness legislation on Gypsies
         and Travellers 229
     Conclusion 248

7   **Education and healthcare   249**
     by Marc Willers
     Introduction 250

Education   250
Healthcare   266
Conclusion   276

8   Race discrimination   277
by Sasha Barton and Marc Willers
Introduction   279
The CRE and the Commission for Equalities and Human
   Rights 280
The legal framework   281
Scope of RRA 1976   287
Racial groups – protection for Gypsies and Travellers   289
Ethnicity, normadism and the meaning of the words 'Gypsy'
   and 'Traveller'   292
Enforcing the RRA 1976   292
The CEHR's powers 297
The race equality duty   299
Opportunities and recommendations for the future   308
Other levers for change   310
Conclusion   312

9   Conclusion   313
by Marc Willers and Chris Johnson
Conclusion   314

APPENDICES

A   Procedure   317
Judicial review   317
Town and Country Planning Act 1990 s288 applications   319
Town and Country Planning Act 1990 s289 appeals   321
Homeless reviews and appeals   322

B   Statutes, circulars and guidance   324

Statutes
Caravan Sites Act 1968 ss2–4   324
Mobile Homes Act 1983   327
Town and Country Planning Act 1990 (extracts)   343
Criminal Justice and Public Order Act 1994   367
Human Rights Act 1998   377
Housing Act 2004 ss 225, 226   400

Circulars
Planning for Gypsy and Traveller Caravan Sites
(ODPM Circular 1/06)   402
Gypsy Sites Policy and Unauthorised Camping
(DoE Circular 18/94)   425

Guidance
Guidance on Managing Unauthorised Camping
(ODPM 2004)   431
Supplement to 'Managing unauthorised camping: a good
practice guide' (ODPM 2005)   488
Guide to effective use of enforcement powers –
Part 1: unauthorised encampments (ODPM 2006)   492

C   Useful organisations   509

D   Bibliography   521

Index   525

Table of cases

A v Head Teacher and Governors of Lord Grey School
  [2006] UKHL 14; [2006] 2 All ER 457; [2006] 2 WLR 690
  Reversing [2004] EWCA Civ 382; [2004] QB 1231; [2004]
  4 All ER 628; *Reversing in Part* [2003] EWHC 1533 (QB);
  [2003] 4 All ER 1317   7.8, 7.43
Anguelova v Bulgaria Application no 38361/97, judgment
  13 June 2002; (2004) 38 EHRR 31, ECHR   2.70
Arlidge v Islington Corp; *sub nom* Arlidge v Mayor,
  Aldermen, & Councillors of the Metropolitan Borough
  of Islington; Arlidge v the Metropolitan Borough of
  Islington [1909] 2 KB 127; 7 LGR 649, KBD   5.102
Arlidge v The Metropolitan Borough of Islington *See*
  Arlidge v Islington Corp—
Arrowsmith v Jenkins [1963] 2 QB 561; [1963] 2 WLR 856;
  [1963] 2 All ER 210, DC   5.85
Associated Provincial Picture Houses Ltd v Wednesbury
  Corp [1948] 1 KB 223; [1947] 2 All ER 680, CA   2.44, 2.46, 4.58
Aston Cantlow and Wilmcote with Billesley Parochial
  Church Council v Wallbank; *sub nom* Wallbank v
  Aston Cantlow [2003] UKHL 37; [2004] 1 AC 546; [2003]
  3 WLR 283; [2003] 3 All ER 1213, HL; reversing [2001]
  EWCA Civ 713; [2002] Ch 51; [2001] 3 WLR 1323;
  [2001] 3 All ER 393, CA   5.153
Barnfather v Islington Education Authority; Barnfather v
  Islington London Borough Council [2003] EWHC 418
  Admin; [2003] 1 WLR 2318; [2003] ELR 263, QBD   7.24
Barnfather v Islington London Borough Council *See*
  Barnfather v Islington Education Authority—
Basildon District Council v First Secretary of State and
  Rachel Cooper *See* R (on the application of Basildon
  District Council) v First Secretary of State—
Basildon District Council v First Secretary of State and
  Temple [2004] EWHC 2759 Admin   4.97
Basildon District Council v Secretary of State for the
  Environment and Appelby, 21 December 2000
  (unreported), Admin Ct   2.95, 7.64
Bath and North East Somerset District Council v Warman
  [1999] ELR 81, QBD   7.22

Beard v United Kingdom (2001) 33 EHRR 442   4.104
Belgian Linguistic Case (No2) (1968) 1 EHRR 252,
    ECHR   7.8, 7.10
Berry v National Assembly of Wales *See* Wrexham CBC v
    National Assembly for Wales—
Berry v Wrexham Maelor County Borough Council August
    2001 *Legal Action* 25   3.35
Bleaklow Industries Ltd v Peak District National Park
    Authority [2006] EWHC 3387 Admin   4.46
Boddington v British Transport Police [1999] 2 AC 143;
    [1998] 2 WLR 639; [1998] 2 All ER 203, HL   5.107, 5.108
Bolton MBC v Secretary of State for the Environment;
    sub nom R v Secretary of State for the Environment
    ex p Bolton MDC (1990) 61 P&CR 343; [1991]
    JPL 241, CA   4.138
Bolton MBC v Secretary of State for the Environment
    [1995] 3 PLR 37   4.138, 4.140
Boyland and Son v Rand [2006] EWCA Civ 1860   5.22, 5.23
Bradford-Smart v West Sussex County Council [2002]
    EWCA Civ 7; [2002] 1 FCR 425; [2002] BLGR 489,
    CA   7.55
Britannia Developments Ltd v Secretary of State for
    Communities and Local Government [2007]
    EWHC 812 Admin   4.102
Buckinghamshire County Council v Hall Aggregates
    (Thames Valley) [1985] JPL 634, CA   4.57
Buckley v United Kingdom (20348/92) (1996) 23 EHRR
    101; [1997] 2 PLR 10; [1996] JPL 1018; (1996) *The Times*,
    9 October, ECtHR (Commission); [1994] JPL 536;
    [1995] JPL 633; 19 EHRR CD20   2.14, 2.17, 2.30,
                                                        2.31, 2.34, 2.36,
                                                        2.39, 2.40, 2.42,
                                                        4.100, 4.107, 4.110,
                                                        4.178
Butler v Bath and North East Somerset District Council
    See R (on the application of Butler) v Bath and North
    East Somerset District Council—
Cambridgeshire and Isle of Ely County Council v Rust
    [1972] 2 QB 426; [1972] 3 WLR 226; [1972] 3 All ER 232,
    District Council   5.85
Campbell v Mirror Group Newspapers Ltd; *sub nom*
    Campbell v MGN Ltd [2004] UKHL 22; (2004) 154
    NLJ 733; (2004) 148 SJLB 572, HL   5.49
Campbell and Cosans v United Kingdom (No2) (1982) 4
    EHRR 293, ECHR   7.10
Carson v Secretary of State for Work and Pensions *See* R
    (on the application of Carson) v Secretary of State for
    Work and Pensions—

Chapman v United Kingdom (2001) 33 EHRR 399; (2001)
    10 BHRC 48, (2001) *The Times*, 30 January, ECtHR   2.8, 2.14, 2.17, 2.20,
                                                           2.23, 2.25, 2.28,
                                                           2.30–2.36, 2.39,
                                                           2.40, 2.42, 2.43,
                                                           2.59, 2.61, 2.92,
                                                           3.55, 4.3, 4.79, 4.90,
                                                           4.104, 4.106, 4.107,
                                                           4.109–4.118, 4.124,
                                                           4.178, 6.54
Chichester District Council v First Secretary of State and
    Grant Doe [2004] EWCA Civ 1248; [2005] 1 WLR 279   4.118
Christchurch Borough Council v McDonagh (2002) 11 July,
    Bournemouth County Court   5.164
City of Edinburgh v Secretary of State for Scotland *See*
    Edinburgh City Council v Secretary of State for
    Scotland—
Clarke v Secretary of State for the Environment, Transport,
    Local Government and the Regions and Tunbridge
    Wells Borough Council; *sub nom* R (on the application
    of Clarke) v Secretary of State for Transport, Local
    Government and the Regions; Clarke v Secretary of
    State for the Environment, Transport and the Regions
    [2002] EWCA Civ 819; [2002] JPL 1365, CA; affirming
    [2001] EWHC 800 Admin; [2002] JPL 552; [2001]
    NPC 164, QBD (Admin Ct); July 2002 *Legal Action* 23;
    (2001) *The Times*, 9 November   2.90, 2.91,
                                                          4.120–4.122, 4.124,
                                                          6.52, 6.53
Coates v South Buckinghamshire District Council [2004]
    EWCA Civ 1378   2.63, 4.188
Codona v Mid-Bedfordshire District Council [2004] EWCA
    Civ 925; [2005] HLR 1; [2005] LGR 241; 148 Sol Jo
    LB 910; [2004] All ER (D) 278 (Jul) (Application
    no 485/05, 7 September 2006; September 2006
    Legal Action 21   2.91, 6.89–6.91,
                                                          6.93, 6.97, 6.103
Commission for Racial Equality v Dutton [1989] QB 783;
    [1989] 2 WLR 17; [1989] 1 All ER 306, CA   4.67, 7.47, 8.20,
                                                          8.47, 8.49, 8.50, 8.71
Connors v United Kingdom (2005) 40 EHRR 9; (2004) 40
    EHRR 189   2.36, 2.84, 2.85,
                                                          3.16, 3.19, 3.21,
                                                          3.24, 3.26, 3.62
Coster v United Kingdom (2001) 33 EHRR 479   4.104
Crump v Gilmore [1968] LGR 56; (1969) 113 SJ 998, DC   7.22
D v United Kingdom (30240/96) (1997) 24 EHRR 423;
    2 BHRC 273, ECHR   7.90

DPP v Jones [1999] 2 AC 240; [1999] 2 WLR 625; [1999]
   2 All ER 257; [1999] 2 CR App R 348, HL   5.83, 5.86
Davis v Tonbridge and Malling Borough Council *See*
   Tonbridge and Malling Borough Council v Davis—
Dawkins v Department of Environment [1993] LCR 517;
   [1993] IRLR 284 CA   8.51
Day v Sheffield City Council August 1988 *Legal Action* 19   3.48
De Freitas v Permanent Secretary of Ministry of
   Agriculture, Fisheries, Lands and Housing [1999] 1
   AC 69; [1998] 3 WLR 675, PC (Ant)   2.46
Demetri v Westminster City Council [2000] 1 WLR 772;
   (2000) 32 HLR 470, CA   6.44
Din v Wandsworth London Borough Council [1983]
   1 AC 657; [1981] 3 WLR 918; [1981] 3 All ER 881, HL   6.75
Doherty v Birmingham City Council and The Secretary of
   State for Communities and Local Government [2006]
   EWCA Civ 1739   3.21, 3.25, 3.27, 5.3
Doncaster MBC v First Secretary of State and
   Angela Smith [2007] EWHC 1034 Admin   4.90
Doncaster MBC v Secretary of State for the Environment,
   Transport and the Regions [2002] EWHC 808
   Admin; [2002] JPL 1509; [2002] 16 EGCS 181, QBD
   (Admin Ct)   4.96, 4.98
Drury v Secretary of State for the Environment, Food and
   Rural Affairs; *sub nom* Secretary of State for the
   Environment, Food and Rural Affairs v Drury [2004]
   EWCA Civ 200; (2004) 101(12) LSG 35; April 2004
   Legal Action 34, CA   5.161, 5.162
Dudgeon v United Kingdom (A/45) (1982) 4 EHRR 149,
   ECHR   2.26
Edinburgh City Council v Secretary of State for Scotland;
   Revival Properties Ltd v Edinburgh City Council;
   Secretary of State for Scotland v Revival Properties Ltd;
   sub nom City of Edinburgh v Secretary of State for
   Scotland [1997] 1 WLR 1447; [1998] 1 All ER 174;
   1998 SC (HL) 33; 1998 SLT 120, HL   4.138
First Secretary of State v Simmons [2005] EWCA
   Civ 1259   4.100
Fleet Mortgage Ltd v Lower Maisonette 46 Eaton Place
   [1972] 1 WLR 765   5.25
Floyd v Scott (2007) (adjourned pending the decision
   in Malcolm)   3.34
Galer v Morrissey *See* Morrissey v Galer—
Gaskin v United Kingdom (A/160); *sub nom* Gaskin v
   United Kingdom (10454/83); Gaskin v
   United Kingdom [1990] 1 FLR 167; (1990)
   12 EHRR 36, ECHR   7.100
Gayford v Chouler [1898] 1 QB 316, QBD   5.44

George v Devon County Council *See* R v Devon County
  Council ex p George—
Ghaidan v Godin-Mendoza; *sub nom* Ghaidan v Mendoza;
  Godin-Mendoza v Ghaidan; Mendoza v Ghaidan [2004]
  UKHL 30, [2004] 2 AC 557; [2004] 3 All ER 411; [2004]
  3 WLR 113; *Affirming* [2002] EWCA Civ 1533; [2003]
  Ch 380; [2003] 2 WLR 478; [2002] 4 All ER 1162, CA   2.65, 2.66, 2.74
Great Portland Estates Plc v Westminster City Council
  See Westminster City Council v Great Portland
  Estates Plc—
Greenwich London Borough Council v Powell [1989]
  AC 995; [1989] 2 WLR 7; [1989] 1 All ER 65, HL   4.70
Gypsy Council v United Kingdom Application no
  66336/01   2.93
Hallam and Smith v Avery and Lambert; Hallam v Avery;
  Smith v Cheltenham Borough Council; *sub nom*
  Hallam v Cheltenham Borough Council [2001]
  UKHL 15; [2001] 1 WLR 655; [2001] ICR 408, HL   8.12
Hambleton District Council v Bird [1995] 3 PLR 8;
  [1996] JPL 675, CA   2.54, 2.58, 4.170
Harrow London Borough Council v Qazi *See* Qazi v
  Harrow London Borough Council—
Hart District Council v Bedford [2006] EWHC 240 (QB)   4.185
Hearne v National Assembly for Wales; *sub nom* Hearne v
  Secretary of State for Wales (1999) 22 October
  (QBENF 1999/0648/C) (1999) *The Times*,
  10 November; (1999) *Independent*, 11 November,
  CA; affirming [2000] JPL 161, QBD   4.72
Hedges v Secretary of State for the Environment and East
  Cambridgeshire District Council (1996) 73 P&CR 534;
  [1996] EGCS 191, QBD   4.85, 4.86
Jarmain v Secretary of State for the Environment,
  Transport and the Regions (No2) [2001] EWHC 1140
  Admin; [2002] 3 EGCS 124, QBD (Admin Ct)   4.161
Kay and others v Lambeth London Borough Council,
  Leeds City Council v Price and others [2006] UKHL 10;
  [2006] 2 AC 465; [2006] 2 WLR 570, *Affirming* [2004]
  EWCA Civ 926; [2005] QB 352; [2004] 3 WLR 1396   3.23–3.26, 3.30,
                                                          5.4 – 5.7, 5.23
Krumpa v DPP [1989] Crim LR 295, DC   5.48
Kruse v Johnson; *sub nom* Knise v Johnson [1898] 2 QB 91,
  QBD   5.94, 5.103
L v Governors of J School *See* R (on the application of
  L (A Child)) v J School Governors—
Lee v First Secretary of State *See* R (on the application of
  Lee) v First Secretary of State—
Lee v United Kingdom (2001) App No 25289/94   4.104
Leicester City Council v Aldwinkle [1991] HLR 40, CA   5.25
Lewis, ex p (1888) LR 21 QBD 191, QBD   5.83

Lewisham London Borough Council v Malcolm (2007)
(unreported to date)   3.34
Lisa Smith and others v Secretary of State for Trade and
Industry and the London Development Agency [2007]
EWHC 1013 Admin   2.53, 3.53–3.55
Lough v The First Secretary of State [2004] 1 WLR 2557   2.49, 2.53
McPhail v Persons, Names Unknown; Bristol Corp v Ross
[1973] Ch 447; [1973] 3 WLR 71; [1973]
3 All ER 393, CA   5.22, 5.23, 5.116
Machado v Secretary of State for the Home Department
[2005] EWCA Civ 597   2.63
Maidstone Borough Council v Secretary of State for the
Environment and Dunn [1996] JPL 584   4.74
Malone v United Kingdom (A/82) (1985) 7 EHRR 14,
ECHR   2.23, 2.24
Manchester Airport Plc v Dutton [2000] QB 133; [1999]
3 WLR 524; [1999] 2 All ER 675, CA   5.10
Manchester City Council v Romano [2004] EWCA Civ 834;
[2004] HLR 87   3.33
Mandla (Sewa Singh) v Dowell Lee [1983] 2 AC 548; [1983]
2 WLR 620; [1983] 1 All ER 1062, HL   8.45
Mendoza v Ghaidan *See* Ghaidan v Godin-Mendoza—
Michalak v Wandsworth London Borough Council *See*
Wandsworth London Borough Council v Michalak—
Mid-Bedfordshire District Council v Smith [2003]
EWHC 932 (QB)   4.186
Miller-Mead v Minister of Housing and Local Government
[1963] 2 QB 196, CA   4.146
Mills v Cooper [1967] 2 QB 459; [1967] 2 WLR 1343; [1967]
2 All ER 100, DC   1.33, 4.69
Mole Valley District Council v Smith; Reigate and
Banstead Borough Council v Brown (1992)
24 HLR 442; 90 LGR 557; (1992) 64 P&CR 491; [1992]
3 PLR 22, CA   2.54
Morrissey v Galer; *sub nom* Galer v Morrissey [1955]
1 WLR 110; [1955] 1 All ER 380, DC   5.96
Myhill and Faith v Wealden District Council [2004] EWCA
Civ 224; April 2004 *Legal Action* 34,
Tunbridge Wells County Court   6.69, 6.71, 6.73
Nachova v Bulgaria, App nos 43577/98–43579/98,
judgment 6 July 2005   2.71, 2.72
Nagy v Weston [1965] 1 WLR 280; [1965] 1 All ER 78, DC   5.85
Newham London Borough Council v Khatun *See* R
(on the application of Khatun) v Newham London
Borough Council—
North Devon Homes Ltd v Brazier [2003] EWHC 574;
[2003] HLR 59; (2003) 6 CCL Rep 245, QBD   3.33
O'Leary v Allied Domecq Case No CL 950275-79 29 August
2000 (unreported), Central London County Court   4.67, 7.47, 8.48, 8.50

Ozbek v Ipswich Borough Council [2006] EWCA Civ 534;
   [2006] HLR 41; [2006] LGR 853, (2006) *The Times*,
   7 June, [2006] All ER (D) 51 (May)   6.86
P v National Association of School Masters Union of
   Women Teachers (NASUWT); *sub nom* P v National
   Association of Schoolmasters Union of Women
   Teachers (NASUWT); P (FC), Re [2003] UKHL 8;
   [2003] 2 AC 663; [2003] 2 WLR 545; [2003] 1 All
   ER 993, HL   7.42
Pearce v Governing Body of Mayfield School [2003]
   UKHL 24   8.27
Percy v Hall [1997] QB 924; [1997] 3 WLR 573; [1996]
   4 All ER 523, CA   5.101
Petrovic v Austria (2001) 33 Crim LR 14   2.67
Piggott v Sheffield CC, 23 January 1998 (unreported),
   Sheffield CC   3.45
Polkingham v Wright [1845] 8 QB 197   5.111
Poplar Housing and Regeneration Community
   Association Ltd v Donaghue [2002] QB 48; [2001]
   3 WLR 183; [2001] 4 All ER 604   5.153
Powell v May [1946] KB 330, KBD   5.100
Price v Carmarthenshire County Council *See* R
   (on the application of Margaret Price) v
   Carmarthenshire County Council—
Price and others v Leeds City Council *See* Kay and others
   v Lambeth London Borough Council, Leeds City
   Council v Price and others—
Qazi v Harrow London Borough Council; *sub nom* Harrow
   London Borough Council v Qazi; Harrow London
   Borough Council v Qazi [2003] UKHL 43; [2003]
   3 WLR 792; [2003] 4 All ER 461; [2004] 1 AC 983, HL   3.21, 3.22, 3.24, 5.5
R v Basingstoke and Deane District Council ex p Bassett
   (1983) 10 HLR 125; [1984] Fam Law 90   6.77
R v Brighton and Hove Borough Council ex p Marmont
   (1998) 30 HLR 1046; [1998] 2 PLR 48, QBD   5.125
R v Cambridge Health Authority ex p B (No 1) [1995] 1
   WLR 898; [1995] 2 All ER 129, CA   7.67
R v Camden London Borough Council ex p Pereira (No2)
   (1999) 31 HLR 317; [1998] NPC 94, CA   6.70
R v Chiltern District Council ex p Roberts (1991) 23
   HLR 387; [1991] COD 214, QBD   6.59, 6.65
R v Clarke (Thomas George) [2002] EWCA Crim 753;
   [2002] JPL 1372, CA (Crim Div)   4.163
R v Cleveland County Council ex p Commission for
   Racial Equality [1993] 1 FCR 597; [1992] LGR 139, CA   8.118
R v Devon County Council ex p George; Devon County
   Council v George; G's application, Re; George v
   Devon County Council [1989] AC 573; [1988] 3
   WLR 1386; [1988] 3 All ER 1002, HL   7.30

R v Epping Forest District Council ex p Strandmill Ltd
[1990] JPL 415, QBD   4.21
R v Governors of W School and West Sussex County
Council ex p K [2001] ELR 311   7.39
R v Gwent County Council ex p Perry (1985)
129 SJ 737, CA   7.59
R v Hackney London Borough Council ex p Ajayi (1998)
30 HLR 473; [1997] COD 371, QBD   6.78
R v Hammersmith and Fulham London Borough Council
ex p Duro-Rama (1983) 9 HLR 71   6.8
R v Harrow London Borough Council ex p Fahia [1998]
1 WLR 1396; [1998] 4 All ER 137,HL   6.76
R v Harrow London Borough Council ex p M [1997]
3 FCR 761; (1997) 34 BMLR 12; [1997] ELR 62, QBD   7.32
R v Hillingdon London Borough Council ex p McDonagh
[1999] EHLR 169; (1999) 31 HLR 531; (1999) 1 LGLR
232, QBD   5.125
R v Hillingdon London Borough Council ex p Ward *See*
R (on the application of Martin Ward) v Hillingdon
London Borough Council; *sub nom* Ward v Hillingdon
London Borough Council; R v Hillingdon London
Borough Council ex p Ward—
R v Kerrier District Council ex p Uzell Blythe (1996)
71 P&CR 566; [1996] JPL 837; [1996] COD 97, QBD   4.145, 5.118, 5.125
R v Lambeth London Borough Council ex p Ly (1986)
19 HLR 51   6.68
R v Leeds City Council ex p Maloney (No1) (1999)
31 HLR 552, QBD   5.125
R v Lincolnshire County Council ex p Atkinson;
R v Wealden District Council ex p Wales and Stratford,
(1996) 8 Admin LR 529; [1997] JPL 65; (1995)
The Times, 22 September, QBD   1.34, 4.144, 5.1,
5.118, 5.119, 5.121, 5.125
R v MAFF ex p Callaghan and others (2000) 32 HLR 8   5.156
R v Metropolitan Police ex p Small (1998) (unreported)
27 August   5.147
R v Ministry of Defence ex p Elias [2005] EWHC 1435
Admin   8.79, 8.102
R v Ministry of Defence ex p Smith [1996] QB 517   2.46, 2.47, 2.50
R v Newham East Justices ex p Hunt; R v Oxted Justices
ex p Franklin [1976] 1 WLR 420; [1976] 1
All ER 839, DC   3.47
R v Newham London Borough Council ex p Ojuri (No 3)
(1998) 31 HLR 452   6.91
R v Newham London Borough Council ex p Sacupima
[2001] HLR 2, CA; [2001] HLR 1, QBD   6.94
R v North and East Devon HA ex p Coughlan [2001]
QB 213; [2000] 2 WLR 622; [2000] 3 All ER 850; (2000)
2 LGLR 1; [1999] BLGR 703; (1999) 2 CCLR 285, CA   7.67

R v Secretary of State for Education and Science ex p E
[1992] 1 FLR 377; [1993] 2 FCR 753, CA   7.32

R v Secretary of State for Education and Science
ex p Talmud Torah Madizikei Hedass School Trust
(1985) *The Times* 12 April   7.18

R v Secretary of State for the Environment ex p Lee;
R v Secretary of State for the Environment ex p Bond
(1987) 54 P&CR 311; [1985] JPL 724, QBD   4.106

R v Secretary of State for the Home Department ex p Daly
See R (on the application of Daly) v Secretary of State
for the Home Department; *sub nom* R v Secretary of
State for the Home Department ex p Daly—

R v Shropshire County Council ex p Bungay (1991) 23
HLR 195; [1990] COD 392   4.71, 4.78

R v South Hams District Council ex p Gibb;
R v Gloucestershire County Council ex p Davies;
R v Dorset County Council ex p Rolls; Rolls v Dorset CC;
Davies v Gloucestershire CC; Gibb v Devon County
Council and South Hams District Council;
R v Warwickshire County Council ex p Waller [1995]
QB 158; [1994] 3 WLR 1151; [1994] 4 All ER 1012, CA   1.40, 4.73, 4.77

R v South Herefordshire District Council ex p Miles (1985)
17 HLR 82, DC   4.122

R v Surrey Quarter Sessions Appeals Committee
ex p Tweedie (1963) 61 LGR 464; [1963] Crim LR 639;
107 SJ 555, DC   7.59

R v Swansea City Council ex p Hearn (1990) 23 HLR 372   6.8

R v Tunbridge Wells Borough Council ex p The Gypsy
Council for Education, Culture, Welfare and
Civil Rights and Eli Frankham, 7 September 2000
(unreported), Admin Ct   2.93

R v Wicks [1998] AC 92; [1997] 2 WLR 876; [1997]
2 All ER 801, HL   4.163

R v Wood (1855) 5 E&B 49   5.99

R v Wood (David) [2001] EWCA Crim 1395; [2002] JPL 219,
CA (Crim Div)   4.163

R (on the application of Albert Smith) v Barking and
Dagenham London Borough Council; *sub nom*
Smith v Barking and Dagenham London Borough
Council [2003] EWCA Civ 385, CA; affirming [2002]
EWHC 2400 Admin; [2002] 48 EGCS 141; (2002)
99(46) LSG 35; [2002] NPC 146; [2003] EHLR Dig 4,
QBD(Admin Ct)   2.81, 2.82, 2.84, 3.15

R (on the application of Aweys and others) v Birmingham
City Council [2007] EWHC 52 Admin   6.64, 6.65, 6.96

R (on the application of B (A Child)) v Head Teacher and
Governing Body of Alperton Community School;
R (on the application of T (A Child)) v Wembley High
School Head Teacher; R (on the application of

C (A Child)) v Cardinal Newman Roman Catholic
School Governing Body; *sub nom* R v Secretary of State
for Education and Employment ex p B; R (on the
application of B) v Secretary of State for Education and
Employment [2001] EWHC 229 Admin; [2002]
BLGR 132; [2001] 1 ELR 359, QBD (Admin Ct)   7.11, 7.40
R (on the application of Basildon District Council) v
First Secretary of State and Rachel Cooper [2004]
EWCA Civ 473, CA   4.74
R (on the application of Butler) v Bath and North East
Somerset District Council; *sub nom* Butler v Bath and
North East Somerset District Council [2003] EWCA
Civ 1614; [2004] JPL 941; (2003) 100(46) LSG 25; [2003]
NPC 129; (2003) *The Times*, 4 November, CA   4.15, 4.39
R (on the application of Caroline Stephenson) v
East Derbyshire Magistrates' Court and Amber Valley
Borough Council [2003] EWHC 903 Admin   5.75, 5.79
R (on the application of Casey and others) v Crawley
Borough Council and the Office of the Deputy
Prime Minister [2006] EWHC 301 Admin   5.142, 5.143
R (on the application of Carson) v Secretary of State for
Work and Pensions; R (on the application of Reynolds)
v Secretary of State for Work and Pensions; *sub nom*
Carson v Secretary of State for Work and Pensions
[2005] UKHL 37; [2006] 1 AC 173; [2005] 4 All ER 545;
Affirming [2003] EWCA Civ 797; [2003] 3 All ER 577;
[2002] EWHC 978 Admin, CA   2.64, 2.73, 2.75
R (on the application of Chelmsford Borough Council) v
First Secretary of State and Draper [2003] EWHC 2978
Admin, QBD (Admin Ct)   4.96, 4.98
R (on the application of Clare Wilson) v Wychavon District
Council and the First Secretary of State [2007] EWCA
Civ 52; [2005] EWHC 2970 Admin   2.77, 2.86–2.89,
          4.149
R (on the application of Daly) v Secretary of State for the
Home Department; [2001] UKHL 26;
[2001] 2 AC 532; [2001] 2 WLR 1622; [2001]
3 All ER 433, HL   2.46, 2.48, 2.50,
          2.63
R (on the application of Egan) v Secretary of State for
Transport, Local Government and the Regions and
Hertsmere Borough Council [2002] EWHC 389
Admin   2.51
R (on the application of Fuller and others) v Chief
Constable of Dorset Constabulary and Secretary of
State for the Home Department [2001] EWHC 1057
Admin ; [2003] QB 480; [2002] 3 WLR 1133; [2002]
3 All ER 57, QBD (Admin Ct)   5.41, 5.42, 5.48,
          5.145, 5.148

R (on the application of Holub and Holub) v Secretary of
State for the Home Department; *sub nom* Holub v
Secretary of State for the Home Department; R v
Secretary of State for the Home Department ex p
Holub [2001] 1 WLR 1359; [2001] HRLR 24, CA   7.8

R (on the application of Jeeves and Baker) v Gravesham
Borough Council [2006] EWHC 1249 Admin; [2006]
JPL 1743   4.25

R (on the application of Kanssen) v Secretary of State for
the Environment, Food and Rural Affairs (SSEFRA)
[2005] EWHC 1024 Admin; [2005] EWCA Civ 1453   5.158, 5.159

R (on the application of Khatun) v Newham London
Borough Council; R (on the application of Zeb) v
Newham London Borough Council; R (on the
application of Iqbal) v Newham London Borough
Council; *sub nom* Khatun v Newham London Borough
Council; Newham London Borough Council v Khatun
[2005] QB 37; [2004] EWCA Civ 55; (2004)
148 SJLB 268; (2004) LS Gaz 13 May, CA   3.36

R (on the application of L (A Child)) v J School Governors;
R (on the application of W (A Child)) v B School
Governors; *sub nom* L v J; W v B; R v B School
Governors ex p W, R v J School Governors ex p L; L
(A Child), Re; L v Governors of J School [2003]
UKHL 9; [2003] 2 AC 633; [2003] 2 WLR 518; [2003] 1
All ER 1012,HL   7.42

R (on the application of L (A Child)) v Manchester City
Council; R (on the application of R (A Child)) v
Manchester City Council [2001] EWHC 707
Admin ; [2002] 1 FLR 43; (2002) 5 CCL Rep 268,
QBD (Admin Ct)   5.124

R (on the application of Lee) v First Secretary of State;
sub nom Lee v First Secretary of State [2003] EWHC
3235 Admin; [2003] NPC 161,QBD (Admin Ct)   2.51, 4.138

R (on the application of Lisa Smith) v South Norfolk
Council [2006] EWHC 2772 Admin   2.52, 4.168, 8.102,
8.104

R (on the application of Lynes) v West Berkshire District
Council [2002] EWHC 1828 Admin; [2003] JPL 1137,
QBD (Admin Ct)   4.147

R (on the application of McCarthy) Chief Constable of the
Sussex Constabulary and the Secretary of State for the
Home Department [2007] EWHC 1520 Admin   5.145

R (on the application of McCarthy and Others) v Basildon
District Council (CO/5225/05)   8.79, 8.102

R (on the application of Mahmood) v Secretary of State for
the Home Department [2001] 1 WLR 840   2.45–2.47

R (on the application of Mitchell and Hearne) v Horsham
District Council [2003] EWHC 234 Admin   4.166

R (on the application of O'Brien and Casey) v Basildon
District Council [2006] EWHC 1346 Admin   2.52, 4.167
R (on the application of O'Donoghue) v Brighton and
Hove City Council [2003] EWCA Civ 459   6.61, 6.62
R (on the application of Piggott) v Bedfordshire County
Council [2002] EWHC 77 Admin; (2002) 99(10)
LSG 31; *The Times,* January 29,2002, QBD
(Admin Ct)   3.29, 3.30
R (on the application of Margaret Price) v Carmarthenshire
County Council [2003] EWHC 42 Admin; [2003]
ACD 39; March 2003 *Legal Action* 30, QBD
(Admin Ct)   2.91, 5.144, 6.51,
                                                       6.54, 6.56, 6.57,
                                                       6.89, 6.95, 6.101
R (on the application of Prokopp) v London
Underground Ltd [2003] EWCA Civ 961; [2004]
Env LR 8; [2004] 1 P&CR 31; [2004] JPL 44; (2003)
New Law Property Digest 103076201, 7 July, CA   4.190
R (on the application of S) v Brent London Borough
Council [2002] EWCA Civ 693   7.40
R (on the application of S) v The Governors of YP School
[2003] EWCA Civ 1306; [2004] ELR 37, CA   7.38
R (on the application of SD) v The Governors of Denbeigh
High School [2006] 2 WLR 719   2.50
R (on the application of Samaroo) v Secretary of State for
the Home Department [2001] EWCA Civ 1139; [2001]
UKHHR 1150   2.48–2.50, 2.53,
3.55
R (on the application of Smith) v LDA [2007] EWHC 636
Admin   3.55
R (on the application of Smith) v South Norfolk Council
See R (on the application of Lisa Smith) v
South Norfolk Council—
R (on the application of Martin Ward) v Hillingdon London
Borough Council; *sub nom* Ward v Hillingdon London
Borough Council; R v Hillingdon London Borough
Council ex p Ward [2001] EWHC Admin 91 ; [2002]
EHLR 4; [2001] HRLR 40; [2001] LGR 457, QBD
(Admin Ct)   5.8, 5.125
Restormel Borough Council v Secretary of State for the
Environment [1982] JPL 785   4.26
Rolls v St George the Martyr, Southwark Vestry (1880)
LR 14 Ch D 785, CA   5.92
Save Britain's Heritage v Number 1 Poultry Ltd; *sub nom*
Save Britain's Heritage v Secretary of State for the
Environment [1991] 1 WLR 153; [1991] 2 All ER 10;
89 LGR 809, HL   4.139
Scott-Higgs v Brighton and Hove City Council [2003]
3 All ER 753, CA   6.72, 6.101

Seddon Properties Ltd v Secretary of State for the
    Environment (1981) 42 P&CR 26; (1978) 248 EG 951;
    [1978] JPL 835, QBD   4.137
Simpson v United Kingdom (1989) 64 DR 188   7.40
Smith v First Secretary of State and Mid Bedfordshire
    District Council [2005] EWCA Civ 859   4.91
Smith v Secretary of State for the Environment,
    Transport and Regions and Wyre Forest District
    Council [2001] EWCA Civ 1550   4.135
Smith v Wokingham District Council April 1980
    LAG Bulletin 92, CC   6.60
Smith and Grady v United Kingdom (1999)
    29 EHRR 493   2.47, 2.50
Smith and Smith v Cheltenham Borough Council and
    Others (CN755478) 7 June 1999 (unreported),
    Bristol CC   8.11, 8.33, 8.39
Smith (Jane) v United Kingdom (2001) 33 EHRR 712   4.104
Somerset County Council v Isaacs; *sub nom* Isaacs v
    Secretary of State for Transport, Local Government
    and the Regions [2002] EWHC 1014 Admin; [2002]
    EHLR 18; [2002] 25 EGCS 151, QBD (Admin Ct)   2.80, 2.84, 3.15
South Bedfordshire District Council v Price [2006]
    EWCA Civ 493   4.188
South Buckinghamshire District Council v Porter;
    Chichester District Council v Searle; Wrexham CBC v
    Berry; Hertsmere Borough Council v Harty; *sub nom*
    South Bucks District Council v Porter [2003] EWCA
    Civ 835; [2003] UKHL 26; [2003] 2 AC 558; [2003]
    2 WLR 1547; [2003] 3 All ER 1, HL; *affirming* [2001]
    EWCA Civ 1549; [2002] 1 WLR 1359; [2002]
    1 All ER 425; July 2002 *Legal Action* 22, CA   2.55, 2.56–2.61, 4.3,
        4.111, 4.115, 4.170,
        4.171, 4.173–4.185,
        4.187, 4.189, 4.193,
        5.166
South Buckinghamshire District Council v Secretary of
    State for Transport, Local Government and the
    Regions and Porter (No 2) [2004] 1 WLR 1953;
    Reversing [2003] EWCA Civ 687; (2003) *The Times*,
    23 May   4.96, 4.139
South Buckinghamshire District Council v Smith [2006]
    EWHC 281. (QB); [2006] All ER (D) 333 (Feb)   4.188
South Cambridgeshire District Council v Flynn [2006]
    EWHC 1320 (QB)   4.188
South Cambridgeshire District Council v Gammell,
    Bromley London Borough Council v Maughan [2005]
    EWCA Civ 1429; (2005) *The Times*, 3 November   4.189
Steward v Royal Borough of Kingston-Upon-Thames
    [2007] EWCA Civ 565, CA   2.39, 6.62, 6.81

Stirrup v Secretary of State for the Environment
CO/383/93 (1993) 3 December,
Local Authority Law 1/94 2   4.58
Stoke on Trent City Council v B&Q (Retail) Ltd;
Wolverhampton Borough Council v B&Q (Retail) Ltd;
Barking and Dagenham London Borough Council v
Home Charm Retail [1984] AC 754; [1984] 2 WLR 929; [
1984] 2 All ER 332, HL   5.166
Stratford-upon-Avon District Council v Ditchman [2002]
Env LR 7   4.185
Stringer v Minister for Housing and Local Government
[1970] 1 WLR 1281; [1971] 1 All ER 65, QBD   4.65
Taylor and Sons (Farms) v Secretary of State for the
Environment, Transport and the Regions; *sub nom* R
(on the application of Taylor (t/a David Taylor & Sons))
v Secretary of State for the Environment, Transport and
the Regions [2001] EWCA Civ 1254; [2002] PLCR 11;
(2001) 98(38) LSG 40; [2001] NPC 134; *New Law Digest*
101088201; (2001) *The Times*, 16 October, CA   4.159
Thlimmenos v Greece (2001) 31 EHRR 15   2.67
Timishev v Russia Application Nos 55762/00 and
55974/00, judgment 13 March 2006   2.66, 2.69, 2.77
Tithe Redemption Commissioners v Runcorn Urban
District Council [1954] Ch 383; [1954] 2 WLR 518;
[1954] 1 All ER 653, CA   5.92
Tonbridge and Malling Borough Council v Davis; *sub nom*
Davis v Tonbridge and Malling Borough Council
[2004] EWCA Civ 194; (2004) 101(10) LSG 30; (2004)
148 SJLB 270, CA   2.60–2.62
Truckell v Stock [1957] 1 WLR 161; [1957] 1 All ER 74, CA   5.92
Varey v United Kingdom (26662/95) (2000) 30 EHRR
CD39; (2001) *The Times*, 30 January, ECHR; (1998)
25 EHRR CD49, Eur Comm HR   4.104
Wandsworth London Borough Council v Michalak;
sub nom Michalek v Wandsworth London Borough
Council; Michalak v Wandsworth London Borough
Council [2002] EWCA Civ 271; [2003] 1 WLR 617;
[2002] 4 All ER1136,CA   2.73–2.75
Waverley Borough Council v Lee [2003] EWHC 29 (Ch)   4.186
West Glamorgan County Council v Rafferty; R v Secretary
of State for Wales ex p Gilhaney [1987] 1 WLR 457;
[1987] 1 All ER 1005 CA   5.1
Westminster City Council v Great Portland Estates Plc;
sub nom Great Portland Estates Plc v Westminster City
Council [1985] AC 661; [1984] 3 WLR 1035; [1984]
3 All ER 744; (1985) 50 P&CR 34, HL   4.92
Westminster City Council and the First Secretary of
State v Morris [2005] EWCA Civ 1184   2.76

Wiltshire County Council v Fraser [1986] 1 WLR 109   5.27, 5.28

Wrexham CBC v National Assembly for Wales; Wrexham
    CBC v Berry; *sub nom* Berry v National Assembly of
    Wales [2003] EWCA Civ 835; [2003] EHLR 20; [2004]
    JPL 65, CA; reversing [2002] EWHC 2414 Admin,
    QBD (Admin Ct)   4.77, 4.78, 4.79, 4.81

Wychavon District Council v Rafferty [2006]
    EWCA Civ 628   4.188

Wycombe District Council v Wells [2005] EWHC 1012
    Admin   4.163

Wyre Forest District Council v Secretary of State for the
    Environment and Allen's Caravans (Estates) [1990]
    2 AC 357; [1990] 2 WLR 517; [1990] 1 All ER 780, HL   4.27

YL v Birmingham City Council [2007] UKHL 27   5.153

Z v Finland (1997) 25 EHRR 371   7.99

Table of statutes

Access to Health Records
    Act 1990   7.92
Access to Justice Act 1999—
    s6(8)(b)   4.191
    s27(1)   3.47
Access to Medical Reports
    Act 1988   7.92
Acquisition of Land Act 1981—
    s24   3.55
Ancient Monuments and
    Archaeological Areas
    Act 1979   5.39
Anti-Social Behaviour
    Act 2003   5.52
Asylum and Immigration
    Act 1996   6.4
Caravan Sites
    Act 1968   1.34, 1.39, 1.45,
        2.80, 3.3, 3.4,
        3.6, 3.7, 3.11,
        3.58, 4.1, 6.41
    Pt I   2.81
    Pt II   1.34, 1.38
    s1   3.57
    s2   3.11
    s2–4   App B
    s3   3.11
    s4   3.11, 3.18
    s6   3.3, 4.1, 4.2
    s7   3.3
    s8   3.3
    s13   4.28
    s16   1.40, 4.69
Caravan Sites and Control of
    Development
    Act 1960   1.33, 3.57, 5.57
    s1   3.58
    s5(6)   3.43
    s23   1.34

Caravan Sites and Control of
    Development Act 1960 *continued*
    s24   1.34, 3.3–3.6
    s24(2)   3.40
    s24(2)(b)   3.40
    s24(2)(c)   3.40
    s24(2A)   3.42
    s24(3)   3.37
    s24(8)   1.33, 1.40, 3.5,
        4.69
    s29(1)   3.5, 4.27, 5.46
    Sch 1   3.58
Children Act 1989   3.51, 6.11
    Pt III   5.123
    s1(1)   3.51
    s17   7.104
    s17(3)   3.51
    s17(6)   3.51
    s17(7)   3.51
    s17(11)   3.51
    s20   6.11
    s24B(3)   6.11
    s36   7.29
Chronically Sick and Disabled
    Persons Act 1970—
    s1   7.88
Countryside Act 1968 5.158
Courts Act 2003—
    s99   5.24
Crime and Disorder
    Act 1998   5.166
Criminal Damage Act 1971—
    s10(1)   5.44
Criminal Justice and Public Order
    Act 1994   1.34, 1.35, 3.4,
        3.40, 3.49, 4.2,
        5.1, 5.44,
        5.152, 5.171,
        6.69, 6.73, 9.3

Criminal Justice and Public Order
Act 1994 *continued*

s61	5.32, 5.34, 5.35, 5.37, 5.38, 5.40, 5.41, 5.46, 5.47, 5.50, 5.52, 5.53, 5.55, 5.57, 5.65, 5.66, 5.70, 5.71, 5.76, 5.146, 5.147, 5.149, App B
s61(1)	5.32, 5.33, 5.36, 5.37, 5.41
s61(1)(a)	5.32, 5.38, 5.41
s61(1)(b)	5.32, 5.41
s61(3)	5.36, 5.37
s61(4)	5.33
s61(4)(a)	5.78
s61(5)	5.33
s61(6)	5.47
s61(9)	5.38, 5.39, 5.44–5.46
s62	5.33, App B
s62A	5.52, 5.53, 5.57, 5.59, 5.65, 5.68, 5.71, 5.72, 5.137, 5.171, App B
s62A(1)	5.68
s62A(2)(a)	5.55
s62A(6)	5.57, 5.62
s62B	5.58, 5.137, 5.171, App B
s62B(1)	5.68
s62B(2)	5.68
s62B(3)	5.69
s62B(5)	5.70
s62C	5.58, 5.69, 5.71, 5.137, 5.171, App B
s62D	5.58, 5.137, 5.171, App B
s62E	5.58, 5.137, 5.171, App B

Criminal Justice and Public Order
Act 1994 *continued*

s62E(6)	5.68
s70	2.93, 5.86
s77	4.144, 5.38, 5.70, 5.73, 5.75, 5.77, 5.81, 5.119, 5.124, 5.125, App B
s77(1)	5.73, 5.77
s77(3)	5.73, 5.78, 5.82, 5.82
s77(5)	5.80
s78	4.144, 5.81, 5.119, App B
s79	4.144, 5.77, 5.79, 5.119, App B
s79(2)	5.77
s79(3)	5.77
s80	3.2, 3.6, App B
s80(1)	1.34
s80(2)(a)	3.40

Criminal Law
Act 1977

s6	5.40
s7	5.117
	5.117
s12(1)(a)	5.117
s12(2)	5.117

Cycle Tracks
Act 1984

	5.39

Data Protection
Act 1998

	7.92–7.94
s7	7.95
s7(1)(a)	7.93
s7(1)(b)	7.93
s7(4)	7.97
s7(9)	7.98
s8(2)	7.96
s10(4)	7.98
s11(2)	7.98
s12(8)	7.98
s15(1)	7.98
ss40–44	7.98
s68	7.94
Sch 11	7.94
Sch 12	7.94

Disability Discrimination
    Act 1995   3.1, 3.33, 3.34,
    7.56
    s1(1)   3.33
    s22(3)(c)   3.33
    s24   3.33
    s28A   7.56
    s68(1)   3.33
Education Act 1980   8.118
Education Act 1996   7.7, 7.31, 7.49
    s7   7.17
    s9   7.10
    s14   7.9
    s14A   7.11
    s19   7.57
    s19(1)   7.45
    s19(2)   7.35
    s312(1)   7.31
    s312(2)   7.31
    s321(1)   7.32
    s323   7.32
    s324(1)   7.32
    s324(5)(a)(i)   7.32
    s437   7.20
    s437(1)   7.60
    s437(3)   7.60
    s443   7.29, 7.60
    s443(1)   7.20
    s444   7.17, 7.25,
        7.29, 7.30
    s444(1)   7.21, 7.22,
        7.24, 7.25
    s444(1A)   7.17, 7.23
    s444(1B)   7.23
    s444(6)   7.26
    s446   7.19
    s447   7.29
    s509   7.30
Education Act 2002   7.7, 7.49
    s52   7.35
Education and Inspections
    Act 2006   7.20
    s2   7.9
    s3   7.11
    s42   7.11
    s82   7.17, 7.30
    s109   7.17, 7.23
Environmental Protection
    Act 1990   3.35, 3.47

Environmental Protection
    Act 1990 *continued*
    s79(1)(a)   3.45
    s79(7)   3.46
    s80   3.46, 7.106
    s80(4)   7.106
    s82   3.45–3.48,
        7.107
    s82(4)(a)   3.46
    s82(4)(c)   3.46
Equality Act 2006   2.96, 8.3, 8.55
    s3   8.3
    s8   8.4, 8.78
    s9   2.97, 8.4, 8.78
    s10   8.4, 8.78
    s11   8.4
    s15(4)(a)   8.85
    s16   8.78
    s16(2)   8.78
    s16(3)   8.78
    s20   2.98, 8.78
    s20(1)(a)   8.72
    s21   2.98
    s21(1)   8.76
    s21(4)   8.76
    s21(6)   8.76
    s22   8.76
    s23   8.76
    s24   2.98, 8.77
    s24(2)   8.76
    s24(3)   8.76
    s25   8.30–8.32
    s28   8.55
    s28(1)   8.55
    s28(4)   8.55
    s30   2.98, 8.79,
        8.101
    s31   8.105
    s32(2)   8.106
    s32(3)   8.107
    s32(8)   8.108
    s32(9)   8.108
    s33   8.77
    s34(2)   8.77
Forestry Act 1967   5.158
    s46(1)   5.106
Health Services and Public Health
    Act 1968—
    s45   7.88

Highways Act 1959	1.33	**Housing Act 1996** *continued*	
Highways Act 1980	5.39, 5.83	s188(1)	6.19, 6.86, 6.87
s137(1)	5.84	s188(2)	6.19
s149	5.90	s188(3)	6.19, 6.45, 6.86
s155(1)	5.89	s189	6.9
Homelessness		s189(1)	6.9
Act 2002	6.2, 6.37	s189(1)(c)	6.69
s1(1)	6.37	s189(1)(d)	6.72
s1(3)	6.37	s189(2)	6.9
s2(1)	6.38	s189(2)(a)	6.10, 6.11
s2(2)	6.39	s190	6.33
s3(1)	6.40	s190(2)	6.21, 6.87
s5(2)	6.24	s190(4)	6.21
Sch 1 para 10	6.21	s190(5)	6.21
Sch 1 para 14	6.23	s191	6.12
Homelessness etc (Scotland)		s191(1)	6.12, 6.74
Act 2003	6.2	s191(2)	6.12
Housing Act 1980	5.23	s191(3)	6.12
s89	5.22	s192(3)	6.24
s89(2)	5.22	s193	6.33
Housing Act 1985	3.12, 3.13,	s193(1)	6.26
	3.15, 6.28, 6.87	s193(2)	6.26, 6.87, 6.96
Pt III	5.123	s193(5)	6.30
s84	3.13	s193(6)	6.30
Sch 1 para 4	6.22, 6.29	s193(7)	6.30
Sch2	3.13	s193(7A)	6.30
Housing Act 1996	6.3, 6.14, 6.42	s193(8)	6.30
Pt I, Ch1	5.62	s195	6.33
Pt VI	3.29, 6.22, 6.30	s195(2)	6.25, 6.87
Pt VII	5.123, 6.2	s195(3)	6.25
s175	6.5	s195(5)	6.23
s175(2)(b)	6.6, 6.51, 6.58	s195(6)	6.23
s175(3)	6.6	s195(9)	6.24
s176	6.7, 6.19, 6.26,	s196	6.12
	6.68	s198(2)	6.31
s177	6.8	s198(4)	6.31
s179	6.4	s198(5)	6.32
s182	6.42	s199(1)	6.13
s184	6.16, 6.64, 6.86	s199(2)	6.14
s184(1)	6.15, 6.64	s199(3)(a)	6.14
s184(2)	6.17	s199(3)(b)	6.14
s184(3)	6.16	s199(5)	6.14
s184(4)	6.17	s200	6.33
s184(5)	6.16	s200(1)	6.87
s184(6)	6.16, 6.18	s200(2)	6.32
s185(1)	6.4	s202	6.43
s185(2)	6.4	s202(1)(d)	6.32
s186(1)	6.4	s202(1)(e)	6.32
s188	6.33	s202(2)	6.44

Housing Act 1996 *continued*
s204(1)	6.46, 6.47
s204(4)	6.48, 6.86
s204A	6.48
s206(1)	6.27
s208(1)	6.28
s208(2)	6.28
s208(3)	6.28
s208(4)	6.28
s209	6.22
s210	6.87
s210(1)	6.28
s210(2)	6.28
s211(1)	6.34
s211(2)	6.33
s211(3)	6.35
s211(4)	6.35
s211(5)	6.33
s214(1)	6.50
Sch 17 para 3	6.22
Housing Act 2004	5.137, 6.28, 9.4
s211	3.18
s224	3.50
s225	4.36, 4.82, 6.93, 6.103, App B
s226	App B

Housing Grants, Construction
   and Regeneration
Act 1996	3.50
s1	3.50

Housing (Scotland)
Act 1987	6.2

Housing (Scotland)
Act 2001	6.2

Human Rights
Act 1998	1.51, 2.1, 2.2, 2.26, 2.43, 2.45, 2.49, 2.54, 2.55, 2.58, 2.60, 2.78, 2.94, 2.99, 3.1, 3.15, 3.24, 4.76, 4.103, 4.111, 4.117, 4.119, 4.174, 4.193, 5.4, 5.22, 5.23,

Human Rights Act 1998 *continued*
	5.145, 5.153, 5.157, 5.164, 7.6, App B
s2	2.45
s3	3.24, 3.26, 5.6
s3(1)	2.3, 2.5
s4	2.3
s6	2.13, 2.97, 5.1, 5.153, 7.91
s6(1)	2.4, 2.56, 2.58, 4.103, 4.174
s6(3)	4.103
s6(3)(a)	2.2

Land Registration
Act 2002	5.75

Landlord and Tenant Act 1985—
s11	3.35

Local Government Act 1972—
s222	5.165
s235(1)	5.95
s236(3)	5.94
s236(6)	5.97

Local Government Finance Act 1988—
Sch 5 paras 3–8	5.39

Local Government (Wales)
   Act 1994—
s66(5)	5.95
Sch15 para 49	5.95

Mental Health Act 1983
	3.15, 7.88
s117	7.88

Mobile Homes Act 1975—
s9(1)	4.28

Mobile Homes Act 1983
	2.80, 3.2, 3.12, 3.13, 3.58, 3.60, 3.61, App B
s1	3.60
s5	3.59
s5(1)	4.28
Sch 1	3.20
Sch 1 Pt 1	3.61

National Assistance Act 1948—
s21	7.88
s29	7.88

National Health Service Act 1977—
  s1   7.67
  s3   7.67
  s 16A   7.73
  s21   7.88
  Sch 8   7.88
National Health Service and
    Community Care Act 1990—
  s46   7.88
  s47   7.89
Planning and Compensation Act
    1991—
  s6   4.155
  s9   2.86
Planning and Compulsory Purchase
    Act 2004   4.6, 4.11
  Pt 1   4.9
  Pt 2   4.9
  Pt 3   4.9
  s15(4)   4.39
  s37   4.17
  s38(6)   4.14, 4.29, 4.59
  s43   4.24
Planning (Hazardous Substances)
    Act 1990   8.37
Planning (Listed Buildings and
    Conservation Areas)
    Act 1990   8.37
Police and Criminal Evidence
    Act 1984
  s24   5.33
Public Order Act 1986
                        5.48, 5.86,
                        5.152, 5.171,
                        8.43
  s14A   2.93, 5.86
Race Relations Act 1976
                        1.32, 4.67,
                        7.16, 7.47,
                        7.48, 7.51, 8.5,
                        8.6, 8.9,
                        8.11–8.13,
                        8.18, 8.22,
                        8.26, 8.28,
                        8.29, 8.33,
                        8.34,
                        8.41–8.45,
                        8.48, 8.52,
                        8.54, 8.56,

Race Relations Act 1976 *continued*
                        8.63, 8.71,
                        8.77, 8.80,
                        8.98, 8.117,
                        8.118
  Pt II   8.18
  Pt IV   8.18
  s1(1)(b)   8.14
  s1A   8.15
  s3A(1)   8.23, 8.25
  s3A(2)   8.24
  s4   8.35
  s11   8.41
  ss17-18D   8.18
  s17   8.36, 8.69
  s18   7.49, 8.36
  s19A   4.67, 4.135,
                        8.37
  s19B   8.18, 8.19, 8.38
  ss20–24   8.18
  s20   8.11, 8.39
  s21   8.11, 8.39,
                        8.40
  s25   8.42
  s26A   8.18
  s26B   8.18
  s29   8.28, 8.71
  s30   8.31
  s31   8.32, 8.75
  s33   8.11, 8.33
  s35   7.49
  s54A   8.63, 8.65
  s57(5)   8.69
  s57ZA   8.63, 8.65
  s65(1)   8.61
  s65(2)   8.62
  s66(1)   8.55
  s68(6)   8.70
  s71   4.67, 7.51,
                        8.77, 8.80,
                        8.104
  s71(1)   7.82, 8.108
  s76   8.18
  s76A   8.18
  Sch 1A   7.82, 8.80
Race Relations (Amendment)
    Act 2000   7.16, 8.5
Road Traffic Act 1988—
  s22   5.88

School Standards and Framework		Town and Country Planning	
Act 1998	7.40	Act 1990 *continued*	
s86	7.11	s172(3)	4.147
s86(2)	7.11	s173–s179	App B
s86(3)	7.11	s173(1)(a)	4.146
s87	7.11	s173(2)	4.146
s119	7.61	s173(4)	4.146
Serious Organised Crime and Police		s173(9)	4.155
Act 2005	5.33	s174(2)	4.155
Sex Discrimination		s178	2.52, 4.165,
Act 1975	4.78		4.167, 8.102
Special Educational Needs and		s179	4.162
Disability Act 2001	7.56	s179(3)	4.163
Town and Country Planning		s179(9)	4.162
Act 1990	4.6, 4.7, 4.18,	s183	2.86, 2.87,
	4.27, 4.136,		4.148, 4.149,
	5.118, 8.37		App B
Pt III	4.7	s183(4)	2.86, 2.87
Pt VII	4.7	s184	App B
Pt XII	4.7	s187	App B
ssl–9	4.17	s187B	2.5, 2.54, 2.56,
s38(6)	4.59		2.58, 2.60,
s54A	4.14		4.170,
s55	App B		4.176–4.178,
s55(1)	4.18		4.180, 4.181,
s55(2)	4.19		4.183, 4.184,
s57	4.20		App B
s62	4.23, App B	s187B(1)	4.169
s70	App B	s187B(2)	4.181
s70(1)(a)	4.127	s191	4.20, 4.22,
s70(2)	4.59		App B
s70A	4.24, App B	s191(2)	4.22
s78	4.132, App B	s192	4.20, App B
s171A–s171H	App B	s285	4.164, App B
s171B	4.22, 4.146	s288	2.51, 4.136,
s171E	4.150		4.137, 4.161,
s171G	4.154		App B
s171H	4.151	s289	4.161, App B
s172	4.155, App B	Wildlife and Countryside Act 1981—	
s172(1)	4.146	s54	5.39

Table of statutory instruments

Civil Procedure Rules 1998, SI No 3132	5.160, 5.161
Pt 2.8(4)	5.19
Pt 3.1(2)(a)	5.20
Pt 19.4	5.24
Pt 39.3	5.24
Pt 40.4	5.25
Pt 50	5.25
Pt 55	5.10, 5.12, 5.14, 5.25, 5.26, 5.77, 5.92, 5.163
Pt 55.1(b)	5.11, 5.12
Pt 55.3(1)	5.13
Pt 55.3(2)	5.17
Pt 55.3(4)	5.13
Pt 55.5(2)	5.18, 5.19
Pt 55.5(3)	5.21
Pt 55.6	5.13
Pt 55.7(2)	5.14
Pt 55 PD para 1.3	5.17
Pt 55 PD para 1.5	5.14
Pt 55 PD para 2.6	5.16
Pt 55 PD para 3.2	5.20
Pt 55 PD para 5	5.163
County Court Rules 1981, SI No 1687	
Ord 24	5.10
Ord.24.6	5.26
Education (Pupil Exclusions and Appeals) (Miscellaneous Amendments) (England) Regulations 2006, SI No 2189	7.36
Employment Act 2002 (Dispute Resolution) Regulations 2004, SI No 2004/752	8.70
Forestry Commission Bye-laws 1982, SI No 648	5.106
Homeless Persons (Priority Need)(Wales) Order 2001, SI No 607	6.10
Homelessness (Priority Need for Accommodation) (England) Order 2002, SI No 2051	6.11

Homelessness (Suitability of Accommodation) (England)
    Order 2003, SI No 3326   6.28, 6.87
    reg 3   6.87
    reg 4   6.87
Homelessness (Suitability of Accommodation)
    Order 1996, SI No 3204   6.28
Homelessness (Suitability of Accommodation) (Wales)
    Order 2006, SI No 650   6.28
    reg 4   6.88
    reg 5   6.88
    reg 6   6.88
    reg 7   6.88
Housing (Assessment of Accommodation Needs)
    (Meaning of Gypsies and Travellers) (England)
    Regulations 2006 SI No 3190   4.82
Housing Benefit and Council Tax (Consequential
    Provisions) Regulations 2006, SI No 217
    Sch 3 para 4(10(b)   3.38
Housing Benefit (General) Regulations 2006,
    SI No 213
    reg 12(1)(g)   3.37
Housing (Northern Ireland) Order 1988   6.2
Housing (Northern Ireland) Order 2003   6.2
Pupil Registration Regulations 2006, SI No 1751   7.28
Race Relations Act 1976 (Amendment) Regulations 2003,
    SI No 1626   8.63, 8.119
    reg 3   8.15
    reg 5   8.23
    reg 41   8.63
    reg 47   8.61
Race Relations Act 1976 (Statutory Duties) Order 2001,
    SI No 3438   8.82
Race Relations (Northern Ireland) Order 1997,
    SI No 869
    art 5   4.67, 8.48
Race Relations (Questions and Replies) Order 1977,
    SI No 842   8.61
    art 4   8.61
Rules of the Supreme Court 1965, SI No 1776
    Ord 45
    r2   5.25
    r4   5.25
    Ord 113   5.10
Town and Country Planning (Appeals) (Determination by
    Inspectors) (Inquiries Procedure) (England) Rules
    2000, SI No 1625   4.133
Town and Country Planning (Appeals) (Written
    Representations Procedure) (England) Regulations
    2000, SI No 1628   4.133

Town and Country Planning (Enforcement)
(Determination by Inspectors) (Inquiries Procedure)
(England) Rules 2002, SI No 2685 .... 4.160
Town and Country Planning (Enforcement) (Hearings
Procedure) (England) Rules 2002, SI No 2684 ... 4.160
Town and Country Planning (Enforcement) (Inquiries
Procedure) (England) Rules 2002, SI No 2686 ... 4.160
Town and Country Planning (Enforcement Notices and
Appeals) (England) Regulations 2002,
SI No 2682 .... 4.160
Town and Country Planning (Enforcement)
(Written Representations Procedure) (England)
Regulations 2002, SI No 2683 ... 4.160
Town and Country Planning (Fees for Applications and
Deemed Applications) Regulations 1989,
SI No 193 .... 4.23
Town and Country Planning (General Permitted
Development) Order 1995, SI No 418 ... 4.21, 4.159
  art 4(1) 4.21
  Class 2 .... 4.21
  Class 4 .... 4.21
  Class 5 .... 4.21
Town and Country Planning (Hearings Procedure)
(England) Rules 2000, SI No 1626 ... 4.133
Town and Country Planning (Inquiries Procedure)
(England) Rules 2000, SI No 1624 ... 4.133
Town and Country Planning (Temporary Stop Notice)
(England) Regulations 2005, SI No 206 ... 4.153
Unfair Contract Terms in Consumer Contracts
Regulations 1999, SI No 2083 ... 3.36
  reg 4 .... 3.36

Table of circulars and guidance

Department of the Environment Circulars

14/89 Caravan Sites and Control of Development
    Act 1960 – Model Standards   3.35, 3.43
14/91 Planning and Compensation Act 1991   4.24, 4.25
21/91Guidance with Regard to Planning Applications by
    Travelling Showpeople   4.82
22/91 Guidance in Respect of Travelling Showpeople   4.69
1/94 Gypsy Sites and Planning   3.9, 4.2, 4.4, 4.5,
                                4.31, 4.32, 4.60,
                                4.79, 4.135, 4.192

      para 4   4.2
      para 13   4.48
18/94 Gypsy Sites Policy and Unauthorised Camping   3.3, 3.7–3.9, 4.144,
                                  4.145,
                                5.119–5.121,
                                5.125, 5.126,
                                5.154, 7.103,
                                App B

      para 6   5.120, 5.121
      para 8   5.154
      para 9   4.144, 5.122
      para 10   4.144, 5.123
      para 11   4.144, 5.123
      para 12   4.144
      para 13   4.144, 5.123
      para 21   3.7
      para 22   3.8
45/94 Welfare Considerations   5.146
11/95 Use of Conditions in Planning Permissions   4.41, 4.129
2/02 Enforcement Appeals Procedures   4.160

Office of the Deputy Prime Minister Circulars

1/06 Planning for Gypsy and Traveller Caravan Sites 3.9, 3.10, 3.40,
3.52, 4.5, 4.30,
4.31, 4.35, 4.37,
4.49, 4.52, 4.54,
4.62, 4.79–4.81,
4.90, 4.126–4.128,
4.167, 4.192, 4.194,
5.136, 5.139, 5.140,
5.143, 5.174, 6.93,
6.103, 7.109, 9.4,
App B

para 2	4.128
para 3	3.9, 4.32
para 5	4.33
para 12	4.34, 5.139
para 13	3.10
para 15	4.80, 4.130, 8.53
para 33	4.39
para 43	4.40
para 45	4.41, 4.188
para 46	4.42, 4.188
para 47	4.43
para 49	4.52
para 50	4.52
para 51	4.52, 4.53
para 52	4.49
para 53	4.49
para 54	4.43, 4.44
para 56	3.40
para 57	3.52
para 63	4.63, 4.143
para 64	4.44
para 66	4.45
para 68	4.142
para 69	4.134
Annex C para 4	4.45

Welsh Office Circulars

2/94 Gypsy Sites and Planning
(*See also* DoE Circular 1/94) 3.40, 4.2, 4.192
76/94 Gypsy Sites Policy and Unauthorised Camping,
See also DoE Circular 18/94 3.3, 5.119, 5.126,
7.103

78/91 Guidance with Regard to Planning Applications by
Travelling Showpeople 4.69, 4.82

Draft Circular (land use): Planning for Gypsy and Traveller
  Caravan Sites in Wales (Welsh Assembly
  Government, 2006)   4.5, 4.192

Reports

Accommodation needs of Gypsy-Travellers in Wales
  (Niner, Welsh Assembly Government, 2006)   1.3, 1.6, 5.34
Breaking the Barriers – Romani Women and Access to
  Public Health Care (Council of Europe, 2003)   7.79
Common Ground: Equality, Good Race Relations and
  Sites for Gypsies and Irish Travellers (CRE/CEHR,
  2006)   5.170, 8.109, 8.129
Counting Gypsies and Travellers: A Review of the Gypsy
  Caravan Count System (Niner, ODPM, 2004)   3.2
Education for All (The Swans Report) (HMSO, 1985)   7.27
Education of Travelling Children: a survey of Educational
  Provision for Travelling Children (Ofsted, 1996)   7.2, 7.34, 7.53
Gypsies and Travellers: A strategy for the CRE, 2004-2007
  (CRE, 2004)   1.3, 1.6, 1.46, 8.129
Gypsies, Travellers and the Health Service
  (Policy Press, 1997)   1.36
Gypsy caravan sites (House of Commons Research
  Note 92/30)   1.38
Health Status of Gypsies and Travellers in England
  (University of Sheffield School of Health and Related
  Research, 2004)   7.78
Issues in School Enrolment, Attendance, Attainment and
  Support for Learning for Gypsy/Traveller and School-
  aged Children and Young People Based in Scottish
  Local Authority Sites (STEP, 2004)   7.53
Local Authority Gypsy/Traveller Sites in England (Niner,
  ODPM, 2003)   5.59, 6.95
Managing Support for the Attainment of Pupils from
  Minority Ethnic Groups (Ofsted, 2001)   7.15, 7.58
Monitoring the government's response to court judgments
  finding breaches of human rights (JCHR, 2007)   2.85
Moving Forward: the provision of accommodation for
  Travellers and Gypsies (IPPR, 2004)   1.28, 5.169, 7.53,
                                                             7.108
Moving On: The Gypsies and Travellers of Britain
  (University of Hertfordshire Press, 1996)   1.6, 1.50
On the Verge: the Gypsies of England (University of
  Hertfordshire Press, 1990)   1.27, 1.30, 1.45
Provision and Condition of Local Authority Gypsy/Traveller
  Sites in England (Niner, ODPM, 2002)   3.2, 3.49
Provision and Support for Traveller Pupils (Ofsted, 2003) 7.2, 7.58, 7.65, 8.1

Raising the Attainment of Minority Ethnic Pupils (Ofsted,
      1999)   7.2
Review of Service Provision for Gypsies and Travellers
      (National Assembly for Wales, 2003)   4.76, 5.129
   para 10.27   5.129
   para 12.21   5.168
Roma/Gypsies: A European Minority (MRG 1995)   7.77
Scrutiny of bills: third progress report (JCHR, 8th
      Report of Session 2003/04)   2.86
Scrutiny of bills: fourth progress report (JCHR, 10th
      Report of Session 2003/04)   2.86
Single Housing Benefit Control for Gypsy and Traveller
      Sites (DWP Research Report No 379, October 2006)   3.39
Sites for Travellers: a study in five London Boroughs
      (London Race and Housing Research Unit, 1989)   1.37
Travellers and Gypsies: An Alternative Strategy
      (CIEH, 1995)   7.103

Guidance

A Better Road (Derbyshire Gypsy Liaison Group, 2003)   7.84
Aiming High: Raising the Achievement of Gypsy Traveller
      Pupils (DfES, 2003, 1018/2004)   7.5, 7.27
Code of Guidance for Local Authorities on Allocation of
      Accommodation and Homelessness (Wales 2003)—
   para 12.22   6.16
   para 18.40   6.56
Draft Guidance on the Design of Sites for Gypsies and
      Travellers (CLG May 2007)   3.10, 3.44
Draft Guidance on the Management of Gypsy and
      Traveller sites (ODPM/CLG May 2007)   3.14, 3.20, 3.31,
                                                                3.32, 3.35, 3.36,
                                                                3.41, 3.44, 5.141
   para 7.15   5.141
Duty to Promote Race Equality; a Guide for Schools
      (CRE, 2002)   7.51, 8.85
Good Practice Guide, Managing Unauthorised Camping
      (DETR/Home Office)   5.125
Guidance on Managing Unauthorised Camping
      (ODPM, 2004)   4.145, 5.58, 5.60,
                                                                5.113, 5.114,
                                                                5.125–5.128, 5.131,
                                                                5.132, 5.134, 5.135,
                                                                5.143, 5.147, 5.148,
                                                                5.150, 5.157, 5.166,
                                                                6.99, 7.65, 7.103,
                                                                App B

Ch 3	5.127
Ch 7	5.135
para 4.2	5.128, 5.167
para 4.3	5.130
para 4.4	5.166
para 4.8	5.60, 6.99
para 5.4	5.132
para 5.7	5.131, 5.157
para 5.8	5.131, 5.157
para 5.9	5.131, 5.157
para 5.10	5.148, 5.157
para 5.14	5.133
para 5.17	5.133
para 5.20	5.134
para 5.22	5.135
para 6.5	5.113, 5.135
para 6.8	5.149
para 6.9	5.147
para 6.16	5.114
para 7.1	5.135
para 7.3	5.135
Guidance on Managing Unauthorised Camping (Welsh Assembly) (2005)	4.145, 5.126, 5.134, 5.150, 5.166
Ch3	5.127
Ch 7	5.135
para 4.2	5.167
para 5.3	5.132
para 5.6	5.131
para 5.7	5.131, 5.157
para 5.8	5.131, 5.157
para 5.9	5.148, 5.157
para 5.13	5.133
para 5.16	5.133
para 5.19	5.134
para 5.21	5.135
para 6.4	5.135
para 6.7	5.149
para 6.8	5.147
para 7.1	5.135
para 7.2	5.135
Guide to Effective Use of Enforcement Powers –Part 1; Unauthorised Encampments (ODPM/ Home Office) (2006)	4.145, 5.37, 5.125, 5.126, 5.131, 5.132, 5.136, 5.138, 5.140, 5.147, 5.150, 5.166, 5.174, 7.103, App B
para 46	5.150

para 47	5.147
para 48	5.37, 5.48
para 59	5.132
para 61	5.136
para 63	5.147
para 72	5.137
para 77	5.131
para 83	5.138
para 97	5.170
Homelessness Code of Guidance for Local Authorities (CLG 2006)	6.42, 6.56, 6.68
para 3.18	6.16
para 16.38	6.56
Local Authority Agreement: Guidelines for Local Authorities and Referees (ALG, CSLA, LGA, WLGA)	6.83
Local Authorities and Gypsies and Travellers: Guide to Responsibilities and Powers (CLG, 2007)	5.140
Managing Unauthorised Camping: a Good Practice Guide (DOETR/HO, 1998)	7.65
Managing Unauthorised Camping: a Good Practice Guide (DOETR/HO, 2000)	7.65

Planning Policy Guidance Notes

PPG 2 (Green Belts) (1995)	4.48, 4.52, 4.96, 4.98
para 1.3	4.47
para 3	4.94
para 3.1	4.50
para 3.2	4.94
PPG 7 (The Countryside and the Rural Economy) (1992)	4.47
PPG 7 (Sustainable Development in Rural Areas) (1997)	4.47
PPG 18 (Enforcing Planning Control) (1991)	4.142
para 5	4.190
para 15	4.142
para 16	4.142

Planning Policy Statements

PPS1 (Delivering Sustainable Development) (2005)	4.44
PPS9 (Biodiversity and Geological Conservation) (2005)	4.30
PPS25 (Development and Flood Risk) (2006)	4.30

Table of European legislation

Conventions

European Communities Treaty—
   art 13   8.119

European Convention for the Protection of
   Human Rights and Fundamental Freedoms (1950)   2.1, 2.3–2.5, 2.7,
                                                  2.9, 2.10, 2.12, 2.14,
                                                  2.16, 2.19, 2.26,
                                                  2.28, 2.34, 2.37,
                                                  2.44–2.48, 2.56,
                                                  2.58, 2.66–2.68,
                                                  2.73, 2.75, 2.93,
                                                  3.15, 4.104, 4.105,
                                                  4.120, 4.124, 4.174,
                                                  5.1, 5.6, 5.42, 7.6,
                                                  7.7, 7.24, 7.40,
                                                  7.90, 7.91, 8.2,
                                                  8.51, 8.122
      art 2   2.72, 2.72, 7.90
      art 3   2.78, 7.90
      art 6   7.40
      art 6(2)   7.24, 7.40
      art 8   2.5, 2.7, 2.13, 2.15,
                                                  2.16, 2.20–2.23,
                                                  2.28, 2.30, 2.35,
                                                  2.36, 2.39, 2.40,
                                                  2.43, 2.46–2.49,
                                                  2.51–2.53, 2.55,
                                                  2.60–2.62, 2.78,
                                                  2.80–2.82, 2.85,
                                                  2.87, 2.90, 2.91,
                                                  2.93, 3.15–3.17,
                                                  3.21, 3.22, 3.24,
                                                  3.55, 4.79, 4.81,
                                                  4.105, 4.110, 4.112,
                                                  4.113, 4.118,

	4.120–4.122, 4.124, 4.135, 4.138, 4.149, 4.178, 4.180, 5.4, 5.6–5.9, 5.22, 5.49, 5.50, 5.166, 6.93, 7.100
art 8(1)	2.7, 2.8, 2.15–2.17,
2.20, 2.22, 2.40, 4.107	
art 8(2)	2.8, 2.16, 2.26, 2.57,
3.24, 4.124, 5.5, 5.8, 5.9	
art 9	7.58
art 10	7.58
art 11	2.92, 2.93
art 14	2.7, 2.9, 2.10, 2.67, 2.68, 2.70, 2.72, 2.73, 2.75, 2.76, 2.78–2.81, 2.85–2.87, 2.90–2.93, 3.15, 4.120–4.122, 4.135, 4.149, 7.16, 8.51
European Convention for the Protection of Human Rights and Fundamental Freedoms Protocol 1—	
art 1	2.49
art 2	2.12, 2.78, 2.94, 7.6, 7.7, 7.10, 7.16, 7.40, 7.43
European Social Charter (1961, revised 1996)—	
art 13	7.67
Framework Convention for the Protection of National Minorities, Strasbourg, 1/2/1195, Council of Europe Doc ETS 157	2.35, 4.109, 8.123–8.127
art 4	8.126, 8.128
art 5	8.126, 8.128
art 6	8.126
art 15	8.126

Directives

Dir 2000/43/EC (Race Equality Directive) 2000 OJ L180/22	4.67, 8.6, 8.119, 8.121, 8.122
art 14	8.120, 8.122

Abbreviations

ACAS	Advisory, Conciliation and Arbitration Service
ACPO	Association of Chief Police Officers
AHRA 1990	Access to Health Records Act 1990
AMRA 1988	Access to Medical Reports Act 1988
AONB	Area of Outstanding National Beauty
CA	Court of Appeal
CA 1989	Children Act 1989
CEHR	Commission for Equality and Human Rights
CJPOA 1994	Criminal Justice and Public Order Act 1994
CLG	Department for Communities and Local Government
CLS	Community Legal Service
CPR	Civil Procedure Rules
CRE	Commission for Racial Equality
CSA 1968	Caravan Sites Act 1968
CSCDA 1960	Caravan Sites and Control of Development Act 1960
DDA 1995	Disability Discrimination Act 1995
DfES	Department for Education and Skills
DFG	Disabled facilities grant
DoE	Department of the Environment
DPA 1998	Data Protection Act 1998
DPD	Development Plan Document
EA 1996	Education Act 1996
EA 2002	Education Act 2002
ECHR	European Convention on Human Rights
ECtHR	European Court of Human Rights
EIA 2006	Education and Inspection Act 2006
EqA 2006	Equality Act 2006
GP	General practitioner
GPDO 1995	Town and Country Planning (General Permitted Development) Order 1995

GTAA	Gypsy and Traveller Accommodation Assessment
GTSG	Gypsy and Traveller Sites Grant
HA 1985	Housing Act 1985
HA 1996	Housing Act 1996
HA 2002	Homelessness Act 2002
HA 2004	Housing Act 2004
HL	House of Lords
HRA 1998	Human Rights Act 1998
LDS	Local Development Scheme
LEA	Local education authority
LPA	Local planning authority
LSC	Legal Services Commission
MHA 1983	Mobile Homes Act 1983
NATT	National Association of Teachers of Travellers
NHS	National Health Service
NHSA 1977	National Health Service Act 1977
ODPM	Office of the Deputy Prime Minister
Ofsted	Office for Standards in Education
PCPA 2004	Planning and Compulsory Purchase Act 2004
PCT	Primary care trust
PD	Practice Direction
PPG	Planning policy guidance
PPS	Planning policy statement
RPB	Regional Planning Body
RRA 1976	Race Relations Act 1976
RR(A)A 2000	Race Relations (Amendment) Act 2000
RSS	Regional Spatial Strategy
SENDA 2001	Special Educational Needs and Disability Act 2001
SHA	Strategic health authority
SSFA 1998	School Standards and Framework Act 1998
SSSI	Site of Special Scientific Interest
TCPA 1990	Town and Country Planning Act 1990
TSN	Temporary Stop Notice

CHAPTER 1

Introduction

1.1   Introduction

1.6   Who are the Gypsies and Travellers?

1.8   Historical context

1.17   Racialising Gypsy people

1.22   Irish Travellers

1.29   The end of the road for nomadism?

1.32   Defining Gypsies in law

1.34   Accommodation for Gypsies and Travellers

1.39   New Travellers

1.46   Culture

1.48   Outline of the book

Introduction

1.1   In 2003, BBC News Online reported:

> Police ... arrested a total of six men on suspicion of inciting racial hatred after a bonfire society torched an effigy of a caravan with a gypsy family painted on the side. The tableau, which was burnt at Firle Bonfire Society's celebrations in East Sussex, caused outrage because of the controversial display. The society denies any claims the caravan, which had PIKEY written on the side ... was designed to be racist.[1]

1.2   The scene described above could easily have been taken from a medieval European genocide, but it was not: the caravan-torching incident took place following problems in the area after a group of Travellers had set up camp near the village. The caravan in question was fortunately not occupied by real people but was made from plywood and adorned to look like a stereotypical modern Gypsy caravan, complete with paintings of Gypsy and Traveller children on the side.

1.3   The Firle bonfire incident sparked a national debate in the media about the treatment of our Gypsy and Traveller population, and about the racism they have experienced for many hundreds of years and which continues to the present day. The Commission for Racial Equality (CRE), subsequent to the Firle incident, launched a four-year strategy[2] aimed specifically at this group. Quoting from a MORI poll conducted in England, the strategy states:

> ... more than one-third of adults who took part admitted to being personally prejudiced against Gypsies and Travellers. This was greater than the levels of prejudice reported towards lesbians and gay men, other ethnic minorities and people with disabilities.[3]

1.4   Romani Gypsies and Irish Travellers are accepted as being racial groups for the purposes of the Race Relations Act 1976 and subsequent amend-

---

1   BBC News Online, 'Six arrests over burnt gypsy effigy', 11 November 2003.

2   *Gypsies and Travellers: a strategy for the CRE, 2004–2007* (CRE, 2004).

3   *Gypsies and Travellers: a strategy for the CRE, 2004–2007*, p6. Reference should also be made to the severely negative comments about Gypsies and Travellers made by Michael Howard MP, then leader of the Conservative party, during the 2005 General Election campaign and the vitriolic campaign in the *Sun* newspaper at the same time under the heading 'Stamp on the Camps' – see the discussion in Clark and Greenfields, *Here to stay: the Gypsies and Travellers of Britain*, University of Hertfordshire Press, 2006, pp1–3. Additionally, in 2006, a group of Irish Travellers on a site in Tamworth were attacked by local residents, solely because they were on an unauthorised encampment, and several caravans were burnt to the ground. This matter, at the date of publication of this book, is subject to ongoing criminal proceedings.

ments.[4] Discrimination against them – as well as inciting racial hatred towards them – is prohibited by law in the United Kingdom. Those involved in the effigy burning defended their actions by saying that their anger was not aimed at the Gypsies and Travellers themselves, but at the local authorities, whose lack of action in providing sufficient sites for Gypsies and Travellers in the area inevitably led to more unsatisfactory locations being occupied. Gypsies and Travellers in their turn argue that the lack of authorised sites means that they have no option but to stop where they can, before being moved on again to some other village or town where another eviction will confront them in the near future.[5]

1.5   The Firle bonfire incident illustrates some of the issues which we will be considering in this book: the implications of the lack of lawful sites for Gypsies and Travellers; the role of the local authorities, the police and the media; and how the law operates in relation to this minority group. However, before we can properly understand the contemporary treatment of Gypsies and Travellers in the United Kingdom, there is a need to place that matter within some kind of historical context. The remainder of this introduction tries to provide just such a context, starting with a brief examination of the vexed question of who the Gypsies and Travellers actually are.

Who are the Gypsies and Travellers?

1.6   The CRE has estimated that:

> [o]f the 200,000 to 300,000 Travellers in England, by far the largest group are Romani Gypsies, who have been in England since the early 16th century. Romani Gypsies have been recognised as a racial group since 1988 ... Irish Travellers, who have been travelling in England as a distinct social group since the 1800s, received legal recognition as a racial group in England and Wales in 2000 ...[6]

There are two other ethnic groups of Travellers in the United Kingdom, the Welsh Gypsy Travellers (or Kale)[7] and Scottish Gypsy

---

4 See chapter 8, below, for an analysis of race relations legislation.
5 See, for example, 'Decent homes for all', pamphlet, Traveller Law Reform Coalition, 2004.
6 *Gypsies and Travellers: a strategy for the CRE,* 2004–2007 (CRE 2004) p3, note 2.
7 There is considerable controversy among Gypsy and Traveller academics and writers about the existence of Kale as a separate type of Traveller group. However, the report by Niner, *Accommodation needs of Gypsy-Travellers in Wales,* Welsh Assembly Government, 2006, differentiates Welsh Gypsies as a separate group from English Gypsies (see, for example, at paragraph 1.8).

Travellers, each of whom have separate origins and histories. Since this book deals with the law as it relates to England and Wales, and given the lack of information on the Kale,[8] the following brief historical overview will concentrate on Romani Gypsies, Irish Travellers and New Travellers.[9]

1.7 Most people have some idea of what is meant by terms such as 'Gypsies' and 'New Age' Travellers. In contemporary, anti-nomadic discourse, 'real Gypsies' occupy the top rung of a sliding scale of authenticity, while 'New Age' Travellers, denied this status, are generally portrayed as pseudo-vagrants, criminals or the dispossessed underclass. While it is not denied that fundamental differences do exist between these groups (particularly in language and customs), the similarities between them – both in terms of their treatment by the state and (relatedly) their economic nomadism – are often overlooked.

Historical context

1.8 The nomads who came to be known as 'Gypsies' were 'the first ... Asian immigrants to Europe'[10] and had migrated from India around 1000 AD, with the first of three main waves arriving in Britain four or five centuries ago (the second at the end of the 19th century and the third in the 1960s). These early Gypsies had an itinerant economy and specialised in metal working, fortune telling, craft-making and musicianship.[11] Their preference for self-employment soon earned them the antipathy of some of the most powerful groups in society at the time, as such economic independence was perceived as a rejection of the master-servant relationship inherent in the Guilds' monopoly of production, as well as 'a carnivalesque incitement to disorder'.[12]

1.9 There is some controversy around why they are called Gypsies, with many claiming that European states believed they had come from

8 See, for example, the discussion in Kenrick and Clark, *Moving on: the Gypsies and Travellers of Britain*, University of Hertfordshire Press, 1996, pp38–39.
9 'New Traveller' is the term preferred by this (non-ethnic) group of Travellers themselves, though we will refer to 'New Age Traveller' where it is relevant in the historical context. See Kenrick and Clark, *Moving On*, pp117–136.
10 Acton, *Gypsy Politics and Social Change*, Routledge, Kegan Paul, 1974, p27.
11 Many Gypsy groups reflect the predominant occupation in which they are involved. For example, the Kalderas, or copperworkers, from whom the word 'cauldron' has been appropriated in English. Liegeois, *Gypsies and Travellers: socio-cultural data, socio-political data*, Council of Europe, 1987, p39.
12 Stewart, *The Puzzle of Roma Persistence*, University of Hertfordshire Press, 1997, p85.

Egypt, perhaps fleeing religious persecution, and that 'Gypsy' is an adaptation of 'Egyptian':

> These long-haired tent-dwellers who appeared among villages and town-dwellers, defied classification, and they were given diverse names connected with an imagined origin or an imperfectly understood identity.[13]

1.10   Their dark skin colour[14] provided a ready focus for discrimination and the 'race' dimension is clearly evident in popular mythology of the time. The subsequent stereotyping of Gypsies invoked fears of the 'Black Heathen' alongside themes of idleness, indiscipline and depravity, themes which persist to this day. Thus, the historical oppression of Gypsy people can be seen to have ethnic, racial and class bases. These three factors are not mutually exclusive in Gypsy history; on the contrary, they are mutually reinforcing. Indeed, the three overlap to the extent that it is impossible to be sure where the influence of one ends and the others begin. Any such obvious deviations from established norms were subject to the most severe social and penal sanctions at the time and Gypsy nomads were particularly vulnerable to such punishment. In this way, their economic skills (which were a fundamental part of their nomadic identity) set them at odds with the dominant ideology of work in both feudal society (as 'masterless men'[15]) and in later capitalist societies (through their continued resistance to proletarianisation).

1.11   Within a short period of time after their arrival, Gypsies became seen as lazy, dirty, parasitic deviants and subject to repressive legislation aimed at expelling and, ultimately, exterminating the Gypsy population. The first such law aimed explicitly against them was Henry VIII's Proclamation of 1530:

> Diverse and many outlandish people calling themselves Egyptians, have gone from place to place and used great and subtle means to deceive the people, bearing them in hand that they by palmistry could tell men's and women's fortunes ... and have deceived the people of their money and have also committed many heinous felonies and robberies.[16]

1.12   Initially, the punishment for being an 'Egyptian' at this time was banishment, but the state had trouble identifying exactly who was and

---

13 Liegeois, *Gypsies and Travellers*, p13.
14 Walvin, *There ain't no black in the Union Jack*, Routledge, 1973, makes the case that British people have 'always found blackness a peculiar and important point of difference', and this is also relevant when considering anti-nomadism.
15 Fraser, *The Gypsies*, Blackwell, 1995, p35.
16 22 Henry VIII c10 of 1530.

who was not a 'Gypsy', as a great many indigenous, dispossessed people roamed the land during the Tudor period. Then, in 1553 Queen Mary passed the Egyptians Act which decreed that the death penalty should be imposed on anyone who was a Gypsy, or anyone 'who shall become of the fellowship or company of Egyptians'. The offence remained on the statute books for over two centuries in Britain.

1.13   The anti-Gypsy ideology combined with the anti-vagrant ideology of the time, a fact clearly reflected in the language of the other draconian legislation, such as the 1554 'Order For the Avoiding of All Doubts and Ambiguities' which re-asserted the intended victims of the legislation as:

> all such sturdy and false vagabonds of that sort living only upon the spoil of the simple people [including those] in any company or fellowship of vagabonds commonly called or calling themselves 'Aegyptians'.

These laws had a populist reflection in contemporary folk tales and mythology which demonstrate that, as early as the 16th century, the stereotype was firmly fixed in the sedentary imagination that Gypsies were work-shy parasites worthy only of contempt:

> The local people, disconcerted by such unclassifiable originality in dress, language, way of life and possible mode of association, accused them of witchcraft, banditry and of spreading disease. In this way there grew up the dark and fearful image of a nomad with a soul as black as his skin, damned for all time in the eyes of a frightened society.[17]

1.14   It is important to underline the fact that the persecution of Gypsy people was not restricted to Britain but was a pan-European affair: during the 16th, 17th and 18th centuries, laws were passed in every single European state to control the 'Gypsy problem' in similarly repressive ways:

> For the next 200 years ... there is a depressing uniformity about the response of most European powers to the presence of Gypsies. They continued to be viewed as criminals simply because of their position in society and, on top of that, the special racial prejudices remained, together with religious hostility towards what was seen as their heathenish practices and sorcery. More generally, they suffered from the tide of repression that was arising everywhere against vagabondage and the 'sturdy beggar'. The authorities could not come to terms with masterless men, with no fixed domicile and useless as a workforce: in their eyes, that status was in itself an aberration, at odds with the established order, and had to be put right by coercion

---

17 Liegeois, *Gypsies and Travellers*, p44.

and pressure of the gyves.[18] Yet when the Gypsies offered legitimate services to the settled population, they were at risk from the ill-will attracted by transient traders and artisans who violated local monopolies, or from the abhorrence that occupations such as peddler or tinker or entertainer aroused among those in power.[19]

1.15 For the Gypsies who had migrated to Britain (as well as indigenous Travellers) commerce formed an important dimension of their economic survival, and while they may have strived to remain culturally independent of their sedentary neighbours, the fact that they traded goods and services with sedentary society meant that economic interdependence became (and has remained) a feature of Gypsy life. Not only did nomadic groups hawk the wares they had made (or bought) in towns and villages which they passed on the road, but they frequently made their nomadic habits coincide with traditional horse and harvest fairs and other meeting places. Here, not only were their skills in trade and craftsmanship in demand, but their musical and entertainment abilities could also earn them a living. By the 19th century, Gypsies had become familiar sights at these fairs, and many would arrange their annual travel routes so that they could attend fairs following the harvest, thus making a living from both:

> Fairs and race-meetings formed a major part of the Gypsy calendar, giving some structure to the timing and direction of their travels, and providing a meeting place for families and friends as well as allowing them to engage in the serious business of horse-dealing ... Once the harvests were in, the movement from town to country was reversed.[20]

1.16 Once again, it can be seen how their nomadism (while fundamental to their identity) is permeated with economic dimensions, primarily in terms of the historical bases of their persecution, but, also, in the fact that the patterns of their nomadism in Britain evolved in relation to the availability of viable economic niches in the wider society. This is demonstrated by the fact that many Gypsies moved with and for the harvest as agricultural workers and used these routes to ply their other trades, for example, at the fairs. These sites in turn became a focus of cultural celebration for Gypsy and Traveller people themselves, thus reinforcing the economic centrality of nomadism for their identity:

> For the Gypsy and the Traveller travelling has many functions. It permits social organisation, it sanctions adaptability and flexibility and makes the

18 'Gyves' meaning shackles or fetters (*The Chambers Dictionary*, 1994).
19 Fraser, *The Gypsies*, p129.
20 Fraser, *The Gypsies*, p110.

practice of trading possible ... Apart from its social function, travel has an equally important economic role. This is evident for certain occupations: nomadic trades observe the dates of holidays and fairs, cattle dealers those of cattle markets, agricultural workers the season for picking fruit, grapes and olives [in Europe]. Generally speaking, the essential characteristic of the occupations practised is self-employment, which in turn necessitates extensive prospecting with frequent journeying, sometimes to distant parts in search of custom, for artisan or trader, for artist or merchant. Gypsies and Travellers cling to their occupational independence, which has so far guaranteed their adaptability.[21]

Racialising Gypsy people

1.17   Well into the 19th century, the persecution of Gypsy people by the populace at large was still encouraged by many European states. For example, in Holland, 'Gypsy hunts' were organised on a regional basis, and not only was it an offence to be a Gypsy, but it was also perfectly lawful to kill one. The racial dimension in this persecution is revealed in the vocabulary of intolerance used against them. Both the Dutch and Italian languages share the simile 'as black as a Gypsy'.[22]

1.18   In the 19th century, a new stereotype, the 'real Romani' or 'genuine Gypsy' evolved, alongside contemporary concerns with racial purity. In time, the pseudo-science of racial hygiene would come to concur with ill-informed 'Gypsyologists' and posit the existence of small, racially pure groups of 'genuine Gypsies' in the midst of a population of congenitally degenerate subproletariat people who had taken to the travelling life in order to avoid work, taxes and other social responsibilities.[23] In other words, the 'Gypsy problem' had become overtly racialised:

> From now onwards alongside the stereotype dirty, dishonest, child-stealing villain we have the dark, handsome, violin-playing lover-Gypsy, a 'noble savage', camping in the woodlands and living off the Earth ... It is allowed that there exists somewhere ... the true Romanies ... racially pure, clean in habits, noble in spirit. But they are never found; they are, of course, a phantom people. Parliamentary debates, in Britain and elsewhere, contain many references to these imaginary beings.[24]

---

21 Liegeois, *Gypsies and Travellers*, pp52–53, note 13.
22 Kenrick and Puxon, *The destiny of Europe's Gypsies*, Chatto-Heinemann, 1972, p113.
23 Kenrick and Puxon, *The destiny of Europe's Gypsies*, p54.
24 Kenrick and Puxon, *The destiny of Europe's Gypsies*, p30 and p41.

1.19 The Nazi Holocaust provides the clearest example of how the articulation of this ancient hatred of nomads became translated into a national policy of racial hygiene. Ethnic Gypsies became the target of genocidal policies under the Third Reich and half a million of them lost their lives precisely because they were Gypsies. While the methods of mass destruction employed by the Nazis may have been unprecedented,[25] the targets of their repression were not. What was unique was that Nazi ideology was able to provide an inescapable biological racism which legitimised existing prejudices.

1.20 For example, the scientist in charge of 'Race Hygiene and Population Biology' at the Reich Department of Health, Dr Ritter, conducted 'research' on Gypsy genealogy, which ultimately formed part of the legitimation for the extermination policies which followed. His findings confirmed his belief that:

> Most gypsies are not gypsies at all, but rather the products of matings with the German criminal asocial subproletariat ... More than 90 per cent of so-called 'gypsies' are of mixed-blood. It has been demonstrated that gypsies, in their racial crosses in our homeland, have mated predominantly with Yenisch [non-Gypsy Travellers] and with asocial criminal elements and that this has lead to the formation of a Yenisch-gypsy lumpenproletariat which costs the state enormous sums in welfare costs ... The gypsy question can only be considered solved when the main body of asocial and good-for-nothing gypsy individuals of mixed-blood is collected together in large labour camps and kept working there, and when the further breeding of this population of mixed-blood is stopped once and for all.[26]

1.21 Thus the ideology of Gypsy romanticism was contrasted with the savage treatment of nomads in the real world. What the myth of the 'real Romani' legitimated, both in Britain and in Europe, was the persecution of Gypsies and Travellers who did not conform to the stereotypical notions of Gypsyhood held by the dominant society. As Okely puts it 'real Gypsies are those who best fit the stereotype of the observer'.[27] An important legacy from this period is that it remains a continuing 'sedentary obsession'[28] to attempt to distinguish these 'genuine Gypsies' from other nomads, and the state's attempts to divide nomads along these arbitrary lines continues to today. To take just one example, in a radio interview in 1999, the then Home Secretary, Jack Straw MP, sought to draw a distinction between genuine Romani

25 See Bauman, *Modernity and the Holocaust*, Polity Press, 1989.
26 Cited in Muller-Hill, *Murderous Science*, Methuesen, New York, 1988, p69.
27 Okely, *The Traveller-Gypsies* (Cambridge University Press, 1983) p27.
28 Fraser, *The Gypsies*, Blackwell, 1995, p27.

Gypsies and 'travellers masquerading as law-abiding gypsies',[29] when referring to an incident involving Travellers in the West Midlands.

Irish Travellers

1.22   There is a common misconception that Irish Travellers originated as the 'dispossessed' of the 'Great Famine' in the mid-19th century whereas, in fact, there is reference to Travellers in Ireland long before the Romanies arrived on the shores of Britain. O'Riain states:

> There is evidence which points to the existence from the fifth century of indigenous nomadic groups in Ireland. In the twelfth century the name Tynkler or Tynker was given to a group of nomads who for a long time had maintained a separate identity, social organisation and dialect.[30]

1.23   Irish Travellers and Romani Gypsies share the reliance on 'self-employment' and each has a distinct language (Shelta and Romani, respectively).[31] However, Irish Travellers have had a different experience of prejudice and discrimination. It has been made clear above how the prejudice against Romani Gypsies in Britain has continued unabated since they first came there. For Irish Travellers, the prejudice increased over time and now continues unabated. An important example of latter-day prejudice within Ireland is the very presumption that Travellers first appeared at the time of the Great Famine. In this way, they can be seen as 'failed settled people'[32] rather than as a distinct ethnic group.

1.24   A large part of this different experience can be traced back to the colonial experience in Ireland and the history of mass emigration. MacLaughlin states:

> [U]nlike Elizabethan England ... those forced from relatively prestigious positions in Gaelic Ireland into vagrancy and mendicancy in colonial Ireland often retained the respect of the native dispossessed well into the eighteenth century.[33]

---

29   *Guardian*, 'Scattergun Straw', 20 August 1999.

30   O'Riain, *Solidarity with Travellers*, Roadside Books, Dublin, 2000, p8.

31   These languages have different origins. Shelta is derived from Gaelic and Romani from Sanskrit.

32   McDonagh, 'Origins of the Travelling People' in *Travellers: citizens of Ireland*, Parish of the Travelling People, Dublin, 2000, p22.

33   MacLaughlin, *Travellers and Ireland: whose country, whose history?*, Cork University Press, 1995, p11.

1.25   Yet that 'respect' was not to last:

> In the case of Ireland, the radical disavowal of 'tinkers'[34] and Travellers probably occurred much later than elsewhere in western Europe. It was particularly exacerbated by the decimation of plebeian agrarian society from the late nineteenth century onwards and the growth of a bourgeois Irish nationalism and clericalism after the Famine.[35]

1.26   Paradoxically, the Irish nationalism of the 19th century and the (eventual) independence of the south of Ireland in the 20th century led not to the inclusion but to the exclusion of Irish Travellers, who were subject to the same assumptions, prejudices and mythology as beset their nomadic counterparts in Britain:

> Nomadism on the other hand, and Travelling communities within Ireland, were looked on as social anomalies, relics from a 'barbarous' past that was best forgotten because they represented all that was backward, unstable and evil about Irish society.[36]

1.27   The experience that Irish Travellers did share with the poor in Ireland was emigration. Thus, they arrived in Britain:

> Although Irish emigration to England began several centuries ago, the first reliable report of Irish Travellers dates from 1850.[37]

1.28   Once in Britain, Irish Travellers experienced the same prejudice that the Romani Gypsies had long been experiencing and that the Irish Travellers had already experienced in Ireland itself. Without repeating the history of persecution and prejudice borne by Gypsies in Britain (as outlined above) the story can be brought up to date by reference to an incident that occurred in the same year, 2003, as the Firle bonfire:

> [T]hat year saw what most believed from the evidence was the racially motivated murder of Johnny Delaney, a teenage [Irish] Traveller, who was attacked in the vicinity of an unauthorised encampment, where members of his family lived and who he had been visiting. In court proceedings the jury were technically unable to identify a racial motive and punish the perpetrators accordingly.[38]

---

34   Nowadays a derogatory name for Irish Travellers.
35   MacLaughlin, *Travellers and Ireland*, p15.
36   MacLaughlin, *Travellers and Ireland*, p28.
37   Kenrick and Bakewell, *On the verge: the Gypsies of England*, University of Hertfordshire Press, 1990, p10.
38   Crawley, *Moving forward: the provision of accommodation for Travellers and Gypsies*, The Institute for Public Policy Research, 2004, p60.

The end of the road for nomadism?

1.29 Stewart[39] argues that successive generations have prematurely rung the funeral knell for nomadism and have prophesied its impending destruction. We have been told that Gypsies in particular are anachronistic throwbacks whose allegedly pre-industrial employment patterns – such as fruit-picking, peg-making and horse-trading – have been made increasingly obsolete through technological and social change:

> Every age, ours as much as its predecessors, believes it will be the last to be blessed (or cursed) by the presence of Gypsies. Well-wishers and hostile commentators, romantics and cynics alike are of fixed opinion that the 'wanderers of the world' have at last been 'domesticated', their way of life finally outmoded and that the 'time of the Gypsies' has run out ... In truth, Gypsies all over Europe have been remarkably successful in preserving their way of life, adapting to changed conditions in order to remain the same.[40]

1.30 As Kenrick and Bakewell observe:

> [For Gypsy people] work is not an end in itself but a means of earning money while staying independent. Independence requires mobility and adaptability. The Gypsies ... have adapted their trades successfully to growing industrialisation. [They] rarely have one single occupation but practice a combination of trades, such as scrap-collecting, tarmacking, hawking, fortune-telling and so on. These trades also require minimum equipment which enables them to stay mobile ... Work patterns distinguish the Gypsy and Travelling people from other groups. There may be migrant workers but rarely do these remain as independent of wage labour as the Gypsies.[41]

1.31 Fraser provides a good example of some of the ways in which social change has been absorbed by Gypsies and Travellers:

> In the face of urbanisation, industrialisation and other European pressures, Gypsies showed themselves able to maintain their autonomy by exploiting opportunities created by the dominant system. They resisted temptations to go over to wage-labour, as so many others were doing. Most – even when settled – seem to have clung tenaciously to some ideal of community and independence and self-employment. In Britain, urbanisation did not prove incompatible with maintaining a degree of nomadism ... they moved from village to town where necessary and abandoned old trades in favour of new activities more suited to the times, but without

39 Stewart, *The puzzle of Roma persistence*.
40 Stewart, *The puzzle of Roma persistence*, p82.
41 Kenrick and Bakewell, *On the verge*, pp14–15.

compromising their freedom, their ethnic identity or their occupational and residential flexibility ... A less resilient culture might have succumbed completely; the Gypsies did not.[42]

Defining Gypsies in law

1.32 The relative influence of race, ethnicity and class in the history of the treatment of Gypsy and Traveller people has a contemporary reflection in the sometimes contradictory ways in which the British state has attempted to define who is and who is not a Gypsy in law. For the purposes of the Race Relations Act (RRA) 1976, for example, Gypsies are defined, by reference to belonging to a 'racial group' through birth or marriage and thus by ethnic criteria. In planning law, however, Gypsies (sometimes referred to as 'gipsies' in statutes and reported cases) are defined as:

> persons of a nomadic habit of life, whatever their race or origin[43]

and the law is concerned with how the Gypsy or Traveller concerned makes their living, rather than the circumstances of their birth.

1.33 The Highways Act 1959 created an offence that could only be committed by Gypsies or Travellers, that of living on or hawking goods on the roadside. The courts, convinced that parliament could not have intended to explicitly discriminate against ethnic Gypsies or Travellers, decided that the term 'Gypsy' must be concerned with one's lifestyle rather than ethnicity.[44] Similarly, the definition contained in the Caravan Sites and Control of Development Act (CSCDA) 1960 was that 'Gypsies' were 'persons of nomadic habit of life, whatever their race or origin'.[45]

Accommodation for Gypsies and Travellers

1.34 In one of the leading cases involving Gypsies and Travellers (relating to the Criminal Justice and Public Order Act (CJPOA)1994), *R v Lincolnshire CC ex p Atkinson; R v Wealden DC ex p Wales and Stratford*,[46]

---

42 Fraser, *The Gypsies*, p93.
43 For a full discussion of the definition of 'Gypsy' for planning law purposes, see chapter 4 at paras 4.67–4.84, below.
44 *Mills v Cooper* [1967] 2 All ER 100.
45 Caravan Sites and Control of Development Act 1960 s24(8). This analysis is continued further at para 1.38 et seq, below.
46 (1996) 8 Admin LR 529; [1997] JPL 65.

Sedley J (as he then was) gave a useful potted history of the post-war legislative history:

> It is relevant to situate this new and in some ways draconic legislation [CJPOA 1994] in its context. For centuries the commons of England provided lawful stopping places for people whose way of life was or had become nomadic. Enough common land had survived the centuries of enclosure to make this way of life still sustainable, but by section 23 of the Caravan Sites and Control of Development Act 1960 local authorities were given the power to close the commons to travellers. This they proceeded to do with great energy, but made no use of the concomitant power given to them by section 24 of the same Act to open caravan sites to compensate for the closure of the commons. By the Caravan Sites Act 1968, therefore, Parliament legislated to make the section 24 power a duty, resting in rural areas on county councils rather than district councils (although the latter continued to possess the power to open sites). For the next quarter of a century there followed a history of non-compliance with the duties imposed by the Act of 1968, marked by a series of decisions of this court holding local authorities to be in breach of their statutory duty; but to apparently little practical effect. The default powers vested in central government, to which the court was required to defer, were rarely if ever used. The culmination of the tensions underlying the history of non-compliance was the enactment of the sections of the Act of 1994 ... There followed, in section 80(1), the wholesale repeal of the material part, Part II, of the Caravan Sites Act 1968.[47]

1.35   The government's position on the repeal of the duty to provide sites by the CJPOA 1994 was that, henceforth, Gypsy and Traveller sites would be provided solely through private endeavour by Gypsies and Travellers themselves utilising the planning system.[48] With no duty in place, public site provision effectively ground to a halt and the number of pitches available began to decline.[49] Private site provision, in the meantime, has manifestly failed to keep up with the demand and Gypsies and Travellers have continued to encounter enormous hurdles in their way when trying to establish private sites.

1.36   The cumulative effect of poverty and the steady diminution of stopping places has impacted on Britain's nomadic populations in serious ways. Allied with the loss of traditional sites has been a concomitant decline in the health of Gypsies and Travellers,[50] due to the extremely poor environmental conditions that often exist on unauthorised sites,

---

47   *Atkinson* (1996) 8 Admin LR 529 at 533–534.
48   See chapter 4, below.
49   See chapter 3, below.
50   See chapter 7, below.

most of which will be without basic services, such as water, refuse collection or sanitation. An analysis of research conducted on Gypsy and Traveller health found:

> high levels of perinatal mortality, still-birth and infant mortality. Traveller children are between one-and-a-half and two times more likely to die in the first year of life than the children of settled communities. Generally ... travelling families [are] seriously disadvantaged in health and healthcare ...[51]

1.37 A significant element of the Travelling community has also been impoverished, both through a reduction in trade with settled society and through the loss of traditional stopping places. Even for those on official sites, restrictive licence conditions have often denied Gypsies and Travellers the opportunity of remaining economically active.[52]

1.38 This brings us back to the question of defining 'Gypsies' at law, since to qualify for provision under the relevant (and now repealed) Part II of the Caravan Sites Act (CSA) 1968, Gypsies and Travellers had to demonstrate that they were within the legal definition of 'Gypsy'. Over the years the courts have continued to emphasise the centrality of economy over ethnicity. The association in the sedentary mind between Gypsies and this type of economic nomadism has now become so strong that such travel has become the essential element of Gypsy status in law. The implications of institutionalising the legal definition of 'Gypsy' in this way remain unresolved. This brings us to a consideration of 'New Travellers', since, arguably, it was this group which the definition was ultimately intended to exclude from provision.

New Travellers

> Many people feel that the law operates unfairly in that it was intended to support the traditional way of life of Romani peoples but has been used by several groups of hippies, drug-takers and law-breakers who drive around in old cars and vans ...[53]

1.39 Quite in what way these 'hippies' were supposed to have used the CSA 1968 (which introduced a duty on certain local authorities to provide sites) is not made clear by the authors of the above statement, but it is

---

51 Hawes, *Gypsies, Travellers and the Health Service*, Policy Press, 1997.

52 See, for example, Hyman, *Sites for Travellers: a study in five London boroughs*, London Race and Housing Research Unit, 1989, p12.

53 Barclay, *Gypsy caravan sites*, House of Commons Research Note 92/30.

untenable to suggest that any significant number of them benefited from site provision under the Act.[54] Local authorities had failed to provide anywhere near adequate provision for traditional Gypsies and Travellers, let alone this new type of Traveller – who were, if anything, even more despised than traditional (ethnic) Gypsies and Travellers. Elsewhere, various arms of the state reinforced the view that the 'hippies' should be treated differently than traditional nomads:

> The situation has become more complex in recent years with the emergence of groups who do not wish to use the sites that are provided, may travel in large numbers, may not be nomadic and for whom the 1968 Act provisions may not have been provided. These may include some of the group colloquially known as New Age Travellers.[55]

1.40   The meaning of the word 'nomadic' was at the centre of a court case in 1992 in which South Hams District Council in Devon argued that a group of 'New Age' Travellers encamped in their area were not Gypsies and were therefore owed no duty regarding site provision.[56] The court confirmed the economic meaning of nomadism, namely that to be a statutory Gypsy one's travel must be related to how one makes a living:

> ... the definition of 'gypsies' [in CSCDA 1960 s24(8) and CSA 1968 s16] imports the requirement that there should be some recognisable connection between the wandering or travelling and the means whereby the persons concerned make or seek their livelihood. Persons, or individuals, who move from place to place merely as the fancy may take them and without any connection between the movement and their means of livelihood fall outside these statutory definitions.[57]

1.41   This case established that Gypsy status could be gained and lost depending on the lifestyle of the individual Gypsy or Traveller. As such the case failed to exclude 'New Age' Travellers as a group – as many local authorities had hoped – but rather established a somewhat paradoxical situation wherein a Romani Gypsy or Irish Traveller by birth living on a static caravan site could well fall outside the definition. An additional implication is that some New Travellers clearly might qualify as statutory 'Gypsies', provided their travel had an economic purpose.

---

54   There are currently believed to be two New Traveller local authority sites in England and none in Wales. The two sites were established after the repeal of the duty to provide sites – information from the Travellers' Advice Team at the Community Law Partnership. No official statistics are available.

55   Consultation Paper, *Reform of the Caravan Sites Act*, Department of the Environment (DoE), March 1992.

56   *R v South Hams DC ex p Gibb* [1994] 4 All ER 1012.

57   [1994] 4 All ER 1012 at 1012.

1.42   Kenrick and Puxon discern a historical pattern here:

> When the racial theories are swept aside, we find that the detractors have
> once more changed ground. Once again, they assert that the majority of
> people who call themselves gypsies are not gypsies at all. They are social
> misfits, the drop-outs of society who have taken up a pseudo-gypsy way of
> life to avoid social responsibilities, taxes and other inconveniences of
> modern life.[58]

1.43   As Fraser has stated:

> If excuse is needed for having plunged here into such legal niceties, it
> lies in the fact that we shall find the question of Gypsy identity has attended
> their passage through Europe ever since they first arrived, and these legal
> debates in the English courts serve very well to illustrate an important
> dilemma which refuses to go away in any discussion of Gypsies. Is it the
> way of life that is paramount in definition?[59]

1.44   While the media-hype around what became known (to everyone apart
from themselves) as 'New Age Travellers' focused heavily on one particular group, the 'Peace Convoy', even by the early 1980s there were
many 'alternative' Travelling groups staging festivals and fairs throughout the summer months. As well as performing as jugglers, musi-
cians, clowns and fire-eaters, and trading things they had made or
bought, many of these New Travellers also focused their nomadism
around the fruit-picking and the fairs, and, like the Gypsies before
them, their rejection of fixed-wage labour attracted particular prejudice.
Free festivals themselves ultimately became expressly prohibited and
were subject to repressive measures by the state – including a para-
military assault against New Travellers by the police at the so-called
'Battle of the Beanfield' near Stonehenge in 1985.[60] By these actions, the
economic and social basis of the New Traveller community itself
became criminalised.

1.45   There are profound similarities between the function of nomadism
for traditional Gypsy and Traveller people and for New Travellers.[61]
The courts have recognised these similarities since the earliest days of
New Traveller culture, although both central and local government
have been loathe to accept this reality in practice:

58 Kenrick and Puxon, *The destiny of Europe's Gypsies*, pp30–31.
59 Fraser, *The Gypsies*, p5.
60 See Worthington, ed, *The Battle of the Beanfield*, Enabler Publications, 2005.
61 This fact is increasingly recognised in planning appeals. Many of the New
    Travellers discussed in chapter 4, below, on planning law have been officially
    accepted as 'gipsies' due to their employment patterns.

In 1986, a Yorkshire court ruled that a group known as 'The Mutants' were Gypsies within the meaning of the [1968 Caravan Sites] Act. In Avon, a New Age Traveller, Mr Rexworthy, was ruled to be a Gypsy. [Yet] the Government has stated ... in Parliament that it does not on the whole see New Age Travellers as Gypsies, to be helped by the 1968 Act.[62]

...

The distinction being made between acceptable 'true Gypsies' and unacceptable other travellers is akin to the 19th century concerns over the 'genuine Romani'. Like previous dividing practices, spoken tolerance for 'real Gypsies' is always expressed in relation to another, less defined group, be it 'half-breeds', Didicois, Irish travellers, tinkers, vagrants or New Age Travellers.[63]

Culture

1.46   It is important, when advising Gypsies and other ethnic Travellers of the law in this area, to have regard to their cultural values (a lot of which are shared). Some areas of commonality include:

- nomadism;
- the dominant position of the family and extended families;
- early and close kin marriage;
- work patterns;
- rituals surrounding death and marriage;
- relationship with the dominant settled society;
- language;
- the experience of discrimination.[64]

1.47   Where relevant, reference is made to Gypsy and ethnic Traveller culture throughout this book.

Outline of the book

1.48   This book is intended as a comprehensive coverage of the law as it relates to Gypsies and Travellers. It only covers the law as it relates to England and Wales.

---

62 Kenrick and Bakewell, *On the verge*, p50.
63 Kenrick and Bakewell, *On the verge*, p52.
64 See, for example, Clark and Greenfields, *Gypsies and Travellers*, pp28–56; McDonagh, 'Ethnicity and culture' in *Travellers: citizens of Ireland*, pp26–31.

1.49   Reference is made throughout to Gypsies (meaning 'Romani Gypsies') and Travellers (encompassing Irish, Scottish, Welsh and New Travellers) except where specific reference is made to a particular group. It is made clear in the text when a statutory definition of 'Gypsy' is being discussed.

1.50   Travelling Showpeople are discussed where relevant.[65] This book does not deal with houseboat dwellers or bargees ('Water Gypsies') since the law relating to them is very different and outside the scope of this work.[66] However some of the discussion of the law (for example, on homelessness, education and health) will be of use to these groups.

1.51   Since it came into force on 2 October 2000, the Human Rights Act (HRA) 1998 has had an effect on all the areas of law covered in this book and its impact is discussed in chapter 2. Public rented provision of sites remains an essential subject and is dealt with in chapter 3, together with a discussion of private rented provision. Planning law is of vital importance to those Gypsies and Travellers attempting to set up their own sites and is dealt with in chapter 4. The need for adequate site provision of all sorts stems from the large numbers of Gypsies and Travellers who remain on unauthorised encampments and the law on this subject is dealt with in chapter 5. Over recent years the potential importance and use of homelessness legislation has come to the fore and the law on this area is dealt with in chapter 6. Education and health are central concerns for Gypsies and Travellers and the law relating to these two areas is discussed in chapter 7. As with the HRA 1998, race discrimination legislation has an impact on all the areas of law discussed and is considered in chapter 8.

1.52   Each chapter flags up potential or expected changes to the law and 'grey areas' where they exist. There is a brief round-up of points for the future in chapter 9, the conclusion.

1.53   The appendices contain useful matters for reference. Appendix A deals with court and other procedures and should be referred to in conjunction with relevant parts of the various chapters.

1.54   The law as it relates to Gypsies and Travellers in England and Wales is correct as at 1 August 2007.

---

65 For a discussion of Travelling Showpeople, see Kenrick and Clark, *Moving On*, pp35–37.
66 For a discussion of Water Gypsies, see Sandford, *Rokkering to the Gorjios*, University of Hertfordshire Press, 1973, pp75–78.

CHAPTER 2

How the Human Rights Act 1998 affects Gypsies and Travellers

2.1   **The duties on public authorities under the Human Rights Act 1998**

2.7   **The most relevant Convention rights**

2.13   **Article 8 decision-making**

2.15   Article 8(1): the nature of the rights in issue

2.20   Nature and extent of interference with article 8 rights

2.22   Article 8(2): justification for interference

Interference in accordance with the law • Legitimate aim • Necessary in a democratic society

2.30   **The European Court of Human Rights' approach to proportionality – general principles derived from *Buckley* and *Chapman***

A wide 'margin of appreciation' • Factors affecting the width of the margin of appreciation • The importance of procedural safeguards • Recognition of a positive obligation • Relevant factual matters

2.43   **Article 8 and relevant domestic decisions post-Human Rights Act 1998**

2.44   Daly approach: where domestic courts review the decisions of public bodies

2.51   Application of the Daly approach in specific cases involving Gypsies and Travellers

Statutory review of planning appeals • Direct action • Compulsory purchase

2.54   Porter approach: the exercise of the domestic court's original jurisdiction to grant planning enforcement injunctions

2.63   Reasons given by domestic courts for decisions on proportionality

2.64   Article 14: general principles

2.67   The European Court of Human Rights' approach to article 14 complaints

2.73   The assessment of article 14 claims by domestic courts

2.78   Article 14 and relevant discrimination cases post-Human Rights Act 1998

Eviction from rented local authority sites • Planning enforcement and the use of stop notices • Planning permission for Gypsy and Traveller sites and the relevance of offers of conventional housing

2.92   Articles 11 and 14: culture and traditional horse fairs

2.94   Article 2 of Protocol 1: education

2.96   Commission for Equality and Human Rights

2.99   Conclusion

The duties on public authorities under the Human Rights Act 1998

2.1   The European Convention on Human Rights[1] (ECHR, or 'the Convention') requires that states which are signatories to the Convention, including the United Kingdom, shall secure to everyone within their jurisdiction a number of rights and freedoms. The Convention also provides individuals with the right to complain to the European Court of Human Rights (ECtHR) in Strasbourg when they consider that their rights and freedoms gauranteed by the Convention have been violated. The main purpose of the Human Rights Act (HRA) 1998,[2] which came into force on 2 October 2000, is to make the Convention a part of UK law – giving our domestic courts the duty to protect individuals human rights – thereby making the Convention directly accessible to people in this country.

2.2   The HRA 1998 imposes new duties on all of the 'public authorities' with which Gypsies and Travellers are frequently in contact, including: government ministers and departments; the Planning Inspectorate; local authorities; the police; education authorities; health authorities; social services departments; and the courts.[3]

2.3   HRA 1998 s3(1) requires all legislation to be read and given effect in a way which is compatible with Convention rights, 'so far as it is possible to do so' and HRA 1998 s4 gives the High Court, Court of Appeal and House of Lords the power to make a declaration of incompatibility in circumstances where it is concluded that a statutory provision is incompatible with a Convention right.

2.4   HRA 1998 s6(1) makes it unlawful for a 'public authority' to act in a way which is incompatible with a Convention right, unless mandated to do so by legislation which cannot itself be read compatibly with Convention rights.

2.5   Most of the powers exercised by public authorities which most directly affect Gypsies and Travellers are broad discretionary powers conferred by statutes in wide and open-ended terms (and clarified or further detailed in government guidance). Such powers must now be interpreted so as to be compatible with Convention rights, which means that the discretion which they give to public authorities must be exercised in a way which respects the Convention rights of Gypsies and Travellers. To give an example, Town and Country Planning Act

1 See appendix B.
2 See appendix B.
3 HRA 1998 s6(3)(a).

(TCPA) 1990 s187B confers very broad discretions on a local planning authority and the court to, respectively, apply for and grant injunctions to restrain breaches of planning control. To the extent that those discretions are each capable of being exercised incompatibly with the article 8 Convention rights of Gypsies and Travellers, HRA 1998 s3(1) requires that they be interpreted restrictively so as not to authorise such breaches of Convention rights. Since the discretion-conferring language of TCPA 1990 s187B is in very broad terms, and nothing in it compels a planning authority or court to apply for or grant injunctions in breach of article 8, it is clearly 'possible' for the provision to be interpreted compatibly with article 8.

2.6   Though this chapter concentrates on case-law relating to the grant of planning permission and the enforcement of planning control, the principles that can be derived from cases decided by the ECtHR and domestic courts are of wider application and will be of relevance to cases involving evictions from authorised sites and unauthorised encampments.

The most relevant Convention rights

2.7   The two Convention rights which are of most particular relevance to Gypsies and Travellers living in the United Kingdom are articles 8 and 14. Article 8(1) provides that:

> (1) Everyone has the right to respect for his private and family life, his home and his correspondence.

> (2) There shall be no interference by a public authority with the exercise of this right except such as is in accordance with the law and is necessary in a democratic society in the interests of national security, public safety or the economic well-being of the country, for the prevention of disorder or crime, for the protection of health or morals, or for the protection of the rights and freedoms of others.

2.8   Article 8(1) has also been interpreted as guaranteeing the right to respect for the traditional way of life of a minority.[4] However, the right protected by article 8(1) is subject to justified limitations (under article 8(2)), where such interference is necessary in a democratic society in the service of various other enumerated interests, including most relevantly 'the protection of the rights of others', which has been interpreted to include the protection of the environment for others' enjoyment.[5]

---

4 *Chapman v United Kingdom* (2001) 33 EHRR 399 at paras 71–74.
5 *Chapman* (2001) 33 EHRR 399 at para 82.

2.9   Article 14 provides that:

> The enjoyment of the rights and freedoms set forth in this Convention shall be secured without discrimination on any ground such as sex, race, colour, language, religion, political or other opinion, national or social origin, association with a national minority, property, birth or other status.

Thus, it requires that no one shall be discriminated against in the enjoyment of their Convention rights on any ground, including matters such as race, sex, national origin, or any other status. Article 14 is in principle relevant to any action or inaction by a public body which treats different categories of people in different ways.

2.10   The right in article 14 is a right not to be discriminated against in the enjoyment of a Convention right. It is not therefore a free-standing equality provision, but relates only to differential treatment in relation to Convention rights. It is also important to appreciate that differences of treatment, even in relation to Convention rights, are capable of being objectively justified under article 14. Not every difference of treatment therefore amounts to a breach of article 14. What has to be established in order to make out a breach of article 14 is that other people in an analogous or relevantly similar situation have been treated more favourably, and that there is no objective or reasonable justification for such difference of treatment.

2.11   In deciding whether a difference of treatment is justified in this sense, a court will look to see whether the difference of treatment serves a legitimate aim, and whether the means employed to achieve that aim are proportionate.

2.12   Another Convention right which is of considerable relevance to Gypsies and Travellers is the right to education protected by article 2 of Protocol 1.[6]

Article 8 decision-making

2.13   HRA 1998 s6 requires public authorities to consider carefully the proportionality of their actions when making decisions which interfere with article 8 rights. Thus public authorities are required to undertake a systematic analysis of the relevant issues and to ensure that they have taken into account the answers to a properly articulated framework of questions before reaching such decisions.

2.14   Translating this requirement into practical reality for decision-makers on the ground is notoriously difficult. In order to make the

6 See paras 2.94–2.95 and chapter 7, below.

task more intelligible, it is possible to distil from the most relevant Convention case-law (in particular *Buckley v United Kingdom*[7] and *Chapman v United Kingdom*[8]) a number of discrete questions which public authorities must ask themselves and answer when deciding whether a particular decision or step would be compatible with the Convention rights of those Gypsies and Travellers affected.

Article 8(1): the nature of the rights in issue

2.15   It is clear that enforcement action against unauthorised development which provides someone with a home constitutes an interference with their article 8(1) rights which requires justification. It is also clear that article 8 is engaged wherever there is an interference with a de facto home: the fact that the home was established unlawfully in the first place does not prevent it from being within the scope of article 8. It is merely a factor to be taken into account in the overall balancing exercise in deciding whether or not the interference is justified (ie proportionate).

2.16   However, the precise nature of the rights which are in issue under article 8(1) is important, because it will affect the approach which should be taken in assessing whether any interference with those rights is justified under article 8(2). In particular, it will affect the 'margin of appreciation'[9] that the ECtHR will accord to the balancing exercise conducted by a national authority. Just as it is well established in Convention case-law that the nature of the right protected, and the nature of the activities being regulated, are important criteria in determining the appropriate scope of the 'margin of appreciation' in a particular set of circumstances, so those factors will also be relevant to the degree of deference which is due to the judgment of the authority in making its own decision about whether the action proposed (for example, enforcement action) breaches article 8.

7 *Buckley v United Kingdom* (1996) 23 EHRR 101.

8 *Chapman* (2001) 33 EHRR 399. See also *Connors v United Kingdom* (2005) 40 EHRR 9 and the commentary in chapter 3 at para 3.16 et seq, below.

9 The 'margin of appreciation' is the concept developed by the ECtHR to give a certain latitude to states in exercising the above-mentioned balancing exercise, especially since the ECtHR itself is a supranational tribunal and at one stage removed from the matters involved. See also paras 2.31–2.35, below. Our domestic courts do not give decision makers the same latitude but have developed a concept known as the 'margin of discretion' – see para 2.45, below.

2.17   On this question of how to characterise the rights in issue under article 8(1), the ECtHR in *Chapman*[10] made a very clear finding which goes significantly beyond its earlier decision in *Buckley*. Whereas in *Buckley*[11] the court held that the case concerned the applicant's right to respect for her 'home' and considered it unnecessary to decide whether it also concerned the applicant's right to respect for her 'private life' and 'family life', in *Chapman* the court expressly held that:

> The applicant's occupation of her caravan is an integral part of her ethnic identity as a Gypsy, reflecting the long tradition of that minority of following a travelling lifestyle ... Measures which affect the applicant's stationing of her caravans have therefore a wider impact than on the right to respect for home. They also affect her ability to maintain her identity as a Gypsy and to lead her private and family life in accordance with that tradition.[12]

2.18   The ECtHR also observed that this was the case even though many Gypsies no longer live a wholly nomadic existence and increasingly settle for longer periods in one place in order to facilitate, for example, the education of their children.

2.19   The ECtHR's clear finding that measures affecting Gypsies' stationing of their caravans affect not merely the right to respect for their 'home' in the narrow sense, but their ability as members of an ethnic minority to continue to live according to their traditional travelling lifestyle, is of considerable significance to the approach which should be taken by public authorities when determining whether any interference with such an important right is justified in all the circumstances: the more important the Convention right, the greater the onus of justification on the public authority and therefore the greater the scrutiny that should be afforded to such justification by the courts.

Nature and extent of interference with article 8 rights

2.20   In *Chapman* the ECtHR found that the decisions of the planning authorities refusing to allow the applicant to remain on her land in her caravans constituted an interference with her article 8(1) rights as identified above.[13] It is not enough, however, for the public authority to end its inquiry into the interference question there. It must also

10 *Chapman* (2001) 33 EHRR 399 at para 73.
11 *Buckley* (1996) 23 EHRR 101 at para 54.
12 *Chapman* (2001) 33 EHRR 399 at para 73.
13 *Chapman* (2001) 33 EHRR 399 at para 78.

go on to consider the nature and extent of the interference with the article 8 rights of the Gypsy or Traveller.

2.21   This should involve the authority in deciding how serious the interference is in the circumstances of the particular case. For example, the interference would be serious if a measure was taken imposing criminal sanctions if the Gypsies or Travellers continue to use their land for the stationing of their caravans without planning permission, in circumstances where there are no alternative sites available and there is no other way in which they can continue to lead their traditional lifestyle within the law. Such a measure would affect the very essence of their rights under article 8 and as such the onus of justification upon the public authorities for such an interference would be a heavy one.

Article 8(2): justification for interference

2.22   Any decision taken by a public authority which clearly constitutes an interference with an individual's article 8(1) rights calls for justification under article 8(2) as being 'in accordance with the law', pursuing a legitimate aim and as being 'necessary in a democratic society' in pursuit of that aim.

Interference in accordance with the law

2.23   In *Chapman* it was conceded that the various measures which had been taken by the planning authorities that interfered with the applicant's article 8 rights were 'in accordance with the law' for the purposes of article 8.[14] The requirement that any interference with article 8 rights be in accordance with the law means that there must not only exist a formal legal basis for the interference (for example, a statutory discretion), but that any law which confers a broad discretion must also give sufficient indication as to the scope of that discretion. As the ECtHR stated in *Malone v United Kingdom*:

> It would be contrary to the rule of law for the legal discretion granted to the executive to be expressed in terms of an unfettered power. Consequently, the law must indicate the scope of any such discretion conferred on the competent authorities and the manner of its exercise with sufficient clarity, having regard to the legitimate aim of the measure in question, to give the individual adequate protection against arbitrary interference.[15]

14 *Chapman* (2001) 33 EHRR 399 at para 79.
15 *Malone v United Kingdom* (1985) 7 EHRR 14 at para 68.

2.24 Generally, a public authority's powers in relation to Gypsies and Travellers, for example, its powers of enforcement in relation to unauthorised developments, will satisfy both aspects of this requirement. If the authority is in any doubt as to whether a particular power which it intends to exercise satisfies this requirement, however, it should ask itself whether the provision in question satisfies the *Malone* test; that is, whether the provision indicates the scope of the discretion conferred on the authority, and the manner of its exercise, with sufficient clarity to give individuals in the position of those affected adequate protection against arbitrary interference.

Legitimate aim

2.25 In *Chapman*, the government argued that the measures in question pursued the enforcement of planning controls which were in the interests of the economic well-being of the country and the preservation of the environment and public health. The ECtHR accepted the applicant's argument that the government had not put forward any detail to substantiate the aims allegedly pursued but relied on a general assertion; it found that the measures pursued the legitimate aim of protecting the 'rights of others' through preservation of the environment, and did not find it necessary to determine whether any other aims were involved.[16]

2.26 As with the nature of the rights in issue, the precise aim pursued by a measure is a matter of importance when it comes to justification, because as a matter of Convention case-law the nature of the aim pursued is recognised to be one of the criteria which may affect the scope of the 'margin of appreciation' to be afforded to the national decision maker:

> ... the scope of the margin of appreciation is not identical in respect of each of the aims [in article 8(2)] justifying restrictions on a right.[17]

Similarly, as a matter of domestic law under the HRA 1998, the precise aim pursued by a measure may affect the degree of deference which is considered by a court to be due to the authority concerned.

2.27 Generally, the planning enforcement powers available to local authorities will pursue the legitimate aim of protecting the rights of others in the sense of environmental protection. However, it remains necessary for the authority to be satisfied in any particular case that a

16 *Chapman* (2001) 33 EHRR 399 at para 82.
17 *Dudgeon v United Kingdom* (1982) 4 EHRR 149 at para 52. See footnote 9 above for an explanation of the concept of the 'margin of appreciation'.

particular enforcement measure is genuinely pursued for such a legitimate aim, and not for some other illegitimate purpose such as merely
appeasing a vociferous or politically important local population or
group which is objecting to the particular development.

Necessary in a democratic society

2.28   The next stage in the structured analysis required by the Convention
involves consideration of the question whether an interference with article 8 rights is 'necessary in a democratic society'. The abstract formu-
lation of the test to be applied at this stage was restated in *Chapman* in
familiar terms: an interference will be considered 'necessary in a democratic society' for a legitimate aim if it answers a 'pressing social
need' and, in particular, if it is proportionate to the legitimate aim
pursued.[18] This is what is often referred to as the 'proportionality
requirement'.

2.29   Although the proportionality test is easily formulated in the abstract,
in practice precisely what proportionality requires in a particular context turns on the application to the facts of each case of general principles for assessing the proportionality of the interference. The general
principles will be identified first before returning to consider the relevant factual matters which are to be taken into account by public
authorities when deciding whether or not an interference with a
Convention right is justified.

The European Court of Human Rights' approach to proportionality – general principles derived from *Buckley* and *Chapman*

2.30   The following general principles can be extracted from both the *Buckley* and *Chapman* decisions and will be followed by the ECtHR when
assessing the proportionality of an interference with article 8 rights
and particularly those which concern measures taken against Gypsies
and Travellers to enforce planning control.

---

18 *Chapman* (2001) 33 EHRR 399 at para 90.

A wide 'margin of appreciation'

2.31   In principle, the national authorities enjoy a wide margin of appreciation 'insofar as the exercise of discretion involving a multitude of local factors is inherent in the choice and implementation of planning policies'.[19]

2.32   The rationale for this is also explained,[20] and is principally the commonsense reason familiar to any court (whether exercising a reviewing or appellate jurisdiction), namely that, compared with the primary fact-finder, the ECtHR is not well equipped to challenge judgments which have been made on detailed questions of local fact by a decision maker who has visited the site and heard the evidence. Planning inspectors, in short, are much better placed to assess the impact of a particular use on the particular locality and, therefore, to assess the legitimacy of planning objections to that use. It is primarily a matter of relative institutional competence.

2.33   The effect of a presumptively wide margin of appreciation is that, in most cases concerning the exercise of planning judgment, the ECtHR will confine itself to a standard of review which is not at all intense and which centres on whether there has been a 'manifest error of appreciation by the national authorities'.[21]

Factors affecting the width of the margin of appreciation

2.34   Although the ECtHR's starting point is a presumptively wide margin of appreciation in this context, it also explicitly recognised in *Buckley*[22] and *Chapman*[23] that certain factors will affect the width of the margin of appreciation to be accorded in any particular case. These factors include:

(1) the nature of the Convention right in issue;
(2) its importance for the individual;
(3) the nature of the activities restricted; and
(4) the nature of the aim pursued by the restrictions.

---

19 *Chapman* (2001) 33 EHRR 399 at para 92 and *Buckley* (1996) 23 EHRR 101 at para 75. See footnote 9 above for an explanation of the concept of the 'margin of appreciation'.
20 *Chapman* (2001) 33 EHRR 399 at para 92.
21 *Chapman* (2001) 33 EHRR 399 at para 92.
22 *Buckley* (1996) 23 EHRR 101 at para 76.
23 *Chapman* (2001) 33 EHRR 399 at para 91.

2.35   The ECtHR in *Chapman*[24] also considered, but did not accept, the argument that a fifth factor should also be recognised as narrowing the
margin of appreciation to be accorded to national authorities, namely
the emerging international consensus among Council of Europe
member states recognising the special needs of minorities and an
obligation to protect their security, identity and lifestyle.[25] The court
accepted that such an international consensus was indeed emerging,
'not only for the purpose of safeguarding the interests of the minorities themselves but to preserve a cultural diversity of value to the whole
community',[26] and this clearly informed its analysis of the nature of the
article 8 rights in issue, but it was not persuaded that the consensus was
sufficiently concrete for it to derive any guidance as to the conduct or
standards which states considered desirable in any particular situation. It, therefore, declined to reduce the margin of appreciation
accorded to states in light of that conclusion.

The importance of procedural safeguards

2.36   In determining whether the state has remained within its margin of
appreciation when fixing the regulatory framework, the ECtHR regards
the procedural safeguards available to the individual as being 'especially
material'.[27] In particular, it will 'examine whether the decision-making
process leading to measures of interference was fair and such as to
afford due respect to the interests safeguarded to the individual by
article 8'.[28]

2.37   Particular attention is paid to procedural safeguards in the decision-making process to compensate for the less intense standard of
review adopted in relation to the substance of the measure which interferes with Convention rights.

2.38   Whether, in a particular case, an individual has yet had the opportunity of taking a procedural step which they wish to take, such as
exercising a right of appeal to the secretary of state against the refusal
of planning permission, should, therefore, be carefully considered by

---

24 *Chapman* (2001) 33 EHRR 399 at paras 93–94.
25 The Framework Convention for the Protection of National Minorities,
    Strasbourg, 1/2/1195, Council of Europe Doc ETS 157.
26 *Chapman* (2001) 33 EHRR 399 at para 93.
27 *Chapman* (2001) 33 EHRR 399 at para 92 and *Buckley* (1996) 23 EHRR 101 at
    paras 76–77. See also *Connors v United Kingdom* (2005) 40 EHRR 9 and the
    commentary in chapter 3 at para 3.16 et seq, below.
28 *Chapman* (2001) 33 EHRR 399 at para 92 and *Buckley* (1996) 23 EHRR 101 at
    paras 76–77.

a local planning authority when deciding whether or not to take enforcement action. Proceeding straight to enforcement, before allowing the Gypsy or Traveller an opportunity to persuade a planning inspector to grant planning permission may, therefore, be found to be precipitative.

Recognition of a positive obligation

2.39   The ECtHR has expressly recognised that the vulnerable position of Gypsies and Travellers as a minority means that some special consideration should be given to their needs and their different lifestyle both in the relevant regulatory planning framework and in arriving at decisions in particular cases,[29] and that to this extent there is a positive obligation imposed on states by article 8 to 'facilitate the Gypsy way of life'.[30]

Relevant factual matters

2.40   The general principles set out above should always guide any assessment of the proportionality of a given interference with article 8 rights in cases which concern measures taken against Gypsies and Travellers to enforce planning control. Against that background, the following can be identified as the most important factual matters which are taken into account by the ECtHR when applying its general principles to the concrete facts of a particular case in order to assess the proportionality of the interference:

- the seriousness of the impact of the measure on the most basic rights of the individuals concerned, including on the security of their accommodation, their family life, health, children's education and ability to maintain their traditional travelling way of life;[31]
- the availability of an alternative site, including its suitability for the individuals' particular needs, the financial circumstances of those affected and the efforts made to find alternative sites;[32]

---

29 *Buckley* (1996) 23 EHRR 101 at paras 76, 80, 84.

30 *Chapman* (2001) 33 EHRR 399 at para 96. But note that in the homelessness case of *Steward v Royal Borough of Kingston Upon Thames* [2007] EWCA Civ 565, the Court of Appeal was not convinced that the positive obligation to facilitate the Gypsy way of life could be extended to cover the lifestyle of New Travellers – see chapter 6 at paras 6.81–6.82, below, for more detail.

31 *Chapman* (2001) 33 EHRR 399 at para 105.

32 *Chapman* (2001) 33 EHRR 399 at paras 103–104, 111–112 and *Buckley* (1996) 23 EHRR 101 at para 81.

- whether there has been a full and fair opportunity for the individuals concerned to make their case for respecting their article 8(1) rights, including those arising from their Gypsy status, before the relevant administrative authorities, including a planning inspector;[33]
- whether the site was established unlawfully;[34]
- the strength of the reasons relied on as the justification for the interference (usually this will be the protection of the environment);[35]
- the seriousness of the enforcement measures taken, and whether other, less restrictive enforcement measures were available.[36]

2.41 A properly conducted assessment of the proportionality of an interference should, therefore, involve consideration of evidence relating to as many of the above factual matters as are relevant in the particular case.

2.42 The approach of the ECtHR in both *Buckley* and *Chapman* was that the initial assessment of the necessity for a particular interference must be for 'the national authorities, who by reason of their direct and continuous contact with the vital forces of their countries are in principle better placed than an international court to evaluate local needs and conditions'.[37]

Article 8 and relevant domestic decisions post-Human Rights Act 1998

2.43 The combined effect of both the duties imposed on public authorities by the HRA 1998 and the decision of the ECtHR in *Chapman* has been considered in a number of cases before our domestic courts. As will be seen below, the approach taken by domestic courts in each of those cases has depended to a very great extent upon whether the court has been asked to review the proportionality of a decision taken by a public body (for example, a decision to compulsorily purchase land on which Gypsies or Travellers are encamped) or whether it has been asked to exercise its own original jurisdiction (for example, in a case where a local authority seeks a planning injunction to prevent Gypsies or Travellers from living on their land in breach of planning control).

---

33 *Chapman* (2001) 33 EHRR 399 at paras 106–109 and *Buckley* (1996) 23 EHRR 101 at para 80.
34 *Chapman* (2001) 33 EHRR 399 at para 102.
35 *Chapman* (2001) 33 EHRR 399 at para 110.
36 *Buckley* (1996) 23 EHRR 101 at para 83.
37 *Chapman* (2001) 33 EHRR 399 at para 91.

Daly approach: where domestic courts review the decisions of public bodies

2.44　There have been a number of cases in which the House of Lords and the Court of Appeal have explained how domestic courts should review a decision taken by a public body which interferes with an individual's Convention rights and it is now clear that the approach that must be adopted in such cases is more sophisticated than the traditional *Wednesbury* grounds of review.

2.45　In *R (Mahmood) v Secretary of State for the Home Department,*[38] an immigration case, Laws LJ stated that, even where the courts are in as good a position as the Secretary of State to decide an issue which engages Convention rights, they must not do so as if they were his or her surrogate. What he called a 'margin of discretion' must be allowed to the statutory decision-maker. In the same case Lord Phillips of Maltravers MR identified the following three principles:

(1) Even where human rights were at stake, the role of the court was supervisory. The court would only intervene where the decision fell outside the range of responses open to a reasonable decision-maker.

(2) In conducting a review of a decision affecting human rights, the court would subject the decision to most anxious scrutiny.

(3) Where the decision interfered with human rights, the court would require substantial justification for the interference in order to be satisfied that the response fell within the range of responses open to a decision-maker. The more substantial the interference, the more that was required to justify it.

Lord Phillips explained his first principle as follows:

> The court does not substitute its own decision for that of the executive. It reviews the decision of the executive to see whether it is permitted by law – in this instance the Human Rights Act 1998. In performing this exercise the court will bear in mind that, just as individual states enjoy a margin of appreciation which permits them to respond, within the law, in a manner which is not uniform, so there will often be an area of discretion permitted to the executive of a country before a response can be demonstrated to infringe the Convention.

Expanding on his third principle, Lord Phillips said:

> When anxiously scrutinising an executive decision that interferes with human rights, the court will ask the question, applying an objective test,

38 [2001] 1 WLR 840.

whether the decision-maker could reasonably have concluded that the interference was necessary to achieve one or more of the legitimate aims recognised by the Convention. When considering the test of necessity in the relevant context, the court must take into account the European jurisprudence in accordance with section 2 of the 1998 Act.[39]

2.46   In *R v Secretary of State for the Home Department ex parte Daly*,[40] a case where the House of Lords was asked to consider whether a policy relating to the search of prisoners' cells breached the article 8 right of prisoners to respect for their correspondence, Lord Steyn clarified what had been said in *Mahmood* by Lord Phillips in the first sentence of the last passage quoted above. Lord Steyn said:

> 26. The explanation of the Master of the Rolls in the first sentence of the cited passage requires clarification. It is couched in language reminiscent of the traditional Wednesbury ground of review (*Associated Provincial Picture Houses Ltd v Wednesbury Corporation* [1948] 1 KB 223), and in particular the adaptation of that test in terms of heightened scrutiny in cases involving fundamental rights as formulated in *R v Ministry of Defence Ex p Smith* [1996] QB 517 554E–G per Sir Thomas Bingham MR. There is a material diference between the *Wednesbury* and *Smith* grounds of review and the approach of proportionality applicable in respect of review where convention rights are at stake.

Having provided that clarification Lord Steyn stated that:

> 27. The contours of proportionality are familiar. In *de Freitas v Permanent Secretary of Ministry of Agriculture, Fisheries, Lands and Housing* [1999] 1 AC 69 the Privy Council adopted a three stage test. Lord Clyde observed, at p 80, that in determining whether a limitation (by an act, rule or decision) is arbitrary or excessive the court should ask itself:
>
> > Whether: (i) the legislative objective is sufficiently important to justify limiting a fundamental right; (ii) the measures designed to meet the legislative objective are rationally connected to it; and (iii) the means used to impair the right or freedom are no more than is necessary to accomplish the objective.

2.47   Whilst Lord Steyn remarked that most cases would be decided the same way whichever approach was adopted, he made the point that the intensity of review is somewhat greater under the proportionality approach and highlighted three particular differences between them:

> 27. ... First, the doctrine of proportionality may require the reviewing court to assess the balance which the decision-maker has struck, not merely

39 [2001] 1 WLR 840 at paras 37–40.
40 [2001] 2 AC 532.

whether it is within the range of rational or resonable decisions. Secondly, the proportionality test may go further than traditional grounds of review inasmuch as it may require attention to be directed to the relative weight accorded to interests and considerations. Thirdly, even the heightened scrutiny test developed in *R v Ministry of Defence, Ex p Smith* [1996] QB 517, 554 is not necessarily appropriate to the protection of human rights. It will be recalled that in *Smith* the Court of Appeal reluctantly felt compelled to reject a limitation on homosexuals in the army. The challenge based on article 8 of the Convention for the Protection of Human Rights and Fundamental Freedoms (the right to respect for private and family life) foundered on the threshold required even by the anxious scrutiny test. The European Court of Human Rights came to the opposite conclusion: *Smith and Grady v United Kingdom* (1999) 29 EHRR 493. The court concluded, at p543, para 138:

> The threshold at which the High Court and the Court of Appeal could find the Ministry of Defence policy irrational was placed so high that it effectively excluded any consideration by the domestic courts of the question of whether the interference with the applicants' rights answered a pressing social need or was proportionate to the national security and public order aims pursued, principles which lie at the heart of the court's analysis of complaints under article 8 of the Convention.

In other words, the intensity of the review, in similar cases, is guaranteed by the twin requirements that the limitation of the right was necessary in a democratic society, in the sense of meeting a pressing social need, and the question whether the interference was really proportionate to the legitimate aim being pursued.

28. The differences in approach between the traditional grounds of review and the proportionality approach may therefore sometimes yield different results. It is therefore imprtant that cases involving convention rights must be analysed in the correct way. This does not mean that there has been a shift to merits review. On the contrary, as Professor Jowell [2000] PL 671, 681 has pointed out the respective roles of judges and administrators are fundamentally distinct and will remain so. To this extent the general tenor of the observations in *Mahmood* [2001] 1 WLR 840 are correct. And Laws LJ rightly emphasised in *Mahmood* at p847, para 18 'that the intensity of review in a public law case will depend on the subject matter in hand'. This is so even in cases involving Convention rights. In law context is everything.

2.48   In *R (Samaroo) v Secretary of State for the Home Department*[41] the Court of Appeal considered whether a decision to deport the claimant breached his rights protected by article 8 of the Convention. Having

41 [2001] EWCA Civ 1139.

referred to the House of Lords decision in *Daly*, Dyson LJ concluded that the issue of proportionality:

> will usually have to be considered in two distinct stages. At the first stage, the question is: can the objective of the measure be achieved by means which are less interfering of an individual's right? ... At the second stage, it is assumed that the means employed to achieve the legitimate aim are necessary in the sense that they are the least intrusive of Convention Rights that can be devised in order to achieve the aim. The question at this stage of the consideration is: does the measure have an excessive or disproportionate effect on the interests of affected persons.[42]

2.49   However, it is important to note that the two-stage approach advocated by Dyson LJ in *Samaroo* has not been uniformly adopted in subsequent cases and that its application to cases involving planning decisions is somewhat debatable. In *Lough v The First Secretary of State*[43] a local authority refused planning permission to the owners of a site for proposed development which involved the demolition of existing buildings and redevelopment on the basis that the proposals conflicted with the authority's unitary development plan in that it caused harm to the amenity of local residents. The owners of the site appealed and a planning inspector appointed by the secretary of state allowed their appeal. Members of a local unincorporated residents' association applied to the High Court to quash the grant of planning permission on the grounds that the proposed development breached their rights protected by article 8 to respect for their private, family life and homes and by article 1 of Protocol 1 (their right to peaceful enjoyment of their possessions). The application was dismissed by the High Court and a subsequent appeal to the Court of Appeal was rejected. When giving the lead judgment in the Court of Appeal Pill LJ said:

> 49. The concept of proportionality is inherent in the approach to decision making in planning law. The procedure stated by Dyson LJ in the Samaroo case [2001] UKHHR 1150, as stated, is not wholly appropriate to decision making in the present context in that it does not take account of the right, recognised in the Convention, of a landowner to make use of his land, a right which is, however, to be weighed against the rights of others affected by the use of the land and of the community in general. The first stage of the procedure stated by Dyson LJ does not require, nor was it intended to require that, before any development of land is permitted, it must be established that the objective of the development cannot be achieved in some other way or on some other site. The effect of the proposal

---

42 [2001] EWCA Civ 1139 at paras 19 and 21.
43 [2004] 1 WLR 2557.

on adjoining owners and occupants must however be considered in the context of Article 8, and a balancing of interests is necessary. The question whether the permission has 'an excessive or disproportionate effect on the interests of affected persons' (Dyson LJ at paragraph 20) is, in the present context, no different from the question posed by the Inspector, a question which has routinely been posed by decision-makers both before and after the enactment of the 1998 Act. Dyson LJ stated, at paragraph 18, that 'it is important to emphasise that the striking of a fair balance lies at the heart of proportionality'.

50. ... The need to strike a balance is central to the conclusion in each case. There may be cases where the two-stage approach to decision making necessary in other fields is also appropriate to a decision as to land use, and the concept of proportionality undoubtedly is, and always has been, a useful tool in striking a balance, but the decision in the *Samaroo* case does not have the effect of imposing on planning law the straight-jacket advocated ...

In a short concurring judgment Keene LJ added:

55. ... the process outlined in *Samaroo* while appropriate where there is direct interference with Article 8 rights by a public body, cannot be applied without adaptation in a situation where the essential conflict is between two or more groups of private interests.

2.50   Whether or not domestic courts adopt the two-stage *Samaroo* approach to the assessment of proportionality, the fact remains that the approach laid down by Lord Steyn in *Daly* remains good law. That point was recently illustrated in the case of *R (SD) v The Governors of Denbeigh High School*[44] where Lord Bingham said:

30. ... it is clear that the court's approach to an issue of proportionality under the Convention must go beyond that traditionally adopted to judicial review in a domestic setting. The inadequacy of that approach was exposed in *Smith and Grady v The United Kingdom* (1999) 29 EHRR 493, para 138, and the new approach required under the 1998 Act was described by Lord Steyn in *R (Daly) v The Secretary of State for the Home Department* [2001] 2 AC 532, paragraphs 25–28, in terms which have never to my knowledge been questioned. There is no shift to a merits review, but the intensity of review is greater than was previously appropriate, and greater even than the heightened scrutiny test adopted by the Court of Appeal in *R v Ministry of Defence, Ex p Smith* [1996] QB 517. The domestic court must now make a value judgment, an evaluation, by reference to the circumstances prevailing at the relevant time ... Proportionality must be judged objectively, by the court ...

44 [2006] 2 WLR 719.

Application of the Daly approach in specific cases involving Gypsies and Travellers

Statutory review of planning appeals

2.51   In *R (Egan) v Secretary of State for Transport, Local Government and the Regions and Hertsmere BC*[45] Sullivan J dismissed an application made under the Town and Country Planning Act (TCPA) 1990 s288 to quash a decision made by the Secretary of State to dismiss the claimant's appeal against the council's refusal of planning permission for a Gypsy site in the Green Belt. When doing so Sullivan J concluded that a considerable measure of deference should be accorded to the judgment of the decision-maker in respect of proportionality, given:

> the fact that the court did not have particular expertise in the planning field, that the balancing exercise does involve matters of planning policy, and the court does not have the opportunity of looking at the site and hearing evidence about special circumstances first hand ...[46]

He rejected the proposition that the court should satisfy itself that the decision maker struck the right balance between Green Belt and other policy considerations, on the one hand, and the claimant's article 8 rights, on the other.[47]

Direct action

2.52   In both *R (O'Brien and Casey) v Basildon DC*[48] and in *R (Smith) v South Norfolk Council*[49] the Administrative Court was asked to review the use by local authorities of their powers under TCPA 1990 s178 to take direct action to evict Gypsies and Travellers from sites which had been developed without planning permission. In each case the court rejected the claimants' case that the use of direct action in such circumstances was necessarily disproportionate and incompatible with article 8 –

45   [2002] EWHC 389 Admin.

46   [2002] EWHC 389 Admin at para 51.

47   [2002] EWHC 389 Admin at para 49. See also *R (Lee) v First Secretary of State* [2003] EWHC 3235 Admin at paras 23–27 for another example of a court's consideration of proportionality in the context of a statutory review. In that case the Secretary of State's decision refusing a Gypsy planning permission was quashed on basis that one sentence in a paragraph dealing with human rights was not sufficient to dispose of the claimant's argument that a refusal of temporary planning permission would amount to a disproportionate interference with his and his family's rights under article 8.

48   *R (O'Brien and Casey) v Basildon DC* [2006] EWHC 1346 Admin and for further discussion of this case see chapter 4 at para 4.167, below.

49   *R (Smith) v South Norfolk Council* [2006] EWHC 2772 Admin and see chapter 4, below.

though the decision to take direct action in the case of *O'Brien* was quashed on other grounds.

Compulsory purchase

2.53 In *Lisa Smith and Others v Secretary of State for Trade and Industry and the London Development Agency*[50] the Administrative Court dismissed a challenge to the Secretary of State's confirmation of a compulsory purchase order (CPO) which encompassed land required for the development of the London 2012 Olympic Games site. The challenge had been brought by Gypsies and Travellers who were living on authorised Gypsy/Traveller sites within the CPO lands. The claimants argued that the decision to confirm the CPO in circumstances where relocation sites had not yet been provided was disproportionate and breached their rights protected by article 8 of the Convention. They also argued that the court should adopt the two-stage *Samaroo* approach and ask itself the question whether the Secretary of State's decision was the least intrusive measure that could be taken to achieve what was acknowledged to be a legitimate aim. In his judgment, Wyn Williams J made reference to the decision in *Lough* and indicated that he did not consider it necessary for the court to adopt the *Samaroo* approach when considering the proportionality of the Secretary of State's decision. However, the judge also recognised that it was arguable that the approach advocated by the Court of Appeal in *Lough* was one which should only be followed in cases where, as Keene LJ had said in that case, there was a conflict between two or more groups of private interests, and so he applied the two-stage *Samaroo* approach in any event. Having done so, he nevertheless concluded that the Secretary of State's decision was proportionate.

Porter approach: the exercise of the domestic court's original jurisdiction to grant planning enforcement injunctions

2.54 A local planning authority that wishes to evict Gypsies and Travellers from an unauthorised site that they have established on their own land may apply for an injunction to restrain a breach of planning control.[51] Before the HRA 1998, the well-established approach of the

---

50 *Lisa Smith v Secretary of State for Trade and Industry and the London Development Agency* [2007] EWHC 1013 Admin and see chapter 3 at paras 3.52–3.55, below.
51 See TCPA 1990 s187B and chapter 4, paras 4.169–4.186, below.

judiciary when dealing with such applications for injunctive relief was to treat the court's discretion as being narrowly circumscribed by the fact that the local planning authority had already decided what constituted a breach of planning control.[52] The judiciary in such cases regarded the planning authority as having already struck the balance between the general public interest, on the one hand, and the interests of the individuals who were to be evicted, on the other, and saw any role for the courts in considering questions such as the availability of alternative sites, or the hardship which would be caused by an injunction, as a usurpation of that policy-making function, and contrary to the will of parliament which had entrusted those powers to the local planning authorities. In other words, the courts adopted an entirely submissive approach to the decisions made by local planning authorities, subject only to a residual power to correct manifest errors or perverse decisions. That approach was exemplified by the decision of Hoffmann J at first instance in *Mole Valley DC v Smith*:[53]

> There can be no doubt that requiring [the Gypsies] to leave the site would cause considerable hardship. This court, however, is not entrusted with a general jurisdiction to solve social problems. The striking of a balance between the requirements of planning policy and the needs of these defendants is a matter which, in my view, has been entrusted to other authorities.

2.55   The central issue in the case of *South Buckinghamshire DC v Porter*[54] was whether that approach survived the coming into force of the HRA 1998, or whether the fact that the article 8 rights of Gypsies and

---

52 The leading authorities were two Court of Appeal decisions, *Mole Valley DC v Smith* [1992] 3 PLR 22 (decided under the predecessor power to grant injunctions) and *Hambleton DC v Bird* [1995] 3 PLR 8.

53 Cited with approval in the Court of Appeal in the same case, [1992] 3 PLR 22 at 31. See, to similar effect, Lord Donaldson MR at 32: '[I]t is not for the courts to usurp the policy decision-making functions of the Secretary of State … by a side-wind', and Balcombe LJ at 33: '[T]he court is being asked to reverse the decisions of the authorities to whom Parliament has entrusted the relevant decision, not on grounds of illegality, but on grounds of policy'. The reasoning of Pill LJ in *Hambleton* at 15 was to precisely the same effect and he stated that the fact that the granting of an injunction is dependent on the court's discretion 'does not however entitle a judge … to act as a court of appeal against a planning decision or to base a refusal to grant an injunction upon his view of the overall public interest'. The judge below in that case was criticised for having taken upon himself the role of assessing the benefits and disbenefits to the public as a whole, thereby 'taking upon himself the policy function of the planning authorities and housing authorities and their powers and duties'.

54 [2003] UKHL 26, [2003] 2 WLR 1547.

Travellers were engaged in such cases, meant that a court must now make an independent judgment in deciding whether or not to grant an injunction. *Porter* was a consolidated appeal against the decisions made in four separate cases by judges in the High Court. In each case, the judge at first instance had granted injunctions to restrain the use by Gypsies and Travellers of land for residential purposes in breach of planning control, and the question for the Court of Appeal and the House of Lords was, therefore, whether those judges had directed themselves correctly about the approach they should take in the exercise of their discretion.

2.56   In a judgment which was subsequently unanimously approved by the House of Lords, the Court of Appeal[55] set out the approach which is to be applied by a court considering an application for an injunction brought under TCPA 1990 s187B in order to be consistent with the court's duty under HRA 1998 s6(1) to act compatibly with Convention rights. The Court of Appeal held that the judge hearing an application for an injunction under section 187B is not entitled to reach his or her own independent view of the planning merits of the case, which he or she is required to take as having been decided within the planning process.[56] However, in deciding whether or not to grant injunctive relief, the Court of Appeal held that the judge must consider a variety of factors which must be weighed in the balance, including:

- questions of hardship for the defendant and his or her family, including the impact on the family's health and education;
- the availability of alternative sites;
- the planning history of the site;
- the need to enforce planning control in the general interest;
- the degree and flagrancy of the breach of planning control;
- whether other enforcement measures had been tried in the past;
- whether there was any urgency in the situation;
- health and safety considerations;
- previous planning decisions;
- the local planning authority's decision to seek injunctive relief;
- the degree of environmental damage resulting from the breach of planning control; and
- the possibility that planning permission would be granted for the residential use of the site in the future.

---

55 [2001] EWCA Civ 1549, [2002] 1 WLR 1359, [2002] 1 All ER 425 at paras 38D–42.
56 [2001] EWCA Civ 1549 at para 38.

2.57   The Court of Appeal also recognised that the weight to be given to these considerations in the balancing exercise may vary depending on a number of other factors. For example, the relevance of, and weight to be attached to, previous planning decisions will depend on matters such as how recent they are, the extent to which considerations of hardship and availability of alternative sites were taken into account, and the strength of the conclusions reached on land use and environmental issues.[57] Similarly, the relevance and weight of the local planning authority's decision will depend on the extent to which it can be shown to have had regard to all the material considerations and to have properly posed and approached the article 8(2) questions as to necessity and proportionality.[58]

2.58   Having identified these various factors as being relevant to the striking of the necessary balance between the competing interests, the Court of Appeal held[59] that the approach to TCPA 1990 s187B that it had adopted in the earlier decision in *Hambleton DC v Bird*[60] – which precluded consideration by the judge of questions of hardship – was not consistent with the court's duty to act compatibly with Convention rights contained in HRA 1998 s6(1). The Court of Appeal concluded that proportionality requires that the injunction not only be appropriate and necessary for the attainment of the public interest objective sought (the safeguarding of the environment), but also that it does not impose an excessive burden on the individual whose private interests (the Gypsy's private life and home and retention of his ethnic identity) are at stake. It was acknowledged by the Court of Appeal that a court's task in answering that question would not be an easy one, involving as it inevitably would the striking of a balance between competing interests of a very different character. The Court of Appeal stated that the task was unavoidable under the HRA 1998, and that 'provided it is undertaken in a structured and articulated way, the appropriate conclusion should emerge'.[61]

57 [2001] EWCA Civ 1549 at para 38.

58 [2001] EWCA Civ 1549 at para 39.

59 [2001] EWCA Civ 1549 at para 41.

60 [1995] 3 PLR 8.

61 [2001] EWCA Civ 1549 at para 42. Applying the new approach to the facts of the particular cases, the Court of Appeal held that in three of the four cases the judges below had determined the applications for an injunction by reference to the old approach which involved them in deferring excessively to the planning authorities' own views as to how the balance between the competing interests fell to be struck. In those three cases the injunction orders were quashed.

2.59   The Court of Appeal's approach in *Porter* was approved unanimously by the House of Lords.[62] The effect of these important decisions has been to require much more careful and explicit consideration of why measures taken against Gypsies and Travellers are justified.[63]

2.60   The decisions of the Court of Appeal and House of Lords in *Porter* represent an important advance on the position before the HRA 1998 came into force.[64] However, the limitations of relying on article 8 to mitigate the effects of the overall shortfall of suitable sites are shown by the decision of the Court of Appeal in *Davis v Tonbridge and Malling BC*.[65] The case concerned an appeal by Travelling Showpeople against an injunction granted pursuant to TCPA 1990 s187B requiring them to leave the site which they had occupied in the absence of any alternative site being available for them in the whole of South East England. The evidence that, despite comprehensive searches, there was no alternative site for the Travelling Showpeople in South East England was clear and undisputed. It was also clear on the evidence that the Travelling Showpeople would suffer 'undoubted', 'real' and 'great' hardship if the injunction was granted. The judge at first instance therefore acknowledged that the case posed 'the stark question whether the appellants should be compelled to leave the site when they have nowhere else to go'. Nevertheless, he held that granting the injunction was not a disproportionate response to the continuing unlawful use of the site.

2.61   The Court of Appeal, after considering in full the decisions of the Court of Appeal and House of Lords in *Porter* and the decision of the ECtHR in *Chapman*, upheld the judge's decision. It held that the judge had correctly distinguished between the decision on the planning merits, which was for the local planning authority, and the decision on enforcement, which was for the court itself. Although there was inevitably considerable overlap between these two stages, because the same circumstances fell to be considered at each stage,[66] in the Court

---

62 [2003] UKHL 26, [2003] 2 WLR 1547.

63 See Chapter 4 at paras 4.185–4.186, below, for reference to other cases where consideration of the principles derived from *Chapman* and the approach taken in *Porter* have led courts to delay or postpone enforcement action.

64 Although it is worth noting that Lord Bingham of Cornhill expressed the view that it was 'very questionable whether article 8 of the European Convention has any bearing on the court's approach to an application under [TCPA s187B]' if the section is interpreted and applied in accordance with the approach enunciated by Simon Brown LJ in the Court of Appeal: see [2003] 2 WLR 1547 at 1565.

65 [2004] EWCA Civ 194.

66 [2004] EWCA Civ 194 at para 40.

of Appeal's view, the judge had exercised his own jurisdiction on the issue of enforcement, and his reasoning in reaching his conclusion that enforcement was not disproportionate could not be faulted.[67] The decision that it was not a disproportionate interference with the article 8 rights of the Travelling Showpeople was, therefore, upheld, notwithstanding that this enforcement decision would cause them great personal hardship due to there being no alternative site available to them in the whole of South East England.[68]

2.62   The decision in *Davis* provides a salutary reminder that the protections against disproportionate enforcement action afforded by article 8 are no substitute for a legislative solution to the chronic under-provision of suitable sites for Gypsies and Travellers.

Reasons given by domestic courts for decisions on proportionality

2.63   In *Coates v South Buckinghamshire DC*,[69] an appeal against the grant of a planning injunction which had the effect of forcing Romani Gypsies to leave their land, the Court of Appeal commented upon the reasons that should be given by a court considering the issue of proportionality. Lord Phillips of Maltravers MR said:

> 7. In my judgment there is only one cardinal rule. The judge's reasons should make clear to the parties why he has reached his decision. Where he has had to balance competing factors it will usually be possible to explain why he has concluded that some have outweighed others. Even where the competition is so unequal that the factors speak for themselves it is desirable to say so.

Sedley LJ went further and said:

> 28. ... I may perhaps add this to what Lord Phillips MR has said in paragraphs 6 and 7 of his judgment. The practical significance of the cardinal rule which he sets out, and with which I respectfully agree, is well illustrated by the remainder of his judgment. Its legal importance has been plain since the seminal decision in the House of Lords in *R (Daly) v Home Secretary* [2001] 2 WLR 1622: see in particular Lord Bingham at paragraph

---

67 [2004] EWCA Civ 194 at paras 42D–55 and 59D–65.

68 It is a curious feature of this case, however, that it was not expressly argued that the underlying planning decision, refusing planning permission for the development, was in breach of article 8: see, for example, [2004] EWCA Civ 194 at para 46. This concession inevitably made it more difficult to argue that enforcement of that underlying decision was in breach of article 8.

69 [2004] EWCA Civ 1378.

23 and Lord Steyn at paragraph 27. Proportionality is rarely a simple yes or no issue. Except in cases where the answer is obvious (for instance where no intelligible justification has been put forward, or where the need is plain and the invasion trivial) it requires a structured consideration of the questions now well established in Strasbourg jurisprudence: is the objective sufficiently important to justify limiting a basic right; is the measure sensibly directed to the objective; does it impair the right more than necessary?

More recently, Sedley LJ returned to the same theme in the case of *Machado v Secretary of State for the Home Department*[70] and said:

> 41. ... I would add that proportionality is not an issue that can ordinarily be addressed in one sentence. It does not demand complexity, but it calls for a structured approach.

Article 14: general principles

2.64   It was said by Lord Walker of Gestingthorpe in *R (Carson) v Secretary of State for Work and Pensions* that:

> In the field of human rights, discrimination is regarded as particularly objectionable because it disregards fundamental notions of human dignity and equality before the law. Discrimination on the ground of sex or race demeans the victim by using a sexual or racial stereotype as a sufficient ground for unfavourable treatment, rather than treating her as an individual to be judged on her own merits.[71]

2.65   Baroness Hale of Richmond explained the point very clearly in *Ghaidan v Godin-Mendoza*:

> My Lords, it is not very long ago in this country that people might be refused access to a so-called 'public' bar because of their sex or the colour of their skin; that a woman might automatically be paid three quarters of what a man was paid for doing exactly the same job; that a landlady offering rooms to let might lawfully put a 'no blacks' notice in her window. We now realise that this was wrong. It was wrong because the sex or colour of the person was simply irrelevant to the choice which was being made: to whether he or she would be a fit and proper person to have a drink with others in a bar, to how well she might do the job, to how good a tenant or lodger he might be. It was wrong because it depended on stereotypical assumptions which had nothing to do with the qualities of the individual involved: even if there was any reason to believe that more

---

70 [2005] EWCA Civ 597.
71 [2006] 1 AC 173 at para 49.

women than men made bad customers this was no justification for discriminating against all women. It was wrong because it was based on an
irrelevant characteristic which the woman ... did not choose and could do
nothing about.[72]

2.66   The Court of Appeal in *Ghaidan v Godin-Mendoza*[73] went further and
stated that article 14 imposes a positive obligation on states to secure
that their citizens enjoy Convention rights without discrimination.
Whilst the point was not discussed in their Lordships' judgments
when the case was considered by the House of Lords, the ECtHR confirmed that such a positive obligation existed, at least in relation to
the eradication of race discrimination when it delivered its judgment
in the case of *Timishev v Russia*:[74]

> Racial discrimination is a particularly invidious kind of discrimination
> and, in view of its perilous consequences, requires from the authorities spe-
> cial vigilance and a vigorous reaction. It is for this reason that the author-
> ities must use all available means to combat racism, thereby reinforcing
> democracy's vision of a society in which diversity is not perceived as a
> threat but as a source of enrichment.

The European Court of Human Rights' approach to article 14 complaints

2.67   As has already been noted, article 14 is not a free-standing right. It
only protects the individual from discrimination in relation to the
enjoyment of other Convention rights. In essence article 14 guarantees
that persons in similar situations should be treated in a similar manner
with respect to their enjoyment of their Convention rights unless there
are objective and reasonable justifications for different treatment, that
is: whether the measure has a legitimate aim; and whether there is a
reasonable relationship of proportionality between the means employed
and the aim sought to be achieved.[75] However, it is important to note
that article 14 also guarantees the right of persons in different situations
to be treated differently[76] – a point that may well be of significance in
cases involving Gypsies and Travellers.

---

72 [2004] 3 WLR 113 at para 130.

73 [2003] Ch 380 at para 5.

74 Application nos 55762/00 and 55974/00, judgment 13 March 2006.

75 *Petrovic v Austria* (2001) 33 EHRR 14 at para 307.

76 *Thlimmenos v Greece* (2001) 31 EHRR 15 at para 411.

2.68   When determining article 14 complaints the ECtHR generally affords states a 'margin of appreciation'. The width of such a margin of appreciation in any given case will depend upon:

- the nature of the Convention right involved – more latitude is allowed in social and economic fields, whereas the margin is very narrow in cases which concern fundamental rights;
- the extent of the interference with a Convention right – if the measure has no more than a limited impact on the enjoyment of a Convention right, then the margin of appreciation is likely to be wider than if the measure prevents the individual from exercising the right;
- the category of alleged discrimination – the ECtHR considers there to be a strong public interest in combatting discrimination on grounds of sex, race, nationality (other than in immigration cases), illegitimacy and religion, and consequently will require states to provide very weighty reasons for discrimination on any of those grounds.

2.69   The burden is on the complainant to establish a difference in treatment. It is then for the respondent state to show that the difference in treatment is justified.[77]

2.70   The standard of proof adopted for article 14 complaints is 'beyond reasonable doubt'. However, as one might imagine, the application of such a high standard presents considerable difficulties for complainants. For example, in *Anguelova v Bulgaria*,[78] the ECtHR was asked to consider an article 14 claim in circumstances where the complainant's son, a Roma Gypsy, had died whilst in police custody. The ECtHR accepted that the complainant's claim that his son had been tortured whilst in custody because of his ethnicity raised a 'serious argument' and noted that the state had not given any plausible explanation for the death in custody. Nevertheless, the ECtHR felt unable to conclude beyond reasonable doubt that the deceased had been treated differently as a consequence of racial prejudice – a decision which led one of the dissenting judges, Judge Bonello, to note that:

> Kurds, coloureds, Muslims, Roma and others are again and again killed, tortured or maimed, but the Court is not persuaded that their race, colour or nationality or place of origin has anything to do with it.

---

77 *Timishev*, Application nos 55762/00 and 55974/00 at para 57.
78 Application no 38361/97, judgment 13 June 2002.

2.71   In *Nachova v Bulgaria*[79] the ECtHR considered a case where two Roma
conscripts had been shot dead by military police officers. The men
had recently absconded from a military construction crew, were known
to be unarmed and were not considered to be dangerous. Nevertheless
both men were killed by automatic weapon fire in broad daylight when
they were found in a Roma neighbourhood where the grandmother of
one of the victims lived. Immediately after the shootings a military
police officer yelled 'You damn Gypsies!' at one of the other residents
of the neighbourhood.

2.72   Complaints were made to the ECtHR under article 2 (the right to
life) and article 14. It was argued before the Grand Chamber that the
'beyond reasonable doubt' standard was simply too high for complainants to meet. The ECtHR disagreed with that point. However,
whilst the court reiterated its adherence to the 'beyond reasonable
doubt' standard of proof it did state that:

> Proof may follow from the co-existence of sufficiently strong, clear and
> concordant inferences or of similar unrebutted presumptions of fact.[80]

Having done so, the ECtHR indicated that there was an obligation on
states to investigate possible racist motives behind acts of violence
and found that Bulgaria had breached its obligation to do so in violation of articles 2 and 14.

The assessment of article 14 claims by domestic courts

2.73   The task of formulating an approach that domestic courts should take
when considering discrimination claims brought under article 14 of the
Convention has proved problematic. The decisions in *Wandsworth
LBC v Michalak*[81] and *R (Carson) v Secretary of State for Work and
Pensions*[82] resulted in the adoption of an approach which required five
questions to be posed by a judge dealing with such a claim:

(1) Do the facts fall within the ambit of one or more of the Convention
rights?
(2) Was there a difference in treatment in respect of that right between
the complainant and others put forward for comparison?

---

79 Application nos 43577/98–43579/98, judgment 6 July 2005.
80 *Nachova v Bulgaria*, Application no 43577/98 at para 147, judgment 6 July
2005.
81 [2003] 1 WLR 617.
82 [2002] EWHC 978 (Admin).

(3) If so, was the difference in treatment on one or more of the prescribed grounds under article 14?

(4) Were those others in an analogous situation?

(5) Was the difference in treatment objectively justifiable in the sense that it had a legitimate aim and bore a reasonable relationship of proportionality to that aim?

2.74 However, in *Ghaidan v Godin-Mendoza*[83] Baroness Hale of Richmond issued a word of warning, making the point that, whilst the Michalak questions were a useful tool of analysis, there was considerable overlap between them and that a rigidly formulaic approach should be avoided.

2.75 The House of Lords revisited the issue when it considered *R (Carson) v Secretary of State for Work and Pensions*[84] on appeal. Having referred to the Michalak questions, Lord Nicholls of Birkenhead said:

> 3. ... I prefer to keep the formulation of the relevant issues in these cases as simple and non-technical as possible. Article 14 does not apply unless the alleged discrimination is in connection with a Convention right and on a ground stated in article 14. If this pre-requisite is satisfied, the essential question for the court is whether the alleged disrcimination, that is, the difference in treatment of which complaint is made, can withstand scrutiny. Sometimes the answer to this question will be plain. There may be such an obvious, relevant difference between the claimant and those with whom he seeks to compare himself that their situations cannot be regarded as analogous. Sometimes, where the position is not so clear, a different approach is called for. Then the court's scrutiny may best be directed at considering whether the differentiation has a legitimate aim and whether the means chosen to achieve the aim is appropriate and not disproportionate in its adverse impact.

Likewise Lord Hoffman and Lord Walker of Gestingthorpe concluded that the question whether there had been a breach of article 14 could be best answered without adopting the *Michalak* approach.

2.76 In addition, their Lordships indicated that a distinction was to be drawn between grounds of discrimination under article 14 which prima facie appeared to offend respect due to the individual, as in the case of sex or race, where very weighty reasons are required to justify the difference in treatment, and those which merely required some rational justification.[85]

83 [2004] 3 WLR 113 at para 134.
84 [2006] 1 AC 173.
85 See also *Westminster City Council and the First Secretary of State v Morris* [2005] EWCA Civ 1184 at para 82.

2.77   Generally domestic courts will afford public bodies a margin of discretion or a discretionary area of judgment when considering whether a difference in treatment is justified. However, the width of the margin of discretion will depend on the nature of the alleged discrimination and ought not to have any application in cases of direct discrimination on grounds of race.[86]

Article 14 and relevant discrimination cases post-Human Rights Act 1998

2.78   Gypsies and Travellers are among the most socially excluded groups in society and frequently suffer discrimination in their access to the most basic necessities of life. Although in theory Gypsies and Travellers enjoy the same entitlements to public services as the settled community, in practice they frequently experience discrimination in their access to such services. Some of the rights and interests which are protected by those basic services (for example, health and education) fall within the scope of other Convention rights, such as the right not to be subjected to inhuman and degrading treatment (article 3), the right to respect for family life (article 8) and the right to education (article 2 of Protocol 1). The article 14 guarantee against discrimination in the enjoyment of Convention rights can therefore be relied upon where discriminatory access to basic services impinges on these Convention rights. However, attempts by Gypsies and Travellers to invoke article 14 in our domestic courts have had mixed results to date.

Evictions from rented local authority sites

2.79   One of the most striking differences of treatment suffered by the Gypsy and Traveller population relates to the terms under which they are permitted to occupy local authority sites. Residents of Gypsy and Traveller sites run by local authorities have no security of tenure and only the most basic legal protection against harassment and eviction; a position which contrasts starkly with that of those living on privately run mobile home parks and those living in local authority housing. This difference of treatment is increasingly anomalous now that the majority of Gypsies and Travellers no longer pursue a wholly nomadic way of life. Article 14 would appear to provide a means of challenging such differential treatment.

---

86 See *Timishev* Application nos 55762/00 and 55974/00 and a fuller discussion on the topic in *R (Clare Wilson) v Wychavon DC and the First Secretary of State* [2007] EWCA Civ 52.

2.80   In *Somerset County Council v Isaacs and Secretary of State for Trans-port, Local Government and the Regions*,[87] article 14 was relied on to challenge the differential treatment of Gypsy caravan occupiers on council sites compared with occupants of mobile homes sites. Caravan dwellers on mobile homes sites have security of tenure under the Mobile Homes Act (MHA) 1983, but occupiers of local authority Gypsy/Traveller sites were not covered by that protection. It was argued that such differential treatment in relation to the enjoyment of the right to respect for home lacked objective justification and was there-fore in breach of article 14 in conjunction with article 8. The High Court gave the discrimination argument short shrift, however, holding that the exemptions from protection in the Caravan Sites Act (CSA) 1968 depended on the status of the site owner as a local authority, and not on any personal quality of the licensee or tenant, and it therefore raised no question of discrimination contrary to article 14.[88]

2.81   In *R (Albert Smith) v Barking and Dagenham LBC and Secretary of State for the Office of the Deputy Prime Minister*,[89] a Gypsy family who were seeking to prevent their eviction from a council site sought a declaration that the provisions of CSA 1968 Pt I were incompatible with ECHR articles 8 and 14. The argument was that Gypsies and Travellers are not given the same protection against eviction by local authorities in CSA 1968 Pt I as is given to secure tenants of con-ventional housing let by local authorities, that this differential treatment of Gypsies and Travellers was without objective and reasonable justification and, therefore, was in breach of article 14.

2.82   It was not disputed that the issue of security of tenure for Gypsies' and Travellers homes on caravan sites fell within the scope of article 8; eviction from a site clearly interfered with the right to respect for their home.[90] The differential treatment also could not be denied; Gypsies and Travellers clearly enjoy lesser legal protection than that available to tenants of conventional housing. The court also rejected the secretary of state's argument that the chosen comparators, council tenants in con-ventional housing, were not in an analogous situation to a Gypsy or Traveller living in a caravan on a council site.

2.83   On the question of whether the difference of treatment was justi-fied, however, the High Court held that the secretary of state had dis-charged the onus he bore of demonstrating that there was an objective and reasonable justification for continuing the absence of security of

---

87 [2002] EWHC 1014 Admin.
88 [2002] EWHC 1014 Admin at para 39.
89 [2002] EWHC 2400 Admin.
90 [2002] EWHC 2400 Admin at para 6.

tenure for Gypsy and Traveller caravan dwellers on council sites. The High Court accepted the secretary of state's argument that he was justified in maintaining the current position of a lack of security of tenure on local authority sites to allow for flexibility in meeting the accommodation needs of Gypsies and Travellers and to facilitate their nomadic way of life. If security of tenure were given to all long-term occupiers, the court held, this might make matters worse for Gypsies and Travellers by reducing the number of sites available for them to enable them to pursue a nomadic way of life.[91]

2.84   However, in 2004 the ECtHR delivered its judgment in *Connors v United Kingdom*[92] and in doing so effectively overruled both *Isaacs* and *Smith*.

2.85   In *Connors*, the ECtHR concluded that the UK government was in breach of article 8.[93] However, the court did not go on to consider whether there was also a breach of article 14.

Planning enforcement and the use of stop notices

2.86   Where a local authority has issued an enforcement notice to restrain a breach of planning control it may also issue a 'stop notice' under TCPA 1990 s183(4) prohibiting the carrying out of a specified activity on the land to which the enforcement notice relates.[94] In its original form TCPA 1990 s183 could not be used to prohibit individuals living in caravans on land or those that used a building as a dwellinghouse. However, the provision was amended by the Planning and Compensation Act (PCA) 1991 s9 and the caravan use exemption was removed though the dwellinghouse exemption was retained. In *R (Clare Wilson) v First Secretary of State and Wychavon DC*[95] the appellant, a Gypsy,

91 Although the discrimination challenge ultimately failed in this case, the court made clear in its judgment that its decision on justification was based on the evidence then available, and that it expected the government to continue to monitor the position and to obtain the necessary evidence to decide whether or not the difference in treatment continued to be justifiable.

92 *Connors v United Kingdom* (2005) 40 EHRR 9. For further discussion on this topic, see chapter 3, below.

93 On 27 June 2007 the Joint Committee on Human Rights (JCHR) published its Sixteenth Report of Session 2006–07 entitled *Monitoring the government's response to court judgments finding breaches of human rights*. In paras 100–103 of the Report the JCHR made it clear that it considered the government should take urgent action to comply with the ECtHR's judgment in Connors. See chapter 3, below, for more discussion on this topic.

94 See chapter 4 at paras 4.148–4.149, below.

95 [2007] EWCA Civ 52. See also the two JCHR Reports on the issue: paras 5.5–5.7 of the Eighth Report of Session 2003–04, *Scrutiny of bills: third progress report*; and paras 3.2–3.4 of the Tenth Report of Session 2003–04, *Scrutiny of bills: fourth progress report*.

challenged the legislation by way of judicial review on grounds that it unlawfully discriminated against Romani Gypsies and Irish Travellers in breach of article 14 of the Convention and she also sought a declaration of incompatibility to that effect. Crane J dismissed the claim and the appellant appealed against that decision.

2.87   In his judgment Richards LJ explained the issues that the Court of Appeal had to determine in the following way:

> The Secretary of State has very properly made a number of concessions which serve greatly to reduce the area of contention. It is not in dispute that (a) the operation of section 183 falls within the ambit of article 8, so as to engage article 14; (b) a higher proportion of gypsies and travellers than of any other relevant group would be likely to be affected by stop notices served under section 183 on caravans used for residential purposes; (c) therefore, although the exemption in section 183(4) appears on its face to be a neutral provision, its greater impact on gypsies and travellers than on the general population means that it is indirectly discriminatory in its effect in relation to a status falling within the scope of article 14; and (d) hence there is an onus on the State to give an objective justification for the rule as formulated. The point for decision is whether the Secretary of State has discharged the onus of justifying the provision.[96]

2.88   Thus it was common ground that the secretary of state had the burden of justifying the admitted discrimination that occurred in 1991 (when the legislation was amended) and continues to date. In addition it was accepted by the Court of Appeal that the standard of proof was a high one for the secretary of state to meet, and that any discretionary area of judgment will be narrow in cases such as this, which involved discrimination on particularly sensitive grounds such as gender or race.[97]

2.89   In the event, the Court of Appeal concluded that: there was a clear distinction between the unauthorised stationing of a residential caravan on land and unauthorised development to which the dwellinghouse exemption applies; and that the use of buildings as dwellinghouses will cause less environmental damage than the stationing of residential caravans on land. In the circumstances the Court of Appeal was satisfied that the difference in treatment was justified and the appeal was dismissed.[98]

---

96 [2007] EWCA Civ 52 at para 27.
97 [2007] EWCA Civ 52 at para 46.
98 [2007] EWCA Civ 52 at paras 66–68. The appellant has been refused permission to appeal to the House of Lords and, having exhausted all domestic remedies, she is now likely to take her case to the ECtHR.

Planning permission for Gypsy and Traveller sites and the relevance of offers of conventional housing

2.90   The protection of article 14 has been invoked rather more success-fully in relation to the relevance of an offer of conventional housing to Gypsies and Travellers when making decisions about planning per-mission or consequential enforcement. In *Clarke v Secretary of State for the Environment, Transport and the Regions and Tunbridge Wells BC*,[99] a planning inspector had found that conventional housing accommo-dation had been offered to the Gypsy family in question, and that they found the prospect distressing, having never lived in a conventional house. Nevertheless, the inspector went on to state that the offer of that accommodation detracted somewhat from the contention that the only alternative to the appeal site was an illegal roadside pitch. The High Court held that:

> ... in certain appropriate circumstances it can amount to a breach of arti-cles 8 and 14 to weigh in the balance and hold against a Gypsy applying for planning permission, or indeed resisting eviction from Council or pri-vate land, that he or she has refused conventional housing accommodation as being contrary to his or her culture.[100]

To treat such refusal as a relevant consideration in reaching a deci-sion was just as impermissible as penalising a religious or strictly observant Christian, Jew or Muslim because they will not work on certain days, or as penalising a strictly observant Buddhist, Muslim, Jew or Sikh because they will not eat certain foods or wear certain clothing.

2.91   The onus was on the individual concerned to satisfy the planning inspector that they or their family do indeed have a genuine aversion to conventional housing, but once that has been established:

> ... it would be contrary to articles 8 and 14 to expect such a person to accept conventional housing and to hold it against him or her that he has not accepted it, or is not prepared to accept it, even as a last resort factor.[101]

99 [2001] EWHC 800 Admin; [2002] JPL 552; July 2002 *Legal Action* 23.
100 [2001] EWHC 800 Admin at para 30.
101 [2001] EWHC 800 Admin at para 34. The decision was upheld on appeal by a unanimous Court of Appeal (see *Clarke v Secretary of State for Transport, Local Government and the Regions and Tunbridge Wells BC* [2002] EWCA Civ 819 at paras 5 and 15 of the judgment, where the Court of Appeal endorsed the important point that an aversion to conventional housing may be grounded in a belief or understanding which is an integral part of a cultural identity as a Gypsy or Traveller). See also *Price v Carmarthenshire County Council* [2003] EWHC 42 Admin and *Codona v Mid-Bedfordshire DC* [2004] EWCA Civ 925. See the further discussion of these issues in chapter 6 at paras 6.51–6.57 and 6.89–6.93, below.

Articles 11 and 14: culture and traditional horse fairs

2.92   In *Chapman*,[102] the ECtHR recognised that Gypsies and Travellers have a right to respect for their traditional way of life and their culture and held that 'the applicant's occupation of her caravan is an integral part of her ethnic identity as a Gypsy, reflecting the long tradition of that minority of following a travelling lifestyle'.

2.93   In the case of *R v Tunbridge Wells BC ex p The Gypsy Council for Education, Culture, Welfare and Civil Rights and Eli Frankham*,[103] the High Court was asked to consider a case concerning the right of Gypsies to attend a traditional 'Horse Fair' that had been held in the village of Horsmonden, in Kent, for many years. A decision had been taken by the local authority to prohibit the holding of the annual Horse Fair on grounds that it would give rise to health and safety considerations.[104] It was the subject of an application for judicial review made by a respected elder of the Gypsy community and an organisation that works for the preservation of the Gypsy way of life. The decision was challenged on the basis that it breached articles 8, 11 (the right to freedom of association and assembly) and 14 of the Convention. However, the High Court accepted that the local authority had taken account of all relevant considerations and had struck the correct balance between the interests of the Romani Gypsy community and the interests of society in general. In addition, the High Court held that the decision was necessary and proportionate, given the circumstances of the case and the fact that an alternative venue had been proposed some 20 miles away from Horsmonden.[105]

Article 2 of Protocol 1: education

2.94   The HRA 1998 gives added weight to an important consideration which is all too frequently neglected in decisions affecting Gypsies and Travellers: the impact of those decisions on the education of Gypsy and Traveller children. Article 2 of Protocol 1 to the Convention provides that no person shall be denied the right to education, which has been interpreted as guaranteeing a right of access to such educational facil-

---

102 *Chapman v UK* (2001) 33 EHRR 399 at para 73.

103 7 September 2000 (unreported), Admin Court.

104 The decision was made under the provisions of Public Order Act 1986 s14A (as amended by Criminal Justice and Public Order Act 1994 s70) and was approved by the Secretary of State.

105 The subsequent complaint made to the ECtHR was ruled inadmissible – see *Gypsy Council v United Kingdom* Application no 66336/01.

ities as exist.[106] In order for this right to education to be practical and effective, the children of Gypsies and Travellers require a minimum degree of stability in order to be able to attend the same school and receive continuous education.

2.95   On the traditional approach to planning law, which looked narrowly at land use considerations with only a narrow exception to consider 'personal circumstances' as a material consideration, the educational interests of Gypsy and Traveller children rarely, if ever, influenced decisions about whether or not to grant planning permission, or whether or not to enforce against unauthorised developments. The enhanced status now given to the right to education means that this is a consideration which might make a real, practical difference in the circumstances of a particular case. In *Basildon DC v Secretary of State for the Environment*,[107] for example, the court upheld a decision of the secretary of state in which the environmental harm caused by a Gypsy caravan site in the Green Belt was considered to be outweighed by the need for stable educational facilities for the younger children of the families concerned.

Commission for Equality and Human Rights

2.96   The Equality Act (EqA) 2006 established the Commission for Equality and Human Rights (CEHR) which will come into being in October 2007. The CEHR is intended to be an independent advocate for equality and human rights in the United Kingdom and its aim will be to reduce inequality, eliminate discrimination, strengthen good relations between people and protect and promote human rights. The CEHR will bring together the work of the Commission for Racial Equality (CRE) the Disability Rights Commission (DRC) and the Equal Opportunities Commission (EOC) in one body and will take on all the powers currently vested in the existing bodies as well as new powers to enforce legislation more effectively and promote equality for all.[108]

2.97   EqA 2006 s9 provides that:

>   (1) The Commission shall, by exercising the powers conferred by this Part –
>
>   (a) promote understanding of the importance of human rights,

106 See chapter 7, below, for a full discussion of issues with regard to education.
107 21 December 2000 (unreported), Admin Court.
108 See chapter 8, below, for a more in-depth discussion of the function and powers of the CRE and CEHR.

    (b) encourage good practice in relation to human rights,

    (c) promote awareness, understanding and protection of human rights, and

    (d) encourage public authorities to comply with section 6 of the Human Rights Act 1998 ...

2.98   EqA 2006 s20 gives the CEHR the power to investigate whether a person has committed an unlawful act and EqA 2006 s21 entitles the CEHR to issue an 'unlawful act notice' in the event that it is satisfied that such an act has been committed. Significantly, EqA 2006 s24 enables the CEHR to apply to the courts for an injunction in circumstances where it is thought that a person is likely to commit an unlawful act. In addition, EqA 2006 s30 provides that the CEHR may institute, or intervene in legal proceedings, whether for judicial review or otherwise, if it appears to the Commission that the proceedings are relevant to a matter in connection with which the Commission has a function.

Conclusion

2.99   The HRA 1998 offers Gypsies and Travellers some important resources to be used in their struggle against the systemic discrimination and exclusion which they face. Requiring public authorities to justify interferences with Gypsies' and Travellers' way of life, and to demonstrate the necessity of treating members of those communities differently from the settled community, is a potentially empowering step for this most marginalised of groups. Used wisely, in a carefully thought-out litigation strategy, and at appropriate points in the policy-making and legislative process, the rights outlined above ought to help to hasten the day when public policy towards Gypsies and Travellers is no longer driven by the ignorance, fear and prejudices of some of the settled population. It is essential that the CEHR uses its powers to help achieve that goal.

CHAPTER 3

Rented Gypsy/Traveller sites

3.1	**Introduction**
3.3	**Provision of sites**
3.11	**Local authority sites – the legal regime**
3.11	Security of tenure
3.15	Security of tenure and the Human Rights Act 1998
3.29	Allocation of pitches
3.33	The Disability Discrimination Act 1995
3.35	Conditions of occupancy and repairs
3.37	Rent/site fee
3.40	Provision of facilities
3.42	Fire precautions
3.46	Environmental Protection Act 1990
3.49	Grants
3.52	Redevelopment of sites
3.56	**Non-local authority sites**
3.62	**Conclusion**

Introduction

3.1   This chapter seeks to explain:

- what security of tenure Gypsies and Travellers have on local authority sites;
- the effect of the Human Rights Act (HRA) 1998 (especially in the light of recent court cases) and the Disability Discrimination Act (DDA) 1995 on security of tenure;
- the role of judicial review in relation to the allocation of and eviction from pitches on local authority sites;
- the law affecting conditions of occupancy and repairs on Gypsy/Traveller sites;
- what security of tenure Gypsies and Travellers have on non-local authority sites.

'Rented Gypsy/Traveller sites' are sites owned by a local authority, another organisation (including, registered social landlords) or private individuals where the pitches on the site are rented out to Gypsies and/or Travellers. According to the Communities and Local Government (CLG) Count of Gypsy caravans (CLG being the government department with responsibility for Gypsy and Traveller accommodation issues), some 40 per cent of the Gypsy and Traveller population at any one time will be accommodated on authorised local authority encampments. For example, in January 2007, the CLG Gypsy Count showed that there were:

- 6,564 caravans on authorised council sites;
- 6,509 caravans on authorised private sites;
- 3,538 caravans on unauthorised sites; and
- a total of 16,611 caravans counted.

3.2   Although the Gypsy Count cannot be taken as completely accurate[1] it gives an idea of the significance of council-provided sites so far as the accommodation of the Gypsy and Traveller population is concerned. This is so despite the closure of local authority sites since the repeal of the duty to provide accommodation by Criminal Justice and Public Order Act (CJPOA) 1994 s80.[2] The legal regime as it affects authorised council sites is, therefore, an important factor in the lives of

---

1   See Niner, *Counting Gypsies and Travellers: a review of the Gypsy Caravan Count System*, ODPM, 2004.

2   For example, since 1994, by 2002 139 residential pitches were lost due to site closure. See Niner, *The provision and condition of local authority Gypsy/Traveller sites in England*, ODPM, 2002, p17.

nearly half of the Gypsy and Traveller population who live in caravans. Though there are no accurate figures available, it is known that only a small minority of authorised private sites are rented sites. Nevertheless, and somewhat ironically given the current lack of security of tenure on local authority sites, those sites are protected under the Mobile Homes Act 1983 and that is also discussed briefly at the end of this chapter.

Provision of sites

3.3   The local authority sites currently in existence have been established under different legal powers or duties. Under the Caravan Sites Act (CSA) 1968, it was the duty of a county council, London borough, or (in Wales) a county borough to exercise its powers under Caravan Sites and Control of Development Act (CSCDA) 1960 s24 to 'provide adequate accommodation for gypsies residing in or resorting to their area'.[3] The CSA 1968 placed an obligation on county councils to determine what sites were to be provided and to acquire the land (subject to consultation and consideration of any objection through the planning process).[4] The district councils were obliged to exercise the other powers under CSCDA 1960 s24, and particularly the management of sites. The county councils were also expected to fix the charges made by the district councils for their provision and to pay the district councils any shortfall between their expenditure and receipts.[5] As a consequence 'the majority of public sites in non-metropolitan districts are owned by county councils and managed by district councils'.[6]

3.4   The CSA 1968 duty was repealed in 1994 by the CJPOA 1994, and now only the powers under CSCDA 1960 s24 remain. Those powers are wide:

(1) A local authority shall have power within their area to provide sites where caravans may be brought, whether for holidays or some other temporary purposes or for use as permanent residences, and to manage the site or lease them to some other person.

(2) ... a local authority shall have power to do anything appearing to them desirable in connection with the provision of such sites ...

3 CSA 1968 s6.
4 CSA 1968 ss7 and 8.
5 CSA 1968 s7.
6 Department of the Environment (DoE) Circular 18/94, Welsh Office 76/94 (hereafter DoE Circular 18/94) *Gypsy sites policy and unauthorised camping* para 19.

3.5 For the purposes of CSCDA 1960 s24 the term 'local authority' is defined as including a county council, a district council, the Common Council of the City of London, the Council of the Isles of Scilly, a London borough and, in Wales, a Welsh county council or county borough.[7]

3.6 When the government repealed the CSA 1968 it envisaged that CSCDA 1960 s24 would become the vehicle for the provision of local authority caravan sites for Gypsies and amended CSCDA 1960 s24 by inserting a power to provide 'working spaces' for Gypsies and facilities for their normal activities.[8]

3.7 The government also envisaged that the network of existing sites would continue to be maintained after the repeal of the CSA 1968 duty. In DoE Circular 18/94 local authorities were advised that:

> The Secretaries of State consider it appropriate that authorities should maintain their existing gypsy caravan sites, or should make suitable arrangements for their maintenance by leasing them to other persons who are willing and able to maintain them.[9]

3.8 The advice in Circular 18/94 also made it clear that the government expected that additional sites would continue to be provided by local authorities:

> The Secretaries of State also expect authorities to continue to consider whether it is appropriate to provide further permanent caravan sites for gypsies in their areas.[10]

3.9 The government has now moved to a more proactive approach to site provision, both public and private, as envisaged in Office of the Deputy Prime Minister (ODPM) Circular 01/2006 (hereafter Circular 1/06) *Planning for Gypsy and Traveller caravan sites*. This starts with a recognition of the failure of the previous policies:

> A new Circular is necessary because evidence shows that the advice set out in [DoE] Circular 1/94 has failed to deliver adequate sites for gypsies and travellers in many areas of England over the last 10 years. Since the issue of Circular 1/94, and the repeal of local authorities' duty to provide gypsy and traveller sites there have been more applications for private gypsy and traveller sites, but this has not resulted in the necessary increase in provision.[11]

---

7 CSCDA 1960 ss24(8) and 29(1).
8 CJPOA 1994 s80.
9 DoE Circular 18/94 para 21.
10 DoE Circular 18/94 para 22.
11 ODPM Circular 1/06 para 3. For further discussion of this circular, see chapter 4, below.

3.10   Circular 1/06 moves on to a recognition of the need for more public site provision:

> The Government recognizes that many gypsies and travellers wish to find and buy their own sites to develop and manage. An increase in the number of approved private sites may also release pitches on local authority sites for gypsies and travellers most in need of public provision. However, there will remain a requirement for public site provision above the current levels. Such sites are needed for gypsies and travellers who are unable to buy and develop their own sites, or prefer to rent, and to provide transit sites and emergency stopping places where gypsies and travellers may legally stop in the course of travelling.[12]

Local authority rented sites – the legal regime

Security of tenure

3.11   A Gypsy or Traveller living on a local authority caravan site has no real protection against eviction provided that he or she has been given four weeks' written notice and a court order has been obtained.[13] However, the CSA 1968 does afford residents some protection from eviction without a court order by making such an act a criminal offence. Similarly, the CSA 1968 protects residents from harassment by making acts calculated to affect the peace or comfort of the occupier and the withdrawal or withholding of services or facilities reasonably required a criminal offence.[14]

3.12   The lack of real protection against a 'lawful' eviction afforded to Gypsies and Travellers occupying local authority sites should be contrasted with the protection from eviction enjoyed by the occupiers of caravan sites covered by the Mobile Homes Act (MHA) 1983.

3.13   The protection enjoyed by MHA 1983 occupiers has some similarity to that of secure tenants of local authorities under the Housing Act (HA) 1985 (which provides that no possession order can be granted except on proof of grounds and the most used grounds being subject to it being reasonable to make an order).[15] The HA 1985 does not apply

---

12 ODPM Circular 1/06 para 13. The CLG *Draft Guidance on the design of sites for Gypsies and Travellers* (May 2007), at chapters 8 and 9, contains detailed recommendations concerning location, layout, services and facilities on both transit sites and emergency stopping places.

13 CSA 1968 ss2, 3 and 4, which remain in force.

14 CSA 1968 s3.

15 HA 1985 s84 and Sch 2.

to caravan sites as it concerns only tenancies or licences of a dwelling-house.

3.14   It should be pointed out that the *Draft Guidance on the management of Gypsy and Traveller sites* produced (in May 2007) by Communities and Local Government envisages court action as being very much a last resort. Thus, at paragraph 9.9, it states:

> Where a licence or agreement has been breached, depending on the severity of the breach, the first aim should normally be to remedy the breach. Appropriate steps might be:
>
> • Collect evidence demonstrating the breach;
> • Verbal negotiation;
> • Written communication with timescale in which to remedy the breach;
> • Second written communication with notification of subsequent actions which could ultimately lead to termination of the licence or agreement.

Security of tenure and the Human Rights Act 1998

3.15   The differences in security of tenure enjoyed by those living on authorised Gypsy sites and those living on sites protected by MHA 1983, on the one hand, and local authority secure tenants under the HA 1985, on the other, might be thought to be incompatible with the European Convention on Human Rights (ECHR); in particular articles 8 (right to respect for private and family life and the home) and 14 (prohibition of discrimination). However, in two cases, the High Court, backed by the Court of Appeal, determined that there was no such incompatibility: *Somerset CC v Isaacs and Secretary of State for Transport, Local Government and the Regions*[16] and *R (Albert Smith) v Barking and Dagenham LBC and Secretary of State for the Office of the Deputy Prime Minister.*[17] Both cases concerned possession proceedings brought by the respective councils against the occupiers of pitches on official Gypsy caravan sites, who had been given notice terminating their occupation agreements.

3.16   The European Court of Human Rights (ECtHR) addressed this issue, subsequent to the above domestic cases, in *Connors v UK.*[18] Mr Connors and his family were Irish Travellers and they had lived for many years on a local authority site. Their licence to occupy the site was terminated as a result of allegations of nuisance. Mr Connors disputed

16 [2002] EWHC 1014 Admin, and see Chapter 2, paras 2.79–2.85.
17 [2002] EWHC 2400 Admin and [2003] EWCA Civ 385, and see Chapter 2, paras 2.79–2.85.
18 (2004) 40 EHRR 189.

these allegations and judicially reviewed the council's decision to seek their eviction. That application for judicial review failed, the council obtained a possession order and Mr Connors and his family were evicted from the site. Mr Connors complained to the ECtHR that the eviction breached his rights under article 8.

3.17   In its judgment, the ECtHR held that:

- there was a positive obligation on the United Kingdom to facilitate the Gypsy way of life;
- the eviction was a serious interference with Mr Connors' article 8 rights and it required particularly weighty reasons of public interest by way of justification;
- it was not persuaded that there was any particular feature about local authority Gypsy/Traveller sites which would render their management unworkable if they were required to establish reasons for evicting long-standing occupants;
- the power to evict without the burden of giving reasons which were liable to be examined on their merits by an independent tribunal had not been convincingly shown to respond to any specific goal or to provide any particular benefit to members of the Gypsy/Traveller community;
- the eviction could not be justified by a 'pressing social need' or be said to be proportionate to the legitimate aim pursued;
- judicial review was not an adequate remedy as it provided no opportunity for examination of the facts in dispute.

As a consequence the ECtHR held that there had been a violation of article 8 and awarded Mr Connors damages.

3.18   Housing Act 2004 s211 (by amending CSA 1968 s4) had made provision for judges to suspend possession orders against Gypsies and Travellers on official sites for periods of up to 12 months (potentially this can be consecutive periods, not just one period). This amendment does not, of course, provide the Gypsy or Traveller concerned with a method of defending the possession action itself. In a memorandum to the Council of Ministers of November 2004,[19] the government has stated that:

> Ministers have accepted during the passage of the Housing Act 2004 that tenure on local authority Gypsy and Traveller sites is out of line with tenure in bricks and mortar social housing, and that public sites have strong similarities to social housing in terms of client profile, landlord profile and

---

19 This memorandum was exhibited to a witness statement in a court case but has never been formally published by the government.

management needs ... Ministers have indicated that the most suitable way to take any proposals forward would be as part of future legislation on tenure reform relating to bricks and mortar housing.

Despite this positive indication, at the date of publication of this book, no formal government proposals have been brought forward.

3.19   Gypsy and Traveller campaigning groups have been pressing the government on this issue since the *Connors* decision. The Gypsy and Traveller Law Reform Coalition commissioned the preparation of a bill, the Caravan Sites (Security of Tenure) Bill 2006, which was given its first (and only) reading as a Ten Minute Rule Bill by Julie Morgan MP on 4 July 2006. Though this bill will, obviously, go no further, it has been used as a campaigning and publicity tool. In July 2005, when introducing new licence agreements for their six sites, Oxfordshire County Council included a clause that brought in a form of security of tenure analogous to that enjoyed by secure tenants of council houses and flats.[20]

3.20   The CLG *Draft Guidance on the management of Gypsy and Traveller sites* (May 2007) makes reference to the government position on the need to change the law but also contains very important recommendations about what the government feels local authorities should be doing in the meantime:

> 9.14 The Government is committed to improving the security of tenure for Gypsies and Travellers on local authority sites and will be consulting on proposals for legislative change to address the issues raised in the Connors case ...

> 9.15 In the meantime, in order to comply with the Connors judgment, we would recommend local authorities avoid asserting a right to summary possession and we would encourage them to provide additional protection to licensees on Gypsy and Traveller sites. We set out below examples of ways in which this might be achieved:

> - Include express terms in licence agreements giving licensees additional protection from eviction. We are aware that some local authority licences have been redrafted so that the authority can only seek possession on certain grounds, for example those which they may rely on against secure tenants. Alternatively they could include some of the protections and privileges given to residents on private sites under Schedule 1 of the Mobile Homes Act 1983;
> - Set up an internal appeals procedure whereby the decision of a local authority to terminate a licence could be challenged by licensees threatened with eviction. The appeal could be considered by a panel which

could decide factual disputes between the site manager and licensee and consider whether it was reasonable for the licence to be terminated.

9.16 Broadly, we suggest that local authorities should follow procedures and safeguards aligned to those expected in other social housing to tackle breaches of tenancy agreements. Failure to do so may result in an evicted licensee taking action against the authority, citing the Connors judgment. Local authorities are, therefore, urged to work with their legal advisers to review their Gypsy and Traveller licence agreements and procedures.

3.21 Whilst a change to the law is awaited, and unless the local authority in question has amended its licence agreements in line with the above draft guidance so as to incorporate security of tenure, Gypsies and Travellers on local authority sites find themselves in a strange state of legal limbo. The case of Mr Doherty illustrates this. The council, stating that it wished to refurbish its official site and to turn it into a transit site, terminated Mr Doherty's licence and sought a possession order. In December 2004, the Birmingham High Court granted the order. In so doing, HHJ McKenna decided that he was bound to follow the House of Lords decision in *Harrow LBC v Qazi*,[21] rather than the ECtHR decision in *Connors v UK*. The central question was whether it would be possible for the defendant in a possession action brought by a public authority to raise a defence under article 8 before the court of first instance.

3.22 Mr Qazi had held a joint tenancy with his wife. His wife left the property and handed in notice to quit. The notice to quit acted so as to (lawfully) terminate the tenancy. Mr Qazi then, effectively, became a trespasser. He pleaded article 8 in his subsequent defence to the possession proceedings. A majority (3 to 2) of the Law Lords held that people without any proprietary interest in the land in question would be unable to rely on such a defence. Lord Millet stated:

> [O]nce [the court] concludes that the landlord is entitled to an order for possession, there is nothing further to investigate. The order is necessary to protect the rights of the landlord; and making or enforcing it does not show a want of appropriate respect for the applicant's home ... In the exceptional case where the applicant believes that the local authority is acting unfairly or from improper or ulterior motives, he can apply to the High Court for judicial review.[22]

3.23 Mr Doherty appealed the High Court decision to the House of Lords. The House of Lords refused permission for the appeal to proceed and

21 [2003] UKHL 43; [2004] 1 AC 983.
22 [2003] UKHL 43 at paras 108–109.

re-directed the appeal to the Court of Appeal to await its own decision
in *Kay & ors v Lambeth LBC, Leeds CC v Price & ors*.[23]

3.24   The *Kay* case involved former tenants who had had their tenancies lawfully terminated and were now, effectively, trespassers. The
Price case involved Irish Travellers who had been evicted more than 50
times by the local authority over the past year from various unauthorised encampments. Both the former tenants in *Kay* and the Travellers in *Price* sought to raise article 8 as a defence to the respective
possession actions. They argued that the earlier judgment of the House
of Lords in Qazi was inconsistent with the ECtHR judgment in *Connors*.
Since they were being asked to depart from their own previous judgment, seven Law Lords heard the case. All seven were agreed that:

- in a possession action taken by a public landowner, article 8 is
  engaged;[24]
- when commencing such a possession action, the public landowner
  does not have to provide justification in terms of article 8(2) in
  every case;
- It is for the defendant to raise the article 8 defence;
- in the vast majority of cases, the proper application of domestic
  law will provide automatic justification in terms of article 8(2).

Connors was seen by the Lords as an example of an exceptional case
where an article 8 defence might be raised against the possession
action.

The majority of the Lords were all in agreement with paragraph
110 of the judgment of Lord Hope, where he stated:

> I would hold that a defence which does not challenge the law under which
> the possession order is sought as being incompatible with article 8 but is
> based only on the occupier's personal circumstances should be struck out
> ... Where domestic law provides for personal circumstances to be taken into
> account, as in a case where the statutory test is whether it would be rea-
> sonable to make a possession order, then a fair opportunity must be given
> for the arguments in favour of the occupier to be presented. But if the
> requirements of the law have been established and the right to recover
> possession is unqualified, the only situations in which it would be open to
> the court to refrain from proceeding to summary judgment and making
> the possession order are these:
>
> (a) if a seriously arguable point is raised that the law which enables the
>   court to make the possession order is incompatible with article 8, the

23 [2006] UKHL 10; [2006] 2 AC 465; [2006] 2 WLR 570.
24 As to whether right to respect for the home is engaged at all in the case of an
    unauthorised encampment, see chapter 5 at paras 5.4–5.9, below.

county court in the exercise of its jurisdiction under the Human Rights Act 1998 should deal with the argument in one or other of two ways: (i) by giving effect to the law, so far as it is possible for it to do so under section 3 [of the HRA 1998], in a way that is compatible with article 8,or (ii) by adjourning the proceedings to enable the compatibility issue to be dealt with in the High Court;

(b) if the defendant wishes to challenge the decision of a public authority to recover possession as an improper exercise of its powers at common law on the ground that it was a decision that no reasonable person would consider justifiable, he should be permitted to do this provided again that the point is seriously arguable ...[25]

3.25 Following the Lords' decision in *Kay and Price*, the Court of Appeal (CA) heard Mr Doherty's case and delivered judgment.[26] The CA decided that Mr Doherty's case could be distinguished from the case of Mr Connors on the basis that the latter involved factual issues (nuisance allegations) whereas the former involved policy issues (the local authority's decision to refurbish the site and turn it into a transit site). This was despite the fact that it had been argued on behalf of Mr Doherty that there were several factual disputes involved in his case. On this point, Carnwath LJ, giving the sole judgment of the CA, said:

> It is true that one aspect was an issue about whether the Doherty's presence 'deterred' others. However, this was not in the context, as in Connors, of an allegation of breach of a licence condition (analogous to a private law cause of action), but simply one part of its overall assessment of the various factors in play. That seems to us well within the margin of appreciation allowed by the Strasbourg jurisprudence in the exercise of an administrative discretion ...[27]

The CA concluded that, though Mr Doherty could have applied for judicial review (which would now be dealt with by way of a defence in the court of first instance rather than by way of application to the High Court), the decision of the local authority was (according to the CA) clearly a reasonable one.

3.26 In the meantime, a distinction has to be drawn between a possession claim involving 'factual issues' and a claim involving 'policy/administrative issues'. In the latter case, the CA has held that judicial review by way of defence is the only possible challenge. In the former case, the position is somewhat more complex. The CA interpreted the Lords' decision in *Kay and Price* as saying that, where one was dealing with a

---

25 [2006] 2 WLR 570 at 610.
26 *Doherty v Birmingham CC and The Secretary of State for Communities and Local Government* [2006] EWCA Civ 1739.
27 [2006] EWCA Civ 1739 at para 61.

Connors type (factual) situation, there were two (as it put it) 'gateways' by which a possession action might be challenged:

(1) by interpreting the statutory provision using HRA 1998 s3 or, alternatively, by seeking a declaration of incompatibility in the High Court;
(2) by applying for judicial review by way of defence in the action in the court of first instance.

3.27   Carnwath LJ, applying the above reasoning in retrospect to the case of Mr Connors, stated:

> On the facts of Connors itself:
> a)   Gateway (a) would have remained closed, because of the inflexibility of the statutory scheme (the only potential remedy being a declaration of incompatibility, which would not have saved the Connors family, but might have helped others in the future);
> b)   Gateway (b) might have been open for a defence based on broader judicial review grounds than those actually advanced.[28]

The reasoning of the CA here is somewhat confusing. On the one hand, it acknowledges that Mr Connors unsuccessfully attempted to take a judicial review challenge before being evicted. It also, of course, acknowledges that the ECtHR made it clear that, in such a case, judicial review was not an adequate remedy. On the other hand, it seems to suggest that a judicial review application using different grounds might have been successful.

3.28   It had also been pointed out on behalf of Mr Doherty that any possession order obtained against a former licensee of a local authority site is obtained by relying on the common law. It was, therefore, argued on his behalf that the court ought to interpret the common law to ensure that it was compliant with the Convention. On this point, the CA concluded that the fact that Gypsies and Travellers are excluded from any of the main statutes that confer security of tenure on certain classes of people, is itself an expression of the will of parliament. Mr Doherty has received leave to appeal the CA decision to the House of Lords.

Allocation of pitches

3.29   Unlike with local authority houses and flats, where Housing Act 1996 Pt VI applies, there is no specific statutory regime that applies to the allocation of pitches on local authority sites. Nevertheless, as a public authority, a local authority will be expected to organise and manage

28   [2006] EWCA Civ 1739 at para 22.

this process in a reasonable and transparent fashion. This is exemplified by the case of *R (Piggott) v Bedfordshire CC*.[29]

3.30   After occupying the pitch as a trespasser, Mrs Piggott applied for a pitch on the local authority site in question (she wanted to be on that particular site as her daughter and other members of her family were living there, she was seriously ill and needed their care and support). It was agreed that the fact that Mrs Piggott was a squatter did not prevent her from making an application (although the council had initially taken that view). Burton J held that the council should have considered three matters: (1) the needs of the applicant; (2) the needs and requirements of others (also applicants) 'who should not be prejudiced by the unauthorised jumping of the gun of the applicant'; and (3) the jumping of the gun itself to see whether it should make any difference at all or how far it should make a difference.[30] The council had failed to make a comparison of her position with that of the others on the waiting list for a pitch. Even though the council had offered Mrs Piggott a pitch on another site, it was held that she was entitled to be considered for a pitch on the site where she was camped. Mrs Piggott sought to challenge the decision to take possession proceedings by way of judicial review. Following *Kay and Price*, such challenges will be raised as a defence to the claim for possession itself.[31]

3.31   Most local authorities operate a waiting list system regarding allocation and will have written policies. An adviser dealing with a query from a Gypsy or Traveller as to allocations will need to have regard to these written policies. The CLG *Draft Guidance on the management of Gypsy and Traveller sites* contains important recommendations on allocations:

> 7.1 It is recommended that local authorities and registered social landlords have and publish a scheme which sets out the policies and procedures for allocating pitches. While landlords are free to devise allocation schemes which make the best use of available resources in the light of local circumstances, the priority for the allocation of a suitable pitch should be given to applicants who are in greatest need and all those on the waiting list should receive due consideration on the basis of an assessment of their needs.

> 7.2 The policy for allocating pitches should be clear, fair and transparent and common across all Gypsy and Traveller sites owned by the landlord.

29 [2002] EWHC 77 Admin.
30 [2002] EWHC 77 Admin at para 34.
31 [2002] EWHC 77 Admin at para 40. Mrs Piggott was subsequently offered and accepted a licence of a pitch on the site.

The waiting list should be regularly reviewed and kept up to date.

...

7.5 Although sites are often occupied by extended family groups and this can help to ensure good community relations on the site, family connections should not override other allocation criteria designed to give priority to those in greatest need. That said, the landlord in consultation with the site manager will want to take account of factors which may affect the suitability of a site as a social unit.

3.32   The CLG *Draft Guidance* also contains recommendations (at p20) as to who might be given priority in an allocations system:

- people who have a need for accommodation on medical or welfare grounds, including those who are mentally ill, or with a physical or learning disability, and need a pitch to receive care;
- people who have a particular need for a stable base, including older people and families with children;
- people occupying unsanitary or overcrowded conditions or who have nowhere to live and are seeking permanent authorised site accommodation for the first time.

The Disability Discrimination Act 1995

3.33   The DDA 1995 makes it unlawful by reason of his or her disability to discriminate against a disabled person by evicting him or her.[32] A disabled person is someone who has a disability defined, for the purposes of the DDA 1995, as a 'physical or mental impairment which has a substantial and long-term adverse effect on his ability to carry out normal day-to-day activities'.[33] However, a landlord can argue that the action is 'justified'[34] and that the eviction is necessary 'in order not to endanger the health or safety of any person (which may include that of the disabled person)' and that 'it is reasonable in all the circumstances of the case' for the landlord to hold that opinion.[35] The DDA 1995 applies to 'premises', the definition of which 'includes land of any description'.[36] A local authority or non-local authority Gypsy or Traveller site will come within the provisions of the DDA 1995. In a case involving a tenant of a dwellinghouse, *North Devon Homes Ltd v*

---

32   DDA 1995 s22(3)(c).
33   DDA 1995 s1(1). See also DDA 1995 Sch 1.
34   DDA 1995 s24.
35   DDA 1995 s24.
36   DDA 1995 s68(1).

Brazier,[37] Mrs Brazier was involved in persistent anti-social behaviour. At first instance, the landlord obtained a possession order. Mrs Brazier successfully appealed against this order on the basis that evicting her was contrary to the above provisions of the DDA 1995. The High Court noted that there was no evidence that the landlord had ever directed its mind to these requirements. However, the High Court also stated that:

> The respondent [landlord], having adopted a proper review of the situation in accordance with the express terms of the Act, may conclude in the future that the health and safety of her neighbours are prejudiced and thus steps should be taken to evict the appellant [tenant].[38]

3.34 Thus, it is important to note that the DDA 1995 does not prohibit the eviction of a person with a disability. Nevertheless, it seems clear that a local authority will not be able to take possession proceedings against a Gypsy or Traveller who suffers from a disability (as defined in the DDA 1995) unless and until proper consideration of the provisions of the DDA 1995 has taken place.[39]

Conditions of occupancy and repairs

3.35 While local authorities have powers as to the provision of facilities, organisation and management and there is guidance from central government,[40] there is little by way of obligations owed to Gypsies or Travellers by local authorities, which can be enforced by them in respect of the conditions of their occupation of authorised sites. Virtually the only obligations are those referred to in para 3.11, above. There are no obligations implied to carry out repairs to what is provided on the pitch (for example, the amenity block containing day room, toilet, bathroom/shower or kitchen) or to repair or maintain the facilities on the site (for example, lighting or access ways). There is no equivalent to Landlord and Tenant Act 1985 s11 which puts repairing obligations on landlords of dwellinghouses let for less than seven years.[41] However,

---

37 [2003] HLR 59 at 905; (2003) 6 CCLR 245.

38 [2003] HLR 59 at 913. This case was followed by the Court of Appeal in *Manchester CC v Romano* [2004] EWCA Civ 834; [2004] HLR 87.

39 There are two cases pending in the Court of Appeal, *Lewisham LBC v Malcolm* (judgment reserved at the date of printing of this book) and *Floyd v Scott* (adjourned pending the decision in *Malcolm*), in which the issue of the application of the DDA 1995 to tenancies where there is no reasonableness requirement for possession has been raised.

40 DoE Circular 14/89, (*Caravan Sites and Control of Development Act 1960 – Model Standards*).

41 Although see para 3.46, below, on the Environmental Protection Act 1990.

it has been possible to imply terms putting obligations on local authority landlords by using the principle of 'necessary implication' from
contract law (this principle could equally apply to non-local authority
sites). Using that principle, Gypsies and Travellers have argued successfully that terms as to the maintenance of the site were to be implied
into their agreements and they were able to recover damages for breach
of them.[42] In the *Berry* case, the court eventually held that the following obligations on the local authority should be implied: to mark out
pitches; to provide hardstanding; to provide chemical toilets and an
emptying point for them; to provide waste receptacles; and to manage
the site. The CLG *Draft Guidance on the management of Gypsy and Traveller sites* recommends (at p24) that landlord's repairing obligations
should be included in the information provided for new arrivals to a
site. The *Draft Guidance* also (at p25 and at paragraph 9.20) recommends that succession to a licence or agreement should be dealt with
in the information provided and in the licence agreement itself.

3.36   Usually the Gypsy's or Traveller's obligations will be set out in a
written agreement provided when he or she agrees to occupy a pitch.
The terms of such an agreement may deal with: the length of time of
occupation (for example, for a year); consideration of renewal; termination; the number of caravans on a pitch; the maximum time permitted away from the site before the right to return is lost; restricting
the use of the pitch (for example, no business use); and conduct on the
pitch and site.[43] They rarely, if at all, impose obligations on the local
authority but simply detail the Gypsy's or Traveller's obligations. Many
adult Gypsies or Travellers are not literate or have poor literacy skills and
this fact can create problems in itself as they may be unaware as to
what they have agreed unless it is also explained verbally to them. The
CLG *Draft Guidance on the management of Gypsy and Traveller sites*
recommends (at paragraph 8.7) that:

> New arrivals should also be provided with a more detailed information
> pack, in writing, and ideally also on CD, DVD or audiocassette, setting

42 *Berry v Wrexham Maelor CBC* August 2001 *Legal Action* 25.
43 It should be noted, however, that in *Newham LBC v Khatun* [2004] EWCA Civ
    55; [2005] QB 37 (a case involving a 'settled' homeless applicant), the Court of
    Appeal decided that the Unfair Contract Terms in Consumer Contracts
    Regulations 1999 SI No 1999/2083 applied to contracts relating to land. These
    regulations will, therefore, apply to Gypsies and Travellers who are licensees
    on local authority (and other) sites. Under the regulations an unfair term is
    one which, contrary to the requirement of good faith, causes a significant
    imbalance in the parties' rights and obligations to the detriment of the Gypsy
    or Traveller concerned (the 'consumer' in terms of the regulations – reg 4).

out the range and standards of services provided, what can be expected from the site management and what is expected of the residents. These should be produced in clear and simple language.

Additionally, the *Draft Guidance* (at paragraph 9.2) states:

> The resident should ... have the terms [of the licence] clearly explained verbally before signing.

Rent/site fee

3.37 Caravan Sites and Control of Development Act (CSCDA) 1960 s24(3) provides that:

> The local authority shall make in respect of the use of sites managed by them, and of any services or facilities provided or made available under this section, such reasonable charges as they may determine.

This provision enables local authorities to charge rent or site fees. Those financially eligible can apply for housing benefit to meet the charge in whole or part, depending on their income and the calculations carried out under the housing benefit regulations.[44] Practical difficulties can arise when Gypsies or Travellers try to claim housing benefit. The fact that the work of many Gypsies and Travellers is of a seasonal/casual nature and that payment is often by cash can complicate the calculation of housing benefit entitlement.

3.38 There has long been a problem for residents of county council sites who are claiming housing benefit. Unlike residents of district or unitary authority sites, county council residents receive a rent allowance as opposed to a rent rebate. The general rule is that claims for rent allowances must be referred to a rent officer for a rent determination. Such a determination serves to fix the amount of housing benefit that is paid and this, almost inevitably, leads to a large shortfall between the actual rent and the housing benefit that is paid. However, in a case in 2006 that was settled without the need for court action, it was recognised that where residents are in receipt of Supporting People payments as part of their rent, then their claim for housing benefit should not be referred to the rent officer. This is because a caravan site will be exempt from the rent restriction rules if:

(1) the site is provided by a non-metropolitan county council; and

---

44 Housing Benefit (General) Regulations 2006 SI No 2006/213 reg 12(1)(g) in particular.

(2) that body, or a person acting on its behalf, also provides the claimant with care, support or supervision.[45]

3.39   The Supporting People scheme provides a range of housing-related support services to vulnerable and disabled people, such as: advice on claiming welfare benefits; support with budgeting; enabling access to services; and support to develop life skills. The terms 'care, support or supervision' are not defined within the regulations but the Supporting People scheme is clearly covered by these terms.[46]

Provision of facilities

3.40   The CSCDA 1960 s24(2) states that local authorities have specific powers 'to provide for the use of those occupying caravan sites any services or facilities for their health or convenience',[47] and 'to provide, in or in connection with sites for the accommodation of gypsies, working space and facilities for the carrying on of such activities as are normally carried on by them'.[48] Those are powers, however, not duties – so the local authority is not obliged to make such provision. The power in respect of the provision of working space was introduced by the CJPOA 1994.[49] However, in practice it is quite common for local authorities to impose restrictions on the business use of their sites, despite the recommendations contained in ODPM Circular 1/06 *Planning for Gypsy and Traveller Caravan Sites*:

> Local planning authorities should, wherever possible, identify in their DPDs [Development Plan Documents] gypsy and traveller sites suitable for mixed residential and business uses, having regard to the safety and amenity of the occupants and their children, and neighbouring residents.[50]

3.41   It is also part of Gypsy and Traveller culture to keep animals such as horses or ponies. This can lead to problems about obtaining a pitch on a local authority site – the agreements often do not permit a resident

---

45 Housing Benefit and Council Tax (Consequential Provisions) Regulations 2006 SI No 217 Sch 3 para 4(10)(b).
46 Uniform treatment of housing benefit claims for residents on all rented Gypsy/Traveller sites has been recommended in Department for Work and Pensions *A single housing benefit control for Gypsy and Traveller sites* Research Report No 379, October 2006.
47 CSCDA 1960 s24(2)(b).
48 CSCDA 1960 s24(2)(c).
49 CJPOA 1994 s80(2)(a).
50 ODPM Circular 1/06 para 56. The circular only applies to England. The National Assembly for Wales is working on a new circular to replace Welsh Office Circular 2/94 – see further chapter 4 at para 4.192, below.

to keep more than a dog or a cat and sometimes prohibit all pets. The CLG *Draft Guidance on the management of Gypsy and Traveller sites* (May 2007) recommends:

> 13.35 [A]s for other forms of social housing, keeping domestic pets (dogs, cats, small birds etc) should be permitted, subject to number and health and safety considerations. In the case of dogs, ownership must be properly identified and conditional upon the animals being properly controlled within the pitch. Any animals in excess of those agreed within the licence or agreement should be agreed with the site manager beforehand ...

> 13.37 Where there is demand for such facilities and where the landlord is satisfied that it may be reasonable and practicable to do so, a grazing area for horses and ponies may be provided, adjoining the site or nearby, to reflect the cultural use of the horse as a traditional means of transport ...

Fire precautions

3.42 The only other specific statutory provision relating to conditions on sites refers to fire precautions. CSCDA 1960 s24(2A) states that:

> Before exercising the power to provide a site ... the local authority shall consult the fire authority, if they are not themselves the fire authority –
>
> (a) as to measures to be taken for preventing and detecting the outbreak of fire on the site; and
> (b) as to the provision and maintenance of means of fighting fire on it.

Somewhat surprisingly, local authorities need only consult with the fire authority and do not necessarily have to follow the advice given to them as a result of such consultation.

3.43 The secretary of state has published model standards under CSCDA 1960 s5(6) making precise recommendations as to the facilities to be provided on caravan sites, for example, as to the provision of fire alarms, fire extinguishers, water supply and the distance of caravans from each other. However, none of them apply to Gypsy caravan sites and there is no obligation on local authorities to abide by the recommendations.[51]

3.44 The CLG *Draft Guidance on the management of Gypsy and Traveller sites* (May 2007) contains strong recommendations with regard to fire safety on sites (at paragraph 13.10):

> The site manager must maintain regular monitoring and testing of fire equipment, alarm-raising equipment, fire reporting and evacuation

---

51 DoE Circular 14/89 *Caravan Sites and Control of Development Act* 1960 – *Model Standards.*

procedures ... All site residents should be told of these procedures on arrival and on a regular basis subsequently.

Further strong recommendations as to fire safety are contained in the CLG *Draft Guidance on the design of sites for Gypsies and Travellers*:

4.3.4 **Essential**: There must be a clear gap of 3 metres within the inside of all site boundaries as a fire prevention measure, unless a risk assessment has determined that alternative arrangements can achieve an adequate level of safety ...

4.10.1 **Essential**: To ensure fire safety, every trailer, caravan or park home must be not less than 6 metres from any other trailer, caravan or park home that is occupied separately ...

6.3.1 **Essential**: Pitches must be no more than 30 metres from a fire point. Fire points must be housed in a weather proof structure, easily accessible and clearly and conspicuously marked 'Fire Point'. A clearly written and conspicuous notice must be provided and maintained at each 'Fire Point' to indicate the action to be taken in the case of fire, including details of the muster point ...

6.3.2 **Essential**: Water standpipes, hydrants or fire extinguishers must be provided on each site as determined by the risk assessment and as informed by consultation with the local fire officer. All equipment must conform to relevant British/European standards ...

6.3.3 **Essential**: A means of raising the alarm in the case of fire must be provided at each fire point. This must be appropriate to the size and layout of the site and informed by consultation with the local fire officer ...

3.45   An example of an attempt to sue a council for failure to provide/maintain fire-fighting equipment on its Gypsy caravan site, allegedly resulting in the destruction of the claimant's caravan and contents, was *Horace Piggott v Sheffield CC*.[52] HHJ Mettyear dismissed the claim finding:

(1) there was no duty of care imposed by law in the circumstances of the case;
(2) had there been a duty of care he would have found a breach of duty;
(3) however, on the facts, he found that the loss would have occurred even if there had been no breach of duty, that is, the breach of duty made no difference.

This was a case in which the council had decided to carry out major renovation works to the site and all fire-fighting equipment was removed

---

52 23 January 1998 (unreported), Sheffield County Court, HHJ Mettyear.

from the site, including fire-extinguishers and means of alarm, leaving only two standpipes. The judge accepted the council's contention that the purpose of measures for dealing with fire on a caravan site (for example, fire extinguishers, a telephone or alarm system) was not to protect the occupier or property of the occupier of the caravan in which the fire started but to prevent the spread of fire from one caravan to another. Accordingly, there was not proximity sufficient to establish a duty of care, nor was it fair, just and reasonable to impose liability, although the reduction of ability to fight fires as a result of the council's actions was foreseeable (an appeal would have been pursued against this part of the learned judge's findings had it not been for (3) above). If there had been a duty of care, he would have found a breach as the water pressure in the standpipes was too low for fire-fighting. However, on the evidence, he found that even if the water pressure had been sufficient, the caravan would still have been destroyed.

Environmental Protection Act 1990

3.46   In relation to the conditions on a site, a Gypsy or Traveller can prosecute the local authority as the person responsible for a statutory nuisance under Environmental Protection Act (EPA) 1990 s82. A statutory nuisance within the meaning of EPA 1990 s79(1)(a) includes 'premises in such a state as to be prejudicial to health'. The phrase 'prejudicial to health' is further defined as 'injurious or likely to cause injury to health'.[53] The defendant in (what are commonly known as) 'section 82 proceedings' is 'the person responsible for the nuisance' defined as 'the person to whose act, default or sufferance [permission] the nuisance is attributable'.[54] The owner of the premises is the proper defendant if the person responsible cannot be found.[55] Statutory nuisance proceedings are often brought by local authorities against private owners[56] but by EPA 1990 s82, a private individual who is 'aggrieved' (that is, affected) by the conditions can bring a prosecution. A notice specifying the problem must first be served 21 days before the proceedings can be commenced. Section 82 proceedings are dealt with by the magistrates' court. The court can convict, fine[57] and order compensation, works and costs. Tenants or other occupiers of houses have frequently

53   EPA 1990 s79(7).
54   EPA 1990 s82(4)(a) and s79(7) respectively.
55   EPA 1990 s82(4)(c).
56   EPA 1990 s80.
57   Up to level 5 on the standard scale.

used these proceedings in respect of conditions not covered by their tenancy agreements, for example, damp caused by excessive condensation.

3.47   Section 82 proceedings can be problematic. The burden of proof is to the criminal standard ('beyond a reasonable doubt') rather than the civil standard ('the balance of probability').[58] No public funding is available for representation although proceedings may be conducted by a lawyer paid on a conditional fee basis, that is, on the basis that the representative will only be paid if successful.[59] However, a lawyer instructed on such a basis is not entitled to charge an additional success fee in cases brought under the EPA 1990. In addition, it should be remembered that the prosecutor may well be ordered to pay the local authority's costs if the case is rejected. Though public funding is available to obtain an expert's report (for example, from an independent environmental health officer) before the trial, it will not cover the cost of the expert's attendance at court. Additionally, the Gypsy or Traveller prosecuting the case needs to consider any possible effect on his or her continuing occupation of the site bearing in mind what has been said above about security of tenure. However, if it could be shown that a local authority's motivation for seeking eviction was that the Gypsy or Traveller had prosecuted the local authority under the EPA 1990, then a 'public law challenge' would lie on the basis that such action was unreasonable (that is, an action that no reasonable local authority would take). Such a challenge would now be made by way of a defence to the claim for possession.

3.48   A Gypsy or Traveller might use section 82 proceedings when the local authority has failed to deal with dampness caused by condensation in an amenity block or has failed to properly deal with rodent infestation, to give just two examples. Gypsies and Travellers have gained advantages by using such proceedings. For example, in *Day v Sheffield CC*,[60] a wide-ranging order was achieved, requiring a programme to deal with rat infestation, internal site lighting, hard surfacing, provision of a dustbin for each pitch and weekly refuse collection.

Grants

3.49   The CJPOA 1994 also repealed the secretary of state's power to pay grants to local authorities for the provision of sites. However, since

---

58   *R v Newham East Justices ex p Hunt* [1976] 1 WLR 420.
59   Access to Justice Act 1999 s27(1).
60   August 1988 *Legal Action* 19.

2001/02, the government has made available £52.4m for repair and maintenance works to existing sites (now including, since 2005/06, for the provision of new sites) and has invited local authorities to submit tenders for grants on an annual basis. This is known as the Gypsy and Traveller Site Grant (GTSG – formerly known as the Gypsy Sites Refurbishment Grant). The GTSG has now continued beyond the initial three-year period. In 2006/07, the government spent £20.4m, providing 140 new pitches, ensuring a further 40 pitches remained in use and refurbishing 76 sites. The Niner report on *The provision and condition of local authority Gypsy/Traveller Sites in England*, commented that:

> ... the GSRG [now the GTSG] will have made a very valuable contribution to bringing sites up to standard, but that expenditure needs to be sustained.[61]

The report calculated that a grand total of £123.5m was needed to bring sites up to standard over a 30-year period.[62]

3.50   Disabled facilities grants (DFGs) are mandatory grants administered by local authorities under the Housing Grants, Construction and Regeneration Act (HGCRA) 1996. Housing Act 2004 s224 amended HGCRA 1996 s1 to extend DFGs to all occupiers of caravans including Gypsies and Travellers on local authority sites (who had not previously been covered).

3.51   Social services have a general duty to assist disabled children within their area under Children Act (CA) 1989 by 'providing a range and level of services appropriate to their needs'.[63] CA 1989 defines a disabled person as a person who '[is] blind, deaf or dumb, suffers from mental disorder of any kind or is substantially and permanently handicapped by illness, injury or congenital deformity or other such disability as may be prescribed'.[64] A service may (in other words, it is for the local authority to decide) include the provision of accommodation, and assistance in kind or in cash (and may be provided for the family of the child as well).[65] It is suggested that these provisions of the CA 1989 could be used to improve conditions for a disabled Gypsy or Traveller child whether they live on local authority or non-local authority sites.

---

61   ODPM, 2002, p22.
62   At p21, table 3.
63   CA 1989 s1(1).
64   CA 1989 s17(11).
65   CA 1989 s17(3), (6) and (7).

Redevelopment of sites

3.52   Major redevelopment projects are dealt with in ODPM Circular 1/06:

> A major development or redevelopment project may require the permanent or temporary relocation of a gypsy or traveller site. An onus should be placed on the planning applicant to identify and provide an alternative site, providing the original site has a legal status. The local planning authority should work with the planning applicant and the gypsy and traveller community to identify a site (or sites) that would be suitable for relocating this community. In proposing relocation and in seeking a relocation site regard will need to be paid both to the gypsy and traveller community's social, economic and environmental needs and identified social, economic, and environmental benefits that the major development/ redevelopment project will bring to the locality and the broader area.[66]

3.53   Reliance was placed on this paragraph by the Gypsy and Traveller claimants in *Lisa Smith and ors v The Secretary of State for Trade and Industry and the London Development Agency.*[67] The London Development Agency (LDA) is the body charged with delivering the necessary land for the London Olympics 2012. Two local authority Gypsy/Traveller sites have to be relocated because of the Olympics. In 2006 a public inquiry took place into the enormous compulsory purchase order (CPO) that the LDA sought. The two sites were included in the CPO. Following the conclusion of the inquiry, the planning inspector made recommendations to the secretary of state. With regard to the two sites, he stated:

> In my opinion, although the benefits of [the CPO] are very compelling, a small group should not be left to pay any excessive personal and social cost for those benefits to be achieved ... Against this background, I consider that [the CPO] should not be confirmed until the Secretary of State is satisfied that suitable relocation sites will be available to meet the reasonable needs of the Gypsies and Travellers that would be displaced.[68]

3.54   Despite that recommendation the secretary of state confirmed the CPO before alternative sites had been found for the Gypsies and Travellers. In his decision letter, the secretary of state noted that potential relocation sites were under consideration and stated that:

> [he was] confident that the LDA are fully aware of the issues involved and ... will make strenuous effort to deal with them so as to ensure the satisfactory relocation of the gypsies and travellers. However ... the Secretary of State appreciates that there is a risk of failure on the relevant timescale that

---

66   ODPM Circular 1/06 para 57.
67   [2007] EWHC 1013 Admin.
68   [2007] EWHC 1013 Admin at para 8.

cannot be eliminated but having regard in particular to the clear and over-whelming importance of [the CPO] and the urgency of the timing issues ... considers it right to confirm the Order now.[69]

3.55 One Gypsy from one site and two Irish Travellers from the other site appealed against the confirmation of the CPO.[70] They claimed that the confirmation of the order was an unlawful interference with their rights under article 8 of the Convention, that the Secretary of State had failed to properly take account of their right to respect for their traditional way of life and the positive obligation on the state to facilitate that way of life[71] and that the secretary of state had failed to use the least intrusive means of achieving the legitimate aim.[72] Wyn Williams J dismissed the appeal, stating:

> I do not find that [the secretary of state's] decision to confirm the order was unjustified or disproportionate. In my judgment, it was the least intrusive measure available to him. Realistically, the only way of ensuring that a substantial proportion of the Order lands (which included the sites) was under the control of the LDA by mid 2007 was to make the order. No other measure, in my judgment would have achieved that objective. Further, the need for the land to be under the control of the LDA by that date was unchallenged and, indeed, on the evidence before both the Inspector and [the secretary of state], unchallengeable.[73]

It should be pointed out that the London Olympics is, self-evidently, an exceptional project and that it is unlikely that other development/redevelopment work will be on that scale or of that importance.

Non-local authority sites

3.56 This section seeks to explain what security of tenure Gypsies and Travellers have on non-local authority sites. Whether or not the Gypsy or Traveller occupier of the caravan owns or rents the caravan, security of tenure on non-local authority sites will still vary depending on whether the site has a site licence and is a 'protected site'.

69 [2007] EWHC 1013 Admin at para 10.
70 Appeal brought under Acquisition of Land Act 1981 s24.
71 Reliance being placed in that regard on *Chapman v UK* (2001) 33 EHRR 399.
72 Reliance being placed in that regard on *R (Samaroo) v SSHD* [2001] EWCA Civ 1139; [2001] UKHRR 1150.
73 [2007] EWHC 1013 Admin at para 50. An earlier challenge to the withdrawal by the LDA of a potential relocation site which had been favoured by the Gypsies concerned was also dismissed: *R (Smith) v LDA* [2007] EWHC 636 Admin.

3.57   The basic definition of 'protected site' is contained in CSA 1968 s1. A protected site is any land which is required to have a site licence by CSCDA 1960, and where the relevant planning permission or site licence is not for holiday use only, or otherwise limited such that there are times of the year when no caravan may be stationed on the land for human habitation.

3.58   Thus any occupier on a site which satisfies those criteria, whether he or she owns or rents the caravan, will have the protection given by CSA 1968.[74] The CSCDA 1960 s1 makes it an offence for a person to cause or permit land to be used as a caravan site unless he or she has a site licence. The CSCDA 1960 Sch 1 lists various exceptions to the requirement to hold a site licence, thereby taking people who come within those exceptions outside the protection of either CSA 1968 or MHA 1983.

3.59   There is a definition of the phrase 'protected site' given in MHA 1983 s5:

> [P]rotected site does not include any land occupied by a local authority as a caravan site providing accommodation for gipsies ...

3.60   Therefore, under MHA 1983 s1, if there is an agreement to station a mobile home on a protected site (which will not include a local authority Gypsy/Traveller site), the MHA 1983 applies. However, the MHA 1983 will not offer any protection to occupiers who rent their mobile home from the site owner, as the agreement will not usually entitle them to station a mobile home on the land.

3.61   The consequences of having an agreement to which MHA 1983 applies is that the terms set out in MHA 1983 Sch 1 Pt 1 are implied.[75] These terms are wide ranging but, most importantly, they include security of tenure. A possession order can only be made on limited grounds, those being:

- breach of the terms of the site licence where the occupier has not remedied that breach within a reasonable period of time;
- that the occupier is not occupying the mobile home as his or her only or main residence; or
- that the mobile home, due to its condition, is having a detrimental effect on the amenity of the site.

74 See para 3.11, above, for the limited protection given by CSA 1968.
75 See appendix B, below. The MHA 1983 also implies certain other terms into agreements and further deals with assignment and succession. Reference should be made to the MHA 1983 itself.

Additionally, and very importantly, even if one or more of those grounds of possession are proven, a court will not grant a possession order unless it is reasonable to do so.

Conclusion

3.62   Given the ECtHR's decision in *Connors v UK* and the security of tenure enjoyed on non-local authority rented sites, it is hoped that the government will make every effort to give those Gypsies and Travellers living on local authority sites proper security of tenure without further delay. It appears that the government now accepts that other matters (such as succession, assignment, the right to exchange and implied repairing obligations) will flow from the introduction of security of tenure.[76]

---

76 Letter to Andrew Dismore MP from Meg Munn MP minister, at that time, with responsibility for Gypsy and Traveller issues, 2007 (undated).

CHAPTER 4

Planning law

4.1   **Introduction**

4.6   **Structure of the planning system**

4.6   Legislation

4.8   National planning policy

4.9   Regional and local planning policy – the development plan

4.17   Planning authorities

4.18   Development

4.20   Planning permission

4.21   Permitted development

4.22   Immunity from enforcement

4.26   Development and the stationing of caravans on land

4.27   The meaning of caravan

4.29   Matters to be taken into account when determining planning applications for Gypsy and Traveller sites
Relevant government policy and advice • Circular 1/06 • Designated areas and site location • Development plan policies for Gypsy and Traveller sites • Other material considerations • Ethnic Gypsies and Travellers and Gypsy status

4.69   Gypsy status and pre-2006 case-law

4.79   Gypsy status and Circular 1/06
The need for Gypsy and Traveller sites • The availability of alternative sites • Fear of crime • Personal circumstances • Human rights as a material consideration • Human rights and offers of conventional housing

4.125   **Making an application for planning permission**

4.127   Conditions

4.132   Appealing against a refusal of planning permission

4.136   An application to the High Court

4.141   Enforcement
4.141   Statutory provisions
4.142   Government guidance on enforcement
4.144   Considerations of common humanity
4.146   Enforcement notices
4.148   Stop notices
4.150   Temporary stop notices
4.155   Enforcement notice appeals
4.162   Prosecution for breach of an enforcement notice
4.165   Direct action
4.169   Planning injunctions
           Suspension • Contempt/applications to vary
4.190   The option to take no action

4.191   Funding for planning inquiries
4.192   Wales

4.193   Conclusion

Introduction

4.1   In 1968, the Caravan Sites Act (CSA) was passed. The Act imposed a
duty on local authorities to provide public sector sites. CSA 1968 s6
required local authorities 'so far as may be necessary to provide adequate accommodation for gipsies residing in or resorting to their area
...'. From 1970 to 1994 a significant number of sites for Gypsies and
Travellers were established in accordance with that duty. However, the
duty was widely flouted and many authorities failed to comply with
their obligation to make adequate provision.

4.2   The Criminal Justice and Public Order Act (CJPOA) 1994 repealed
CSA 1968 s6, and, at that time, the government rightly forecast that the
repeal of the duty was 'expected to lead to more applications for private
gypsy sites'. It had already published planning advice on the provision of sites for Gypsies and Travellers in the form of Department of
Environment (DoE) Circular 1/94, *Gypsy sites and planning*, which
advised local planning authorities (LPAs) that they should assess the
needs of Gypsies and Travellers within their areas and then produce a
plan which identified locations suitable for sites; and that they should
only rely on criteria-based policies where it was impossible to identify suitable sites within their areas.[1]

4.3   Since then planning law has played an increasingly important role
in the provision of sites where Gypsies and Travellers can place their
caravans and live in them. However, statistics show that while, in general, LPAs allow most planning applications for settled members of the
public, they refuse most applications by Gypsies and Travellers, forcing a disadvantaged section of the population to go to the trouble and
expense of appealing these refusals. As Lord Bingham said in his judgment in *South Buckinghamshire DC v Porter:*[2]

> In the case of Gypsies, the problem was compounded by features peculiar
> to them. Their characteristic lifestyle debarred them from access to con-
> ventional sources of housing provision. Their attempts to obtain plan-
> ning permission almost always met with failure: statistics quoted by the
> European Court of Human Rights in *Chapman v United Kingdom*[3] ...

---

1   Department of the Environment (DoE) Circular 1/94, Welsh Office 2/94
    (hereafter Circular 1/94) para 4.
2   *South Buckinghamshire DC v Porter; Chichester DC v Searle; Wrexham CBC v
    Berry; Hertsmere BC v Harty* [2003] UKHL 26; [2003] 2 AC 558, [2003] 2 WLR
    1547, [2003] 3 All ER 1.
3   *Chapman v United Kingdom* (2001) 33 EHRR 399, (2001) 10 BHRC 48, (2001)
    Times, 30 January, ECtHR, at para 66.

showed that in 1991, the most recent year for which figures were available, 90 per cent of applications made by Gypsies had been refused whereas 80 per cent of all applications had been granted. But for many years the capacity of sites authorised for occupation by Gypsies has fallen well short of that needed to accommodate those seeking space on which to station their caravans.[4]

4.4   The advice in Circular 1/94 that LPAs assess need and cater for that need by identifying land on which Gypsy sites could be established was largely ignored and the vast majority of LPAs failed to assess the needs of Gypsies and Travellers within their areas, simply adopting criteria-based policies without giving any reason why it was impossible to adopt location-based ones.

4.5   The government recognised that the advice in Circular 1/94 had not been followed by LPAs, and, in 2006, it issued new and more positive planning advice on the provision of sites for Gypsies and Travellers in England in the form of ODPM Circular 1/06 *Planning for Gypsy and Traveller caravan sites*.[5] The new advice is detailed below and this chapter aims to ensure that Gypsies and Travellers and those who represent them are aware of key points of current planning law and policy.

Structure of the planning system

Legislation

4.6   Since 1948 the development of land in England and Wales has been subject to controls imposed by the Town and Country Planning Acts. The present law is contained in the Town and Country Planning Act (TCPA) 1990 – though it has been amended by subsequent legislation, particularly the Planning and Compulsory Purchase Act (PCPA) 2004.[6] Similar regimes exist in Scotland and Northern Ireland and a broadly similar regime also exists in the Republic of Ireland.

---

4   [2003] 2 WLR 1547 at 1554.
5   A very similar draft circular is still under preparation by the National Assembly for Wales at the date of publication of this book. See *Draft circular: planning for Gypsy and Traveller caravan sites*, Welsh Assembly Government, 2006.
6   The provisions of the PCPA 2004 commenced on a variety of dates and the Act is now almost fully in force.

4.7   TCPA 1990 is divided into 14 parts, of which the most important for Gypsies and Travellers are:

- Part III – control over development, which includes the need for planning permission, consideration of applications for planning permission and appeals against refusal of planning permission;
- Part VII – enforcement, which provides for various means of enforcing against breaches of planning control; and
- Part XII – validity, which provides for High Court challenges to various decisions related to planning, including the decisions of planning inspectors on development control and enforcement appeals.

National planning policy

4.8   The government's national planning policy is contained in planning policy statements (PPSs), planning policy guidance notes (PPGs) (which are being replaced by PPSs) and circulars.

Regional and local planning policy – the development plan

4.9   Local planning policy is contained in what is known as the development plan, which, despite its name, always (in England) consists of more than one document. In 2004, a new system for the production of development plans was introduced by the government.[7]

4.10   The old system for the production of development plans has only been replaced in a few districts and so it is still important to outline how it worked in practice:

- in London boroughs, metropolitan district councils and some other unitary authorities, the development plan consisted of a 'unitary development plan' and, in London, the London Plan or, elsewhere, the regional spatial strategy.
- in parts of the country where there are both county councils and district councils (and in some unitary authorities) there are structure plans prepared by the county council (sometimes with a unitary authority or a group of unitary authorities) and local plans prepared by the district council or unitary authority, which, together with the regional spatial strategy (along with minerals and waste plans), constitute the development plan.

7   PCPA 2004 Pts 1–3.

4.11   However, the PCPA 2004 introduces a new development plan system. In future, in England (but not Wales), development plans will consist of:

- regional spatial strategies (RSSs) prepared by the regional planning bodies (RPBs) or, in London, the spatial development strategy prepared by the Mayor of London ('the London Plan');
- development plan documents prepared by district councils, unitary authorities, The Broads Authority, National Park authorities and, in the case of minerals and waste development plan documents, by county councils.

The government's aim is for the new system to be in place as quickly as possible. In the meantime, adopted structure and local plans and unitary development plans will retain development plan status and have automatically been saved for a period of three years from the commencement of the PCPA 2004. For plans in preparation, the three-year period will commence from the adoption or approval of the draft plan.

4.12   RSSs cover the whole of a standard government region in England (subject to alterations for cross-boundary national parks) and set out the policy of the Secretary of State for Communities and Local Government in relation to the development and use of land within the region.

4.13   LPAs are required to produce: a local development scheme (LDS) giving details of the development plan documents (DPDs) and other documents that it will be preparing. The secretary of state can direct the LPA to make amendments. Such a direction has been made against South Gloucestershire Council in respect of its failure to deal adequately with Gypsies and Travellers within its LDS. DPDs form part of the development plan.

4.14   PCPA 2004 s38(6) provides that planning applications should be determined in accordance with the development plan, unless material considerations indicate otherwise.[8] Given the importance placed upon development plans when it comes to the determination of planning applications, it is not surprising that major economic concerns, such as housebuilders and the minerals industry, keep an eye on their preparation in order to ensure that their interests are fully borne in mind.

4.15   A major cause of inequality between the planning system's provision of accommodation for house-dwellers and its provision of accommodation for Gypsies and Travellers is that, while powerful and

---

8   Formerly TCPA 1990 s54A.

well-financed bodies ensure that the interests of housebuilders are recognised, Gypsies' and Travellers' organisations do not have the resources to monitor emerging development plans and to challenge the absence of adequate policies to meet the needs of Gypsies and Travellers.[9] As a result, while the amendment of Green Belt boundaries to meet the need for housing has taken place on many occasions, it has never been changed to meet the needs of Gypsies and Travellers.

4.16   In the future Gypsies and Travellers and those advising them should consider objecting to the absence of appropriate policies in revised development plan documents before they are adopted.[10]

Planning authorities

4.17   Most planning decisions are taken by the LPA for the area concerned. In most English Gypsy and Traveller cases the relevant LPA will be the district council, metropolitan borough, London borough or national park authority. Under the new system, county councils, where they exist, will only have responsibility for minerals and waste development plan documents. Planning in national parks is the sole responsibility of national park authorities.[11] In Wales the LPA will be the county council, county borough council or national park authority.

Development

4.18   The meaning of 'development' is central to the system of development control:

> Subject to the following provisions of this section, in this Act, except where the context otherwise requires, 'development', means the carrying out of building, engineering, mining or other operations in, on, over or under land, or the making of any material change in the use of any buildings or other land.[12]

9   The only case in which a Gypsy or Traveller has successfully challenged a development plan is *Butler v Bath and North East Somerset DC and others* [2003] EWCA Civ 1614; [2004] JPL 941; (2003) *Times*, 4 November. There have been many successful challenges by housebuilders and other developers.

10   These objections may include, for example: that the DPD makes inadequate provision for Gypsies and Travellers; that some land adjoining existing sites should be allocated for expansion; and that existing sites (together with some land for expansion) within the Green Belt should no longer be designated as such.

11   See TCPA 1990 ss1–9 and PCPA 2004 s37.

12   TCPA 1990 s55(1).

4.19 This definition is divided into two limbs:

- 'building, engineering, mining or other operations', known as 'operational development'; and
- material change of use.

Various operations and uses are deemed not to be development, including use of land for the purposes of agriculture or forestry.[13] The stationing of a residential caravan on land for the purposes of agriculture, for example, fruit or hop picking or to attend ewes during lambing, will therefore not constitute development.

Planning permission

4.20 Planning permission is required for the carrying out of any development of land[14] unless the operation or use is lawful or immune from enforcement.[15]

Permitted development

4.21 Some matters (mainly of a minor nature) are granted planning permission by statutory instruments, known as development orders, the most important of which is the Town and Country Planning (General Permitted Development) Order (GPDO) 1995.[16] These include:

- certain minor operations, such as the erection of gates, walls and fences below specified heights;[17]
- certain temporary buildings and uses, such as moveable structures required in connection with building or engineering operations;[18] and

---

13 TCPA 1990 s55(2).

14 TCPA 1990 s57.

15 TCPA 1990 s191 provides that 'uses and operations are lawful at any time if – (a) no enforcement action may then be taken in respect of them (whether because they did not involve development or require planning permission or because the time for enforcement action has expired or for any other reason); and (b) they do not constitute a contravention of any of the requirements of any enforcement notice then in force'. A person wishing to find out whether an existing use or operation is lawful may apply to the LPA for a certificate of lawfulness under TCPA 1990 s191 (or TCPA 1990 s192 in the case of a proposed use or operation) and see para 4.22 below.

16 SI 1995 No 418.

17 GPDO Class 2.

18 GPDO Class 4.

- certain caravan uses, such as use by a person travelling with a caravan for one or two nights.[19]

They are subject to conditions, which are contained in the GPDO and which must be checked before relying on them. These permitted development rights may be withdrawn by a direction under GPDO 1995 article 4(1) made in respect of a specified area or removed by a planning condition. This will not affect the legality of development that has already been carried out under the GPDO.[20] The most important practical consequence of the GPDO for Gypsies and Travellers is that (unless there is an article 4 direction or a planning condition to the contrary) they are allowed to erect gates, fences, walls or other means of enclosure up to one metre in height where they adjoin a highway used by vehicular traffic and up to two metres high elsewhere on the boundary of their land.[21]

Immunity from enforcement

4.22   TCPA 1990 s171B establishes two different limitation periods for enforcement action that can be taken by an LPA in circumstances where a breach of planning control has occurred:

(1) Where there has been a breach of planning control consisting in the carrying out without planning permission of building, engineering, mining or other operations in, on, over or under land, no enforcement action may be taken after the end of the period of four years beginning with the date on which the operations were substantially completed.

(2) Where there has been a breach of planning control consisting in the change of use of any building to use as a single dwellinghouse, no enforcement action may be taken after the end of the period of four years beginning with the date of the breach.

(3) In the case of any other breach of planning control, no enforcement action may be taken after the end of ten years beginning with the date of the breach.

....

TCPA 1990 s191(2) makes it clear that failure to take enforcement action within the appropriate period will result in any use or operation, in respect of which action might have been taken, becoming lawful.

---

19 GPDO Class 5.

20 *R v Epping Forest DC ex p Strandmill Ltd* [1990] JPL 415.

21 Those advising Gypsies and Travellers in respect of these issues should check the exact wording of the GPDO.

Those Gypsies and Travellers who can prove that they have used land for residential purposes in breach of planning control for more than ten years, without enforcement action having been taken against them, may make an application under TCPA 1990 s191 for a certificate of lawful use.

4.23   In most cases it will be necessary to apply for planning permission to the LPA for the proposed development.[22] A fee must be paid to cover the cost of such an application.[23]

4.24   In general there is no limit to the number of times that an application for planning permission can be made. However, TCPA 1990 s70A gives an LPA the power to decline to determine applications where within the last two years, either the secretary of state has dismissed an appeal in respect of a similar application or the LPA has itself refused a similar application; and the LPA thinks that there 'there has been no significant change since the refusal or ... dismissal'.[24] The power is discretionary and in DoE Circular 14/91 *Planning and Compensation Act 1991* at Annex 2, Part 1, paragraph 5, the government advised that it should only be used by an LPA where it believes that:

> The applicant is intending to exert pressure by submitting repeated similar applications. If an application has been revised in a genuine attempt to take account of objections to an earlier proposal, it should not be regarded as 'similar' for the purposes of this section.

4.25   There is no right of appeal against an LPA's refusal to determine an application; but the exercise of the power is susceptible to judicial review. In the recent case of *R (Jeeves and Baker) v Gravesham Borough Council*,[25] the court considered a judicial review brought by Gypsies against such a decision. Collins J had regard to the guidance in Circular 14/91 and quashed the LPA's decision. When doing so he reiterated the point that the power to decline to determine a second application should only be used in narrow circumstances such as a situation where the applicant is abusing the right to apply for planning permission by attempting to exert pressure on the planning authority. It follows that an applicant who wishes to make a further planning application after the refusal of planning permission by the LPA or the dismissal of an appeal against such a refusal, should, therefore, consider whether he

---

22   TCPA 1990 s62.
23   Town and Country Planning (Fees for Applications and Deemed Applications) Regulations 1989 SI No 193, as amended.
24   TCPA 1990 s70A. PCPA 2004 s43 has extended this power to decline to determine applications.
25   [2006] EWHC 1249 Admin; [2006] JPL 1743.

or she can wait until the expiry of the two-year period or whether the application can be changed significantly in a genuine attempt to meet the objections to the original proposal.

Development and the stationing of caravans on land

4.26   A common mistake in Gypsy and Traveller planning cases is to treat the placing of a caravan on land as an operational development. In itself, it is not, although it may involve associated operational development, such as the construction of roadways, hardstanding and amenity blocks. The stationing of a caravan on land for residential purposes, where the planning unit has previously had a wholly non-residential use (for example, a field in agricultural use), will be a material change of use and thus constitute development.[26] Usually this will require express planning permission.[27] If the previous use of the land was for another type of caravan site, such as a site for Travelling Showpeople or a touring caravan site, it will be a question of fact and degree whether the change of its use to a site for Gypsies and Travellers is sufficient to be material.

The meaning of caravan

4.27   The definition of 'caravan' that applies in TCPA 1990 is that contained in the Caravan Sites and Control of Development Act (CSCDA) 1960 s29(1), namely:

> 'caravan' means any structure designed or adapted for human habitation which is capable of being moved from one place to another (whether by being towed, or by being transported on a motor vehicle or trailer) and any motor vehicle so designed or adapted, but does not include –
>
> (a) any railway rolling stock which is for the time being on rails forming part of a railway system,
> (b) any tent.[28]

4.28   The word 'caravan' also covers certain structures composed of not more than two sections capable, when disassembled, of being moved by road.[29] The phrase 'mobile home' as used in mobile homes

---

26 *Restormel BC v Secretary of State for the Environment* [1982] JPL 785.
27 For circumstances where express provision is not required for the stationing of a caravan see para 4.21, above.
28 *Wyre Forest DC v Secretary of State for the Environment* [1990] 2 AC 357; [1990] 2 WLR 517; [1990] 1 All ER 780, HL. CSCDA 1960 s29(1) also defines 'caravan site'.
29 For the full extended definition, see CSA 1968 s13.

legislation has the same meaning as 'caravan' in caravan sites legislation.[30] It follows that, while 'caravan' and 'mobile home' convey different meanings in everyday English, in law they are synonymous and cover almost everything that would be called a caravan, a caravanette, a trailer-home or a mobile home.

Matters to be taken into account when determining planning applications for Gypsy and Traveller sites

4.29   As has already been mentioned, PCPA 2004 s38(6) provides that:

> planning applications are determined in accordance with the Development Plan unless material considerations indicate otherwise.

The paragraphs that follow consider the main 'material considerations' that affect applications for planning permission for Gypsy and Traveller caravan sites.

Relevant government policy and advice

4.30   Planning applications for Gypsy and Traveller sites may engage all manner of policy considerations covered by PPSs and PPGs. For example: the location of a proposed caravan site within or nearby to a Site of Special Scientific Interest (SSSI) or an area of regional or local biodiversity and geological interest will bring into play the advice contained within PPS9: *Biodiversity and geological conservation* (2005); whilst a proposed development in a flood plain will bring into play national policy contained in PPS25: *Development and flood risk* (2006). Government guidance contained in circulars will also be of relevance and the most important advice in any case where a Gypsy or Traveller seeks planning permission for a caravan site will usually be that contained in Circular 1/06.

Circular 1/06

4.31   Office of the Deputy Prime Minister Circular 1/06 was issued on 2 February 2006. It replaced Circular 1/94, provided updated guidance on the planning aspects of finding sites for Gypsies and Travellers and indicated how local authorities could work with them to achieve that aim. Those representing Gypsies and Travellers need to ensure that they are familiar with this Circular as the guidance it contains is likely to be of great importance in any case where a Gypsy or Traveller seeks planning permission for a caravan site.

---

30   Mobile Homes Act 1975 s9(1) and Mobile Homes Act 1983 s5(1).

4.32   In paragraph 3 of Circular 1/06 the government stated that:

A new Circular is necessary because evidence shows that the advice set out in Circular 1/94 has failed to deliver adequate sites for gypsies and travellers in many areas of England over the last 10 years. Since the issue of Circular 1/94, and the repeal of local authorities' duty to provide gypsy and traveller sites there have been more applications for private gypsy and traveller sites, but this has not resulted in the necessary increase in provision.

4.33   In paragraph 5 of Circular 1/06 the government acknowledged the poor health and low level of educational attainment amongst Gypsies and Travellers and expressed the view that the new circular should enhance their health and education outcomes.

4.34   In paragraph 12 the government indicated that it is intended that Circular 1/06 will, inter alia:

- create and support sustainable, respectful and inclusive communities where Gypsies and Travellers have fair access to suitable accommodation, education, health and welfare provision;
- reduce the number of unauthorised encampments and developments;
- increase significantly the number of Gypsy and Traveller sites in appropriate locations with planning permission in order to address under-provision over the next three to five years;
- recognise, protect and facilitate the traditional travelling way of life of Gypsies and Travellers, whilst respecting the interests of the settled community;
- underline the importance of assessing needs at regional and sub-regional level and for local authorities to develop strategies to ensure that needs are dealt with fairly and effectively;
- identify and make provision for the resultant land and accommodation requirements;
- promote more private Gypsy and Traveller site provision in appropriate locations through the planning system, while recognising that there will always be those who cannot provide their own sites;
- help avoid Gypsies and Travellers becoming homeless through eviction from unauthorised sites without an alternative to move to.

4.35   Circular 1/06 explains how the new planning system will work in the context of the provision of Gypsy and Traveller sites.

4.36   Local authorities are required by Housing Act 2004 s225 to carry out an assessment of the accommodation needs of Gypsies and Travellers.

4.37   Circular 1/06 makes it clear that LPAs should begin the process by complying with their statutory duty to assess the accommodation needs of Gypsies and Travellers and produce Gypsy and Traveller accommodation assessments (GTAAs).

4.38   The information from GTAAs will be fed to the RPBs, who will then be responsible for preparing RSSs which will identify the number of pitches required (but not their location) for each LPA and a strategic view of needs across the region.

4.39   It is then for individual LPAs to produce their own DPDs which set out site-specific allocations for the number of pitches that the RSSs have specified they need to accommodate within their areas. Paragraph 33 of Circular 1/06 states that LPAs will need to demonstrate that sites are suitable and that there is a realistic likelihood that specific sites allocated in DPDs will be made available for that purpose. DPDs will also need to explain how the land required will be made available for a Gypsy or Traveller site and the timescales for such provision. An important point is that LPAs will no longer be able to simply rely on criteria-based policies.[31] In the event that LPAs fail to comply with these requirements, PCPA 2004 s15(4) gives the Secretary of State the power to direct the relevant LPA to do so.

4.40   Clearly, it will take some time for LPAs to complete GTAAs, for RPBs to produce RSSs which accurately identify the number of pitches that individual LPAs should be required to provide, and for LPAs then to adopt site-specific DPDs. Paragraph 43 of Circular 1/06 states that where there is a clear and unmet need for additional site provision, then LPAs should bring forward DPDs containing site allocations in advance of the regional consideration of pitch numbers and completion of their GTAAs.

4.41   Paragraph 45 of Circular 1/06 refers to the advice in DoE Circular 11/95: *The use of conditions in planning permissions* that a temporary permission may be justified where it is expected that the planning circumstances will change in a particular way at the end of the period of temporary permission; and indicates that where there is unmet need and no available alternative Gypsy and Traveller site provision in an area, but there is a reasonable expectation that new sites are likely to become available at the end of that period in the area which will meet that need, LPAs should give consideration to granting temporary planning permission.

4.42   Paragraph 46 states that, in such circumstances, LPAs:

---

31   See *Butler v Bath and North East Somerset Council* [2003] EWCA Civ 1614; [2004] JPL 941, (2003) *Times*, 4 November, for the Court of Appeal's view of the situation pre-Circular 1/06.

are expected to give substantial weight to the unmet need in considering whether a temporary planning permission is justified.

4.43 In paragraph 47, the government recognises that Gypsies and Travellers in rural areas often face difficulties in securing an adequate supply of affordable land for their needs and advises LPAs in rural areas that they should include a 'rural exception site policy' in the relevant DPD. In paragraph 54 the government states that:

> Rural settings, where not subject to special planning constraints are acceptable in principle.

4.44 Sustainable development is a core principle which underpins the government's planning policy[32] and one of the key aims of the government is to reduce the need for individuals to travel by private motor vehicle. However, in paragraph 54 of Circular 1/06 the government states that:

> In assessing the suitability of [sites in rural settings], local authorities should be realistic about the availability, or likely availability, of alternatives to the car in accessing local services; ...

In paragraph 64 the government advises local authorities that a holistic approach should be taken to the issue of sustainability when considering whether to grant planning permission for a Gypsy or Traveller site:

> Issues of sustainability are important and should not only be considered in terms of transport mode and distances from services. Such considerations should include:
> (a) the promotion of peaceful and integrated co-existence between the site and the local community;
> (b) the wider benefits of easier access to GP and other health services;
> (c) children attending school on a regular basis;
> (d) the provision of a settled base that reduces the need for long-distance travelling and possible environmental damage caused by unauthorised encampment; and
> (e) not locating sites in areas at high risk of flooding, including functional floodplains, given the particular vulnerability of caravans.[33]

4.45 Highway considerations may also be relevant in a case where a Gypsy or a Traveller wishes to establish a site. Paragraph 66 of Circular 1/06 states that:

> Sites, whether public or private, should be identified having regard to highways considerations. In setting their policies, local planning authorities

32 See PPS1: *Delivering sustainable development* (2005).
33 In fact most Gypsies and Travellers are highly skilled at moving caravans very quickly when there is a risk of flooding.

should have regard to the potential for noise and other disturbance from the movement of vehicles to and from the site, the stationing of vehicles on the site, and on-site business activities. However, projected vehicle movements for gypsy and traveller sites should be assessed on an individual basis for each site. Proposals should not be rejected if they would only give rise to modest additional daily vehicle movements and/or the impact on minor roads would not be significant.[34]

4.46   A failure to point out relevant government advice to members of a planning committee or incorrect information as to the meaning of that advice may lead to the High Court quashing a decision made by that committee.[35]

Designated areas and site location

4.47   Much of England and Wales is designated, usually under an adopted development plan. In 1995, approved Green Belts covered 12 per cent of England.[36] In 1992, National Parks and Areas of Outstanding Natural Beauty (AONB) alone covered about 22 per cent of England and Wales.[37] The overlap between Green Belts, on the one hand, and National Parks and AONB, on the other, is comparatively small. In addition to these designations, there are SSSI, world heritage sites and many other (principally local) designations.

4.48   Formerly, paragraph 13 of Circular 1/94 provided:

> As a rule it will not be appropriate to make provision for gypsy sites in areas of open land where development is severely restricted, for example, Areas of Outstanding Natural Beauty, Sites of Special Scientific Interest, and other protected areas. Gypsy sites are not regarded as being among those uses of land which are normally appropriate in Green Belts. Green Belt land should therefore not be allocated for gypsy sites in development plans. PPG 2 gives guidance on Green Belt policy.

4.49   The old guidance did not distinguish between an area of sufficient national importance to be an AONB and 'other protected areas' which might merely be of district-level importance. In practice, many more permissions were granted in locally designated areas than in AONB.

---

34   See also Circular 1/06 Annex C para 4.
35   *Bleaklow Industries Ltd v Peak District National Park Authority* [2006] EWHC 3387 Admin.
36   PPG 2: *Green Belts* (1995) para 1.3.
37   PPG 7: *The countryside and the rural economy* (1992), since replaced by PPS 7: *Sustainable development in rural areas* (1997). The percentage of land now covered by National Parks and AONB has increased since 1992 as a result of further designations.

However, Circular 1/06 draws a very clear distinction between national and local designations, a point that should be borne in mind when considering old decisions on locally designated or undesignated land. Paragraphs 52 and 53 now provide:

> 52. In areas with nationally recognised designations (Sites of Special Scientific Interest, National Nature Reserves, National Parks, Areas of Outstanding Natural Beauty, Heritage Coasts, Scheduled Monuments, Conservation Areas, Registered Historic Battlefields and Registered Parks and Gardens), as with any other form of development, planning permission for gypsy and traveller sites should only be granted where it can be demonstrated that the objectives of the designation will not be compromised by the development.

> 53. However, local landscape and local nature conservation designations should not be used in themselves to refuse planning permission for gypsy and traveller sites.

4.50 It has long been policy that inappropriate development in a Green Belt should only be allowed if 'very special circumstances' exist. Paragraph 3.1 of Planning Policy Guidance Note 2: *Green Belts* begins:

> The general policies controlling development in the countryside apply with equal force in Green Belts but there is, in addition, a general presumption against inappropriate development within them. Such development should not be approved, except in very special circumstances ...

4.51 Gypsy and Traveller sites are considered to be inappropriate development in the Green Belt. The consequence is that Gypsies and Travellers seeking planning permission for a site within a Green Belt face a far greater burden than those seeking planning permission in undesignated or locally designated countryside. They will have to show 'very special circumstances'. Over the years this had led to numerous appeals, in some of which 'very special circumstances' have been established, and in some of which they have not. Court cases have considered whether such determinations involved an error of law. Recent cases and appeal decisions have continued this long-established pattern.[38]

4.52 However, Circular 1/06 has, to some extent, relaxed the policy which protects the Green Belt against the establishment of Gypsy and Traveller sites. Paragraphs 49–51 of Circular 1/06 provide:

> 49. There is a general presumption against inappropriate development within Green Belts. New gypsy and traveller sites in the Green Belt are normally inappropriate development, as defined in Planning Policy

---

38 See cases mentioned in the 'other material considerations' section from para 4.64, below.

Guidance 2: 'Green Belts' (PPG2). National planning policy on Green Belts applies equally to applications for planning permission from gypsies and travellers, and the settled population. Alternatives should be explored before Green Belt locations are considered. Pressure for development of sites on Green Belt land can usually be avoided if the local planning authority allocates sufficient sites elsewhere in its area, in its LDF, to meet identified need. Criteria-based policies in DPDs for the location of gypsy and traveller sites ... should not depart from national planning policy as set out in PPG2.

50. The presence of Green Belt will constrain and limit opportunities for identifying gypsy and traveller sites in some areas. The general extent of the Green Belt should be addressed through the RSS in the first instance. PPG2 makes clear that once the general extent of Green Belt has been approved, and once detailed Green Belt boundaries have been established in adopted development plans, they should only be altered exceptionally.

51. Alterations to the Green Belt boundary can be used in exceptional circumstances for housing and other types of development inappropriate for the Green Belt. Such alterations have often been used in cases where a local authority's area contains a high proportion of Green Belt land and no other suitable sites outside the Green Belt exist. Such an exceptional limited alteration to the defined Green Belt boundary (which might be to accommodate a site inset within the Green Belt) could be considered to meet a specific, identified need for a gypsy and traveller site in the same way such an alteration could be used for any other type of development. Such a proposal should be brought forward through the plan-making process. Where land is removed from the Green Belt in this way, it should be specifically allocated in a DPD as a gypsy and traveller site only.

4.53   Paragraph 51 is of particular interest. Those making representations on behalf of Gypsies and Travellers in respect of development plan documents should consider proposing alterations to Green Belt boundaries to allow for both existing and proposed Gypsy and Traveller sites. In the case of existing Gypsy or Traveller sites in a Green Belt, consideration should be given to excluding them together with a modest area for future expansion (perhaps a further 50 per cent) from the Green Belt.

4.54   The reality is that most Gypsies and Travellers want to live in rural areas and will, in any event, be unable to live elsewhere. Circular 1/06 recognises this fact and allows for Gypsy and Traveller sites in the countryside (particularly those areas of countryside not subject to a national designation or in a Green Belt). Gypsies and Travellers would be best advised to avoid trying to establish sites on land which is situated within the Green Belt, an AONB or other area which is covered by some form of national designation in parts of the country where other land not subject to such designation can be found to meet their needs.

However, in parts of the country where all the land is Green Belt or subject to some other form of national designation (such as in many areas around Greater London) it is inevitable that land for Gypsy and Traveller sites will have to be found in the Green Belt.

4.55 In areas where there is a substantial amount of undesignated rural land it ought, with goodwill from all concerned, to be relatively easy to locate suitable sites for Gypsies and Travellers. Unfortunately, that goodwill is often lacking. In other areas, the fact that most land is designated will not remove the need to provide for Gypsies' and Travellers' accommodation. In such circumstances, it is suggested that three approaches might be considered by all those concerned with the provision of sites.

4.56 First, there are sites that are naturally screened so that they have little or no visual impact: former military sites such as anti-aircraft emplacements and redundant utility sites, such as a former substation, may well have natural screening that has developed over the years and may be available at a price that Gypsies and Travellers could afford. Although these may in many respects be suitable for Gypsy and Traveller sites, advisers should be aware that such sites may be contaminated and should give their clients a clear warning of this possibility. They should firmly advise site investigation before purchase.[39] Some former quarries may also be suitable, although physical safety in them should be given particular consideration.

4.57 Secondly, a 'sieve map' process may be adopted to determine preferred areas. Under this process the land of greatest importance within the LPA's area is excluded first. In assessing importance, national designations such as AONB and SSSI are clearly of greater importance than local designations or landscape character areas. Further areas may be excluded in order of importance, but the process stops before the area of land remaining is too small to permit a realistic search for sites. In an area that was mainly undesignated land, all designated land might be excluded by this method. In an area that was wholly designated land, sites would be permitted in areas carrying the designation(s) of least importance. This is an entirely appropriate method of meeting a planning need.[40]

4.58 Thirdly, an approach based on the needs of Gypsies and Travellers can be adopted. This is likely to lead to a search for sites reasonably close to (but not immediately adjoining) settlements of sufficient size to

---

39 Gypsies and Travellers should be advised to instruct a conveyancing solicitor or a licensed conveyancer.

40 *Buckinghamshire CC v Hall Aggregates* [1985] JPL 634, CA.

contain basic facilities such as a primary school, doctor's surgery and shop(s), with access to a road appropriate for a lorry towing a caravan. At its best, such an approach can lead to the identification of sites where Gypsies and Travellers' accommodation needs can be met in areas where they wish to live. However, if not done properly, such an approach can result in the adoption of a policy consisting of so many mandatory criteria that it is unrealistic to expect that a site could be found which would comply with its requirements. The criteria used should be reasonable. Thus in *Stirrup v Secretary of State for the Environment*,[41] a district council had interpreted a county council's policy as meaning that all Gypsy and Traveller sites should have mains services readily and economically available. The High Court held that 'a requirement of mains services for a single caravan might well be *Wednesbury*[42] unreasonable'.

Development plan policies for Gypsy and Traveller sites

4.59   As has already been said,[43] PCPA 2004 s38(6) provides that planning applications should be determined in accordance with the development plan, unless material considerations indicate otherwise.[44]

4.60   Formerly, Circular 1/94 required LPAs to carry out a quantitative assessment of the need for Gypsy and Traveller sites within their areas and identify, wherever possible, locations suitable for Gypsy and Traveller sites, whether local authority or private sites, in their development plans. Where it was not possible to do so, LPAs were required to set out clear, realistic criteria for suitable locations, as a basis for site provision policies.

4.61   In fact, few, if any, LPAs in England and Wales carried out a quantitative assessment of need, and almost all the LPAs adopted criteria-based policies without looking to see whether they could identify sites in their areas.

4.62   Until Gypsy and Traveller DPDs are produced by LPAs, planning applications will continue to be assessed against existing (often inadequate) development plans. It should, however, be remembered that development plan policies that predate and are in conflict with Circular 1/06 will be treated as being out of date. In such circumstances, LPAs should appreciate that, when planning inspectors determine

41   (1993) 3 December, CO/383/93, Local Authority Law 1/94 2.
42   *Associated Provincial Picture Houses Ltd v Wednesbury Corporation* [1948] 1 KB 223; [1947] 2 All ER 680, CA.
43   See para 4.14, above.
44   PCPA 2004 s38(6) read with TCPA 1990 s70(2).

appeals against the refusal of planning permission for a Gypsy or Traveller site, they are likely to give significantly greater weight to Circular 1/06 than to, for example, an unrealistic and out-of-date, criteria-based local plan policy.

4.63   Paragraph 63 of Circular 1/06 warns LPAs that the absence of existing provision may prejudice enforcement action, or give rise to grounds for appeal against refusal of an application for a new site. At planning appeals, it has been the well-established practice of those representing Gypsies and Travellers to adduce evidence of under-provision and evidence that the need for Gypsy and Traveller sites in the area is unlikely to be met in the foreseeable future. The advice in paragraph 63 of Circular 1/06 makes that evidence all the more important.

Other material considerations

4.64   LPAs are required to have regard to all considerations which are material to an application but the legislation does not provide LPAs with any guidance on what considerations might be regarded as material. It has, therefore, been left to the courts to determine what is capable of amounting to a material consideration. In general, the courts have avoided placing limits on what might constitute a material consideration in any given case.

4.65   In the majority of cases concerning Gypsies and Travellers, the proposed use of a piece of land as a Gypsy caravan site will conflict with some policies contained in the development plan. In such circumstances, Gypsies and Travellers will only be granted planning permission if they can show that there are material considerations that outweigh the development plan policy objections and justify the grant of planning permission. The phrase 'material considerations' is broad. As Cooke J stated in *Stringer v Minister of Housing and Local Government*:

> In principle ... any consideration which relates to the use and development of land is capable of being a planning consideration. Whether a particular consideration falling within that broad class is material in any given case will depend on the circumstances.[45]

4.66   Considerations that may be of particular relevance to applications for planning permission made by Gypsies and Travellers include:

- Gypsy status;
- the general need for Gypsy and Traveller sites and the availability of alternative sites;

45 [1971] 1 All ER 65 at 77.

- the applicant's need for a Gypsy or Traveller site;
- personal circumstances; and
- human rights.

Ethnic Gypsies and Travellers and Gypsy status

4.67   There is no doubt that Romani Gypsies are a separate racial group for the purposes of the Race Relations Act (RRA) 1976.[46] Irish Travellers are also recognised as a separate ethnic group.[47] Moreover, RRA 1976 ss19A and 71, when read together, provide that local authorities must ensure that they exercise their planning functions with due regard to the need to eliminate unlawful discrimination, including discrimination against Romani Gypsies and Irish Travellers.

4.68   However, in order to benefit from the positive government guidance on the provision of Gypsy and Traveller sites, it is not enough for an applicant to prove that he or she is an ethnic Gypsy or Traveller; an applicant must show that he or she is entitled to what has become known as 'Gypsy status'.

Gypsy status and pre-2006 case-law

4.69   Somewhat confusingly, the word 'Gypsies' was defined for the purposes of the provision of caravan sites for Gypsies and Travellers in legislation not on grounds of ethnicity but as meaning:

> ... persons of nomadic habit of life, whatever their race or origin, but does not include members of an organised group of travelling showmen, or persons engaged in travelling circuses, travelling together as such.[48]

and as a consequence the issue has generated a substantial amount of litigation.

46   *Commission for Racial Equality v Dutton* [1989] QB 783; [1989] 1 All ER 306, CA.

47   *O'Leary v Allied Domecq* (2000) 29 August (unreported) (Case No CL 950275–79), Central London County Court, HHJ Goldstein. For further consideration of this point see chapter 8, below. In addition see the Race Relations (Northern Ireland) Order 1997 article 5, which, for the avoidance of doubt, makes express provision for Irish Travellers. Note also that since 19 July 2003 both Romani Gypsies and Irish Travellers have been protected by the EU Race Equality Directive (Directive 2000/43/EC; 2000 OJ L180/22). For a detailed consideration of this Directive see [2003] EHRLR 515.

48   CSCDA 1960 s24(8). The same definition was formerly contained in CSA 1968 s16 and stems from the decision of the Divisional Court in *Mills v Cooper* [1967] 2 WLR 1343. For guidance in respect of Travelling Showpeople, see DoE Circular 22/91 (Welsh Office Circular 78/91).

4.70   In *Greenwich LBC v Powell*,[49] Lord Bridge of Harwich stated that a person could be a statutory Gypsy if he led a nomadic way of life only seasonally.

4.71   The case of *R v Shropshire CC ex p Bungay*,[50] concerned a Gypsy family that had not travelled for some 15 years in order to care for its elderly and infirm parents. An aggrieved local resident in the area of the family's recently approved Gypsy site sought judicial review of the local authority's decision to accept that the family had retained their Gypsy status even though it had not travelled for some considerable time. Dismissing the claim, the judge held that a person could remain a Gypsy even if he or she did not travel, provided that their nomadism was held in abeyance and not abandoned.

4.72   In the later case of *Hearne v National Assembly for Wales*,[51] a traditional Gypsy was held not to be a Gypsy for the purposes of planning law as he had stated that he intended to abandon his nomadic habit of life, lived in a permanent dwelling and was taking a course that led to permanent employment.

4.73   In *R v South Hams DC ex p Gibb*,[52] the Court of Appeal considered the statutory definition further and qualified it by holding that there should be some recognisable connection between the travelling of those claiming to be Gypsies and the means whereby they made or sought their livelihood:

> ... the definition of 'Gypsies' ... imports the requirement that there should be some recognisable connection between the wandering or travelling and the means whereby the persons concerned make or seek their livelihood. Persons, or individuals, who move from place to place merely as the fancy may take them and without any connection between the movement and their means of livelihood fall outside these statutory definitions ...[53]

4.74   The latter part of the Court of Appeal's interpretation of the statutory definition of 'Gypsy' involves a consideration of whether the individual concerned travels to seek or make their livelihood and this point has been considered further in a number of cases. For example, in *Maidstone BC v Secretary of State for the Environment and Dunn*,[54] it was held that a Romani Gypsy who bred horses and travelled to horse fairs at

49   [1989] 1 AC 995; [1989] 2 WLR 7 at 15.
50   [1991] 23 HLR 195.
51   22 October 1999, (QBENF 1999/0648/C); (1999) *Times*, 10 November.
52   [1995] QB 158; [1994] 4 All ER 1012, CA.
53   [1994] 4 All ER 1012 at 1021.
54   [1996] JPL 584.

Appleby, Stow-in-the-Wold and the New Forest, where he bought and sold horses, and who remained away from his permanent site for up to two months of the year, at least partly in connection with this traditional Gypsy activity, was entitled to be accorded Gypsy status. More recently, in *Basildon DC v First Secretary of State and Rachel Cooper*,[55] the Court of Appeal accepted that a Romani Gypsy woman was a statutory Gypsy, in circumstances where she travelled to traditional Gypsy fairs during the summer months and sold craft items at those events.

4.75   In the past, LPAs often went to considerable lengths to try to 'prove' that the Gypsies or Travellers seeking planning permission were not entitled to Gypsy status.

4.76   The Welsh Assembly's Equality of Opportunity Committee[56] has recognised this tendency and has argued that the weaknesses in the planning system are indicated by the increasing consideration of the provisions of the Human Rights Act (HRA) 1998 in relation to legal action being taken by Gypsies and Travellers on planning issues. The Committee noted the:

> ... apparent obsession with finding ways to prove that an individual is not a 'Gypsy' for the purposes of the planning system. This approach is extremely unhelpful ... and there can be no doubt that actual mobility at any given time is a poor indicator as to whether someone should be considered a Gypsy or a Traveller.[57]

4.77   In *Wrexham CBC v The National Assembly for Wales and Berry*,[58] the courts considered once more the question of whether an individual can lose her or his Gypsy status, particularly in relation to cases where old age and ill-health has led to Gypsies and Travellers not being able to travel. In *Berry*, a planning inspector had allowed a planning enforcement appeal for an ethnic Irish Traveller family in Wrexham, only to see the decision challenged in the High Court on the grounds that the elder breadwinner in the family, Mr Berry, was no longer a 'Gypsy' because he had become too ill to continue to travel for work. In his judgment, Sullivan J decided that he could not see anything in *R v South Hams DC ex p Gibb*[59] to suggest that, had the Court of Appeal been confronted with what might be described as a 'retired' Gypsy, it

---

55   [2004] EWCA Civ 473.
56   *Review of service provision for Gypsies and Travellers*, National Assembly for Wales, 2003.
57   *Review of Service Provision for Gypsies and Travellers* at p58.
58   [2002] EWHC 2414 Admin.
59   [1995] QB 158; [1994] 4 All ER 1012, CA.

would have said that he had ceased to be a statutory Gypsy because he had become too ill and/or too old to travel in order to search for work. Indeed, Sullivan J stated that he believed:

> ... such an approach would be contrary to common sense and common humanity ... It would be inhuman pedantry to approach the policy guidance ... upon that basis ...[60]

4.78 Wrexham CBC appealed against the decision of Sullivan J and the Court of Appeal allowed the appeal.[61] In doing so, Auld LJ stated that the following propositions of law should be applied:

...

(2) Whether applicants for planning permission are of a 'nomadic way of life' as a matter of planning law and policy is a functional test to be applied to their normal way of life at the time of the determination. Are they at that time following such a habit of life in the sense of a pattern and/or a rhythm of full time or seasonal or other periodic travelling? The fact that they may have a permanent base from which they set out on, and to which they return from, their periodic travelling may not deprive them of nomadic status. And the fact that they are temporarily confined to their permanent base for personal reasons such as sickness and/or possibly the interests of their children, may not do so either, depending on the reasons and the length of time, past and projected, of the abeyance of their travelling life. But if they have retired permanently from travelling for whatever reason, ill health, age or simply because they no longer wish to follow that way of life, they no longer have a 'nomadic way of life'. That is not to say they cannot recover it later, if their circumstances and intention change ... But that would arise if and when they made some future application for permission on the strength of that resumption of the status.

(3) Where, as here, a question is raised before a Planning Inspector as to whether applicants for planning permission are 'gypsies' for the purpose of planning law and policy, he should: (i) clearly direct himself to, and identify, the statutory and policy meaning of that word; and (ii) as a second and separate exercise, decide by reference to that meaning on the facts of the case whether the applicants fall within it ...

(4) In making the second, factual, decision whether applicants for planning permission are gypsies, the first and most important question is whether they are – to use a neutral expression – actually living a travelling life, whether seasonal or periodic in some other way, at the time

---

60 [2002] EWHC 2414 Admin at para 20. Note that the decision of Sullivan J was overturned by the Court of Appeal – see para 4.78, below.

61 [2003] EWCA Civ 835.

of the determination. If they are not, then it is a matter of fact and degree whether the current absence of travelling means that they have not acquired or no longer follow a nomadic habit of life.

(5) On such an issue of fact and degree, the decision-maker may find any one or more of the following circumstances relevant and, if so, of varying weight: (i) the fact that the applicants do or do not come from a traditional gypsy background and/or have or have not followed a nomadic way of life in the past – the possible relevance in either case being that respectively they may be less or more likely to give it up for very long or to abandon it entirely; (ii) the fact that the applicants do or do not have an honest and realistically realisable intention of resuming travelling and, if they do, how soon and in what circumstances; (iii) the reason or reasons for the applicants not living a travelling way of life at the time of the determination and their likely duration.[62]

Gypsy status and Circular 1/06

4.79   The decision in *Berry* left ethnic Gypsies and Travellers who had been forced to cease travelling on grounds of old age or ill-health in a particularly unfortunate position – in effect they were precluded from relying on the positive government guidance in Circular 1/94 on the provision of Gypsy and Traveller sites at the very time when they needed a settled base on which to station their caravans in which they had lived for all their lives. The Court of Appeal's decision did not reflect the fact that the state owed a positive duty under article 8 of the European Convention on Human Rights (ECHR or 'the Convention') to facilitate the Gypsy way of life[63] and Mr Berry took his case to the European Court of Human Rights (ECtHR). However, before the ECtHR could consider Mr Berry's case, his re-determined planning and enforcement appeals were allowed, meaning he was no longer a 'victim' for ECHR purposes. As a consequence, the court found his case to be inadmissible.

4.80   The question whether a person could retain their nomadic status, notwithstanding illness or old age, was dealt with head-on when the

---

62 Gypsy and Traveller women who are single parents may be faced with LPA decisions that they are not statutory 'Gypsies' since they do not travel for an economic purpose. In such circumstances, they may be able to argue that their economic nomadism is in abeyance (see *R v Shropshire CC ex p Bungay* (1991) 23 HLR 195). Alternatively, they may be able to argue that such a conclusion amounts to indirect sex discrimination under the Sex Discrimination Act 1975, though there is currently no case-law on this matter.

63 *Chapman v UK* (2001) 33 EHRR 399; (2001) 10 BHRC 48; (2001) *Times*, 30 January, at para 73.

government published Circular 1/06 and, in doing so, changed the policy definition of the term 'Gypsies and Travellers'. Paragraph 15 of Circular 1/06 states that:

> For the purposes of this Circular 'gypsies and travellers' means
>
> Persons of nomadic habit of life whatever their race or origin, including such persons who on grounds only of their own or their family's or dependants' educational or health needs or old age have ceased to travel temporarily or permanently, but excluding members of an organised group of travelling show people or circus people travelling together as such.

4.81 To a substantial extent this reverses the effect of the Court of Appeal's judgment in *Berry*; although clearly it does not follow that all Gypsies and Travellers who wish to seek planning permission for a caravan site will be able to rely upon the positive government guidance in Circular 1/06. For example, if an applicant has willingly given up travelling, for example, to take up employment, then he or she will not be able to do so – a situation which the courts may yet conclude amounts to a breach of article 8 of the Convention.

4.82 The fact remains that disputes concerning 'Gypsy status' still arise in planning appeals. To add to the confusion on this topic, on 2 January 2007, the government issued the Housing (Assessment of Accommodation Needs) (Meaning of Gypsies and Travellers) (England) Regulations 2006,[64] which state that yet another definition of 'Gypsies and Travellers' is to be used by local authorities for the purposes of carrying out their Gypsy and Traveller accommodation assessments (GTAAs), in accordance with duties imposed by Housing Act 2004 s225. The Regulations state that:

> 'Gypsies and Travellers' means –
>
> (a) persons with a cultural tradition of nomadism or of living in a caravan; and
> (b) all other persons of a nomadic habit of life, whatever their race or origin, including –
>   (i) such persons who, on grounds only of their own or their family's or dependant's educational or health needs or old age, have ceased to travel temporarily or permanently; and
>   (ii) members of an organised group of travelling showpeople or circus people (whether or not travelling together as such).[65]

---

64 SI No 3190.

65 This definition thus includes Travelling Showpeople. Guidance with regard to planning applications by Travelling Showpeople is contained in DoE Circular 22/91 (Welsh Office Circular 78/91).

4.83   It is not clear how the government expect the two inconsistent definitions to be applied, or why the definition in the Regulations should not be applied throughout planning law and practice. What is clear is that the Regulations' definition embraces those Gypsies and Travellers who have resorted to conventional bricks and mortar accommodation due to the scarcity of lawful sites but whose culture, traditions and preference would be to live on a site in a caravan. Given the central role of GTAAs as the evidential basis for future site allocations through the RSS, this is a significant consideration.

4.84   Some Gypsy and Traveller campaigners argue that the time has come for the government to accept – as they say it must do if it is to pay due regard to the right that Gypsies and Travellers have to respect for their traditional way of life – that all those with a cultural tradition of nomadism or of living in a caravan, as well as all other persons of a nomadic habit of life whatever their race or origin, should be entitled to Gypsy status for the purpose of seeking planning permission for a site.

The need for Gypsy and Traveller sites

4.85   The case of *Hedges and Hedges v Secretary of State for the Environment and East Cambridgeshire DC*[66] is authority for the fact that the national, regional and local need for additional site provision is capable of being a material consideration in planning applications made by Gypsies and Travellers.

4.86   *Hedges* is also an authority for the proposition that the personal need of a Gypsy or Traveller for a site is a material consideration that should be considered independently of the question of personal circumstances and hardship.[67]

4.87   The fact that there is a significant national need for additional sites is beyond doubt. However, the level of need does vary across the regions.

4.88   The regional and local need can be roughly deduced from the bi-annual Gypsy count figures conducted by LPAs. However, many of these counts have been shown to underestimate need to a considerable degree, with authorities undercounting and in some cases misreporting figures. In the future, GTAAs will be far more accurate in assessing levels of need for such accommodation.

4.89   Meanwhile, those advising Gypsies and Travellers should remember that the bi-annual counts are only a 'snapshot in time' and be

---

66   [1996] 73 P&CR 534 at 545.
67   [1996] 73 P&CR 534 at 545.

careful not to give the information which they contain too much weight, particularly in circumstances where an LPA suggests that the Gypsy count shows a very low level of need for more sites in its area. If possible advisers should test the information that they provide. Often Gypsies and Travellers living in an area or local Gypsy and Traveller support groups[68] will be able to give more accurate information about the existence of caravan sites and the level of unauthorised camping that takes place in the area and it is important that planning inspectors are informed of the true level of need.

The availability of alternative sites

4.90   More recently, in the case of *Doncaster MBC v First Secretary of State and Angela Smith*,[69] the approach to be adopted to the issue of the availability of alternative sites was considered. In that case, the local authority challenged the grant of planning permission for a Gypsy site in the Green Belt and, in particular, the planning inspector's view that:

> The absence of any alternative, available, affordable, acceptable and suitable land to which the site occupants could move has to be afforded considerable weight in favour of the development.

The local authority argued that the inspector had set too high a threshold when considering whether there were alternative sites which could accommodate the occupants. Bartlett J disagreed. He noted that, in *Chapman*, the ECtHR had said that the evaluation of suitable alternative accommodation for Gypsies would involve a consideration of the particular needs of the person concerned, his or her family requirements and financial resources; and he concluded that the inspector's assessment of that issue had been entirely in accord with both the decision in *Chapman* and the policy contained within Circular 1/06.

Fear of crime

4.91   The case of *Smith v First Secretary of State and Mid-Bedfordshire District Council*[70] represented a welcome rejection of prejudice against Gypsies and Travellers. In that case, the Court of Appeal quashed an inspector's decision to refuse planning permission for a Gypsy site in circumstances where he had based his decision, in part, on local residents' fears that crime would increase in the area if planning permission was granted. Rather than being based on extrapolation from

68   See appendix C, below, for a list of some such groups.
69   [2007] EWHC 1034 Admin.
70   [2005] EWCA Civ 859.

past events, this fear arose from assumptions as to the characteristics of the future occupiers that were unsupported by evidence. The Court of Appeal held that 'fear' had to have a reasonable basis and the object of that fear had to be the use of the land. Unlike a polluting factory or a bail hostel, a caravan site was not inherently likely to cause difficulties to neighbours. It was wrong to view the use of the land as a Gypsy or Traveller site as creating the concern that attached to an institution such as a bail hostel. Where concern for the future rested not on extrapolation from past events, but at least partly on assumptions unsupported by evidence as to the characteristics of the future occupiers, then it must not be taken into account. The decision was remitted to the secretary of state for reconsideration and the families have since been granted five years' temporary planning permission.

Personal circumstances

4.92   The traditional approach in planning law to land-use factors and personal circumstances is contained in Lord Scarman's speech in *Great Portland Estates plc v Westminster CC*:

> ... the principle ... is now well settled. It was stated ... in one sentence in East Barnet Urban District Council v British Transport Commission ... Lord Parker CJ said ... 'what is really to be considered is the character of the use of the land, not the particular purpose of a particular occupier.' These words have rightly been recognised as extending beyond the issue of change of use: they are accepted as a statement of general principle in planning law. They apply to development plans as well as to planning control ... However, like all generalisations, Lord Parker CJ's statement has its own limitations. Personal circumstances of an occupier, personal hardship, the difficulties of businesses which are of value to the character of a community are not to be ignored in the administration of planning control. It would be inhuman pedantry to exclude from the control of our environment the human factor. The human factor is always present, of course, indirectly as the background to the consideration of the character of land use. It can, however, and sometimes should, be given direct effect as an exceptional or special circumstance. But such circumstances, when they arise, fall to be considered not as a general rule but as exceptions to a general rule to be met in special cases. If a planning authority is to give effect to them, a specific case has to be made and the planning authority must give reasons for accepting it.[71]

4.93   While personal circumstances carry little or no weight in the vast majority of planning cases, they are often of crucial importance when

---

71 [1985] AC 661 at 669–670; [1984] 3 All ER 744, HL.

Gypsies and Travellers apply for planning permission. This is particularly so where the proposed site is situated within a Green Belt.

4.94 As has already been noted, PPG 2 paragraph 3 states that there is a general presumption against inappropriate development within the Green Belt. Paragraph 3.2 states that inappropriate development is, by definition, harmful to the Green Belt and such development should not be approved, except in 'very special circumstances'. It is for the applicant to justify inappropriate development and 'very special circumstances' will not exist unless the harm by reason of inappropriateness, and any other harm, is clearly outweighed by other considerations.

4.95 Gypsy and Traveller sites are not categorised as 'appropriate development' and, in practice, a Gypsy or Traveller seeking planning permission for a site within the Green Belt will have to show that there is a pressing need for further sites and/or that their personal circumstances justify the grant of planning permission.

4.96 In *Doncaster MBC v Secretary of State for the Environment, Transport and the Regions*[72] and *R (Chelmsford BC) v First Secretary of State and Draper*,[73] Sullivan J emphasised the importance of the guidance in PPG 2 and, in *Doncaster*, he emphasised the fact that it is important that the need to establish the existence of '"very special circumstances" ... is not watered down'.[74] That approach has since been endorsed by the Court of Appeal.[75]

4.97 However, it should be noted that a combination of factors, none of them very special in their own right, can, when taken together, amount to very special circumstances. In *Basildon DC v First Secretary of State and Temple*,[76] the local authority challenged a decision taken by a planning inspector to grant a Gypsy family planning permission for a site in the Green Belt. The planning inspector had concluded that very special circumstances existed having taken account of a number of factors, including:

- the local authority's failure to assess the needs of Gypsies and Travellers within its area;
- the severe shortage of suitable alternative and available sites within the area;

72 [2002] EWHC 808 Admin.
73 [2003] EWHC 2978 Admin.
74 [2002] EWHC 808 Admin at para 74.
75 *South Buckinghamshire DC v Secretary of State for Transport, Local Government and the Regions and Porter* (No 2) [2003] EWCA Civ 687; (2003) *Times*, 23 May.
76 [2004] EWHC 2759 Admin.

- the educational needs of the children of the family; and
- the fact that the dismissal of the appeal would force the family to chose between abandoning their traditional way of life by accepting local authority housing in order to keep their children in school and a return to life on the road.

4.98   The local authority argued that very special circumstances could not merely be factors that weigh in favour of granting planning permission but that each factor relied upon had to be of such a quality that it could reasonably be called 'very special'. Sullivan J disagreed and made it clear that:

> 10 ... There is no reason why a number of factors ordinary in themselves cannot combine to create something very special. The claimant's approach flies in the face of the approach normally adopted to the determination of planning issues: to consider all relevant factors in the round ...

> 17. The short answer to the claimant's argument is that in planning, as in ordinary life, a number of ordinary factors when combined together result in something very special. Whether any particular combination amounts to very special circumstances for the purposes of PPG2 will be a matter for the planning judgment of the decision-taker.

Sullivan J added that the case could be distinguished from the *Doncaster* and *Draper* cases – in both those cases only the apparently unexceptional educational needs of children living on the site had been relied upon as 'very special circumstances'.

4.99   The education of the children of Gypsies and Travellers may be of particular relevance in a planning application and if those needs are sufficiently strong (for example, because a child has special educational needs that can only be met whilst the child is living on a settled site), then they may be sufficient to clearly outweigh the objections to the use of land within the Green Belt as a caravan site (on their own or in conjunction with other considerations). Similarly, health considerations are often a very important factor in planning cases and can prove to be crucial.

4.100   *First Secretary of State v Simmons*[77] was yet another case where the courts considered a decision-maker's conclusion on the issue of whether 'very special circumstances' existed to justify development in a Green Belt. The local planning authority issued an enforcement notice requiring Mr Simmons to discontinue the use of Green Belt land for stationing caravans on the basis that the use of the land as a Gypsy caravan site constituted inappropriate development in the Green Belt. On appeal against the enforcement notice, the secretary of state found that there

---

77 [2005] EWCA Civ 1295.

was an unmet need for sites in the locality, but did not consider that this was sufficient to amount to 'very special circumstances'. The secretary of state noted that Mr Simmons' pattern of travel took him to areas of the country which were not within the Green Belt, that there had been no real effort to find an alternative site outside the Green Belt, and that this weighed against his case.[78] The Court of Appeal upheld the secretary of state's decision. It follows that Gypsies and Travellers seeking planning permission for a site on land in an area within the Green Belt or covered by some form of national designation, should present evidence to show that they need to live in that area, for example, because of local connections or other commitments, or that they have searched for alternative sites beyond the designated area in vain. Typically, evidence of a search having been carried out will include correspondence with local estate agents and local authorities as well as evidence of actual searches that have been undertaken.

4.101　　Where personal circumstances tip the balance in favour of a grant of planning permission, the permission is likely to be subject to a condition making its benefit personal to the applicants.

4.102　　Where there is an application for retrospective permission or a decision whether an enforcement notice should be issued or upheld, the disruption that would be caused to the occupiers of the accommodation is a material consideration.[79]

Human rights as a material consideration

4.103　Local authorities, planning inspectors, the secretary of state and the courts are all public bodies for the purposes of HRA 1998 s6(3) and are, therefore, subject to the duty imposed by HRA 1998 s6(1) to act compatibly with the Convention when dealing with applications for planning permission made by Gypsies and Travellers.[80]

4.104　　In 2001, the ECtHR gave its judgment in five cases brought by British Gypsies who had been refused planning permission to place their caravan homes on their own land.[81] The UK government settled

---

78　See also *Buckley v UK* (1996) 23 EHRR 101; [1997] 2 PLR 10; [1996] JPL 1018.

79　*Britannia Developments Ltd v Secretary of State for Communities and Local Government* [2007] EWHC 812 Admin.

80　For a detailed consideration of the HRA 1998 as it affects Gypsies and Travellers see chapter 2, above.

81　*Chapman v United Kingdom* (2001) 33 EHRR 399; (2001) 10 BHRC 48; (2001) *Times*, 30 January, ECtHR (Commission [1998] HRDC IX 386). See also *Beard v United Kingdom* (2001) 33 EHRR 442; *Coster v United Kingdom* (2001) 33 EHRR 479; *Smith (Jane) v United Kingdom* (2001) 33 EHRR 712; and *Lee v United Kingdom* (2001) Application No 25289/94.

a sixth case, in which the European Commission of Human Rights had previously found a breach of the Convention, by a payment of £60,000 and full costs.[82]

4.105   The applicants in each case had complained of breaches of various Convention rights, notably article 8. This provides:

(1) Everyone has the right to respect for his private and family life, his home and his correspondence.

(2) There shall be no interference by a public authority with the exercise of this right except such as is in accordance with the law and is necessary in a democratic society in the interests of national security, public safety or the economic well-being of the country, for the prevention of disorder or crime, for the protection of health or morals, or for the protection of the rights and freedoms of others.

4.106   The lead case, *Chapman v United Kingdom*,[83] concerned a Gypsy woman who had bought land in the Three Rivers District of Hertfordshire. This district contained no provision for Gypsies and Travellers and was in a county that had a history of under-provision for Gypsies and Travellers. This had led to a High Court declaration that the local authority was in breach of the (now repealed) statutory duty to provide Gypsy caravan sites.[84] Mrs Chapman's land was, however, situated in a Green Belt.

4.107   The ECtHR first considered whether the prima facie rights contained in article 8(1) were in issue. It unanimously held that they were, not only in the case of the right to respect for home (which in the light of an earlier decision of the ECtHR in *Buckley v United Kingdom*[85] the government had conceded), but also in the case of the right to respect for private and family life. As the ECtHR said:

... the applicant's occupation of her caravan is an integral part of her ethnic identity as a Gypsy, reflecting the long tradition of that minority of following a travelling lifestyle. This is the case even though, under the pressure of development and diverse policies or from their own volition, many Gypsies no longer live a wholly nomadic existence and increasingly settle for long periods in one place in order to facilitate, for example, the education of their children. Measures which affect the applicant's stationing of her caravans have therefore a wider impact than on the right to respect for

---

82   *Varey v United Kingdom* (Application No 26662/95).

83   *Chapman v United Kingdom* (2001) 33 EHRR 399, (2001) 10 BHRR 48.

84   *R v Secretary of State for the Environment ex p Lee* (1987) 54 P&CR 311.

85   (1996) 23 EHRR 101; [1997] 2 PLR 10; [1996] JPL 1018, (1996) *Times*, 9 October, ECtHR (Commission) [1994] JPL 536; [1995] JPL 633; 19 EHRR CD20.

home. They also affect her ability to maintain her identity as a Gypsy and to lead her private and family life in accordance with that tradition.[86]

4.108   The judges of the ECtHR disagreed on whether the interference by the state was justified as 'necessary in a democratic society'. A majority of 10 of the 17 judges held that it was, while a minority dissented. There was a distinct difference between the Western European judges, a majority of whom found in the applicants' favour, and the Eastern European ones who, with the exception of the Slovak judge, found in favour of the UK government. Schiemann LJ, the ad hoc UK judge, also found in the government's favour.

4.109   The majority recognised that:

> ... there may be said to be an emerging international consensus amongst the Contracting States of the Council of Europe recognising the special needs of minorities and an obligation to protect their security, identity and lifestyle [see in particular the Framework Convention for the Protection of Minorities[87]], not only for the purpose of safeguarding the interests of the minorities themselves but to preserve a cultural diversity of value to the whole community.[88]

However they were 'not persuaded that the consensus is sufficiently concrete for it to derive any guidance as to the conduct or standards which Contracting States consider desirable in any particular situation'.[89] In so stating, they left open the possibility that the consensus may harden sufficiently for the ECtHR to bear it in mind in future judgments.

4.110   The majority also held that:

> As intimated in the *Buckley* judgment, the vulnerable position of Gypsies as a minority means that some special consideration should be given to their needs and their different lifestyle both in the relevant regulatory planning framework and in arriving at the decisions in particular cases ... To this extent there is thus a positive obligation imposed on the Contracting States by virtue of Article 8 to facilitate the Gypsy way of life ...[90]

---

86   *Chapman v United Kingdom* (2001) 33 EHRR 399, (2001) 10 BHRR 48 at para 73.

87   Framework Convention for the Protection of National Minorities, Strasbourg, 1/2/1195, Council of Europe Doc ETS 157.

88   *Chapman v United Kingdom* (2001) 33 EHRR 399, (2001) 10 BHRR 48 at para 93.

89   (2001) 33 EHRR 399 at para 94.

90   (2001) 33 EHRR 399 at para 96.

4.111   However, the majority relied upon the doctrine of 'margin of appreciation'[91] to find for the government, holding:

> ... a margin of appreciation must, inevitably, be left to the national authorities, who by reason of their direct and continuous contact with the vital forces of their countries are in principle better placed than an international court to evaluate local needs and conditions.[92]

It should be noted that this doctrine depends on the international nature of the ECtHR. It will, therefore, not apply to a national court acting under the HRA 1998.[93]

4.112   While the government succeeded, it did not escape criticism from the majority, who commented:

> ... the issue for determination ... is not the acceptability or not of a general situation, however deplorable, in the United Kingdom in the light of the United Kingdom's undertakings in international law, but the narrower one whether the particular circumstances of the case disclose a violation of the applicant's, Mrs Chapman's, right to respect for her home under article 8 ...[94]

4.113   The minority delivered a strong dissenting judgment in respect of article 8. They accepted:

> that the examination of planning objections to a particular use of a site is not a role for which this Court is well-suited ... Where town and country planning is concerned, the Court has previously noted that this involves the exercise of discretionary judgment in the implementation of policies adopted in the interest of the community ...[95]

4.114   However, the dissenting judges took a different approach to the treatment of minorities stating:

> There is an emerging consensus amongst the member States of the Council of Europe recognising the special needs of minorities and an obligation to protect their security, identity and lifestyle, not only for the purpose of safeguarding the interests of the minorities themselves but also in order to preserve a cultural diversity of value to the whole community. This consensus includes a recognition that the protection of the rights of minorities, such as Gypsies, requires not only that Contracting States refrain

---

91   See chapter 2 at paras 2.31–2.35, above.

92   *Chapman* (2001) 33 EHRR 399 at para 91.

93   See the Court of Appeal decision in *South Buckinghamshire DC v Porter; Chichester DC v Searle; Wrexham CBC v Berry; Hertsmere BC v Harty* [2001] EWCA Civ 1549; [2002] 1 All ER 425; [2002] 1 WLR 1359; July 2002 *Legal Action* 22, at para 25, per Simon Brown LJ. See also footnote 97 below.

94   *Chapman v United Kingdom* (2001) 33 EHRR 399 at para 100.

95   (2001) 33 EHRR 399, joint dissenting opinion at p435.

from policies or practices which discriminate against them but that also, where necessary, they should take positive steps to improve their situation through, for example, legislation or specific programmes. We cannot therefore agree with the majority's assertion that the consensus is not sufficiently concrete or with their conclusion that the complexity of the competing interests renders the Court's role a strictly supervisory one ...[96]

4.115 The dissenting judges bore in mind the difficulties of Gypsies, stating:

The long-term failures of local authorities to make effective provision for Gypsies in their planning policies is evident from the history of implementation of measures concerning Gypsy sites, both public and private ... the Government is already well aware that the legislative and policy framework does not provide in practice for the needs of the Gypsy minority and that their policy of leaving it to local authorities to make provision for Gypsies has been of limited effectiveness ... it is in our opinion disproportionate to take steps to evict a Gypsy family from their home on their own land in circumstances where there has not been shown to be any other lawful, alternative site reasonably open to them. It would accordingly be for the authorities to adopt such measures as they consider appropriate to ensure that the planning system affords effective respect for the home, private life and family life of Gypsies such as the applicant.[97]

4.116 In addition to joining the dissenting opinion, Judge Bonello emphasised Hertfordshire County Council's proven non-compliance with the law. In a separate opinion he stated:

A public authority owes as great an obligation to comply with the law as any individual. Its responsibility is eminently more than that of individuals belonging to vulnerable classes who are virtually forced to disregard the law in order to be able to exercise their fundamental right to a private and family life – individuals who have to contravene the law due to the operation of the prior failures of the public authorities. In the present case, both the public authorities and the individual had undoubtedly trespassed the boundaries of legality. But it was the public authority's default in observing the law that precipitated and induced the subsequent default by the individual. That failure of the authorities has brought about a situation which almost justifies the defence of necessity. Why a human rights court should look with more sympathy at the far-reaching breach of law committed by the powerful, than at that forced on the weak, has not yet been properly explained.[98]

---

96 (2001) 33 EHRR 399 at pp435–436.

97 (2001) 33 EHRR 399 at p438. In granting leave to appeal in *South Buckinghamshire DC v Porter* [2001] EWCA Civ 1549; [2002] 1 WLR 1359; [2002] 1 All ER 425,CA, Sedley LJ stated that our domestic courts could refer to the minority decision in *Chapman v United Kingdom*.

98 (2001) 33 EHRR 399 at p441.

4.117   Though the applicants in *Chapman* were unsuccessful, the HRA 1998 principles derived from that case are of general application and will be relevant in almost every case where Gypsies and Travellers seek planning permission for use of land as a caravan site.

4.118   The decision in *Chapman* can be contrasted with the case of *Chichester DC v First Secretary of State and Grant Doe*,[99] where the Court of Appeal upheld the decision of a planning inspector in circumstances where he had concluded that the refusal of planning permission would breach the article 8 rights of a Gypsy family.

Human rights and offers of conventional housing

4.119   Significantly, the provisions of the HRA 1998 and the Convention have been applied by the domestic courts to determine whether the availability of conventional housing should be taken into consideration (that is, a material consideration) when Gypsies and Travellers seek planning permission for their own caravan sites.

4.120   In *Clarke v Secretary of State for the Environment, Transport and the Regions and Tunbridge Wells BC*,[100] an inspector dismissed an appeal against the local planning authority's refusal of planning permission to site a Gypsy caravan in a special landscape area. Mr Clarke argued that the inspector had wrongly taken into account an offer by the authority of conventional housing accommodation and that this was in breach of articles 8 and 14 of the ECHR.[101]

4.121   At first instance Burton J held:

> ... it can amount to a breach of articles 8 and 14 to weigh in the balance and hold against a Gypsy applying for planning permission, or indeed resisting eviction from ... land, that he or she has refused conventional housing accommodation as being contrary to his or her culture. Such circumstances ... are and should be, limited, just as they are if, for example, it is to be alleged similarly to be impermissible, in relevant circumstances, to hold it against or penalise a religious or strictly observant Christian, Jew or Muslim because he or she will not, and thus cannot work on certain days, or to hold it against, or penalise, a strictly observant Buddhist, Muslim, Jew or Sikh because he eats or will not eat certain foods, or will not wear

---

99   [2004] EWCA Civ 1248; [2005] 1 WLR 279.

100 [2001] EWHC 800 Admin; [2002] JPL 552; July 2002 *Legal Action* 23; (2001) *Times*, 9 November.

101 See para 4.105, above, for article 8. Article 14 provides: 'The enjoyment of the rights and freedoms set forth in this Convention shall be secured without discrimination on any ground such as sex, race, colour, language, religion, political or other opinion, national or social origin, association with a national minority, property, birth or other status.'

certain clothing. It is not, and cannot be, a formality to establish this, and the onus is upon the person such as a Gypsy who seeks to establish it.[102]

4.122 After considering the need to establish Gypsy status, he said:

> ... if such be established then ... bricks and mortar, if offered, are unsuitable, just as would be the offer of a rat-infested barn.[103] It would be contrary to articles 8 and 14 to expect such a person to accept conventional housing and to hold it against him or her that he has not accepted it, or is not prepared to accept it, even as a last resort factor.[104]

4.123 The inspector's decision was quashed on the basis that he either took into account impermissible factors relating to conventional housing or made insufficient findings in respect of such factors.

4.124 The LPA's appeal was dismissed and the Court of Appeal held that the approach of Burton J was entirely in accord with the approach of the ECtHR in *Chapman*.[105] Buxton LJ held:

> What the judge seems to me to be ... rightly directing the inspector to, is a careful examination of the objections of the Clarke family to living in conventional housing in order to determine the extent to which article 8 is truly engaged, and the nature of its engagement by the combination of their Gypsy identity and their opposition to conventional housing. Only when the inspector has made that determination in clearer terms than he adopted in his present letter will it be possible for him properly to engage in the balancing consideration that Burton J envisages ... This was a case where a Convention right was potentially engaged and in such cases a more intense scrutiny of the facts upon which that right is asserted needs to be engaged in before the court can indulge in the balancing exercise that article 8(2) imposes on it.[106]

Making an application for planning permission

4.125 Advisers assisting with an application for planning permission should include the following:

- a plan showing the boundaries of the site; and
- the application fee.

---

102 [2001] EWHC 800 Admin at para 30.

103 As to which see *R v South Herefordshire DC ex p Miles* (1983) 17 HLR 82, per Woolf J (as he then was).

104 [2001] EWHC 800 Admin at para 34.

105 *Chapman v United Kingdom* (2001) 33 EHRR 399, (2001) 10 BHRR 48.

106 [2002] EWCA Civ 819 at para 15.

The site area should be specified in the application form, preferably in square metres or hectares. Although a high degree of mathematical precision is seldom essential, guesses can cause difficulty at a later stage.

4.126   Advisers may also wish to consider submitting information on the following matters:

- Evidence of the applicant's Circular 1/06 Gypsy status and of Gypsy ethnicity, including details of travelling by the applicant and by family members for the purpose of work and copies (not originals in case they are lost) of family photographs.
- Where applicants and their families have ceased travelling temporarily, evidence of any intention to resume travelling or of the health or educational reasons for ceasing to travel.
- Details and evidence of any factors relevant to the personal circumstances of members of the family, in particular any health, educational or other welfare needs. Ill-health should be evidenced by a detailed letter or report from the relevant GP or consultant. Letters from headteachers and/or Traveller education support staff can also be of considerable benefit.
- Details and evidence of attempts to find alternative sites, including, for example, letters to local estate agents and evidence of inquiries of local authorities.
- Evidence of any aversion to conventional housing.
- Occupational needs.
- Any specific need for accommodation that would assist Romani Gypsies and Irish Travellers who keep animals, particularly horses and ponies.

Conditions

4.127   TCPA 1990 s70(1)(a) enables LPAs to grant planning permissions subject to conditions. In practice all planning permissions include some conditions. In Gypsy and Traveller cases these may include, among others, the following:

- a condition limiting the occupation of the site to Gypsies as defined in Circular 1/06;
- a condition making the planning permission temporary; and
- a condition making the planning permission personal to certain specific individuals.

4.128   Conditions can be very useful, enabling permission to be granted where it would otherwise be refused. As paragraph 2 of Circular 1/06 states:

If used properly, conditions can enhance the quality of development and enable many development proposals to proceed where it would otherwise have been necessary to refuse planning permission.

4.129 Government advice on conditions is contained in DoE Circular 11/95, *The use of conditions in planning permissions*. Conditions should meet each of the following six tests. They should be: (i) necessary; (ii) reasonable; (iii) relevant to the development to be permitted; (iv) enforceable; (v) precise; and (vi) reasonable in all other respects. The Circular contains model conditions in its appendix A. Advisers should consider whether to suggest such conditions when seeking planning permission or appealing against the refusal of permission. For example, if a business use of part of the site is proposed, a condition against working at night and on Sundays and bank and public holidays might be appropriate.

4.130 If planning permission would not have been granted for a caravan, but for the fact that it is to meet the needs of Gypsies and Travellers, a condition limiting occupancy to Gypsies as defined in paragraph 15 of Circular 1/06 may be appropriate. If permission is granted in an unsatisfactory location because of a need for sites that it is anticipated will be met within a few years, a temporary permission may be appropriate. Similarly, if the site is only justified by personal circumstances, a personal permission may be appropriate. In practice, most applicants gladly accept the imposition of a condition which limits occupation to Gypsies and Travellers. However, it is not uncommon for applicants to give reasons why a personal or temporary permission is not necessary but for them to state, in the alternative, that they would be willing to accept the imposition of such a condition rather than suffer an outright refusal.

4.131 Where an LPA refuses an application on a ground that could be overcome by a condition, this is often the basis for an application at appeal for a partial award of costs to cover the costs of fighting that ground. Where it has been necessary to employ expert witnesses to challenge such a ground, for example, in the case of a highway or flooding objection, these costs may be considerable.

Appealing against a refusal of planning permission

4.132 If the local planning authority refuses permission the applicant may appeal to the secretary of state[107] within six months of the date of refusal of permission.

107 TCPA 1990 s78.

4.133   Most appeals are determined by an inspector from the Planning Inspectorate. A small proportion are determined by the Secretary of State for Communities and Local Government or the Welsh Assembly (in reality, a civil servant acting on their behalf) after consideration of a report prepared by an inspector. There are four procedures for an appeal:

- the appeal is determined by an inspector having taken account of written representations submitted by the parties;[108] or
- a hearing is held and the appeal is determined by an inspector;[109] or
- an inquiry is held and the appeal is determined by an inspector;[110] or
- the appeal is determined by the secretary of state following an inquiry held by an inspector.[111]

The four different types of appeal are governed by different procedural rules. The time limits imposed by these must be obeyed. Failure to do so may disadvantage the appellant considerably.

4.134   An appeal is a fresh determination of the merits of an application. As such, although the history of the matter may be of relevance, the principal matters are likely to be the factual situation and the current policy at the date of the appeal. Paragraph 69 of Circular 1/06 states that:

> A Planning Inspector considering any subsequent appeal will have regard to the development plan so far as is relevant, and will take into account all material considerations, which should already have been addressed at the application stage. These will include the existing and planned provision of, and need for, sites in the area, the accuracy of the data used to assess need, the methodology employed in the assessment of how up-to-date it is, information on pitch availability on public and private sites, personal circumstances and alternative accommodation options.

4.135   Advisers assisting Gypsies and Travellers should, therefore, include in the appeal documentation the material adduced in support of the application. In addition they should also answer the reasons given by the LPA for refusing planning permission and bring their evidence up to date (particularly where a case is reliant on personal

108 Town and Country Planning (Appeals) (Written Representations Procedure) (England) Regulations 2000 SI No 1628.
109 Town and Country Planning (Hearings Procedure) (England) Rules 2000 SI No 1626.
110 Town and Country Planning (Appeals) (Determination by Inspectors) (Inquiries Procedure) (England) Rules 2000 SI No 1625.
111 Town and Country Planning (Inquiries Procedure) (England) Rules 2000 SI No 1624.

circumstances and welfare needs). Where the LPA is relying upon policies that conflict with government advice (for example, an old criteria-based policy that, in practice, included criteria that are too difficult to meet), then that point should be explicitly made. Where racist material is included in the papers before the inspector, for example, objectors' letters containing offensive assertions against Romani Gypsies or Irish Travellers, the inspector's attention should be drawn to RRA 1976 s19A.[112] Thorough preparation is necessary. If a point is omitted it will not normally be possible to raise it before the High Court in any appeal.[113]

An application to the High Court[114]

4.136   An appeal decision taken in respect of the refusal of a planning application may itself be challenged under TCPA 1990 s288 by an application to the High Court on the ground that the appeal decision was not within the powers of, or did not comply with, the relevant requirements of the TCPA 1990.[115] Such a challenge can only be made within six weeks of the date on the decision letter. This period cannot be extended under any circumstances.

4.137   The principles affecting a statutory review under TCPA 1990 s288 were conveniently summarised in *Seddon Properties v Secretary of State for the Environment*:[116]

- decision makers must not act perversely;
- they must not take into account irrelevant matters or fail to take into account that which is relevant;
- they must abide by statutory procedures; and
- they must not depart from the principles of natural justice.

4.138   Case-law has made it clear that:

- questions of planning judgment are for the decision maker not the court;[117]

112   Similarly, New Travellers may be able to object to discriminatory material by reference to ECHR articles 8 and 14.

113   *Smith v Secretary of State for the Environment, Transport and the Regions and Wyre Forest DC* [2001] EWCA Civ 1550. In that case it had not been argued at the planning inquiry that the development plan did not comply with DoE Circular 1/94.

114   And see appendix A, below, on procedures.

115   TCPA 1990 s288.

116   (1981) 42 P&CR 26–28, per Forbes J.

117   *City of Edinburgh v Secretary of State for Scotland* [1997] 1 WLR 1447 at 1458–1459, per Lord Clyde.

- the requirement to take into account all relevant considerations is limited to those matters which might cause the decision-maker to reach a different decision;[118] and
- the decision-maker, while required to have regard to every material consideration, need only state reasons in respect of the principal controversial issues.[119]

So, for example, a secretary of state's decision was quashed where he had to deal with the issue of the grant of temporary planning permission and proportionality in the context of article 8 but had failed to do so.[120]

4.139   Decision-makers have a duty to give adequate and intelligible reasons. That fact was reiterated by the House of Lords when it upheld a decision to grant a Gypsy family planning permission in the case of *South Buckinghamshire District Council v Porter (No 2)*.[121] In that case Lord Brown summarised the case-law on the adequacy of reasons as follows:

> The reasons for a decision must be intelligible. They must enable the reader to understand why the matter was decided as it was and what conclusions were reached on the principle important controversial issues, disclosing how any issue of law or fact was resolved. Reasons can be briefly stated, the degree of particularity required depending entirely on the nature of the issues falling for decision. The reasoning must not give rise to a substantial doubt as to whether the decision-maker erred in law, for example by misunderstanding some relevant policy or some other important matter or by failing to reach a rational decision on relevant grounds. But such adverse inference will not readily be drawn. The reasons need refer only to the main issues in the dispute, not to every material consideration. They should enable disappointed developers to assess their prospects of obtaining some alternative development permission, or, as the case may be, their unsuccessful opponents to understand how the policy or approach underlying the grant of planning permission may impact upon future such applications. Decision letters must be read in a straightforward manner, recognising that they are addressed to parties well aware of the issues involved and the arguments advanced. A reasons challenge will only succeed if the party aggrieved can satisfy the court that he has genuinely been substantially prejudiced by the failure to provide an adequately reasoned decision.[122]

---

118   *Bolton MBC v Secretary of State for the Environment* (1990) 61 P&CR 343, at 352–353, CA, per Glidewell LJ.

119   *Bolton MBC v Secretary of State for the Environment* (1995) 3 PLR 37 at 42–43, HL.

120   *Lee v First Secretary of State* [2003] EWHC 3235 Admin.

121   [2004] 1 WLR 1953.

122   See also *Save Britain's Heritage v No 1 Poultry Ltd* [1991] 1 WLR 153 at 165–168, per Lord Bridge of Harwich.

4.140   In applications where only one party appears on each side, costs normally follow the event. Where there is multiple representation, costs are in the discretion of the court and there are no absolute rules.[123]

Enforcement

Statutory provisions

4.141   If a development is carried out without the grant of the required planning permission, the local planning authority may:

- issue an enforcement notice (with or without a stop notice) if it considers it expedient to do so having regard to the provisions of the development plan and to any other material considerations;
- issue a temporary stop notice;
- seek a planning enforcement injunction;
- take direct action and execute the works required by an enforcement notice;
- take no action.

Government guidance on enforcement

4.142   The principal guidance on enforcement against Gypsies and Travellers who are using land for residential purposes in breach of planning control can be found in PPG 18: *Enforcing planning control* (1991) and various circulars and other publications.[124] The guidance in PPG 18 relating to small businesses applies to Gypsy and Traveller sites.[125] PPG 18 requires the LPA:

> ... to explore – in discussion with the owner or operator – whether the [use] can be allowed to continue operating acceptably on the site at its current level of activity, or perhaps less intensively. The LPA should carefully explain the planning objections to the current operation ... and, if it is practicable, suggest ways to overcome them. This may result in the grant of a mutually acceptable conditional planning permission, enabling the owner or operator to continue ... at the site without harm to local amenity ...[126]

---

123   Normal practice is however set out in *Bolton MBC v Secretary of State for the Environment* [1995] 3 PLR 37 at 51.

124   See Circular 1/06 para 68.

125   PPG 18 at para 15.

126   PPG 18 at para 16.

In addition PPG 18 advises LPAs that:

> Unless it is urgently needed, formal enforcement action should not come as a 'bolt from the blue'... It should be preceded by informal discussion about possible means of minimising harm to local amenity caused by the ... activity; and, if formal action will clearly be needed, by discussion of the possible relocation ... to another site ...[127]

4.143   It should not be forgotten that Circular 1/06 paragraph 63 states that:

> Local planning authorities should also have regard to whether the absence of existing provision may prejudice enforcement action ...

It follows that those representing Gypsies and Travellers in enforcement proceedings should draw attention to any such deficiency, for example, as a defence to injunction proceedings or as mitigation.

Considerations of common humanity

4.144   *R v Lincolnshire CC ex p Atkinson*[128] concerned the exercise of powers under CJPOA 1994 s77 in relation to unauthorised encampments.[129] Commenting on DoE Circular 18/94, *Gypsy sites policy and unauthorised camping* paragraphs 9–13, Sedley J said:

> Detailed analysis of these passages and debate about what legal force, if any, an advisory circular of this kind possesses has been made unnecessary by the realistic concession of counsel for both local authorities that whether or not they were spelt out in a departmental circular the matters mentioned in the paragraphs ... would be material considerations in the public law sense that to overlook them in the exercise of a local authority's powers under sections 77 to 79 of the Act ... would be to leave a relevant matter out of account and so jeopardise the validity of any consequent step. The concession is rightly made because those considerations in the material paragraphs which are not statutory are considerations of common humanity, none of which can properly be ignored when dealing with one of the most fundamental human needs, the need for shelter with at least a modicum of security.[130]

4.145   Case-law has made it clear that the considerations of common humanity identified in DoE Circular 18/94 must be taken into account in reaching decisions in relation to enforcement action.[131] The ODPM

127   PPG 18 at para 16.
128   *R v Lincolnshire CC ex p Atkinson; Wealden DC ex p Wales and Stratford* [1997] JPL 65; (1996) 8 Admin LR 529; (1995) *Times*, 22 September.
129   See chapter 5 at para 5.119, below.
130   [1997] JPL 65 at 72; [1995] 8 Admin LR 529.
131   *R v Kerrier DC ex p Uzell Blythe* (1996) 71 P&CR 566 at 571.

guidance issued in 2004 and 2006 regarding unauthorised encampments (and the Welsh Assembly guidance issued in 2005 on the same
issue) will also have some relevance.[132]

Enforcement notices

4.146 An LPA may issue an enforcement notice where it appears to it that
there has been a breach of planning control and that it is expedient to
issue the notice, having regard to the provisions of the development
plan and to any other material considerations.[133] As has been stated
above,[134] TCPA 1990 s171B deals with time limits for the enforcement
of planning control. Its effect is that:

- an enforcement notice must be issued within four years of the date
  of the breach of planning control where it relates to a breach consisting of –
  (i) the carrying out without planning permission of building, engi-
      neering, mining or other operations in, on, over or under land;
      or
  (ii) the making without planning permission of a change of use of
       any building to use it as a single dwelling house;
- in the case of any other breach of planning control, no enforcement action may be taken more than ten years after the date of the
  breach.

Enforcement notices should state 'the matters which appear to the
local planning authority to constitute the breach of planning control'
and 'specify the steps which the authority require to be taken, or the
activities which the authority require to cease, in order to achieve
whole or partial remediation'.[135] If an enforcement notice fails to comply
with these requirements then it may be held to be a nullity and therefore of no effect.[136]

4.147 An enforcement notice must specify the date on which it is to take
effect and service of the notice shall take place not more than 28 days
after its date of issue and not less than 28 days before the date specified
in it, as the date on which it is to take effect.[137] It has been held that an

132 See chapter 5, below.
133 TCPA 1990 s172(1).
134 See para 4.22, above.
135 TCPA 1990 s173(1)(a), (2) and (4).
136 *Miller-Mead v Minister of Housing and Local Government* [1963] 2 QB 196, CA.
137 TCPA 1990 s172(3).

enforcement notice that required immediate compliance was a nullity, without legal effect and incapable of amendment.[138]

Stop notices

4.148   Where an LPA has issued an enforcement notice, TCPA 1990 s183 provides that it can also issue a stop notice requiring that any activity which contravenes planning control ceases immediately. There is no right of appeal against a stop notice though one can challenge the LPA's decision to issue such a notice by way of judicial review.

4.149   In *R (Clare Wilson) v First Secretary of State*,[139] the claimant argued that TCPA 1990 s183 was incompatible with articles 8 and 14 of the Convention and she sought a declaration of incompatibility. The claimant pointed to the fact that stop notices cannot be used to prohibit the use of any building as a dwelling house, but can be so used in circumstances where Gypsies and Travellers use caravans for residential purposes without planning permission. She argued that this difference in treatment had an unjustifiable and disproportionate effect on Gypsies and Travellers. At first instance, Crane J disagreed; he took the view that greater harm was likely to occur when a caravan was brought onto a piece of land than that which was likely to occur when a building was used as a dwelling house and that the difference in treatment was justified on that basis. The Court of Appeal upheld that decision and the claimant was refused permission to appeal to the House of Lords.[140]

Temporary stop notices

4.150   TCPA 1990 s171E gives LPAs the power to issue a temporary stop notice (TSN) to prohibit the carrying on of an activity that it considers to be a breach of planning control. A TSN may not last for more than 28 days. There is no need for an LPA to have issued an enforcement notice before issuing a TSN

4.151   TCPA 1990 s171H provides for compensation for the effect of a temporary stop notice in certain circumstances. These include those situations where the activity which is specified in the notice is authorised by planning permission or a development order. So, for example, if a TSN

---

138   *R (Lynes) v West Berkshire DC* [2002] EWHC 1828 Admin.

139   [2005] EWHC 2970 Admin.

140   [2007] EWCA Civ 52. At the date of publication of this book, it is understood that the claimant will be lodging an application with the ECtHR.

prevented the erection of gates and fencing permitted by the GPDO, there would be grounds for someone with an interest in the land to claim compensation in respect of any loss or damage directly attributable to the TSN prohibition. Claims should be made within 12 months of the date of the decision in respect of which the claim is being made.

4.152　A TSN may not prohibit the use of a building as a dwelling house. Nor may it prohibit use of a caravan as a main residence:

> unless the local planning authority consider that the risk of harm to a compelling public interest arising from the stationing of the caravan is so serious as to outweigh any benefit, to the occupier of the caravan, in the stationing of the caravan for the period for which the temporary stop notice has effect.

4.153　That exception was introduced by the Town and Country Planning (Temporary Stop Notice) (England) Regulations 2005.[141] The explanatory memorandum to the Regulations gives, as examples of compelling public interest, a serious traffic hazard or the fact that the site is a protected habitat.

4.154　TCPA 1990 s171G provides that a person who breaches a TSN is liable to a fine.[142]

Enforcement notice appeals

4.155　There is a right of appeal against an enforcement notice to the Secretary of State on one or more of the following seven grounds:

(a) that, in respect of any breach of planning control which may be constituted by the matters stated in the notice, planning permission ought to be granted or, as the case may be, the condition or limitation concerned ought to be discharged;

(b) that those matters have not occurred;

(c) that those matters (if they occurred) do not constitute a breach of planning control;

(d) that, at the date when the notice was issued, no enforcement action could be taken in respect of any breach of planning control which may be constituted by those matters;

(e) that copies of the enforcement notice were not served as required by TCPA 1990 s172;

(f) that the steps required by the notice to be taken, or the activities required by the notice to cease, exceed what is necessary to remedy

---

141　SI No 206.
142　Up to £20,000 in a magistrates' court and unlimited in the Crown Court.

any breach of planning control which may be constituted by those matters or, as the case may be, to remedy any injury to amenity which has been caused by any such breach;

(g) that any period specified in the notice in accordance with TCPA 1990 s173(9) falls short of what should reasonably be allowed.[143]

4.156   It is common for Gypsies and Travellers who are served with an enforcement notice, requiring them to cease the use of land for residential purposes, to appeal against the notice on ground (a). An appeal brought under ground (a) will be determined by a planning inspector having regard to exactly the same matters that would be taken into account on a planning appeal and it should be prepared in much the same way.[144]

4.157   In addition, it is common for Gypsies and Travellers to appeal against such an enforcement notice on ground (g). Those advising Gypsies and Travellers should always consider whether the enforcement notice should be appealed on ground (g). If the time for compliance is too short, for example, because it will take the occupant of the site longer to find alternative accommodation, then a ground (g) appeal could be brought. If extensive works, such as the removal of hardstanding, are required and the appellant is impecunious, a ground (g) appeal will probably be appropriate.

4.158   Appeals brought under grounds (b), (c), (d) and (e) depend on the facts and the evidence available to prove the point in issue.

4.159   When deciding whether to appeal on ground (f), it is important to consider whether the enforcement notice enforces against existing rights such as fencing and gates permitted by the GPDO.[145] An appellant who wishes to rely on ground (f) should specify, without prejudice to his or her position on other grounds, the arguments in relation to existing rights and indicate the variations of the notice that would be appropriate if the other grounds of appeal failed.[146]

4.160   The enforcement appeal system was reformed to bring it in line with development control appeals with effect in England from

---

143   TCPA 1990 s174(2) as substituted by the Planning and Compensation Act 1991 s6.

144   A ground (a) appeal costs a fee equivalent to twice that for a planning appeal (which is, at the date of publication of this book, £265), unless an appeal against a refusal of planning permission is lodged before the enforcement notice comes in to effect.

145   See para 4.21, above.

146   *Taylor v Secretary of State for the Environment, Transport and the Regions* [2001] EWCA Civ 1254; *New Law Digest* 101088201; (2001) *Times*, 16 October.

23 December 2002.[147] As with all planning appeals, the timetable for these appeals should be strictly observed. If it is not, the appellant may be seriously disadvantaged.

4.161 There is a further appeal (for which permission is required) on a point of law to the High Court against a decision on an appeal against an enforcement notice pursuant to TCPA 1990 s289.[148] Such an appeal may be brought in circumstances where it can be argued that:

- the decision was perverse;
- there was a breach of the rules of natural justice;
- there was an absence of evidence to support a finding of fact;
- the decision-maker took account of irrelevant factors or failed to bear in mind relevant factors.

The appeal must be brought within 28 days.[149]

Prosecution for breach of an enforcement notice

4.162 Non-compliance with an enforcement notice is a criminal offence contrary to TCPA 1990 s179. It is an offence triable either way and is punishable in the magistrates' court with a fine not exceeding £20,000 and in the Crown Court with an unlimited fine. When determining the amount of any fine to be imposed the court 'shall in particular have regard to any financial benefit which has been accrued or appears likely to accrue to [the defendant] in consequence of the offence'.[150]

---

147 This has been brought about through five statutory instruments: the Town and Country Planning (Enforcement Notices and Appeals) (England) Regulations 2002 SI No 2682; the Town and Country Planning (Enforcement) (Written Representations Procedure) (England) Regulations 2002 SI No 2683; the Town and Country Planning (Enforcement) (Hearings Procedure) (England) Rules 2002 SI No 2684; the Town and Country Planning (Enforcement) (Determination by Inspectors) (Inquiries Procedure) (England) Rules 2002 SI No 2685; and the Town and Country Planning (Enforcement) (Inquiries Procedure) (England) Rules 2002 SI No 2686. Advice on these is contained in DoE Circular 2/02 *Enforcement appeals procedures*. There are almost identical rules for Wales.

148 See appendix A, below, on procedures, and note the different procedure depending on whether it is an appeal against a refusal of planning permission or an appeal against an enforcement notice.

149 In *Jarmain v Secretary of State for the Environment, Transport and the Regions* [2001] EWHC 1140 Admin, Gibbs J, it was held that an appeal against a decision made in respect of an enforcement notice appeal must be made pursuant to TCPA 1990 s289 and not s288.

150 TCPA 1990 s179(9).

4.163   In such a prosecution it must be shown that the 'enforcement notice' issued by the LPA is formally valid (and has not been set aside) and that it is not possible to challenge its lawfulness.[151] Where owners of land are prosecuted for breach of an enforcement notice, they have a defence if they can show that everything that could be expected to be done to secure compliance with the notice was done.[152] However, in *Wycombe District Council v Wells*,[153] a case involving a Gypsy who had been prosecuted for failing to comply with an enforcement notice which required him to cease using his land as a caravan site, Newman J held that the defence could not be established by demonstrating that the reason for non-compliance with the enforcement notice was that no alternative site was available. The decision in *Wells* only serves to emphasise the importance of producing full evidence in support of one's case for planning permission or on appeal against the refusal of permission or an enforcement notice.

4.164   Finally, it should be noted that it is not open to a defendant to challenge the validity of the enforcement notice on any of the grounds upon which appeal may be made to the Secretary of State other than by such an appeal.[154]

Direct action

4.165   Where any steps required by an enforcement notice are not taken within the period for compliance with the notice, the LPA may enter the land and take those steps. It may then recover from the owner of the land any expenses reasonably incurred by them in doing so.[155]

4.166   In *R (Mitchell and Hearne) v Horsham District Council*,[156] it was decided that LPAs should only resort to such action having given careful consideration to the personal circumstances of those who will be affected and having taken account of all relevant government planning policy.

4.167   In *R (O'Brien) v Basildon District Council*,[157] Ouseley J quashed the defendant LPA's decision to take direct action against a number of

---

151   *R v Wicks* [1998] AC 92, HL.
152   TCPA 1990 s179(3). See also *R v Clarke* [2002] JPL 1372 and *R v Wood* [2001] EWCA Crim 1395; [2002] JPL 219.
153   [2005] EWHC 1012.
154   TCPA 1990 s285.
155   TCPA 1990 s178.
156   [2003] EWHC 234 Admin.
157   [2006] EWHC 1346 Admin.

families on the ground that the LPA had failed to take account of the claimants' prospects of success at a forthcoming planning inquiry, given: the new and positive advice in Circular 1/06; and the difference between the views of the planning inspectorate and the LPA on the level of need within the district. When doing so, the judge said:

> The power given by section 178, when used as I conclude the Act permits, for residential eviction is a drastic power ... It is in my view necessary for a local planning authority in deciding whether to use section 178 to consider and weigh various factors: the degree of harm done to the interests protected by planning control; the need for a swift or urgent remedy; the need to uphold and enforce planning control embodied in an effective enforcement notice and the criminal law; the personal circumstances and impact on the individuals of removal. Part of that will involve the question of whether they have somewhere else to go or whether inevitably they will have to camp on the roadside, or in some other unauthorised Green Belt location of indeterminate harm. But it is also relevant, and the more plainly so where the conclusion is that the occupants have nowhere lawful or suitable to go, to consider the prospects of success which they might have on a planning application or on appeal, and the time scale over which that might be resolved ... an appeal decision might be imminent with obvious good prospects of success in the light of other decisions nearby; the removal of a group of gypsies for them shortly after to be reinstated after a successful appeal would be plainly disproportionate ... I consider that for a decision to use section 178 to be lawful, consideration of the occupiers' prospects of success in a planning application or appeal and the timing of the resolution of that issue is necessary. If that is not done, a material consideration will have been ignored and action may well be disproportionate, depending on the prospects, the timing of the decision, the degree of harm, and so on.

4.168   However, the same judge rejected another challenge to a decision to take direct action against a number of Gypsy families living on their own land without planning permission in Norfolk.[158]

Planning injunctions

4.169   TCPA 1990 s187B(1) provides that where an LPA considers 'it necessary or expedient for any actual or apprehended breach of planning control to be restrained by injunction, they may apply to the court for an injunction'.

4.170   The judgment of the House of Lords in *South Buckinghamshire DC v Porter (No 1)*[159] is not only the leading decision on the use of TCPA

---

158   *R (Smith) v South Norfolk Council* [2006] EWHC 2772 Admin.
159   [2003] UKHL 26; [2003] 2 AC 558, [2003] 3 All ER 1, [2003] 2 WLR 1547.

0 s187B against Gypsies and Travellers, but it is also a helpful source of dicta in other fields of planning law and practice. This judgment related to four consolidated appeals. In each case Gypsies and Travellers, who were living in caravans on land without the requisite planning permission, were defendants to proceedings brought by the LPAs for planning injunctions under section s187B. At first instance, each court had granted an injunction requiring the Gypsies or Travellers to move off their land. The Gypsies and Travellers appealed to the Court of Appeal raising human rights arguments as to why the injunctions should not have been granted. The Court of Appeal unanimously allowed their appeals, holding that *Hambleton DC v Bird*,[160] which had greatly limited the power of a judge to refuse a section 187B injunction, was no longer good law (if it ever had been such).[161]

4.171 Simon Brown LJ giving the leading judgment in that case, stated that a judge:

> should not grant injunctive relief unless he would be prepared if necessary to contemplate committing the defendant to prison for breach of the order, and that he would not be of this mind unless he had considered for himself all questions of hardship for the defendant and his family if required to move, necessarily including therefore, the availability of suitable alternative sites.[162]

4.172 Simon Brown LJ indicated that a judge was entitled to take account of countervailing considerations against the need to enforce planning control, for example:

- the degree and the flagrancy of the (postulated) breach;
- whether conventional enforcement measures had been tried;
- the urgency of the situation;
- health and safety considerations;
- whether the injunction was intended to remove a Gypsy or Traveller from a site or prevent him moving on to a site; and
- previous planning decisions – the relevance of which would depend upon a variety of matters including their age, the extent to which considerations of hardship and the availability of alternative sites was taken into account, the strength of the conclusions reached on the land use and environmental issues and whether a defendant had the

160 [1995] 3 PLR 8, CA.
161 *South Buckinghamshire DC v Porter; Chichester DC v Searle; Wrexham CBC v Berry; Hertsmere BC v Harty* [2001] EWCA Civ 1549; [2002] 1 All ER 425; [2002] 1 WLR 1359; July 2002 *Legal Action* 22.
162 [2002] 1 WLR 1359 at 1377.

opportunity to make his or her case for at least a temporary personal planning permission.

4.173   Simon Brown LJ added that:

> ... whilst it is not for the court to question the correctness of the existing planning status of the land, the court in deciding whether or not to grant an injunction (and if so, whether and for how long to suspend it) is bound to come to some broad view as to the degree of environmental damage resulting from the breach and the urgency or otherwise of bringing it to an end. In this regard the court need not shut its mind to the possibility of the planning authority itself coming to reach a different planning judgment in the case.[163]

4.174   Finally, Simon Brown LJ stated that:

> ... the court's discretion is absolute and injunctive relief is unlikely unless properly thought to be 'commensurate' – in today's language, proportionate ... whatever view one takes of the correctness of the *Hambleton* approach in the period prior to the coming into force of the Human Rights Act 1998, to my mind it cannot be thought consistent with the court's duty under section 6(1) to act compatibly with Convention rights. Proportionality requires not only that the injunction be appropriate and necessary for the attainment of the public interest objective sought – here the safeguarding of the environment – but also that it does not impose an excessive burden on the individual whose private interests – here the gypsy's private life and home and the retention of his ethnic identity – are at stake.[164]

4.175   The House of Lords unanimously dismissed the LPA's appeals and endorsed the guidance given by the Court of Appeal.[165]

4.176   Having considered the arguments and previous decisions, Lord Bingham stated that the power to grant an injunction under TCPA 1990 s187B was a discretionary power, and that 'the court is not obliged to grant an injunction because a local authority considers it necessary or expedient for any actual or apprehended breach of planning control to be restrained by injunction' and that 'the court must decide whether in all the circumstances it is just to grant the relief sought'.[166]

4.177   Lord Bingham added:

> ... the Secretary of State was entitled to have regard to the personal circumstances of the Gypsies ... When application is made ... under section

163   [2002] 1 WLR 1359 at 1377–1378.
164   [2002] 1 WLR 1359 at 1378.
165   *South Buckinghamshire DC v Porter and others (No 1)* [2003] UKHL 26; [2003] 2 AC 558, [2003] 3 All ER 1, [2003] 2 WLR 1547.
166   [2003] 2 WLR 1547 at 1562.

187B, the evidence will usually make clear whether, and to what extent, the local planning authority has taken account of the personal circumstances of the defendant and any hardship an injunction may cause. If it appears that these aspects have been neglected and on examination they weigh against the grant of relief, the court will be readier to refuse it. If it appears that the local planning authority has fully considered them and nonetheless resolved that it is necessary or expedient to seek relief, this will ordinarily weigh heavily in favour of granting relief, since the court must accord respect to the balance which the local planning authority has struck between public and private interests. It is, however, ultimately for the court to decide whether the remedy sought is just and proportionate in all the circumstances ...[167]

4.178   Lord Bingham continued, explaining that:

The court should ordinarily be slow to make an order which it would not at that time be willing, if need be, to enforce by imprisonment.[168]

He doubted that article 8 of the Convention added to domestic law, stating in respect of the *Buckley*[169] and *Chapman*[170] judgments:

... when asked to grant injunctive relief under section 187B the court must consider whether, on the facts of the case, such relief is proportionate in the Convention sense, and grant relief only if it judges it to be so. Although domestic law is expressed in terms of justice and convenience rather than proportionality, this is in all essentials the task which the court is in any event required by domestic law to carry out.[171]

4.179   Lord Bingham concluded his judgment by stating that:

The guidance given by the Court of Appeal in the judgment of Simon Brown LJ ... was in my opinion judicious and accurate in all essential respects and I would endorse it.[172]

4.180   Lord Steyn agreed, adopting similar reasoning to Lord Bingham, and stated, having referred to article 8:

Even if it had previously been possible to ignore great or marked hardship in the exercise of discretion under section 187B – a hypothesis which I do not accept – such an approach is no longer possible.[173]

---

167   [2003] 2 WLR 1547 at 1564.
168   [2003] 2 WLR 1547 at 1565.
169   *Buckley v United Kingdom* (1996) 23 EHRR 101, [1997] 2 PLR 10, [1996] JPL 1018.
170   *Chapman v United Kingdom* (2001) 33 EHRR 399, (2001) 10 BHRC 48.
171   [2003] 2 WLR 1547 at 1566.
172   [2003] 2 WLR 1547 at 1566.
173   [2003] 2 WLR 1547 at 1572.

4.181 Commenting on the fact that TCPA 1990 s187B empowers an LPA to apply for an injunction, whether or not it has exercised or is proposing to exercise any of its other planning enforcement powers, Lord Clyde said:

> ... that does not mean that the court may not take account of the facts regarding any other remedy which the authority have pursued or the fact that they have not pursued any other remedy.

The key words of his opinion are:

> ... section 187B(2) allows and has always allowed the court in the exercise of its discretion in granting an injunction to weigh up the public interest in securing the enforcement of planning policy and planning decisions against the private interests of the individuals who are allegedly in breach of planning control. In particular I would hold that it is open to the court to consider questions of hardship, particularly as regards health, arising out of the effect on such individuals of a grant of an injunction.[174]

Lord Clyde also pointed out that in Gypsy and Traveller cases 'considerations of humanity may be particularly acute owing to their particular traditions and lifestyle'.[175]

4.182 Lord Hutton said:

> ... it is not for the court to act merely as a rubber stamp to endorse the decision of the local planning authority to stop the use by the particular defendant in breach of planning control. Moreover the court is as well placed as the local planning authority to decide whether the considerations relating to the human factor outweigh purely planning considerations; the weight to be attached to the personal circumstances of a defendant in deciding whether a coercive order should be made against him is a task which is constantly performed by the courts.[176]

4.183 Lord Scott of Foscote dealt with the criteria that govern the grant of section 187B injunctions:

> ... the court must take into account all or any circumstances of the case that bear upon the question whether the grant would be 'just and convenient'. Of particular importance, of course, will be whether or not the local planning authority can establish not only that there is a current or apprehended breach of planning control but also that the ordinary statutory means of enforcement are not likely to be effective in preventing the breach or bringing it to an end. In a case in which the statutory procedure of enforcement notice, prosecution for non-compliance and

---

174 [2003] 2 WLR 1547 at 1574 and 1576.
175 [2003] 2 WLR 1547 at 1577.
176 [2003] 2 WLR 1547 at 1580.

exercise by the authority of such statutory self-help remedies as are available had not been tried and where there was no sufficient reason to assume that, if tried, they would not succeed in dealing with the breach, the local planning authority would be unlikely to succeed in persuading the court that the grant of an injunction would be just and convenient.[177]

4.184   He also stated that the jurisdiction to grant TCPA 1990 s187B injunctions 'is one of great delicacy and to be used with caution'.[178]

4.185   Since *Porter (No 1)*, LPAs have met with varying success in applications for planning injunctions. For example, in *Hart DC v Bedford*[179] the LPA's evidence was equivocal and challenged and the court concluded that the grant of an injunction would not be proportionate. In *Stratford-upon-Avon DC v Hitchman*,[180] the High Court refused an application for a planning injunction because of lack of precision.

4.186   In some cases the court has granted an injunction but allowed an extended period of time for compliance.[181]

Suspension

4.187   In *Porter (No 1)*, Lord Scott of Foscote said:

> ... If the court thought that there was a real prospect that an appeal against an enforcement notice or a fresh application by the defendant for the requisite planning permission might succeed, the court could adjourn the injunction application until the planning situation had become clarified. But where the planning situation is clear and apparently final the court would, in my opinion, have no alternative but to consider the injunction application without regard to the merits of the planning decisions.[182]

4.188   Given the new advice in paragraphs 45 and 46 of Circular 1/06 Gypsies and Travellers defending injunction and other enforcement action can now argue that they should not be forced to leave their land until they have had the opportunity to seek at least the grant of temporary planning permission. Such an argument was successful in *South Bucks DC v Smith*,[183] a case where the Gypsy defendants had been living on their land in the Green Belt in breach of planning control

---

177   [2003] 2 WLR 1547 at 1584.
178   [2003] 2 WLR 1547 at 1584–1585.
179   [2006] EWHC 240, QB.
180   [2002] Env LR 7.
181   See, for example, *Waverley BC v Lee* [2003] EWHC 29, Ch; *Mid-Bedfordshire DC v Smith* [2003] EWHC 932, QB.
182   *South Buckinghamshire DC v Porter and others (No 1)* [2003] UKHL 26; [2003] 2 AC 558; [2003] 3 All ER 1; [2003] 2 WLR 1547, at para 100.
183   [2006] EWHC 281 QB.

for a period of 32 years and had made a fresh application for planning permission. They argued that they had a realistic chance of being granted temporary planning permission. However, a similar argument failed in other cases where Gypsies and Travellers had moved on to land in knowing breach of injunctions and enforcement notices.[184]

Contempt/applications to vary

4.189　In *South Cambridgeshire DC v Gammell, Bromley LBC v Maughan*,[185] the Court of Appeal considered the position of Gypsies and Travellers who had entered land subject to a planning injunction where they were aware of that injunction. The Court of Appeal stated that:

> the correct course for a person subject to an injunction was to apply to vary or discharge it. At that stage the principles in *South Buckinghamshire v Porter* ... as to bearing in mind personal circumstances would apply. It was not to take action in breach of it. A person in breach of the injunction should apply immediately to vary or discharge it. If he had knowledge of the injunction, he should give an explanation for his breach. The Court would then bear all the circumstances in mind, including the reason for the breach, the order and the personal circumstances.[186]

The option to take no action

4.190　LPAs are not obliged to take enforcement action.[187] Rather, they are only entitled to take enforcement action where they consider it expedient.[188]

Funding for planning inquiries

4.191　Community Legal Service funding ('legal aid') is not available to cover the cost of representation at planning inquiries. However, Access to Justice Act 1999 s6(8)(b) empowers the Lord Chancellor to authorise funding in individual cases, following a request from the Legal Services

---

184　*South Bedfordshire DC v Price* [2006] EWCA Civ 493; *Wychavon DC v Rafferty* [2006] EWCA Civ 628; *South Cambridgeshire DC v Flynn* [2006] EWHC 1320, QB, but see Sedley LJ's dissenting judgement in *Coates v South Bucks DC* [2004] EWCA Civ 1378.

185　*South Cambridgeshire DC v Gammell, Bromley LBC v Maughan* [2005] EWCA Civ 1429; (2005) *Times*, 3 November.

186　[2005] EWCA Civ 1429 at para 33.

187　PPG 18: *Enforcing planning control*, para 5.

188　*R (Prokopp) v London Underground Ltd* [2003] EWCA Civ 961; *New Law Property Digest* 103076201, 7 July 2003.

Commission (LSC) so long as the person seeking funding is financially eligible for legal aid. The Lord Chancellor's Guidance indicates that the client must show that no alternative means of funding is available. Under the Guidance, the Lord Chancellor will be prepared to consider funding (known as 'exceptional funding') where:

(i)   there is significant wider public interest; or
(ii) the case is of overwhelming importance to the client; or
(iii) there is convincing evidence that there are other exceptional circumstances such that without public funding for representation it would be practically impossible for the client to bring or defend the proceedings, or the lack of public funding would lead to obvious unfairness in the proceedings.[189]

'Exceptional funding' has been obtained under these provisions for Gypsies and Travellers for representation at planning inquiries. The provisions are complex and solicitors or advisers should refer to the details in the latest edition of the LSC Manual. Applications will need to be made to the LSC area office in London.[190] Relevant factors include lack of literacy and the need for complex technical evidence, for example, in respect of highways objections or flood risks associated with the proposed development.

Wales

4.192   On 13 December 2006, the Welsh Assembly published its *Draft Circular (land use) planning for Gypsy and Traveller caravan sites in Wales*. The Draft Circular includes much of the advice in Circular 1/06 – although there are one or two notable exceptions such as the lack of any advice on the removal of land from Green Wedges (the Welsh equivalent of Green Belts) in order to facilitate site provision. The consultation period has now ended and a new circular to replace Welsh Office Circular 2/94 (the equivalent of DoE Circular 1/94) is awaited.

---

189   As contained in LSC *The Funding Code: The Manual* (2007) Volume 3, Part C 352–3, paras 13–15.
190   And see Murdoch, 'Gypsies and planning appeals: the right to a fair and impartial hearing' [2002] JPL 1056.

Conclusion

4.193 HRA 1998 has led to a series of far-reaching legal cases concerning Gypsies and Travellers and the planning system that, in the main, have supported their attempts to continue to follow their traditional way of life. Perhaps most significantly, the House of Lords in *Porter (No 1)* held that the vulnerable position of Gypsies and Travellers as a minority group deserves more sympathetic attention than had hitherto been the case and stated that:

> ... there is force in the observation attributed to Vaclav Havel, no doubt informed by the dire experience of central Europe: 'The Gypsies are a litmus test not of democracy but of civil society.'[191]

4.194 If LPAs comply with their statutory requirements to assess the accommodation needs of Gypsies and Travellers and the advice in Circular 1/06, then we should see real progress in the provision of sites in the next few years.

4.195 Whilst it is appreciated that the provision of more sites may give rise to local opposition, LPAs will no doubt be able to explain to their electorate that the case for making additional provision is overwhelming, given the fact that:

- there is a moral obligation to do so in order to address the deprivation suffered by those without a stable and secure base from which to travel;
- the provision of more sites will minimise expenditure of public funds on enforcement;
- plan-led provision is likely to result in the establishment of sites which are situated in suitable locations and which are sustainable; and
- failure to comply with the requirements will result in the intervention of central government.

191 [2003] 2 WLR 1547 at 1564.

CHAPTER 5

Evictions from unauthorised encampments

5.1   Introduction

5.10   Methods of eviction and substantive defences

5.10   Civil Procedure Rules Part 55

Who can use it? • Has title been proved? • Should the matter have been commenced in the High Court? • Was sufficient notice given and has service been properly effected? • The hearing • Warrants of possession and restitution

5.32   Criminal Justice and Public Order Act 1994 s61

Who can use it? • 'The senior police officer present' • 'Two or more persons ... with the common purpose of residing' • 'Trespassing on land' • 'Reasonable steps ... by or on behalf of the occupier to ask them to leave' • Has one of the additional three criteria been met? • 'Damage to land or property on land' • 'Threatening, abusive or insulting words or behaviour' • 'Six or more vehicles' • The statutory defence • Obtaining a court order

5.52   CJPOA 1994 s62A

Who can use it? • 'The senior police officer present' • 'Trespassers' • 'Common purpose of residing there' • 'Caravans' • 'Suitable pitch' • 'Occupier' • 'Communicated to the person' • 'Consult every local authority' • Offences • Statutory defence

5.73   CJPOA 1994 s77

Who can use it? • 'Consent of the occupier' • 'Vehicle or vehicles' • 'Written notice' • 'As soon as practicable' • 'Again enters the land ... within the period of three months' • Statutory defence • Obtaining a court order

5.83   Highways Act 1980

Who can use it?

5.94   Bye-laws

Who can use them?

5.109   Common law powers
        Who can use them?

5.118   Planning enforcement
        Who can use it?

5.119   Public law challenges

5.119   Local authorities

5.145   The police

5.153   Government departments and other public authorities

5.160   Other matters

5.160   Width of possession orders

5.165   Injunctions

5.167   Conclusion

Introduction

5.1   Before the duty to provide caravan sites was repealed by the Criminal Justice and Public Order Act (CJPOA) 1994,[1] it was possible to challenge a local authority's decision to take eviction action against an unauthorised encampment by making an application for judicial review and arguing that the local authority in question had failed to provide sufficient (or any) sites.[2] At the same time as the CJPOA 1994 repealed the duty, it armed local authorities with 'draconic'[3] new eviction powers. The use of these far-reaching powers has been circumscribed, to some extent, by the effect of government guidance and the fact that public bodies have had to comply with their duty to act compatibly with the European Convention on Human Rights (ECHR or 'the Convention') since October 2000.[4] Recent developments in homelessness legislation[5] have also had a significant impact on the use of eviction powers by local authorities.

5.2   There are many other bodies and individuals that may be involved in the eviction of Gypsies and Travellers from unauthorised encampments, including: the police; government departments; other public authorities; and private landowners.

5.3   This chapter begins by detailing the different 'methods' that can be used in the eviction of those living on unauthorised encampments and by explaining which method is available to which body or individual and what 'substantive defences' might be available to those facing eviction in each case. The term 'substantive defence' is used to indicate a defence that can be raised in any court of first instance. The chapter then moves on to indicate what (if any) 'public law challenges' might be available to those facing eviction, that is, challenges that could be made by way of judicial review in an attempt to prevent eviction taking place.[6] It should

---

1   For further discussion, see chapter 1, above.
2   See, for example, *West Glamorgan CC ex p Rafferty; R v Secretary of State for Wales* ex p Gilhaney [1987] 1 WLR 457.
3   Described as such by Sedley J in *R v Lincolnshire CC ex p Atkinson; Wealden DC ex p Wales and Stratford* (1995) 8 Admin LR 529 (hereafter referred to as 'the *Atkinson* case').
4   HRA 1998 s6.
5   See chapter 6, below.
6   Following *Doherty v Birmingham CC and the Secretary of State for Communities and Local Government* [2006] EWCA Civ 1736, it is now clear that, where possession action is taken in the county court or the High Court, the public law challenge will be taken by way of defence in that same action – see para 5.119 et seq, below. A 'public law challenge' will not be available against an individual. For more detail on judicial review, see appendix A, below.

be emphasised at the outset that 'substantive defences' will not often be of practical use in cases where a public body uses its powers to evict Gypsies and Travellers from unauthorised encampments and that it is much more likely that the eviction will be prevented or at least postponed if a 'public law challenge' is mounted and it can be shown that the public body's decision to seek eviction was unlawful.

5.4   One starts from the position that a landowner has a basic right to obtain possession against people who are trespassing on his or her land. It is not necessary to discuss the political, philosophical and cultural clashes between nomadism and sedentarism but clearly some of those issues colour the legal position.[7] After the introduction of the Human Rights Act (HRA) 1998 in October 2000, the question arose as to whether it would be possible for a trespasser to raise a defence under ECHR article 8 (the right to respect for private and family life and the home) before the court of first instance in eviction proceedings. In *Price and ors v Leeds CC*,[8] the Court of Appeal rejected the possibility of using article 8 as a defence in such proceedings. The Travellers in that case then appealed to the House of Lords (HL), which heard the case, together with a case involving former tenants (*Kay and ors v Lambeth LBC; Price & ors v Leeds CC*[9]).

5.5   Since the HL was being asked to depart from its own previous judgment in *Harrow LBC v Qazi*,[10] seven Law Lords heard the case. All seven were agreed that:

- in a possession action taken by a public landowner, article 8 is engaged;
- when commencing such a possession action, the public landowner does not have to provide justification in terms of article 8(2) in every case;
- it is for the defendant to raise the article 8 defence;
- in the vast majority of cases, the proper application of domestic law will provide automatic justification in terms of article 8(2).

5.6   The majority of the Lords were all in agreement with the judgment of Lord Hope, where he stated (at paragraph 110):

7   For a wider discussion of these issues see Hawes and Perez, *The Gypsy and the state: the ethnic cleansing of British society*, The Policy Press, 1996; Clark and Greenfields, *Here to stay: the Gypsies and Travellers of Britain*, University of Hertfordshire Press, 2006.

8   [2005] QB 352.

9   [2006] UKHL 10; [2006] 2 AC 465; [2006] 2 WLR 570. For a more extensive discussion of the *Kay and Price* case, see chapter 3 at paras.3.23–3.26, above.

10   [2003] UKHL 43; [2004] 1 AC 983.

I would hold that a defence which does not challenge the law under which the possession order is sought as being incompatible with article 8 but is based only on the occupier's personal circumstances should be struck out ...

The majority held that the only possibility of a defence for trespassers such as the Travellers in the *Price* case would be: where the law which enables the court to make the order for possession is incompatible with article 8, either the court would interpret the law so that it was compatible with the Convention applying HRA 1998 s3 or, if the case was in the county court, adjourn the case so that the High Court could deal with the compatibility issue; or a challenge on judicial review grounds, though they also made it clear that such a challenge would now be taken by way of defence in the court of first instance (where the possession action is commenced in the county court or the High Court).

5.7　　There was some disagreement amongst the Lords as to if and when article 8 (in terms of right to respect for the home) might be engaged at all in a case involving Gypsies or Travellers on an unauthorised encampment. The Travellers in the *Price* case had only been on the land in question for two days when the possession action was commenced (albeit that they had been evicted over 50 times from unauthorised encampments in the previous year). Lord Hope referred to the Strasbourg case-law from which he derived the principle that:

Sufficient and continuous links are required for a house to be considered a 'home' for the purposes of article 8 ...[11]

He concluded that the applicants in *Price* had not established such continuous links. Lord Scott agreed that the Travellers had not established a 'home' but, importantly, he also stated:

It is clearly possible for a trespasser to establish a 'home' in property that belongs to someone else but whether and when he has done so must be a matter of degree.[12]

5.8　　However, it is also important to note that article 8 is, in any event, probably engaged in such circumstances due to the other aspect of the article, the right to respect for private and family life. Thus Stanley Burnton J in *R v Hillingdon LBC ex p Ward* stated:

So far as Article 8 is concerned, I do not think that plot 8, which Mr Ward had occupied as a trespasser for about a fortnight, could be said to be 'his home', but his private and family life are affected by the Council's decision.

11　[2006] UKHL 10 at para 90.
12　[2006] UKHL 10 at para 128.

It is therefore necessary to consider whether the Council's decision satisfies the requirements of Article 8(2).[13]

5.9   It remains unclear what the circumstances are in which a court, if a Gypsy or Traveller is taking a public law challenge to a possession action, will feel that article 8 cannot, effectively, be relied on because article 8(2) will be automatically justified. We will return to public law challenges further below.

Methods of eviction and substantive defences

Civil Procedure Rules Part 55[14]

Who can use it?

Anyone with sufficient interest in the land including, potentially, a licensee.[15]

5.10   Civil Procedure Rules (CPR) Part 55 has taken the place of County Court Rules Order 24 (in the county court) and Rules of the Supreme Court Order 113 (in the High Court), both of which had previously provided the procedures for the eviction of trespassers.

5.11   CPR 55.1(b) states:

> ... 'a possession claim against trespassers' means a claim for the recovery of land which the claimant alleges is occupied only by a person or persons who entered or remained on the land without the consent of a person entitled to possession of that land but does not include a claim against a tenant or subtenant whether his tenancy has been terminated or not.

5.12   A tenant whose tenancy is terminated will not become a 'trespasser' for the purposes of CPR Part 55 but a licensee, whose licence is terminated, will do so. Gypsies or Travellers residing on rented caravan sites will normally be licensees. If a Gypsy or Traveller lives in caravans or vehicles on land with the consent of the owner or occupier of the land, even if a rent or fee is paid to the owner or occupier, they will be a licensee. Once such a licence is terminated,[16] they will come within the scope of CPR 55.1(b).

---

13   [2001] LGR 457 at 463G, H; [2001] EWHC 91 Admin at para 29.

14   Throughout this section on CPR Part 55, reference should be made to *Civil Procedure ('The White Book')*, Sweet & Maxwell, 2007.

15   *Manchester Airport Authority v Dutton* [1999] 2 All ER 675.

16   See chapter 3 at paras 3.11–3.28, above, for a discussion of the law relating to the termination of a licence on an official site.

5.13 Possession claims must normally be commenced in the county court[17] but exceptionally they can be commenced in the High Court.[18] CPR 55.6 deals with service of claims against 'trespassers':

> Where, in a possession claim against trespassers, the claim has been issued against 'persons unknown' [as it usually is[19]], the claim form, particulars of claim and any witness statements must be served on those persons by –
>
> (a) (i) attaching copies of the claim form, particulars of claim and any witness statements to the main door or some other part of the land so that they are clearly visible; and
>
> (ii) if practicable, inserting copies of those documents in a sealed transparent envelope addressed to 'the occupiers' through the letter box;[20] or
>
> (b) placing stakes in the land in places where they are clearly visible and attaching to each stake copies of the claim form, particulars of claim and any witness statements in a sealed transparent envelope addressed to 'the occupiers'.[21]

5.14 A CPR Part 55 claim is commenced by using claim form N5 and, in a claim against trespassers, the standard particulars of claim form, N121. Both these forms must be used.[22] However, in practice, if they have not been used, the judge may simply adjourn the matter for the correct forms to be produced rather than strike the claim out. The 'trespasser' does not have to file a defence,[23] but clearly would want to do so if he or she wishes to argue that he or she is not a 'trespasser' or wishes to raise one of the other 'substantive defences' listed below.

5.15 A solicitor or adviser instructed by a Gypsy or Traveller who is threatened with eviction should carefully consider whether the claimant has complied with the procedural rules and proved that he or she is entitled to possession. If there is no 'substantive defence' to a claim brought by a public body but the decision to evict is susceptible to public law challenge (see further below), then a defence will have to be filed and

---

17 CPR 55.3(1).
18 See para 5.17, below.
19 See CPR 55.3(4).
20 This method of service may be relevant to Gypsies or Travellers parked within the curtilage of a building (area of land attached to a dwelling-house), especially where there are also 'trespassers' residing in the building itself.
21 This is the method of service normally employed for unauthorised encampments but it is also common for notices to be attached to vehicles on a site.
22 See CPR Practice Direction (PD) 55.1.5.
23 CPR 55.7(2).

served as soon as feasible. If there is time, it is best to have a defence available for the first hearing of the matter.

Has title been proved?

5.16   The claimant will need to prove title to, or sufficient interest in, the land,[24] usually by the production of a witness statement or affidavit (from a person who has authority to give such evidence) which will have attached to it either office copy entries from the Land Registry, conveyances, leases or other relevant official documents proving title to the land. In the absence of such proof, the Gypsies' or Travellers' adviser may wish to do a Land Registry search themselves. Alternatively, the Gypsies or Travellers may wish to make inquiries of local residents who may be able to cast some light on the question of ownership of, or legal interest in, a piece of land.

Should the matter have been commenced in the High Court?

5.17   If brought in the High Court, a separate certificate from the claimant (verified by a statement of truth) explaining why this has been done is required.[25] CPR Practice Direction (PD) paragraph 1.3 states:

> Circumstances which may, in an appropriate case, justify starting a claim in the High Court are if –
> (1) there are complicated disputes of fact;
> (2) there are points of law of general importance; or
> (3) the claim is against trespassers and there is a substantial risk of public disturbance or of serious harm to persons or property which properly require immediate determination.

Was sufficient notice given and has service been properly effected?

5.18   CPR Part 55.5(2) states:

> In a possession claim against trespassers the defendant must be served with the claim form, particulars of claim and any witness statements –
> (a) in the case of residential property, not less than five days; and
> (b) in the case of other land, not less than two days, before the hearing date.

Simple failure of service may not be enough, in itself, to defend the claim. The defendant may need to show some prejudice to his or her case or disadvantage as a result of the failure of service, for example,

---

24   CPR PD 55.2.6.
25   CPR 55.3(2).

inability to investigate the question of title in the time allowed. It has to be said that the court is more likely to adjourn the hearing, rather than dismiss the claim, where service has been defective.

5.19   Gypsies or Travellers who are 'trespassers' and who are occupying land within the curtilage of a residential building (for example, in the yard of a disused house) will have to be served five clear working days before the hearing date while those camping on 'other land' will only have to be given two clear working days' notice.[26] For example, in an action taken against Gypsies and Travellers camping on a car park where the hearing date is on:

- a Thursday, then service should be effected on the Monday, provided that is a working day;
- a (working) Monday, then service should be effected on the previous Wednesday.[27]

5.20   There is provision for the court to shorten the above time limits.[28] CPR PD 55.3.2 states:

> Particular consideration should be given to the exercise of this power if:
> (1) the defendant, or a person for whom the defendant is responsible, has assaulted or threatened to assault:
>   (a) the claimant;
>   (b) a member of the claimant's staff;
>   (c) another resident in the locality;
> (2) there are reasonable grounds for fearing such an assault; or
> (3) the defendant, or a person for whom the defendant is responsible, has caused serious damage or threatened to cause serious damage to the property or to the home or property of another resident in the locality.

5.21   In such a case the claimant should make an application for abridgement of time on form N244.[29] If the application is allowed by the court, service could be shortened to the day before the hearing. Self-evidently, an adviser or solicitor assisting a Gypsy or Traveller on an unauthorised encampment who is facing such a short deadline will have to make a

---

26 Notes to CPR Part 55, 55.5(2). CPR 2.8(4) states: 'Where the specified period is – (a) five days or less and (b) includes (i) a Saturday or Sunday; or (ii) a Bank Holiday, Christmas Day or Good Friday, that day does not count.'

27 Defendants are given at least two clear working days' notice so that they can obtain legal advice, if it is required. If the hearing date was on a Monday and service was effected on the Friday, then the defendant might be unable to obtain such advice.

28 CPR 3.1(2)(a).

29 Notes to CPR Part 55, 55.5(3).

very quick assessment of possible 'substantive defences' or 'public law challenges' and may be able to set aside an order for abridgement in circumstances where:

- the allegations are denied;
- responsibility for the persons who have caused or threatened to cause serious damage is denied, for example, the Gypsy or Traveller may be encamped with others over whom he or she has no responsibility or control;
- any assertion that the damage caused or threatened involves 'serious damage' is denied.

The hearing

5.22   If there is no defence to the claim for possession of land occupied by trespassers, or if the court rejects any defence raised, then it has long been held by the courts that there is no discretion and the court must order possession forthwith. This principle has become known as the rule in *McPhail*.[30] Recently this 'rule' has been seriously questioned. In the case of *Boyland & Son v Rand*,[31] a Traveller on an unauthorised encampment on private land sought a suspension of the possession order due to her pressing personal circumstances, her daughter being severely disabled. Reliance was placed on her behalf on Housing Act (HA) 1980 s89, which relates to any land and which states:

> (1) Where a court makes an order for possession of any land in a case not falling within the exceptions mentioned in subsection (2) below, the giving up of possession shall not be postponed (whether by the order or any variation, suspension or stay of execution) to a date not later than 14 days after the making of the order, unless it appears to the court that exceptional hardship would be caused by requiring possession to be given up by that date; and shall not in any event be postponed to a date later than six weeks after the making of the order.

None of the exceptions in HA 1980 s89(2) applied to Gypsies or Travellers on unauthorised encampments.

Reliance was also placed on the fact that the HRA 1998 had been brought into force since the *McPhail* judgment and it was argued that, in order to have regard to article 8 of the Convention, the court must now have some discretion to suspend an order against trespassers.

---

30   The principle was first stated by the Court of Appeal in *McPhail v Persons Unknown* [1973] 3 All ER 393.
31   [2006] EWCA Civ 1860.

5.23   The Court of Appeal (CA), in a permission hearing, rejected those arguments. With regard to the HA 1980 argument, the CA felt that the power to postpone or suspend only related to those cases where there already was a power to postpone. Neuberger LJ stated:

> There is no reason to think that, by a side wind, the legislature intended to grant squatters rights which did not previously exist.[32]

In rejecting the HRA 1998 argument, the CA referred to the four Law Lords in the *Kay and Price* case[33] who felt that the rule in *McPhail* remained good law (a point that Lord Bingham, in the minority in *Kay and Price*, disagreed with). It is possible that this issue may return to the CA at a later date in terms of unauthorised encampments on local or other public authority land.

5.24   In a claim against trespassers, the court has no power to suspend the enforcement of the possession order unless the claimant agrees. However, in practice there will clearly be a delay before the bailiff (in the case of a county court order) or the High Court enforcement officer (in the case of a High Court order)[34] sets an eviction date. Moreover, while the court can only, with the claimant's agreement, give a suspension before the possession order comes into effect, the claimant retains a discretion as to when to apply for a warrant (or writ in the High Court) of possession (which entitles the claimant to enforce the possession order and evict the trespassers). Failure by a local authority or other public authority to take into account new welfare considerations that arise after the date of the possession order could give rise to a 'public law challenge'.[35] Though notice by the bailiff or High Court enforcement officer is not required,[36] it is common practice for the bailiff or High Court enforcement officer to notify the 'trespassers' of the date they have set for eviction. Nevertheless, this practice is not always followed and it is, therefore, a good idea to be proactive and to contact the bailiff or High Court enforcement officer and ask whether a warrant (or writ) of possession has been issued and, if so, when they will be carrying out the

---

32 [2006] EWCA Civ 1860 at para 9.
33 [2006] UKHL 10; [2006] 2 AC 465; [2006] 2 WLR 570.
34 Previously a sheriff executed High Court writs but this practice was repealed by Courts Act (CA) 2003 s99. For further discussion of this change see [2004] LS Gaz, 22 April, p31.
35 For a full discussion of 'public law challenges' see paras 5.119–5.159, below.
36 The Courts Service provides a form N54 to notify those subject to possession orders of impending eviction but there is no obligation to use it.

eviction.[37] At the hearing, the Gypsy or Traveller could apply to be joined as a named party to the proceedings.[38] However, unless they have a defence to the proceedings, there is no point in applying to be joined since it will merely open up the possibility of an order for costs.

Warrants of possession and restitution

5.25 After obtaining a possession order under CPR Part 55 in the county court, the order must be served on the defendants.[39] Unless the defendants voluntarily vacate the land in question, the claimant will have to obtain a warrant of possession. The claimant will then have to request the county court bailiff to execute the warrant (in the High Court, the claimant will obtain a writ of possession and execution will be effected by the High Court enforcement officer). The usual High Court practice is for the claimant to apply for the writ of possession on notice to the defendant, as was held to be the requirement of RSC Ord 45 r2 and r4 (preserved by CPR Part 50) in *Fleet Mortgage Ltd v Lower Maisonette* 46 *Eaton Place*.[40] In the county court, no notice is required. This difference has been commented on by the Court of Appeal.[41] If a new incident of trespass occurs more than three months after the date on which the original possession order was granted, the claimant will have to apply for a warrant of restitution (writ of restitution in the High Court). Permission is required for a warrant (or writ) of possession which is sought more than three months after the date of the order and is also required for a warrant (or writ) of restitution regardless of when it is sought.[42] However, no notice of any of the above applications needs to be given to the defendants.[43]

---

37 CPR Part 39, 39.3 sets out the circumstances in which a party who fails to attend the hearing may apply to set aside the order. The party must: act promptly; have a good reason for not attending; and, have a reasonable prospect of success at trial.

38 CPR Part 19, 19.4.

39 CPR Part 40, 40.4.

40 [1972] 1 WLR 765.

41 See *Leicester CC v Aldwinkle* [1991] HLR 40.

42 However, note that if the new incident of trespass (even if it does not involve all of the original trespassers) occurs within the three months following the order, a warrant (or writ) of possession can be sought without the need for permission.

43 For circumstances where a warrant (or writ) might be set aside, see *Leicester CC v Aldwinkle* [1991] HLR 40, CA. Though this case involved the tenancy of a dwellinghouse, the principles outlined in it (especially with regard to oppressive use of warrants) may occasionally be of use to Gypsies or Travellers faced with a warrant, for example, if there was not a sufficient nexus or link with the previously obtained possession order.

5.26   Under CCR Order 24.6:[44]

(1) Subject to paragraphs (2) and (3), a warrant of possession to enforce an order for possession, in a possession claim against trespassers under Part 55, may be issued at any time after the making of the order and ... a warrant of restitution may be issued in aid of the warrant of possession.

(2) No warrant of possession shall be issued after the expiry of three months from the date of the order without the permission of the court, and an application for such permission may be made without notice being served on any other party unless the court otherwise directs.

(3) Nothing in this rule shall authorise the issue of a warrant before the date on which possession is ordered to be given.

5.27   In *Wiltshire CC v Fraser*,[45] it was held that a warrant (or writ) of restitution will be issued to recover land from occupants who were neither parties to the original proceedings nor dispossessed by the original order, provided there is a plain and sufficient nexus (or link) between the order for possession and the need to effect further recovery of the land. In Fraser, a possession order against trespassers was obtained and executed in 1983. In 1985 there was a new incident of trespass and, among the trespassers, were two of the defendants named in the original proceedings. This was held to be a sufficient nexus.

5.28   Simon Brown J (as he then was) stated:

Given that the writ of restitution can be issued to recover land from occupants who were neither party to the original proceedings nor dispossessed by the earlier writ of possession, in what circumstances should this be permitted? In my judgment this will always depend upon the particular facts of the individual case ... The writ of restitution being in aid of execution, it would be appropriate to permit its issue only in those cases where there was a plain and sufficient nexus between the original recovery of possession and the need to effect further recovery of the same land. Putting it another way, the court will be bound to ask itself: are the acts or episodes of trespass of which the owners complain during the overall period in question properly to be regarded as essentially one transaction?[46]

5.29   Clearly, therefore, where at least one defendant who was on the land in question at the time of the original order, returns to the same piece of land, the claimant will be able to obtain a warrant (or writ) of restitution. However, it is also common for a claimant to seek to obtain a warrant (or writ) in other circumstances. For example:

(1) where the trespassers involved in the later incident of trespass are

---

44   Retained in force – see *Civil Procedure ('The White Book')* 2007, Vol 1, p2168.

45   [1986] 1 WLR 109.

46   [1986] 1 WLR 109 at 113.

acquaintances of a defendant or defendants who were involved in the original possession action;

(2) where the trespassers involved in the later incident of trespass were directed to the land or told about the land by a previous defendant or defendants;

(3) where a registration plate on a vehicle present on the land in question at the time the original possession order was obtained, is the same as the registration plate on a vehicle present at the later incident of trespass.

With regard to these examples, and ones like them, it is questionable whether a court would hold that there was 'essentially one transaction'.

5.30   Clearly, if there is no nexus or link between the original and the subsequent incidents of trespass, the claimant will not be able to obtain a warrant (or writ) of restitution and will have to seek a fresh possession order.

5.31   Regardless of whether a warrant (or writ) of restitution can be obtained, and regardless of whether some or all of the original defendants are involved in the subsequent incident of trespass, provided there is a sufficient period of time between the two incidents of trespass, the government guidance on welfare inquiries, applicable to local authorities and other public authorities, will still be relevant.[47] For example, even if exactly the same group of trespassers have returned to the same piece of land, there may have been a significant change of circumstances that the local authority or other public authority ought now to take into account before deciding whether to proceed with further eviction action.

Criminal Justice and Public Order Act 1994 s61

Who can use it?

The police

5.32   CJPOA 1994 s61 states:

(1) If the senior police officer present at the scene reasonably believes that two or more persons are trespassing on land and are present there with the common purpose of residing there for any period, that

---

47   For further discussion of the need for welfare inquiries, see paras 5.119–5.139, below.

reasonable steps have been taken by or on behalf of the occupier to ask them to leave and –

(a) that any of those persons has caused damage to the land or to property on the land or used threatening, abusive or insulting words or behaviour towards the occupier, a member of his family or an employee or agent of his, or

(b) that those persons have between them six or more vehicles on the land,

he may direct those persons, or any of them, to leave the land and to remove any vehicles or other property they have with them on the land.

5.33 Failure to comply with such a direction to leave may result in arrest without a warrant[48] and impoundment of vehicles.[49] Section 61(4) contains the details of the 'offence':

If a person knowing that a direction under subsection (1) above has been given which applies to him –

(a) fails to leave the land as soon as reasonably practicable, or

(b) having left again enters the land as a trespasser within the period of three months beginning with the day on which the direction was given,

he commits an offence and is liable on summary conviction to imprisonment for a term not exceeding three months or a fine not exceeding level 4 on the standard scale, or both.

5.34 The CJPOA 1994 s61 powers are regularly used by the police in England. The report by Niner, *Accommodation needs of Gypsy-Travellers in Wales* (Welsh Assembly Government, April 2006) found no use of section 61 powers by Welsh police over the previous three year period (at paragraphs 5.13–5.14). The Association of Chief Police Officers (ACPO) Guidance for Scotland, states:

There is a general presumption against prosecution of the unauthorised encampment of Gypsy Travellers relating to trespassory offences, although this presumption may be overridden by public interest considerations, dependent upon the circumstances ... Prosecution ... should only be considered as a last resort when all other options have been exhausted.

5.35 There are several 'hurdles' which the police must cross before being able to properly justify a CJPOA 1994 s61 eviction. Effectively each of these 'hurdles' presents the possibility for a 'substantive defence'.

---

48 The power of arrest was originally contained in CJPOA 1994 s61(5) but is now to be found in the Police and Criminal Evidence Act 1984 s24 (as inserted by the Serious Organised Crime and Police Act 2005 as of 1 January 2006).

49 CJPOA 1994 s62.

'The senior police officer present'

5.36   CJPOA 1994 s61(3) states:

> A direction under subsection (1) above, if not communicated to the persons referred to in subsection (1) by the police officer giving the direction, may be communicated to them by any constable at the scene.

5.37   Since CJPOA 1994 s61(1) makes clear that the senior police officer must be present at the scene of the trespass, it must follow (if section 61(3) is to have any meaning) that the 'senior police officer present' must be above the rank of constable, even if he or she does not personally communicate the direction to leave. It should be noted that there is no requirement for a section 61 removal direction to be in writing and commonly it is given verbally. However, some police forces have a policy of giving a written notice and it can be important to be aware of any such written policies that exist. The Office of the Deputy Prime Minister (ODPM)/Home Office *Guide to effective use of enforcement powers – Part 1: Unauthorised encampments*[50] (hereafter 'the 2006 Encampment Guidance'), with regard to the police powers of eviction, states:

> Once a decision to use police powers is made, a uniformed police officer visits the encampment and advises the occupiers that they are required to leave by a certain date and time, and provides them with a copy of the legislation. The police may determine the period of notice to the unauthorised campers to leave, and this may be hours or days. The police may also videotape their visit to the encampment in case of later challenge or dispute.[51]

The recommendation that a copy of the relevant legislation should be provided is an important one. It would now seem logical for all police forces to incorporate the relevant piece of legislation within a formal, written notice.[52]

'Two or more persons ... with the common purpose of residing'

5.38   Very occasionally one meets with a Gypsy or Traveller travelling alone. The police cannot use their CJPOA 1994 s61 powers against such a person. Additionally, if the Gypsies or Travellers have stopped for some

---

50   Issued in February 2006.
51   2006 Encampment Guidance para 48.
52   It should also be noted that 'days' may be given for the Gypsies and Travellers concerned to leave.

purpose other than 'residing' (for example, to make a hot drink or to change a flat tyre) then section 61 cannot be used. This is regardless of the perceived inconvenience of the location (for example, a supermarket car park). It should also be noted that, under section 61(9) – the definition section:

> ... a person may be regarded for the purposes of this section as having a purpose of residing in a place notwithstanding that he has a home elsewhere.

Thus, Gypsies and Travellers who, for example, have a pitch on an official site but are in the process of travelling for seasonal work, might be caught by section 61 if they stop on land without permission despite the existence of their 'home' elsewhere. It should also be noted that, unlike with the local authority powers of eviction under CJPOA 1994 s77,[53] the Gypsies or Travellers do not have to be in vehicles. Thus Gypsies and Travellers in tents or benders, for example, can be served with a direction even if they do not have a vehicle.[54]

'Trespassing on land'

5.39   Trespass has its ordinary meaning. By CJPOA 1994 s61(9):

> 'land' does not include –
>   (a) buildings other than –
>   (i) agricultural buildings within the meaning of, in England and Wales, paragraphs 3 to 8 of Schedule 5 to the Local Government Finance Act 1988 ...
>   (ii) scheduled monuments within the meaning of the Ancient Monuments and Archaeological Areas Act 1979;
>   (b) land forming part of –
>   (i) a highway unless it falls within the classifications in section 54 of the Wildlife and Countryside Act 1981 (footpath, bridleway or byway open to all traffic or road used as a public path) or is a cycle track under the Highways Act 1980 or the Cycle Tracks Act 1984 ...

5.40   Therefore, the police will not be able to serve a removal direction under CJPOA 1994 s61 on Gypsies and Travellers who are camping within the curtilage of a building or are camping on the highway (subject to the exceptions detailed above). With regard to 'buildings', it is not

---

53 See para 5.73, below.
54 Providing CJPOA 1994 s61(1)(a) is satisfied. A 'bender' is a dome-shaped, tent-like structure, constructed by fixing tarpaulin over wooden rods or poles.

uncommon in urban areas for Gypsies or Travellers[55] to be encamped within the yard or curtilage of a disused or empty building. CJPOA 1994 s61 could not be used in such circumstances. It is also quite common for Gypsies or Travellers to be encamped at the end of dead-end roads, in cul-de-sacs, on lay-bys or on highway verges. Once again, section 61 cannot be used to evict them from such a site.

'Reasonable steps ... by or on behalf of the occupier to ask them to leave'

5.41   The leading case on this issue is *R (Fuller) v Chief Constable of the Dorset Constabulary and Secretary of State for the Home Department.*[56] This case involved an unauthorised encampment on a former rubbish tip owned by Weymouth BC. After a period of 'toleration', and following an incident at the site concerning a confrontation between two police officers and certain of the Travellers, the police and the local authority simultaneously served removal directions which expired at the same time. This action was quashed by the High Court. Giving judgment, Stanley Burnton J gave a useful summary of the effect of CJPOA 1994 s61:

> In construing section 61 of the 1994 Act on the basis of common law principles, it is necessary to bear in mind that because it creates a criminal offence it is to be narrowly construed. Indeed, it creates a draconian procedure. I accept the claimants' point that Travellers are likely to comply with a direction under section 61 through fear of arrest and the forcible removal and detention of their vehicles although they may have an arguable justification for remaining on the land. Section 61 must, I think, be all the more narrowly construed for that reason.
>
> The claimants submitted ... that section 61(1) assumes that the steps taken by the occupier to ask the trespassers to leave have been ineffective: ie, they have refused to leave. Whereas section 61(1)(a) applies to persons who have already been guilty of criminal or other misconduct, section 61(1)(b) applies to persons who may have been perfectly well-behaved. It seems to me that Parliament was unlikely to have intended to bring the criminal law to bear on such trespassers who had not refused to leave when asked. On this basis, section 61(1) is to be read as impliedly requiring that the trespassers have not complied with the occupier's request

---

55   Especially New Travellers – based on the casework of the Travellers' Advice Team at Community Law Partnership. For the potential relevance of Criminal Law Act 1977 for Gypsies or Travellers who are residing within the 'curtilage' of a building, see para 5.117, below

56   [2002] 3 All ER 57.

that they leave as a condition of the making of a direction by the police under the section.[57]

In other words, the occupier must give notice to leave before there can be any question of the police serving a section 61 removal direction. Thus, for example, a private landowner might give 48 hours' notice for the Gypsies or Travellers to leave. If they have not left at the end of that 48-hour period, then the police can decide to use section 61. However, what is the position if the landowner or occupier is a local authority or other public authority?

5.42   In order to answer this question it is necessary to consider the extent to which local authorities and other public authorities must take account of welfare or humanitarian considerations before evicting trespassers from their land.[58] If a local authority (or other public authority) has failed to take account of humanitarian considerations before deciding to evict Gypsies or Travellers residing on their land without permission, then it is arguable that their failure to do so may, in itself, mean that reasonable steps have not yet been taken by the occupier. In the *Fuller* case, Stanley Burnton J stated:

> In my judgment, a local authority must consider the Convention rights of trespassers and their human needs generally when deciding whether or not to enforce its right to possession of that land.[59]

It must be fairly clear, therefore, that a local authority must make inquiries into welfare issues before it can come to a decision on eviction.[60]

Has one of the additional three criteria been met?

5.43   A removal direction cannot be issued unless the senior police officer present at the scene reasonably believes that the trespassers:

- have caused damage to land or property on the land;
- have used threatening, abusive or insulting words or behaviour; or
- have six or more vehicles between them on the land.

57   [2002] 3 All ER 57 at 69.
58   See 'public law challenges' at paras 5.119–5.144, below.
59   *Fuller* [2002] 3 All ER 57 at 74.
60   Other public authorities will also be required to take account of welfare inquiries, as discussed at paras 5.153–5.159, below.

'Damage to land or property on land'

5.44   In terms of 'damage to land', CJPOA 1994 s61(9) defines 'property' as:

> (a) in England and Wales, property within the meaning of section 10(1) of the Criminal Damage Act 1971 ...

Criminal Damage Act 1971 s10(1) defines 'property' as:

> ... property of a tangible nature, whether real or personal, including money and – including wild creatures ... not including mushrooms growing wild on any land or flowers, fruit or foliage of a plant growing wild on any land.

Additionally, CJPOA 1994 s61(9), states that 'damage':

> ... includes the deposit of any substance capable of polluting the land.

Thus, fly-tipping is probably within the definition. However, it is unclear precisely what might be encompassed by the phrase 'damage to land'. In an old nineteenth-century case, *Gayford v Chouler*, a farmer gained damages from someone who walked across his hay meadow thus damaging the crop.[61] It might be hoped that a modern court would consider 'damage' to mean something more significant than squashed grass. Some possibilities might include:

- the breaking of a lock to a gate;
- damage to a height barrier;
- cutting wood for fires.

However, without any extensive definition within CJPOA 1994 and with a dearth of case-law on this issue, it is very difficult to predict what might be encompassed by the phrase.

'Threatening, abusive or insulting words or behaviour'

5.45   Any 'threatening, abusive or insulting words or behaviour' must be directed to 'the occupier, a member of his family or an employee or agent of his'. 'Occupier', under CJPOA 1994 s61(9), means:

> ... in England and Wales, the person entitled to possession of the land by virtue of an estate or interest held by him ...

The rest of this criterion has its ordinary meaning and will turn on the evidence presented and the answers the Gypsies or Travellers have to any allegations that are made. It will be important for police officers

---

61   *Gayford v Chouler* [1898] 1 QB 316.

to make sure that they treat Gypsies and Travellers fairly and that they do not jump to the conclusion that the evidence of the occupier or his or her agent should be preferred to that of the trespassers unless there are reasonable grounds for reaching such a conclusion.

'Six or more vehicles'

5.46 The definition of 'vehicle' is extremely wide. CJPOA 1994 s61(9) states:

> 'vehicle' includes –
>
> (a) any vehicle, whether or not it is in a fit state for use on roads, and includes any chassis or body, with or without wheels, appearing to have formed part of such a vehicle, and any load carried by, and anything attached to, such a vehicle; and
>
> (b) a caravan as defined in section 29(1) of the Caravan Sites and Control of Development Act 1960.

Thus, a caravan and its towing vehicle will constitute two vehicles. Three caravans and three towing vehicles will make the requisite six. Taking the ordinary meaning of the word 'vehicle' it can be implied that it is 'constructed'. Thus a motor-bike, barrel-top wagon or even a bicycle or derelict car may be covered by the term but clearly the horse that pulls the wagon will not. A 'caravan' is defined, under Caravan Sites and Control of Development Act (CSCDA) 1960 s29(1), as:

> ... any structure designed or adapted for human habitation which is capable of being moved from one place to another (whether by being towed, or by being transported on a motor vehicle or trailer) and any motor vehicle so designed or adapted, but does not include –
>
> (a) any railway rolling stock which is for the time being on rails forming part of a railway system, or
>
> (b) any tent ...

Thus, the term 'caravan' not only includes caravans as such but also camper vans, motor vehicles designed or adapted for human habitation (such as buses, lorries or removal vans) and mobile homes. Some Gypsies and Travellers have been known to park five or less vehicles on the land in question and to park the rest of their vehicles off the land, for example, on a nearby road, so as to avoid falling foul of section 61.

The statutory defence

5.47 The statutory defence to CJPOA 1994 s61 evictions is contained in section 61(6):

> In proceedings for an offence under this section it is a defence for the accused to show –

(a) that he was not trespassing on the land, or
(b) that he had a reasonable excuse for failing to leave the land as soon as reasonably practicable or, as the case may be, for again entering the land as a trespasser.

If Gypsies or Travellers can show that they have permission from the occupier of land to remain there, they are clearly not trespassers and the section cannot be used.

5.48   In the case of *Krumpa v DPP*,[62] the Divisional Court considered the meaning of the phrase 'reasonably practicable'[63] and concluded that the question whether something was 'reasonably practicable' should be considered objectively and was not a matter that could be determined solely by the police officer's view of what was reasonable. However, in *Fuller*,[64] Stanley Burnton J adopted a very narrow interpretation of the phrase in the context of removal directions and stated that:

> If the trespassers have failed to comply with the occupier's request, there is no reason for a direction not to take immediate effect.[65]

5.49   It is not uncommon for the police to use video evidence when dealing with an unauthorised encampment. Clearly, if the police were to take more intrusive video evidence (for example, by filming the interior of vehicles, as has been known to happen in the past) then they may commit an unjustified interference with the rights of the trespassers to respect for their private and family life and their homes protected by article 8 of the ECHR.[66]

Obtaining a court order

5.50   As has been seen above, Gypsies or Travellers who fail to comply with a valid removal direction under CJPOA 1961 s61 or who return to the land within the specified three-month period can face arrest and impoundment of their vehicles (that is, their homes) without the need for any court order to be obtained. If arrest or impoundment has

---

62   [1989] Crim LR 295.
63   In the context of the Public Order Act 1986 which first introduced the police powers of eviction against Gypsies, Travellers and other trespassers.
64   [2002] 3 All ER 57 at 70.
65   Nevertheless, as mentioned at para. 5.37, above, para 48 of the 2006 Encampment Guidance contemplates the police giving notice which may last 'days'.
66   See *Campbell v MGN Limited* [2004] UKHL 22. For further discussion of ECHR article 8, see chapter 2, above.

occurred, or if the Gypsies or Travellers remain on the land in defiance of the removal direction, the police will have to seek a further order from a magistrates' court. When the matter comes to court, the Gypsies or Travellers will have the opportunity of putting forward the 'substantive defences' mentioned above, if any apply. The very real practical problem for Gypsies or Travellers is that the threat of arrest and/or impoundment before the matter comes to court may (understandably) force them to leave the land on which they are encamped even where they or their advisers believe there is a 'substantive defence'. In such circumstances, a 'public law challenge' by way of judicial review may be mounted if the police have acted unlawfully, for example, by:

- failing to take into account a relevant matter;
- acting unreasonably in failing to properly address a defence raised by the trespassers; or
- acting 'disproportionately' in terms of article 8 of the ECHR.

In practice such a 'public law challenge' will need to be lodged very swiftly.[67]

5.51   There may be grounds (other than the above) for a 'public law challenge' which will be examined later in this chapter.

CJPOA 1994 s62A

Who can use it?

The police

5.52   The Anti-Social Behaviour Act 2003 introduced a new section 62A to CJPOA 1994.[68] Section 62A exists alongside CJPOA 1994 s61. In other words, the police can use either power provided, of course, the necessary criteria are met. Section 62A, which is entitled 'Power to remove trespassers: alternative site available', states as follows:

(1) If the senior police officer present at a scene reasonably believes that the conditions in subsection (2) are satisfied in relation to a person and land, he may direct the person –
(a) to leave the land;

---

67 For further discussion of judicial review see appendix A, below. For further discussion of article 8 and 'proportionality', see chapter 2, above.

68 The Traveller Law Reform Coalition, when making submissions during the passage of the Anti-Social Behaviour Bill, pointed out that it was extremely insulting to Gypsies and Travellers to include unauthorised encampments per se within the scope of a measure designed to tackle anti-social behaviour.

     (b) to remove any vehicle and other property he has with him on the land.

  (2) The conditions are –

     (a) that the person and one or more others ('the trespassers') are trespassing on land;

     (b) that the trespassers have between them at least one vehicle on the land;

     (c) that the trespassers are present on the land with the common purpose of residing there for any period;

     (d) if it appears to the officer that the person has one or more caravans in his possession or under his control on the land, that there is a suitable pitch on a relevant caravan site for that caravan or each of those caravans;

     (e) that the occupier of the land or a person acting on his behalf has asked the police to remove the trespassers from the land.

  (3) A direction under subsection (1) may be communicated to the person to whom it applies by any constable at the scene.

  (4) Subsection (5) applies if –

     (a) a police officer proposes to give a direction under subsection (1) in relation to a person and land, and

     (b) it appears to him that the person has one or more caravans in his possession or under his control on the land.

  (5) The officer must consult every local authority within whose area the land is situated as to whether there is a suitable pitch for the caravan or each of the caravans on a relevant caravan site which is situated in the local authority's area.

5.53   Though the provisions in section 62A are very similar to those in section 61 there are some subtle and important differences and these will be emphasised, where they occur, below.

'The senior police officer present'

5.54   It seems that a police constable could give such a direction though there will have to be a more senior officer present.[69]

'Trespassers'

5.55   CJPOA 1994 s62A(2)(a) refers to 'the person and one or more others'. The presence of 'and' seems to indicate, as is the case with section 61, that a single Gypsy or Traveller encamped on their own cannot be caught by this section.[70]

---

69 See the discussion at paras 5.36–5.37, above, which applies equally here.
70 See para 5.38, above.

'Common purpose of residing there'

5.56   If the Gypsies or Travellers are simply stopping on the way to somewhere else, for example, to have a meal, then the section would not apply.[71]

'Caravans'

5.57   CJPOA 1994 s62A refers to identifying a suitable pitch for a 'caravan'. The definition section[72] gives the word 'caravan' the same meaning as that given to it in the CSCDA 1960.[73] If the Gypsies or Travellers are residing in benders or tents the section does not apply. This differs from section 61, which can be used against Gypsies or Travellers residing solely in benders or tents.[74] However, it is nowadays rare to come across Gypsies or Travellers residing in benders or tents, so there will be few cases where this issue arises in practice.

'Suitable pitch'

5.58   The inclusion of the word 'suitable' is important. No case-law exists at present to help in the definition of 'suitable pitch'. The ODPM *Guidance on Managing Unauthorised Camping* (February 2004, hereafter the '2004 Encampment Guidance')[75] states:

> The meaning of suitable pitch is not defined in the legislation. Of course, it is for the courts to interpret legislation, but the Secretary of State considers that a *suitable pitch* is one that provides basic amenities including water, toilets and waste disposal facilities. Other factors include the potential for community tension and issues of public order/anti-social behaviour need to be considered especially where the trespasser intends to remain on the site for the three month period. This could include an authorised transit site or stopping place. There should be a reasonable expectation that the pitch will be available for peaceful occupation for at least three months, except where the trespasser is expecting to move on before that time (emphasis in the text).

Additionally, the 2004 Encampment Guidance states that:

> A suitable pitch will only be available if there are currently no waiting lists for that site.

71   See para 5.38, above.
72   CJPOA 1994 s62A(6).
73   For the definition of 'caravan', see para 5.46, above.
74   See para 5.38, above.
75   The guidance on sections 62A–62E was released as an add-on to the 2004 Encampment Guidance on 7 March 2005.

5.59   It seems unlikely that the police will be able to use CJPOA 1994 s62A to evict Gypsies and Travellers until local authorities provide sufficient sites for them. The report by Niner, *Local authority Gypsy/Traveller sites in England*[76] indicated that, on the 324 local authority Gypsy sites recorded by the January 2002 Gypsy Count, there were only 307 transit pitches. Additionally, not all these transit pitches will have sufficient amenities for them to be deemed to be 'suitable'.

5.60   A pitch may not be suitable for a number of reasons. For example, it may be on a site occupied by people that are in dispute with the Gypsies and Travellers that the police wish to evict. The 2004 Encampment Guidance states:

> There must be close working between site managers and local authority and police officers dealing with unauthorised camping over allocations of pitches on sites. Site managers may be aware of issues around Gypsy/Traveller group and family compatibility, which must be taken into account when allocating pitches on residential sites.[77]

5.61   Therefore, the question of 'compatibility' of groups or families will also be relevant to the issue of whether the pitch offered is 'suitable'. Another important factor relevant to the issue of suitability will be related to the location of the pitch and its distance from schools, work and healthcare provision. Local authorities will also have to have regard to their allocations policy for any particular site to which it is suggested that a Gypsy or Traveller should be directed and ensure that that is also being followed.

5.62   The pitch must be on a 'relevant caravan site' which is defined as:

> ... a caravan site which is –
> (a) situated in the area of a local authority within whose area the land is situated, and
> (b) managed by a relevant site manager.[78]

Therefore, if a Gypsy or Traveller is encamped in the area of a district council, the site could be anywhere within the relevant county council area.

'Relevant site manager' is defined as:

> (a) a local authority within whose area the land is situated;
> (b) a registered social landlord.[79]

---

76   ODPM, 2003.
77   The 2004 Encampment Guidance at para 4.8.
78   CJPOA 1994 s62A(6).
79   CJPOA 1994 s62A(6). A housing association would be an example of a registered social landlord. To be a registered social landlord the body in question must be registered as such under Chapter 1 of Part 1 of the Housing Act 1996.

5.63   Therefore the site must either be managed by the local authority or by a registered social landlord, such as a housing association. If the site is managed by some other organisation, even if it is owned by the local authority in question, it will not be a 'relevant caravan site'. This is an important point for advisers or solicitors to be aware of.

5.64   It may also be the case that suitable pitches can only be identified for some of the Gypsies or Travellers parked on an unauthorised encampment and it is possible for the section to be applied to only a part of the group of Gypsies or Travellers in question. However, if the group is an extended family[80] or if certain members of the group require special support from others within the group, those factors will also have to be taken into account, it is suggested, in assessing the suitability of a pitch or pitches offered.

'Occupier'

5.65   CJPOA 1994 s61 provided that the occupier must take 'reasonable steps'.[81] Under section 62A the occupier (or someone acting on his behalf) merely has to ask the police to remove the trespassers and he or she does not have to give any notice to the Gypsies or Travellers or make any request for them to leave. However, if the occupier is a local authority or other public authority, it seems that it will still have to take account of welfare considerations before making a request to the police to use section 62A.[82]

'Communicated to the person'

5.66   As with CJPOA 1994 s61, there is no need for written notice to be given.[83] It appears that a Gypsy or Traveller, who is away from the land or otherwise not present when a direction to leave is communicated, may not be subject to the direction.

'Consult every local authority'

5.67   In England, this could involve not only a district council but also the relevant county council. No doubt local authorities and the police will need to have in place policies for liaison and sharing of information.

---

80   As is very common among Irish Travellers: see, for example, McDonagh 'Nomadism' in *Travellers: Citizens of Ireland*, The Parish of the Travelling People, Dublin, 2000, pp33–46.

81   See paras 5.41–5.42, above.

82   See further the discussion at paras 5.119–5.144, below.

83   But see the discussion at para 5.37, above.

Additionally, this implies that the pitch offered could be on a county council site. If the latter site was a considerable distance away from the encampment, that factor raise the question of whether the pitch was 'suitable'.[84] Where the county council area is extremely large, it might be doubted, in relation to distance from schools or healthcare, whether anywhere in the area would automatically be 'suitable'.

Offences

5.68 A person commits an offence if he knows that a direction under CJPOA 1994 s62A(1) has been given which applies to him or her and:

(a) he fails to leave the relevant land as soon as reasonably practicable,[85] or

(b) he enters any land in the area of the relevant local authority as a trespasser before the end of the relevant period with the intention of residing there.[86]

The 'relevant period' is three months from the day on which the direction is given.[87] Importantly, it should be noted that this applies to all land in the relevant local authority area. However, the word 'relevant' qualifies 'local authority' in this context (contrast the position of an officer consulting the local authority or local authorities in the context of 'suitable pitch'). 'Relevant local authority' means:

(a) if the relevant land is situated in the area of more than one local authority (but is not in the Isles of Scilly), the district council or county borough council within whose area the relevant land is situated;

(b) ... the Council of the Isles of Scilly;

in any other case, the local authority within whose area the relevant land is situated.[88]

Thus failure to comply with a direction under section 62A could result in an effective three-month ban from that local authority area (and not some wider county council area). However, if the Gypsies or Travellers, who have received a direction, stop on land in the area with the permission of the occupier, then they will not commit an offence.

5.69 A person guilty of an offence is liable on summary conviction to imprisonment for a term not exceeding three months or a fine or

---

84 See para 5.61, above.
85 For a discussion of the meaning of 'reasonably practicable' see para 5.48, above.
86 CJPOA 1994 s62B(1).
87 CJPOA 1994 s62B(2).
88 CJPOA 1994 s62E(6).

both.[89] A constable may arrest a person committing an offence under this section.[90] A constable may also seize and remove any vehicles.[91]

Statutory defence

5.70   CJPOA 1994 s62B(5) states:

> In proceedings for an offence under this section it is a defence for the accused to show –
>
> (a) that he was not trespassing on the land in respect of which he is alleged to have committed the offence, or
> (b) that he had a reasonable excuse –
>   (i) for failing to leave the relevant land as soon as reasonably practicable, or
>   (ii) for entering the land in the area of the relevant local authority as a trespasser with the intention of residing there, or
> (c) that, at the time the direction was given, he was under the age of 18 years and was residing with his parent or guardian.

There is no case-law on the definition of 'reasonable excuse' in this context but it can be surmised that this might include mechanical breakdown or illness.[92] The exclusion of Gypsies or Travellers aged under 18 simply protects them from prosecution but will not normally (presuming they are travelling with adults) protect them from eviction. Again, as with section 61, it is likely that the section will normally be effective without the need to take the matter to court, since the threat of eviction and impoundment of their homes will usually be sufficient to persuade the Gypsies or Travellers to move.

5.71   As with CJPOA 1994 s61, if Gypsies or Travellers had been arrested[93] or have had their vehicles impounded[94] for failing to comply with a direction to leave under section 62A, or if they have not yet left the land (or have returned to other land in the area) in defiance of such a direction, the police would have to obtain a further order from the magistrates' court.[95]

---

89   The fine should not exceed level 4 on the standard scale: CJPOA 1994 s62B(3).
90   See footnote 48 above.
91   CJPOA 1994 s62C.
92   By analogy with CJPOA 1994 s77 – see further at para 5.73 et seq, below.
93   See footnote 48, above.
94   Under CJPOA 1994 s62C.
95   See further the discussion at para 5.50, above.

5.72   Gypsy and Traveller support groups have voiced serious concerns about the use of CJPOA 1994 s62A.[96] The short deadlines that the police can give to Gypsies and Travellers mean that in practice it will be very unlikely that a court will hear a public law challenge before eviction takes place. However, the fact that the eviction has been carried out will not render a public law challenge academic, because the Gypsies or Travellers may wish to challenge the use of section 62A in order to avoid committing an offence if they return to the area or remain in the area within three months of the day when the direction was given.

CJPOA 1994 s77

Who can use it?

Local authorities

5.73   CJPOA 1994 s77 states:

> (1) If it appears to a local authority that persons are for the time being residing in a vehicle or vehicles within that authority's area –
>
> (a) on any land forming part of a highway;
> (b) on any other unoccupied land; or
> (c) on any occupied land without the consent of the occupier,
>
> the authority may give a direction that those persons and any others with them are to leave the land and remove the vehicle or vehicles and any other property they have with them on the land.

The offence is defined by CJPOA 1994 s77(3) as follows:

> If a person knowing that a direction under subsection (1) above has been given which applies to him –
>
> (a) fails, as soon as practicable, to leave the land or remove from the land any vehicle or other property which is the subject of the direction, or
> (b) having removed any such vehicle or property again enters the land with a vehicle within the period of three months beginning with the day on which the direction was given,
>
> he commits an offence and is liable on summary conviction to a fine not exceeding level 3 on the standard scale.

5.74   This is a very wide-ranging power and, though there is a specific statutory defence that is discussed at para 5.80, below, there are very few 'substantive defences'. Almost inevitably, it is the question of potential 'public law challenges' that is much more significant.[97] Nevertheless, the following 'substantive defences' may be available.

96 See further the conclusion at para 5.167–5.174, below.
97 See paras 5.119–5.159, below.

'Consent of the occupier'

5.75   Virtually all land, regardless of whether or not it is owned by the local authority, is potentially covered by CJPOA 1994 s77. The section cannot be used where the Gypsies or Travellers have the consent of the occupier to be there. However, as can be seen below,[98] local authorities can utilise planning enforcement powers in those circumstances. An attempt to argue that land where there was no known owner or occupier was not within the section because the Gypsies themselves were the (adverse) occupiers, was unsuccessful at permission stage in the High Court.[99]

'Vehicle or vehicles'

5.76   In contrast to CJPOA 1994 s61, the Gypsies or Travellers must be residing in a vehicle or vehicles. Gypsies or Travellers who are not residing in vehicles (for example, in benders or tents) will not be covered by the section. However this is subject to the exception mentioned in the next paragraph.

'Written notice'

5.77   With regard to service of the required written notice of a removal direction under CJPOA 1994 s77, section 79 states:

>   (2) Where it is impracticable to serve a relevant document on a person named in it, the document shall be treated as duly served on him if a copy of it is fixed in a prominent place to the vehicle concerned; and where a relevant document is directed to the unnamed occupants of vehicles, it shall be treated as duly served on those occupants if a copy of it is fixed in a prominent place to every vehicle on the land in question at the time when service is thus effected.

>   (3) A local authority shall take such steps as may be reasonably practicable to secure that a copy of any relevant document is displayed on the land in question (otherwise than by being fixed to a vehicle) in a manner designed to ensure that it is likely to be seen by any person camping on the land.

---

98   At para 5.118.

99   *R (Caroline Stephenson) v East Derbyshire Magistrates' Court and Amber Valley BC* [2003] EWHC 903 Admin, Sullivan J. In certain (rare) cases, where a Gypsy or Traveller has been residing on land that he or she did not own for 12 years or more without permission, he or she may be able to claim adverse possession of that land. However, the law on adverse possession is complex and has changed dramatically since the bringing into force of the Land Registration Act 2002. See Jourdan, *Adverse Possession*, Butterworths, 2003.

If a written notice is not placed on the vehicle(s) of a Gypsy or Traveller, that may constitute a defence. The catch-all phrase in section 77(1), 'any others with them', means that Gypsies or Travellers living on the land in tents or benders will be subject to the removal direction if they are with others who are residing in vehicles on the land. In those circumstances, section 79(3) makes similar provision to that which covers CPR Part 55 proceedings for display of notices on stakes or by other prominent methods.

'As soon as practicable'

5.78   It should be noted that, in contrast to CJPOA 1994 s61(4)(a), the word 'reasonably' has been omitted from CJPOA 1994 s77(3)[100] and Gypsies and Travellers can be prosecuted if they fail to leave the land 'as soon as practicable' after a removal direction has been given. What is 'practicable' in any given case will depend upon the facts but it is likely that a magistrates' court would convict a Gypsy or Traveller who had failed to comply with a short deadline in all but exceptional cases.

'Again enters the land ... within the period of three months'

5.79   The question whether a Gypsy or Traveller has returned to the land within three months of the original removal direction will be a simple matter of fact. In a case where Gypsies had ignored a removal direction and remained on the land for more than three months before being prosecuted under CJPOA 1994 s79 it was unsuccessfully argued that a removal direction could only be effective for a period of three months and that there was no power to prosecute a person after that period of time had expired.[101]

Statutory defence

5.80   The statutory defence is contained within CJPOA 1994 s77(5) and can be relied on, like the other potential defences, if and when the matter comes before the magistrates' court. It states:

> In proceedings for an offence under this section it is a defence for the accused to show that his failure to leave or to remove the vehicle or other property as soon as practicable or his re-entry with a vehicle was due to illness, mechanical breakdown or other immediate emergency.

---

100   See further para 5.33, above.

101   *R (Caroline Stephenson) v East Derbyshire Magistrates' Court and Amber Valley BC* [2003] EWHC 903 Admin.

This is a fairly self-explanatory defence though there is currently no case-law to help us with the breadth (or otherwise) of the phrase 'other immediate emergency'. However, the practicalities of raising this statutory defence and any other substantive defence (and thus turning up at court and risking a removal order and a fine) are dealt with in the conclusion to this chapter.[102]

Obtaining a court order

5.81 Under CJPOA 1994 s78:

(1) A magistrates' court may, on a complaint made by a local authority, if satisfied that persons and vehicles in which they are residing are present on land within that authority's area in contravention of a direction given under section 77, make an order requiring the removal of any vehicle or other property which is so present on the land and any person residing in it.

(2) An order under this section may authorise the local authority to take such steps as are reasonably necessary to ensure that the order is complied with and, in particular, may authorise the local authority, by its officers and servants –

(a) to enter upon the land specified in the order; and

(b) to take, in relation to any vehicle or property to be removed in pursuance of the order, such steps for securing entry and rendering it suitable for removal, as may be so specified.

(3) The local authority shall not enter upon any occupied land unless they have given to the owner or occupier at least 24 hours' notice of their intention to do so, or unless after reasonable enquiries they are unable to ascertain their names and addresses.

5.82 Normally, therefore, such a removal order will ensure that the Gypsies or Travellers who are subject to the order will have at least 24 hours after the order is obtained within which to leave the land. This will not be the case, however, if the local authority is both the owner and the occupier of the land, or if the local authority cannot reasonably ascertain the identity of the owner or occupier. It has been the normal practice of local authorities, since this power of eviction was brought into force, to only seek a removal order and not to seek a conviction for the potential criminal offence under CJPOA s77(3).[103]

---

102 At paras 5.167–5.174, below.
103 See para 5.73, above.

Highways Act 1980

Who can use it?

Local authorities and the police

5.83   A 'highway' is a way over which there exists a public right of passage, that is a right for all, at all seasons of the year, freely and at their will, to pass and re-pass without let or hindrance.[104] It should also be noted that a highway will include any footpaths or cycle tracks as well as the carriageway, and also any verge enjoyed by the public as part of the highway.[105]

5.84   If a person, without lawful authority or excuse, in any way wilfully obstructs the free passage along a highway, he or she is guilty of an offence.[106]

5.85   A lawful excuse will be established if it can be shown that the person causing the obstruction honestly but mistakenly believed, on reasonable grounds, that the facts were such as would make the conduct lawful.[107] However, proof of mens rea is not required to act wilfully, that is, one does not have to intend to cause an obstruction – if an obstruction is caused and the person responsible for the obstruction acted of their own free will, that is sufficient.[108] Thus the person responsible for the obstruction probably has a 'substantive defence' if their car has broken down and is thus causing an obstruction. Indeed, where the obstruction is of a temporary nature (as in the latter example), it will only be an offence if it is shown that the obstruction arose from unreasonable use of the highway.[109]

5.86   The case of *DPP v Jones*[110] raises an interesting question with regard to the use of highways legislation to 'move on' Gypsies or Travellers. The case did not involve action for breach of the highways legislation but

---

104   *Ex p Lewis* (1888) 21 QBD 191 at 197, per Wills J.

105   See *DPP v Jones* [1999] 2 WLR 625.

106   Highways Act 1980 s137(1). A person guilty of an offence is liable to a fine not exceeding level 3 on the standard scale.

107   *Cambridgeshire and Isle of Ely CC v Rust* [1972] 2 QB 426; [1972] 3 All ER 232.

108   *Arrowsmith v Jenkins* [1963] 2 QB 561.

109   *Nagy v Weston* [1965] 1 All ER 78, [1965] 1 WLR 280.

110   [1999] 2 WLR 625.

for 'trespassory assembly'.[111] The defendants took part in a peaceful, non-obstructive assembly on a highway. They were campaigning for the right to hold a festival at Stonehenge and were on the roadside verge, adjacent to the perimeter fence of the monument at Stonehenge. The Court of Appeal allowed the defendants' appeal against the Divisional Court finding that this amounted to a 'trespassory assembly'. The Court of Appeal held that the public had the right to use the highway for such reasonable and usual activities, including peaceful assembly, as was consistent with the primary right to use it for passage and repassage, it being a matter of fact and degree for the court in each case to decide whether the user was reasonable and not inconsistent with that primary right. Lord Irvine of Lairg stated:

> It is neither desirable in theory nor acceptable in practice for commonplace activities on the public highway not to count as breaches of the criminal law of wilful obstruction of the highway, yet to count as trespasses ... and therefore form the basis for a finding of trespassory assembly for the purposes of the Act of 1986. A system of law sanctioning these discordant outcomes would not command respect.[112]

5.87   Gypsies or Travellers do not usually face actions on the basis of 'trespassory assemblies' but they do frequently stop for short periods on the verges of highways (which are, in terms of highways legislation, part of the highway). Indeed, Gypsies and Travellers have been stopping in such locations, for short periods, for hundreds of years in the United Kingdom. It could be argued that such an incident, where the Gypsies or Travellers are not obstructing any footpath or cycle track and are acting peaceably, comes within the ambit of a 'commonplace activity', as mentioned by Lord Irvine. Nevertheless, it is common for Gypsies and Travellers on the verges of a carriageway to be moved on for allegedly obstructing the highway. However, there is, as yet, no case-law on this situation.

5.88   It is also an offence for any person in charge of a vehicle to cause or permit it, or a trailer (which could include a caravan) drawn by it, to

111   A 'trespassory assembly' is defined by Public Order Act 1986 s14A, as inserted by CJPOA 1994 s70, as: 'an assembly ... intended to be held in any district at a place on land to which the public has no right of access or only a limited right of access [which] is likely to be held without the permission of the occupier of the land or to conduct itself in such a way as to exceed the limits of any permission of his or the limits of the public's rights of access and ... may result – (i) in serious disruption to the life of the community, or (ii) where the land, or a building or monument on it, is of historical, architectural, archaeological or scientific importance, in significant damage to the land, building or monument ...'
112   [1999] 2 WLR 625 at 633F; [1999] 2 AC 240 at 258B.

remain at rest on any road in such position, condition or circumstances as to be likely to cause danger to other road users.[113]

5.89   On certain highways the keeper of any horses, cattle, sheep, goats or swine found straying on or lying on or at the side of the highway is guilty of an offence.[114]

5.90   The only possibility of impoundment of vehicles under the highways legislation is contained in Highways Act 1980 s149, as follows:

(1) If anything is so deposited on a highway as to constitute a nuisance, the highway authority for the highway may by notice require the person who deposited it there to remove it forthwith [and can apply to magistrates for a removal and disposal order].

(2) If the highway authority for any highway have reasonable grounds for considering –

(a) that anything unlawfully deposited on the highway constitutes a danger (including a danger caused by obstructing the view) to users of the highway, and

(b) that the thing in question ought to be removed without the delay involved in giving notice or obtaining a removal and disposal order

...

the authority may remove the thing forthwith.

5.91   The 'thing unlawfully deposited' could include vehicles. If sufficient danger is caused, impoundment could occur. Other than this circumstance, impoundment without an order is not possible.

5.92   Where a highway is created through the acquisition of land over which it passes, either by agreement or through the exercise of compulsory purchase powers, the highway authority is the owner both of the surface of the highway and the subsoil. However, where a highway is created by dedication (that is, with the permission of the landowner without releasing his or her rights over the land), the subsoil[115] beneath the highway remains in the ownership of the 'dedicating landowner'.[116] Moreover, in the case of those highways which are not maintainable at

---

113   Road Traffic Act 1988 s22. A person guilty of an offence is liable to a fine not exceeding level 3 on the standard scale and also discretionary disqualification.

114   Highways Act 1980 s155(1). A person guilty of an offence is liable to a fine not exceeding level 3 on the standard scale. The animal in question can also be removed to the common pound.

115   The surface of the road was defined by Denning LJ, in *Tithe Redemption Commission v Runcorn UDC* [1954] 2 WLR 518, as: 'the top spit, or perhaps ... the top two spits, of the road' (at 530).

116   See *Truckell v Stock* (1957) 1 WLR 161; *Rolls v St George the Martyr, Southwark, Vestry* (1880) 14 Ch D 785.

public expense, both the surface of the highway and the subsoil remain within the ownership of the dedicating landowner.[117] Where the dedicating landowner retains ownership of the surface of the highway and/or the subsoil, he or she will be able to take possession action (for example, CPR Part 55 proceedings) against any trespassers on the highway.

5.93   In a case where a Gypsy or Traveller is prosecuted under any of the above statutory provisions he or she will be able to defend the proceedings successfully if the prosecuting authority are unable to satisfy the magistrates' court that all the elements of the alleged offence have been proved.

Bye-laws

Who can use them?

Local authorities and certain other public authorities

5.94   A bye-law is an ordinance affecting the public and laid down by an authority which has been given statutory powers to do so.[118] If validly made, a bye-law has the force of law within its sphere of operation. Bye-laws made by local authorities must be confirmed by some central authority before they can have the force of law.[119]

5.95   A local authority can either be given power to deal with specific matters or may make bye-laws for the good rule and government of the whole or any part of the area they cover, as well as for the prevention and suppression of nuisances.[120]

5.96   Bye-laws may not be made if they duplicate the provisions of other enactments.[121]

5.97   A copy of a bye-law or part of a bye-law must be provided to any person on request on payment of such sum as the authority may determine.[122]

---

117 See *Encyclopaedia of Highway Law and Practice*, Sweet & Maxwell, 2007, 1-002.

118 *Kruse v Johnson* [1898] 2 QB 91.

119 Local Government Act 1972 s236(3).

120 This applies to the council of a district, the council of a principal area in Wales, the council of a London borough and the Council of the Isles of Scilly: Local Government Act 1972 s235(1) as amended by the Local Government (Wales) Act 1994 s66(5), Sch 15 para 49.

121 See, for example, *Galer v Morrissey* [1955] 1 All ER 380.

122 Local Government Act 1972 s236(6) – currently the sum must not exceed 10p for every 100 words.

5.98   A bye-law requires four elements for it to be valid:

(a) it must be intra vires (that is, within the power of the authority making it);
(b) it must not be 'repugnant' to the general law;
(c) it must be certain;
(d) it must be reasonable.

5.99   A bye-law must be intra vires. A local authority cannot take upon itself powers by means of a bye-law beyond the powers conferred on it by statute.[123]

5.100   A bye-law must not be repugnant to the general law. Therefore, a bye-law must not make something unlawful which the general law does not make unlawful.[124]

5.101   A bye-law must be certain. To be certain, a bye-law must contain a clear statement of the course of action required (or that should be avoided) and must contain sufficient information to allow people to know what is expected of them.[125]

5.102   A bye-law must be reasonable. To be reasonable, a bye-law must not be manifestly unjust, capricious, inequitable or partial in its operation, or involve oppressive interference with the rights of those subject to it. For example, in one case bye-laws imposing on landlords a duty to clean certain houses were held unreasonable where they applied to a landlord who had not reserved a right of entry to the property in question.[126]

5.103   A local authority may not waive the requirements of its bye-laws unless it has reserved the right to do so. Bye-laws made by local authorities should be interpreted benevolently and upheld if possible.[127]

5.104   The production of a printed copy of a bye-law made by a local authority which is endorsed with a certificate signed by the proper officer of the authority is prima facie evidence of the bye-law, provided the certificate states that:

(a) it was made by the local authority;
(b) the copy is a true copy;
(c) on a specified date the bye-law was confirmed.

---

123 See, for example, *R v Wood* (1855) 5 E&B 49.
124 See, for example, *Powell v May* [1946] KB 330.
125 See, for example, *Percy v Hall* [1997] QB 924.
126 *Arlidge v The Metropolitan Borough of Islington* [1909] 2 KB 127.
127 *Kruse v Johnson* (1989) 2 QB 91 at 99, per Lord Russell of Killowen CJ.

5.105   Bye-laws may be enforced by the imposition of fines, the removal of offenders from the place to which the bye-law relates or by injunction.

5.106   Other public authorities may be empowered to make bye-laws. For example, the Forestry Commission may make bye-laws:

- for the preservation of trees, timber and the Commissioners' property;
- for prohibiting or regulating any act or thing tending to injure or disfigure Forestry Commission land or amenities; and
- for regulating the reasonable use of the land by the public for the purposes of exercise or recreation.[128]

5.107   All of the principles with regard to validity and scope mentioned above also apply to bye-laws produced by other public authorities.[129]

5.108   If a local or other public authority prosecutes a Gypsy or Traveller for allegedly breaching a bye-law, the matters mentioned above with regard to validity may provide a 'substantive defence'.[130] However, it should be emphasised that the practice of local and other public authorities tends to be to rely on other forms of possession action to evict Gypsies or Travellers from land, while at the same time quoting relevant bye-laws (sometimes as a way of justifying their action as being 'proportionate' or 'reasonable').

Common law powers

Who can use them?

Anyone entitled to possession of the land, for example, landowner, tenant, licensee

5.109   If a trespasser peaceably enters or is on land, the person who is in, or is entitled to, possession may require him or her to leave, and, if the trespasser refuses to leave, may remove that person from the land, using no more force than is reasonably necessary.[131] The request to leave could, potentially, be a request to leave forthwith.

5.110   Such powers are available to all landowners. But an attempt to use these powers by a local or other public authority could give rise to a public law challenge by way of judicial review.[132]

---

128   Forestry Act 1967 s46(1). The Forestry Commission bye-laws currently in force are Forestry Commission Bye-laws 1982 SI No 648.

129   *Boddington v British Transport Police* [1999] 2 AC 143.

130   *Boddington v British Transport Police* [1999] 2 AC 143.

131   Halsbury, *Laws of England*, Butterworths, 4th edn, 1999, Vol 45(2), para 522.

132   See paras 5.119–5.159, below.

5.111   However, if a trespasser enters with force and violence, the person in possession may remove that person without a previous request to depart.[133] Once again, in the case of local or other public authorities, a potential public law challenge is not precluded, though the fact of the use of force or violence by the trespasser may assist the authority to argue that its decision to evict is 'proportionate' or 'reasonable'.

5.112   The use of more force than is 'reasonably necessary' could result in an action for trespass to the person or property and a compensation claim for any damage caused. The person(s) carrying out the eviction or the person in possession could also be charged with having committed a criminal offence, such as assault or criminal damage, if the trespasser is injured or property is damaged during the course of the eviction.

5.113   The 2004 Encampment Guidance states:

> The Government believes that local authorities should always follow a route which requires a court order. As local authorities and public bodies, authorities must have regard to considerations of common humanity or other statutory duties, and must ensure that the human rights of unauthorised campers are safeguarded.[134]

This would seem to effectively preclude the use of common law powers by local and other public authorities.

5.114   The 2004 Encampment Guidance also contains recommendations for other landowners using common law powers of eviction:

> Good practice guidelines for common law evictions would seek to ensure that no more than necessary 'reasonable force' is used and might include:
> * Police should always be notified of an eviction and called in to stand by to prevent a breach of the peace.
> * If police advise that it is inappropriate to carry out an eviction, it should always be delayed until an agreed time.[135]

5.115   If the person using common law powers is subsequently prosecuted for wrongful use of those powers (see para 5.112, above), failure to follow the above guidance may be used in evidence against them.

5.116   It is also noted that Lord Denning stated that these powers were 'not to be recommended' to landowners due to the 'possible disturbance' which might be caused.[136]

---

133   See, for example, *Polkingham v Wright* [1845] 8 QB 197.
134   2004 Encampment Guidance at para 6.5.
135   2004 Encampment Guidance at para 6.16.
136   *McPhail v Persons Unknown* [1973] 3 All ER 393 at 396.

5.117 Gypsies or Travellers who are encamped on an unauthorised encampment which is within the 'curtilage' of a building may be able to rely on Criminal Law Act (CLA) 1977 s6. Section 6 makes it a summary offence[137] for a person without lawful authority to use or threaten violence for the purpose of securing entry to premises, in which, to his or her knowledge, someone is present who is opposed to the entry.[138] Squatters in buildings or on land ancillary to buildings will often post notices (sometimes called 'section 6 notices') on the outside of the building to draw to the attention of the owner or someone attempting to gain entry of their presence and of the fact that they are opposed to any forceful entry. However, if entry can be gained without the use of violence (for example, by simply climbing over a wall or fence), then the offence will not have been committed. 'Premises' includes land 'ancillary to a building'.[139] 'Premises' also includes 'any movable structure, vehicle or vessel designed or adapted for use for residential purposes'.[140] Therefore, section 6 will apply to violent entry upon a caravan, mobile home or houseboat.[141]

Planning enforcement

Who can use it?

Local authorities

5.118 The Town and Country Planning Act (TCPA) 1990 enables local authorities to take enforcement action against unauthorised developments by the use of enforcement notices, stop notices or injunctions. Very often, the Gypsies or Travellers on such encampments may also be trying to obtain planning permission. On other occasions, the Gypsies or Travellers may be on land with the consent of the owner but may not have the requisite planning permission. Action may be threatened by the local authority against the owner and/or the Gypsies and Travellers.[142] The existence of these powers does not preclude a potential

---

137 Punishable with six months' imprisonment or a fine or both.
138 CLA 1977 s6 does not apply to a 'displaced residential occupier' or to a 'protected intending occupier' – see CLA 1977 s7.
139 CLA 1977 s12(1)(a).
140 CLA 1977 s12(2).
141 For advice on the law relating to 'squatting', contact the Advisory Service for Squatters – see appendix C, below – which also produces a Squatters' Handbook.
142 For a full discussion of planning matters as they affect Gypsies and Travellers, see chapter 4, above.

public law challenge by way of judicial review by the Gypsies or Travellers.[143]

Public law challenges

Local authorities

5.119   In the *Atkinson* case,[144] Sedley J (as he then was) made it clear that local authorities, when considering the eviction of unauthorised encampments, ought to comply with Department of the Environment (DoE) Circular 18/94, Welsh Office Circular 76/94 (hereafter DoE Circular 18/94).[145] Sedley J stated:

> Detailed analysis of [passages from the Circular] and debate about what legal force, if any, an advisory circular of this kind possesses has been made unnecessary by the realistic concession of counsel for both local authorities that whether or not they were spelt out in a departmental circular the matters mentioned ... would be material considerations in the public law sense that to overlook them in the exercise of a local authority's powers under sections 77 to 79 of the Act of 1994 would be to leave relevant matters out of account and so jeopardise the validity of any consequent step. The concession is rightly made because those considerations in the material paragraphs which are not statutory are considerations of common humanity, none of which can be properly ignored when dealing with one of the most fundamental human needs, the need for shelter with at least a modicum of security.[146]

5.120   DoE Circular 18/94 is, therefore, a vital tool for those advising on this area of the law. At paragraph 6 it states:

> While it is a matter for local discretion to decide whether it is appropriate to evict an unauthorised gypsy encampment, the Secretary of State believes that local authorities should consider using their powers to do so wherever the gypsies concerned are causing a level of nuisance which cannot be effectively controlled. They also consider that it would usually be legiti-

---

143   And see the case of *R v Kerrier DC ex p Uzell Blythe* [1996] JPL 837, where Latham J (as he then was) applied the principles of the *Atkinson* case (see para 5.119 et seq, below) to a situation involving planning enforcement powers.

144   *R v Lincolnshire CC ex p Atkinson; Wealden DC ex p Wales and Stratford* (1996) 8 Admin LR 529.

145   *Gypsy sites policy and unauthorised camping*, issued 23 November 1994 and amended 26 July 2000. The Welsh Office Circular is identical to the DoE Circular. See appendix B, below.

146   (1995) 8 Admin LR 529 at 535.

mate for a local authority to exercise these powers wherever gypsies who are camped unlawfully refuse to move onto an authorised local authority site. Where there are no such sites, and the authority reaches the view that an unauthorised gypsy encampment is not causing a level of nuisance which cannot be effectively controlled, it should consider providing basic services, such as toilets, a refuse skip and a supply of drinking water at that site.

5.121   The *Atkinson* case made it clear that local authorities must have regard to humanitarian considerations (and this is emphasised later in the Circular, as we will see below). Paragraph 6 lays emphasis on the question of 'nuisance'. It follows that, if the unauthorised encampment is situated on a disused piece of land and not causing any problems, the local authority may wish to consider 'toleration' of the encampment. Eviction may lead to the group of Gypsies or Travellers moving to a less appropriate, more high-profile site. 'Toleration' might certainly be appropriate where the local authority cannot suggest an authorised permanent site, transit site or emergency stopping place that the Gypsies or Travellers could go to. On the other hand, if the encampment was in the town hall car park, there would need to be the most extreme welfare circumstances before a court might expect the local authority to hold back from eviction.

5.122   At paragraph 9 of Circular 18/94 it is stated:

> [Local authorities] should use [their] powers in a humane and compassionate way, taking account of the rights and needs of the gypsies concerned, the owners of the land in question, and the wider community whose lives may be affected by the situation.

5.123   Local authorities are also reminded of their obligations under Children Act 1989 Pt III (regarding the welfare of 'children in need'), Housing Act 1985 Pt III (now Housing Act 1996 Pt VII, covering duties to homeless people), and concerning the provision of education for school-age children.[147] Local authorities should also bear in mind possible assistance from local health and/or welfare services.[148]

5.124   DoE Circular 18/94 is intended to give local authorities guidance on the use of CJPOA 1994 s77. Local authorities clearly need to carry out some form of inquiry process in order to gather the necessary information and then adopt a suitable method by which to analyse and consider such information. They will also need to be able to show that the decision maker has proper delegated authority. For example, in a

---

147   DoE Circular 18/94 paras 10 and 11.
148   DoE Circular 18/94 para 13.

case involving remuneration for long-term foster carers,[149] the policy of
the local authority was quashed, among other things, because the
preparation of the policy had not been lawfully delegated to the officers
who had, in fact, devised it. Solicitors or advisers assisting Gypsies or
Travellers who are facing eviction from an unauthorised encampment
by a local authority, should consider requesting details of who made the
decision to evict and whether that person or persons had properly delegated powers to do so.

5.125   Following the *Atkinson* case, some local authorities sought to test
whether the general thrust of DoE Circular 18/94 would apply to other
methods of eviction and there followed a line of somewhat conflicting
High Court judgments.[150] However, the position was clarified in October 1998 by the publication of the Department of the Environment,
Transport and the Regions (DETR)/Home Office *Good practice guide,
managing unauthorised camping.*[151] This guidance was the result of
research commissioned by the government from the University of
Birmingham. The guidance made clear that local authorities should
take into account welfare issues regardless of the method of eviction
being contemplated. The guidance has now been superseded by the
ODPM *Guidance on managing unauthorised camping* ('the 2004 Encampment Guidance').[152] The 2004 Encampment Guidance only applies to

149   *R (L) v Manchester CC* [2001] EWHC 707 Admin; [2002] 1 FLR 43, Munby J.
150   *R v Kerrier DC ex p Uzell Blythe* [1996] JPL 837; *R v Brighton and Hove Council
       ex p Marmont* (1998) 30 HLR 1046; *R v Hillingdon LBC ex p McDonagh* (1999)
       31 HLR 531; and *R v Leeds CC ex p Maloney* [1999] HLR 552. Broadly
       speaking, the judgments in *Uzell Blythe* and *Maloney* stated that Circular
       18/94 (or, at least, the spirit of it) should apply to enforcement/eviction
       action other than just evictions under CJPOA 1994 s77, and the judgments
       in *Marmont* and *McDonagh* stated the contrary view, though it was at least
       accepted in those cases that there must be some reference to 'humanitarian
       considerations'.
151   This Guidance was amended in 2000. The fact that welfare inquiries should
       be carried out regardless of the type of eviction action was effectively
       confirmed in *R (Martin Ward) v Hillingdon LBC* [2001] LGR 457, where
       Stanley Burnton J at 460, stated:
          [A] local authority considering exercising its powers to evict travellers ...
          from an unauthorised encampment must not act in an uninformed,
          precipitate and inconsiderate manner. It must make adequate inquiries to
          elicit relevant information, including the number, age, health and needs
          of the travellers concerned, and make its decision having properly taken
          that information into account. The guidance expressly envisages that
          there will be circumstances in which a local authority may properly decide
          not to evict travellers from an unauthorised encampment.
152   The ODPM Guidance also resulted from further research by the University
       of Birmingham headed (as with the previous guidance) by Pat Niner of the
       Centre for Urban and Regional Studies. The Guidance came into effect on 27
       February 2004. See appendix B, below.

England. It has now been supplemented by further guidance for England from the ODPM/Home Office, namely the *Guide to effective use of enforcement powers – Part 1: Unauthorised encampments*[153] (the 2006 Encampment Guidance). Thus, in England, those dealing with Gypsy and Traveller encampments and those advising Gypsies and Travellers on such encampments must have reference to all three codes of guidance: DoE Circular 18/94; the 2004 Encampment Guidance; and the 2006 Encampment Guidance.

5.126 As we have already mentioned, Welsh Office Circular 76/94 is identical to DoE Circular 18/94. This guidance was supplemented, in January 2005, by the Welsh Assembly Government/Home Office *Guidance on managing unauthorised camping* (hereafter the Welsh Encampment Guidance). Both of these sets of guidance must be considered together when dealing with Welsh cases. The Welsh Encampment Guidance is very similar to the 2004 Encampment Guidance but has certain differences. When referring from here on in this chapter to the 2004 Encampment Guidance, footnotes will refer to the position with regard to the Welsh Encampment Guidance where either the paragraph number is different or the wording is significantly different. Otherwise it should be noted that the paragraph numbers are the same in the Welsh Encampment Guidance and the wording is the same or virtually the same.[154] The Welsh Assembly Government has not yet indicated whether it will be producing an equivalent of the 2006 Encampment Guidance.

5.127 The 2004 Encampment Guidance stresses the importance for local authorities of the information-gathering process and the importance of strategies being put in place.[155] It will be important, therefore, for advisers to obtain copies of the relevant strategies on unauthorised camping from local authorities and police authorities in order to check that they have been followed.

5.128 The 2004 Encampment Guidance makes clear the government's emphasis on the need for site provision. At paragraph 4.2 it is stated:

> Site provision is an essential element in any strategy. In a context where the number of Gypsy caravans exceeds the number of authorised places where they can stop – which is the case in England – provision of suitable accommodation for Gypsies and Travellers must be seen as a vital part of an approach to dealing with unauthorised camping. Population increase and family growth among Gypsies and Travellers must also be considered.

---

153 Issued in February 2006.
154 See www.wales.gov.uk/dsjr/publications/localgov/guidecamping/?lang=en
155 See, in both the 2004 Encampment Guidance and the Welsh Encampment Guidance, chapter 3, 'Developing a strategy for unauthorised camping'.

5.129   With regard to Wales, the Equality of Opportunity Committee of the National Assembly for Wales has stated:

> Put bluntly, providing services to Gypsy-Travellers tends to be unpopular with the wider public, and given that there is no longer a requirement to provide sites, the issue is given a low priority. The service providers [including local authorities] were strongly in favour of a new national framework for sites, even a reintroduction of a duty to provide sites as the only way to make progress on this issue.[156]

5.130   The 2004 Encampment Guidance, at paragraph 4.3, continues:

> All local authorities should review the provision of sites for Gypsies and Travellers.

The lack of a clear and coherent written strategy in itself may be a factor in a potential public law challenge.

5.131   The 2004 Encampment Guidance also emphasises the importance of welfare inquiries and the need for public bodies to take account of considerations of common humanity.[157] This is also emphasised in the 2006 Encampment Guidance. For example, at paragraph 77 it is stated:

> Local authorities should ensure that, in accordance with their wider obligations, and to ensure that they comply with Human Rights legislation, proper welfare enquiries are carried out to determine whether there are pressing needs presented by the unauthorised campers and that, where necessary, the appropriate agencies are involved as soon as possible.

5.132   However, the 2004 Encampment Guidance also makes it clear that the location of an encampment will be an important consideration. For example, at paragraph 5.4 it is stated:

> Unauthorised encampments are almost always, by definition, unlawful. However, while there are insufficient authorised sites, it is recognised that some unauthorised camping will continue. There are locations, however, where encampment will not be acceptable under any circumstances. Each encampment location must be considered on its merits against criteria such as health and safety considerations for the unauthorised campers, traffic hazard, public health risks, serious environmental damage, genuine nuisance to neighbours and proximity to other sensitive land-uses.[158]

---

156   *Review of service provision for Gypsies and Travellers,* National Assembly for Wales, May 2003, para 10.27.

157   See the 2004 Encampment Guidance paras 5.7–5.10; Welsh Encampment Guidance paras 5.6–5.9.

158   Welsh Encampment Guidance para 5.3.

Thus, to take the extreme example of an encampment in the town hall car park, the location of the encampment, in such a case, may preclude any question of a public law challenge due to lack of inquiries.[159] In the 2006 Encampment Guidance examples are given of locations that cause serious disruption and may need to be moved, for example, school grounds during term time, urban parks and business parks.[160]

5.133   It will be important for local authorities to keep written records of the inquiry process and, for this purpose, pro formas might be used.[161] At paragraph 5.17 of the 2004 Encampment Guidance it is stated that:

> Reasonable attempts should be made to get information from unauthorised campers not present at the time of a visit. Other members of the group may sometimes be able to provide information. A letter or self-completion form may be left with clear instructions for its return (at no cost to the unauthorised camper). All such actions should be clearly recorded, and if there is still no response, this should be noted.[162]

Usually Gypsies and Travellers will not be aware in advance of the time of a visit. More than one visit may therefore be required. Reliance on pro formas or self-completion forms may also be dependent on questions of literacy. Additionally, Gypsies and Travellers may be reluctant to give their names for fear that they will be named in court proceedings and may face court costs. Advisers and solicitors assisting Gypsies and Travellers could encourage local authorities (and, indeed, other public authorities) to confirm to the Gypsies and Travellers concerned that no such adverse consequences will arise if they give their names. Alternatively, the Gypsies and Travellers should be urged to provide relevant information, even if it is provided anonymously.

5.134   It is important, however, that the inquiry process is more than just a paper exercise. A proper decision-making process is required. Paragraph 5.20 of the 2004 Encampment Guidance states:

> Any welfare needs of unauthorised campers are a material consideration

---

159 This is not to say that inquiries should not be made in such a case. However, if the Gypsies or Travellers are unlawfully encamped on a location such as the town hall car park, only the most extreme of personal circumstances might lead to a decision to 'tolerate' the encampment for a short period.

160 2006 Encampment Guidance para 59.

161 2004 Encampment Guidance para 5.14; Welsh Encampment Guidance para 5.13.

162 Welsh Encampment Guidance para 5.16 (reference to 'no cost to the unauthorised camper' removed).

for local authorities when deciding whether to start eviction proceedings or to allow the encampment to remain longer. Welfare needs do not give an open-ended 'right' for unauthorised campers to stay as long as they want in an area. For example, the presence of a pregnant woman or school age children does not, per se, mean that an encampment must remain indefinitely. To defer an eviction which is justified on other grounds, the need must be more immediate and/or of a fixed term.[163]

The 2004 Encampment Guidance gives some specific examples of situations where good practice suggests that eviction should be delayed:

- advanced pregnancy – a period shortly before and after birth in normal circumstances, longer on medical advice if there are complications;
- ill health – indicators might include a hospital appointment booked; in-patient treatment of a close family member; period during which a condition can be diagnosed, stabilised and a course of treatment started;
- educational needs – children in school if within four weeks of the end of term or if access to special education has been gained.[164]

5.135   It is important for local authorities to identify who is responsible for taking decisions (as is also the case for the police).[165] A decision being taken by the wrong officer or employee may lead to a successful challenge.[166] As mentioned above,[167] the government stresses that it wants local authorities to follow a route that ultimately requires a court order.[168] If the local authority decides to 'tolerate' an encampment for the time being, it must take a 'management' role.[169] The 2004 Encampment Guidance makes it clear that the same standards of behaviour should be expected of the occupants of an unauthorised encampment as might be expected of the settled community.[170] Examples of

---

163   Welsh Encampment Guidance para 5.19.
164   2004 Encampment Guidance Box 18 p31; Welsh Encampment Guidance Box 16 p20.
165   2004 Encampment Guidance para 5.22; Welsh Encampment Guidance para 5.21.
166   See para 5.124, above.
167   At para 5.113, above.
168   2004 Encampment Guidance para 6.5; Welsh Encampment Guidance para 6.4.
169   See 2004 Encampment Guidance and Welsh Encampment Guidance, chapter 7 'Managing unauthorised encampments'.
170   2004 Encampment Guidance and Welsh Encampment Guidance para 7.1.

unacceptable behaviour are given such as over-large encampments, aggressive or threatening behaviour, failure to control dogs, persistent and disturbing noise, littering/fly-tipping, damage to property or criminal activity.[171]

5.136 The 2006 Encampment Guidance and the ODPM Circular 1/06, *Planning for Gypsy and Traveller caravan sites* (hereafter Circular 1/06),[172] both place emphasis on the need for alternative locations, even if of a temporary nature, to be identified for Gypsies and Travellers who do not have or cannot locate authorised stopping places. For example, the 2006 Encampment Guidance, at paragraph 61 states:

> [A]ction will be more effective if there is an alternative site to which Gypsies and Travellers can be directed, either pitches on an authorised transit site, or a location which is deemed to be a more 'acceptable' unauthorised site.

5.137 Similarly, the 2006 Encampment Guidance at paragraph 72 states:

> Enforcement action will be quicker and more effective, and a wider range of powers can be used, where appropriate authorised provision is made for Gypsies and Travellers within the area. The Housing Act 2004 requires local authorities to undertake accommodation needs assessment for Gypsies and Travellers who reside in or resort to their areas, and then to set out a strategy to meet those needs. Adequate provision will have wide benefits in the management of unauthorised camping as:
> - There will be less unauthorised camping in the first place;
> - The police will not be restricted in the use of ss 62A-E CJPOA if suitable pitches are available;
> - Legal challenges are less likely to occur or succeed;
> - The courts are more likely to grant possession orders to local authorities who show they are acting responsibly in carrying out their wider duties and who deal with each incident of unauthorised camping on its merits.

5.138 There is also an important emphasis in the 2006 Encampment Guidance on local authorities considering whether an encampment can be 'tolerated' in combination with consideration of alternative locations. Thus at paragraph 83, under the heading 'Avoiding unnecessary enforcement action', it is stated:

> Before taking action, landowners should consider whether enforcement is

---

171 2004 Encampment Guidance para 7.3; Welsh Encampment Guidance para 7.2.

172 Also issued in February 2006. See chapter 4, above, for a detailed discussion of ODPM Circular 01/06. The Welsh Assembly Government has put a very similar draft circular out for consultation and its finalised version is awaited.

absolutely necessary. It may be that in certain circumstances, alternatives to eviction action are appropriate, for example:

- Where unauthorised campers have chosen an unobtrusive location in which to camp it may be preferable to agree a departure date with them;
- Where unauthorised campers have chosen to stop in an unacceptable location, but where the local authority has also identified a location in the vicinity which would be much less damaging or obtrusive, unauthorised campers could be encouraged to move to this location.

5.139   In similar vein, Circular 1/06, at paragraph 12, gives as one of its main intentions:

> ... to help to avoid gypsies and travellers becoming homeless through eviction from unauthorised sites without an alternative to move to.

5.140   At the same time as the 2006 Encampment Guidance and Circular 1/06 were published,[173] the ODPM also published *Local authorities and Gyspies and Travellers: Guide to responsibilities and powers*. This states, at page 12:

> Many unauthorised sites are not contentious and are trouble-free. In these circumstances, some authorities choose not to take enforcement action. However, a 'toleration' approach does not negate the need for local authorities to allocate land for authorised sites.

5.141   The theme of alternative provision is continued in the ODPM *Draft Guidance on the Management of Gypsy and Traveller Sites* (May 2007). At paragraph 7.15 of this consultation document, it is stated:

> In circumstances involving an unauthorised encampment, the household concerned should be found authorised site accommodation as soon as possible for the short term with more suitable authorised accommodation as soon as possible thereafter.

5.142   In summary, local authorities faced with an unauthorised encampment (certainly when it is on their own land) must make welfare inquiries and must take careful account of the information gleaned from those inquiries. Questions of nuisance, obstruction, inappropriate location and anti-social behaviour have to be taken into account. There is an important new emphasis on identifying an alternative location for the Gypsies and Travellers concerned, even if this is for a temporary period of time. In many ways, these were the issues at the forefront of the court's mind in *R(Casey & ors) v Crawley BC and the ODPM*.[174]

173   February 2006.
174   [2006] EWHC 301 Admin.

5.143   It should be emphasised that *Casey* involved a post-February 2006 (ie post the publication of the guidance discussed above) judgment but a pre-February 2006 decision to evict. The case involved a group of Irish Travellers who were originally split between two unauthorised encampments, both on the same local authority's land. It was accepted that the sites of the encampments were not ideal locations. Burton J concluded that the welfare inquiries that had been carried out were sufficient to comply with the 2004 Encampment Guidance. He also took account of the fact that the local authority had been trying to identify a location for an authorised site and, in all the circumstances, he concluded that the decision to evict was not unlawful. Very importantly, Burton J framed three options that were available to the defendant local authority:

> i) Seek and obtain possession of the sites [Option 1].
> ii) Tolerate the Claimants, if only for a short time, until an alternative could be found [Option 2].
> iii) Find an alternative site, if only on a temporary basis, and offer the [Claimants] a move to it [Option 3].[175]

Burton J continued:

> If, in a given situation, *reactively* the Council can find for travellers on an unauthorised site another temporary toleration site where lawfully, and notwithstanding the lack of planning permission, they can be temporarily sited, that would be a suitable administrative decision and exercise of Option 3: but there is no need for them to have a pro-actively identified pool [of such sites] ready, even if that were feasible.[176]

It might now be argued, post the publication of Circular 1/06 and the accompanying guidance, that we might now be on the move from the reactive to the proactive position.

5.144   If a Gypsy or Traveller has made a homeless application to a local authority relying on the case of *R (Margaret Price) v Carmarthenshire CC*,[177] and is camping on a piece of the same local authority's land, then it can be argued that he or she should be allowed to remain there while the homelessness application is progressed, providing that he or she is not causing any nuisance or obstruction.

---

175 [2006] EWHC 301 Admin at para 50.
176 [2006] EWHC 301 Admin at para 55(ii).
177 [2003] EWHC 42 Admin; March 2003 *Legal Action* 30. For full discussion of this case, see chapter 6 at para 6.51 et seq, below.

The police

5.145   It should be noted that attempts in two court cases to argue that the police powers of eviction were incompatible with the HRA 1998 failed.[178]

5.146   The police must also take account of welfare considerations. Home Office Circular 45/94 states, in relation to CJPOA 1994 s61:

> The decision whether or not to issue a direction to leave is an operational one for the police alone to take in the light of all the circumstances of the particular case. But in making this decision, the senior officer at the scene may wish to take account of the personal circumstances of the trespassers; for example, the presence of elderly persons, invalids, pregnant women, children and other persons whose well-being may be jeopardised by a precipitate move.

5.147   The 2004 Encampment Guidance makes reference to the case of *R v Metropolitan Police ex p Small.*[179] summing up the case-law position thus:

> Case law (Small) has established that, while police officers do not have to undertake welfare enquiries as such, they must be aware of humanitarian considerations in reaching their decisions and must ensure that all decisions are proportionate. A decision may be taken to explicitly exclude individuals or families with serious welfare needs from a section 61 direction to leave.[180]

This is further emphasised in the 2006 Encampment Guidance which states at paragraph 63 that:

> If the anti-social behaviour is focused amongst particular individuals in the group, or if a member of the group is ill, it may be appropriate to take action to evict some people but not others.

It is difficult to see how the police officers present can take account of humanitarian considerations without making some form of inquiry. However, it is suggested that it will be difficult to argue that the police have failed to comply with their duty if they request that the Gypsies or Travellers provide details of the existence of any welfare concerns and

---

178   *R (Fuller & ors) v Chief Constable of the Dorset Constabulary and the Secretary of State for the Home Department* [2002] 3 All ER 57; *R (McCarthy) v Chief Constable of the Sussex Constabulary and the Secretary of State for the Home Department* [2007] EWHC 1520 Admin.

179   Unreported leave application in the (as it then was) Crown Office List before Collins J, 27 August 1998.

180   2004 Encampment Guidance para 6.9; Welsh Encampment Guidance para 6.8.

then take account of any relevant information when deciding whether to issue a removal direction.

5.148 The 2004 Encampment Guidance indicates that, where a local authority is involved, the police can probably rely on the inquiries conducted by the local authority.[181] Equally it can be argued that, if it is local authority land, the local authority ought to go through its correct processes before even considering police involvement.[182]

5.149 At paragraph 6.8, the 2004 Encampment Guidance provides some examples of factors which might prompt police eviction action:

- unacceptable behaviour by unauthorised campers at the encampment, including individual criminal activity, which cannot be controlled by means other than eviction;
- significant disruption to the life of the surrounding community;
- serious breaches of the peace or disorder caused by the encampment.

The same paragraph continues:

Police forces/commands should not adopt blanket policies or presumptions either for or against the use of [CJPOA 1994] section 61.[183]

5.150 The 2006 Encampment Guidance also contains very important guidance for the police. At paragraph 46 it is stated that:

A senior police officer then considers whether it is appropriate to use the power, based on various factors:
- Whether there are other activities on the encampment, such as serious breaches of the peace, disorder, criminal activity or anti-social behaviour which would necessitate police involvement under their wider powers;
- Given the impact of the unauthorised encampment on the environment and the local settled community, is it reasonable and proportionate to use police powers;
- Is action by the police legally sustainable;
- Are sufficient resources available.

As with the 2004 Encampment Guidance and the Welsh Encampment Guidance, the clear implication is that the police powers of eviction should really only be utilised in more extreme or pressing circumstances.

5.151 It must be said that, if the local authority in whose area the encampment occurs is not involved in the process, it is difficult to see how

---

181 2004 Encampment Guidance para 5.10; Welsh Encampment Guidance para 5.9.
182 See paras 5.41–5.42, above, and the discussion of the *Fuller* case, above.
183 Welsh Encampment Guidance para 6.7.

the police can ensure that they take account of 'humanitarian considerations' without carrying out some kind of inquiry process themselves. Indeed, some police forces have specific policies that recommend just such a procedure.

In any event, it will be important for advisers to have a copy of the relevant police authority's policy on unauthorised encampments. Flagrant failure to follow written policies may also enable a public law challenge to be made.

5.152 Police powers of eviction were first introduced in the Public Order Act (POA) 1986. It is clear from the debates during the passage of POA 1986 and CJPOA 1994 through parliament, that the Conservative government intended that the legislation would primarily be used to deal with incidents of 'mass trespass'[184] and this fact gives weight to the argument that police powers of eviction should not be used as a matter of course or following every request from a landowner or occupier of land.

Government departments and other public authorities

5.153 Clearly, local authorities, which have certain powers and duties with regard to Gypsies and Travellers encamped in their area, are 'public authorities' for the purposes of the HRA 1998 and for the purpose of any potential public law challenge. What other bodies or organisations might come within the definition of 'public authority' in this context? A 'public authority', for the purposes of HRA 1998 s6, can either be a 'core public authority' which exercises functions which are broadly governmental or a 'hybrid public authority', some of whose functions are of a public nature.[185] It is not possible to give a definitve list of organisations that will be seen as 'public authorities' with regard to the eviction of an unauthorised encampment. In some cases it will be clear. The Forestry Commission comes under the auspices of the Department of the Environment, Food and Rural Affairs and will, therefore, be seen as a 'core public authority'. A housing association which manages Gypsy/Traveller sites for a local authority may be seen as a relevant 'public authority' with regard to encampments. Whether

---

184 For example, during the passage of CJPOA 1994, the Home Secretary stated: 'Local communities should not have to put up with, or even fear the prospect of, mass invasions by those who selfishly gather, regardless of the rights of others.' *Hansard, HC Debates*, col 29, 11 January 1994.

185 See *Poplar Housing and Regeneration Community Association Ltd v Donaghue* [2002] QB 48; [2001] 3 WLR 183; [2001] 4 All ER 604; *Aston Cantlow and Wilmcote with Billesley Parochial Church Council v Wallbank* [2003] UKHL 37; [2003] 3 WLR 283; and *YL v Birmingham CC* [2007] UKHL 27.

other organisations or bodies can come within the definition will depend on the particular circumstances, for example: the powers they are using; whether those powers are statutory or otherwise; the source of their finances; and the nature of their dealings with a particular encampment.

5.154   Up until recently, there was a long-running debate about the extent to which other public bodies needed to have regard to considerations of common humanity before deciding to evict Gypsies and Travellers from their land. DoE Circular 18/94 states, at paragraph 8:

> Where gypsies are unlawfully encamped on government-owned land, it is for the local authority, with the agreement of the land-owning department, to take any necessary steps to ensure that the encampment does not constitute a hazard to public health. It will continue to be the policy of the Secretary of State that government departments should act in conformity with the advice that unauthorised encampments should not normally be allowed to continue where they are causing a level of nuisance which cannot be effectively controlled, particularly where local authority authorised sites are available. The National Assembly for Wales will act in the same way.

5.155   It had been argued that government departments also have a duty to make direct inquiries themselves and to take into account humanitarian considerations and should not take eviction action in circumstances where an encampment on land that they own or occupy is not causing a nuisance.

5.156   Over recent years there has been a series of cases involving the Forestry Commission.[186] The Forestry Commission practice, when it becomes aware of an unauthorised encampment, has been to write to the local authority to bring the encampment to its attention and to suggest that the authority may like to investigate whether there are any welfare concerns. The standard letter used invites the authority (or authorities) to revert to the Forestry Commission if they want to make any submissions about the encampment following on from any welfare inquiries.[187] The problem with this procedure, as has been pointed out over the years to the Forestry Commission by Gypsies' and Travellers' solicitors and advisers, is that the local authority concerned is, perhaps, unlikely to take a proactive approach when the

---

186 Now part of the Department of the Environment, Food and Rural Affairs (DEFRA) but formerly part of the Ministry of Agriculture, Fisheries and Food (MAFF).

187 This approach was effectively approved in the case of *R v MAFF ex p Callaghan and others* (2000) 32 HLR 8.

encampment is not on its own land. This may result in no welfare inquiries being carried out.

5.157   The 2004 Encampment Guidance states:

> 5.7 ... The police and other public bodies who might be involved in dealing with unauthorised encampments do not have comparable duties [to local authorities] but must still, as public servants, show common humanity to those they meet.
>
> 5.8 The Human Rights Act (HRA) applies to all public bodies including local authorities (including town and parish councils), police, public bodies and the courts. With regard to eviction, the issue that must be determined is whether the interference with Gypsy/Traveller family life and home is justified and proportionate. Any particular welfare needs experienced by unauthorised campers are material in reaching a balanced and proportionate decision. The human rights of members of the settled community are also material if any authority fails to act to curb nuisance from an encampment.
>
> 5.9 Case law is still developing with regard to the sorts of welfare enquiries, which the courts consider necessary to properly taken decisions in relation to actions against unauthorised encampments. Cases are testing the requirements under different powers, and the requirements placed on different agencies (authorities, police, and other public landowners). Very generally, court decisions to date suggest:
> - All public authorities need to be able to demonstrate that they have taken into consideration any welfare needs of unauthorised campers prior to making a decision to evict.
> - The courts recognise that the police and other public bodies have different resources and welfare duties from local authorities. Generally the extent and detail of appropriate enquiries is less for police and non-local authority 'public authorities' ...
>
> 5.10 Because local authorities have appropriate skills and resources to enable them to make (or to co-ordinate) welfare enquiries, it is considered good practice for local authorities to respond positively to requests for assistance in making enquiries from the police or other public bodies.[188]

5.158   In *R (Kanssen) v Secretary of State for the Environment, Food and Rural Affairs (SSEFRA)*,[189] Owen J concluded that the Forestry Commission's practice of writing to the relevant local authorities was sufficient to comply with its obligations under common law and under government guidance. This is despite the fact that he also made it clear that the Forestry Commission must take account of any 'humanitarian

---

188   Welsh Encampment Guidance paras 5.7–5.9.
189   [2005] EWHC 1024 Admin.

considerations' that are put in front of it. Owen J also concluded that the Forestry Commission does not have power under the Forestry Act 1967 and the Countryside Act 1968 to provide sites for Gypsies and Travellers. Mr Kanssen's appeal to the Court of Appeal was refused permission to proceed.[190]

5.159   In light of the decision in *Kanssen* it will be important for advisers and solicitors who are assisting Gypsies or Travellers who are faced with eviction from non-local authority public authority land to bring welfare issues to the attention of the authority concerned. The authority will then need to consider those welfare issues before deciding whether to evict the encampment or whether to continue with any eviction process that is already commenced. It would also seem to be incumbent on local authorities and other public authority landowners in the area to develop joint strategies for dealing with unauthorised encampments and incumbent on local authorities to take a proactive approach to welfare inquiries when an encampment is on another public authority's land.

Other matters

Width of possession orders

5.160   It had been the practice of certain large landowners, when seeking a possession order against Gypsies or Travellers on an unauthorised encampment, to obtain an order not only covering the piece of land on which the encampment is situated but also covering other land in their ownership in the surrounding area. Recognition of this practice was to be found in the former notes to the CPR:

> Where a claimant, such as the Forestry Commission, owns a number of parcels of land in a particular area which are susceptible to unlawful occupation and is seeking possession in respect of one such parcel which is unlawfully occupied but apprehends that if the order is made the unlawful occupiers will move to one or more of the other parcels and seeks to include them in the possession order such other areas must be clearly defined ... The court can then include in the possession order those parcels to which on the evidence and the law the claimants are found to be entitled.[191]

---

190   *R (Kanssen) v SSEFRA* [2005] EWCA Civ 1453.

191   *Civil Procedure ('the White Book')* 2003, Vol 1, p1748. Reference is also made to the previous Forestry Commission practice of seeking orders covering a 20-mile radius around the encampment.

5.161   It is now clear from the decision in the case of *Drury v Secretary of State for the Environment, Food and Rural Affairs*[192] that the law as previously propounded in the notes to the CPR was incorrect. Ms Drury and other Travellers were encamped on a piece of woodland owned by the Forestry Commission. The Forestry Commission obtained a possession order covering the piece of woodland in question, but also 30 other pieces of woodland within a 20-mile radius of the encampment on the basis of an assertion made by the Forestry Commission that further unauthorised encampments would occur on other pieces of woodland in the area. The evidence adduced by the Forestry Commission in support of their assertion was minimal: reference was made to the fact that the registration plate on one of the vehicles involved in the current encampment was the same as the registration plate on a vehicle involved in an encampment on the same piece of woodland some five years previously and the fact that there had been a number of other unlawful encampments in the area over recent years (but no evidence was provided that these other encampments involved the Travellers on the encampment that was the subject of the action in *Drury*).

5.162   The Court of Appeal quashed the possession order obtained for the other 30 pieces of woodland. Wilson J stated:

> [I]f a claimant entitled to an order for possession of a certain area of land contends that its occupants are likely to decamp to a separate area of land owned by him, the separate area should in my view be included in the order for possession if, but only if, he would have been entitled to an injunction quia timet[193] against the occupants in relation to the separate area … It follows that the inclusion in a possession order of an area of land owned by the claimant which has not yet been occupied by the defendants should be exceptional. Although it would be foolish to be prescriptive about the nature of the necessary evidence, it seems safe to say that it will usually take the form either of an expression of intention to decamp to the other area or of a history of movement between the two areas from which a real danger of repetition can be inferred or … of such propinquity and similarity between the two areas as to command the inference of a real danger of decampment from one to the other.[194]

5.163   Though this decision is to be welcomed, it is suggested that it does not go far enough and that the legality of wide possession orders may require further consideration by the higher courts. Many advisers

192   [2004] EWCA Civ 200, April 2004 *Legal Action* 34.

193   In other words, an injunction in anticipation of an unlawful event or action. Such an injunction requires a very high level of cogent evidence.

194   [2004] EWCA Civ 200 at paras 20 and 21.

acting for Gypsies and Travellers consider that CPR Part 55 simply does not permit a court to grant possession for any land other than that on which an unauthorised encampment is situated. CPR Part 55 refers to the land occupied.[195] It should also be noted that an order covering other areas of land may encompass other Gypsies or Travellers who happen to be encamped on one of those other areas and who will, therefore, have no opportunity of putting their case forward. Nevertheless, for the moment, wide orders can be obtained, but only following the production of very cogent evidence and only in exceptional circumstances.

5.164   If a claimant is seeking a wide possession order covering parcels of land other than the area of land where the encampment is situated, they will also have to properly identify those other areas of land. In other words, certainty as to the identification of all areas of land concerned is essential. In *Christchurch BC v Thomas McDonagh*,[196] the borough council sought an order for possession of the car park where the Travellers were unlawfully encamped and for all other land in the borough council's ownership. The land, other than the car park, was not specified or described in the claim form or at court. At first instance, an order was made covering both the car park and all other land in the ownership of the borough council. On appeal in the county court the latter part of the order, with regard to all the other land, was quashed. The judge stated:

> The resulting order made by the court ... did not sufficiently identify the land to which it referred. It was suggested on behalf of Christchurch that the order could be amended to add to the order the words 'as shown on the terriers'.[197] This would not be sufficient to remedy the deficiency. It is unrealistic to expect travellers to be able to refer to records held by a local authority to discover whether land is owned by that authority.

The court also felt that the wider order originally obtained was 'disproportionate' having regard to the HRA 1998.

Injunctions

5.165   Occasionally local authorities will seek injunctions against Gypsies or Travellers who frequent their area and have no authorised place to stay. Sometimes the motivation for such an action by the local

---

195 CPR PD 55.5.
196 11 July 2002, Bournemouth County Court, HHJ Mastin.
197 The local authority records of land in its ownership.

authority will be allegations of nuisance or anti-social behaviour made against the Gypsies or Travellers concerned. However, sometimes the motivation will be simply to try to prevent the Gypsies or Travellers stopping on any land in the area on the basis of frequency or number of unauthorised encampments by the group of Gypsies or Travellers in question. Such injunctions will be brought under the powers contained in Local Government Act 1972 s222.

5.166   It is suggested that a decision to seek such an injunction may be susceptible to judicial review (though no definitive case-law on the matter exists as yet with regard to unauthorised encampments).[198] In *Stoke-on-Trent CC v B&Q (Retail) Ltd,*[199] it was held that it must be established that the defendant is not merely infringing the law but that he or she is deliberately or flagrantly flouting it before an injunction will be granted. It is also suggested that such an order would be disproportionate in terms of article 8 of the ECHR, especially since a less severe form of action[200] could be taken. Moreover, local authorities who seek such orders will ignore the government's recommendations in the 2004 Encampment Guidance which states at paragraph 4.4:

> All local authorities experiencing unauthorised encampments should provide either transit sites or stopping places to cater for Gypsies and Travellers moving within or passing through their area.

It is suggested that local authorities should not be allowed to ignore this recommendation and other similar recommendations contained within the 2004, 2006 and Welsh, Encampment Guidance by simply seeking to obtain injunctions banning certain groups of Gypsies or Travellers from their area.

Conclusion

5.167   The government position on unauthorised camping is made clear in the 2004 Encampment Guidance which at paragraph 4.2 states:

198   However, with regard to unauthorised developments (ie where the Gypsies or Travellers have not obtained planning permission to reside on the land) there is very extensive case-law, culminating in the case of *South Buckinghamshire DC v Porter* [2003] UKHL 26; [2004] 1 WLR 1953. For full discussion of this case, see chapter 4 at paras 4.169–4.189, above.

199   [1984] 2 All ER 332.

200   Such as, in the case of anti-social behaviour, an anti-social behaviour order under the Crime and Disorder Act 1998, or, in the case of an unauthorised encampment, a possession order.

In a context where the number of Gypsy caravans exceeds the number of authorised places where they can stop – which is the case in England – provision of suitable accommodation for Gypsies and Travellers must be seen as a vital part of an approach to dealing with unauthorised camping.[201]

5.168   The sometimes dire effects on Gypsies and Travellers of the lack of sites (of all sorts, including transit and emergency stopping places) are well documented. For example, the report from the Equality of Opportunity Committee of the National Assembly for Wales stated:

[S]ervice providers in the education and health fields both identified accommodation issues as one of the barriers to successful service provision in their area. Undoubtedly the lack of appropriate accommodation can be a significant barrier to education. Evictions from unauthorised sites can lead to a lack of continuity in education and discourage parents from seeking to register their children in the first place.[202]

5.169   The Institute for Public Policy Research (IPPR) has stated:

There is an unacceptable and persistent culture of linking anti-social behaviour and the accommodation needs of Travellers and Gypsies. Accommodation needs and anti-social behaviour are two completely separate issues and they must be dealt with as such, irrespective of the pressure, both political and social, to link the two. As was pointed out by many of those with whom we consulted ... this is not done with any other section of the community and would be considered racist under any other circumstances.[203]

5.170   The government now recognise the need to put the horse before the cart and to ensure that sites are provided in order to deal with the 'problem' of unauthorised encampments:

The most effective method of combating unauthorised camping is to provide sites in accessible locations for those Gypsies and Travellers who pass through their area. This may not be limited to official residential and transit sites; it might also include particular locations which have been identified in the district where Gypsies and Travellers can stop for limited and agreed short periods of time, without having any adverse impact on the settled community.[204]

---

201   Welsh Encampment Guidance para 4.2 is in virtually identical terms.
202   *Review of service provision for Gypsies and Travellers,* National Assembly for Wales, 2003, para 12.21. For further discussion of this, in the context of the law relating to education and health, see chapter 7, below.
203   Crawley, *Moving forward: the provision of accommodation for Travellers and Gypsies,* IPPR, 2004, p13.
204   2006 Encampment Guidance para 97.

5.171　Given the current lack of transit sites that the police can direct Gypsies or Travellers to, it remains to be seen how the police deal with their new powers under CJPOA 1994 ss62A–62E. Current indications are that police forces appreciate that these new powers cannot realistically be used until sufficient transit sites have been provided. In general, with regard to the CJPOA 1994 powers of eviction conferred on both the police and local authorities, the criminalisation of trespass[205] has often, due to the speed with which evictions can take place, precluded Gypsies and Travellers from effectively challenging such eviction actions where they believe that substantive defences or public law challenges may lie.

5.172　The law on how public bodies should deal with the conduct of welfare inquiries and the legality of wide possession orders is ripe for further development.

5.173　The following chapter looks at the homelessness legislation as it relates to Gypsies and Travellers. Where Gypsies or Travellers are on an unauthorised encampment on local authority land (where that encampment is not causing severe nuisance or disruption), and where the same Gypsies and Travellers have made a homeless application in the hope of obtaining an authorised pitch or piece of land, there is a strong argument for allowing that encampment to remain where it is while the homelessness application is progressed.[206]

5.174　Following the publication in February 2006 of Circular 1/06[207] and the 2006 Encampment Guidance, Gypsy and Traveller campaigners hope that all public bodies concerned will take a proactive approach to the provision of sites and thereby reduce the need to resort to the eviction of those camped on unauthorised sites.

205　First brought in, in terms of police powers, by the Public Order Act 1986.
206　For a full discussion of these issues, see chapter 6 at paras 6.86–6.95, below.
207　And with the new Welsh Planning Circular awaited.

CHAPTER 6

Homelessness as it relates to Gypsies and Travellers

6.1   Homelessness legislation

6.1   Introduction

6.5   Homelessness

6.9   Priority need

6.12   Intentional homelessness

6.13   Local connection

6.15   Preliminary duties

6.20   Principal duties

         Limited duties • Full duties

6.31   Local connection

6.33   Protection of property

6.37   Homelessness strategies

6.42   Code of guidance

6.43   Reviews and appeals

6.50   Criminal offences

6.51   Effect of the homelessness legislation on Gypsies and Travellers

6.51   *R (Margaret Price) v Carmarthenshire CC*

6.58   When is a Gypsy or Traveller regarded as being homeless?

6.63   Making a homeless application

6.69   Priority need

6.74   Intentional homelessness

6.83   Local connection
6.86   Suitable interim accommodation
6.96   The full duty to accommodate

6.103   Conclusion

Homelessness legislation

Introduction

6.1   This chapter aims to highlight aspects of the homelessness legislation in England and Wales which are of specific interest to and importance for Gypsies and Travellers. However, some broad idea of the law in this area is required and the first part of this chapter aims to provide that.[1]

6.2   The relevant statutory provisions are to be found in the Housing Act (HA) 1996 Pt VII, as amended by the Homelessness Act 2002.[2]

6.3   The HA 1996 places an obligation on local housing authorities to secure that suitable accommodation is available for a person who is:

- homeless;
- eligible for assistance;
- in priority need of accommodation;
- and who did not become homeless intentionally.

There are also other obligations imposed by HA 1996 which will be discussed further below.

6.4   There are two categories of person who are ineligible for assistance[3] (although they may still benefit from the general 'advice and information' duty):[4]

- 'persons from abroad', which means persons who are subject to immigration control under the Asylum and Immigration Act 1996, unless they are re-qualified by regulations;[5]

---

1   For a full coverage of homelessness, see Arden, Hunter and Johnson, *Homelessness and allocations*, Legal Action Group, 7th edn, 2006; and Luba and Davies, *Housing allocations and homelessness: law and practice*, Jordans, 2006.

2   For Scotland the relevant statute is the Housing (Scotland) Act 1987 as amended by the Housing (Scotland) Act 2001 and the Homelessness etc (Scotland) Act 2003. There is a widening gap between the situation in England and Wales and that in Scotland. The 2003 Act provides for the eventual abolition of categories of priority need and also provides for continuing duties towards intentionally homeless applicants. For Northern Ireland reference should be made to the Housing (Northern Ireland) Order 1988 as amended by the Housing (Northern Ireland) Order 2003.

3   The question of 'eligibility' can be a complex one and is beyond the scope of this book. For a full discussion of this issue see note 1, above.

4   HA 1996 s179.

5   HA 1996 s185(1) and (2).

- those asylum-seekers, or dependants of asylum-seekers, who are not excluded as 'persons from abroad', but who will still be ineligible for assistance if they have accommodation in the United Kingdom, however temporary, which is available for their occupation;[6]

This obviously may be of relevance to Roma from Eastern Europe. If an applicant is not within these categories or is within the first category ('persons from abroad') but is 're-included' by regulation, he or she will be 'eligible for assistance'.

Homelessness

6.5   HA 1996 s175 defines homelessness:

(1) A person is homeless if he has no accommodation available for his occupation, in the United Kingdom or elsewhere, which he –
   (a) is entitled to occupy by virtue of an interest in it or by virtue of an order of a court,
   (b) has an express or implied licence to occupy, or
   (c) occupies as a residence by virtue of any enactment or rule of law giving him the right to remain in occupation or restricting the right of another person to recover possession.
(2) A person is also homeless if he has accommodation but –
   (a) he cannot secure entry to it, or
   (b) it consists of a moveable structure, vehicle or vessel designed or adapted for human habitation and there is no place where he is entitled or permitted both to place it and reside in it.
(3) A person shall not be treated as having accommodation unless it is accommodation which it would be reasonable for him to continue to occupy.
(4) A person is threatened with homelessness if it is likely that he will become homeless within 28 days.

6.6   HA 1996 s175(2)(b) will be the most relevant provision for Gypsies and Travellers, though HA 1996 s175(3) may also be relevant for those Gypsies and Travellers that have left conventional housing.[7]

6.7   'Accommodation available for occupation' is defined by HA 1996 s176 thus:

Accommodation shall be regarded as available for a person's occupation only if it is available for occupation by him together with –

---

6   HA 1996 s186(1).
7   'Conventional housing', in this context, means bricks and mortar accommodation.

(a) any other person who normally resides with him as a member of his family, or

(b) any other person who might reasonably be expected to reside with him.[8]

6.8 The phrase 'reasonable to continue to occupy' is defined by HA 1996 s177 as follows:

(1) It is not reasonable for a person to continue to occupy accommodation if it is probable that this will lead to domestic violence or other violence against him, or against –

(a) a person who normally resides with him as a member of his family, or

(b) any other person who might reasonably be expected to reside with him ...

(2) In determining whether it would be, or would have been, reasonable for a person to continue to occupy accommodation, regard may be had to the general circumstances prevailing in relation to housing in the district of the local housing authority to whom he has applied for accommodation or for assistance in obtaining accommodation.

It is important to note that considerations of violence and the general housing circumstances of the area are not exhaustive of the matters to be taken into account when determining whether it is reasonable to continue to occupy accommodation or not.[9]

Priority need

6.9 HA 1996 s189 deals with 'priority need for accommodation':

(1) The following have a priority need for accommodation –

(a) a pregnant woman or a person with whom she resides or might reasonably be expected to reside;

(b) a person with whom dependent children reside or might reasonably be expected to reside;

(c) a person who is vulnerable as a result of old age, mental illness or handicap or physical disability or other special reason, or with whom such a person resides or might reasonably be expected to reside;

(d) a person who is homeless or threatened with homelessness as a result of an emergency such as flood, fire or other disaster.

---

8 The question of extended Gypsy and Traveller families is discussed at para 6.68, below

9 *R v Hammersmith & Fulham LBC ex p Duro-Rama* (1983) 9 HLR 71; *R v Swansea CC ex p Hearn* (1990) 23 HLR 372.

(2) The Secretary of State may by order –
  (a) specify further descriptions of persons as having a priority need for accommodation, and
  (b) amend or repeal any part of subsection (1).[10]

6.10   In Wales, the HA 1996 s189(2)(a) power has been used to specify:[11]

  (i) all those who are aged 18 or over, and under 21, if at any time while they were a child they were looked after, accommodated or fostered, or they are at particular risk of sexual or financial exploitation;
  (ii) all 16- and 17-year olds;
  (iii) those without dependent children who have been subject to domestic violence, who are at risk of such violence or would be if they returned home;
  (iv) those who formerly served in the regular armed forces and have been homeless since leaving those forces;
  (v) former prisoners who have been homeless since leaving custody, provided they have a local connection with the local housing authority.

6.11   In England, the section 189(2)(a) power has been used to specify:[12]

  (i) all 16- and 17-year olds, provided they are not a relevant child (as defined by the Children Act (CA) 1989), or a child to whom the local authority owes a duty to provide accommodation under CA 1989 s20;
  (ii) any person who is aged 18 to 20, other than a relevant student,[13] who at any time after reaching the age of 16 but while still under 18 was, but is no longer, looked after, accommodated or fostered;
  (iii) those who are vulnerable because they have previously been looked after, accommodated or fostered;
  (iv) those who are vulnerable as a result of service in Her Majesty's regular armed forces;
  (v) those who are vulnerable as a result of having served a custodial sentence, having been committed for contempt of court or having been remanded in custody;
  (vi) those who are vulnerable because they have had to cease to occupy accommodation because of violence or threats of violence which are likely to be carried out.

---

10 For a discussion of extended Gypsy and Traveller families, see para 6.68, below. 'Other special reason' is a category that may have specific relevance to single homeless Gypsies and Travellers, as discussed at paras 6.69–6.71, below.

11 Homeless Persons (Priority Need) (Wales) Order 2001 SI No 607.

12 Homelessness (Priority Need for Accommodation) (England) Order 2002 SI No 2051.

13 As defined by CA 1989 s24B(3).

Intentional homelessness

6.12   The phrase 'intentional homelessness' is defined in HA 1996 s191 as:

(1) A person becomes homeless intentionally if he deliberately does or fails to do anything in consequence of which he ceases to occupy accommodation which is available for his occupation and which it would have been reasonable for him to continue to occupy.

(2) For the purposes of subsection (1) an act or omission in good faith on the part of a person who was unaware of any relevant fact shall not be treated as deliberate.

(3) A person shall be treated as becoming homeless intentionally if –

(a) he enters into an arrangement under which he is required to cease to occupy accommodation which it would have been reasonable for him to continue to occupy, and

(b) the purpose of the arrangement is to enable him to become entitled to assistance under this Part,

and there is no other good reason why he is homeless.

There is a similar definition to cover the situation of becoming threatened with homelessness intentionally.[14]

Local connection

6.13   A person has a local connection with the district of a local housing authority if he or she has a connection with it because:

• he or she is, or was, normally resident there of his or her own choice;

• he or she is employed there;

• of family associations; or

• of special circumstances.[15]

6.14   A person in the regular armed forces will not be considered as either employed in the district or as resident in the district.[16] A person is not resident in a district if he or she is detained under the authority of an Act of parliament, for example, a prisoner or a patient in a mental hospital.[17] The secretary of state may specify other circumstances when someone will not be treated as either resident or employed in a district but this power has not been used to date.[18]

14 HA 1996 s196.
15 HA 1996 s199(1).
16 HA 1996 s199(2) and (3)(a).
17 HA 1996 s199(3)(b).
18 HA 1996 s199(5). The particular position of Gypsies and Travellers who may be moving around several districts or forced by frequent evictions to move around several districts, will be discussed at para 6.83, below.

Preliminary duties

6.15   Where a local authority has reason to believe that an applicant may be homeless or threatened with homelessness, it shall make such inquiries as are necessary to see whether:

- he or she is eligible for assistance; and
- if so, what duty, if any, might be owed to him or her.[19]

6.16   On completion of its inquiries, the local authority must notify the applicant of its decision in writing and, if it is against the interests of the applicant, must also notify him or her of the reasons for that decision.[20] The notification should also tell the applicant about his or her right to request a review of the decision (within 21 days).[21] Paragraph 3.18 of the English *Homelessness Code of Guidance*[22] states that:

> Wherever possible, it is recommended that housing authorities aim to complete their enquiries and notify the applicant of their decision within 33 working days of accepting a duty to make enquiries under s184. In many cases it should be possible for authorities to complete the inquiries significantly earlier.

Paragraph 12.22 of the Welsh *Code of Guidance for Local Authorities on Allocation of Accommodation and Homelessness*[23] recommends targets of 33 working days to decision and three working days for notification.

6.17   The local authority may also make inquiries into whether the applicant has a local connection with the district of another local housing authority in England, Wales or Scotland.[24] If the local authority decides to make a local connection referral to another authority,[25] it shall still notify the applicant of this decision and of the reasons for it.[26]

6.18   The notice required to be given to the applicant, if not received by him or her, shall be treated as having been given to him or her if it is made available at the authority's office for a reasonable period for collection by him or her.[27] In other words, the burden is on the applicant who does not receive the decision to go to the local authority's office and ask for it.

---

19   HA 1996 s184(1).
20   HA 1996 s184(3) and (6).
21   HA 1996 s184(5).
22   See further at para 6.56, below.
23   Issued April 2003.
24   HA 1996 s184(2).
25   See further at paras 6.13–6.14, above.
26   HA 1996 s184(4).
27   HA 1996 s184(6).

6.19   Inquiries might take some time to complete. Meanwhile, if the local housing authority has reason to believe that the applicant may be homeless, eligible for assistance and has a priority need, it has a duty to secure that accommodation is available for his or her occupation pending a decision as to what duty, if any, is owed to him or her.[28] The duty is placed on the authority to whom the applicant applies, regardless of any question about local connection.[29] The accommodation available must be available for occupation by the applicant, together with any other person who normally resides with him or her as a family member or any other person who might reasonably be expected to reside with him or her.[30] The duty to provide interim accommodation will end once an applicant has been notified of the local authority's decision. However, if the applicant requests a review of the decision then the local authority has the power to provide interim accommodation pending that review.[31]

Principal duties

6.20   The principal duties that may be owed to an applicant by a local housing authority can be divided into limited duties and full duties.

Limited duties

6.21   If the authority is satisfied that the applicant is homeless and in priority need but that he or she is intentionally homeless, it shall secure that accommodation is available for his or her occupation for such period as it considers will give the applicant a reasonable opportunity of securing accommodation for his or her occupation and provide him or her with appropriate advice and assistance to try and locate such accommodation.[32] Such advice and assistance should include information about the likely availability in the authority's district of types of accommodation appropriate to the applicant's housing needs.[33] This advice and assistance should be provided after the applicant's housing needs have been assessed.[34] In the case of Gypsies and Travellers, such infor-

28   HA 1996 s188(1) and see paras 6.86–6.95, below, for a more detailed discussion on the interim accommodation duty and its relevance to homeless applications made by Gypsies and Travellers.
29   HA 1996 s188(2).
30   HA 1996 s176.
31   HA 1996 s188(3).
32   HA 1996 s190(2).
33   HA 1996 s190(5), inserted by HA 2002 Sch 1 para 10.
34   HA 1996 s190(4), inserted by HA 2002 Sch 1 para 10.

mation should presumably include details of local authority or private Gypsy/Traveller sites in the district.

6.22   If the authority provides its own accommodation in order to comply with the above duty, it will not be secure unless and until the authority notifies the applicant otherwise under the allocation provisions.[35] If the authority fulfils its duty by arranging for accommodation with a private landlord, a tenancy granted in this way cannot be an assured tenancy before the end of the period of 12 months beginning with the date when the applicant was notified of the local authority's decision or the date of notification of the decision on review or appeal, unless during that period the landlord notifies the applicant otherwise.[36]

6.23   If the authority:

- is not satisfied that the applicant has a priority need; or
- is so satisfied but also concludes that he or she became threatened with homelessness intentionally,

it shall secure that he or she is provided (whether by the authority or by someone else) with advice and assistance in any attempts he or she may make to secure that accommodation does not cease to be available to him or her.[37] This advice and assistance should be provided after the applicant's housing needs have been assessed.[38] If homelessness does then occur, and the applicant is in priority need but intentionally homeless, a period of temporary accommodation[39] will then be available.

6.24   If the authority is satisfied that the applicant did not become homeless intentionally but is also satisfied that he or she is not in priority need, it may nevertheless secure that accommodation is available for occupation by the applicant.[40] If satisfied that the applicant is not in priority need but that he or she is threatened with homelessness, though not intentionally, the authority may take reasonable steps to secure that accommodation does not cease to be available.[41]

35   HA 1985 Sch 1 para 4, substituted by HA 1996 Sch 17 para 3. The allocation provisions under HA 1996 Pt VI are outside the scope of this book – see further in Arden, Hunter and Johnson, *Homelessness and allocations* and Luba and Davies *Housing allocations and homelessness*. No doubt, in terms of Gypsy sites under local authority control, there will usually be specific allocation policies that the local authority operates – see also chapter 3, above.
36   HA 1996 s209.
37   HA 1996 s195(5).
38   HA 1996 s195(6), inserted by HA 2002 Sch 1 para 14.
39   See para 6.21, above.
40   HA 1996 s192(3).
41   HA 1996 s195(9), inserted by HA 2002 s5(2).

6.25   Similarly, if the authority is satisfied that the applicant has a priority need and is threatened with homelessness, but not intentionally, it shall take reasonable steps to ensure that accommodation does not cease to be available for his or her occupation.[42] However, this duty cannot affect the right of the authority to obtain possession of its own accommodation.[43]

Full duties

6.26   Where a local authority is satisfied that an applicant is homeless, in priority need and not intentionally homeless, it shall secure that accommodation is available for occupation by the applicant.[44] The accommodation must also be available for any other family member who normally resides with him or her, or anyone else who might reasonably be expected to reside with him or her.[45]

6.27   A local housing authority may discharge this duty as follows:

- by securing that suitable accommodation provided by the authority is available;
- by securing that the applicant obtains suitable accommodation from some other person (which may include another local authority or a housing association); or
- by giving the applicant such advice and assistance as will secure that suitable accommodation is available from some other person.[46]

6.28   In deciding whether accommodation is 'suitable' for a person, the local housing authority shall have regard to certain provisions of the HA 1985 and the Housing Act (HA) 2004 which relate to hazardous housing, slum clearance, overcrowding and houses in multiple occupation.[47] The secretary of state can add to the definition of what is 'suitable' and has done so, particularly with regard to affordability of the accommodation.[48] So far as reasonably practicable, the authority shall ensure

---

42   HA 1996 s195(2).
43   HA 1996 s195(3).
44   HA 1996 s193(1) and (2).
45   HA 1996 s176 and see para 6.19, above.
46   HA 1996 s206(1).
47   HA 1996 s210(1).
48   HA 1996 s210(2). See the Homelessness (Suitability of Accommodation) Order 1996 SI 1996 No 3204; the Homelessness (Suitability of Accommodation) (England) Order 2003 SI No 3326; and the Homelessness (Suitability of Accommodation) (Wales) Order 2006 SI No 650. For a full discussion of 'suitable accommodation' as it relates to Gypsies and Travellers, see paras 6.86–6.102, below.

that accommodation is available for the occupation of the applicant in its district.[49] If an applicant is placed in another area, the authority must give notice to the local housing authority with responsibility for that area; any such notice must contain certain specified details[50] and must be given in writing within two weeks of the accommodation being made available.[51]

6.29   Where a local authority provides its own accommodation in discharge of the duty, it is not secure.[52] This is not normally relevant to a Gypsy or Traveller seeking other than bricks and mortar accommodation, since occupants of local authority Gypsy or Traveller sites currently have minimal security of tenure.[53]

6.30   The 'full duty' owed to the applicant can be brought to an end if:

- the applicant, having been informed by the authority of the possible consequences of refusal and his or her right to request a review, refuses an offer of accommodation which the authority is satisfied is suitable for him or her and the authority then notifies him or her that it considers that it has discharged its duty;
- the applicant ceases to be eligible for assistance;
- the applicant becomes homeless intentionally from the accommodation made available for his or her accommodation;
- the applicant accepts an offer under HA 1996 Pt VI (the allocation provisions);
- the applicant accepts an offer of an assured (not an assured shorthold) tenancy from a private landlord;
- the applicant otherwise voluntarily ceases to occupy as his or her only or principal home the accommodation made available for his or her occupation;
- the applicant, having been informed of the possible consequences of refusal and his or her right to request a review of the suitability of the accommodation, refuses a final offer (which is defined as an offer 'made in writing' stating 'that it is a final offer for the purposes of [HA 1996 s193(7)]'[54]) and the authority is satisfied that the

49   HA 1996 s208(1).
50   HA 1996 s208(2) and (3).
51   HA 1996 s208(4).
52   HA 1985 Sch 1 para 4.
53   See chapter 3, above.
54   HA 1996 s193(7A).

offer is suitable and that it is reasonable for the applicant to accept the offer;
• the applicant, in certain circumstances, accepts the offer of an assured shorthold tenancy from a private landlord.[55]

Local connection

6.31 The local connection provisions allow one local housing authority to transfer the responsibility of ensuring that accommodation becomes available to another authority where:

• the applicant was placed in accommodation in that area by another local housing authority in the first place;[56] or
• neither the applicant nor any person who might reasonably be expected to reside with him or her has a local connection with the district of the authority they are applying to, and the applicant or a person who might reasonably be expected to reside with him or her has a local connection with the district of another authority, and neither the applicant nor a person who might reasonably be expected to reside with him or her will run the risk of domestic violence in that other area.[57]

6.32 The definition of what amounts to 'local connection' is supplemented by the Local Authority Agreement, which is discussed in further detail at paras 6.83–6.85, below. The applicant can request a review of a local authority's decision that she or he has a local connection.[58] There is an arbitration system put in place to deal with disagreements between local authorities.[59] The arbitration decision itself can be subject to review and appeal.[60]

Protection of property

6.33 Where a local authority is or has been under a duty under HA 1996 ss188, 190, 193, 195 or 200,[61] it may also be under a duty to take

55 HA 1996 s193(5)–(8). For fuller details see Arden, Hunter and Johnson, *Homelessness and allocations* and Luba and Davies *Housing allocations and homelessness*.
56 HA 1996 s198(4). See para 6.13, above.
57 HA 1996 s198(2).
58 HA 1996 s200(2).
59 HA 1996 s198(5).
60 HA 1996 s202(1)(d) and (e).
61 See paras 6.19, 6.21, 6.23, 6.26 and 6.32, above.

reasonable steps to prevent the loss of an applicant's property, or prevent or mitigate damage to it.[62] An applicant's property includes the personal property of any person reasonably expected to reside with him or
her.[63]

6.34   The duty arises where the local authority has reason to believe that
there is a danger of loss of, or damage to, any personal property of an
applicant by reason of his or her inability to protect it or deal with it, and
no other suitable arrangements have been or are being made.[64]

6.35   In other circumstances, the local authority has a power to protect
property.[65] The local authority, when agreeing to protect property under
these provisions, can impose reasonable charges and conditions as to
the disposal of property.[66] These provisions are not reviewable but
could be subject to public law challenge by way of judicial review.[67]

6.36   These provisions might be most relevant to Gypsies and Travellers
who have decided to seek conventional housing. For example, such
applicants may require storage for their caravans pending the provision
of suitable accommodation.

Homelessness strategies

6.37   The Homelessness Act (HA) 2002 imposed a new duty on local authorities to carry out a homelessness review and to formulate and publish
a homelessness strategy based on the results of that review.[68]

6.38   A homelessness review means a review by a local authority of:

(a) the levels, and likely future levels, of homelessness in its district;
(b) the activities which are carried out for any purpose mentioned in
   para 6.39, below, (or which contribute to their achievement); and
(c) the resources available to the housing authority, the social services
   authority for their district, other public authorities, voluntary organisations and other persons for such activities.[69]

6.39   The purposes of the review are:

(a) preventing homelessness in the district of the authority;

---

62   HA 1996 s211(2).
63   HA 1996 s211(5).
64   HA 1996 s211(1).
65   HA 1996 s211(3).
66   HA 1996 s211(4).
67   For a fuller discussion of judicial review, see appendix A, below.
68   HA 2002 s1(1) and (3).
69   HA 2002 s2(1).

(b) securing that accommodation is or will be available for people in the district who are or may become homeless;

(c) providing support for people in the district –
- who are or may become homeless; or
- who have been homeless and need support to prevent them becoming homeless again.[70]

6.40　A homelessness strategy is a strategy formulated by a local housing authority to deal with those matters mentioned in para 6.39, above.[71]

6.41　Research by Lord Avebury[72] has shown that the majority of local authorities that had recorded unauthorised encampments in their district[73] had failed to even mention Gypsies and Travellers in their review and strategy. It is difficult to see how local authorities can properly deal with applications from homeless Gypsies and Travellers if they have failed to even address those needs in their strategy. It is further suggested that the strategy should include an assessment of available land in the local authority area and the possibility of assistance from other public authorities, neighbouring local authorities or (where relevant) the county council.[74]

Code of guidance

6.42　In the exercise of their functions under the homelessness provisions of HA 1996, local authorities are bound to have regard to such guidance as may from time to time be given by the secretary of state.[75] The secretary of state has issued a code of guidance.[76]

70　HA 2002 s2(2).

71　HA 2002 s3(1).

72　The peer who, as Eric Lubbock MP, sponsored the private members bill that became the Caravan Sites Act 1968. The research showed that, of 152 local authorities whose strategies were checked, 107 (70.4 %) did not mention Gypsies or Travellers.

73　According to the Gypsy Count figures at that time carried out by the Office of the Deputy Prime Minister (ODPM) but now carried out by Communities and Local Government (CLG).

74　See para 6.98, below.

75　HA 1996 s182.

76　English *Homelessness Code of Guidance for Local Authorities*. The latest code was issued by CLG on 2 September 2006.

Reviews and appeals

6.43   Applicants have a statutory right to request an internal review[77] of any
of the following decisions regarding:

- eligibility for assistance;
- what duty is owed to an applicant found to be homeless or threatened with homelessness;
- referral to another authority under the local connection provisions;
- whether the conditions for local connection referral are met;
- what duty is owed following a local connection referral; or
- any decision about the suitability of accommodation offered in discharge of duty.

6.44   The right to a review does not include the right to a review of an earlier
decision made following a review.[78] If the local authority in question has
a procedure involving a further 'review' stage, it is important that the
Gypsy or Traveller (or their adviser or solicitor) obtain confirmation
that the previous decision no longer stands, otherwise, it will be necessary to appeal to the county court within the necessary time limit
from the original review decision.[79]

6.45   Pending the outcome of the review, the local authority has a discretion to provide accommodation for the applicant.[80]

6.46   An appeal can be made to the county court if the applicant either:

- is dissatisfied with the outcome of the review; or
- has not been notified of the outcome within the time limit prescribed.[81]

6.47   Appeal lies only on a point of law, whether arising from the original
decision (if the local authority has failed to conclude the review within
the time prescribed) or from the decision on review.[82]

6.48   Pending an appeal, the local authority has a discretion to provide
accommodation for the applicant.[83] If the authority refuses or fails to
do so, the applicant may also appeal that decision to the county court.[84]

---

77   HA 1996 s202.
78   HA 1996 s202(2).
79   *Demetri v Westminster CC* [2000] 1 WLR 772.
80   HA 1996 s188(3).
81   HA 1996 s204(1).
82   HA 1996 s204(1).
83   HA 1996 s204(4).
84   HA 1996 s204A.

6.49   The procedures to be adopted on review and on appeal to the county court are detailed in appendix A, below.

Criminal offences

6.50   It is a criminal offence knowingly or recklessly to make a statement which is false in a material particular, or knowingly to withhold information which an authority has reasonably required in connection with the exercise of its functions under the homelessness legislation, with intent to induce an authority to believe that the person making the statement or withholding the information, or any other person, is entitled to accommodation or assistance.[85]

Effect of the homelessness legislation on Gypsies and Travellers

R (Margaret Price) v Carmarthenshire CC[86]

6.51   Mrs Price and her family are Irish Travellers and were homeless in terms of the legislation because they were living on an unauthorised encampment and did not have an authorised pitch for their caravans.[87] The family had been resorting to Carmarthenshire for several years and applied to the local authority for homeless persons accommodation. In 2001 Mrs Price had made an inquiry about conventional (that is, bricks and mortar) accommodation. When she made her subsequent homeless application to the local authority, Mrs Price explained that she had made her earlier inquiry purely because of pressure from a local authority officer and that she had had no intention of moving into conventional housing.

6.52   In the planning case of *Clarke v Secretary of State for the Environment Transport and the Regions*,[88] the High Court (later upheld by the Court of Appeal) had overturned the decision of a planning inspector who had refused planning permission to Mr Clarke, a Romani Gypsy, in circumstances where the inspector had taken into account a previous

---

85 HA 1996 s214(1).
86 [2003] EWHC 42 Admin; March 2003 *Legal Action* 30.
87 HA 1996 s175(2)(b) – see para 6.5, above.
88 *Clarke v Secretary of State for the Environment, Transport and the Regions and Tunbridge Wells BC* [2001] EWHC 800 Admin; [2002] JPL 552; July 2002 *Legal Action* 23. For full discussion of this case see chapter 2 at paras 2.90–2.91 and chapter 4 at paras 4.120–4.124, above.

offer of settled accommodation that had been made to him by the local authority. Burton J, at first instance, stated that, if an 'aversion to conventional housing' were established then 'bricks and mortar, if offered, are unsuitable, just as would be the offer of a rat-infested barn'.[89]

6.53   In Mrs Price's case, the local authority had regard to the *Clarke* decision, but concluded from the facts of Mrs Price's case (including the fact that her mother, who had previously travelled, now lived in a bungalow due to ill-health, and her sister, who travelled with her, had previously lived in settled accommodation for a short period of time) that she did not have a 'cultural aversion to conventional housing'. It offered her a house which she refused. It then sought to evict her from the piece of its own land where it had, until then, been 'tolerating' her encampment. Mrs Price sought judicial review of the local authority's decision.

6.54   In the High Court, Newman J quashed the decision to evict, stating:

> In order to meet the requirements and accord respect, something more than 'taking account' of an applicant's gypsy culture is required. As the court in Chapman[90] stated, respect includes the positive obligation to act so as to facilitate the gypsy way of life, without being under a duty to guarantee it to an applicant in any particular case.[91]

6.55   Newman J also found that, in seeking to respect her Gypsy way of life, the local authority's approach was flawed because it had given too much weight to the fact that she had seemingly been prepared to give it up to live in conventional housing in 2001 and had used this as sufficient reason for disregarding her Gypsy way of life altogether when considering her wishes. Equally he found that, had the local authority reached the conclusion that her cultural commitment to traditional life was so powerful as to present great difficulty in her living in conventional housing, the local authority was not bound by duty to find her a pitch, but her cultural commitment would have been a significant factor in considering how far the authority should go to facilitate her traditional way of life.

6.56   Following on from the *Margaret Price* case, the government has, in its most recent version of the English *Homelessness Code of Guidance for Local Authorities*,[92] amended the section that deals with homeless Gypsies and Travellers. That section now states:

---

89 [2001] EWHC 800 Admin at para 34.
90 *Chapman v UK* (2001) 33 EHRR 399 and see chapter 2, above.
91 *R (Margaret Price) v Carmarthenshire CC* [2003] EWHC 42 Admin at para 19.
92 Issued by CLG on 2 September 2006.

Where a duty to secure accommodation [for a Gypsy or Traveller] arises but an appropriate site is not immediately available, the housing authority may need to provide an alternative temporary solution until a suitable site or some other suitable option, becomes available. Some Gypsies and Travellers may have a cultural aversion to the prospect of 'bricks and mortar' accommodation. In such cases, the authority should seek to provide an alternative solution.[93]

The reference in the previous English Code to homeless Gypsies and Travellers had been criticised in the *Price* case. Unfortunately a very similar reference remains in paragraph 18.40 of the Welsh *Code of Guidance for Local Authorities on Allocation of Accommodation and Homelessness* where it is stated that:

[A]pplications [by Gypsies and Travellers] must be considered on the same basis as all other applicants. If no pitch or berth is available to enable them to resume occupation of their moveable home, it is open to the housing authority to discharge its homelessness obligations by arranging for some other form of suitable accommodation to be made available.

6.57   There is no reason why houseboat dwellers might not be able to avail themselves of the court's decision in the *Price* case.

When is a Gypsy or Traveller regarded as being homeless?

6.58   A Gypsy or Traveller is homeless if there is no place where he or she is entitled or permitted to place his or her caravan or vehicle.[94] In this context, what do the words 'entitled' or 'permitted' mean?

6.59   In *R v Chiltern DC ex p Roberts et al*,[95] the applicants were Travelling Showpeople who had lost their winter accommodation. They were travelling in connection with their work during the summer months when they made their application. When travelling from fair to fair, they were permitted to stay on land provided by the organisers of the fairs. They were held not to be 'homeless' since, at the time of the application, they were 'permitted' to stop in various places.

6.60   In *Smith v Wokingham DC*,[96] the applicants were parked in a caravan on land belonging to the county council. Though they had no express permission or licence, they had lived at this encampment for

93   CLG English *Homelessness Code of Guidance for Local Authorities* para 16.38.
94   HA 1996 s175(2)(b).
95   (1990) 23 HLR 387, QBD.
96   April 1980 *LAG Bulletin* 92, CC.

two-and-a-half years. The county court judge decided that this amounted
to 'permission' and, accordingly, that they were not homeless.

6.61   In *R (O'Donoghue) v Brighton and Hove CC*,[97] the applicant had
been allowed to place her caravans on a piece of land owned by the
local authority for a 'tolerated' period of 30 days. Once that period had
ended, she made a homelessness application to the authority. The
authority decided that she was not homeless and, therefore, that it did
not, at that stage, owe her any duty to provide interim accommodation. No eviction action had yet been commenced by the local authority. In refusing permission to proceed with a judicial review application
concerning the failure to provide interim accommodation, Jackson J
held that the applicant had effectively been given implicit permission
to remain before eviction action was commenced and that the judicial review application was premature. When refusing permission to
appeal that decision, the Court of Appeal agreed that the application for
judicial review was premature because no eviction action had been
taken but accepted that it was arguable that the applicant no longer
had permission to remain on the land and that she was homeless at the
time that she made her application.

6.62   *Steward v Royal Borough of Kingston-upon-Thames*[98] was a case taken
by a homeless New Traveller who challenged a finding that she had
made herself intentionally homeless when she had left conventional
housing some years previously.[99] Reliance was placed upon the
O'Donoghue decision, since Ms Steward had managed to remain on a
number of unauthorised sites for long periods of time (in one case
for over a year) before any eviction action was commenced. Ms Steward argued: that her encampment on those sites had been 'permitted'; that each occasion on which she was evicted from those sites
amounted to a new incidence of homelessness; and that the investigation of any potential intentionality should relate to that new incident. In rejecting that argument, the Court of Appeal gave the word
'permitted' a restricted meaning. For an encampment to be 'permitted',
there would need to be some positive indication from the landowner
that the Gypsies or Travellers could remain for the time being (rather
than simply inaction or failure to commence eviction action), albeit
that such indication might fall short of amounting to a licence. Buxton
LJ accepted the finding of the judge at first instance who had stated:

97 [2003] EWCA Civ 459.
98 [2007] EWCA Civ 565.
99 See further at para 6.81, below.

I accept the submissions of counsel [for the local authority], that unlawful occupation of disused sites as [a] trespasser, from which he could have been evicted at any time if the landowner chose, is far removed from settled accommodation.[100]

Making a homeless application

6.63   A homeless Gypsy or Traveller has to make a homelessness application to a local authority before any of these matters can be considered.

6.64   Gypsies and Travellers can encounter considerable problems when first trying to make an application. Some authorities may try to put them on the ordinary housing register or may say that they are not homeless because they have their caravan or caravans. They might be turned away because they are told that the authority only has conventional housing. This is unlawful. A local authority that has reason to believe that an applicant may be homeless or threatened with homelessness must investigate the matter further and must accept and process an application from that applicant.[101] In *R (Aweys and ors) v Birmingham CC*, Collins J stated:

> It is apparent that the threshold for the duty of Councils to act under s184 is a low one ... since it arises if they have reason to believe the applicant may be homeless or threatened with homelessness. In the vast majority of cases, the making of the application will mean that it is difficult if not impossible for the Council not to believe that the applicant may be homeless or threatened with homelessness. Furthermore, no particular form of application is prescribed. This is not surprising since the provisions are dealing with people who are likely to be vulnerable and who cannot be expected to have obtained legal advice or to have an acquaintance with the statutory provisions. If it is apparent from what is said by an applicant (for there is no requirement that an application be in writing) or from anything in writing that he may be homeless or threatened with homelessness, the duty is triggered.[102]

6.65   Many Gypsies and Travellers are illiterate or have limited literacy skills. As a consequence, they may encounter difficulties when making homelessness applications. It is important to remember that an application under the homelessness legislation does not have to be made in any particular form (as Collins J explained in *Aweys*). In the earlier case

---

100   [2007] EWCA Civ 565 at para 11.
101   HA 1996 s184(1) – and see para 6.15, above.
102   [2007] EWHC 52 Admin at para 8.

of *Roberts*,[103] a letter from the applicants' solicitors, giving appropriate particulars in a schedule, was held to amount to an application. Though *Aweys* makes it clear that applications can be made orally, it is advisable that they are made in writing so as to ensure that there is a record of the application having been made and the details of the application. It is suggested that a written application could include some or all of the following information:

- details and dates of birth of the applicant and his or her family (if any);
- previous accommodation over, say, the last five years[104] – in many cases, the applicant will have been moving frequently from one unauthorised encampment to another and it is suggested that a general history of encampments, concentrating in particular on the districts or areas in which he or she had been residing, would be sufficient;
- details of health problems if 'priority need' is in question;
- details of schools, colleges and employment (to ensure that the local authority focuses on the provision of suitable accommodation within a reasonable distance of such educational establishments and/or areas in which work is undertaken);
- details of local connections, including reference to other family members in the area (to address the issue of 'local connection');
- if the applicant has previously occupied conventional housing, then the local authority should be told why that accommodation was vacated (to address the question whether the applicant is intentionally homeless).[105]

6.66   Though a local authority may insist, as part of its own homelessness procedures, on an interview and/or the completion of an application form, the important point here is that a letter written by the applicant's advisers will clearly be sufficient to ensure that the local authority investigates whether the applicant is eligible for assistance and whether it owes any duty to him or her. Additionally, application forms that are used typically do not cater for the needs of Gypsies and Travellers. For example, there may be no optional box for indicating that the applicant requires an authorised site or pitch for their caravan or vehicle. It may be wise for a solicitor or adviser to assist their client in

---

103   *R v Chiltern DC ex p Roberts et al* (1990) 23 HLR 387, QBD, and see para 6.59, above.

104   See the discussion of 'local connection' at paras 6.83–6.85, below.

105   See paras 6.74–6.82, below.

Member of the Rawlings family and wagon 1990   ©Barry Lewis/Alamy

Romani Gypsy wagons at Appleby Horse Fair ©Ian Simpson/Alamy

Appleby Horse Fair ©Janine Wiedel Photolibrary/Alamy

Appleby Horse Fair 2006 © Vic Pigula / Alamy
Inset: Study of two Travellers at Appleby Horse Fair © John Baxter / Alamy

Southall Horse Market, West London © Niall McDiarmid / Alamy

Irish Travellers in County Kerry, Ireland in 1961 © POPPERFOTO / Alamy

Road sign outside Clays Lane Gypsy site © Jeremy Trew, Trewimage / Alamy

Clays Lane Gypsy Site, East London – the site was compulsorily purchased to make way for the 2012 Olympic Games © LondonPhotos – Homer Sykes / Alamy

Photo taken by a child on an
unauthorised site in East London
© Caroline Christie and Bobby Lloyd,
On Site Arts

Johnny Delaney 1988-2003
© Delaney family

Mrs Porter's grandson – two for the pot! © Porter family

Woman and children inside caravan, Chelston Meadows, Plymouth 1984 © Sara Hannant

New Traveller at Braypool/Horsdean unauthorised encampment, East Sussex, 2000
© Neil Ansell

Man sitting in front of Mongolian Yurt at Tinker's Bubble, a low impact living community near Yeovil, Somerset © Sara Hannant

Gypsy man at Stow in the Wold Fair in 2000 © Andrew Fox / Alamy

filling in such a form to ensure that no misunderstandings arise. The local authority to whom the application is made could be asked to send any application form to the adviser or solicitor so that they can assist their client in completing it.

6.67   If a local authority insists on a formal interview taking place where a Gypsy or Traveller has made a homeless application then it may be wise, if possible, for someone (for example, from a local Gypsy or Traveller support group) to accompany the applicant to the interview to ensure, once again, that the local authority processes the application correctly. Those advising Gypsies and Travellers have met with many instances where, for example, applicants have simply been turned away by local authorities without a formal application having been accepted or where it transpires that the local authority has processed the application on the basis that it is for conventional, 'bricks and mortar' accommodation when the applicants specifically requested a site for their caravans. Practical support for the applicant can, therefore, be very important.

6.68   Some Gypsy and Traveller families travel around as an extended family group. This is especially so with Irish Travellers.[106] If an extended family group has always travelled together, it could be argued that one application should be taken from the whole group rather than a series of applications from each 'household'. This argument is based on HA 1996 s176:

> Accommodation shall be regarded as available for a person's occupation only if it is available for occupation by him together with –
> (a) *any other person who normally resides with him as a member of his family* or
> (b) *any other person who might reasonably be expected to reside with him...* (emphasis added).

The Homelessness Code of Guidance does not refer to 'extended families'. There is, as yet, no case-law on this particular point except that, in the context of a decision as to which family members of an extended family were to be accommodated in discharge of duty as persons who 'might reasonably be expected to reside with' the applicant, Simon Brown J in *R v Lambeth LBC ex p Ly* stated:

> [I]t is a question of fact to be decided by the local authority. Moreover, in determining this question of fact, it seems to me that many different considerations may well come into play. Certainly it will be pertinent always

---

106   See, for example, McDonagh, 'Nomadism' in *Travellers: citizens of Ireland, The Parish of the Travelling People*, Dublin, 2000, pp33–46.

to consider the true nature and ambit of the family unit concerned and questions of blood relationship, dependency and so forth within the family; dependency, that is, both emotional and financial.[107].

Priority need[108]

6.69　In the case of _Myhill and Faith v Wealden DC_,[109] the applicants, who were single men, argued that they were 'vulnerable' for some 'other special reason' for the purposes of HA 1996 s189(1)(c) on the basis that:

- as Travellers they were statistically far more likely to be homeless than the general population – the government statistics presented to the court, which were not challenged by the local authority, indicated that whereas 1.2 per cent of settled households were homeless, 18 per cent (at that time) of Gypsies and Travellers were homeless;
- Gypsies and Travellers were much less likely to be able to find accommodation due to the acknowledged lack of sites;
- while on unauthorised encampments, Gypsies and Travellers faced possible criminal prosecution under the Criminal Justice and Public Order Act 1994.

6.70　The county court judge rejected these arguments. He relied on the following quote from the judgment of Hobhouse LJ in one of the leading cases on 'priority need', _R v Camden LBC ex p Pereira_:

> The Council must ask itself whether the applicant is, when homeless, less able to fend for himself than an ordinary homeless person so that injury or detriment to him will result when a less vulnerable person would be able to cope without harmful effects ...[110]

6.71　In refusing permission to appeal to the Court of Appeal, Buxton LJ stated:

> The focus [in the above quote] is quite clearly on the ability of the individual to deal with the condition of homelessness, rather than on the question to which the statistics and oral arguments in this case go, of how likely it is that the persons when they become homeless will remain such.[111]

6.72　A person who is homeless or threatened with homelessness as a result of an emergency, such as flood, fire or other disaster, is also in

---

107 (1986) 19 HLR 51 at 55.
108 See paras 6.9–6.11, above, for the details of the categories of 'priority need'.
109 [2004] EWCA Civ 224; April 2004 _Legal Action_ 34; 23 November 2003, Tunbridge Wells County Court.
110 (1999) 31 HLR 317 at 330.
111 _Myhill and Faith v Wealden DC_ [2004] EWCA Civ 224 at para 5.

'priority need'.[112] In the case of *Scott-Higgs v Brighton and Hove CC*,[113] the single applicant had been residing in his caravan on an unauthorised encampment. The local authority obtained a possession order against him but had not yet enforced the order when, after going out one day, the applicant returned to find his caravan had disappeared (it was never established what happened to the caravan). He applied as a homeless person to the local authority for accommodation. He claimed that the loss of his caravan should mean that he was in priority need. The local authority found him not to be in priority need. The judge at first instance upheld this decision. On appeal, the Court of Appeal stated that the loss of one's caravan in such circumstances could come within the definition of 'flood, fire or other disaster', but that his homelessness was not as a result of this event. He was already homeless since he did not have an authorised place to pitch his caravan. He could not, therefore, be said to be in priority need. It should be noted that, if Mr Scott-Higgs had been on an authorised encampment (for example a licensee on a local authority site) and his caravan had disappeared, then he would have been in priority need. In other words, in such a situation, the loss of the caravan would have caused his homelessness.

6.73   In the absence of any duty to provide sites,[114] there remains a huge problem for homeless Gypsies and Travellers who (especially in the light of the *Myhill and Faith* case) are not considered to be in priority need.

Intentional homelessness

6.74   A local authority will only conclude that a person is intentionally homeless if he or she has deliberately done or failed to do something in consequence of which he or she has ceased to occupy accommodation which is available for his or her occupation and which it would have been reasonable for him or her to continue to occupy.[115] Thus, it is clear that there must be a causal link between a person's deliberate act or omission and the loss of accommodation; a person can only be considered to be intentionally homeless if his or her deliberate act or omission caused the homelessness.

6.75   There have been a number of cases where the courts have had to consider whether the causal link or 'chain of causation' has been broken by an intervening event. For example, in *Din v Wandsworth*

---

112   HA 1996 s189(1)(d).

113   [2003] 3 All ER 753, CA.

114   Repealed by the Criminal Justice and Public Order Act 1994.

115   See para 6.12, above, and HA 1996 s191(1).

LBC,[116] the House of Lords held that the chain of causation will be broken in circumstances where a person has lived in 'settled accommodation'[117] for a period of time.

6.76   More recently, in *R v Harrow LBC ex p Fahia*,[118] the applicant had been found intentionally homeless and was placed in a guest-house where she remained for over a year. She was evicted from the guest house when her housing benefit was cut (through no fault of her own) and she could no longer afford the rent. The local authority did not accept that the period of time in the guest house amounted to 'settled accommodation'. However, the Court of Appeal allowed the homeless applicant's appeal. It held that events other than securing settled accommodation could break the chain of causation and ordered that the local authority reconsider whether the change in the applicant's entitlement to housing benefit amounted to such an event.

6.77   Similarly, in *R v Basingstoke and Deane DC ex p Bassett*,[119] the fact that the applicant had spent a period of time staying with her sister-in-law (an arrangement which it was accepted the applicant was entitled to believe would continue but ceased when her sister-in-law separated from her husband and left the accommodation) was held to break the chain of causation.

6.78   By way of contrast, in *R v Hackney LBC ex p Ajayi*,[120] the applicant had left accommodation in Nigeria to come to London. After staying with various friends for short periods, she moved in with another friend in January 1996, just as she discovered that she was pregnant. When the baby was born, her friend asked her to leave. It was held that the chain of causation had not been broken and that the decision that she was 'intentionally homeless' because of leaving the accommodation in Nigeria, was correct.

6.79   These cases indicate that it will very much be a matter of fact and degree, based on the circumstances of an individual case, as to whether the chain of causation has been broken.

6.80   It is not uncommon for homeless Gypsies and Travellers to have previously lived in 'bricks and mortar' accommodation for a period of time and the vast majority of New Travellers will, at one time or another,

---

116   [1983] 1 AC 657.
117   The question of what constitutes 'settled accommodation' has been considered by the courts in a number of cases. For further discussion see Arden, Hunter and Johnson, *Homelessness and allocations* and Luba and Davies *Housing allocations and homelessness*.
118   [1998] 1 WLR 1396.
119   (1983) 10 HLR 125, QBD.
120   (1997) 30 HLR 473, QBD.

have lived in conventional housing.[121] When considering whether a Gypsy or Traveller is intentionally homeless a local authority will pay particular attention to any periods that he or she spent living in bricks and mortar to see whether the applicant ceased to occupy the accommodation as a result of a deliberate act or omission or whether he or she left such accommodation in circumstances where it was reasonable for him or her to continue to occupy it.

6.81   In *Steward v Royal Borough of Kingston-upon-Thames*,[122] Ms Steward had left conventional housing some years previously to move onto the road. On applying as homeless to the local authority, she was found to be intentionally homeless. The Court of Appeal held that Ms Steward's encampment on a number of unauthorised sites for lengthy periods of time without eviction action did not break the 'chain of causation'. However, the chain might be broken, in other circumstances, if it could be said that an encampment was 'permitted', for example, if a local authority or landowner gives a Gypsy or Traveller a positive indication that he or she will be able to stay on an unauthorised site for a lengthy period of time.

6.82   Where a Gypsy or Traveller has been found intentionally homeless because he or she left conventional housing, the solicitor or adviser assisting them on a review or appeal will have to examine the past history of accommodation carefully and avoid taking matters at face value. For example:

- if a Gypsy or Traveller leaves conventional housing because it transpires that he or she has a psychological aversion to 'bricks and mortar', it may not be possible to say that he or she left the accommodation and became homeless as a result of a deliberate act or omission and it can be argued that it was not reasonable for him or her to continue to occupy the accommodation – in such a case expert evidence from a psychologist or other relevant professionals should be obtained;
- if a New Traveller only ever lived in insecure accommodation (such as a 'squat') it may be argued that the accommodation did not amount to settled accommodation;
- a previous eviction from conventional housing may not have been the fault of the Gypsy or Traveller applicant, for example, it may

121 The casework of the Travellers' Advice Team at the Community Law Partnership demonstrates that there are now adult New Travellers who were born on the road and have never lived in conventional housing, though they remain very much a minority of the New Traveller population – there are no official statistics available.

122 [2007] EWCA Civ 565. See also para 6.62, above.

have been because of housing benefit department errors which led
to rent arrears in circumstances where the Gypsy or Traveller applicant did not realise that the problem could have been resolved without the need for eviction to take place.

Local connection

6.83   The statutory provisions relating to 'local connection'[123] are further
explained in the guidance known as the Local Authority Agreement.[124]
The guidance states that:

- 'normal residence' in an area should be residence for at least six
  months in the area during the previous 12 months, or for not less
  than three years during the previous five-year period;
- regarding employment in an area, it is recommended that confirmation should be obtained from the applicant's employer and it
  should be established that the employment is not of a casual nature;
- 'family associations' normally arise when an applicant or member
  of the household has parents, adult children or brothers or sisters
  who have been resident in the area for at least five years at the date
  of the application and the applicant indicates a wish to be near
  them. Only in exceptional circumstances would the residence of relatives other than those listed above be taken to establish a local
  connection. The residence of children in another area from that
  of their parents cannot be taken to be residence of their own choice
  and therefore does not constitute a local connection. However, a
  referral should not be made to another local authority on the
  grounds of family association if the applicant objects;
- there may be special circumstances which the local authority considers give rise to a local connection in the area. The fact that an
  applicant seeks to return to an area where he or she was brought up
  or lived in the past may be grounds for finding a local connection.

6.84   The Local Authority Agreement also lists certain exceptions to the
above categories:

- time spent in the service of the regular armed forces;
- time spent in detention under the authority of an Act of parliament (for example, prisons, mental hospitals);

123   See paras 6.13–6.14, above.
124   *Guidelines for Local Authorities and Referees* agreed by Association of London
Government, Convention of Scottish Local Authorities, Local Government
Association and the Welsh Local Government Association.

- time spent as a result of an earlier homeless application, in accommodation secured by another local authority under the homelessness legislation within the last five years;
- time spent in hospital;
- time spent in an institution in which households are accepted only for a limited period (for example, refuges and rehabilitation centres).

It should be stressed that if a homeless applicant has a local connection with the area of the local authority to which he or she applies, then a referral to another local authority will not be possible even if the applicant also has a local connection with that other authority's area.

6.85   The Local Authority Agreement is not a statute but is strong guidance and cannot be ignored. Nevertheless, it is suggested that the guidance should not be applied too rigidly by local authorities in the case of homeless Gypsies and Travellers and that their particular circumstances and the difficulties they face should also be taken into account. By way of example it is perhaps worth looking at the guidance on 'normal residence' and 'family associations':

- According to the guidance, a Gypsy or Traveller would have to have spent at least six months in the area during the last 12 months to have a local connection, but it is suggested that a local authority should not apply the guidance too rigidly in the case of Gypsies or Travellers who have been frequently forced to move from one unauthorised encampment to another, particularly when eviction action taken by the local authority itself forced them to spend a period of time in a neighbouring local authority's area.
- The extended family is an essential part of Irish Traveller culture[125] and the list of relatives in the guidance, by which an applicant can establish a local connection with an area, may be too narrow in the case of an Irish Traveller. For example, it has been held to be too narrow in a case concerning a former asylum-seeker.[126]

Suitable interim accommodation[127]

6.86   It can be seen above that if a local authority has reason to believe that an applicant may be homeless, eligible for assistance and in priority need, it has a duty to secure that accommodation is available

---

125   See, for example, McDonagh, 'Nomadism' in *Travellers: citizens of Ireland,* pp33–46.

126   *Ozbek v Ipswich BC* [2006] EWCA Civ 534; [2006] HLR 41.

127   See paras 6.51–6.62, above.

pending its final decision.[128] If, having conducted inquiries, the local authority decides that a full duty is not owed to the applicant,[129] then the local authority has a power to ensure that accommodation is available pending any review of that decision requested by the applicant.[130] If the original decision is upheld on review, the local authority, once again, then has a power to secure that accommodation is available pending a county court appeal.[131]

6.87   Interim accommodation must be suitable.[132] When deciding what is suitable, a local authority must have regard to the slum clearance, overcrowding and 'houses in multiple occupation' provisions of the HA 1985. The case-law and statutory instruments to date have almost entirely related to the provision of conventional housing. In England, the government has provided that bed and breakfast (B&B) accommodation is not to be regarded as suitable for an applicant with family commitments[133] where the accommodation is secured for:

- a homeless applicant pending final decision;[134]
- a homeless applicant in priority need but intentionally homeless;[135]
- an applicant who is owed the full duty to secure accommodation;[136]
- an applicant who is to be referred to another local authority under the local connection provisions,[137] or
- an applicant who is threatened with homelessness.[138]

However, in England, where no accommodation other than B&B is available for such an applicant and he or she occupies the B&B accommodation for a period, or a total of periods, not exceeding six weeks, then such accommodation will be considered 'suitable'.[139]

6.88   In Wales, the National Assembly for Wales has indicated that B&B accommodation is not to be regarded as suitable unless it meets certain

128   HA 1996 s188(1).
129   HA 1996 s184.
130   HA 1996 s188(3).
131   HA 1996 s204(4).
132   HA 1996 s210.
133   The Homelessness (Suitability of Accommodation) (England) Order 2003 SI No 3326 reg 3.
134   HA 1996 s188(1).
135   HA 1996 s190(2).
136   HA 1996 s193(2).
137   HA 1996 s200(1).
138   HA 1996 s195(2).
139   The Homelessness (Suitability of Accommodation) (England) Order 2003 SI No 3326 reg 4.

basic standards and is not to be regarded as suitable for a homeless person who is a minor or a pregnant woman.[140] This does not apply if the homeless person occupies the B&B accommodation for a total of periods which does not exceed two weeks or occupies a 'higher standard' B&B accommodation for a total of periods which does not exceed six weeks (unless an offer of suitable alternative accommodation is made and the homeless person chooses to remain in that B&B accommodation).[141] From 7 April 2008, in Wales, B&B accommodation will not be regarded as suitable for a homeless person in priority need (with the same exceptions as outlined above).[142]

6.89   *Codona v Mid-Bedfordshire DC*[143] involved the offer of B&B accommodation to a homeless Gypsy and her extended family. Leanne Codona rejected the offer on the basis of her 'cultural aversion to conventional housing', which was accepted as being of the strongest form. The Court of Appeal (CA) approved the decision in *R (Margaret Price) v Carmarthenshire CC.*[144] However, the CA also held that the offer of B&B accommodation was not 'unsuitable' despite the fact that the local authority had simply investigated three authorised Gypsy/Traveller sites in the area (none of which had any vacancies) before making the offer of B&B.

6.90   The CA in *Codona* approved the following relevant considerations when assessing a Gypsy's or Traveller's application for accommodation:

- whether the applicant and, if relevant, his or her family, live in a caravan or caravans;
- whether they are Romani or subscribe to a Gypsy culture;
- whether they are nomadic for a substantial part of the year;
- whether the nomadism is linked to their livelihood;[145]
- whether they subscribe to the relevant features of the Gypsy life in question, such as an aversion to conventional housing.[146]

---

140 The Homelessness (Suitability of Accommodation((Wales) Order 2006 SI No 650 regs 4 and 5.

141 The Homelessness (Suitability of Accommodation) (Wales) Order 2006 reg 6.

142 The Homelessness (Suitability of Accommodation) (Wales) Order 2006 reg 7.

143 [2005] HLR 1.

144 2003] EWHC 42 Admin; March 2003 *Legal Action* 30, and see paras 6.51–6.62, above.

145 Though it is now clear that this nomadism can have ceased either temporarily or permanently. See chapter 4 at paras 4.79–4.84, above.

146 [2005] HLR 1 at 17.

6.91   The CA stressed the minimum line of suitability as established in cases involving settled people.[147] However, Auld LJ concluded:

> [T]his was a case in which the Council was required as a matter of relative urgency to find accommodation for an extended family occupying some six or seven caravans, who were insisting, because of their aversion to conventional housing, on being provided an alternative site for all of their caravans on which they could continue to live together. Despite careful enquiries by the Council it could find no such site. Nor could it provide at short notice long-term conventional bricks and mortar housing for the extended family. It was driven, therefore, as a short-term measure, to offer short-term accommodation of a bed and breakfast nature. In doing so, it was clearly acting as a matter of last resort and with the clear understanding ... that the duration of their stay in such accommodation was to be kept as short as possible.[148]

6.92   It is important to notice the stress the CA placed on the issues of 'urgency' and 'last resort'. If the homeless Gypsy or Traveller has somewhere to stay in the meantime or if a 'temporary', 'tolerated' site (perhaps on the local authority's own land) can be identified in the interim, then there may be no need to act so swiftly and more time can be taken over the process of locating a suitable pitch or site. Elsewhere in the judgment the CA seems to suggest that evidence of psychiatric as opposed to psychological harm might be required to show aversion to conventional housing. There seems little justification for such a preference since psychiatric and psychological harm in this context would appear to be two sides of the same coin.

6.93   Upon dismissal of her appeal (and upon the House of Lords refusing her permission to appeal further), Leanne Codona made an application to the European Court of Human Rights (ECtHR). The ECtHR found her application to be inadmissible.[149] The ECtHR stated:

> The Court recalls that article 8 does not in terms recognise the right to be provided with a home ... let alone a specific home or category of home ... It recalls that the scope of any positive obligation to house the homeless is limited ... It therefore considers that that obligation must be even more limited as regards an obligation to house a homeless person in a specific class of accommodation chosen by that person and where the person has previously been living on land in breach of planning regulations ... Against this, the Court recalls that there is a positive obligation imposed on the Contracting States by virtue of article 8 to facilitate the gypsy way of life (see Chapman at 96). It notes that the domestic courts in the instant case found

---

147   For example, *R v Newham LBC ex p Ojuri* (No 3) (1998) 31 HLR 452.
148   [2005] HLR 1 at 20.
149   Application no 485/05, 7 February 2006; September 2006 *Legal Action* 21.

that the applicant had a 'cultural aversion' to living in bricks and mortar accommodation and is prepared to accept that this aversion can be identified as forming part of the applicant's gypsy way of life. Following Chapman the Court does not rule out that, in principle, article 8 could impose a positive obligation on the authorities to provide accommodation for a homeless gypsy which is such that it facilitates their 'gypsy way of life'. However, it considers that this obligation could only arise where the authorities had such accommodation at their disposal and were making a choice between offering such accommodation or accommodation which was not 'suitable' for the cultural needs of a gypsy. In the instant case, however, it appears to be common ground that there were, in fact, no sites available upon which the applicant could lawfully place her caravan. In the premises, the Court cannot conclude that the authorities were then under a positive obligation to create such a site for the applicant (and her extended family) ... Finally, the Court does not consider that the apparent change in the policy of the respondent State[150] regarding the provision of caravan sites relied upon by the applicant is in fact of relevance to the present case. Although it welcomes any steps taken to increase the number of caravan sites, it must consider the situation by reference to facts as they stand ...

6.94 Accommodation outside the local authority's area may be suitable depending on the circumstances of the case. In deciding the question of suitability, the local authority must consider the individual needs of the applicant and his or her family, including those relating to work, education and health.[151] It will be important, therefore, that the homeless Gypsy or Traveller supplies the local authority with all relevant information with regard to work in the area, schools attended and whether this involves special educational needs, registration with a local general practitioner or attendance at a local hospital, the need for support from relatives or friends in the area and any other relevant matters.

6.95 The report by Niner, *Local authority Gypsy/Traveller sites in England*[152] indicated that, on the 324 local authority Gypsy sites recorded by the January 2002 Gypsy Count, there were only 307 transit pitches. Given the severe shortfall in suitable pitches, it is suggested that in cases where a homeless Gypsy or Traveller is camping on local authority land and the encampment is not causing any undue nuisance, then it would be reasonable for the local authority to permit him or her to

---

150 Namely the introduction of HA 2004 s225 and the new ODPM Circular 01/06, and see the discussion at para 6.103, below.

151 See, for example, *R v Newham LBC ex p Sacupima* [2001] HLR 2, CA, [2001] HLR 1, QBD.

152 ODPM, 2003.

remain on the land while his or her homelessness application is processed. Alternatively, the local authority could seek to identify temporary sites, perhaps on disused or underused land[153] where facilities could be provided.[154] Indeed, a local authority's decision to proceed with the eviction from its own land of a homeless Gypsy or Traveller when the local authority had failed to comply with the duty to secure that accommodation is available pending their final decision could well result in a public law challenge by way of judicial review.[155]

The full duty to accommodate

6.96   It now appears clear that a local authority which has decided that it has a full duty to accommodate a homeless applicant under HA 1996 s193(2)[156] must comply with the duty immediately.[157]

6.97   Where a local authority is satisfied that a homeless Gypsy or Traveller has a sufficient degree of 'cultural aversion to conventional housing' such that it should use its best endeavours to seek a suitable pitch or site, it will be incumbent on that authority to show that it has taken all reasonable steps to do so. Following the CA's decision in *Codona*, the claimant, Leanne Codona refused an offer of B&B accommodation and the local authority then offered her extended family three houses next to each other in purported compliance with the full duty. Ms Codona appealed to the county court, following an unsuccessful review of the decision to offer the family permanent housing.[158] Ms Codona's appeal was subsequently dismissed; the county court considered that the local authority had done what it could and that the offer was suitable.[159]

6.98   Local authorities are no longer obliged to keep registers of disused or underused land. However, the National Land Use Database[160] may

---

153   This could include other public authority land or even private land.

154   By way of example, a tap could be installed for water, refuse collection services set up and portaloos provided.

155   As, indeed, occurred in the *Price* case itself. For a discussion of judicial review procedures, see appendix A, below.

156   See para 6.26, above.

157   See Collins J in *R (Aweys and ors) v Birmingham CC* [2007] EWHC 52 Admin at para 24.

158   20 March 2006, Luton County Court, HHJ Farnworth.

159   See para 6.103, below, for a discussion on whether the position on this issue might now be changing.

160   A partnership project between CLG, English Partnerships and Ordnance Survey. The National Land Use Database is not yet publicly accessible though the aim is that it should be in the future. However, it can be accessed by local authorities.

be of great assistance to a local authority, combined with its own knowledge of land in its area. Additionally, the Gypsy or Traveller applicant may have good local knowledge of the area and may be able to provide the local authority with examples of pieces of land that might be suitable. It is also suggested that it will not be sufficient for the local authority simply to have regard to any vacant pitches on authorised sites in the area. If there are vacant pitches on a site, the local authority may also have to have regard to the allocations policy for that particular site before offering a pitch to a homeless applicant.[161]

6.99   The ODPM *Guidance on managing unauthorised camping*[162] states:

> There must be close working between site managers and local authority ... dealing with unauthorised camping over allocations of pitches on sites. Site managers may be aware of issues around Gypsy/Traveller group and family compatibility, which must be taken into account when allocating pitches on residential sites.[163]

In other words, the question of 'compatibility' of groups or families will also be relevant to the issue of suitability. Another relevant matter may be the location of the accommodation and its distance from schools, employment and healthcare facilities.

6.100   Obviously, New Travellers who are homeless can also make homeless applications. When it comes to the duty to accommodate, it should be remembered that the central issue is 'suitability'. Therefore, in the case of New Travellers, they may not be able to show a 'cultural aversion to conventional housing', but it should be sufficient if they can show an 'aversion to conventional housing'. It is accepted that it may be more difficult for a New Traveller to show such an aversion. Nevertheless, it should be remembered that many New Travellers have spent many years travelling and some were born on the road.

6.101   The vast majority of homeless Gypsies or Travellers will have their own caravan or living vehicle but will not have an authorised pitch where they can place it. If a Gypsy or Traveller no longer has his or her caravan or living vehicle,[164] it is arguable that the duty to secure that accommodation becomes available might include the provision of a suitable caravan or vehicle.[165]

---

161 See further the discussion on 'allocation' in chapter 3 at paras 3.30–3.33, above.

162 *Guidance on managing unauthorised camping*, ODPM, February 2004.

163 *Guidance on managing unauthorised camping* at para 4.8.

164 See the *Scott-Higgs* case for an example at para 6.72, above.

165 This argument was raised in *Price* but was not referred to in the judgment.

6.102   Those advising homeless Gypsies or Travellers who are owed the duty to secure accommodation, may have to consider obtaining expert reports on the question of 'aversion to housing' (for example, from a psychologist or other medical practitioner) and/or from a planning consultant or land surveyor on the question of available land in an area. Those providing reports on the availability of land will have to have regard to the relevant development plans and government guidance.[166]

Conclusion

6.103   It is to be noted that the cases fought by Leanne Codona (see above) all referred to decisions taken before policy changes which took place in February 2006. Local authorities now have a duty to assess and make provision for the accommodation needs of Gypsies and Travellers by identifying land which would be suitable for caravan sites (see HA 2004 s225 and Circular 1/06, *Planning for Gypsy and Traveller caravan sites*[167]). The government's aim is that the exercise will be completed by 2011. As we approach that date it is our view that local authorities will find it increasingly difficult to avoid providing homeless Gypsies and Travellers with anything other than land on which to place their caravans. In the meantime, it would seem both humane and cost effective for local authorities to identify locations within their areas where homeless Gypsies and Travellers could camp on a temporary basis.

166   For detailed discussion of these and other planning issues, see chapter 4, above.
167   For full discussion of these matters, see chapter 4, above.

CHAPTER 7

Education and healthcare

7.1 Introduction

7.2 Education
7.2 Attendance and achievement amongst Gypsy and Traveller pupils
7.6 The right to education
7.14 Admission to school
7.17 Attendance at school
7.30 Transport to school
7.31 Special educational needs
7.34 Exclusion from school
7.47 Racial discrimination
7.53 Bullying at school
7.56 Disability discrimination
7.57 Education otherwise than at school
7.61 Education of children under school age
7.63 Raising the achievement of Gypsy and Traveller pupils

7.67 Healthcare
7.67 The right to healthcare
7.68 NHS structure
7.77 Gypsy and Traveller health research
7.79 Access to healthcare
7.87 Mental health and care in the community
7.90 Healthcare and the ECHR
7.92 Medical records, privacy and the ECHR
7.101 Environmental health

7.108 Conclusion

Introduction

7.1   This chapter is designed to provide the reader with an overview of the law relating to education and healthcare insofar as it may affect the lives of Gypsies and Travellers and their children.

Education

Attendance and achievement amongst Gypsy and Traveller pupils

7.2   Evidence gathered in 1996[1] and 1999[2] led the Office for Standards in Education (Ofsted) to report its view that Gypsy and Traveller pupils have the lowest level of attainment of any ethnic minority group and that they are most at risk in the education system. More recent inspection evidence compiled by Ofsted revealed the fact that there were between 10,000 and 12,000 Gypsy and Traveller children of secondary school age that were not registered and did not attend school. This led Ofsted to state in its report in 2003 that:

> The vast majority of Traveller pupils linger on the periphery of the education system. The situation has persisted for too long and the alarm bells rung in earlier reports have yet to be heeded.[3]

7.3   There are a number of reasons for the poor levels of attendance and achievement of Gypsy and Traveller pupils. Perhaps the most obvious reason stems from enforced mobility; children that live on unauthorised sites are bound to suffer considerable disruption to their schooling when their families are evicted and it is not surprising that those that are subject to numerous evictions are the least likely to attend school.

7.4   When commenting on the poor levels of attendance, Ofsted also noted the fact that Gypsy and Traveller children tend to come from very caring and protective families, that some parents fear that their children will be subjected to racist bullying at school and that schooling will lead to potential erosion of their community's moral codes and values.[4]

---

1   *The Education of travelling children: a survey of educational provision for travelling children*, Ofsted, 1996.
2   *Raising the attainment of minority ethnic pupils*, Ofsted, 1999.
3   *Provision and support for Traveller pupils*, Ofsted, 2003.
4   For more information on the culture and customs of Romani Gypsies and Irish Travellers, see: Vesey-Fitzgerald, *Gypsies of Britain*, Readers Union, 1973; Sheehan, ed, *Travellers: citizens of Ireland*, The Parish of the Travelling People, Dublin, 2000.

In addition, Ofsted noted that there is a very strong tradition of starting work in the family business at a young age within the Travelling community and that some Gypsy and Traveller parents regard the somewhat inflexible school curriculum as having little relevance to their traditional way of life.

7.5   In 2003, and in an attempt to tackle these findings, the Department for Education and Skills (DfES) published '*Aiming high: raising the achievement of Gypsy Traveller pupils*' in order to give all those involved in education a broad overview of good practice which was designed to tackle the under-achievement of Gypsy and Traveller pupils.[5] In 2004 the government published 'Every child matters: change for children' which set out a new approach to the well-being of children and young people from birth to age 19 and indicated that it was the government's aim for every child, whatever their background or their circumstances, to have the support they need to:

- be healthy;
- stay safe;
- enjoy and achieve;
- make a positive contribution; and
- achieve economic well-being.[6]

Though of general application, the principles underpinning Every Child Matters will have a particular relevance for those working with Gypsy and Traveller children.

The right to education

7.6   The Human Rights Act (HRA) 1998 came into force on 2 October 2000 and incorporates most of the European Convention on Human

---

5   It can be obtained from DfES Publications: by post at PO Box 5050, Sherwood Park, Annesley, Nottingham NG15 0DJ; by telephone on 0845 6022260; or by email at dfes@prolog.uk.com, and by quoting the reference DfES/0443/2003. In addition, in 2005 the DfES published '*Aiming high: partnerships between schools and Traveller Education Support Services in raising the achievement of Gypsy Traveller pupils*', a paper which emphasised the need for the adoption of effective partnership strategies. Though all references in this work to the government department responsible for schools will be to the DfES, it should be noted that on 28 June 2007 the government abolished the DfES and replaced it with two new departments, the Department for Children, Schools and Families (DCSC) and the Department of Innovations, Universities and Skills (DIUS).

6   DfES 1018/2004.

Rights (ECHR or 'the Convention') into UK law. Of particular relevance to education is ECHR Protocol 1 article 2 which provides that:

> No person shall be denied the right to education. In the exercise of any functions which it assumes in relation to education and to teaching, the state shall respect the right of parents to ensure such education and teaching in conformity with their own religious and philosophical convictions.

7.7   However, when the United Kingdom ratified the Convention it entered the following reservation with regard to the second sentence of Protocol 1 article 2:

> ... in view of certain provisions of the Education Acts in the United Kingdom, the principle affirmed in the second sentence of article 2 is accepted by the United Kingdom only so far as it is compatible with the provision of efficient instruction and training, and the avoidance of unreasonable public expenditure.

7.8   Thus, it has been held that the general right to education comprises a number of rights (none of which is absolute):

(i)   a right of access to such educational establishments as exist;
(ii)   a right to effective (but not the most effective possible) education;
(iii) a right to official recognition of academic qualifications.

As regards the right to an effective education, for the right to education to be meaningful the quality of the education must reach a minimum standard.[7]

7.9   Local education authorities (LEAs) have a statutory duty to ensure that education is available for all children of compulsory school age (5- to 16-year-olds) in their area that is appropriate to their age, abilities, aptitudes and any special educational needs that they might possess.[8]

7.10   LEAs have a duty to have regard to the:

> ... general principle that pupils are to be educated in accordance with the wishes of their parents, so far as this is compatible with the provision of efficient instruction and training and the avoidance of unreasonable expenditure.[9]

LEAs have a duty to respect parents' religious and philosophical convictions. 'Respect' means more than simply 'acknowledge' or 'take

---

7   *R (Holub and Holub) v Secretary of State for the Home Department* [2001] 1 WLR 1359. See also *Belgian Linguistics Case (No 2)* (1968) 1 EHRR 252 at 281; and *A v Head Teacher and Governors of Lord Grey School* [2003] 4 All ER 1317.

8   Education Act (EA) 1996 s14 as amended by Education and Inspections Act (EIA) 2006 s2.

9   EA 1996 s9.

into account' such views but does not require LEAs to cater for all parents' convictions; parents do not have an absolute right to choose the manner in which their children are to be educated at school.[10]

7.11   LEAs also have a duty to give parents the opportunity to express a preference as to which school they wish their child to attend.[11] LEAs must comply with parental preference unless to do so would be prejudicial to efficient education or the efficient use of resources.[12] These duties are owed to all of the children residing in the area of an LEA, whether permanently or temporarily and must, therefore, apply to Gypsy and Traveller children residing with their families on unauthorised sites on a temporary basis.

7.12   Although Gypsy and Traveller children of school age have the same legal right to education as anyone else, it is difficult in practical terms for them to exercise that right without a permanent or legal place to stop. Most LEAs provide specialist Traveller educational support services to help Gypsy and Traveller pupils and parents to access education and to provide practical advice and support to schools admitting them. When a Gypsy or Traveller family with children of school age moves into a new area, they should contact the local Traveller education support service for assistance.

7.13   The National Association of Teachers of Travellers (NATT) produces an annual booklet listing the local Traveller education support services, and can also provide information about books and other educational resources designed specifically for Gypsy and Traveller children.[13]

Admission to school

7.14   Gypsy and Traveller children should be admitted to schools on the same basis as any other children. However, some schools may still rely upon admissions policies that disadvantage Gypsy and Traveller children: for instance, an admissions policy which gives preference

10   *The Belgian Linguistics Case (No 2)* (1968) 1 EHRR 252. But see also *Campbell and Cosans v United Kingdom* (1982) 4 EHRR 293, for an example of a case where there was found to be a breach of both the first and the second sentence of article 2 of Protocol 1 of the ECHR.

11   School Standards and Framework Act 1998 s86 as amended by EIA 2006 s42.

12   School Standards and Framework Act 1998 ss86(2), (3) and 87; and *R (B) v Head Teacher and Governing Body of Alperton Community School* [2001] EWHC 229 Admin; [2001] 1 ELR 359; and see the Education Act 1996 s14A, inserted by EIA 2006 s3.

13   NATT can be contacted by visiting its website at www.natt.org.uk. See also appendix C, below, for a list of other useful organisations.

to children whose older brothers and sisters have already attended the school could be argued to unfairly disadvantage Gypsy and Traveller families who have recently moved into the area. Such a policy may be susceptible to legal challenge on grounds that it is discriminatory and/or unreasonable.[14]

7.15   There is anecdotal evidence of some schools having refused admission to Gypsy and Traveller pupils, whether through racism, fear that school league tables will be affected or concern that non-Travelling parents will resent such admission. In a report published in 2001 Ofsted noted that:

> ... a few schools in a small number of the LEAs inspected had expressed reservations to Traveller education services about taking on pupils from Traveller families, such schools [are] clearly failing to recognise their legal responsibilities.[15]

7.16   If it can be proved that a Gypsy or Traveller child has been refused admission on any such grounds then it may be possible to bring a claim under the Race Relations Act (RRA) 1976[16] and/or article 2 of Protocol 1 (the right to education) combined with article 14 (the prohibition of discrimination) of the ECHR.

Attendance at school

7.17   Education Act (EA) 1996 s7 provides that:

> It shall be the duty of the parent of every child of compulsory school age to cause him to receive efficient full-time education suitable to his age, ability and aptitude and to any special educational needs he may have either by regular attendance at school or otherwise.

Failure to do so is an offence and can lead to prosecution.[17]

7.18   In *R v Secretary of State for Education and Science ex p Talmud Torah Madizikei Hedass School Trust*,[18] it was held that education is 'suitable' if it primarily equips a child for life in a community of which he or she

---

14   The DfES published a new Schools Admissions Code which came into force on 28 February 2007 and can be found at www.dfes.gov.uk. The code places an emphasis on ensuring that admissibility criteria are as clear and fair as possible and that particular social groups are not disadvantaged.

15   *Managing support for the attainment of pupils from minority ethnic groups*, Ofsted, 2001.

16   As amended by the Race Relations (Amendment) Act 2000. See paras 7.47–7.50 and chapter 8, below.

17   EA 1996 s444 or s444(1A) as amended by EIA 2006 ss82 and 109.

18   (1985) *Times*, 12 April.

is a member as long as it does not foreclose the child's option later to adopt some other form of life if he or she wishes to do so.

7.19　Schools must report all unauthorised absences and LEAs have a responsibility to prosecute parents in appropriate cases.[19]

7.20　If a child is not registered at a school and the LEA considers that the child is not receiving suitable education, then it may issue a 'school attendance order' requiring the parent to register the child at a named school.[20] The Education Act (EA) 1996 s443(1) provides that a parent who fails to comply with a school attendance order will be guilty of a criminal offence unless he or she can prove that the child is receiving suitable education out of school.

7.21　Where a child is registered at a school but fails to attend that school regularly, an LEA has the power to prosecute the parent. The EA 1996 s444(1) provides that:

> If a child of compulsory school age who is a registered pupil at a school fails to attend regularly at the school, his parent is guilty of an offence.

7.22　A parent convicted of an offence under EA 1996 s444(1) can be punished with a fine. The offence is one of 'strict liability' and parents cannot defend a prosecution by claiming that they had no knowledge of their child's non-attendance or by claiming that they had done all that they could reasonably be expected to do to ensure that their child attended school.[21]

7.23　The EA 1996 s444(1A) provides that a parent will be guilty of a more serious offence and be liable to a fine or to imprisonment for a term not exceeding three months, if he or she knows that his or her child is failing to attend regularly at school and he or she fails to cause the child to do so. However, the parent will have a defence to such a charge if he or she can prove that there was a reasonable justification for the failure to cause the child to attend regularly.[22]

7.24　It had been thought that the offence created by EA 1996 s444(1) might breach ECHR article 6(2)[23] because it is a strict liability offence which does not require proof of any knowledge or fault on the part of the parent. However, in the case of *Barnfather v Islington LBC and the*

19　EA 1996 s446.
20　EA 1996 s437 as amended by EIA 2006.
21　*Bath and North East Somerset DC v Warman* [1999] ELR 81 and *Crump v Gilmore* [1968] LGR 56.
22　The defence is set out in EA 1996 s444(1B), a provision inserted by EIA 2006 s109.
23　ECHR article 6(2) provides that: 'Everyone charged with a criminal offence shall be presumed innocent until proved guilty according to law.'

Secretary of State for Education and Skills,[24] it was held that EA 1996 s444(1) did not engage article 6(2) and that the offence was compatible with the Convention.

7.25   However, EA 1996 s444 does provide parents with a number of statutory excuses or defences to a prosecution brought under section 444(1). For example, a child will not be taken to have failed to attend regularly at school if he or she:

- has been given authorised leave of absence;
- was unable to attend due to sickness;
- did not attend school on any day of religious observance;
- was unable to attend because the school was not within walking distance and no suitable transport arrangements had been made by the LEA.[25]

7.26   More particularly, Gypsy and Traveller parents are protected from conviction for the non-attendance of their children at school where they can demonstrate, in accordance with the EA 1996 s444(6), that:

- they are engaged in a trade or business of such a nature that requires them to travel from place to place;
- the child has attended at a school as a registered pupil as regularly as the nature of that trade permits; and
- where the child has attained the age of six years, they have attended school for at least 200 half-day sessions during the preceding school year (September to July).

7.27   However, there is some concern that this statutory exception may, in practice, deny Gypsy and Traveller children equality of access in education. For example, the authors of the Swann Report wrote:

> We are concerned that the specific provision ... although presumably intended originally to protect travelling parents from unreasonable prosecution for failing to send their children to school, may in practice serve to deprive travellers' children of equality of access to education; LEAs may see this provision in the Act as offering a convenient excuse for not enforcing school attendance for travellers' children, rather than, as we would wish, striving to achieve full time attendance by all school age children in their areas.[26]

---

24   [2003] ELR 263.
25   See paragraph 7.30, below.
26   Committee of Inquiry into the Education of Children from Ethnic Minority Groups, *Education for all* ('The Swann Report'), HMSO, 1985, paras 26–27.

More recently the DfES has emphasised the fact that Gypsy and Traveller parents should not regard the 200 half-day sessions as the norm but should continue to comply with their legal duty to ensure that their children are receiving efficient, suitable, full-time education even when not at school.[27]

7.28   To protect the continuity of learning for Gypsy and Traveller children, the DfES has introduced the concept of 'dual registration'. If parents inform their 'base' school or the Traveller education support service that the family will be travelling and intend to return by a given time, the school may keep the child's place for them and record their absence as authorised. The child can then register at other schools while the family is travelling. Gypsy and Traveller parents can also take advantage of 'school-based distance learning' whereby teachers and the Traveller education support service work together to provide pupils with a package of curriculum-based material to be taken away and studied by them while the family are travelling.[28]

7.29   Before an LEA can prosecute a parent under either EA 1996 s443 or s444, it must first consider whether to apply to a family proceedings court for an 'education supervision order'.[29] Such an order will be made where a child 'is of compulsory school age and is not being properly educated',[30] or, in other words, is not receiving a suitable education. Education supervision orders last 12 months but can be extended for up to three years. They are designed to ensure that both the parent and the child receive support and advice from a supervisor such as an education welfare officer or an educational social worker.

Transport to school

7.30   The EA 1996 s509 provides that LEAs have a duty to make appropriate arrangements to provide free transport for children to attend school unless the school is within walking distance, that is two miles (or three miles where the child is over eight years old). Alternatively, LEAs may 'as they think fit' provide funding for 'reasonable travelling expenses' for children for whom they have not made arrangements to provide free transport. As has already been noted, parents will have a defence to the charge of failing to send their children to school under EA 1996 s444, if the school at which their children are registered is not within

---

27 *Aiming high: raising the achievement of Gypsy Traveller pupils*, DfES, 2003.
28 See the Pupil Registration Regulations 2006 SI No 1751.
29 EA 1996 s447.
30 Children Act 1989 s36.

walking distance and no suitable arrangements have been made by the LEA for their transportation to and from school.[31]

Special educational needs

7.31   A child has 'special educational needs', for the purposes of the EA 1996, if he or she has a 'learning difficulty' that requires special educational provision to be made.[32] A child will have a learning difficulty if he or she:

- has a significantly greater difficulty in learning than the majority of children of the same age;
- has a disability which either prevents or hinders him or her from making use of educational facilities of a kind generally provided for children of the same age in schools within the area of the LEA; or
- is under the age of five years and is, or would be, if special educational provision was not made, likely to fall within the above categories when over that age.[33]

7.32   LEAs have a duty to identify those children with special educational needs for whom they are responsible and to make special educational provision to address those needs.[34] Where an LEA is of the opinion that a child for whom it is responsible is, or probably is, a child with special educational needs, it must follow the procedure for the assessment of the needs of a child laid down by EA 1996 s323. If, in the light of such an assessment, it is necessary for an LEA to determine the special educational provision that is required to address the needs of a child found to have a learning difficulty, then it must make and maintain a statement of the child's special educational needs.[35] Having done so, the LEA must then arrange for the special educational provision specified in the statement to be made for the child.[36]

7.33   If a Gypsy or Traveller child has started school late or attended school irregularly, he or she may be judged to have special needs and parents should contact their local Traveller education support service

---

31   See *George v Devon CC* [1988] 3 All ER 1002 and EA 1996 s444 as amended by EIA 2006 s82.

32   EA 1996 s312(1).

33   EA 1996 s312(2).

34   EA 1996 s321(1).

35   EA 1996 s324(1).

36   EA 1996 s324(5)(a)(i); *R v Secretary of State for Education and Science ex p E* [1992] 1 FLR 377; and *R v Harrow LBC ex p M* [1997] ELR 62.

for advice and assistance on the decision-making process relating to the assessment of the special needs of their child.

Exclusion from school

7.34   In 1996 Ofsted found that Gypsy and Traveller children suffer a disproportionately high level of school exclusion.[37]

7.35   The Education Act (EA) 2002 s52 states that:

(1) The headteacher of a maintained school may exclude a pupil from the school for a fixed period or permanently.

(2) The teacher in charge of a pupil referral unit[38] may exclude a pupil from the unit for a fixed period or permanently.

7.36   In late 2005, the DfES published a tranche of documents which gave schools and local authorities advice and guidance on the management of pupils' attendance and behaviour.[39] That guidance was supplemented in 2006 by the Education (Pupil Exclusions and Appeals) (Miscellaneous Amendments) (England) Regulations and yet further guidance entitled '*Improving behaviour and attendance: guidance on exclusion from schools and Pupil Referral Units*'.[40]

7.37   There is a duty on headteachers, teachers in charge of pupil referral units, governing bodies and independent appeal panels to have regard to the guidance and abide by the regulations when considering whether to exclude a pupil, and failure to do so may well give rise to a successful legal challenge.

7.38   When a decision maker has to consider whether a pupil has misbehaved the standard of proof to be applied is the 'balance of probabilities'. However, case-law suggests that the seriousness of the alleged conduct must be taken into account in making decisions on the 'balance of probabilities' and the more serious the allegation the more convincing the evidence will need to be.[41]

---

37   *Report on the education of Travelling children,* Ofsted, 1996.

38   Any school established and maintained by an LEA which is not a 'community school' or a 'special school' but is specially organised to provide education for children who, by reason of illness, exclusion from school or otherwise, may not for any period receive suitable education will be known as a 'pupil referral unit': see EA 1996 s19(2).

39   See www.dfes.gov.uk/behaviourandattendance/guidance/IBAGuidance/index.cfm.

40   For a full resume of all the guidance see *Recent developments in education law, Legal Action,* May 2006 and November 2006. The next edition of the DfES exclusion guidance is due to be published later in 2007.

41   See *R (S) v The Governors of YP School* [2003] EWCA Civ 1306.

7.39   Exclusion hearings conducted by governing bodies or independent appeal panels are also open to challenge on the basis that they have been conducted in breach of the rules of evidence and natural justice. For example, in *R v Governors of W School and West Sussex CC ex p K*,[42] the court held that the decision of the governing body to exclude K should be quashed on the basis that it had been unfair and procedurally flawed in circumstances where: K had been handicapped in the presentation of his defence; the 'evidence' included the verbal opinions of an anonymous police officer; and only lip service had been paid to the standard of proof at the hearing.

7.40   However, it has been held that exclusion proceedings are not subject to ECHR article 6 (which guarantees the right to a fair trial in the determination of civil rights and obligations and criminal charges).[43] In the case of *R (B) v Head Teacher and Governing Body of Alperton Community School*,[44] several claimants sought judicial review of decisions regarding admission to and exclusion from schools and they alleged that certain provisions of the School Standards and Framework Act (SSFA) 1998 breached the Convention. In the event, the court held that, as no private right to an education existed in English law, ECHR article 6 was not applicable to independent appeal panel exclusion proceedings, and the relevant provisions of SSFA 1998 did not breach ECHR Protocol 1 article 2 (the right to education).[45]

7.41   Where an independent appeal panel upholds an appeal and quashes a decision to exclude a child from school, the child will be reinstated. However, reinstatement will not necessarily result in a return to mainstream classes.

7.42   In *L v Governors of J School*,[46] the House of Lords considered a case where a school had imposed terms and conditions on a child's reinstatement which required him to receive tuition in isolation from other pupils, prohibited him from socialising with his former classmates and restricted his movements in the school in circumstances where staff threatened strike action if the child returned to mainstream classes. By a majority, the House of Lords held that reinstatement (that is, the re-establishment of the 'school-pupil relationship')

---

42 [2001] ELR 311.

43 ECHR article 6(2) provides that: 'Everyone charged with a criminal offence shall be presumed innocent until proved guilty according to law.'

44 [2001] EWHC 229 Admin, [2001] 1 ELR 359; but compare *R (S) v Brent LBC* [2002] EWCA Civ 693.

45 See also *Simpson v United Kingdom* (1989) 64 DR 188 for a similar decision in relation to special educational needs.

46 [2003] UKHL 9.

occurred when a school resumed responsibilities and obligations towards a pupil and that, on the facts of the case, the regime imposed by the school was sufficient to amount to reinstatement. When doing so, the House of Lords made it clear that a school must always act in good faith and that reinstatement must be genuine and not a sham. However, Lord Bingham expressed specific concern that the special arrangements failed to facilitate the child's actual reintegration into the school.[47]

7.43   The exclusion of a pupil from school will not violate ECHR Protocol 1 article 2 (the right to education) unless the pupil is given no effective access to alternative educational facilities. Everything will depend upon the circumstances of the case.[48]

7.44   If the child of a Gypsy or Traveller is threatened with exclusion then he or she should contact the local Traveller education support service or the National Association of Teachers of Travellers for initial assistance but may also need to seek specialist legal advice.[49]

7.45   A child who has been excluded from school should still receive a suitable education and EA 1996 s19(1) provides that:

> Each local education authority shall make arrangements for the provision of suitable full-time or part-time education at school or otherwise than at school for those children of compulsory school age who, by reason of illness, exclusion from school or otherwise, may not for any period receive suitable education unless such arrangements are made for them.

7.46   Where a Gypsy or Traveller parent has concerns regarding the provision of education to an excluded child, he or she may wish to challenge the school or the LEA by bringing a claim for judicial review and/or damages.

Racial discrimination

7.47   Romani Gypsies and Irish Travellers are recognised as members of separate racial groups under the RRA 1976.[50] Although there is, as yet, no case-law on the matter, it is suggested that Welsh and Scottish

---

47   See also the case of *P v NASUWT* [2003] UKHL 8.
48   See, for example, *A v Head Teacher and Governors of Lord Grey School* [2006] UKHL 14.
49   See appendix C, below, for a full list of useful organisations.
50   See chapter 8, below, and the cases of *Commission for Racial Equality v Dutton* [1989] 1 QB 783; and *O'Leary v Allied Domecq* (unreported) (CL950275–79), 29 August 2000, HHJ Goldstein, Central London County Court.

Gypsy Travellers should also be recognised under the RRA 1976 as separate racial groups.[51]

7.48   The RRA 1976 outlaws both direct and indirect racial discrimination in education. Specifically, RRA 1976 s17 provides that it is unlawful for a body in charge of an educational establishment to discriminate against a person:

(a) in the terms on which it offers to admit him to the establishment as a pupil;

(b) by refusing or deliberately omitting to accept an application for his admission to the establishment as a pupil; or

(c) where he is a pupil of the establishment –

  (i) in the way that it affords him access to any benefits, facilities or services, or by refusing or deliberately omitting to afford him access to them; or

  (ii) by excluding him from the establishment or subjecting him to any other detriment.

7.49   More generally, RRA 1976 s18 states that it is unlawful for LEAs and other responsible bodies to discriminate in the performance of any of their other functions under the Education Acts, although there is an exception made in the case of establishments that afford persons of a particular racial group access to facilities or services to meet the special needs of that group with regard to their education, training or welfare or any ancillary benefits.[52]

7.50   If an ethnic Gypsy or Traveller parent believes that their child has been the subject of discrimination then legal advice should be sought. A claimant must notify the secretary of state before proceedings are commenced and a claim should be brought in the county court within six months of the alleged act of discrimination.

7.51   The RRA 1976 now imposes a statutory duty on public bodies including LEAs and schools to promote race equality.[53] Schools are now required to:

• prepare a race equality policy, that is, a written statement of their policies for promoting race equality, and act upon it;

• assess the impact of their policies on pupils, staff and parents from different racial groups, in particular the impact on attainment levels of these pupils; and

---

51 So the points made in paragraphs 7.48–7.50, below, may also apply with equal force to Scottish and Welsh Gypsy Travellers.

52 RRA 1976 s35.

53 RRA 1976 s71 (as amended).

- monitor the operation of all the school's policies, in particular their impact on the attainment levels of pupils from different racial groups.[54]

7.52   Ofsted will inspect schools' compliance with their new duties as part of its regular inspections.

Bullying at school

7.53   In 1996 Ofsted found that Gypsy and Traveller children are often subject to bullying of a racist nature and, more recently, the Scottish Traveller Education Project indicated that bullying is an endemic problem in schools in Scotland.[55]

7.54   Schools should have clear policies and strategies to deal with the prevention of bullying and the punishment of such behaviour. The fact that schools must now comply with the duty to promote racial equality should cause them to address bullying and racist behaviour directed against Romani Gypsies and Irish Travellers.

7.55   If an LEA or a school fails to respond to bullying against Gypsies and Irish Travellers at all, or as effectively as when such behaviour is directed against pupils from other ethnic minority groups, then it could be guilty of discrimination.[56] Alternatively, if an LEA or a school fails to take reasonable steps to investigate bullying behaviour and to prevent its recurrence, then it may be liable in negligence to pay a pupil damages for breach of its duty to take care of the child's health and safety.[57]

Disability discrimination

7.56   The Special Educational Needs and Disability Act (SENDA) 2001 amended the Disability Discrimination Act (DDA) 1995 so as to

---

54 The Commission for Racial Equality (CRE) has published a useful document, *The duty to promote race equality: a guide for schools*, available at www.cre.gov.uk.

55 See *The education of Travelling children: a survey of educational provision for Travelling children*, Ofsted, 1996; and Crawley, *Moving forward: the provision of accommodation for Travellers and Gypsies*, The Institute for Public Policy Research, 2004, p33. For a more wide-ranging discussion of the education of Gypsy and Traveller children in Scotland, see the STEP report, *Issues in school enrolment, attendance, attainment and support for learning for Gypsy/Traveller and school-aged children and young people based in Scottish local authority sites*, 2004.

56 See also chapter 8, below.

57 See, for example, *Bradford-Smart v West Sussex CC* [2002] EWCA Civ 7.

introduce the duty not to discriminate on grounds of disability in education. Schools are now prohibited from discriminating against disabled children in their admission arrangements, in the provision of education and associated services and in relation to exclusions from school.[58]

Education otherwise than at school

7.57   Parents do have the option of educating their children at home. However, a child educated at home must still receive a 'suitable education', that is efficient full-time education suitable to the child's age, ability and aptitude and any special educational needs he or she may have.[59]

7.58   The right to educate one's child at home is clearly in keeping with ECHR article 9 (the right to freedom of thought, conscience and religion) and article 10 (the right to freedom of expression), but must be balanced against the right of the child to receive an effective education. In 2001, Ofsted indicated that the lack of monitoring and support undertaken by LEAs of the education of children outside school is a matter of some concern:

> In about half of the LEAs in which services were inspected there was a growing trend among Traveller families to opt for education other than at school (that is, education at home), particularly in the secondary phase. Services responded with appropriate advice, but the practice on registration and monitoring varied significantly among LEAs. The lack of evaluative monitoring typified the poorest provision.[60]

7.59   Parents need only inform an LEA of their intention to provide a child with 'education otherwise than at school' if the child has been registered at a school. The national curriculum need not be followed and formal testing is not required. However, LEAs may inspect education being provided at home in order to monitor and assess whether a child is receiving a 'suitable education'.[61]

7.60   If it appears to an LEA that a child of school age is not receiving suitable education at home it must serve the parents with a notice in writing requiring them to satisfy it that the child is receiving such

---

58   DDA 1995 s28A; and see Palmer et al, *Discrimination law handbook*, 2nd edn, Legal Action Group, 2007 for a more detailed explanation of the DDA 1995 in the education field.

59   EA 1996 s19.

60   *Managing support for the attainment of pupils from minority ethnic groups*, *Ofsted*, 2001; see also *Provision and support for Traveller pupils*, Ofsted, 2003.

61   See *R v Surrey Quarter Sessions Appeal Committee ex p Tweedie* [1963] 61 LGR 464; and *R v Gwent CC ex p Perry* (1985) 129 Sol Jo 737.

62   EA 1996 s437(1) as amended.

education.[62] If the LEA is not satisfied by the parents that the child is receiving a suitable education, then it must serve the parents with a 'school attendance order' requiring the parents to register the child at a named school.[63] It is a criminal offence to fail to comply with a school attendance order and a parent convicted by the magistrates' court is liable to a fine.[64]

Education of children under school age

7.61   LEAs also have a duty to secure sufficient provision in their area for nursery education.[65]

7.62   Children that have not had the benefit of any form of pre-school learning experience are at risk of under-achievement when at school. Gypsy and Traveller parents with 3- to 4-year-old children should contact their LEA or local Traveller education support service for details of the facilities available in their area and should make inquiries about local Sure Start programmes in order to gain access to affordable childcare and pre-school education.[66]

Raising the achievement of Gypsy and Traveller pupils

7.63   If LEAs and schools follow the guidance in Aiming High,[67] then it is hoped by the government that they will begin to address many of the issues identified in this chapter and raise the level of achievement of Gypsy and Traveller children within the education system, thus ensuring that they experience real equality of opportunity.

7.64   Nevertheless, it is difficult to see how much will change for those Gypsy and Traveller children still living on unauthorised sites under the threat of constant eviction unless and until both local authorities and the courts place greater weight on their educational needs.[68]

63   EA 1996 s437(3) as amended.
64   EA 1996 s443.
65   SSFA 1998 s119.
66   More information on Sure Start programmes can be found at www.surestart.gov.uk. Parents may also wish to obtain a copy of the booklet *'Early years: Traveller children training at home and school'*, published by Educational Services and North Yorkshire County Council.
67   See footnote 5 above.
68   See *Basildon DC v Secretary of State for the Environment and Appelby* (unreported) 21 December 2001, Admin Ct and chapter 2 at para 2.95, above, for an example of a planning case where a court upheld the decision of the secretary of state to grant planning permission for a Gypsy site in the Green Belt. In that case it was considered that the educational needs of the children living on the site clearly outweighed the objections based on conflicts with planning policy and the environmental harm caused by the development.

7.65   In February 2004, the government published new *Guidance on managing unauthorised camping*,[69] which stipulates that all public authorities need to be able to demonstrate that they have taken the welfare needs of unauthorised campers into consideration before making a decision to evict. The educational needs of children camping with their parents on an unauthorised site will clearly be relevant to such a decision.[70] Yet, as Ofsted stated in its 2003 report:[71]

> Many authorities have clear statements about the inclusion of all pupils in education. However, in too many authorities, the ways in which they deal with unauthorised encampments contradict the principles set out in their public statements on inclusion, educational entitlement and race equality. Such contradictions undermine relationships and inhibit the effectiveness of the Traveller Education Support Services and other agencies.

7.66   It is very important, therefore, that Gypsies and Travellers who are living with their children and wish to challenge a local authority's decision to evict them from an unauthorised encampment should place great emphasis upon the educational needs of their children (highlighting any special educational needs) and, if the matter comes to court, ask that the local authority's justification for eviction be subjected to close and careful scrutiny.

Healthcare

The right to healthcare

7.67   In effect, everyone has a right to healthcare provided by the National Health Service (NHS).[72] What this means in practice is that no hospital should ever turn away an individual who is in need of treatment. However, that does not mean that a patient is entitled to insist upon a particular type of treatment. A number of cases in which individuals have sought to challenge decisions taken by healthcare professions

---

69   The *Guidance* was effective from 27 February 2004 and published by the Office of the Deputy Prime Minister (ODPM) and replaces the earlier guidance contained in *Managing unauthorised camping: a good practice guide*, that had been published by the Department of Environment, Transport and the Regions and the Home Office in 1998 (and was amended in 2000). See also chapter 5 at para 5.125, above.
70   See para 5.20 of the Guidance.
71   *Provision and support for Traveller pupils*, Ofsted, 2003, p5.
72   National Health Service Act (NHSA) 1977 ss1 and 3 and article 13 of the European Social Charter (1961, revised 1996).

with regard to a patient's treatment and, more generally, with regard to the management and allocation of resources to fund certain types of treatment have been unsuccessful.[73]

NHS structure

7.68   The structure of the NHS has changed in recent years and a number of bodies have been created in an attempt to improve the provision of health and care services to the public.[74]

7.69   The Department of Health is responsible for:

- setting overall direction and leading transformation of the NHS and social care;
- setting national standards to improve quality of services;
- securing resources and making investment decisions to ensure that the NHS and social care are able to deliver services; and
- working with key partners (such as with strategic health authorities, the Commission for Healthcare Improvement, the Commission for Social Care Inspection, the NHS Modernisation Agency and the Social Care Institute for Excellence) to ensure quality of services.

7.70   The Modernisation Agency has been created to support NHS clinicians and managers in their efforts to deliver improvements to their services. The best-performing organisations will be rewarded with more power to make decisions at a local level. The Agency will also support NHS organisations where services are poor or failing – identifying problems and helping to get these organisations back on track.

7.71   In April 2002, 28 new strategic health authorities (SHAs) were created to cover larger areas, to develop strategies for the NHS and to make sure their local NHS organisations were performing well. SHAs are responsible for:

- developing plans for improving health services in their local area;
- making sure local health services are of a high quality and are performing well;

---

73 See, for example, *R v Cambridge Health Authority ex p B* [1995] 2 All ER 129, CA and compare with *R v North East Devon HA ex p Coughlan* [2000] 3 All ER 850; (1999) 2 CCLR 285, where a patient was given a 'legitimate expectation' that she would be entitled to reside in a particular home for life and the court concluded that the health authority's subsequent decision to close the home was unlawful.

74 This chapter explains the structure of the NHS in England – different organisational structures are in place in Wales, Scotland and Northern Ireland.

- increasing the capacity of local health services – so they can provide more services;
- making sure national priorities – for example, programmes for improving cancer services – are integrated into local health service plans.

They manage the NHS locally and are a key link between the Department of Health and the NHS.

7.72 There are also a number of special health authorities (SpHAs) which provide a health service to the whole of the country, not just to the local community; for example, the National Blood Authority.

7.73 Locally based primary care trusts (PCTs) have also been created and given the role of running the NHS, improving health and managing health services in their areas.[75] They work with local authorities and other agencies that provide health and social care to make sure the community's needs are being met.

7.74 PCTs are now at the centre of the NHS and receive 75 per cent of the NHS budget. As they are local organisations, they are expected to be in the best position to understand the needs of their community, so that they can make sure that the organisations providing health and social care services are working effectively. For example, PCTs must ensure that there are enough services for people in their area and that they are accessible to patients. They are also responsible for ensuring that health and social care systems work together to the benefit of patients.

7.75 'Primary care' is the care provided by people such as general practitioners (GPs), opticians and pharmacists. NHS walk-in centres and NHS Direct[76] are also providers of primary care. All those offering primary care are now managed by PCTs. If a medical or other problem cannot be resolved by a provider of primary care, then it will be referred to a 'secondary care' specialist. NHS hospitals provide acute and specialist secondary care services. PCTs are responsible for assessing the health needs of the local community and decide which secondary care services to commission to meet the needs of the people within their areas.

7.76 Hospitals are managed by NHS Trusts, which are expected to ensure that hospitals provide high-quality healthcare, and that they spend their money efficiently. They also decide on a strategy for how the hospitals will develop, so that services can improve. Trusts employ most of the NHS workforce, including nurses, doctors, dentists, pharmacists,

---

75 See NHSA 1977 s16A.
76 NHS Direct is a 24-hour telephone service and can be contacted on 0845 4647.

midwives and health visitors, as well as people doing jobs related to medicine and other non-medical staff.

Gypsy and Traveller health research

7.77 In 1995, the Minority Rights Group (MRG) identified the following particular concerns about the health of the Gypsy population:

- the life expectancy of Gypsies is poor and significantly less than the sedentary population;
- the Gypsy birth rate is high and perinatal mortality, stillbirth mortality and infant mortality is significantly higher than the national average;
- there are numerous chronic illnesses suffered by Gypsies (for example, respiratory and digestive diseases, rheumatism);
- many Gypsies have an unbalanced diet, leading to deficiencies;
- smoking is very common among Gypsies;
- Gypsies have little, if any, dental care, with access to such care being more difficult as a result of many dental practices opting out of the NHS.[77]

7.78 In 2004 a research team from the University of Sheffield School of Health and Related Research, supported by an advisory group, published a report submitted to the Department of Health entitled *The health status of Gypsies and Travellers in England*. The report is essential reading for those working with Gypsies and Travellers and particularly healthcare providers, managers, planners and policy makers. Having undertaken extensive research, the authors of the report found that:

- Gypsies and Travellers have significantly poorer health status and significantly more self-reported symptoms of ill-health than other UK residents;
- health problems amongst Gypsies and Travellers are between two and five times more common than in the settled community;
- Gypsies and Travellers are more likely to be anxious, have breathing problems (including asthma and bronchitis) and chest pain;
- Gypsies and Travellers are also more likely to suffer from miscarriages, still births, the death of young babies and older children;
- the health beliefs and attitudes to health services of Gypsy and Travellers demonstrate a cultural pride in self-reliance;

77 *Roma/Gypsies: a European minority*, MRG 1995.

- there is a stoicism and tolerance of chronic ill-health amongst Gypsies and Travellers and a deep-rooted fear of cancer and other terminal illnesses which tends to lead to the avoidance of screening;
- Gypsies and Travellers place more trust in family carers than in professional care.

The report concluded that the health needs of Gypsies and Travellers are not being met through current provision and it made a number of important recommendations aimed at improving the health of Gypsies and Travellers and their access to health services. In particular it stressed the need for partnerships to be developed between Gypsies and Travellers and healthcare workers. In addition it suggested that PCTs should employ specialist Gypsy and Traveller healthcare workers. Having gathered anecdotal evidence from Gypsies and Travellers which revealed instances of blatant discrimination, bad communication and cultural ignorance on the part of healthcare professionals, the report also recommended that cultural awareness training be provided to healthcare workers and that Gypsies and Travellers be identified in ethnic monitoring in order to ensure that their needs are recognised by policy makers.[78]

Access to healthcare

7.79   There are a number of reasons why Gypsies and Travellers experience difficulty in gaining access to all types of health provision.[79]

7.80   High up on the list is the fact that many Gypsies and Travellers are still subject to a life of continual eviction in circumstances where there are not enough suitable places for them to camp.

7.81   Perhaps not surprisingly, the bureaucracy associated with the NHS also causes many Gypsies and Travellers problems. The completion of forms and the provision of information, such as dates of birth and history of previous healthcare, required by the NHS presents particular difficulties for illiterate Gypsies and Travellers.

7.82   There is a duty on PCTs and NHS Trusts to have 'due regard' to the need to eliminate discrimination in their provision of services and

---

78   The full report can be downloaded from www.shef.ac.uk/scharr/sections/ir/library/publications.html.

79   For a comprehensive European report on the elimination of discrimination and the improvement of access to healthcare for Gypsy and Traveller women and their communities see *Breaking the barriers – Romani women and access to public health care*, Council of Europe, 2003.

to promote equality of opportunity and good relations between persons of different racial groups.[80]

7.83 However, some Gypsies and Travellers do experience discrimination at the hands of healthcare professionals. For example, Gypsies and Travellers living on unauthorised encampments still find that there are some GP surgeries that are reluctant to register them because they do not have a permanent address.

7.84 More generally, there seems to be a lack of cultural awareness on the part of many service providers that can lead to discrimination and prejudice.[81]

7.85 For all those reasons Gypsies and Travellers without a permanent base tend to visit hospital casualty departments or NHS Walk-In centres when they have an accident or illness and, as a consequence, are liable to experience a lack of consistency in healthcare provision. As a result they may be unable to receive the information, advice, support and preventative healthcare that is available to other members of the community.

7.86 Where Gypsies and Travellers can expect to be able to stay in an area for more than a few weeks, it is obviously sensible for them to try to register with a local GP if they have any health problems that need attention. Lists of doctors should be available at main Post Offices or by contacting NHS Direct.[82] Alternatively, information can be provided by health visitors or obtained from the National Association of Health Workers with Travellers.[83]

Mental health and care in the community

7.87 Mental healthcare can be provided by GPs and by other primary care services. More specialist care (such as counselling and other psychological therapies, community and family support) is available in the community and may be provided by local authorities' social services departments. Alternatively, an individual may be admitted to hospital for treatment.

---

80 RRA 1976 s71(1) and Sch 1A.

81 The Derbyshire Gypsy Liaison Group (see appendix C, below, for contact details) has published a useful information booklet for healthcare and other professionals on the culture and customs followed by Gypsies and Travellers called *A better road*, 2003.

82 See footnote 76 above.

83 See appendix C, below, for contact details.

7.88   Local authorities have a duty to prepare and publish plans for community care services in their areas.[84] The term 'community care services' covers a wide range of services, including: the provision of
accommodation for adults who are unable to care for themselves;[85]
services for adults who are blind, deaf, dumb or substantially and permanently handicapped by illness, injury or congenital disability, including the adaptation of homes and the provision of meals and special
equipment;[86] services promoting the welfare of elderly people;[87] non-residential services for pregnant women and mothers; home help and
laundry facilities for households caring for a person who is ill, handicapped or pregnant;[88] and after-care services for those people who
have been detained in hospital under the Mental Health Act (MHA)
1983 and subsequently discharged.[89]

7.89   Local authorities also have an obligation[90] to assess the needs of
anyone who appears to them possibly to be in need of community
care services and to decide whether such services should be provided
in the light of that assessment.[91]

Healthcare and the ECHR

7.90   The ECHR does not give individuals an express right to medical treatment. However, it is clear that there could be circumstances where
the failure to provide such treatment or the withdrawal of services
could amount to a breach of article 2 (the right to life) and/or article 3
(the prohibition of inhuman and degrading treatment) of the ECHR.[92]
Likewise, negligent medical treatment could also engage articles 2
and 3.

7.91   SHAs, SpHAs, NHS Trusts, other regulatory bodies and local
authorities all have a duty as public bodies to comply with the provisions
of the Convention.[93]

---

84   National Health Service and Community Care Act (NHSCCA) 1990 s46.
85   National Assistance Act (NAA) 1948 s21.
86   NAA 1948 s29 and Chronically Sick and Disabled Persons Act 1970 s1.†
87   Health Services and Public Health Act 1968 s45.
88   NHSA 1977 s21 and Sch 8.
89   MHA 1983 s117.
90   NHSCCA 1990 s47.
91   See generally, Clements and Thompson, *Community Care and the Law* (4th
     edn, Legal Action Group, 2007).
92   See, for example, *D v United Kingdom* (1997) 24 EHRR 423.
93   HRA 1998 s6.

Medical records, privacy and the ECHR

7.92   In the United Kingdom, individuals are entitled to obtain access to medical and health records. The Access to Medical Reports Act (AMRA) 1988
gave individuals the right to obtain disclosure of medical reports prepared about themselves for the purposes of employment or insurance
(save in certain circumstances). The Access to Health Records Act (AHRA)
1990[94] gave individuals a general right of access to medical records created
after November 1991 (subject also to exceptions), but most of its provisions
have been superseded by the Data Protection Act (DPA) 1998. AHRA
1990 is now only of any real relevance in cases where disclosure of the medical records of a deceased person is sought.

7.93   The DPA 1998 gives individuals the right, on a written application,
to be informed whether their personal data is being processed, and, if
it is, then they can request a description of the data, the purpose for
which it is being processed, and the people to whom it may be dis-
closed.[95] The DPA 1998 also gives individuals the right to have the
information communicated to them in an intelligible form.

7.94   The DPA 1998 covers all 'accessible records' and, therefore, all
social services and health records,[96] educational records[97] and accessible public records including information held by a local housing
authority and by a local social services authority for any purpose relating to the functions of the authority.[98]

7.95   The written request for information made to the person holding the
data (the 'data controller') must provide such information as the data
controller reasonably requires in order to identify the individual making
the request and locate the information required.[99] The request must also
be accompanied by the payment of a fee.[100] If a valid request has been
made, then disclosure of the information required ought to be made
promptly and in any event within 40 days.[101]

7.96   In practice these provisions entitle patients to a copy of their
records together, if necessary, with an intelligible explanation of
their contents.[102]

94   As amended by the DPA 1998.
95   DPA 1998 s7(1)(a) and (b).
96   DPA 1998 s68 and Schs 11 and 12.
97   DPA 1998 Sch 11.
98   DPA 1998 Sch 12.
99   DPA 1998 s7.
100   DPA 1998 s7.
101   DPA 1998 s7.
102   DPA 1998 s8(2).

7.97   However, there are a number of exceptions to the duty to provide disclosure. For example, disclosure need not be provided of material that would be likely to prejudice criminal investigations, national security or ongoing health education and social work. Nor is there any obligation to disclose information if to do so would involve the disclosure of material relating to another individual, unless that individual consents or it is considered by the data controller to be reasonable in the circumstances to comply with the request without that individual's consent.[103]

7.98   If disclosure is refused by a data controller, then an individual can apply to the county court or High Court for an order that the data controller complies with the request[104] or an application can be made to the Information Commissioner for enforcement action to be taken.[105]

7.99   In *Z v Finland*,[106] it was held that the collection of medical data and the maintenance of medical records fell within the sphere of private life protected by ECHR article 8. In addition, it was said that medical confidentiality was a 'vital principle' crucial to privacy and also to preserving confidence in the medical profession and the health services in general. As a consequence it was held that:

> ... any state measures compelling communication or disclosure of such information without the consent of the patient call for the most careful scrutiny ...[107]

7.100 Likewise, any decision taken by a public body to restrict the disclosure of an individual's medical reports will engage article 8 (right to respect for private and family life, home and correspondence) and it should be possible to challenge such a decision by way of judicial review where it can be said that the restriction is unreasonable or disproportionate.[108]

Environmental health

7.101 Another matter of great concern to Gypsies, Travellers and healthcare practitioners alike is the fact that there is a clear and undeniable link between the poor living environment and poor health of many Gypsies and Travellers.

103   DPA 1998 s7(4).
104   DPA 1998 ss7(9), 10(4), 11(2), 12(8) and 15(1).
105   DPA 1998 ss40–44.
106   (1997) 25 EHRR 371.
107   (1997) 25 EHRR 371 at para 96.
108   See, for example, *Gaskin v United Kingdom* (1989) 12 EHRR 36.

7.102   One particular problem for those Gypsies and Travellers without an authorised site results from the lack of access to fresh water. A variety of health problems can result from the lack of water and poor sanitation including skin diseases, gastro-enteritis, hepatitis and other infections.

7.103   While there is no statutory duty on local authorities to provide water to those living on unauthorised encampments, Department of Environment (DoE) Circular 18/94, (Welsh Office 76/94) *Gypsy sites policy and unauthorised camping*, advises local authorities to consider tolerating the presence of Gypsies and Travellers on temporary or unofficial sites and to examine ways of minimising the level of nuisance on such sites. Local authorities should be encouraged to comply with the advice in DoE Circular 18/94 by providing basic services such as toilets, a refuse skip and a supply of drinking water to those camped on unauthorised sites.[109]

7.104   Alternatively, it may be possible to persuade a local authority to provide water in circumstances where there are children 'in need' living on the site: that is, children who are unlikely to achieve or maintain, or to have the opportunity of achieving or maintaining, a reasonable standard of health or development, without the provision of services by a local authority, or children whose health is likely to be significantly impaired or further impaired without the provision of such services.[110]

7.105   It is not only those living on the roadside that suffer health problems associated with their environment. Many Gypsies and Travellers living on permanent sites may, paradoxically, experience even worse conditions and resultant health complaints. Permanent sites are often found in isolated and environmentally poor areas (by, or sometimes under, major roads or railways, and often near rubbish dumps, on former industrial sites or close to sewage plants) where health problems can stem from poor air quality, poor drainage and the contamination of land.[111]

109 In a report from the Chartered Institute of Environmental Health, *Travellers and Gypsies: an alternative strategy*, 1995, it was stated that: 'Emergency and temporary unofficial encampments can threaten public health. Local authorities must mitigate against this by providing basic sanitation, wholesome water and by removing refuse.' See also the ODPM *Guidance on managing unauthorised camping*, February 2004 and the ODPM *Guide to effective use of enforcement powers. Part 1: Unauthorised encampments*, 2006.
110 Children Act 1989 s17.
111 See also chapter 3, above, and chapter 8 at para 8.2, below.

7.106   Where an authorised site run by a private individual or body is in such a state that it is prejudicial to health or a nuisance, then a resident Gypsy or Traveller is entitled to make a complaint to the local authority. If the local authority is satisfied that a statutory nuisance exists, is likely to occur or is likely to recur in its area, then it has a duty to serve an abatement notice[112] on the 'person' responsible. Contravention of, or failure to comply with, an abatement notice without reasonable excuse is a criminal offence.[113]

7.107   In a case where a local authority site is in such a state that it is prejudicial to health or a nuisance, then a resident Gypsy or Traveller is entitled to make a complaint to the magistrates' court and request that the statutory nuisance be brought to an end.[114] Failure to comply with such an order is a criminal offence.

Conclusion

7.108   In a report published in 2004, the Institute for Public Policy Research (IPPR) made the point that:

> Gypsy [and Traveller] communities continue to be over-represented in nearly all indices of deprivation and social exclusion and to experience widespread prejudice and discrimination. Significant change will be needed in order to make a real impact on the lives of the Travelling community. As with other socially excluded groups it is clear that suitable, good quality, well managed and regulated accommodation is the key to overcoming other social problems.[115]

7.109   The government has clearly recognised this point and intends that the guidance in Circular 1/06 '*Planning for Gypsy and Traveller caravan sites*' will address the acute shortage of suitable accommodation within the next three to five years. Whether that aim is achieved will depend upon the political will of those working in both local and central government.

---

112   Environment Protection Act (EPA) 1990 s80. See chapter 3 at paras 3.46–3.48, above, for a full discussion of this issue and explanation of the various terms.

113   EPA 1990 s80(4).

114   EPA 1990 s82.

115   Crawley, *Moving forward: the provision of accommodation for Travellers and Gypsies*, The Institute of Public Policy Research, 2004, p5.

CHAPTER 8

Race discrimination

8.1	**Introduction**
8.3	**The CRE and the Commission for Equalities and Human Rights**
8.5	**The legal framework**
8.7	Direct discrimination
8.13	Indirect discrimination
	Grounds of 'colour and nationality' • *Grounds of 'race or ethnic or national origins only'*
8.21	Segregation
8.22	Victimisation
8.23	Harassment
8.28	Unlawful advertisements
8.31	Instructions to discriminate
8.32	Pressure to discriminate
8.33	Aiding an unlawful act
8.34	**Scope of RRA 1976**
	Employment • *Education* • *Planning* • *Public functions* • *Goods, facilities or services* • *Housing* • *Discrimination by other bodies*
8.44	**Racial groups – protection for Gypsies and Travellers**
8.52	**Ethnicity, nomadism and the meaning of the words 'Gypsy' and 'Traveller'**

8.54   Enforcing the RRA 1976

8.55   Pursuing a complaint of discrimination

8.61   Obtaining information by using the questionnaire procedure

8.62   Failure to reply or evasive and equivocal replies

8.63   Power of the courts or tribunals to draw inferences

Grounds of race or ethnic or national origin • Grounds of colour or nationality

8.68   Time limits for making a complaint

8.71   'No Traveller' signs and other discriminatory advertisements

8.72   The CEHR's powers

Investigations • Unlawful act notices • Injunctions • Inquiries

8.79   The CEHR's power to institute or intervene in legal proceedings

8.80   The race equality duty

8.86   How can the race equality duty be used in practice?

Local authorities • Police • Schools • Health bodies • Central government and devolved administrations

8.99   Ethnic monitoring

8.101   Sanctions for non-compliance with the race equality duty

Judicial review • The CEHR's power to issue a compliance notice

8.109   Common Ground

8.117   Opportunities and recommendations for the future

Challenging discriminatory legislation • The European Union Race Directive

8.123   Other levers for change

8.129   Conclusion

Introduction

8.1   Romani Gypsies have been resident in Great Britain since the 16th century. Irish Travellers have been resident in mainland Britain since at least the 19th century. Yet they remain two of the most disadvantaged racial groups in Britain. An estimated 12,000 Gypsy and Traveller pupils of secondary school age are not in school.[1] Life expectancy is a decade less for Gypsy and Traveller men than for other racial groups, and still less for Gypsy and Traveller women. A key contributor to their poor socio-economic condition is the fact that thousands of families have no lawful residence: they are routinely refused planning permission and face constant eviction or other enforcement action, including criminal proceedings, when trying to pursue their traditional way of life, living in their caravans.

8.2   Although race relations legislation has been in force in the United Kingdom since 1965 and has developed considerably to protect against increasingly subtle forms of discrimination, Gypsies and Travellers are still experiencing discrimination of the most overt kind: 'No blacks, no Irish, no dogs' signs[2] disappeared decades ago, but the 'No Travellers' signs, used intentionally to exclude Gypsies and Travellers, are still widespread, indicating that discrimination against these groups remains the last 'respectable' form of racism in the United Kingdom.[3] This is supported by the findings of a 2003 Mori poll conducted in England[4] in which 34 per cent of respondents admitted to being personally prejudiced against Gypsies and Travellers. In 2004, Trevor Phillips, the former Chair of the Commission for Racial Equality (CRE) and now the Chair of the Commission for Equality and Human Rights (CEHR), compared the situation of Gypsies and Travellers living in Great Britain to that of black people living in the American Deep South in the 1950s and, in 2005, Sarah Spencer, one of the CRE's Commissioners, drew further attention to their plight in an article entitled '*Gypsies and Travellers: Britain's forgotten minority*':[5]

---

1   *Provision and support for Traveller pupils*, Ofsted, 2003, available at www.ofsted.gov.uk.
2   See, for example, the discussion by McVeigh 'Nick, nack, paddywhack: anti-Irish racism and the racialisation of Irishness' in Lentin and McVeigh, eds, *Racism and anti-racism in Ireland*, Beyond the Pale, 2002, pp136–152.
3   See, for example, Hawes and Perez, *The Gypsy and the State: the ethnic cleansing of British society*, The Polity Press, 1996, pp148–155.
4   *Profiles of prejudice: the nature of prejudice in England*, Stonewall, 2003.
5   [2005] EHRLR 335.

The European Convention on Human Rights ... was a key pillar of Europe's response to the Nazi holocaust in which half a million Gypsies were among those who lost their lives. The Convention is now helping to protect the rights of this community in the United Kingdom ...

The majority of the 15,000 caravans that are homes to Gypsy and Traveller families in England are on sites provides by local authorities, or which are privately owned with planning permission for this use. But the location and condition of these sites would not be tolerated for any other section of society. 26 per cent are situated next to, or under, motorways, 13 per cent next to runways. 12 per cent are next to rubbish tips, and 4 per cent adjacent to sewage farms. Tucked away out of sight, far from shops and schools, they can frequently lack public transport to reach jobs and essential services. In 1997, 90 per cent of planning applications from Gypsies and Travellers were rejected, compared to a success rate of 80 per cent for all other applications ... 18 per cent of Gypsies and Travellers were homeless in 2003 compared to 0.6 per cent of the population ... Lacking sites on which to live, some pitch on land belonging to others; or on their own land but lacking permission for caravan use. There follows a cycle of confrontation and eviction, reluctant travel to a new area, new encampment, confrontation and eviction. Children cannot settle in school. Employment and health care are disrupted. Overt discrimination remains a common experience ... There is a constant struggle to secure the bare necessities, exacerbated by the inability of many adults to read and write, by the reluctance of local officials to visit sites, and by the isolation of these communities from the support of local residents ... But we know that these are communities experiencing severe disadvantage. Infant mortality is twice the national average and life expectancy at least 10 years less than that of others in their generation.

The CRE and the Commission for Equality and Human Rights

8.3   The Equality Act (EqA) 2006 established a new body called the Commission for Equality and Human Rights (CEHR) which will take over the responsibilities currently fulfilled by the CRE, the Disability Rights Commission and the Equal Opportunities Commission in October 2007.[6] EqA 2006 s3 provides that:

---

6   As a consequence all references in this chapter to the powers and duties held by the CRE will be to those which the EqA 2006 gives to the CEHR. However, there are references throughout this chapter to the work done by the CRE in the past.

The [CEHR] shall exercise its functions ... with a view to encouraging and supporting the development of a society in which –
  (a) people's ability to achieve their potential is not limited by prejudice or discrimination,
  (b) there is respect for and protection of each individual's human rights,
  (c) there is respect for the dignity and worth of each individual,
  (d) each individual has an equal opportunity to participate in society, and
  (e) there is mutal respect between groups based on understanding and valuing of diversity and on shared respect for equality and human rights.

8.4 The CEHR has a duty to use its powers to:

- promote and encourage good practice and an awareness of rights about equality, diversity and human rights and work to eliminate unlawful discrimination and harassment;[7]
- promote an understanding of the importance of good relations between different groups (especially between different racial and religious groups) and between members of groups and others;[8]
- monitor the effectiveness of the equality and human rights enactments;[9] and
- identify changes that have taken place in society and the results that our society should aim to achieve for the purpose of encouraging and supporting the development of a society which the Commission seeks to promote.

The legal framework

8.5 The Race Relations Act (RRA) 1976[10] makes it unlawful to discriminate on racial grounds in employment, education, housing and planning, the exercise of public functions and in the provision of goods, facilities and services.

8.6 The RRA 1976 defines four main forms of unlawful discrimination: direct discrimination; indirect discrimination; victimisation; and harassment. The definitions of indirect discrimination and harassment vary according to the context in which the discrimination or

---

7 EqA 2006 ss8 and 9.
8 EqA 2006 s10.
9 EqA 2006 s11.
10 As amended by the Race Relations (Amendment) Act (RRAA) 2000.

harassment takes place. This is because of new, improved definitions introduced by the Race Relations Act 1976 (Amendment) Regulations 2003, which provides protection against discrimination on grounds of race, ethnic or national origins, but not on grounds of colour or nationality, in the areas of employment, training and service provision.

Direct discrimination

8.7   Direct discrimination occurs when a person is treated less favourably on racial grounds than another person is or would be treated in the same or similar circumstances. No justification is acceptable for direct racial discrimination.

8.8   Discrimination rarely takes place openly and may not even be conscious. It will, therefore, usually be proved only as a matter of inference.

8.9   The RRA 1976 recognises that a person alleging unlawful racial discrimination may not be able to compare his or her treatment with that of another actual person. In these circumstances, the RRA 1976 permits the comparison to be made with a hypothetical person of a different racial group in a similar situation. The question to be asked is: how would a person from a different racial group be treated, in circumstances that are not identical but not too dissimilar?

8.10   In certain cases involving Gypsies and Travellers, particularly where they live on sites and they feel they have been discriminated against in the way accommodation or ancillary facilities are offered or managed, it may be difficult to find an appropriate comparator. A council tenant is unlikely to be accepted as a comparator because the nature of a caravan on a council site would be considered 'materially different' from a council house.

8.11   The case of *Smith and Smith v Cheltenham Borough Council and others*[11] provides a clear example of direct discrimination against a Gypsy. The applicant, a Gypsy woman, had hired the Pittville Pump Rooms from the council for a reception for her daughter's wedding, and paid a deposit on the booking. Further wedding arrangements were then made, including catering and the printing of invitations. As a result of several allegations of disorder in recent years, and rumours about the forthcoming wedding, the police became concerned that the wedding celebrations might involve public disorder and liaised with the council, including the manager of the venue, to voice these concerns. The council attached conditions to the hire of the venue,

11   (Unreported) 7 June 1999 (CN755478), Bristol County Court, HHJ Rutherford.

including a requirement that entry should be by ticket only, and that a further deposit should be paid. The claimant and her daughter were very upset and booked an alternative venue (where the event took place without incident). They subsequently brought an action against the council for breach of contract and discrimination in the provision of goods and services[12] and against individual police officers for knowingly aiding the council to discriminate.[13]

8.12   HHJ Rutherford found in their favour and awarded damages against the council. He stated:

> I find that there is no foundation for the assertions of the police that the Gypsy problems of 1997 were linked to the Smith family. The truth is that as soon as the word 'Gypsy' appears assumptions are made that large numbers will descend and cause trouble.

However, the judge concluded that the police had not breached the RRA 1976 because they had not knowingly aided the council in discriminating and were not involved in the council's decision.[14]

Indirect discrimination

8.13   The RRA 1976 contains two definitions for indirect discrimination.

Grounds of 'colour and nationality'

8.14   Indirect discrimination occurs when a person applies a 'condition or requirement' which is apparently neutral but which is such that the proportion of people from a particular racial group who can comply with it is considerably smaller than the proportion of people from other groups who could comply, and which cannot be justified on non-racial grounds.[15]

Grounds of 'race or ethnic or national origins only'

8.15   Indirect discrimination also occurs when a 'provision, criterion or practice', which on the face of it has nothing to do with race, puts or would put people of a particular race or ethnic or national origin at a particular disadvantage compared with others, unless it can be shown

---

12 RRA 1976 ss20 and 21.
13 RRA 1976 s33, which prohibits a person from knowingly aiding another to do an act in breach of the RRA 1976.
14 The Court of Appeal upheld the decision of HHJ Rutherford: see *Hallam and Smith v Avery and Lambert* [2001] 1 WLR 655.
15 RRA 1976 s1(1)(b).

that the provision, criterion or practice is a 'proportionate means of achieving a legitimate aim'.[16]

8.16   In practical terms this broader definition will now cover informal practices in addition to more formal requirements and it need not require statistical evidence of disadvantage. The aim of the provision must be justifiable and the provision, criterion or practice needs to be proportionate.

8.17   The concept of 'practice' may be defined as the customary ways in which an intention or policy is actually carried out. It may include attitudes and behaviour that could amount to discrimination through unwitting prejudice, ignorance, thoughtlessness and racist stereotyping.

8.18   It is important to note, however, that this broader definition only applies to certain provisions of the RRA 1976:

- Part II – discrimination in employment;
- sections 17–18D – discrimination in education;
- section 19B – discrimination by public bodies in all functions but only insofar as such functions relate to any form of social security, healthcare, any other form of social protection and any form of social advantage;
- sections 20–24 – goods, facilities and services, disposal or management of premises;
- sections 26A and 26B – barristers and advocates;
- sections 76 and 76A – government appointments;
- Part IV – other unlawful acts: discriminatory advertisements; instructions to discriminate; employer liability; aiding unlawful acts.

8.19   Notable exclusions from the broader definition of indirect discrimination are planning,[17] regulatory and law enforcement functions.

8.20   In *Commission for Racial Equality v Dutton*,[18] the Court of Appeal concluded that a 'no Traveller' sign displayed in a pub was an example of indirect discrimination. It does not directly discriminate against Gypsies, as it applies to a wider nomadic group, but as Nicholls LJ stated:

---

16   RRA 1976 s1A (as amended by Race Relations Act 1976 (Amendment) Regulations 2003 SI 2003 No 1626 reg 3).

17   Though it may be possible to argue that the provision of accommodation for Gypsies and Travellers is a social advantage and therefore falls within RRA 1976 s19B.

18   [1989] 2 WLR 17, CA.

Clearly the proportion of gypsies who will satisfy the 'No Travellers' condition is considerably smaller than the proportion of non-gypsies ... a far higher proportion of gypsies are leading a nomadic way of life than the rest of the population in general or, more narrowly, than the rest of the population who might wish to resort to the Cat and Mutton [public house].[19]

Segregation

8.21 Segregating a person from others on racial grounds automatically means treating him or her less favourably, and constitutes unlawful direct discrimination.

Victimisation

8.22 This occurs when a person is treated less favourably than another because they have brought or are suspected of having brought legal proceedings under RRA 1976; or because they have given evidence or information on behalf of someone else's complaint under RRA 1976; or because they have complained of racial discrimination.

Harassment

8.23 A person harasses another on grounds of race or ethnic or national origin when his or her behaviour is unwanted, and when it has the purpose or effect of:

(a) violating the other person's dignity; or
(b) creating an intimidating, hostile, degrading, humiliating or offensive (working) environment for them.[20]

8.24 For a finding of harassment, it must be reasonable to believe that the behaviour in question would have such an effect, taking all the circumstances into account, including the complainant's view of the behaviour.[21]

8.25 It would be necessary to show that the conduct had, or was intended to have, the effect of violating a person's dignity or creating a degrading, humiliating, hostile, intimidating or offensive working environment for that person.[22]

---

19 [1989] 2 WLR 17 at 29.
20 RRA 1976 s3A(1) (as amended by Race Relations Act 1976 (Amendment) Regulations 2003 reg 5).
21 RRA 1976 s3A(2).
22 RRA 1976 s3A(1).

8.26   Harassment on grounds of colour or nationality amounts to less favourable treatment and may constitute unlawful direct discrimination under the RRA 1976.

8.27   So, for example, if an Irish Traveller was subjected to a campaign of racist comments and taunts from work colleagues, then he or she could make a complaint of harassment against the harassers and the employer, who is liable for the acts of employees. The employer is not, however, liable for the acts of third parties.[23]

Unlawful advertisements

8.28   It is unlawful to publish, or to be responsible for publishing, an advertisement that indicates, or may reasonably be taken to indicate, an intention to discriminate unlawfully.[24] The RRA 1976 applies to all forms of advertising, including internal circulars or newsletters announcing staff vacancies, and displays on notice-boards or in shop windows. This provision would apply to 'No Traveller' signs.

8.29   The RRA 1976 allows a small number of exceptions where discrimination is not unlawful, for example, in the case of a lawful positive action training measure or a genuine occupational requirement or qualification. The advertisement should make it clear that the employer is making use of such an exception.

8.30   Only the CEHR has the power to bring legal action against the publication of an unlawful advertisement.[25]

Instructions to discriminate

8.31   It is unlawful for a person who has authority over another person, or whose wishes that person customarily follows, to instruct him or her to discriminate unlawfully on racial grounds.[26] Only the CEHR has the power to bring legal action in respect of such discrimination.[27]

Pressure to discriminate

8.32   It is also unlawful to induce, or attempt to induce, a person to discriminate unlawfully on racial grounds[28] The courts have expressed the

---

23 *Pearce v Governing Body of Mayfield School* [2003] UKHL 24.
24 RRA 1976 s29.
25 EqA 2006 s25.
26 RRA 1976 s30.
27 EqA 2006 s25.
28 RRA 1976 s31.

view that 'inducement' may be no more than persuasion and that it does not necessarily entail a benefit or detriment. Only the CEHR has the power to bring legal action in respect of such discrimination.[29]

Aiding an unlawful act

8.33   It is unlawful to knowingly aid another person to do an act made unlawful by the RRA 1976.[30]

Scope of RRA 1976

8.34   The RRA 1976 prohibits discrimination in a wide range of areas.

Employment[31]

8.35   It is unlawful for a person: to apply discriminatory recruitment or application procedures; to offer different terms and conditions to employees of different racial groups; to withhold a job offer on racial grounds; to discriminate in offering opportunities for promotion, transfer or training; to discriminate in offering or withholding other benefits, facilities or services; or to dismiss someone on racial grounds.

Education[32]

8.36   Local education authorities and governing bodies are prohibited from discriminating against pupils on racial grounds: by admitting them on different terms to other pupils; by rejecting their application; by withholding benefits, facilities or services or offering such benefits on differential terms; by excluding them or subjecting them to any other detriment and from any other discriminatory act.

Planning[33]

8.37   Local planning authorities are prohibited from discriminating against a person on racial grounds in carrying out their planning

---

29   EqA 2006 s25.
30   RRA 1976 s33 and *Smith and Smith v Cheltenham BC*, 7 June 1999 (CN755478), Bristol County Court, HHJ Rutherford.
31   RRA 1976 s4.
32   RRA 1976 ss17 and 18.
33   RRA 1976 s19A.

functions.[34] So, for example, discrimination would have occurred if a planning authority rejected an application for planning permission for a site where it could be proved that the decision was based on the fact that the applicant was an ethnic Gypsy or Traveller.

Public functions[35]

8.38   It is unlawful for any public authority,[36] including the police, to discriminate in carrying out any of its functions. For example, the discriminatory use of 'stop and search' powers by the police would be unlawful.

Goods, facilities or services[37]

8.39   It is unlawful for anyone who provides goods, facilities or services to the public to refuse provision on racial grounds, or to provide a lesser standard of provision. This provision could be used, for example, where an electricity or water company refuses to provide services for ethnic Gypsies or Travellers living on a site, or provided substandard services on racial grounds. *Smith and Smith v Cheltenham Borough Council*[38] is an example of the successful use of RRA 1976 ss20 and 21.

Housing[39]

8.40   It is unlawful for someone to discriminate in how they dispose of or manage premises, by refusing an application for the premises or treating an applicant differently in relation to any list of persons in need of such premises. It is unlawful for someone to discriminate in how they manage the premises, how they give or withhold benefits or facilities and in the way that an eviction is carried out. This provision applies to site provision and management. So, for example, a Romani Gypsy or ethnic Traveller could bring a claim that a housing authority had

---

34 In England and Wales 'planning functions' means functions under the Town and Country Planning Act 1990, the Planning (Listed Buildings and Conservation Areas) Act 1990, the Planning (Hazardous Substances) Act 1990 and any others which are prescribed.

35 RRA 1976 s19B.

36 In this section, 'public authority' includes any person certain of whose functions are functions of a public nature.

37 RRA 1976 s20.

38 (Unreported) 7 June 1999 (CN755478), Bristol County Court, HHJ Rutherford and see para 8.11, above.

39 RRA 1976 s21.

discriminated against them when allocating council housing or pitches on an official site.

Discrimination by other bodies

8.41 Trade unions, employers' associations and professional and trade associations have a dual role as employers and providers of services specifically covered by the RRA 1976. They are also responsible for making sure that their representatives and members do not discriminate unlawfully, on racial grounds:

- in the way they admit members; or
- in the way they treat them, as colleagues, supervisors or subordinates.[40]

8.42 The Act also applies to membership clubs. It is unlawful for clubs and associations to discriminate on racial grounds in membership and the provision of benefits, facilities or services to members or by subjecting a member to any other detriment. This applies only to clubs and associations of 25 or more members and where admission is regulated by a constitution.[41]

8.43 The RRA 1976 does not apply to racist newspaper articles or to racist broadcasts. However, where it is considered that an article or broadcast amounts to an 'incitement to racial hatred' then the police may prosecute the person(s) responsible for breaching the provisions of the Public Order Act 1986 which outlaw such acts. Any member of the public can refer such material to the police. Although the CEHR has no legal powers to deal with such cases, it may refer matters to the police directly.[42]

Racial groups – protection for Gypsies and Travellers

8.44 The RRA 1976 protects all racial groups from discrimination. 'Racial group' means a group of persons defined by reference to colour, race, nationality or ethnic or national origins.

---

40 RRA 1976 s11.
41 RRA 1976 s25.
42 In October 2003, the CRE referred the burning of an effigy of a Gypsy caravan in Firle, Sussex to the police (see chapter 1 at para 1.1, above). The police subsequently launched an investigation and a number of people were arrested – though no one was ever prosecuted in relation to the incident.

8.45   Romani Gypsies and Irish Travellers have been held to be 'ethnic' groups for the purpose of the RRA 1976. The criteria for determining whether a group constitutes an ethnic group are set out in the House of Lords judgment in the case of *Mandla (Sewa Singh) v Dowell Lee*.[43] The Lords held that to constitute an 'ethnic group' under the RRA 1976 a group had to regard itself, and be regarded by others, as a distinct community by virtue of certain characteristics. Two essential factors are:

- a long, shared history, of which the group is conscious as distinguishing it from other groups, and the memory of which it keeps alive;
- a cultural tradition of its own, including family and social customs and manners, often but not necessarily associated with religious observance.

8.46   Other relevant considerations which are likely to indicate, but are not essential to define, a distinct ethnic group include:

- a common geographical origin or descent from a small number of common ancestors;
- a common language, not necessarily peculiar to that group;
- a common literature peculiar to the group;
- a common religion different from that of neighbouring groups or from the general community surrounding it;
- being a minority or being an oppressed or a dominant group within a larger community.

8.47   In *CRE v Dutton*,[44] the Court of Appeal found that Romani Gypsies were a minority with a long, shared history, a common geographical origin and a cultural tradition of their own.

8.48   In *O'Leary v Allied Domecq*,[45] HHJ Goldstein reached a similar decision in respect of Irish Travellers. Although a county court judgment, it should be noted that, in Northern Ireland, Irish Travellers are explicitly protected from discrimination under Race Relations (Northern Ireland) Order 1997 article 5, and this makes it highly unlikely that their status as members of a separate ethnic group could be open to

---

43 [1983] 2 AC 548.
44 [1989] 2 WLR 17, CA.
45 *P O'Leary and others v Allied Domecq and others* (unreported) 29 August 2000 (Case No CL 950275–79), Central London County Court, Goldstein HHJ.

challenge again in the United Kingdom. As HHJ Goldstein said in *O'Leary*:

> ... if indeed it be the case, as the defence argue, that Irish travellers do not bring themselves within the definition of an ethnic social group under the Act, then we have a very strange anomaly that Irish travellers are protected in Ireland but not protected in England as a result of legislation by a British government.[46]

8.49   The distinct racial identity of Scottish Gypsy Travellers and Welsh Gypsy Travellers has yet to be considered by the courts although there was some recognition of Welsh Gypsy Travellers in the observations made by Nicholls LJ in *Dutton*.[47]

8.50   New Travellers and other occupational Travellers do not come within the definition of a racial group. In *O'Leary*,[48] HHJ Goldstein made it clear that the court's decision would not enable all Travellers to claim ethnic status, and that it should not be seen as 'opening the floodgates to endless applications from amorphous groups seeking to take advantage of this decision'. Furthermore, it was made clear by Stocker LJ in *Dutton*[49] that a strong case would need to be made by others and that 'the fact alone that a group may comply with all or most of the relevant criteria does not establish that such a group is of ethnic origin'.

8.51   Even after hearing expert evidence, the courts may still reject an argument that a group constitutes a racial group. For example, in *Dawkins v Department of the Environment*,[50] the EAT held that Rastafarians were not an ethnic group because, although they share a common religion and meet some of the other criteria, it was considered that they do not have a sufficiently long shared history and that there was not enough to distinguish them from the rest of the African Caribbean community. The same arguments may apply to other Travelling groups.[51]

---

46 *P O'Leary and others v Allied Domecq and others* at p26 of the judgment.
47 [1989] 2 WLR 17 at 27.
48 *P O'Leary and others v Allied Domecq and others* at p39 of the judgment.
49 [1989] 2 WLR 17 at 34.
50 [1993] IRLR 284.
51 Those Travellers that are not recognised members of an ethnic group can still use European Convention on Human Rights (ECHR) article 14 to challenge discrimination in respect of any of the other rights that they enjoy under the Convention. See chapter 2 at paras 2.9–2.11, above.

Ethnicity, nomadism and the meaning of the words 'Gypsy' and 'Traveller'

8.52   Romani Gypsies and Irish Travellers are protected from discrimination by the RRA 1976 whether or not they pursue a nomadic way of life. It is their separate group identities which makes them eligible for protection.

8.53   However, it is important to remember that the meaning of the words 'Gypsy' and 'Traveller' in legislation and government guidance relating to the provision of caravan sites is not based on ethnicity.[52] Paragraph 15 of ODPM Circular 01/06, *Planning for Gypsy and Traveller caravan sites*, states that:

> For the purposes of this Circular 'gypsies and travellers' means
>
> > Persons of nomadic habit of life whatever their race or origin, including such persons who on grounds only of their own or their family's or dependants' educational or health needs or old age have ceased to travel temporarily or permanently, but excluding members of an organised group of travelling show people or circus people travelling together as such.

It follows that a person can be an ethnic Romani Gypsy or Irish Traveller but not be entitled to rely upon the positive advice on the provision of accommodation for Gypsies and Travellers if he or she has ceased travelling for a reason not included in paragraph 15 of the Circular.[53]

Enforcing the RRA 1976

8.54   If a Gypsy or Traveller feels that he or she has been discriminated against directly or indirectly, or victimised or harassed in any of the areas covered by the RRA 1976 on racial grounds, he or she can make a complaint of discrimination.

Pursuing a complaint of discrimination

8.55   A complainant can seek assistance from a Citizens' Advice Bureau (CAB), a local Race Equality Council (which is an independent voluntary organisation), a solicitor or other suitable advice agency. He or she can also approach the CEHR for advice and assistance. EqA 2006

---

52 See chapters 1 and 4, above.
53 See chapter 4, above.

s28 covers the provision of legal assistance by the CEHR and EqA 2006 s28(1) provides that:

> The Commission may assist an individual who is or may become a party to legal proceedings if –
>   (a) the proceedings relate or may relate (wholly or partly) to a provision of the equality enactments, and
>   (b) the individual alleges that he has been the victim of behaviour contrary to a provision of the equality enactments,

and EqA 2006 s28(4) makes it clear that assistance can include the provision of legal advice, legal representation and the facilities for the settlement of a dispute.[54]

8.56 Cases involving racial discrimination in employment are heard in employment tribunals. Other racial discrimination cases are heard in county courts (in England and Wales).[55] In many cases it is advisable to settle a case before it gets to a full hearing, if the terms are acceptable to both parties or are the same or better than what would be granted by a court or tribunal. In practice, a significant proportion of all cases are settled on agreed terms. A settlement may take the form of an agreement to pay a sum of money or an apology and may also contain an undertaking to work with the CEHR to bring the respondent into compliance with the RRA 1976.

8.57 In employment cases, the services of the Advisory, Conciliation and Arbitration Service (ACAS) are automatically offered, to help the complainant reach a settlement. ACAS is an independent body set up to act as a go-between in disputes. There is no obligation to accept ACAS's advice, but, if a settlement is reached through ACAS, the complainant cannot go to the tribunal and the complaint must be withdrawn. ACAS cannot assist with settling county or sheriff court cases.

8.58 If cases do reach hearings, then the employment tribunal can order compensation to be paid to the applicant. The amount may include a sum for lost earnings and benefits and a sum for injury to feelings. There is no ceiling to the amount a tribunal can award, although it will normally follow guidelines and precedents from previous cases. If the case is successful, the tribunal can also recommend that the

---

54 Note that RRA 1976 s66(1) provided a statutory criteria for the CRE to apply when considering whether to provide assistance, and that it would only do so where cases raised a question of principle, or were of such complexity that it would be unreasonable to expect the applicant to deal with the case unaided or by reason of any other special consideration. This provision has been repealed by the EqA 2006.
55 Sheriff court in Scotland.

employer take certain steps to enable the complainant to work without further discrimination.

8.59   If the case is not successful, the applicant will not automatically be ordered to pay the other side's legal costs, but the tribunal may make an applicant pay if it thinks he or she acted unreasonably, frivolously or vexatiously in pursuing the case. An appeal against the tribunal's decision can be made to the Employment Appeal Tribunal, but only on a point of law. An appeal must be lodged within 42 days.

8.60   In the county court,[56] if the case is successful, the court can order compensation to be paid. The amount may include a sum to compensate the claimant for any losses and a sum for injury to feelings. There is no ceiling to the compensation that a court can award, but awards tend to be lower than those made by tribunals. If the case is withdrawn before trial or is ultimately unsuccessful, then the claimant will normally be ordered to pay the defendant's legal costs.

Obtaining information by using the questionnaire procedure

8.61   Where a person suspects that they have been subjected to unlawful discrimination or harassment, they may send a questionnaire to the person or body suspected of discriminating against them.[57] RRA 1976 s65(1) permits the secretary of state by order to prescribe the forms that may be used by the aggrieved person and the respondent. The Race Relations (Questions and Replies) Order 1977 permits an 'aggrieved' person to question a possible 'respondent on his reasons for doing any relevant act, or any other matter which is or may be relevant'. The order permits the use of forms 'to the like effect' with such variations as the circumstances may require.

Failure to reply or evasive and equivocal replies

8.62   Where the aggrieved person questions the respondent, the question and any reply are admissible in evidence in any proceedings that are brought. Where a respondent deliberately and without reasonable excuse omits to reply, or is evasive or equivocal in their reply, RRA

---

56   Sheriff court in Scotland.
57   The time limits for the service of and replies to questionnaires can be found in Race Relations (Questions and Replies) Order 1977 SI No 842 article 4 and Race Relations Act 1976 (Amendment) Regulations 2003 SI No 1626 reg 47.

1976 s65(2) permits a court or tribunal to draw any inference that it considers just and equitable, including an inference that the respondent committed an unlawful act.

Power of the courts or tribunals to draw inferences

8.63 The Race Relations Act 1976 (Amendment) Regulations 2003[58] amend RRA 1976 by inserting two new sections into the Act. RRA 1976 ss54A and 57ZA apply to complaints of discrimination on grounds of race or ethnic or national origins and to complaints of harassment brought before employment tribunals and the courts respectively and change the burden of proof in these cases. Previously, the burden of proof was on the claimant to prove the allegation of discrimination. Since 19 July 2003, the burden of proof has shifted so that, once the complainant has established the facts from which discrimination or harassment could be inferred, the burden of proof is on the respondent to show that they did not discriminate against the complainant.

8.64 An applicant (or claimant in the county court) can take advantage of the questionnaire procedure to obtain information that might assist them in establishing a prima facie case of discrimination before the tribunal (or court). Where a respondent fails to provide evidence to show that they did not discriminate against the complainant, the court or tribunal is directed to find against the respondent or defendant.

8.65 As RRA 1976 ss54A and 57ZA apply to complaints of discrimination on grounds of race or ethnic or national origin and to complaints of harassment, the burden of proof used by the tribunals and courts will now vary according to the grounds of the alleged discrimination.

Grounds of race or ethnic or national origin

8.66 If an applicant or claimant can establish the facts from which a tribunal or court can infer that an act of racial discrimination or harassment on grounds of race or ethnic or national origin has occurred, the employer will have to prove that any difference in treatment was not due in any way to discrimination or harassment. If the explanation is inadequate or unsatisfactory, the tribunal or court must find that unlawful discrimination or harassment has occurred.

---

58 SI No 1626 reg 41.

Grounds of colour or nationality

8.67　If the act of discrimination or harassment is on the grounds of colour or nationality, and the applicant or claimant establishes facts from which a tribunal or court could infer that he or she has suffered racial discrimination, the tribunal or court will ask the employer for an explanation. If the explanation is inadequate or unsatisfactory, the tribunal or court may find that discrimination has occurred.

Time limits for making a complaint

8.68　A discrimination complaint must be made within a fixed period of the discriminatory act occurring, or ceasing to occur. There are separate time limits for county court and tribunal proceedings. Generally, complaints brought in the county court (or sheriff's court in Scotland) must be brought within six months (that is, no later than six months less one day) of the act of discrimination complained of – though if an application is made to the CEHR for assistance within the six-month deadline then the time limit may be extended by two or possibly three months.

8.69　In the case of complaints made under RRA 1976 s57(5) (against education authorities or certain educational bodies that are listed in the table in RRA 1976 s17), the claimant is required to first give notice of the claim to the secretary of state, and the complaint must be made to the county court within eight months of the act complained of.

8.70　Generally, a complaint made to the employment tribunal must be lodged within three months (that is, no later than three months less one day) of the act of discrimination complained of.[59] Exceptionally, and only in very limited circumstances, the court or tribunal will consider a late complaint or claim when it is 'just and equitable' to do so.[60]

59　Though, in a case where the Employment Act 2002 (Dispute Resolution) Regulations 2004 SI No 752 applies the three-month time limit will automatically be extended by three months to six months in order to allow the parties to resolve the dispute. See Palmer et al, *Discrimination law handbook* (2nd edn, Legal Action Group, 2007), for further information on time limits and exceptions to the general rule.

60　RRA 1976 s68(6).

'No Traveller' signs and other discriminatory advertisements

8.71   Such cases do not require a 'victim', and while an individual can bring 'No Traveller' signs to the CEHR's attention, only the CEHR is empowered to take legal action.[61] The practice is to ask the respondent to remove the sign and to seek a formal agreement that the act will not be repeated. Where necessary, proceedings may be brought under the RRA 1976, as in the case of *CRE v Dutton*.[62]

The CEHR's powers

Investigations

8.72   The EqA 2006 s20(1)(a) gives the CEHR the power to investigate whether or not a person or body has committed an unlawful act.The CEHR may only conduct such an exercise if it suspects that the person concerned has committed such an act.

8.73   The CEHR's investigative powers replace those formerly vested in the CRE to conduct 'belief investigations' into discriminatory practices, which could only be undertaken where there was a reasonable belief that discrimination had occurred or was occurring and the complaint was made by or about a specific named body or bodies.

8.74   In 1980, the CRE conducted four named formal investigations into suspected unlawful discrimination against a Gypsy. These investigations examined allegations that certain residents of the village of Brymbo (near Wrexham) had unlawfully sought to influence Wrexham Maelor Borough Council to withhold council housing from an applicant because he was a Gypsy. Two of the investigations examined the conduct of local residents: one, the conduct of a councillor; and the other, the conduct of the local community council.

8.75   One of the residents had organised a petition to the council asking them not to house the Gypsy family in question. The petition stated 'we do not approve of the gypsies coming to live in Brymbo' and further that 'should our objections be ignored we are prepared to take whatever action is appropriate to further our objections'. The resident in question was further quoted in the local newspaper as saying 'the gypsies will move in here over our dead bodies'. Another named subject of

---

61   RRA 1976 s29.
62   [1989] 2 WLR 17, CA.

the investigation made similar comments to a TV reporter. Brymbo Community Council had written to the council following a committee meeting expressing their 'profound dismay at the intentions of Wrexham Maelor Borough Council's Housing Department, to house another family of itinerants in the Brymbo area'. These actions were deemed to be in breach of RRA 1976 s31, which prohibits the use of pressure to discriminate and, of the four subjects of the investigation, three were issued with non-discrimination notices. The CRE concluded that the councillor was not guilty of discrimination.

Unlawful act notices

8.76   If the CEHR has conducted an investigation and is satisfied that the person or body has committed an unlawful act then it may issue an 'unlawful act notice'.[63] The notice must specify the unlawful act and the provision of the equality enactments by virtue of which the act is unlawful. In addition, the unlawful act notice may require the person or body to prepare an action plan for the purpose of avoiding repetition or continuation of the unlawful act and may recommend action to be taken for that purpose.[64] Alternatively, the CEHR may enter into an agreement with a person or body such that an undertaking is given not to commit an unlawful act of a specified kind.[65] The CEHR may apply for an order requiring a party to such an agreement to comply with an undertaking given pursuant to the agreement.[66]

Injunctions

8.77   The EqA 2006 s24 gives the CEHR the power to apply to the county court for an injunction[67] to restrain a person or body that it thinks is likely to commit an act which is contrary to the equality enactments and therefore unlawful.[68]

---

63   See EqA 2006 s21(1), but note that a person or body issued with an unlawful act notice may appeal to the appropriate court or tribunal against the notice and, on appeal, the notice may be affirmed, annulled or varied (EqA 2006 s21(6)).

64   EqA 2006 s21(4) and note that there are specific provisions relating to action plans in EqA 2006 s22.

65   EqA 2006 s23.

66   EqA 2006 s24(2) and (3).

67   Application should be made to a sheriff for an interdict in Scotland.

68   The list of equality enactments is set out in EqA 2006 s33 and includes the RRA 1976. However, it should be noted that EqA 2006 s34(2) states that action is not unlawful by reason only of the fact that it contravenes a duty under or by virtue of RRA 1976 s71.

Inquiries

8.78 EqA 2006 s16 gives the CEHR the power to conduct an inquiry into a matter relating to the duties that it has under EqA 2006 ss8–10.[69] If, in the course of an inquiry, the CEHR suspects that a person or body may have committed an unlawful act, then the CEHR may commence an investigation into that matter using its powers under EqA 2006 s20. However, the CEHR is required, so far as is possible, to exclude consideration of such a matter from its inquiry and should not make any reference to the commission of an unlawful act by a specified person or body in its report of an inquiry.[70]

The CEHR's power to institute or intervene in legal proceedings

8.79 The EqA 2006 s30 gives the CEHR the capacity to institute or intervene in legal proceedings whether for judicial review or otherwise, if it appears to the CEHR that the proceedings are relevant to a matter in connection with which it has a function.[71]

The race equality duty

8.80 The RRA 1976 (as amended) also places a positive legal obligation on over 40,000 public bodies,[72] including local authorities, police, schools, higher and further educational institutions, health bodies and central government to 'have due regard to the need to eliminate unlawful discrimination, to promote equality of opportunity and good relations between persons of different racial groups' in carrying out all their functions ('the race equality duty').[73]

8.81 It is obligatory for all such public bodies to comply with the race equality duty in all functions that have some relevance to race equality.

8.82 In order to assist bodies to better comply with the race equality

---

69 See para 8.4, above.
70 EqA 2006 s16(2) and (3).
71 See by way of example, *R v Ministry of Defence ex p Elias* [2005] EWHC 1435 Admin; and the intervention made by the CRE in *R (McCarthy and Others) v Basildon District Council* (CO/5225/05), an ongoing claim for judicial review of a decision taken to pursue direct action to evict a large number of Irish Travellers from an unauthorised development in Essex.
72 Listed in RRA 1976 Sch 1A.
73 RRA 1976 s71.

duty, certain bodies have been given additional duties.[74] The main public authorities, including local authorities, police, health authorities and central government, have 'specific duties' to prepare and publish a race equality scheme ('the scheme'). In this scheme they are obliged to:

- list the functions and policies they have assessed as being relevant to race equality;
- set out arrangements for consulting on and assessing the impact of new and proposed policies on race equality;
- monitor the impact of existing policies on race equality;
- ensure public access to information and services and train staff on the duty.

In addition, such bodies have a separate duty to monitor their employment practices.

8.83   Schools must comply with slightly different additional duties and must:

- publish a race equality policy instead of a scheme;
- assess and monitor the impact of their policies on pupils, staff and parents of different racial groups, in particular, the impact on the attainment levels of such pupils;
- take reasonably practicable steps to publish annually the results of the school monitoring.

8.84   Some public authorities, such as parish councils, only have to comply with the racial equality duty and are not obliged to comply with any additional duties.

8.85   In order to help public bodies comply with their obligations, the CRE published a *Statutory Code of Practice*[75] and sector-specific guides. The CEHR also has the power to issue codes of practice which shall be admissible as evidence in a court or tribunal.[76]

How can the race equality duty be used in practice?

8.86   In essence, the race equality duty, supported by the additional duties, requires public bodies to be proactive about race equality. Rather than wait for cases of discrimination to be brought against them, public

---

74 The Race Relations Act 1976 (Statutory Duties) Order 2001 SI 2001 No 3438.

75 *Statutory Code of Practice on the Duty to Promote Race Equality*, CRE, 2002.

76 EqA 2006 s15(4)(a).

bodies are advised to collect data on all areas of their employment, service delivery and other functions, to analyse the results, to establish whether there is an adverse impact on certain racial groups and, where this adverse impact cannot be justified within the wider policy aim, to make changes to mitigate this impact. For example, if a local authority was collecting data on user satisfaction of particular relevant services and analysing this by reference to racial groups, it may discover that a particular group or groups was dissatisfied with the services offered, or underrepresented as users of particular services in comparison with local census data. The authority would need to look further into the reasons for this situation and make necessary changes if the reason could not be justified.

8.87   The race equality duty could bring major benefits for Gypsies and Travellers. If implemented effectively, it would mean that all listed public bodies were actively monitoring their policies for adverse impact on all racial groups, including those policies generally affecting Gypsies and Travellers. If they found that Gypsies and Travellers were adversely affected, and if this could not be justified within the wider goals of their policies, then they should change the policy. They should also be actively assessing the impact of any new or proposed policies and consulting Gypsies and Travellers on those policies. Consultation responses and impact assessments should be publicly available to Gypsies and Travellers. Public authority staff should also be trained on the race equality duty and any relevant parts of the additional duties.

8.88   The section below highlights what should be expected of various public authorities in relation to Gypsies and Travellers. It should be noted that the suggestions set out below are not all statutory requirements, but suggested good practice in order to ensure compliance with the race equality duty.

Local authorities

8.89   Where there are Gypsies and Travellers in their area, or where Gypsies and Travellers periodically enter their areas, local authorities should list functions of general or particular relevance to Gypsies and Travellers in their race equality schemes, and set out their arrangements for complying with the duty in respect of these functions. They should consult on and assess the impact of new policies and monitor existing policies that are likely to have a particular impact on Gypsies and Travellers. This might include policies relating to planning, planning enforcement, site provision, site management, eviction and homelessness.

8.90   Local authorities should also assess the impact of wider policies and practices on Gypsies and Travellers, for example, housing allocation or satisfaction with and uptake of the range of public services. Local authorities should also consider how they are promoting good race relations between Gypsies and Travellers and the rest of the community, particularly in the context of planning enforcement and eviction. Authorities will need to consider relevant functions, whether they are providing them directly or securing services from external suppliers through contractual arrangements. If local authorities engage an external supplier to provide services on their behalf then they are still responsible for meeting the duty, even though the supplier has no direct positive legal obligation to do so. This means that the local authorities need to build race equality considerations into the procurement process to the extent necessary to ensure compliance with the duty. Of relevance to Gypsies and Travellers may be the appointment of site managers, the engagement of companies providing electricity and facilities to sites and the use of a private company employed to carry out planning enforcement or eviction.

Police

8.91   Policies adopted by the police for dealing with the management of unauthorised encampments and eviction will impact particularly on Gypsies and Travellers and each police force or authority will need to establish whether their policies have or could have an unjustifiably adverse impact on Gypsies and Travellers.

8.92   They will also need to examine more general policies to assess the impact that they have on Gypsies and Travellers. For example, if monitoring showed that Gypsies and Travellers were overrepresented in records showing the ethnic status of those refused bail at the police station, then the police force would need to conduct a thorough examination of its policies on the grant of bail to see if there was any justification for the statistics. If there was no such justification, then the police force would be obliged to make necessary changes to its policies in order to mitigate the adverse impact of those policies on Gypsies and Travellers.

8.93   The police will also need to ensure that they comply with their duty to promote good race relations, particularly in the event of evictions or enforcement, where there may be issues of public order. It follows that the police will also need to take appropriate action when dealing with complaints of incitement to racial hatred against Gypsies and Travellers.

Schools

8.94   Schools (and local education authorities) will need to consider how their policies, in particular those on exclusion and admission and those relating to attainment, affect Gypsy and Traveller pupils and whether changes could be made to promote equal opportunities for Gypsies and Travellers.

8.95   Schools will also need to consider how good race relations are promoted in the school environment, for example, by developing aspects of the curriculum which celebrate Gypsy and Traveller culture, or through strong leadership, particularly where there may be unauthorised encampments in the local area, and hostility to such encampments. Teachers would need to ensure that they have adequate policies in place on racism and bullying and that complaints made by Gypsy and Traveller pupils are taken seriously.

Health bodies

8.96   Health bodies will need to consider how they are promoting equal opportunities for Gypsies and Travellers, how their staff are trained to be aware of the particular issues facing Gypsies and Travellers and how their general policies could impact on Gypsies and Travellers. If, for example, they established that there were disproportionately low levels of registration or take-up of preventative healthcare by Gypsies and Travellers in comparison with other racial groups, changes should be considered to improve Gypsies' and Travellers' access to and uptake of healthcare.

Central government and devolved administrations

8.97   With their responsibilities for creating law and policy, and providing a leadership role for other public authorities, central government departments, the Scottish Parliament and Executive and the National Assembly for Wales all have a vital role to play through their race equality duty. Each department and devolved body must, like other listed public bodies, produce a race equality scheme.

8.98   Government departments and devolved administrations have an obligation to fulfil their duty in respect of their internal work, and the policies and strategies they produce. Policies and Green and White papers, are all within the scope of the RRA 1976 and arrangements should be made to consult on and assess the impact of, those policies that are relevant to race equality. Government departments also have an important leadership role to play in assisting the bodies in their sector to comply with the duty.

Ethnic monitoring

8.99   The effective implementation of the race equality duty relies on ethnic monitoring – collecting ethnic data, analysing results, identifying disproportionalities and making changes where they cannot be justified. The CRE's advice on monitoring was that authorities should base their monitoring categories on the Census 2001 categories, but adapt their ethnic classification system to the particular local circumstances, so that it includes the particular ethnic groups they employ or serve. So, for example, Romani Gypsies and Irish Travellers could be included as a specific subcategory of 'white other'. However, with the exception of schools, the majority of authorities are not ethnically monitoring Gypsies and Travellers. This is reflected at the national level, including, crucially, the Census itself, meaning that authorities at the local level do not have a baseline against which to compare their own data.

8.100   Public authorities should be encouraged to collect more detailed local data and to ensure that where data is lacking, detailed consultation is used to ascertain the impact of policies. For consultation to be meaningful, it has to be carried out in a way that actively engages the consultees in an appropriate way.

Sanctions for non-compliance with the race equality duty

Judicial review

8.101   Compliance with the duty to 'have due regard to the need to eliminate unlawful discrimination, to promote equality of opportunity and good relations between persons of different racial groups' may be secured by way of judicial review in the High Court[77] by a person who is directly affected or has sufficient interest, such as the CEHR itself.[78]

8.102   The case of *R (Lisa Smith) v South Norfolk Council*[79] concerned the judicial review of the local authority's decision to take direct action pursuant to Town and Country Planning Act 1990 s178 to evict a number of Gypsy families who were living on their own land in breach of planning control and the requirements of a valid enforcement notice.

---

77   For details of judicial review procedures, see appendix A, below.

78   EqA 2006 s 30.

79   [2006] EWHC 2772 Admin. See also *R v Ministry of Defence ex p Elias* [2005] EWHC 1435 Admin and note that this issue will be revisited when the court considers the case of *R (McCarthy and Others) v Basildon District Council* (CO/5225/05).

The facts of the case are somewhat complicated and do not need to be repeated in any detail here. Lisa Smith challenged the decision on a number of grounds and argued that the local authority had failed to have due regard to its race equality duty before reaching its decision to take direct action – despite the fact that the eviction of the families would affect their ability to access essential services, resort to unauthorised sites would generate conflict with the settled population in the vicinity and steps could be taken to minimise those consequences.

8.103   Ouseley J disagreed and dismissed the claim for judicial review. When rejecting the race equality duty point, the judge took account of the fact that the Gypsies had been able to advance their case for planning permission to remain on the site within the planning process and the fact that the local authority had itself tried (albeit in vain) to obtain planning permission for an alternative site for the families before it had taken the decision to take direct action to remove them from their land. In addition, Ouseley J noted that the local authority had carried out a race impact assessment and had identified the fact that the failure to take enforcement action to remove the Gypsies from their land would in itself be likely to provoke hostility towards Gypsies and Travellers amongst the settled population.

8.104   Though Lisa Smith's challenge was dismissed, the argument may well succeed in other cases where decision makers have failed to pay due regard to the race equality duty before taking decisions which affect the lives of Gypsies and Travellers. In his judgment, Ouseley J stressed the importance of compliance with the race equality duty in the following way:

> I do not accept the submission made by [the local authority] that s71 was concerned with outcomes; ultimately of course it is aimed at affecting the way in which bodies act. But it does so through the requirement that a process of consideration, a thought process, be undertaken at the time when decisions which could have an impact on racial grounds or on race relations, to put it broadly, are being taken. That process should cover the three aspects identified in the section. However, that process can be carried out without the section being referred to provided that the aspects to which it is addressed are considered, and due regard is paid to them.[80]

The CEHR's power to issue a compliance notice

8.105   EqA 2006 s31 gives the CEHR the power to assess the extent to which, or the manner in which, a public sector body has complied with the race equality duty.

---

80 [2006] EWHC 2772 Admin at para 87.

8.106   Where the CEHR has carried out an assessment and thinks that a public sector body has failed to comply with the race equality duty (for example, because it has failed to produce a race equality scheme or has produced a scheme that is so poorly drafted that it could not properly assist the body to comply with its race equality duty), then the CEHR may serve a 'compliance notice' on the body requiring it to comply with the duty and within 28 days to inform the CEHR of the steps that it has taken, or is taking, to comply with the duty.[81]

8.107   In addition, EqA 2006 s32(3) gives the CEHR the power to issue a notice which requires a public authority to furnish information so that the CEHR can assess whether it has complied with the race equality duty.

8.108   Where the CEHR thinks that a public sector body has failed to comply with a requirement of a compliance notice, then: in a case where it is considered that a breach of RRA 1976 s71(1) has occurred, the CEHR has the power to apply to the High Court (or in Scotland, the Court of Session) for an order requiring the body to comply; and, in respect of a breach of 'specific duties', it may apply to the county court (or in Scotland, the sheriff's court) for such an order.[82]

Common Ground

8.109   In May 2005, the CRE published *Common Ground Equality, good race relations and sites for Gypsies and Irish Travellers*,[83] a report of an extensive inquiry into the extent to which local authorities and police authorities were meeting their race equality duty, specifically in the context of Gypsy and Traveller sites. In particular, the inquiry looked at planning for Gypsy and Traveller sites, site provision and management, and the management of unauthorised encampments and developments.

8.110   The inquiry included:

- the analysis of the answers to a detailed three-part questionnaire which had been sent to all 410 local authorities in England and Wales, and which resulted in a response rate of 58 per cent;
- a detailed on-site analysis in nine local authority areas, comprising document analysis, interviews with local authority staff and

81   EqA 2006 s32(2).
82   EqA 2006 s 32(8) and (9).
83   *Common Ground* can be obtained from the CRE's website – www.cre.gov.uk – until October 2007, when the CRE ceases to operate and its functions will be taken over by the CEHR.

councillors, relevant police, education and health officials, local Gypsies and Irish Travellers and local residents;
- a public call for evidence, resulting in the consideration of 403 responses from police forces, health authorities, Traveller education support services, Gypsies and Travellers and other interested parties.

8.111   The report identified areas of good practice in every area. A few local authorities showed strong leadership on the issue of Gypsy and Traveller sites: some had taken steps to encourage relationships of trust to develop between those living on Gypsy and Traveller sites and local residents; some resource and manage sites well; and there was evidence of local authorities assisting Gypsies and Travellers to identify land to buy to establish their own sites.

8.112   However, overall, the inquiry gives cause for concern. The report shows that Gypsies and Irish Travellers pass through almost every local authority in England and Wales (91 per cent), and that in over a tenth of local authorities they are the largest ethnic minority group. Despite those facts, the vast majority of local authorities have done little to implement their race equality duty in relation to these groups.

8.113   One of the most important points of concern which the report identified was the significant community tension relating to the establishment of Gypsy and Traveller sites; this issue was acknowledged by the majority of local authorities (67 per cent), but few had taken steps to promote good race relations or taken any other action to investigate and address the root causes of the community tension.

8.114   The vast majority of local authorities that reported community tension said that unauthorised encampments were a cause (94 per cent), whilst almost half also pointed to planning applications and enforcement as another cause (46 per cent). Whilst the CRE's findings on this point are not surprising, it is disturbing to note that only a tenth of local authorities have identified unauthorised encampments as an issue relevant to race equality and race relations in their statutory race equality schemes. While recognising that tensions centre on problems resulting from the lack of authorised Gyspy and Traveller sites, only a small proportion had adequately assessed site needs (34 per cent), and fewer still had developed concrete plans to provide sites, or taken steps to facilitate private provision. This community tension tends to generate considerable public resistance to providing any more public and private sites, thereby creating a vicious circle.

8.115   The report also identifies organisational problems in relation to Gypsy and Traveller sites. It shows a notable lack of council leadership on the issue of Gypsy and Traveller sites at either councillor or officer level, and weak organisational arrangements. Frequently, there is a lack of joined-up working between different departments with responsibility for Gypsy and Traveller sites, leading to counterproductive effects. Often, those with specific responsibility for working with those on Gypsy and Traveller sites are insufficiently senior to have an impact, and are separated from mainstream functions. There is an overall lack of coherent policy framework in relation to Gypsy and Traveller sites, not helped by a failure to collect sufficient data and to conduct meaningful consultation before policies are formulated.

8.116   The inquiry was not a formal investigation and the report's conclusions have no legal implications. Nevertheless, the CRE made 56 recommendations for change which were designed to help achieve the goal of replacing:

> ... the vicious circle of unmet need and public hostility ... with a sustainable approach to planning, providing and managing Gypsy sites in England and Wales.

The recommendations were aimed at the government, local authorities, police forces and other key organisations with a role to play in the provision and management of Gypsy and Traveller sites and were drafted in an attempt to help public bodies comply with their race equality duty in relation to Gypsies and Travellers. One year on, the CRE is in the process of assessing whether, and to what extent, its recommendations have been implemented.

Opportunities and recommendations for the future

Challenging discriminatory legislation

8.117   The RRA 1976 has rarely been used to challenge legislation, for example, planning, eviction and homelessness legislation. Indeed, there is no mechanism or procedure for pre-legislative scrutiny or audits of proposed legislation or for declarations of unlawfulness of primary legislation under the RRA 1976.

8.118   The status of the RRA 1976 was affirmed in the case of *R v Cleveland County Council ex p CRE*,[84] in which the Court of Appeal ruled that the provisions of the Education Act 1980, requiring local education authorities to comply with parental preferences in the allocation of school places, took precedence over the RRA 1976, even though this enabled local education authorities to allow parents to choose schools on the basis of the racial or ethnic composition of their pupil populations.

The European Union Race Directive[85]

8.119 The Race Relations Act 1976 (Amendment) Regulations 2003[86] were designed to insert the provisions of the European Union (EU) Race Directive[87] into our domestic legislation. The Race Directive establishes the principle of equal treatment. It also requires EU member states to introduce legislation to outlaw discrimination on grounds of race and ethnic origin in the fields of: employment and training; education; goods and services; housing; social protection; and social advantages.

8.120 Of particular interest is article 14 of the Race Directive, which imposes an obligation on member states to take the necessary measures to ensure that:

• any laws, regulations and administrative provisions contrary to the principle of equal treatment are abolished; and
• any provisions contrary to the principle of equal treatment which are included in individual or collective contracts or agreements, internal rules or undertakings, rules governing profit-making or non-profit-making associations and rules governing the independent professions and workers' and employers' organisations are or may be declared null and void or are amended.

8.121 The Race Directive may be enforced by the European Commission against a member state upon complaint by another member state or in certain circumstances by a natural and legal person such as the CEHR. Alternatively, judicial review may be brought in the British courts on the basis that legislative provisions contravene an EU Directive.[88] Again, the CEHR may have standing to bring such proceedings, as might other organisations with sufficient interest.

8.122 This is new and untested territory and there has not yet been any such challenge in terms of the Race Directive. Nevertheless, article 14

---

85 Directive No 2000/43/EC.
86 SI No 1626.
87 The Directive implementing the principle of equal treatment between persons irrespective of racial or ethnic origin adopted under article 13 of the European Communities Treaty.
88 For details of judicial review procedures, see appendix A, below.

of the Race Directive provides another useful opportunity for strategic litigation and there are certain areas of law, particularly those that have already been challenged for compatibility with the European Convention on Human Rights, that could be explored afresh under this provision if there was further evidence of discriminatory impact.

Other levers for change

8.123   The Framework Convention for the Protection of National Minorities represents another significant lever for change. This was drawn up within the Council of Europe by the Ad Hoc Committee for the Protection of National Minorities and adopted by the Committee of Ministers of the Council of Europe in 1994. It was opened for signature by the member states of the Council of Europe the following year. Non-member states may also be invited by the Committee of Ministers to become a party to this instrument.

8.124   The Framework Convention is not the only instrument to be developed within the Council of Europe for the protection of national minorities, but it is the most comprehensive, and, importantly, it is the Council's first legally binding multilateral instrument devoted to the protection of national minorities in general.

8.125   The Framework Convention sets out principles to be respected, as well as goals to be achieved, by the signatories, in order to ensure the protection of persons belonging to national minorities, while fully respecting the principles of territorial integrity and political independence of states. The principles contained in the Framework Convention have to be implemented through national legislation and appropriate governmental policies. It is envisaged that the provisions can also be implemented through bilateral and multilateral treaties.

8.126   Certain articles of the Framework Convention are of particular importance to Gypsies and Travellers:

- Article 4 obliges state-parties to 'undertake to guarantee to persons belonging to national minorities the right of equality before the law and of equal protection of the law' and to 'undertake to adopt, where necessary, adequate measures in order to promote, in all areas of economic, social, political and cultural life, full and effective equality between persons belonging to a national minority and those belonging to the majority'.
- Article 5 obliges state-parties to 'undertake to promote the conditions necessary for persons belonging to national minorities to

maintain and develop their culture, and to preserve the essential elements of their identity, namely their religion, language, traditions and cultural heritage'.

- Article 6 obliges state-parties to 'encourage a spirit of tolerance and intercultural dialogue and take effective measures to promote mutual respect and understanding and co-operation among all persons living on their territory, irrespective of those persons' ethnic, cultural, linguistic or religious identity, in particular in the fields of education, culture and the media', and also to 'take appropriate measures to protect persons who may be subject to threats or acts of discrimination, hostility or violence as a result of their ethnic, cultural, linguistic or religious identity'.

- Article 15 requires state-parties to 'create the conditions necessary for the effective participation of persons belonging to national minorities in cultural, social and economic life and in public affairs'.

8.127 As a signatory, the UK government is required to submit periodic reports containing full information on legislative and other measures taken to give effect to the principles of the Framework Convention. The United Kingdom's first report was submitted in July 1999.[89] The report was made public and examined by the Advisory Committee to the Committee of Ministers which prepared an opinion on the measures taken by the United Kingdom.

8.128 Significantly, in the first round of monitoring the Advisory Committee highlighted the need for more effort in the United Kingdom in bridging the socio-economic gap between the majority of the population and Gypsy/Roma and Irish Travellers (article 4) and the need for further steps to provide adequate stopping places for Gypsy/Roma and Irish Travellers (article 5).[90] The UK government must now consider how to meet these recommendations.[91]

---

89 UK report on the Council of Europe Framework Convention for the Protection of National Minorities: available at www.communities.gov.uk.

90 The opinion can be found on the Council of Europe website at www.humanrights.coe.int/minorities/Eng/FrameworkConvention/ AdvisoryCommittee/Opinions/Table.html.

91 See also paras 144–147 of the report dated 8 June 2005, prepared by Mr Alvaro Gil-Robles, Commissioner for Human Rights for the Committee of Ministers following his visit to the United Kingdom in November 2004 (CommDH(2005)6). The report can be found at www.statewatch.org/news/2005/jun/coe-uk-report-pdf.

Conclusion

8.129   While the race equality legislation has developed considerably over the last 25 to 30 years, it has had relatively little impact on the discrimination that Gypsies and Travellers experience within our community. However, there is no doubt that the recent changes to the legislation have strengthened the provisions designed to combat racism and that it could be used in the future to bring significant improvements to the lives of Gypsies and Travellers. In 2004 the CRE adopted a Strategy regarding Gypsies and Travellers[92] which identified the difficulties which they face in our society and called for the implementation of the kind of measures discussed above. More recently, the CRE's report *Common Ground* made a number of recommendations which were designed to address the discrimination suffered by Gypsies and Travellers and to promote good relations between them and the settled community. It is now crucial that the CEHR ensures that these measures and recommendations are brought into force so that the persistent discrimination and prejudice against Gypsies and Travellers can finally be tackled.

---

92   *Gypsies and Travellers: a strategy for the CRE, 2004–2007*, CRE, 2004.

CHAPTER 9

Conclusion

9.1   Conclusion

Conclusion

9.1   Throughout this book the authors have drawn attention to anticipated changes in legislation, 'grey areas' and legal issues that might arise in the future and those points will not be repeated here.

9.2   It is clear that the lack of provision of suitable sites for Gypsies and Travellers is the root cause of most, if not all, of the difficulties that they face living in Great Britain today.

9.3   When the duty to provide sites was repealed by the Criminal Justice and Public Order Act 1994, the government stressed the point that Gypsies and Travellers should be encouraged to provide their own accommodation. However, the fact is that those Gypsies and Travellers who can afford to develop their own sites have been frustrated in their attempts to do so. Meanwhile, there are thousands of other Gypsies and Travellers who remain on unauthorised, roadside encampments without the resources to buy their own land, for whom the provision of additional public sites will be a necessity.

9.4   There is now a new legal framework and new policy designed to address the severe shortage of sites. The Housing Act 2004 has imposed on local authorities in England the duty to assess the need for Gypsy and Traveller sites in their area (and will soon do so in Wales). These assessments will be considered by regional planning boards and will form the basis of their regional spatial strategies. Local planning authorities will then have to identify locations for the number of pitches that regional spatial strategies consider should be found in their areas. ODPM Circular 1/06 makes it clear that both private and public provision is required.

9.5   Previous attempts to provide sufficient sites have failed; government policy has been ignored and, as a consequence, Gypsies and Travellers have no faith in the promises made by politicians.

9.6   This time it is absolutely vital that everyone concerned with the provision of sites makes a concerted effort to tackle the problem, in order to resolve the terrible cycle of eviction, confrontation and deprivation that faces thousands of Gypsies and Travellers. In particular, the government must retain the political will to push through its policy and use its powers to force recalcitrant local authorities to comply with the new requirements in both a vigorous and determined fashion. The government now has a golden opportunity to address the accommodation needs of Gypsies and Travellers and it is crucial that it uses its powers effectively in order to achieve that aim.

APPENDICES

A   **Procedure   317**

Judicial review   317

Town and Country Planning Act 1990 s288
applications   319

Town and Country Planning Act 1990 s289 appeals   321

Homeless reviews and appeals   322

B   **Statutes, circulars and guidance   324**

Statutes   324

Caravan Sites Act 1968 ss2–4   324

Mobile Homes Act 1983   327

Town and Country Planning Act 1990 (extracts)   343

Criminal Justice and Public Order Act 1994 (extracts)   367

Human Rights Act 1998   377

Housing Act 2004 ss 225, 226   400

Circulars   402

Planning for Gypsy and Traveller Caravan Sites
(ODPM Circular 1/06)   402

Gypsy Sites Policy and Unauthorised Camping
(DoE Circular 18/94)   425

Guidance   431

Guidance on Managing Unauthorised Camping
(ODPM/HOME OFFICE 2004)   431

Supplement to 'Managing unauthorised camping: a good practice guide' (ODPM 2005)   488

Guide to effective use of enforcement powers –
Part 1: unauthorised encampments (ODPM 2006)   492

C   **Useful organisations   509**

D   **Bibliography   521**

APPENDIX A

Procedure

In this appendix, the reader is given an outline of the procedure to be followed in respect of:

- judicial review;
- Town and Country Planning Act 1990 s288 applications;
- Town and Country Planning Act 1990 s289 appeals; and
- homeless reviews and appeals.

Judicial review

Generally, public law challenges are taken by way of judicial review in the High Court (Administrative Court).[1] However, the House of Lords has made it clear that where a Gypsy or a Traveller wishes to challenge a public body's decision to seek possession of land on which he or she is camped on public law grounds then such a challenge will be taken by way of defence to the claim for possession in the court of first instance (normally the county court but sometimes the High Court).[2]

Decisions of public bodies, such as local authorities, may be challenged on public law grounds in the courts on the basis that:

- the decision is so unreasonable that no reasonable public authority could have come to the decision (known as *Wednesbury* unreasonableness[3]);
- the public authority failed to take into account relevant material when reaching the decision;
- the public authority took into account irrelevant material when reaching the decision;
- in reaching the decision the public authority misdirected itself in law;

1 Judicial review is, itself, a complex matter and for full details see Manning, *Judicial review: a practitioner's guide*, 2nd edn, Legal Action Group, 2004. It is also essential to have reference to Civil Procedure Rules (CPR) Part 54 (see *Civil Procedure*, known as 'The White Book', Sweet & Maxwell, 2007).
2 *Kay and ors v Lambeth LBC, Leeds CC v Price and ors* [2006] UKHL 10; [2006] 4 AC 465; [2006] 2 WLR 570; and *Doherty v Birmingham CC and the Secretary of State for Communities and Local Government* [2006] EWCA Civ 1739.
3 An expression that derives from *Associated Provincial Picture Houses v Wednesbury Corporation* [1947] 2 All ER 680.

317

- the public authority fettered its discretion by adopting a blanket policy without regard to the facts of the individual case;
- the public authority breached its obligations under the Human Rights Act 1998.

There is a pre-action protocol procedure for judicial review claims[4] which should be followed wherever it is possible to do so. Among other things, the protocol advises that a 'letter before claim' should be sent to the defendant which sets out the grounds for the claim and gives the defendant 14 days to reply. However, the protocol does not have to be followed if the matter is urgent, for example, in the case of an impending eviction.

A judicial review claim must be lodged promptly and, in any event, no later than three months after the date on which the grounds for making the claim (normally the decision of the public authority) arose.[5] The court can extend or abridge time, but can only exercise its discretion in cases where it is satisfied that there are very good reasons for doing so.[6] Any application for an extension or abridgement of time must be made in the claim form and should be supported by written evidence.[7]

A judicial review claim is commenced by filing two copies of a paginated and indexed bundle containing the following documents in the Administrative Court Office of the High Court:[8] a claim form (on form N461); a witness statement attaching all relevant documents; a notice of issue of public funding certificate or undertaking to lodge the same (where relevant); a bundle of statutory instruments and guidance that are relevant to the claim; and a list of essential reading.[9] In addition a fee is payable.[10]

In urgent cases an application for a stay or injunction (for example, to prevent an imminent eviction taking place) should be made in the claim form and a draft order setting out the terms of the stay or injunction sought should also be filed. In addition, an application should be

---

4 See note 1, above; *The White Book*, Vol 1.
5 CPR 54.5.
6 See CPR 54.5 and CPR 3.1(2)(a).
7 CPR Practice Direction (PD) 54.5.6–54.5.7.
8 The vast majority of claims are filed with the Administrative Court Office at the Royal Courts of Justice, Strand, London WC2A 2LL. However, judicial review cases can be brought in the Administrative Court in Wales (Law Courts, Cathays Park, Cardiff CF10 3PG) if the remedy sought involves a devolution issue arising out of the Government of Wales Act 1998 or an issue concerning the National Assembly for Wales, the Welsh Executive or any Welsh public body. Where a claim in such a case is filed in the Administrative Court in London there is discretion to transfer the claim to Cardiff: see CPR PD 54.3.
9 For more detail see CPR 54.6 and CPR PD 54.5.6–54.5.7.
10 £50 at the time of writing.

made on form N463 for the claim to be given urgent consideration by the Administrative Court.

Permission is required before the matter can proceed to a final hearing as a substantive application.[11] Normally, permission is dealt with on the papers (that is, without a hearing). However, the court may, in its discretion, order that a hearing take place. If permission is refused on the papers, the claimant has an automatic right to request renewal of the matter at an oral hearing.[12] Where an application for permission in a civil matter has been refused by a judge after an oral hearing the claimant may appeal to the Court of Appeal within seven days.[13]

If the defendant (public authority) wishes to take part in the proceedings then it must file an acknowledgement of service (form N462) within 21 days of service of the sealed claim form[14] and then serve the acknowledgement of service on the claimant no later than seven days after it has been filed.

If permission is granted, an additional fee is payable[15] and the matter will then proceed to a final hearing. The claimant must file and serve a skeleton argument not less than 21 working days before the date of the hearing. The defendant must file and serve a skeleton argument in response at least 14 days before the hearing date.[16] The claimant must file a paginated and indexed bundle containing all relevant documents at the same time as filing his or her skeleton argument.[17]

In civil matters the court's decision on a substantive application can be appealed with leave to the Court of Appeal, Civil Division.[18]

Town and Country Planning Act 1990 s288 applications[19]

A 'person aggrieved', for example, a person who has been refused planning permission by a planning inspector or the Secretary of State for Communities and Local Government (or a local authority which unsuccessfully opposed the grant of planning permission at a planning inquiry), will have a statutory right to apply to the High Court (Administrative Court) for an order that the decision be quashed on grounds that the decision maker erred in law.

---

11 CPR 54.4.
12 In the case of a publicly funded claimant, the solicitor will have to be able to justify such a step, on the merits of the case, to the Legal Services Commission.
13 CPR 52.15.
14 CPR 54.8. The claimant must lodge a certificate of service upon serving the sealed claim form on the defendant.
15 £180 at the time of writing.
16 CPR PD 54.15.1 and 54.15.2.
17 CPR PD 54.16.1.
18 CPR 52.3.
19 See also chapter 4 at paras 4.136–4.140, above.

An application must be filed within six weeks of the date of the decision letter.[20] The time limit is absolute[21] and will not be extended even if the applicant had not and could not reasonably have been expected to have known of the decision within the six-week period.[22]

Details of the procedure to be followed can be found in RSC Order 94.[23]

The application is made on a CPR Part 8 claim form. The claim form (and three copies for the court to seal) must be filed[24] together with the application fee[25] and a notice of issue of public funding certificate or undertaking to lodge the same (where relevant). It is important to note that the applicant must also serve the claim form on the solicitors acting for the Secretary of State for Communities and Local Government (the Treasury Solicitor) and the relevant local authority within the six-week period.[26]

Any witness statement to be relied upon must be filed and served within 14 days of service of the claim form.[27] The respondents will then have 21 days from service of the applicant's witness statement(s) to file and serve witness evidence in response.[28]

The applicant must file and serve a skeleton argument at least 21 working days before the hearing date, together with a trial bundle. The respondent must serve a skeleton argument in response at least 14 days before the hearing.

An unsuccessful party may appeal to the Court of Appeal with permission of the court below or the Court of Appeal itself. Permission to appeal will only be granted where:

- the court considers that the appeal would have a real prospect of success; or

20 Town and Country Planning Act 1990 s288(3). Time starts to run from the date of the decision, not the date when the decision is received: see *Griffiths v Secretary of State for the Environment* [1983] 1 All ER 439, HL. However, the actual date on which the decision is made is ignored when calculating whether the period of six weeks has expired: see *Okolo v Secretary of State for the Environment* [1997] 4 All ER 242. Thus, if an unsuccessful applicant wishes to challenge a decision made on a Monday, then he or she must file an application before midnight on the Monday six weeks later.

21 *Smith v East Elloe Rural DC* [1956] AC 736.

22 *R v Secretary of State for the Environment ex p Kent* [1988] 3 PLR 17; [1990] 1 PLR 128.

23 See a note 1, above; *The White Book*, Vol 1.

24 The claim form should be filed with the Administrative Court office at the Royal Courts of Justice, Strand, London WC2A 2LL.

25 At the time of writing, £400.

26 CPR Sch 1, RSC Order 94 r2(2). The Treasury Solicitor is based at One Kemble Street, London WC2B 4TS.

27 CPR Sch 1, RSC Order 94 r3(2).

28 CPR Sch 1 RSC Order 94 r3(3).

- there is some other compelling reason why the appeal should be heard.[29]

Town and Country Planning Act 1990 s289 appeals[30]

A decision made in respect of an enforcement notice by a planning inspector or the Secretary of State for Communities and Local Government can be appealed by an unsuccessful appellant, an unsuccessful local authority or any other persons having an interest in the land to which the enforcement notice relates, on a point of law to the High Court (Administrative Court).

Permission (or leave) to appeal is required before a Town and Country Planning Act 1990 s289 appeal can proceed to a final hearing.[31]

An application for permission to appeal must be filed within 28 days of the date on the decision letter.[32] There is power to extend the time limit if there is a good reason to do so.[33] Any application for an extension of time should be made at the same time that the application is filed.

The appellant should file: an appellant's notice (form N161) together with copies for the court and the respondents; a witness statement verifying any facts relied upon; a paginated bundle of documents including the decision letter and any particularly relevant evidence; and a list of essential reading.[34] In addition, the appellant must file a notice of issue of public funding certificate or undertaking to lodge the same (where relevant).

A skeleton argument should be included in the appellant's notice or should follow within 14 days of the date on which it is filed.[35]

Sealed copies of the appellant's notice, witness statement and skeleton argument must then be served on: the solicitor acting for the Secretary of State for Communities and Local Government (the Treasury Solicitor); the local planning authority that served the enforcement notice; and any other person having an interest in the land to which the notice relates, within seven days of the date on which they were filed.[36]

An application fee is required and a further fee is payable if permission is granted.[37]

If permission is refused there is no right of appeal against that decision.

---

29 CPR 52.3(6).
30 See chapter 4 at para 4.161, above.
31 Town and Country Planning Act 1990 s289(6).
32 CPR Sch 1, RSC Order 94 r12.
33 CPR 3.1(2).
34 See CPR PD 52.5.6 for a full list of all the documents that must be filed with an appellant's notice.
35 CPR 52.4(5).
36 CPR 52.4. The address of the Treasury Solicitor is One Kemble Street, London WC2B 4TS.
37 At the time of writing the application fee is £50 and the fee payable on grant of permission is £200.

If permission is granted and a respondent wishes to contest the appeal then a respondent's notice must be filed within 14 days of the service of notification of the grant of permission[38] and it must be served on the appellant and any other respondent within seven days of it being filed.

An unsuccessful party may only appeal to the Court of Appeal against a decision made after a substantive hearing if the Court of Appeal itself grants permission to do so. Permission will only be granted if the Court of Appeal considers that: the appeal would raise an important point of principle or practice; or there is some other compelling reason for the Court of Appeal to determine the appeal.[39]

Homeless reviews and appeals[40]

A request for a review should be made within 21 days of notification of a decision under Housing Act 1996 s184. The applicant must be told of the right to request a review in the letter of notification.[41] The local authority has power to extend time.[42] The current regulations on review procedures are contained in the Allocation of Housing and Homelessness (Review Procedures) Regulations 1999.[43] The regulations specify that the reviewing officer must be someone who was not involved in the original decision and who is senior to the original decision-maker.[44] Where necessary, the reviewing officer will need to undertake further inquiries before reaching a decision and may have to have regard to matters occurring after the original decision was taken.[45] An applicant should be given the opportunity of refuting matters on which the local authority seeks to rely.[46]

The regulations[47] require a local authority to notify applicants of its decision within eight weeks of their request for a review. Where the applicant is seeking to review a decision made by two local authorities that the conditions for a local connection referral are met, the relevant

---

38   CPR 52.5.

39   CPR 52.13.

40   See chapter 6 at paras 6.43–6.48, above, for details of the grounds on which a review or appeal against a negative (for the applicant) decision can be taken. For further details on review and appeal procedures, see Arden, Hunter and Johnson, *Homelessness and allocations*, (7th edn, Legal Action Group, 2006).

41   Housing Act (HA) 1996 s184(5).

42   HA 1996 s202(3).

43   SI No 71.

44   Allocation of Housing and Homelessness (Review Procedures) Regulations 1999 reg 2.

45   *Mohammed v Hammersmith and Fulham LBC* [2002] HLR 7, HL.

46   *Robinson v Brent LBC* [1998] HLR 1015, CA.

47   Allocation of Housing and Homelessness (Review Procedures) Regulations 1999 reg 9(1)(a).

period is ten weeks.[48] The parties may agree a longer period and this may be very useful for applicants where further evidence is being sought.[49]

When assisting a Gypsy or Traveller in such a review, it will be important for any adviser or solicitor involved to request a copy of the local authority's homelessness file. This will be required so that the adviser or solicitor can consider the information that was available to the local authority when it took its decision.

There is a right of appeal to the county court: against a review decision on a point of law; or, if the local authority fails to carry out the review decision within the requisite time limit, against the original decision.[50] 'Point of law' includes not only matters of legal interpretation but also the full range of issues that would be the subject of an application to the High Court for judicial review (see above).

The appeal must be brought within 21 days of the applicant being notified of the decision on review, or when the applicant should have been notified.[51] The court has power to extend this time limit 'for good reason'.[52]

An appeal is lodged using claim form N161 and should be accompanied by a witness statement attaching all relevant documentation and a notice of issue of public funding certificate or undertaking to lodge the same (where relevant). For this and all subsequent procedures in running a county court homeless appeal, advisers and solicitors should have careful reference to CPR Part 52.

48 Allocation of Housing and Homelessness (Review Procedures) Regulations 1999 reg 9(1)(b).
49 Communities and Local Government (CLG), *English Homelessness Code of Guidance* para19.16; *Welsh Code of Guidance for Local Authorities on Allocation of Accommodation and Homelessness* para 21.15.
50 HA 1996 s204(1).
51 HA 1996 s204(2).
52 HA 1996 s204(2A).

Statutes, circulars and guidance

Legislation in appendix B is reproduced as amended up to date to August 2007.
© *Crown Copyright.*

CARAVAN SITES ACT 1968 (EXTRACTS)

Minimum length of notice

2   In any case where a residential contract is determinable by notice given by either party to the other, a notice so given shall be of no effect unless it is given not less than four weeks before the date on which it is to take effect.

Protection of occupiers against eviction and harassment

3(1)   Subject to the provisions of this section, a person shall be guilty of an offence under this section –

(a)   if, during the subsistence of a residential contract, he unlawfully deprives the occupier of his occupation on the protected site of any caravan which the occupier is entitled by the contract to station and occupy, or to occupy, as his residence thereon;

(b)   if, after the expiration or determination of a residential contract, he enforces, otherwise than by proceedings in the court, any right to exclude the occupier from the protected site or from any such caravan, or to remove or exclude any such caravan from the site;

(c)   if, whether during the subsistence or after the expiration or determination of a residential contract, the person–

(i)   does anything likely to interfere with the peace or comfort of the occupier or persons residing with the occupier; or

(ii)   persistently withdraws or withholds services or facilities reasonably required for the occupation of the caravan as a residence on the site,

and (in either case) knows, or has reasonable cause to believe, that that conduct is likely to cause the occupier to abandon the occupation of the caravan or remove it from the site or to refrain from exercising any right or pursuing any remedy in relation to the caravan.

(2)   References in this section to the occupier include references to the person who was the occupier under a residential contract which has expired or been determined and, in the case of the death of the occupier (whether during the subsistence or after the expiration or determination of the contract), to any person then residing with the occupier being –

(a)   the widow, widower or civil partner of the occupier; or

(b) in default of a widow, widower or civil partner so residing, any member of the occupier's family.

(3) A person guilty of an offence under this section shall, without prejudice to any liability or remedy to which he may be subject in civil proceedings, be liable on summary conviction–

(a) in the case of a first offence, to a fine not exceeding the statutory maximum;

(b) in the case of a second or subsequent offence, to a fine not exceeding the statutory maximum or to imprisonment for a term not exceeding 6 months, or to both.

(4) In proceedings for an offence under paragraph (a)or (b)of subsection (1) of this section it shall be a defence to prove that the accused believed, and had reasonable cause to believe, that the occupier of the caravan had ceased to reside on the site.

(4A) In proceedings for an offence under subsection (1)(c) of this section it shall be a defence to prove that the accused had reasonable grounds for doing the acts or withdrawing or withholding the services or facilities in question.

(5) Nothing in this section applies to the exercise by any person of a right to take possession of a caravan of which he is the owner, other than a right conferred by or arising on the expiration or determination of a residential contract, or to anything done pursuant to the order of any court.

Provision for suspension of eviction orders

4(1) If in proceedings by the owner of a protected site the court makes an order for enforcing in relation thereto any such right as is mentioned in paragraph (b) of subsection (1) of section 3 of this Act, the court may (without prejudice to any power apart from this section to postpone the operation or suspend the execution of an order, and subject to the following provisions of this section) suspend the enforcement of the order for such period not exceeding twelve months from the date of the order as the court thinks reasonable.

(2) Where the court by virtue of this section suspends the enforcement of an order, it may impose such terms and conditions, including conditions as to the payment of rent or other periodical payments or of arrears of such rent or payments, as the court thinks reasonable.

(3) The court may from time to time, on the application of either party, extend, reduce or terminate the period of suspension ordered by virtue of this section, or vary any terms or conditions imposed thereunder, but shall not extend the period of suspension for more than twelve months at a time.

(4) In considering whether or how to exercise its powers under this section, the court shall have regard to all the circumstances, and in particular to the questions –

(a) whether the occupier of the caravan has failed, whether before or after the expiration or determination of the relevant residential contract, to observe any terms or conditions of that contract, any conditions of the site licence, or any reasonable rules made by the owner for the management and conduct of the site or the maintenance of caravans thereon;

(b) whether the occupier has unreasonably refused an offer by the owner to renew the residential contract or make another such contract for a reasonable period and on reasonable terms;

(c) whether the occupier has failed to make reasonable efforts to obtain elsewhere other suitable accommodation for his caravan (or, as the case may be, another suitable caravan and accommodation for it).

(5) Where the court makes such an order as is mentioned in subsection (1) of this section but suspends the enforcement of that order by virtue of this section, the court shall make no order for costs unless it appears to the court, having regard to the conduct of the owner or of the occupier, that there are special reasons for making such an order.

(6) The court shall not suspend the enforcement of an order by virtue of this section if–

(a) no site licence under Part 1 of the Caravan Sites and Control of Development Act 1960 (c 62) is in force in respect of the site; and

(b) paragraph 11 of Schedule 1 to that Act does not apply;

and where a site licence in respect of the site is expressed to expire at the end of a specified period, the period for which enforcement may be suspended by virtue of this section shall not extend beyond the expiration of the licence.

MOBILE HOMES ACT 1983

Particulars of agreements

1(1) This Act applies to any agreement under which a person ('the occupier') is entitled–

(a) to station a mobile home on land forming part of a protected site; and

(b) to occupy the mobile home as his only or main residence.

(2) Before making an agreement to which this Act applies, the owner of the protected site ('the owner') shall give to the proposed occupier under the agreement a written statement which–

(a) specifies the names and addresses of the parties;

(b) includes particulars of the land on which the proposed occupier is to be entitled to station the mobile home that are sufficient to identify that land;

(c) sets out the express terms to be contained in the agreement;

(d) sets out the terms to be implied by section 2(1) below; and

(e) complies with such other requirements as may be prescribed by regulations made by the appropriate national authority.

(3) The written statement required by subsection (2) above must be given–

(a) not later than 28 days before the date on which any agreement for the sale of the mobile home to the proposed occupier is made, or

(b) (if no such agreement is made before the making of the agreement to which this Act applies) not later than 28 days before the date on which the agreement to which this Act applies is made.

(4) But if the proposed occupier consents in writing to that statement being given to him by a date ('the chosen date') which is less than 28 days before the date mentioned in subsection (3)(a) or (b) above, the statement must be given to him not later than the chosen date.

(5) If any express term–

(a) is contained in an agreement to which this Act applies, but

(b) was not set out in a written statement given to the proposed occupier in accordance with subsections (2) to (4) above,

the term is unenforceable by the owner or any person within section 3(1) below.

This is subject to any order made by the court under section 2(3) below.

(6) If the owner has failed to give the occupier a written statement in accordance with subsections (2) to (4) above, the occupier may, at any time after the making of the agreement, apply to the court for an order requiring the owner–

(a) to give him a written statement which complies with paragraphs (a) to (e) of subsection (2) (read with any modifications necessary to reflect the fact that the agreement has been made), and

(b) to do so not later than such date as is specified in the order.

(7) A statement required to be given to a person under this section may be either delivered to him personally or sent to him by post.

(8)   Any reference in this section to the making of an agreement to which this Act applies includes a reference to any variation of an agreement by virtue of which the agreement becomes one to which this Act applies.

(9)   Regulations under this section–

(a)   shall be made by statutory instrument;

(b)   if made by the Secretary of State, shall be subject to annulment in pursuance of a resolution of either House of Parliament; and

(c)   may make different provision with respect to different cases or descriptions of case, including different provision for different areas.

Terms of agreements

2(1)   In any agreement to which this Act applies there shall be implied the terms set out in Part I of Schedule 1 to this Act; and this subsection shall have effect notwithstanding any express term of the agreement.

(2)   The court may, on the application of either party made within the relevant period, order that there shall be implied in the agreement terms concerning the matters mentioned in Part II of Schedule 1 to this Act.

(3)   The court may, on the application of either party made within the relevant period, make an order–

(a)   varying or deleting any express term of the agreement;

(b)   in the case of any express term to which section 1(6) above applies, provide for the term to have full effect or to have such effect subject to any variation specified in the order.

(3A)   In subsections (2) and (3) above 'the relevant period' means the period beginning with the date on which the agreement is made and ending–

(a)   six months after that date, or

(b)   where a written statement relating to the agreement is given to the occupier after that date (whether or not in compliance with an order under section 1(6) above), six months after the date on which the statement is given;

and section 1(8) above applies for the purposes of this subsection as it applies for the purposes of section 1.

(4)   On an application under this section, the court shall make such provision as the court considers just and equitable in the circumstances.

(5)   The supplementary provisions in Part 3 of Schedule 1 to this Act have effect for the purposes of paragraphs 8 and 9 of Part 1 of that Schedule.

Power to amend implied terms

2A(1)   The appropriate national authority may by order make such amendments of Part 1 or 2 of Schedule 1 to this Act as the authority considers appropriate.

(2)   An order under this section–

(a)   shall be made by statutory instrument;

(b)   may make different provision with respect to different cases or descriptions of case, including different provision for different areas;

(c) may contain such incidental, supplementary, consequential, transitional or saving provisions as the authority making the order considers appropriate.

(3) Without prejudice to the generality of subsections (1) and (2), an order under this section may–

(a) make provision for or in connection with the determination by the court of such questions, or the making by the court of such orders, as are specified in the order;

(b) make such amendments of any provision of this Act as the authority making the order considers appropriate in consequence of any amendment made by the order in Part 1 or 2 of Schedule 1.

(4) The first order made under this section in relation to England or Wales respectively may provide for all or any of its provisions to apply in relation to agreements to which this Act applies that were made at any time before the day on which the order comes into force (as well as in relation to such agreements made on or after that day).

(5) No order may be made by the appropriate national authority under this section unless the authority has consulted–

(a) such organisations as appear to it to be representative of interests substantially affected by the order; and

(b) such other persons as it considers appropriate.

(6) No order may be made by the Secretary of State under this section unless a draft of the order has been laid before, and approved by a resolution of, each House of Parliament.

Power to amend implied terms: Scotland

2B(1) The Scottish Ministers may by order make such amendments of Part 1 or 2 of Schedule 1 to this Act as they consider appropriate.

(2) An order under this section–

(a) shall be made by statutory instrument;

(b) may make different provision with respect to different cases or descriptions of case;

(c) may contain such incidental, supplementary, consequential, transitional or saving provisions as the Scottish Ministers consider appropriate.

(3) Without prejudice to the generality of subsections (1) and (2), an order under this section may–

(a) make provision for or in connection with the determination by the court of such questions, or the making by the court of such orders, as are specified in the order;

(b) make such amendments of any provision of this Act as the Scottish Ministers consider appropriate in consequence of any amendment made by the order in Part 1 or 2 of Schedule 1.

(4) The first order made under this section may provide for all or any of its provisions to apply in relation to agreements to which this Act applies that were made at any time before the day on which the order comes into force (as well as in relation to such agreements made on or after that day).

(5)   No order may be made under this section unless the Scottish Ministers have consulted–
(a)   such organisations as appear to them to be representative of interests substantially affected by the order; and
(b)   such other persons as they consider appropriate.

(6)   No order may be made under this section unless a draft of the order has been laid before, and approved by a resolution of, the Scottish Parliament.

Successors in title

3(1)   An agreement to which this Act applies shall be binding on and enure for the benefit of any successor in title of the owner and any person claiming through or under the owner or any such successor.

(2)   Where an agreement to which this Act applies is lawfully assigned to any person, the agreement shall enure for the benefit of and be binding on that person.

(3)   Where a person entitled to the benefit of and bound by an agreement to which this Act applies dies at a time when he is occupying the mobile home as his only or main residence, the agreement shall enure for the benefit of and be binding on–
(a)   any person residing with that person ('the deceased') at that time being–
(i)   the widow, widower or surviving civil partner of the deceased; or
(ii) in default of a widow, widower or surviving civil partner so residing, any member of the deceased's fairly ; or
(b)   in default of any such person so residing, the person entitled to the mobile home by virtue of the deceased's will or under the law relating to intestacy but subject to subsection (4) below.

(4)   An agreement to which this Act applies shall not enure for the benefit of or be binding on a person by virtue of subsection (3)(b) above in so far as–
(a)   it would, but for this subsection, enable or require that person to occupy the mobile home; or
(b)   it includes terms implied by virtue of paragraph 5 or 9 of Part I of Schedule 1 to this Act.

Jurisdiction of the court

4   The court shall have jurisdiction to determine any question arising under this Act or any agreement to which it applies, and to entertain any proceedings brought under this Act or any such agreement.

Interpretation

5(1)   In this Act, unless the context otherwise requires–
'the appropriate national authority' means–
(a)   in relation to England, the Secretary of State, and
(b)   in relation to Wales, the National Assembly for Wales;
'the court' means–

(a) in relation to England and Wales, the county court for the district in which the protected site is situated or, where the parties have agreed in writing to submit any question arising under this Act or, as the case may be, any agreement to which it applies to arbitration, the arbitrator;

(b) in relation to Scotland, the sheriff having jurisdiction where the protected site is situated or, where the parties have so agreed, the arbiter ;

'local authority' has the same meaning as in Part I of the Caravan Sites and Control of Development Act 1960;

'mobile home' has the same meaning as 'caravan' has in that Part of that Act ;

'owner', in relation to a protected site, means the person who, by virtue of an estate or interest held by him, is entitled to posse ssion of the site or would be so entitled but for the rights of any persons to station mobile homes on land forming part of the site;

'planning permission' means permission under Part III of the Town and Country Planning Act 1990 or Part III of the Town and Country Planning (Scotland) Act 1997;

'protected site' does not include any land occupied by a local authority as a caravan site providing accommodation for gipsies or, in Scotland, for persons to whom section 24(8A) of the Caravan Sites and Control of Development Act 1960 applies but, subject to that, has the same meaning as in Part I of the Caravan Sites Act 1968.

(2)   In relation to an agreement to which this Act applies–

(a) any reference in this Act to the owner includes a reference to any person who is bound by and entitled to the benefit of the agreement by virtue of subsection (1) of section 3 above; and

(b) subject to subsection (4) of that section, any reference in this Act to the occupier includes a reference to any person who is entitled to the benefit of and bound by the agreement by virtue of subsection (2) or (3) of that section.

(3)   A person is a member of another's family within the meaning of this Act if he is his spouse, parent, grandparent, child, grandchild, brother, sister, uncle, aunt, nephew or niece; treating–

(a) any relationship by marriage or civil partnership as a relationship by blood, any relationship of the half blood as a relationship of the whole blood and the stepchild of any person as his child; and

(b) an illegitimate person as the legitimate child of his mother and reputed father; or if they live together as husband and wife or as if they were civil partners.

(4)   In relation to land in Scotland, any reference in this Act to an 'estate or interest' shall be construed as a reference to a right in, or to, the land.

Short title, repeals, commencement and extent

6(1)   This Act may be cited as the Mobile Homes Act 1983.

(2)   The enactments mentioned in Schedule 2 to this Act are hereby repealed to the extent specified in the third column of that Schedule.

(3)   This Act shall come into force on the expiry of the period of one week beginning with the day on which it is passed.

(4)   This Act does not extend to Northern Ireland.

SCHEDULE 1: AGREEMENTS UNDER ACT

PART I: TERMS IMPLIED BY ACT

Duration of agreement

1   Subject to paragraph 2 below, the right to station the mobile home on land forming part of the protected site shall subsist until the agreement is determined under paragraph 3, 4, 5 or 6 below.

2(1)   If the owner's estate or interest is insufficient to enable him to grant the right for an indefinite period, the period for which the right subsists shall not extend beyond the date when the owner's estate or interest determines.

(2)   If planning permission for the use of the protected site as a site for mobile homes has been granted in terms such that it will expire at the end of a specified period, the period for which the right subsists shall not extend beyond the date when the planning permission expires.

(3)   If before the end of a period determined by this paragraph there is a change in circumstances which allows a longer period, account shall be taken of that change.

Termination by occupier

3   The occupier shall be entitled to terminate the agreement by notice in writing given to the owner not less than four weeks before the date on which it is to take effect.

Termination by owner

4   The owner shall be entitled to terminate the agreement forthwith if, on the application of the owner, the court–

        (a) is satisfied that the occupier has breached a term of the agreement and, after service of a notice to remedy the breach, has not complied with the notice within a reasonable time; and

        (b) considers it reasonable for the agreement to be terminated.

5   The owner shall be entitled to terminate the agreement forthwith if, on the application of the owner, the court–

        (a) is satisfied that the occupier is not occupying the mobile home as his only or main residence; and

        (b) considers it reasonable for the agreement to be terminated.

6(1)   The owner shall be entitled to terminate the agreement forthwith if, on the application of the owner, the court is satisfied that, having regard to its ... condition, the mobile home–

        (a) is having a detrimental effect on the amenity of the site; and

        (b) the court considers it reasonable for the agreement to be terminated.

(2)   [Repealed.]

(3)   Sub-paragraphs (4) and (5) below apply if, on an application under sub-paragraph (1) above–

     (a)   the court considers that, having regard to the present condition of the mobile home, paragraph (a)of that sub-paragraph applies to it, but

     (b)   it also considers that it would be reasonably practicable for particular repairs to be carried out on the mobile home that would result in sub-paragraph (1)(a) not applying to it, and

     (c)   the occupier indicates that he intends to carry out those repairs.

(4)   In such a case the court may make an order adjourning proceedings on the application for such period specified in the order as the court considers reasonable to allow the repairs to be carried out.

The repairs must be set out in the order.

(5)   If the court makes such an order, the application shall not be further proceeded with unless the court is satisfied that the specified period has expired without the repairs having been carried out.

Recovery of overpayments by occupier

7   Where the agreement is terminated as mentioned in paragraph 3, 4, 5 or 6 above, the occupier shall be entitled to recover from the owner so much of any payment made by him in pursuance of the agreement as is attributable to a period beginning after the termination.

Sale of mobile home

8(1)   The occupier shall be entitled to sell the mobile home, and to assign the agreement, to a person approved of by the owner, whose approval shall not be unreasonably withheld.

(1A)   The occupier may serve on the owner a request for the owner to approve a person for the purposes of sub-paragraph (1) above.

(1B)   Where the owner receives such a request, he must, within the period of 28 days beginning with the date on which he received the request–

     (a)   approve the person, unless it is reasonable for him not to do so, and

     (b)   serve on the occupier notice of his decision whether or not to approve the person.

(1C)   The owner may not give his approval subject to conditions.

(1D)   If the approval is withheld, the notice under sub-paragraph (1B) above must specify the reasons for withholding it.

(1E)   If the owner fails to notify the occupier as required by sub-paragraph (1B) (and, if applicable, sub-paragraph (1D)) above, the occupier may apply to the court for an order declaring that the person is approved for the purposes of sub-paragraph (1) above; and the court may make such an order if it thinks fit.

(1F)   It is for the owner–

     (a)   if he served a notice as mentioned in sub-paragraph (1B) (and, if applicable, sub-paragraph (1D) and the question arises whether he served the notice within the required period of 28 days, to show that he did;

(b) [Repealed.]

(c)   if he did not give his approval and the question arises whether it was reasonable for him not to do so, to show that it was reasonable.

(1G)   A request or notice under this paragraph–

(a)   must be in writing, and

(b)   may be served by post.

(2)   Where the occupier sells the mobile home, and assigns the agreement, as mentioned in sub-paragraph (1) above, the owner shall be entitled to receive a commission on the sale at a rate not exceeding such rate as may be specified by an order made by the appropriate national authority.

(2A)   Except to the extent mentioned in sub-paragraph (2) above, the owner may not require any payment to be made (whether to himself or otherwise) in connection with the sale of the mobile home, and the assignment of the agreement, as mentioned in sub-paragraph (1) above.

(3)   An order under this paragraph–

(a)   shall be made by statutory instrument which (if made by the Secretary of State) shall be subject to annulment in pursuance of a resolution of either House of Parliament; and

(b)   may make different provision for different areas or for sales at different prices.

Gift of mobile home

9(1)   The occupier shall be entitled to give the mobile home, and to assign the agreement, to a member of his family approved by the owner, whose approval shall not be unreasonably withheld.

(2)   Sub-paragraphs (1A) to (1G) of paragraph 8 above shall apply in relation to the approval of a person for the purposes of sub-paragraph (1) above as they apply in relation to the approval of a person for the purposes of sub-paragraph (1) of that paragraph.

(3)   The owner may not require any payment to be made (whether to himself or otherwise) in connection with the gift of the mobile home, and the assignment of the agreement, as mentioned in sub-paragraph (1) above.

Re-siting of mobile home

10(1)   The owner shall be entitled to require that the occupier's right to station the mobile home is exercisable for any period in relation to another pitch forming part of the protected site ('the other pitch') if (and only if)–

(a)   on the application of the owner, the court is satisfied that the other pitch is broadly comparable to the occupier's original pitch and that it is reasonable for the mobile home to be stationed on the other pitch for that period; or

(b)   the owner needs to carry out essential repair or emergency works that can only be carried out if the mobile home is moved to the other pitch for that period, and the other pitch is broadly comparable to the occupier's original pitch.

(2)   If the owner requires the occupier to station the mobile home on the other pitch so that he can replace, or carry out repairs to, the base on

which the mobile home is stationed, he must if the occupier so requires, or the court on the application of the occupier so orders, secure that the mobile home is returned to the original pitch on the completion of the replacement or repairs.

(3) The owner shall pay all the costs and expenses incurred by the occupier in connection with his mobile home being moved to and from the other pitch.

(4) In this paragraph and in paragraph 13 below, 'essential repair or emergency works' means–

(a) repairs to the base on which the mobile home is stationed;

(b) works or repairs needed to comply with any relevant legal requirements; or

(c) works or repairs in connection with restoration following flood, landslide or other natural disaster.

Quiet enjoyment of the mobile home

11 The occupier shall be entitled to quiet enjoyment of the mobile home together with the pitch during the continuance of the agreement, subject to paragraphs 10, 12, 13 and 14.

Owner's right of entry to the pitch

12 The owner may enter the pitch without prior notice between the hours of 9 am and 6 pm

(a) to deliver written communications, including post and notices, to the occupier; and

(b) to read any meter for gas, electricity, water, sewerage or other services supplied by the owner.

13 The owner may enter the pitch to carry out essential repair or emergency works on giving as much notice to the occupier (whether in writing or otherwise) as is reasonably practicable in the circumstances.

14 Unless the occupier has agreed otherwise, the owner may enter the pitch for a reason other than one specified in paragraph 12 or 13 only if he has given the occupier at least 14 clear days' written notice of the date, time and reason for his visit.

15 The rights conferred by paragraphs 12 to 14 above do not extend to the mobile home.

The pitch fee

16 The pitch fee can only be changed in accordance with paragraph 17, either–

(a) with the agreement of the occupier, or

(b) if the court, on the application of the owner or the occupier, considers it reasonable for the pitch fee to be changed and makes an order determining the amount of the new pitch fee.

17(1) The pitch fee shall be reviewed annually as at the review date.

(2) At least 28 clear days before the review date the owner shall serve on the occupier a written notice setting out his proposals in respect of the new pitch fee.

(3)   If the occupier agrees to the proposed new pitch fee, it shall be payable as from the review date.

(4)   If the occupier does not agree to the proposed new pitch fee–

    (a) the owner may apply to the court for an order under paragraph 16(b) determining the amount of the new pitch fee;

    (b) the occupier shall continue to pay the current pitch fee to the owner until such time as the new pitch fee is agreed by the occupier or an order determining the amount of the new pitch fee is made by the court under paragraph 16(b); and

    (c) the new pitch fee shall be payable as from the review date but the occupier shall not be treated as being in arrears until the 28th day after the date on which the new pitch fee is agreed or, as the case may be, the 28th day after the date of the court order determining the amount of the new pitch fee.

(5)   An application under sub-paragraph (4)(a) may be made at any time after the end of the period of 28 days beginning with the review date.

(6)   Sub-paragraphs (7) to (10) apply if the owner–

    (a) has not served the notice required by sub-paragraph (2) by the time by which it was required to be served, but

    (b) at any time thereafter serves on the occupier a written notice setting out his proposals in respect of a new pitch fee.

(7)   If (at any time) the occupier agrees to the proposed pitch fee, it shall be payable as from the 28th day after the date on which the owner serves the notice under sub-paragraph (6)(b).

(8)   If the occupier has not agreed to the proposed pitch fee–

    (a) the owner may apply to the court for an order under paragraph 16(b) determining the amount of the new pitch fee;

    (b) the occupier shall continue to pay the current pitch fee to the owner until such time as the new pitch fee is agreed by the occupier or an order determining the amount of the new pitch fee is made by the court under paragraph 16(b); and

    (c) if the court makes such an order, the new pitch fee shall be payable as from the 28th day after the date on which the owner serves the notice under sub-paragraph (6)(b).

(9)   An application under sub-paragraph (8) may be made at any time after the end of the period of 56 days beginning with date on which the owner serves the notice under sub-paragraph (6)(b).

(10)   The occupier shall not be treated as being in arrears–

    (a) where sub-paragraph (7) applies, until the 28th day after the date on which the new pitch fee is agreed; or

    (b) where sub-paragraph (8)(b) applies, until the 28th day after the date on which the new pitch fee is agreed or, as the case may be, the 28th day after the date of the court order determining the amount of the new pitch fee.

18(1) When determining the amount of the new pitch fee particular regard shall be had to–

    (a) any sums expended by the owner since the last review date on improvements–

        (i) which are for the benefit of the occupiers of mobile homes on the protected site;

        (ii) which were the subject of consultation in accordance with paragraph 22(e) and (f) below; and

        (iii) to which a majority of the occupiers have not disagreed in writing or which, in the case of such disagreement, the court, on the application of the owner, has ordered should be taken into account when determining the amount of the new pitch fee;

    (b) any decrease in the amenity of the protected site since the last review date; and

    (c) the effect of any enactment, other than an order made under paragraph 8(2) above, which has come into force since the last review date.

(2)   When calculating what constitutes a majority of the occupiers for the purposes of sub-paragraph (1)(b)(iii) each mobile home is to be taken to have only one occupier and, in the event of there being more than one occupier of a mobile home, its occupier is to be taken to be the occupier whose name first appears on the agreement.

(3)   In a case where the pitch fee has not been previously reviewed, references in this paragraph to the last review date are to be read as references to the date when the agreement commenced.

19   When determining the amount of the new pitch fee, any costs incurred by the owner in connection with expanding the protected site shall not be taken into account.

20(1)   There is a presumption that the pitch fee shall increase or decrease by a percentage which is no more than any percentage increase or decrease in the retail prices index since the last review date, unless this would be unreasonable having regard to paragraph 18(1) above.

(2)   Paragraph 18(3) above applies for the purposes of this paragraph as it applies for the purposes of paragraph 18.

Occupier's obligations

21   The occupier shall–

    (a) pay the pitch fee to the owner;

    (b) pay to the owner all sums due under the agreement in respect of gas, electricity, water, sewerage or other services supplied by the owner;

    (c) keep the mobile home in a sound state of repair;

    (d) maintain–

        (i) the outside of the mobile home, and

        (ii) the pitch, including all fences and outbuildings belonging to, or enjoyed with, it and the mobile home, in a clean and tidy condition; and

(e) if requested by the owner, provide him with documentary evidence of any costs or expenses in respect of which the occupier seeks reimbursement.

Owner's obligations

22   The owner shall–

(a) if requested by the occupier, and on payment by the occupier of a charge of not more than £30, provide accurate written details of–

  (i) the size of the pitch and the base on which the mobile home is stationed; and

  (ii) the location of the pitch and the base within the protected site;

and such details must include measurements between identifiable fixed points on the protected site and the pitch and the base;

(b) if requested by the occupier, provide (free of charge) documentary evidence in support and explanation of–

  (i) any new pitch fee;

  (ii) any charges for gas, electricity, water, sewerage or other services payable by the occupier to the owner under the agreement;

and

  (iii) any other charges, costs or expenses payable by the occupier to the owner under the agreement;

(c) be responsible for repairing the base on which the mobile home is stationed and for maintaining any gas, electricity, water, sewerage or other services supplied by the owner to the pitch or to the mobile home;

(d) maintain in a clean and tidy condition those parts of the protected site, including access ways, site boundary fences and trees, which are not the responsibility of any occupier of a mobile home stationed on the protected site;

(e) consult the occupier about improvements to the protected site in general, and in particular about those which the owner wishes to be taken into account when determining the amount of any new pitch fee; and

(f) consult a qualifying residents' association, if there is one, about all matters which relate to the operation and management of, or improvements to, the protected site and may affect the occupiers either directly or indirectly.

23   The owner shall not do or cause to be done anything which may adversely affect the ability of the occupier to perform his obligations under paragraph 21(c) and (d) above.

24   For the purposes of paragraph 22(e) above, to 'consult' the occupier means–

(a) to give the occupier at least 28 clear days' notice in writing of the proposed improvements which–

  (i) describes the proposed improvements and how they will benefit the occupier in the long and short term;

  (ii) details how the pitch fee may be affected when it is next reviewed; and

    (iii) states when and where the occupier can make representations about the proposed improvements; and

(b) to take into account any representations made by the occupier about the proposed improvements, in accordance with paragraph (a)(iii), before undertaking them.

25   For the purposes of paragraph 22(f) above, to 'consult' a qualifying residents' association means–

(a) to give the association at least 28 clear days' notice in writing of the matters referred to in paragraph 22(f) which–

    (i) describes the matters and how they may affect the occupiers either directly or indirectly in the long and short term; and

    (ii) states when and where the association can make representations about the matters; and

(b) to take into account any representations made by the association, in accordance with paragraph (a)(ii), before proceeding with the matters.

Owner's name and address

26(1) The owner shall by notice inform the occupier and any qualifying residents' association of the address in England or Wales at which notices (including notices of proceedings) may be served on him by the occupier or a qualifying residents' association.

(2)   If the owner fails to comply with sub-paragraph (1), then (subject to sub-paragraph (5) below) any amount otherwise due from the occupier to the owner in respect of the pitch fee shall be treated for all purposes as not being due from the occupier to the owner at any time before the owner does so comply.

(3)   Where in accordance with the agreement the owner gives any written notice to the occupier or (as the case may be) a qualifying residents' association, the notice must contain the following information–

(a) the name and address of the owner; and

(b) if that address is not in England or Wales, an address in England or Wales at which notices (including notices of proceedings) may be served on the owner.

(4)   Subject to sub-paragraph (5) below, where–

(a) the occupier or a qualifying residents' association receives such a notice, but

(b) it does not contain the information required to be contained in it by virtue of sub-paragraph (3) above,

the notice shall be treated as not having been given until such time as the owner gives the information to the occupier or (as the case may be) the association in respect of the notice.

(5)   An amount or notice within sub-paragraph (2) or (4) (as the case may be) shall not be treated as mentioned in relation to any time when, by virtue of an order of any court or tribunal, there is in force an appointment of a receiver or manager whose functions include receiving from the occupier the pitch fee, payments for services supplied or other charges.

(6)   Nothing in sub-paragraphs (3) to (5) applies to any notice containing a demand to which paragraph 27(1) below applies.

27(1)   Where the owner makes any demand for payment by the occupier of the pitch fee, or in respect of services supplied or other charges, the demand must contain–

(a)   the name and address of the owner; and

(b)   if that address is not in England or Wales, an address in England or Wales at which notices (including notices of proceedings) may be served on the owner.

(2)   Subject to sub-paragraph (3) below, where–

(a)   the occupier receives such a demand, but

(b)   it does not contain the information required to be contained in it by virtue of sub-paragraph (1),

the amount demanded shall be treated for all purposes as not being due from the occupier to the owner at any time before the owner gives that information to the occupier in respect of the demand.

(3)   The amount demanded shall not be so treated in relation to any time when, by virtue of an order of any court or tribunal, there is in force an appointment of a receiver or manager whose functions include receiving from the occupier the pitch fee, payments for services supplied or other charges.

Qualifying residents' association

28(1)   A residents' association is a qualifying residents' association in relation to a protected site if–

(a)   it is an association representing the occupiers of mobile homes on that site;

(b)   at least 50 per cent of the occupiers of the mobile homes on that site are members of the association;

(c)   it is independent from the owner, who together with any agent or employee of his is excluded from membership;

(d)   subject to paragraph (c) above, membership is open to all occupiers who own a mobile home on that site;

(e)   it maintains a list of members which is open to public inspection together with the rules and constitution of the residents' association;

(f)   it has a chairman, secretary and treasurer who are elected by and from among the members;

(g)   with the exception of administrative decisions taken by the chairman, secretary and treasurer acting in their official capacities, decisions are taken by voting and there is only one vote for each mobile home; and

(h)   the owner has acknowledged in writing to the secretary that the association is a qualifying residents' association, or, in default of this, the court has so ordered.

(2)   When calculating the percentage of occupiers for the purpose of sub-paragraph (1)(b) above, each mobile home shall be taken to have only one occupier and, in the event of there being more than one occupier

of a mobile home, its occupier is to be taken to be the occupier whose name first appears on the agreement.

Interpretation

29   In this Schedule–

'pitch' means the land, forming part of the protected site and including any garden area, on which the occupier is entitled to station the mobile home under the terms of the agreement;

'pitch fee' means the amount which the occupier is required by the agreement to pay to the owner for the right to station the mobile home on the pitch and for use of the common areas of the protected site and their maintenance, but does not include amounts due in respect of gas, electricity, water and sewerage or other services, unless the agreement expressly provides that the pitch fee includes such amounts;

'retail prices index' means the general index (for all items) published by the Office for National Statistics or, if that index is not published for a relevant month, any substituted index or index figures published by that Office;

'review date' means the date specified in the written statement as the date on which the pitch fee will be reviewed in each year, or if no such date is specified, each anniversary of the date the agreement commenced; and

'written statement' means the written statement that the owner of the protected site is required to give to the occupier by section 1(2)   o f this Act.

PART II: MATTERS CONCERNING WHICH TERMS MAY BE IMPLIED BY COURT

1   [Repealed.]

2   The sums payable by the occupier in pursuance of the agreement and the times at which they are to be paid.

3   The review at yearly intervals of the sums so payable.

4   The provision or improvement of services available on the protected site, and the use by the occupier of such services.

5   The preservation of the amenity of the protected site.

6   [Repealed.]

7   [Repealed.]

PART III: SUPPLEMENTARY PROVISIONS

Duty to forward requests under paragraph 8 or 9 of Part 1

1(1)   This paragraph applies to–

(a) a request by the occupier for the owner to approve a person for the purposes of paragraph 8(1) of Part 1 (see paragraph 8(1A)), or

(b) a request by the occupier for the owner to approve a person for the purposes of paragraph 9(1) of Part 1 (see paragraph 8(1A) as applied by paragraph 9(2)).

(2)   If a person ('the recipient') receives such a request and he–

(a)   though not the owner, has an estate or interest in the protected site, and

(b)   believes that another person is the owner (and that the other person has not received such a request),

the recipient owes a duty to the occupier to take such steps as are reasonable to secure that the other person receives the request within the period of 28 days beginning with the date on which the recipient receives it.

(3)   In paragraph 8(1B) of Part 1 of this Schedule (as it applies to any request within sub-paragraph (1) above) any reference to the owner receiving such a request includes a reference to his receiving it in accordance with sub-paragraph (2) above.

Action for breach of duty under paragraph 1

2(1)   A claim that a person has broken the duty under paragraph 1(2) above may be made the subject of civil proceedings in like manner as any other claim in tort for breach of statutory duty.

(2)   The right conferred by sub-paragraph (1) is in addition to any right to bring proceedings, in respect of a breach of any implied term having effect by virtue of paragraph 8 or 9 of Part 1 of this Schedule, against a person bound by that term.

SCHEDULE 2: REPEALS

Chapter	Short title	Extent of repeal
1975 c. 49	The Mobile Homes Act 1975.	Sections 1 to 6. In section 9, in subsection (1), all definitions except those of 'the Act of 1960', 'the Act of 1968' and 'mobile home', and sub-section (2).

TOWN AND COUNTRY PLANNING ACT 1990 (EXTRACTS)

Meaning of 'development' and 'new development'

55(1) Subject to the following provisions of this section, in this Act, except where the context otherwise requires, 'development,' means the carrying out of building, engineering, mining or other operations in, on, over or under land, or the making of any material change in the use of any buildings or other land.

(1A) For the purposes of this Act 'building operations' includes –

(a) demolition of buildings;

(b) rebuilding;

(c) structural alterations of or additions to buildings; and

(d) other operations normally undertaken by a person carrying on business as a builder.

(2) The following operations or uses of land shall not be taken for the purposes of this Act to involve development of the land –

(a) the carrying out for the maintenance, improvement or other alteration of any building of works which –

(i) affect only the interior of the building, or

(ii) do not materially affect the external appearance of the building,

and are not works for making good war damage or works begun after 5th December 1968 for the alteration of a building by providing additional space in it underground;

(b) the carrying out on land within the boundaries of a road by a local highway authority of any works required for the maintenance or improvement of the road but, in the case of any such works which are not exclusively for the maintenance of the road, not including any works which may have significant adverse effects on the environment;

(c) the carrying out by a local authority or statutory undertakers of any works for the purpose of inspecting, repairing or renewing any sewers, mains, pipes, cables or other apparatus, including the breaking open of any street or other land for that purpose;

(d) the use of any buildings or other land within the curtilage of a dwellinghouse for any purpose incidental to the enjoyment of the dwellinghouse as such;

(e) the use of any land for the purposes of agriculture or forestry (including afforestation) and the use for any of those purposes of any building occupied together with land so used;

(f) in the case of buildings or other land which are used for a purpose of any class specified in an order made by the Secretary of State under this section, the use of the buildings or other land or, subject to the provisions of the order, of any part of the buildings or the other land, for any other purpose of the same class;

(g) the demolition of any description of building specified in a direction given by the Secretary of State to local planning authorities generally or to a particular local planning authority.

(2A)   The Secretary of State may in a development order specify any circumstances or description of circumstances in which subsection (2) does not apply to operations mentioned in paragraph (a) of that subsection which have the effect of increasing the gross floor space of the building by such amount or percentage amount as is so specified.

(2B)   The development order may make different provision for different purposes.

(3)   For the avoidance of doubt it is hereby declared that for the purposes of this section –

    (a) the use as two or more separate dwellinghouses of any building previously used as a single dwellinghouse involves a material change in the use of the building and of each part of it which is so used;

    (b) the deposit of refuse or waste materials on land involves a material change in its use, notwithstanding that the land is comprised in a site already used for that purpose, if –

        (i) the superficial area of the deposit is extended, or

        (ii) the height of the deposit is extended and exceeds the level of the land adjoining the site.

(4)   For the purposes of this Act mining operations include –

    (a) the removal of material of any description –

        (i) from a mineral-working deposit;

        (ii) from a deposit of pulverised fuel ash or other furnace ash or clinker;

        or

        (iii)from a deposit of iron, steel or other metallic slags; and

    (b) the extraction of minerals from a disused railway embankment.

(4A)   Where the placing or assembly of any tank in any part of any inland waters for the purpose of fish farming there would not, apart from this subsection, involve development of the land below, this Act shall have effect as if the tank resulted from carrying out engineering operations over that land; and in this subsection –

    'fish farming' means the breeding, rearing or keeping of fish or shellfish (which includes any kind of crustacean and mollusc);

    'inland waters' means waters which do not form part of the sea or of any creek, bay or estuary or of any river as far as the tide flows; and

    'tank' includes any cage and any other structure for use in fish farming.

(5)   Without prejudice to any regulations made under the provisions of this Act relating to the control of advertisements, the use for the display of advertisements of any external part of a building which is not normally used for that purpose shall be treated for the purposes of this section as involving a material change in the use of that part of the building.

(6)   [Repealed.]

Applications for planning permission

62(1)   A development order may make provision as to applications for planning permission made to a local planning authority.

(2)   Provision referred to in subsection (1) includes provision as to–

      (a)   the form and manner in which the application must be made;

      (b)   particulars of such matters as are to be included in the application;

      (c)   documents or other materials as are to accompany the application.

(3)   The local planning authority may require that an application for planning permission must include–

      (a)   such particulars as they think necessary;

      (b)   such evidence in support of anything in or relating to the application as they think necessary.

(4)   But a requirement under subsection (3) must not be inconsistent with provision made under subsection (1).

(5)   A development order must require that an application for planning permission of such description as is specified in the order must be accompanied by such of the following as is so specified–

      (a)   a statement about the design principles and concepts that have been applied to the development;

      (b)   a statement about how issues relating to access to the development have been dealt with.

(6)   The form and content of a statement mentioned in subsection (5) is such as is required by the development order.

Determination of applications: general considerations

70(1)   Where an application is made to a local planning authority for planning permission –

      (a)   subject to sections 91 and 92, they may grant planning permission, either unconditionally or subject to such conditions as they think fit; or

      (b)   they may refuse planning permission.

(2)   In dealing with such an application the authority shall have regard to the provisions of the development plan, so far as material to the application, and to any other material considerations.

(3)   Subsection (1) has effect subject to section 65 and to the following provisions of this Act, to sections 66, 67, 72 and 73 of the Planning (Listed Buildings and Conservation Areas) Act 1990 and to section 15 of the Health Services Act 1976.

Power of local planning authority to decline to determine applications

70A(1) A local planning authority may decline to determine a relevant application if–

      (a)   any of the conditions in subsections (2) to (4) is satisfied, and

      (b)   the authority think there has been no significant change in the relevant considerations since the relevant event.

(2)   The condition is that in the period of two years ending with the date on which the application mentioned in subsection (1) is received the Secretary of State has refused a similar application referred to him under section 76A or 77.

346 Gypsy and Traveller Law / appendix B

(3)   The condition is that in that period the Secretary of State has dismissed an appeal—
        (a) against the refusal of a similar application, or
        (b) under section 78(2) in respect of a similar application.

(4)   The condition is that—
        (a) in that period the local planning authority have refused more than one similar application, and
        (b) there has been no appeal to the Secretary of State against any such refusal.

(5)   A relevant application is—
        (a) an application for planning permission for the development of any land;
        (b) an application for approval in pursuance of section 60(2).

(6)   The relevant considerations are—
        (a) the development plan so far as material to the application;
        (b) any other material considerations.

(7)   The relevant event is—
        (a) for the purposes of subsections (2) and (4) the refusal of the similar application;
        (b) for the purposes of subsection (3) the dismissal of the appeal.

(8)   An application for planning permission is similar to another application if (and only if) the local planning authority think that the development and the land to which the applications relate are the same or substantially the same.

Right to appeal against planning decisions and failure to take such decisions

78(1)   Where a local planning authority –
        (a) refuse an application for planning permission or grant it subject to conditions;
        (b) refuse an application for any consent, agreement or approval of that authority required by a condition imposed on a grant of planning permission or grant it subject to conditions; or
        (c) refuse an application for any approval of that authority required under a development order *or a local development order*[1] or grant it subject to conditions,
        the applicant may by notice appeal to the Secretary of State.

(2)   A person who has made such an application may also appeal to the Secretary of State if the local planning authority have done none of the following –
        (a) given notice to the applicant of their decision on the application;
             (aa) given notice to the applicant that they have exercised their power under section 70A *or 70B*[2] to decline to determine the application;

---

1   Words in italics not yet in force in Wales.
2   Words in italics not yet in force.

(b) given notice to him that the application has been referred to the Secretary of State in accordance with directions given under section 77, within such period as may be prescribed by the development order or within such extended period as may at any time be agreed upon in writing between the applicant and the authority.

(3) Any appeal under this section shall be made by notice served within such time and in such manner as may be prescribed by a development order.

(4) The time prescribed for the service of such a notice must not be less than –

(a) 28 days from the date of notification of the decision; or

(b) in the case of an appeal under subsection (2), 28 days from the end of the period prescribed as mentioned in subsection (2) or, as the case may be, the extended period mentioned in that subsection.

(5) For the purposes of the application of sections 79(1), 253(2)(c), 266(1)(b) and 288(10)(b) in relation to an appeal under subsection (2), it shall be assumed that the authority decided to refuse the application in question.

PART VII: ENFORCEMENT

INTRODUCTORY

Expressions used in connection with enforcement

171A(1) For the purposes of this Act–

(a) carrying out development without the required planning permission; or

(b) failing to comply with any condition or limitation subject to which planning permission has been granted,

constitutes a breach of planning control.

(2) For the purposes of this Act–

(a) the issue of an enforcement notice (defined in section 172); or

(b) the service of a breach of condition notice (defined in section 187A),

constitutes taking enforcement action.

(3) In this Part 'planning permission' includes permission under Part III of the 1947 Act, of the 1962 Act or of the 1971 Act.

Time limits

171B(1) Where there has been a breach of planning control consisting in the carrying out without planning permission of building, engineering, mining or other operations in, on, over or under land, no enforcement action may be taken after the end of the period of four years beginning with the date on which the operations were substantially completed.

(2) Where there has been a breach of planning control consisting in the change of use of any building to use as a single dwellinghouse, no enforcement action may be taken after the end of the period of four years beginning with the date of the breach.

(3)   In the case of any other breach of planning control, no enforcement
        action may be taken after the end of the period of ten years beginning
        with the date of the breach.

(4)   The preceding subsections do not prevent–

(a)   the service of a breach of condition notice in respect of any breach
        of planning control if an enforcement notice in respect of the
        breach is in effect; or

(b)   taking further enforcement action in respect of any breach of plan-
        ning control if, during the period of four years ending with that
        action being taken, the local planning authority have taken or pur-
        ported to take enforcement action in respect of that breach.

PLANNING CONTRAVENTION NOTICES

Power to require information about activities on land

171C(1) Where it appears to the local planning authority that there may have
        been a breach of planning control in respect of any land, they may
        serve notice to that effect (referred to in this Act as a 'planning contra-
        vention notice') on any person who–

(a)   is the owner or occupier of the land or has any other interest in it;
        or

(b)   is carrying out operations on the land or is using it for any pur-
        pose.

(2)   A planning contravention notice may require the person on whom it is
        served to give such information as to–

(a)   any operations being carried out on the land, any use of the land and
        any other activities being carried out on the land; and

(b)   any matter relating to the conditions or limitations subject to which
        any planning permission in respect of the land has been granted,
        as may be specified in the notice.

(3)   Without prejudice to the generality of subsection (2), the notice may
        require the person on whom it is served, so far as he is able–

(a)   to state whether or not the land is being used for any purpose spec-
        ified in the notice or any operations or activities specified in the
        notice are being or have been carried out on the land;

(b)   to state when any use, operations or activities began;

(c)   to give the name and [postal] address of any person known to him
        to use or have used the land for any purpose or to be carrying out,
        or have carried out, any operations or activities on the land;

(d)   to give any information he holds as to any planning permission
        for any use or operations or any reason for planning permission not
        being required for any use or operations;

(e)   to state the nature of his interest (if any) in the land and the name
        and [postal] address of any other person known to him to have an
        interest in the land.

(4)   A planning contravention notice may give notice of a time and place at
        which–

(a)   any offer which the person on whom the notice is served may wish to make to apply for planning permission, to refrain from carrying out any operations or activities or to undertake remedial works; and

(b)   any representations which he may wish to make about the notice, will be considered by the authority, and the authority shall give him an opportunity to make in person any such offer or representations at that time and place.

(5)   A planning contravention notice must inform the person on whom it is served–

    (a)   of the likely consequences of his failing to respond to the notice and, in particular, that enforcement action may be taken; and

    (b)   of the effect of section 186(5)(b).

(6)   Any requirement of a planning contravention notice shall be complied with by giving information in writing to the local planning authority.

(7)   The service of a planning contravention notice does not affect any other power exercisable in respect of any breach of planning control.

(8)   In this section references to operations or activities on land include operations or activities in, under or over the land.

Penalties for non-compliance with planning contravention notice

171D(1) If, at any time after the end of the period of twenty-one days beginning with the day on which a planning contravention notice has been served on any person, he has not complied with any requirement of the notice, he shall be guilty of an offence.

(2)   An offence under subsection (1) may be charged by reference to any day or longer period of time and a person may be convicted of a second or subsequent offence under that subsection by reference to any period of time following the preceding conviction for such an offence.

(3)   It shall be a defence for a person charged with an offence under subsection (1) to prove that he had a reasonable excuse for failing to comply with the requirement.

(4)   A person guilty of an offence under subsection (1) shall be liable on summary conviction to a fine not exceeding level 3 on the standard scale.

(5)   If any person–

    (a)   makes any statement purporting to comply with a requirement of a planning contravention notice which he knows to be false or misleading in a material particular; or

    (b)   recklessly makes such a statement which is false or misleading in a material particular,

he shall be guilty of an offence.

(6)   A person guilty of an offence under subsection (5) shall be liable on summary conviction to a fine not exceeding level 5 on the standard scale.

TEMPORARY STOP NOTICES[3]

Temporary stop notice

171E(1) This section applies if the local planning authority think–

(a) that there has been a breach of planning control in relation to any land, and

(b) that it is expedient that the activity (or any part of the activity) which amounts to the breach is stopped immediately.

(2) The authority may issue a temporary stop notice.

(3) The notice must be in writing and must–

(a) specify the activity which the authority think amounts to the breach;

(b) prohibit the carrying on of the activity (or of so much of the activity as is specified in the notice);

(c) set out the authority's reasons for issuing the notice.

(4) A temporary stop notice may be served on any of the following–

(a) the person who the authority think is carrying on the activity;

(b) a person who the authority think is an occupier of the land;

(c) a person who the authority think has an interest in the land.

(5) The authority must display on the land–

(a) a copy of the notice;

(b) a statement of the effect of the notice and of section 171G.

(6) A temporary stop notice has effect from the time a copy of it is first displayed in pursuance of subsection (5).

(7) A temporary stop notice ceases to have effect–

(a) at the end of the period of 28 days starting on the day the copy notice is so displayed,

(b) at the end of such shorter period starting on that day as is specified in the notice, or

(c) if it is withdrawn by the local planning authority.

Temporary stop notice: restrictions

171F(1) A temporary stop notice does not prohibit–

(a) the use of a building as a dwelling house;

(b) the carrying out of an activity of such description or in such circumstances as is prescribed.

(2) A temporary stop notice does not prohibit the carrying out of any activity which has been carried out (whether or not continuously) for a period of four years ending with the day on which the copy of the notice is first displayed as mentioned in section 171E(6).

(3) Subsection (2) does not prevent a temporary stop notice prohibiting–

(a) activity consisting of or incidental to building, engineering, mining or other operations, or

(b) the deposit of refuse or waste materials.

(4) For the purposes of subsection (2) any period during which the activity is authorised by planning permission must be ignored.

3   Not yet in force in Wales.

(5)   A second or subsequent temporary stop notice must not be issued in respect of the same activity unless the local planning authority has first taken some other enforcement action in relation to the breach of planning control which is constituted by the activity.

(6)   In subsection (5) enforcement action includes obtaining the grant of an injunction under section 187B.

Temporary stop notice: offences

171G(1) A person commits an offence if he contravenes a temporary stop notice–
    (a)   which has been served on him, or
    (b)   a copy of which has been displayed in accordance with section 171E(5).

(2)   Contravention of a temporary stop notice includes causing or permitting the contravention of the notice.

(3)   An offence under this section may be charged by reference to a day or a longer period of time.

(4)   A person may be convicted of more than one such offence in relation to the same temporary stop notice by reference to different days or periods of time.

(5)   A person does not commit an offence under this section if he proves–
    (a)   that the temporary stop notice was not served on him, and
    (b)   that he did not know, and could not reasonably have been expected to know, of its existence.

(6)   A person convicted of an offence under this section is liable–
    (a)   on summary conviction, to a fine not exceeding £20,000;
    (b)   on conviction on indictment, to a fine.

(7)   In determining the amount of the fine the court must have regard in particular to any financial benefit which has accrued or has appeared to accrue to the person convicted in consequence of the offence.

Temporary stop notice: compensation

171H(1) This section applies if and only if a temporary stop notice is issued and at least one of the following paragraphs applies–
    (a)   the activity which is specified in the notice is authorised by planning permission or a development order or local development order;
    (b)   a certificate in respect of the activity is issued under section 191 or granted under that section by virtue of section 195;
    (c)   the authority withdraws the notice.

(2)   Subsection (1)(a) does not apply if the planning permission is granted on or after the date on which a copy of the notice is first displayed as mentioned in section 171E(6).

(3)   Subsection (1)(c) does not apply if the notice is withdrawn following the grant of planning permission as mentioned in subsection (2).

(4)   A person who at the time the notice is served has an interest in the land to which the notice relates is entitled to be compensated by the local planning authority in respect of any loss or damage directly attributable to the prohibition effected by the notice.

(5)   Subsections (3) to (7) of section 186 apply to compensation payable under this section as they apply to compensation payable under that section; and for that purpose references in those subsections to a stop notice must be taken to be references to a temporary stop notice.

Issue of enforcement notice

172(1) The local planning authority may issue a notice (in this Act referred to as an 'enforcement notice') where it appears to them –

(a) that there has been a breach of planning control; and

(b) that it is expedient to issue the notice, having regard to the provisions of the development plan and to any other material considerations.

(2)   A copy of an enforcement notice shall be served –

(a) on the owner and on the occupier of the land to which it relates; and

(b) on any other person having an interest in the land, being an interest which, in the opinion of the authority, is materially affected by the notice.

(3)   The service of the notice shall take place –

(a) not more than twenty-eight days after its date of issue; and

(b) not less than twenty-eight days before the date specified in it as the date on which it is to take effect.

Contents and effect of notice

173(1) An enforcement notice shall state –

(a) the matters which appear to the local planning authority to constitute the breach of planning control; and

(b) the paragraph of section 171A(1) within which, in the opinion of the authority, the breach falls.

(2)   A notice complies with subsection (1)(a) if it enables any person on whom a copy of it is served to know what those matters are.

(3)   An enforcement notice shall specify the steps which the authority require to be taken, or the activities which the authority require to cease, in order to achieve, wholly or partly, any of the following purposes.

(4)   Those purposes are –

(a) remedying the breach by making any development comply with the terms (including conditions and limitations) of any planning permission which has been granted in respect of the land, by discontinuing any use of the land or by restoring the land to its condition before the breach took place; or

(b) remedying any injury to amenity which has been caused by the breach.

(5)   An enforcement notice may, for example, require –

(a) the alteration or removal of any buildings or works;

(b) the carrying out of any building or other operations;

(c) any activity on the land not to be carried on except to the extent specified in the notice; or

> (d) the contour of a deposit of refuse or waste materials on land to be modified by altering the gradient or gradients of its sides.

(6) Where an enforcement notice is issued in respect of a breach of planning control consisting of demolition of a building, the notice may require the construction of a building (in this section referred to as a 'replacement building') which, subject to subsection (7), is as similar as possible to the demolished building.

(7) A replacement building –

> (a) must comply with any requirement imposed by any enactment applicable to the construction of buildings;
>
> (b) may differ from the demolished building in any respect which, if the demolished building had been altered in that respect, would not have constituted a breach of planning control;
>
> (c) must comply with any regulations made for the purposes of this subsection (including regulations modifying paragraphs (a) and (b)).

(8) An enforcement notice shall specify the date on which it is to take effect and, subject to sections 175(4) and 289(4A), shall take effect on that date.

(9) An enforcement notice shall specify the period at the end of which any steps are required to have been taken or any activities are required to have ceased and may specify different periods for different steps or activities; and, where different periods apply to different steps or activities, references in this Part to the period for compliance with an enforcement notice, in relation to any step or activity, are to the period at the end of which the step is required to have been taken or the activity is required to have ceased.

(10) An enforcement notice shall specify such additional matters as may be prescribed, and regulations may require every copy of an enforcement notice served under section 172 to be accompanied by an explanatory note giving prescribed information as to the right of appeal under section 174.

(11) Where –

> (a) an enforcement notice in respect of any breach of planning control could have required any buildings or works to be removed or any activity to cease, but does not do so; and
>
> (b) all the requirements of the notice have been complied with,

then, so far as the notice did not so require, planning permission shall be treated as having been granted by virtue of section 73A in respect of development consisting of the construction of the buildings or works or, as the case may be, the carrying out of the activities.

(12) Where –

> (a) an enforcement notice requires the construction of a replacement building; and
>
> (b) all the requirements of the notice with respect to that construction have been complied with,

planning permission shall be treated as having been granted by virtue of section 73A in respect of development consisting of that construction.

Appeal against enforcement notice

174(1) A person having an interest in the land to which an enforcement notice relates or a relevant occupier may appeal to the Secretary of State against the notice, whether or not a copy of it has been served on him.

(2) An appeal may be brought on any of the following grounds –

   (a) that, in respect of any breach of planning control which may be constituted by the matters stated in the notice, planning permission ought to be granted or, as the case may be, the condition or limitation concerned ought to be discharged;

   (b) that those matters have not occurred;

   (c) that those matters (if they occurred) do not constitute a breach of planning control;

   (d) that, at the date when the notice was issued, no enforcement action could be taken in respect of any breach of planning control which may be constituted by those matters;

   (e) that copies of the enforcement notice were not served as required by section 172;

   (f) that the steps required by the notice to be taken, or the activities required by the notice to cease, exceed what is necessary to remedy any breach of planning control which may be constituted by those matters or, as the case may be, to remedy any injury to amenity which has been caused by any such breach;

   (g) that any period specified in the notice in accordance with section 173(9) falls short of what should reasonably be allowed.

(3) An appeal under this section shall be made –

   (a) by giving written notice of the appeal to the Secretary of State before the date specified in the enforcement notice as the date on which it is to take effect; or

   (b) by sending such notice to him in a properly addressed and prepaid letter posted to him at such time that, in the ordinary course of post, it would be delivered to him before that date; or

   (c) by sending such notice to him using electronic communications at such time that, in the ordinary course of transmission, it would be delivered to him before that date.

(4) A person who gives notice under subsection (3) shall submit to the Secretary of State, either when giving the notice or within the prescribed time, a statement in writing –

   (a) specifying the grounds on which he is appealing against the enforcement notice; and

   (b) giving such further information as may be prescribed.

(5) If, where more than one ground is specified in that statement, the appellant does not give information required under subsection (4)(b) in relation to each of those grounds within the prescribed time, the Secretary of State may determine the appeal without considering any ground as to which the appellant has failed to give such information within that time.

(6) In this section 'relevant occupier' means a person who –

    (a) on the date on which the enforcement notice is issued occupies the land to which the notice relates by virtue of a licence; and

    (b) continues so to occupy the land when the appeal is brought.

Appeals: supplementary provisions

175(1) The Secretary of State may by regulations prescribe the procedure which is to be followed on appeals under section 174 and, in particular, but without prejudice to the generality of this subsection, may –

    (a) require the local planning authority to submit, within such time as may be prescribed, a statement indicating the submissions which they propose to put forward on the appeal;

    (b) specify the matters to be included in such a statement;

    (c) require the authority or the appellant to give such notice of such an appeal as may be prescribed;

    (d) require the authority to send to the Secretary of State, within such period from the date of the bringing of the appeal as may be prescribed, a copy of the enforcement notice and a list of the persons served with copies of it.

(2) The notice to be prescribed under subsection (1)(c) shall be such notice as in the opinion of the Secretary of State is likely to bring the appeal to the attention of persons in the locality in which the land to which the enforcement notice relates is situated.

(3) Subject to section 176(4), the Secretary of State shall, if either the appellant or the local planning authority so desire, give each of them an opportunity of appearing before and being heard by a person appointed by the Secretary of State for the purpose.

(4) Where an appeal is brought under section 174 the enforcement notice shall subject to any order under section 289(4A) be of no effect pending the final determination or the withdrawal of the appeal.

(5) Where any person has appealed to the Secretary of State against an enforcement notice, no person shall be entitled, in any other proceedings instituted after the making of the appeal, to claim that the notice was not duly served on the person who appealed.

(6) Schedule 6 applies to appeals under section 174, including appeals under that section as applied by regulations under any other provisions of this Act.

(7) Subsection (5) of section 250 of the Local Government Act 1972 (which authorises a Minister holding an inquiry under that section to make orders with respect to the costs of the parties) shall apply in relation to any proceedings before the Secretary of State on an appeal under section 174 as if those proceedings were an inquiry held by the Secretary of State under section 250.

General provisions relating to determination of appeals

176(1) On an appeal under section 174 the Secretary of State may –

    (a) correct any defect, error or misdescription in the enforcement notice; or

    (b) vary the terms of the enforcement notice,

if he is satisfied that the correction or variation will not cause injustice to the appellant or the local planning authority.

(2)   Where the Secretary of State determines to allow the appeal, he may quash the notice.

(2A)   The Secretary of State shall give any directions necessary to give effect to his determination on the appeal.

(3)   The Secretary of State –

(a)   may dismiss an appeal if the appellant fails to comply with section 174(4) within the prescribed time; and

(b)   may allow an appeal and quash the enforcement notice if the local planning authority fail to comply with any requirement of regulations made by virtue of paragraph (a), (b), or (d) of section 175(1) within the prescribed period.

(4)   If the Secretary of State proposes to dismiss an appeal under paragraph (a) of subsection (3) or to allow an appeal and quash the enforcement notice under paragraph (b) of that subsection, he need not comply with section 175(3).

(5)   Where it would otherwise be a ground for determining an appeal under section 174 in favour of the appellant that a person required to be served with a copy of the enforcement notice was not served, the Secretary of State may disregard that fact if neither the appellant nor that person has been substantially prejudiced by the failure to serve him.

Grant or modification of planning permission on appeals against enforcement notices

177(1)   On the determination of an appeal under section 174, the Secretary of State may –

(a)   grant planning permission in respect of the matters stated in the enforcement notice as constituting a breach of planning control, whether in relation to the whole or any part of those matters or in relation to the whole or any part of the land to which the notice relates;

(b)   discharge any condition or limitation subject to which planning permission was granted;

(c)   determine whether, on the date on which the appeal was made, any existing use of the land was lawful, any operations which had been carried out in, on, over or under the land were lawful or any matter constituting a failure to comply with any condition or limitation subject to which planning permission was granted was lawful and, if so, issue a certificate under section 191.

(1A)   The provisions of sections 191 to 194 mentioned in subsection (1B) shall apply for the purposes of subsection (1)(c) as they apply for the purposes of section 191, but as if –

(a)   any reference to an application for a certificate were a reference to the appeal and any reference to the date of such an application were a reference to the date on which the appeal is made; and

(b)   references to the local planning authority were references to the Secretary of State.

(1B)　Those provisions are: sections 191(5) to (7), 193(4) (so far as it relates to the form of the certificate), (6) and (7) and 194.

(2)　In considering whether to grant planning permission under subsection (1), the Secretary of State shall have regard to the provisions of the development plan, so far as material to the subject matter of the enforcement notice, and to any other material considerations.

(3)　The planning permission that may be granted under subsection (1) is any planning permission that might be granted on an application under Part III.

(4)　Where under subsection (1) the Secretary of State discharges a condition or limitation, he may substitute another condition or limitation for it, whether more or less onerous.

(5)　Where an appeal against an enforcement notice is brought under section 174, the appellant shall be deemed to have made an application for planning permission in respect of the matters stated in the enforcement notice as constituting a breach of planning control.

(5A)　Where –

(a)　the statement under subsection (4) of section 174 specifies the ground mentioned in subsection (2)(a) of that section;

(b)　any fee is payable under regulations made by virtue of section 303 in respect of the application deemed to be made by virtue of the appeal; and

(c)　the Secretary of State gives notice in writing to the appellant specifying the period within which the fee must be paid,

then, if that fee is not paid within that period, the appeal, so far as brought on that ground, and the application shall lapse at the end of that period.

(6)　Any planning permission granted under subsection (1) on an appeal shall be treated as granted on the application deemed to have been made by the appellant.

(7)　In relation to a grant of planning permission or a determination under subsection (1) the Secretary of State's decision shall be final.

(8)　For the purposes of section 69 the Secretary of State's decision shall be treated as having been given by him in dealing with an application for planning permission made to the local planning authority.

Execution and cost of works required by enforcement notice

178(1)　Where any steps required by an enforcement notice to be taken are not taken within the period for compliance with the notice, the local planning authority may –

(a)　enter the land and take the steps; and

(b)　recover from the person who is then the owner of the land any expenses reasonably incurred by them in doing so.

(2)　Where a copy of an enforcement notice has been served in respect of any breach of planning control –

(a)　any expenses incurred by the owner or occupier of any land for the purpose of complying with the notice, and

(b) any sums paid by the owner of any land under subsection (1) in respect of expenses incurred by the local planning authority in taking steps required by such a notice to be taken,

shall be deemed to be incurred or paid for the use and at the request of the person by whom the breach of planning control was committed.

(3) Regulations made under this Act may provide that –

(a) section 276 of the Public Health Act 1936, (power of local authorities to sell materials removed in executing works under that Act subject to accounting for the proceeds of sale);

(b) section 289 of that Act (power to require the occupier of any premises to permit works to be executed by the owner of the premises); and

(c) section 294 of that Act (limit on liability of persons holding premises as agents or trustees in respect of the expenses recoverable under that Act),

shall apply, subject to such adaptations and modifications as may be specified in the regulations, in relation to any steps required to be taken by an enforcement notice.

(4) Regulations under subsection (3) applying section 289 of the Public Health Act 1936 may include adaptations and modifications for the purpose of giving the owner of land to which an enforcement notice relates the right, as against all other persons interested in the land, to comply with the requirements of the enforcement notice.

(5) Regulations under subsection (3) may also provide for the charging on the land of any expenses recoverable by a local planning authority under subsection (1).

(6) Any person who wilfully obstructs a person acting in the exercise of powers under subsection (1) shall be guilty of an offence and liable on summary conviction to a fine not exceeding level 3 on the standard scale.

Offence where enforcement notice not complied with

179(1) Where, at any time after the end of the period for compliance with an enforcement notice, any step required by the notice to be taken has not been taken or any activity required by the notice to cease is being carried on, the person who is then the owner of the land is in breach of the notice.

(2) Where the owner of the land is in breach of an enforcement notice he shall be guilty of an offence.

(3) In proceedings against any person for an offence under subsection (2), it shall be a defence for him to show that he did everything he could be expected to do to secure compliance with the notice.

(4) A person who has control of or an interest in the land to which an enforcement notice relates (other than the owner) must not carry on any activity which is required by the notice to cease or cause or permit such an activity to be carried on.

(5) A person who, at any time after the end of the period for compliance with the notice, contravenes subsection (4) shall be guilty of an offence.

(6)   An offence under subsection (2) or (5) may be charged by reference to any day or longer period of time and a person may be convicted of a second or subsequent offence under the subsection in question by reference to any period of time following the preceding conviction for such an offence.

(7)   Where –
   (a)   a person charged with an offence under this section has not been served with a copy of the enforcement notice; and
   (b)   the notice is not contained in the appropriate register kept under section 188,
   it shall be a defence for him to show that he was not aware of the existence of the notice.

(8)   A person guilty of an offence under this section shall be liable –
   (a)   on summary conviction, to a fine not exceeding £20,000; and
   (b)   on conviction on indictment, to a fine.

(9)   In determining the amount of any fine to be imposed on a person convicted of an offence under this section, the court shall in particular have regard to any financial benefit which has accrued or appears likely to accrue to him in consequence of the offence.

STOP NOTICES

Stop notices

183(1)   Where the local planning authority consider it expedient that any relevant activity should cease before the expiry of the period for compliance with an enforcement notice, they may, when they serve the copy of the enforcement notice or afterwards, serve a notice (in this Act referred to as a 'stop notice') prohibiting the carrying out of that activity on the land to which the enforcement notice relates, or any part of that land specified in the stop notice.

(2)   In this section and sections 184 and 186 'relevant activity' means any activity specified in the enforcement notice as an activity which the local planning authority require to cease and any activity carried out as part of that activity or associated with that activity.

(3)   A stop notice may not be served where the enforcement notice has taken effect.

(4)   A stop notice shall not prohibit the use of any building as a dwelling-house.

(5)   A stop notice shall not prohibit the carrying out of any activity if the activity has been carried out (whether continuously or not) for a period of more than four years ending with the service of the notice; and for the purposes of this subsection no account is to be taken of any period during which the activity was authorised by planning permission.

(5A)   Subsection (5) does not prevent a stop notice prohibiting any activity consisting of, or incidental to, building, engineering, mining or other operations or the deposit of refuse or waste materials.

(6)   A stop notice may be served by the local planning authority on any

person who appears to them to have an interest in the land or to be engaged in any activity prohibited by the notice.

(7)   The local planning authority may at any time withdraw a stop notice (without prejudice to their power to serve another) by serving notice to that effect on persons served with the stop notice.

Stop notices: supplementary provisions

184(1) A stop notice must refer to the enforcement notice to which it relates and have a copy of that notice annexed to it.

(2)   A stop notice must specify the date on which it will take effect (and it cannot be contravened until that date).

(3)   That date–

(a)   must not be earlier than three days after the date when the notice is served, unless the local planning authority consider that there are special reasons for specifying an earlier date and a statement of those reasons is served with the stop notice; and

(b)   must not be later than twenty-eight days from the date when the notice is first served on any person.

(4)   A stop notice shall cease to have effect when–

(a)   the enforcement notice to which it relates is withdrawn or quashed; or

(b)   the period for compliance with the enforcement notice expires; or

(c)   notice of the withdrawal of the stop notice is first served under section 183(7).

(5)   A stop notice shall also cease to have effect if or to the extent that the activities prohibited by it cease, on a variation of the enforcement notice, to be relevant activities.

(6)   Where a stop notice has been served in respect of any land, the local planning authority may display there a notice (in this section and section 187 referred to as a 'site notice')–

(a)   stating that a stop notice has been served and that any person contravening it may be prosecuted for an offence under section 187,

(b)   giving the date when the stop notice takes effect, and

(c)   indicating its requirements.

(7)   If under section 183(7) the local planning authority withdraw a stop notice in respect of which a site notice was displayed, they must display a notice of the withdrawal in place of the site notice.

(8)   A stop notice shall not be invalid by reason that a copy of the enforcement notice to which it relates was not served as required by section 172 if it is shown that the local planning authority took all such steps as were reasonably practicable to effect proper service.

Penalties for contravention of stop notice

187(1) If any person contravenes a stop notice after a site notice has been displayed or the stop notice has been served on him he shall be guilty of an offence.

(1A)   An offence under this section may be charged by reference to any day or longer period of time and a person may be convicted of a second or subsequent offence under this section by reference to any period of time following the preceding conviction for such an offence.

(1B) References in this section to contravening a stop notice include causing or permitting its contravention.

(2) person guilty of an offence under this section shall be liable–

(a) on summary conviction, to a fine not exceeding £20,000; and

(b) on conviction on indictment, to a fine.

(2A) In determining the amount of any fine to be imposed on a person convicted of an offence under this section, the court shall in particular have regard to any financial benefit which has accrued or appears likely to accrue to him in consequence of the offence.

(3) In proceedings for an offence under this section it shall be a defence for the accused to prove–

(a) that the stop notice was not served on him, and

(b) that he did not know, and could not reasonably have been expected to know, of its existence.

Injunctions restraining breaches of planning control

187B(1) Where a local planning authority consider it necessary or expedient for any actual or apprehended breach of planning control to be restrained by injunction, they may apply to the court for an injunction, whether or not they have exercised or are proposing to exercise any of their other powers under this Part.

(2) On an application under subsection (1) the court may grant such an injunction as the court thinks appropriate for the purpose of restraining the breach.

(3) Rules of court may provide for such an injunction to be issued against a person whose identity is unknown.

(4) In this section 'the court' means the High Court or the county court.

CERTIFICATE OF LAWFUL USE OR DEVELOPMENT

Certificate of lawfulness of existing use or development

191(1) If any person wishes to ascertain whether–

(a) any existing use of buildings or other land is lawful;

(b) any operations which have been carried out in, on, over or under land are lawful; or

(c) any other matter constituting a failure to comply with any condition or limitation subject to which planning permission has been granted is lawful,

he may make an application for the purpose to the local planning authority specifying the land and describing the use, operations or other matter.

(2) For the purposes of this Act uses and operations are lawful at any time if–

(a) no enforcement action may then be taken in respect of them (whether because they did not involve development or require planning permission or because the time for enforcement action has expired or for any other reason); and

(b) they do not constitute a contravention of any of the requirements of any enforcement notice then in force.

(3) For the purposes of this Act any matter constituting a failure to comply with any condition or limitation subject to which planning permission has been granted is lawful at any time if–

(a) the time for taking enforcement action in respect of the failure has then expired; and

(b) it does not constitute a contravention of any of the requirements of any enforcement notice or breach of condition notice then in force.

(4) If, on an application under this section, the local planning authority are provided with information satisfying them of the lawfulness at the time of the application of the use, operations or other matter described in the application, or that description as modified by the local planning authority or a description substituted by them, they shall issue a certificate to that effect; and in any other case they shall refuse the application.

(5) A certificate under this section shall–

(a) specify the land to which it relates;

(b) describe the use, operations or other matter in question (in the case of any use falling within one of the classes specified in an order under section 55(2)(f), identifying it by reference to that class);

(c) give the reasons for determining the use, operations or other matter to be lawful; and

(d) specify the date of the application for the certificate.

(6) The lawfulness of any use, operations or other matter for which a certificate is in force under this section shall be conclusively presumed.

(7) A certificate under this section in respect of any use shall also have effect, for the purposes of the following enactments, as if it were a grant of planning permission–

(a) section 3(3) of the Caravan Sites and Control of Development Act 1960;

(b) section 5(2) of the Control of Pollution Act 1974; and

(c) section 36(2)(a) of the Environmental Protection Act 1990.

Certificate of lawfulness of proposed use or development

192(1) If any person wishes to ascertain whether–

(a) any proposed use of buildings or other land; or

(b) any operations proposed to be carried out in, on, over or under land,

would be lawful, he may make an application for the purpose to the local planning authority specifying the land and describing the use or operations in question.

(2) If, on an application under this section, the local planning authority are provided with information satisfying them that the use or operations

described in the application would be lawful if instituted or begun at the time of the application, they shall issue a certificate to that effect; and in any other case they shall refuse the application.

(3)   A certificate under this section shall–

(a)   specify the land to which it relates;

(b)   describe the use or operations in question (in the case of any use falling within one of the classes specified in an order under section 55(2)(f), identifying it by reference to that class);

(c)   give the reasons for determining the use or operations to be lawful; and

(d)   specify the date of the application for the certificate.

(4)   The lawfulness of any use or operations for which a certificate is in force under this section shall be conclusively presumed unless there is a material change, before the use is instituted or the operations are begun, in any of the matters relevant to determining such lawfulness.

Validity of enforcement notices and similar notices

285(1)   The validity of an enforcement notice shall not, except by way of an appeal under Part VII, be questioned in any proceedings whatsoever on any of the grounds on which such an appeal may be brought.

(2)   Subsection (1) shall not apply to proceedings brought under section 179 against a person who–

(a)   has held an interest in the land since before the enforcement notice was issued under that Part;

(b)   did not have a copy of the enforcement notice served on him under that Part; and

(c)   satisfies the court–

(i)   that he did not know and could not reasonably have been expected to know that the enforcement notice had been issued; and

(ii)   that his interests have been substantially prejudiced by the failure to serve him with a copy of it.

(3)   Subject to subsection (4), the validity of a notice which has been served under section 215 on the owner and occupier of the land shall not, except by way of an appeal under Chapter II of Part VIII, be questioned in any proceedings whatsoever on either of the grounds specified in section 217(1)(a) or (b).

(4)   Subsection (3) shall not prevent the validity of such a notice being questioned on either of those grounds in proceedings brought under section 216 against a person on whom the notice was not served, but who has held an interest in the land since before the notice was served on the owner an occupier of the land, if he did not appeal against the notice under that Chapter.

Proceedings for questioning the validity of other orders, decisions and directions

288(1) If any person –

(a)   is aggrieved by any order to which this section applies and wishes to question the validity of that order on the grounds –

(i)   that the order is not within the powers of this Act, or

(ii)   that any of the relevant requirements have not been complied with in relation to that order; or

(b)   is aggrieved by any action on the part of the Secretary of State to which this section applies and wishes to question the validity of that action on the grounds –

(i)   that the action is not within the powers of this Act, or

(ii)   that any of the relevant requirements have not been complied with in relation to that action,

he may make an application to the High Court under this section.

(2)   Without prejudice to subsection (1), if the authority directly concerned with any order to which this section applies, or with any action on the part of the Secretary of State to which this section applies, wish to question the validity of that order or action on any of the grounds mentioned in subsection (1), the authority may make an application to the High Court under this section.

(3)   An application under this section must be made within six weeks from the date on which the order is confirmed (or, in the case of an order under section 97 which takes effect under section 99 without confirmation, the date on which it takes effect) or, as the case may be, the date on which the action is taken.

(4)   This section applies to any such order as is mentioned in subsection (2) of section 284 and to any such action on the part of the Secretary of State as is mentioned in subsection (3) of that section.

(5)   On any application under this section the High Court –

(a)   may, subject to subsection (6), by interim order suspend the operation of the order or action, the validity of which is questioned by the application, until the final determination of the proceedings;

(b)   if satisfied that the order or action in question is not within the powers of this Act, or that the interests of the applicant have been substantially prejudiced by a failure to comply with any of the relevant requirements in relation to it, may quash that order or action.

(6)   Paragraph (a) of subsection (5) shall not apply to applications questioning the validity of tree preservation orders.

(7)   In relation to a tree preservation order, or to an order made in pursuance of section 221(5), the powers conferred on the High Court by subsection (5) shall be exercisable by way of quashing or (where applicable) suspending the operation of the order either in whole or in part, as the court may determine.

(8)   References in this section to the confirmation of an order include the confirmation of an order subject to modifications as well as the confirmation of an order in the form in which it was made.

(9)   In this section 'the relevant requirements', in relation to any order or action to which this section applies, means any requirements of this Act or of the Tribunals and Inquiries Act 1992, or of any order, regulations or rules made under this Act or under that Act which are applicable to that order or action.

(10)   Any reference in this section to the authority directly concerned with any order or action to which this section applies –

(a)   in relation to any such decision as is mentioned in section 284(3)(f), is a reference to the council on whom the notice in question was served and, in a case where the Secretary of State has modified such a notice, wholly or in part, by substituting another local authority or statutory undertakers for that council, includes a reference to that local authority or those statutory undertakers;

(b)   in any other case, is a reference to the authority who made the order in question or made the decision or served the notice to which the proceedings in question relate, or who referred the matter to the Secretary of State, or, where the order or notice in question was made or served by him, the authority named in the order or notice.

Appeals to High Court relating to enforcement notices and notices under section 207

289(1) Where the Secretary of State gives a decision in proceedings on an appeal under Part VII against an enforcement notice the appellant or the local planning authority or any other person having an interest in the land to which the notice relates may, according as rules of court may provide, either appeal to the High Court against the decision on a point of law or require the Secretary of State to state and sign a case for the opinion of the High Court.

(2)   Where the Secretary of State gives a decision in proceedings on an appeal under Part VIII against a notice under section 207, the appellant or the local planning authority or any person (other than the appellant) on whom the notice was served may, according as rules of court may provide, either appeal to the High Court against the decision on a point of law or require the Secretary of State to state and sign a case for the opinion of the High Court.

(3)   At any stage of the proceedings on any such appeal as is mentioned in subsection (1), the Secretary of State may state any question of law arising in the course of the proceedings in the form of a special case for the decision of the High Court.

(4)   A decision of the High Court on a case stated by virtue of subsection (3) shall be deemed to be a judgment of the court within the meaning of section 16 of the [Supreme Court Act 1981][4] (jurisdiction of the Court of Appeal to hear and determine appeals from any judgment of the High Court).

4   The words in square brackets in 289(4)are substituted with the words 'Senior Courts Act 1981' by the Constitutional Reform Act 2005. Not yet in force.

(4A) In proceedings brought by virtue of this section in respect of an enforcement notice, the High Court or, as the case may be, the Court of Appeal may, on such terms if any as the Court thinks fit (which may include terms requiring the local planning authority to give an undertaking as to damages or any other matter), order that the notice shall have effect, or have effect to such extent as may be specified in the order, pending the final determination of those proceedings and any re-hearing and determination by the Secretary of State.

(4B) Where proceedings are brought by virtue of this section in respect of any notice under section 207, the notice shall be of no effect pending the final determination of those proceedings and any re-hearing and determination by the Secretary of State.

(5) In relation to any proceedings in the High Court or the Court of Appeal brought by virtue of this section the power to make rules of court shall include power to make rules –

(a) prescribing the powers of the High Court or the Court of Appeal with respect to the remitting of the matter with the opinion or direction of the court for re-hearing and determination by the Secretary of State; and

(b) providing for the Secretary of State, either generally or in such circumstances as may be prescribed by the rules, to be treated as a party to any such proceedings and to be entitled to appear and to be heard accordingly.

(5A) Rules of court may also provide for the High Court or, as the case may be, the Court of Appeal to give directions as to the exercise, until such proceedings in respect of an enforcement notice are finally concluded and any re-hearing and determination by the Secretary of State has taken place, of any other powers in respect of the matters to which such a notice relates.

(6) No proceedings in the High Court shall be brought by virtue of this section except with the leave of that Court and no appeal to the Court of Appeal shall be so brought except with the leave of the Court of Appeal or of the High Court.

(7) In this section 'decision' includes a direction or order, and references to the giving of a decision shall be construed accordingly.

CRIMINAL JUSTICE AND PUBLIC ORDER ACT 1994 (EXTRACTS)

PART V: PUBLIC ORDER: COLLECTIVE TRESPASS OR NUISANCE ON LAND

Power to remove trespassers on land

61(1) If the senior police officer present at the scene reasonably believes that two or more persons are trespassing on land and are present there with the common purpose of residing there for any period, that reasonable steps have been taken by or on behalf of the occupier to ask them to leave and –

(a) that any of those persons has caused damage to the land or to property on the land or used threatening, abusive or insulting words or behaviour towards the occupier, a member of his family or an employee or agent of his, or

(b) that those persons have between them six or more vehicles on the land,

he may direct those persons, or any of them, to leave the land and to remove any vehicles or other property they have with them on the land.

(2) Where the persons in question are reasonably believed by the senior police officer to be persons who were not originally trespassers but have become trespassers on the land, the officer must reasonably believe that the other conditions specified in subsection (1) are satisfied after those persons became trespassers before he can exercise the power conferred by that subsection.

(3) A direction under subsection (1) above, if not communicated to the persons referred to in subsection (1) by the police officer giving the direction, may be communicated to them by any constable at the scene.

(4) If a person knowing that a direction under subsection (1) above has been given which applies to him –

(a) fails to leave the land as soon as reasonably practicable, or

(b) having left again enters the land as a trespasser within the period of three months beginning with the day on which the direction was given,

he commits an offence and is liable on summary conviction to imprisonment for a term not exceeding *51 weeks*[5] or a fine not exceeding level 4 on the standard scale, or both.

(4A) Where, as respects Scotland, the reason why these persons have become trespassers is that they have ceased to be entitled to exercise access rights by virtue of –

(a) their having formed the common purpose mentioned in subsection (1) above; or

---

5 Words in italics not yet in force. See Criminal Justice Act 2003.

(b) one or more of the conditions specified in paragraphs (a) and (b) of that subsection having been satisfied,

the circumstances constituting that reason shall be treated, for the purposes of subsection (4) above, as having also occurred after these persons became trespassers.

(4B) In subsection (4A) above 'access rights' has the meaning given by the Land Reform (Scotland) Act 2003.

(5) [Repealed.]

(6) In proceedings for an offence under this section it is a defence for the accused to show –

(a) that he was not trespassing on the land, or

(b) that he had a reasonable excuse for failing to leave the land as soon as reasonably practicable or, as the case may be, for again entering the land as a trespasser.

(7) In its application in England and Wales to common land this section has effect as if in the preceding subsections of it –

(a) references to trespassing or trespassers were references to acts and persons doing acts which constitute either a trespass as against the occupier or an infringement of the commoners' rights; and

(b) references to 'the occupier' included the commoners or any of them or, in the case of common land to which the public has access, the local authority as well as any commoner.

(8) Subsection (7) above does not –

(a) require action by more than one occupier; or

(b) constitute persons trespassers as against any commoner or the local authority if they are permitted to be there by the other occupier.

(9) In this section –

'common land' means–

(a) land registered as common land in a register of common land kept under Part 1 of the Commons Act 2006; and

(b) land to which Part 1 of that Act does not apply and which is subject to rights of common as defined in that Act;[6]

'commoner' means a person with rights of common as so defined;[7]

'land' does not include –

(a) buildings other than –

(i) agricultural buildings within the meaning of, in England and Wales, paragraphs 3 to 8 of Schedule 5 to the Local Government Finance Act 1988 or, in Scotland, section 7(2) of the Valuation and Rating (Scotland) Act 1956, or

(ii) scheduled monuments within the meaning of the Ancient Monuments and Archaeological Areas Act 1979;

---

6 Words in italics not yet in force. See Commons Act 2006.

7 Words in italics not yet in force. See Commons Act 2006.

(b) land forming part of –
  (i) a highway unless it is a footpath, bridleway or byway open to all traffic within the meaning of Part III of the Wildlife and Countryside Act 1981, is a restricted byway within the meaning of Part II of the Countryside and Rights of Way Act 2000] or is a cycle track under the Highways Act 1980 or the Cycle Tracks Act 1984; or
  (ii) a road within the meaning of the Roads (Scotland) Act 1984 unless it falls within the definitions in section 151(2)(a)(ii) or (b) (footpaths and cycle tracks) of that Act or is a bridleway within the meaning of section 47 of the Countryside (Scotland) Act 1967;

'the local authority', in relation to common land, means any local authority which has powers in relation to the land under section 9 of the *Commons Act 2006*;[8]

'occupier' (and in subsection (8) 'the other occupier') means –

(a) in England and Wales, the person entitled to possession of the land by virtue of an estate or interest held by him; and

(b) in Scotland, the person lawfully entitled to natural possession of the land;

'property', in relation to damage to property on land, means –

(a) in England and Wales, property within the meaning of section 10(1) of the Criminal Damage Act 1971; and

(b) in Scotland, either –
  (i) heritable property other than land; or
  (ii) corporeal moveable property,

and 'damage' includes the deposit of any substance capable of polluting the land;

'trespass' means, in the application of this section –

(a) in England and Wales, subject to the extensions effected by subsection (7) above, trespass as against the occupier of the land;

(b) in Scotland, entering, or as the case may be remaining on, land without lawful authority and without the occupier's consent; and

'trespassing' and 'trespasser' shall be construed accordingly;

'vehicle' includes –

(a) any vehicle, whether or not it is in a fit state for use on roads, and includes any chassis or body, with or without wheels, appearing to have formed part of such a vehicle, and any load carried by, and anything attached to, such a vehicle; and

(b) a caravan as defined in section 29(1) of the Caravan Sites and Control of Development Act 1960;

and a person may be regarded for the purposes of this section as having a purpose of residing in a place notwithstanding that he has a home elsewhere.

---

8   Words in italics not yet in force. See Commons Act 2006.

Supplementary powers of seizure

62(1) If a direction has been given under section 61 and a constable reasonably suspects that any person to whom the direction applies has, without reasonable excuse –

(a) failed to remove any vehicle on the land which appears to the constable to belong to him or to be in his possession or under his control; or

(b) entered the land as a trespasser with a vehicle within the period of three months beginning with the day on which the direction was given, the constable may seize and remove that vehicle.

(2) In this section, 'trespasser' and 'vehicle' have the same meaning as in section 61.

Power to remove trespassers: alternative site available

62A(1) If the senior police officer present at a scene reasonably believes that the conditions in subsection (2) are satisfied in relation to a person and land, he may direct the person –

(a) to leave the land;

(b) to remove any vehicle and other property he has with him on the land.

(2) The conditions are –

(a) that the person and one or more others ('the trespassers') are trespassing on the land;

(b) that the trespassers have between them at least one vehicle on the land;

(c) that the trespassers are present on the land with the common purpose of residing there for any period;

(d) if it appears to the officer that the person has one or more caravans in his possession or under his control on the land, that there is a suitable pitch on a relevant caravan site for that caravan or each of those caravans;

(e) that the occupier of the land or a person acting on his behalf has asked the police to remove the trespassers from the land.

(3) A direction under subsection (1) may be communicated to the person to whom it applies by any constable at the scene.

(4) Subsection (5) applies if –

(a) a police officer proposes to give a direction under subsection (1) in relation to a person and land, and

(b) it appears to him that the person has one or more caravans in his possession or under his control on the land.

(5) The officer must consult every local authority within whose area the land is situated as to whether there is a suitable pitch for the caravan or each of the caravans on a relevant caravan site which is situated in the local authority's area.

(6) In this section –

'caravan' and 'caravan site' have the same meanings as in Part 1 of the Caravan Sites and Control of Development Act 1960;

'relevant caravan site' means a caravan site which is –

(a) situated in the area of a local authority within whose area the land is situated, and

(b) managed by a relevant site manager;

'relevant site manager' means –

(a) a local authority within whose area the land is situated;

(b) a registered social landlord;

'registered social landlord' means a body registered as a social landlord under Chapter 1 of Part 1 of the Housing Act 1996.

(7) The Secretary of State may by order amend the definition of 'relevant site manager' in subsection (6) by adding a person or description of person.

(8) An order under subsection (7) must be made by statutory instrument and is subject to annulment in pursuance of a resolution of either House of Parliament.

Failure to comply with direction under section 62A: offences

62B(1) A person commits an offence if he knows that a direction under section 62A(1) has been given which applies to him and –

(a) he fails to leave the relevant land as soon as reasonably practicable, or

(b) he enters any land in the area of the relevant local authority as a trespasser before the end of the relevant period with the intention of residing there.

(2) The relevant period is the period of 3 months starting with the day on which the direction is given.

(3) A person guilty of an offence under this section is liable on summary conviction to imprisonment for a term not exceeding *51 weeks*[9] or a fine not exceeding level 4 on the standard scale or both.

(4) [Repealed.]

(5) In proceedings for an offence under this section it is a defence for the accused to show –

(a) that he was not trespassing on the land in respect of which he is alleged to have committed the offence, or

(b) that he had a reasonable excuse –

(i) for failing to leave the relevant land as soon as reasonably practicable, or

(ii) for entering land in the area of the relevant local authority as a trespasser with the intention of residing there, or

(c) that, at the time the direction was given, he was under the age of 18 years and was residing with his parent or guardian.

Failure to comply with direction under section 62A: seizure

62C(1) This section applies if a direction has been given under section 62A(1) and a constable reasonably suspects that a person to whom the direction applies has, without reasonable excuse –

9 Words in italics not yet in force. See Criminal Justice Act 2003.

(a) failed to remove any vehicle on the relevant land which appears to the constable to belong to him or to be in his possession or under his control; or

(b) entered any land in the area of the relevant local authority as a trespasser with a vehicle before the end of the relevant period with the intention of residing there.

(2) The relevant period is the period of 3 months starting with the day on which the direction is given.

(3) The constable may seize and remove the vehicle.

Common land: modifications

62D(1) In their application to common land sections 62A to 62C have effect with these modifications.

(2) References to trespassing and trespassers have effect as if they were references to acts, and persons doing acts, which constitute–
(a) a trespass as against the occupier, or
(b) an infringement of the commoners' rights.

(3) References to the occupier –
(a) in the case of land to which the public has access, include the local authority and any commoner;
(b) in any other case, include the commoners or any of them.

(4) Subsection (1) does not –
(a) require action by more than one occupier, or
(b) constitute persons trespassers as against any commoner or the local authority if they are permitted to be there by the other occupier.

(5) In this section 'common land', 'commoner' and 'the local authority' have the meanings given by section 61.

Sections 62A to 62D: interpretation

62E(1) Subsections (2) to (8) apply for the interpretation of sections 62A to 62D and this section.

(2) 'Land' does not include buildings other than –
(a) agricultural buildings within the meaning of paragraphs 3 to 8 of Schedule 5 to the Local Government Finance Act 1988, or
(b) scheduled monuments within the meaning of the Ancient Monuments and Archaeological Areas Act 1979.

(3) 'Local authority' means –
(a) in Greater London, a London borough or the Common Council of the City of London;
(b) in England outside Greater London, a county council, a district council or the Council of the Isles of Scilly;
(c) in Wales, a county council or a county borough council.

(4) 'Occupier', 'trespass', 'trespassing' and 'trespasser' have the meanings given by section 61 in relation to England and Wales.

(5) 'The relevant land' means the land in respect of which a direction under section 62A(1) is given.

(6) 'The relevant local authority' means –

    (a) if the relevant land is situated in the area of more than one local authority (but is not in the Isles of Scilly), the district council or county borough council within whose area the relevant land is situated;

    (b) if the relevant land is situated in the Isles of Scilly, the Council of the Isles of Scilly;

    (c) in any other case, the local authority within whose area the relevant land is situated.

(7) 'Vehicle' has the meaning given by section 61.

(8) A person may be regarded as having a purpose of residing in a place even if he has a home elsewhere.

Powers to remove unauthorised campers

Power of local authority to direct unauthorised campers to leave land

77(1) If it appears to a local authority that persons are for the time being residing in a vehicle or vehicles within that authority's area –

    (a) on any land forming part of a highway;

    (b) on any other unoccupied land; or

    (c) on any occupied land without the consent of the occupier,

the authority may give a direction that those persons and any others with them are to leave the land and remove the vehicle or vehicles and any other property they have with them on the land.

(2) Notice of a direction under subsection (1) must be served on the persons to whom the direction applies, but it shall be sufficient for this purpose for the direction to specify the land and (except where the direction applies to only one person) to be addressed to all occupants of the vehicles on the land, without naming them.

(3) If a person knowing that a direction under subsection (1) above has been given which applies to him –

    (a) fails, as soon as practicable, to leave the land or remove from the land any vehicle or other property which is the subject of the direction, or

    (b) having removed any such vehicle or property again enters the land with a vehicle within the period of three months beginning with the day on which the direction was given,

he commits an offence and is liable on summary conviction to a fine not exceeding level 3 on the standard scale.

(4) A direction under subsection (1) operates to require persons who re-enter the land within the said period with vehicles or other property to leave and remove the vehicles or other property as it operates in relation to the persons and vehicles or other property on the land when the direction was given.

(5) In proceedings for an offence under this section it is a defence for the accused to show that his failure to leave or to remove the vehicle or

other property as soon as practicable or his re-entry with a vehicle was due to illness, mechanical breakdown or other immediate emergency.

(6) In this section –

'land' means land in the open air;

'local authority' means –

(a) in Greater London, a London borough or the Common Council of the City of London;

(b) in England outside Greater London, a county council, a district council or the Council of the Isles of Scilly;

(c) in Wales, a county council or a county borough council;

'occupier' means the person entitled to possession of the land by virtue of an estate or interest held by him;

'vehicle' includes –

(a) any vehicle, whether or not it is in a fit state for use on roads, and includes any body, with or without wheels, appearing to have formed part of such a vehicle, and any load carried by, and anything attached to, such a vehicle; and

(b) a caravan as defined in section 29(1) of the Caravan Sites and Control of Development Act 1960;

and a person may be regarded for the purposes of this section as residing on any land notwithstanding that he has a home elsewhere.

(7) Until 1st April 1996, in this section 'local authority' means, in Wales, a county council or a district council.

Orders for removal of persons and their vehicles unlawfully on land

78(1) A magistrates' court may, on a complaint made by a local authority, if satisfied that persons and vehicles in which they are residing are present on land within that authority's area in contravention of a direction given under section 77, make an order requiring the removal of any vehicle or other property which is so present on the land and any person residing in it.

(2) An order under this section may authorise the local authority to take such steps as are reasonably necessary to ensure that the order is complied with and, in particular, may authorise the authority, by its officers and servants–

(a) to enter upon the land specified in the order; and

(b) to take, in relation to any vehicle or property to be removed in pursuance of the order, such steps for securing entry and rendering it suitable for removal as may be so specified.

(3) The local authority shall not enter upon any occupied land unless they have given to the owner and occupier at least 24 hours notice of their intention to do so, or unless after reasonable inquiries they are unable to ascertain their names and addresses.

(4) A person who wilfully obstructs any person in the exercise of any power conferred on him by an order under this section commits an offence and is liable on summary conviction to a fine not exceeding level 3 on the standard scale.

(5)   Where a complaint is made under this section, a summons issued by the court requiring the person or persons to whom it is directed to appear before the court to answer to the complaint may be directed –

(a)   to the occupant of a particular vehicle on the land in question; or

(b)   to all occupants of vehicles on the land in question, without naming him or them.

(6)   Section 55(2) of the Magistrates' Courts Act 1980 (warrant for arrest of defendant failing to appear) does not apply to proceedings on a complaint made under this section.

(7)   Section 77(6) of this Act applies also for the interpretation of this section.

Provisions as to directions under section 77 and orders under section 78

79(1)   The following provisions apply in relation to the service of notice of a direction under section 77 and of a summons under section 78, referred to in those provisions as a 'relevant document'.

(2)   Where it is impracticable to serve a relevant document on a person named in it, the document shall be treated as duly served on him if a copy of it is fixed in a prominent place to the vehicle concerned; and where a relevant document is directed to the unnamed occupants of vehicles, it shall be treated as duly served on those occupants if a copy of it is fixed in a prominent place to every vehicle on the land in question at the time when service is thus effected.

(3)   A local authority shall take such steps as may be reasonably practicable to secure that a copy of any relevant document is displayed on the land in question (otherwise than by being fixed to a vehicle) in a manner designed to ensure that it is likely to be seen by any person camping on the land.

(4)   Notice of any relevant document shall be given by the local authority to the owner of the land in question and to any occupier of that land unless, after reasonable inquiries, the authority is unable to ascertain the name and address of the owner or occupier; and the owner of any such land and any occupier of such land shall be entitled to appear and to be heard in the proceedings.

(5)   Section 77(6) applies also for the interpretation of this section.

Repeal of certain provisions relating to gipsy sites

80(1), (2) [Repealed.]

(3)   The repeal by subsection (1) above of section 8 of the said Act of 1968 shall not affect the validity of directions given under subsection (3)(a) of that section; and in the case of directions under subsection (3)(c), the council may elect either to withdraw the application or request the Secretary of State to determine the application and if they so request the application shall be treated as referred to him under section 77 of the Town and Country Planning Act 1990.

(4)   The repeal by subsection (1) above of the definition of 'gipsies' in section 16 of the said Act of 1968 shall not affect the interpretation of that word in the definition of 'protected site' in section 5(1) of the Mobile

Homes Act 1983 or in any document embodying the terms of any planning permission granted under the Town and Country Planning Act 1990 before the commencement of this section.

(5)   ... so far as it extends to England and Wales except for the purposes of applications for grant received by the Secretary of State before the commencement of this section.

HUMAN RIGHTS ACT 1998

INTRODUCTION

The Convention Rights

1(1) In this Act 'the Convention rights' means the rights and fundamental freedoms set out in –

(a) Articles 2 to 12 and 14 of the Convention,

(b) Articles 1 to 3 of the First Protocol, and

(c) Articles 1 and 2 of the Sixth Protocol,

as read with Articles 16 to 18 of the Convention.

(2) Those Articles are to have effect for the purposes of this Act subject to any designated derogation or reservation (as to which see sections 14 and 15).

(3) The Articles are set out in Schedule 1.

(4) The Secretary of State may by order make such amendments to this Act as he considers appropriate to reflect the effect, in relation to the United Kingdom, of a protocol.

(5) In subsection (4) 'protocol' means a protocol to the Convention –

(a) which the United Kingdom has ratified; or

(b) which the United Kingdom has signed with a view to ratification.

(6) No amendment may be made by an order under subsection (4) so as to come into force before the protocol concerned is in force in relation to the United Kingdom.

Interpretation of Convention rights

2(1) A court or tribunal determining a question which has arisen in connection with a Convention right must take into account any –

(a) judgment, decision, declaration or advisory opinion of the European Court of Human Rights,

(b) opinion of the Commission given in a report adopted under Article 31 of the Convention,

(c) decision of the Commission in connection with Article 26 or 27(2) of the Convention, or

(d) decision of the Committee of Ministers taken under Article 46 of the Convention,

whenever made or given, so far as, in the opinion of the court or tribunal, it is relevant to the proceedings in which that question has arisen.

(2) Evidence of any judgment, decision, declaration or opinion of which account may have to be taken under this section is to be given in proceedings before any court or tribunal in such manner as may be provided by rules.

(3) In this section 'rules' means rules of court or, in the case of proceedings before a tribunal, rules made for the purposes of this section –

(a) by the Lord Chancellor or the Secretary of State, in relation to any proceedings outside Scotland;

(b) by the Secretary of State, in relation to proceedings in Scotland; or
(c) by a Northern Ireland department, in relation to proceedings before a tribunal in Northern Ireland –
(i) which deals with transferred matters; and
(ii) for which no rules made under paragraph (a) are in force.

LEGISLATION

Interpretation of legislation

3(1) So far as it is possible to do so, primary legislation and subordinate legislation must be read and given effect in a way which is compatible with the Convention rights.

(2) This section –
(a) applies to primary legislation and subordinate legislation whenever enacted;
(b) does not affect the validity, continuing operation or enforcement of any incompatible primary legislation; and
(c) does not affect the validity, continuing operation or enforcement of any incompatible subordinate legislation if (disregarding any possibility of revocation) primary legislation prevents removal of the incompatibility.

Declaration of incompatibility

4(1) Subsection (2) applies in any proceedings in which a court determines whether a provision of primary legislation is compatible with a Convention right.

(2) If the court is satisfied that the provision is incompatible with a Convention right, it may make a declaration of that incompatibility.

(3) Subsection (4) applies in any proceedings in which a court determines whether a provision of subordinate legislation, made in the exercise of a power conferred by primary legislation, is compatible with a Convention right.

(4) If the court is satisfied –
(a) that the provision is incompatible with a Convention right, and
(b) that (disregarding any possibility of revocation) the primary legislation concerned prevents removal of the incompatibility,
it may make a declaration of that incompatibility.

(5) In this section 'court' means –
(a) the House of Lords;
(b) the Judicial Committee of the Privy Council;
(c) the Courts-Martial Appeal Court;
(d) in Scotland, the High Court of Justiciary sitting otherwise than as a trial court or the Court of Session;
(e) in England and Wales or Northern Ireland, the High Court or the Court of Appeal.

(6)   A declaration under this section ('a declaration of incompatibility') –

    (a)   does not affect the validity, continuing operation or enforcement of the provision in respect of which it is given; and

    (b)   is not binding on the parties to the proceedings in which it is made.

Right of Crown to intervene

5(1)   Where a court is considering whether to make a declaration of incompatibility, the Crown is entitled to notice in accordance with rules of court.

(2)   In any case to which subsection (1) applies –

    (a)   a Minister of the Crown (or a person nominated by him),

    (b)   a member of the Scottish Executive,

    (c)   a Northern Ireland Minister,

    (d)   a Northern Ireland department,

is entitled, on giving notice in accordance with rules of court, to be joined as a party to the proceedings.

(3)   Notice under subsection (2) may be given at any time during the proceedings.

(4)   A person who has been made a party to criminal proceedings (other than in Scotland) as the result of a notice under subsection (2) may, with leave, appeal to the House of Lords against any declaration of incompatibility made in the proceedings.

(5)   In subsection (4) –

'criminal proceedings' includes all proceedings before the Courts-Martial Appeal Court; and

'leave' means leave granted by the court making the declaration of incompatibility or by the House of Lords.

PUBLIC AUTHORITIES

Acts of public authorities

6(1)   It is unlawful for a public authority to act in a way which is incompatible with a Convention right.

(2)   Subsection (1) does not apply to an act if –

    (a)   as the result of one or more provisions of primary legislation, the authority could not have acted differently; or

    (b)   in the case of one or more provisions of, or made under, primary legislation which cannot be read or given effect in a way which is compatible with the Convention rights, the authority was acting so as to give effect to or enforce those provisions.

(3)   In this section 'public authority' includes –

    (a)   a court or tribunal, and

    (b)   any person certain of whose functions are functions of a public nature,

but does not include either House of Parliament or a person exercising functions in connection with proceedings in Parliament.

(4)   In subsection (3) 'Parliament' does not include the House of Lords in its judicial capacity.

(5)   In relation to a particular act, a person is not a public authority by virtue only of subsection (3)(b) if the nature of the act is private.

(6)   'An act' includes a failure to act but does not include a failure to –

(a)   introduce in, or lay before, Parliament a proposal for legislation; or

(b)   make any primary legislation or remedial order.

Proceedings

7(1)   A person who claims that a public authority has acted (or proposes to act) in a way which is made unlawful by section 6(1) may –

(a)   bring proceedings against the authority under this Act in the appropriate court or tribunal, or

(b)   rely on the Convention right or rights concerned in any legal proceedings,

but only if he is (or would be) a victim of the unlawful act.

(2)   In subsection (1)(a) 'appropriate court or tribunal' means such court or tribunal as may be determined in accordance with rules; and proceedings against an authority include a counterclaim or similar proceeding.

(3)   If the proceedings are brought on an application for judicial review, the applicant is to be taken to have a sufficient interest in relation to the unlawful act only if he is, or would be, a victim of that act.

(4)   If the proceedings are made by way of a petition for judicial review in Scotland, the applicant shall be taken to have title and interest to sue in relation to the unlawful act only if he is, or would be, a victim of that act.

(5)   Proceedings under subsection (1)(a) must be brought before the end of –

(a)   the period of one year beginning with the date on which the act complained of took place; or

(b)   such longer period as the court or tribunal considers equitable having regard to all the circumstances,

but that is subject to any rule imposing a stricter time limit in relation to the procedure in question.

(6)   In subsection (1)(b) 'legal proceedings' includes –

(a)   proceedings brought by or at the instigation of a public authority; and

(b)   an appeal against the decision of a court or tribunal.

(7)   For the purposes of this section, a person is a victim of an unlawful act only if he would be a victim for the purposes of Article 34 of the Convention if proceedings were brought in the European Court of Human Rights in respect of that act.

(8)   Nothing in this Act creates a criminal offence.

(9)   In this section 'rules' means –

(a)   in relation to proceedings before a court or tribunal outside

Scotland, rules made by the Lord Chancellor or the Secretary of State for the purposes of this section or rules of court,

(b) in relation to proceedings before a court or tribunal in Scotland, rules made by the Secretary of State for those purposes,

(c) in relation to proceedings before a tribunal in Northern Ireland –
   (i) which deals with transferred matters; and
   (ii) for which no rules made under paragraph (a) are in force,

rules made by a Northern Ireland department for those purposes, and includes provision made by order under section 1 of the Courts and Legal Services Act 1990.

(10) In making rules, regard must be had to section 9.

(11) The Minister who has power to make rules in relation to a particular tribunal may, to the extent he considers it necessary to ensure that the tribunal can provide an appropriate remedy in relation to an act (or proposed act) of a public authority which is (or would be) unlawful as a result of section 6(1), by order add to –

(a) the relief or remedies which the tribunal may grant; or

(b) the grounds on which it may grant any of them.

(12) An order made under subsection (11) may contain such incidental, supplemental, consequential or transitional provision as the Minister making it considers appropriate.

(13) 'The Minister' includes the Northern Ireland department concerned.

Judicial remedies

8(1) In relation to any act (or proposed act) of a public authority which the court finds is (or would be) unlawful, it may grant such relief or remedy, or make such order, within its powers as it considers just and appropriate.

(2) But damages may be awarded only by a court which has power to award damages, or to order the payment of compensation, in civil proceedings.

(3) No award of damages is to be made unless, taking account of all the circumstances of the case, including –

(a) any other relief or remedy granted, or order made, in relation to the act in question (by that or any other court), and

(b) the consequences of any decision (of that or any other court) in respect of that act,

the court is satisfied that the award is necessary to afford just satisfaction to the person in whose favour it is made.

(4) In determining –

(a) whether to award damages, or

(b) the amount of an award,

the court must take into account the principles applied by the European Court of Human Rights in relation to the award of compensation under Article 41 of the Convention.

(5) A public authority against which damages are awarded is to be treated –

(a) in Scotland, for the purposes of section 3 of the Law Reform

(Miscellaneous Provisions) (Scotland) Act 1940 as if the award were made in an action of damages in which the authority has been found liable in respect of loss or damage to the person to whom the award is made;

(b) for the purposes of the Civil Liability (Contribution) Act 1978 as liable in respect of damage suffered by the person to whom the award is made.

(6)   In this section –

'court' includes a tribunal;

'damages' means damages for an unlawful act of a public authority; and

'unlawful' means unlawful under section 6(1).

Judicial acts

9(1)   Proceedings under section 7(1)(a) in respect of a judicial act may be brought only –

(a) by exercising a right of appeal;

(b) on an application (in Scotland a petition) for judicial review; or

(c) in such other forum as may be prescribed by rules.

(2)   That does not affect any rule of law which prevents a court from being the subject of judicial review.

(3)   In proceedings under this Act in respect of a judicial act done in good faith, damages may not be awarded otherwise than to compensate a person to the extent required by Article 5(5) of the Convention.

(4)   An award of damages permitted by subsection (3) is to be made against the Crown; but no award may be made unless the appropriate person, if not a party to the proceedings, is joined.

(5)   In this section –

'appropriate person' means the Minister responsible for the court concerned, or a person or government department nominated by him;

'court' includes a tribunal;

'judge' includes a member of a tribunal, a justice of the peace and a clerk or other officer entitled to exercise the jurisdiction of a court;

'judicial act' means a judicial act of a court and includes an act done on the instructions, or on behalf, of a judge; and

'rules' has the same meaning as in section 7(9).

REMEDIAL ACTION

Power to take remedial action

10(1)   This section applies if –

(a) a provision of legislation has been declared under section 4 to be incompatible with a Convention right and, if an appeal lies –

(i) all persons who may appeal have stated in writing that they do not intend to do so;

    (ii) the time for bringing an appeal has expired and no appeal has been brought within that time; or

    (iii) an appeal brought within that time has been determined or abandoned; or

    (b) it appears to a Minister of the Crown or Her Majesty in Council that, having regard to a finding of the European Court of Human Rights made after the coming into force of this section in proceedings against the United Kingdom, a provision of legislation is incompatible with an obligation of the United Kingdom arising from the Convention.

(2)   If a Minister of the Crown considers that there are compelling reasons for proceeding under this section, he may by order make such amendments to the legislation as he considers necessary to remove the incompatibility.

(3)   If, in the case of subordinate legislation, a Minister of the Crown considers –

    (a) that it is necessary to amend the primary legislation under which the subordinate legislation in question was made, in order to enable the incompatibility to be removed, and

    (b) that there are compelling reasons for proceeding under this section,

he may by order make such amendments to the primary legislation as he considers necessary.

(4)   This section also applies where the provision in question is in subordinate legislation and has been quashed, or declared invalid, by reason of incompatibility with a Convention right and the Minister proposes to proceed under paragraph 2(b) of Schedule 2.

(5)   If the legislation is an Order in Council, the power conferred by subsection (2) or (3) is exercisable by Her Majesty in Council.

(6)   In this section 'legislation' does not include a Measure of the Church Assembly or of the General Synod of the Church of England.

(7)   Schedule 2 makes further provision about remedial orders.

OTHER RIGHTS AND PROCEEDINGS

Safeguard for existing human rights

11   A person's reliance on a Convention right does not restrict –

    (a) any other right or freedom conferred on him by or under any law having effect in any part of the United Kingdom; or

    (b) his right to make any claim or bring any proceedings which he could make or bring apart from sections 7 to 9.

Freedom of expression

12(1)   This section applies if a court is considering whether to grant any relief which, if granted, might affect the exercise of the Convention right to freedom of expression.

(2)   If the person against whom the application for relief is made ('the

respondent') is neither present nor represented, no such relief is to be granted unless the court is satisfied –

(a) that the applicant has taken all practicable steps to notify the respondent; or

(b) that there are compelling reasons why the respondent should not be notified.

(3) No such relief is to be granted so as to restrain publication before trial unless the court is satisfied that the applicant is likely to establish that publication should not be allowed.

(4) The court must have particular regard to the importance of the Convention right to freedom of expression and, where the proceedings relate to material which the respondent claims, or which appears to the court, to be journalistic, literary or artistic material (or to conduct connected with such material), to –

(a) the extent to which –

(i) the material has, or is about to, become available to the public; or

(ii) it is, or would be, in the public interest for the material to be published;

(b) any relevant privacy code.

(5) In this section –

'court' includes a tribunal; and

'relief' includes any remedy or order (other than in criminal proceedings).

Freedom of thought, conscience and religion

13(1) If a court's determination of any question arising under this Act might affect the exercise by a religious organisation (itself or its members collectively) of the Convention right to freedom of thought, conscience and religion, it must have particular regard to the importance of that right.

(2) In this section 'court' includes a tribunal.

DEROGATIONS AND RESERVATIONS

Derogations

14(1) In this Act 'designated derogation' means any derogation by the United Kingdom from an Article of the Convention, or of any protocol to the Convention, which is designated for the purposes of this Act in an order made by the Secretary of State.

(2) [Repealed.]

(3) If a designated derogation is amended or replaced it ceases to be a designated derogation.

(4) But subsection (3) does not prevent the Secretary of State from exercising his power under subsection (1) to make a fresh designation order in respect of the Article concerned.

(5) The Secretary of State must by order make such amendments to

Schedule 3 as he considers appropriate to reflect –
(a) any designation order; or
(b) the effect of subsection (3).

(6) A designation order may be made in anticipation of the making by the United Kingdom of a proposed derogation.

Reservations

15(1) In this Act 'designated reservation' means –
(a) the United Kingdom's reservation to Article 2 of the First Protocol to the Convention; and
(b) any other reservation by the United Kingdom to an Article of the Convention, or of any protocol to the Convention, which is designated for the purposes of this Act in an order made by the Secretary of State.

(2) The text of the reservation referred to in subsection (1)(a) is set out in Part II of Schedule 3.

(3) If a designated reservation is withdrawn wholly or in part it ceases to be a designated reservation.

(4) But subsection (3) does not prevent the Secretary of State from exercising his power under subsection (1)(b) to make a fresh designation order in respect of the Article concerned.

(5) The Secretary of State must by order make such amendments to this Act as he considers appropriate to reflect –
(a) any designation order; or
(b) the effect of subsection (3).

Period for which designated derogations have effect

16(1) If it has not already been withdrawn by the United Kingdom, a designated derogation ceases to have effect for the purposes of this Act in the case of any other derogation, at the end of the period of five years beginning with the date on which the order designating it was made.

(2) At any time before the period –
(a) fixed by subsection (1), or
(b) extended by an order under this subsection,
comes to an end, the Secretary of State may by order extend it by a further period of five years.

(3) An order under section 14(1) ceases to have effect at the end of the period for consideration, unless a resolution has been passed by each House approving the order.

(4) Subsection (3) does not affect –
(a) anything done in reliance on the order; or
(b) the power to make a fresh order under section 14(1).

(5) In subsection (3) 'period for consideration' means the period of forty days beginning with the day on which the order was made.

(6) In calculating the period for consideration, no account is to be taken of any time during which –

(a) Parliament is dissolved or prorogued; or

(b) both Houses are adjourned for more than four days.

(7)   If a designated derogation is withdrawn by the United Kingdom, the Secretary of State must by order make such amendments to this Act as he considers are required to reflect that withdrawal.

Periodic review of designated reservations

17(1)   The appropriate Minister must review the designated reservation referred to in section 15(1)(a) –

(a) before the end of the period of five years beginning with the date on which section 1(2) came into force; and

(b) if that designation is still in force, before the end of the period of five years beginning with the date on which the last report relating to it was laid under subsection (3).

(2)   The appropriate Minister must review each of the other designated reservations (if any) –

(a) before the end of the period of five years beginning with the date on which the order designating the reservation first came into force; and

(b) if the designation is still in force, before the end of the period of five years beginning with the date on which the last report relating to it was laid under subsection (3).

(3)   The Minister conducting a review under this section must prepare a report on the result of the review and lay a copy of it before each House of Parliament.

Appointment to European Court of Human Rights

18(1)   In this section 'judicial office' means the office of –

(a) Lord Justice of Appeal, Justice of the High Court or Circuit judge, in England and Wales;

(b) judge of the Court of Session or sheriff, in Scotland;

(c) Lord Justice of Appeal, judge of the High Court or county court judge, in Northern Ireland.

(2)   The holder of a judicial office may become a judge of the European Court of Human Rights ('the Court') without being required to relinquish his office.

(3)   But he is not required to perform the duties of his judicial office while he is a judge of the Court.

(4)   In respect of any period during which he is a judge of the Court –

(a) a Lord Justice of Appeal or Justice of the High Court is not to count as a judge of the relevant court for the purposes of section 2(1) or 4(1) of the Supreme Court Act 1981 (maximum number of judges) nor as a judge of the Supreme Court for the purposes of section 12(1) to (6) of that Act (salaries, etc);

(b) a judge of the Court of Session is not to count as a judge of that court for the purposes of section 1(1) of the Court of Session Act 1988 (maximum number of judges) or of section 9(1)(c) of the Administration of Justice Act 1973 ('the 1973 Act') (salaries, etc);

(c)   a Lord Justice of Appeal or judge of the High Court in Northern Ireland is not to count as a judge of the relevant court for the purposes of section 2(1) or 3(1) of the Judicature (Northern Ireland) Act 1978 (maximum number of judges) nor as a judge of the Supreme Court of Northern Ireland for the purposes of section 9(1)(d) of the 1973 Act (salaries, etc);

(d)   a Circuit judge is not to count as such for the purposes of section 18 of the Courts Act 1971 (salaries, etc);

(e)   a sheriff is not to count as such for the purposes of section 14 of the Sheriff Courts (Scotland) Act 1907 (salaries, etc);

(f)   a county court judge of Northern Ireland is not to count as such for the purposes of section 106 of the County Courts Act Northern Ireland) 1959 (salaries, etc).

(5)   If a sheriff principal is appointed a judge of the Court, section 11(1) of the Sheriff Courts (Scotland) Act 1971 (temporary appointment of sheriff principal) applies, while he holds that appointment, as if his office is vacant.

(6)   Schedule 4 makes provision about judicial pensions in relation to the holder of a judicial office who serves as a judge of the Court.

(7)   The Lord Chancellor or the Secretary of State may by order make such transitional provision (including, in particular, provision for a temporary increase in the maximum number of judges) as he considers appropriate in relation to any holder of a judicial office who has completed his service as a judge of the Court.

PARLIAMENTARY PROCEDURE

Statements of compatibility

19(1)   A Minister of the Crown in charge of a Bill in either House of Parliament must, before Second Reading of the Bill –

(a)   make a statement to the effect that in his view the provisions of the Bill are compatible with the Convention rights ('a statement of compatibility'); or

(b)   make a statement to the effect that although he is unable to make a statement of compatibility the government nevertheless wishes the House to proceed with the Bill.

(2)   The statement must be in writing and be published in such manner as the Minister making it considers appropriate.

SUPPLEMENTAL

Orders, etc, under this Act

20(1)   Any power of a Minister of the Crown to make an order under this Act is exercisable by statutory instrument.

(2)   The power of the Lord Chancellor or the Secretary of State to make rules (other than rules of court) under section 2(3) or 7(9) is exercisable by statutory instrument.

(3)   Any statutory instrument made under section 14, 15 or 16(7) must be laid before Parliament.

(4)   No order may be made by the Lord Chancellor or the Secretary of State under section 1(4), 7(11) or 16(2) unless a draft of the order has been laid before, and approved by, each House of Parliament.

(5)   Any statutory instrument made under section 18(7) or Schedule 4, or to which subsection (2) applies, shall be subject to annulment in pursuance of a resolution of either House of Parliament.

(6)   The power of a Northern Ireland department to make –

(a) rules under section 2(3)(c) or 7(9)(c), or

(b) an order under section 7(11),

is exercisable by statutory rule for the purposes of the Statutory Rules (Northern Ireland) Order 1979.

(7)   Any rules made under section 2(3)(c) or 7(9)(c) shall be subject to negative resolution; and section 41(6) of the Interpretation Act Northern Ireland) 1954 (meaning of 'subject to negative resolution') shall apply as if the power to make the rules were conferred by an Act of the Northern Ireland Assembly.

(8)   No order may be made by a Northern Ireland department under section 7(11) unless a draft of the order has been laid before, and approved by, the Northern Ireland Assembly.

Interpretation, etc

21(1)   In this Act –

'amend' includes repeal and apply (with or without modifications);

'the appropriate Minister' means the Minister of the Crown having charge of the appropriate authorised government department (within the meaning of the Crown Proceedings Act 1947);

'the Commission' means the European Commission of Human Rights;

'the Convention' means the Convention for the Protection of Human Rights and Fundamental Freedoms, agreed by the Council of Europe at Rome on 4th November 1950 as it has effect for the time being in relation to the United Kingdom;

'declaration of incompatibility' means a declaration under section 4;

'Minister of the Crown' has the same meaning as in the Ministers of the Crown Act 1975;

'Northern Ireland Minister' includes the First Minister and the deputy First Minister in Northern Ireland;

'primary legislation' means any –

(a) public general Act;

(b) local and personal Act;

(c) private Act;

(d) Measure of the Church Assembly;

(e) Measure of the General Synod of the Church of England;

(f) Order in Council –

(i) made in exercise of Her Majesty's Royal Prerogative;

(ii) made under section 38(1)(a) of the Northern Ireland Constitution Act 1973 or the corresponding provision of the Northern Ireland Act 1998; or

(iii)amending an Act of a kind mentioned in paragraph (a), (b) or (c);

and includes an order or other instrument made under primary legislation (otherwise than by the National Assembly for Wales, a member of the Scottish Executive, a Northern Ireland Minister or a Northern Ireland department) to the extent to which it operates to bring one or more provisions of that legislation into force or amends any primary legislation;

'the First Protocol' means the protocol to the Convention agreed at Paris on 20th March 1952;

'the Sixth Protocol' means the protocol to the Convention agreed at Strasbourg on 28th April 1983;

'the Eleventh Protocol' means the protocol to the Convention (restructuring the control machinery established by the Convention) agreed at Strasbourg on 11th May 1994;

'remedial order' means an order under section 10;

'subordinate legislation' means any –

(a) Order in Council other than one –

(i) made in exercise of Her Majesty's Royal Prerogative;

(ii) made under section 38(1)(a) of the Northern Ireland Constitution Act 1973 or the corresponding provision of the Northern Ireland Act 1998; or

(iii)amending an Act of a kind mentioned in the definition of primary legislation;

(b) Act of the Scottish Parliament;

(c) Act of the Parliament of Northern Ireland;

(d) Measure of the Assembly established under section 1 of the Northern Ireland Assembly Act 1973;

(e) Act of the Northern Ireland Assembly;

(f) order, rules, regulations, scheme, warrant, byelaw or other instrument made under primary legislation (except to the extent to which it operates to bring one or more provisions of that legislation into force or amends any primary legislation);

(g) order, rules, regulations, scheme, warrant, byelaw or other instrument made under legislation mentioned in paragraph (b), (c), (d) or (e) or made under an Order in Council applying only to Northern Ireland;

(h) order, rules, regulations, scheme, warrant, byelaw or other instrument made by a member of the Scottish Executive, a Northern Ireland Minister or a Northern Ireland department in exercise of prerogative or other executive functions of Her Majesty which are exercisable by such a person on behalf of Her Majesty;

'transferred matters' has the same meaning as in the Northern Ireland Act 1998; and 'tribunal' means any tribunal in which legal proceedings may be brought.

(2) The references in paragraphs (b) and (c) of section 2(1) to Articles are to Articles of the Convention as they had effect immediately before the coming into force of the Eleventh Protocol.

(3) The reference in paragraph (d) of section 2(1) to Article 46 includes a reference to Articles 32 and 54 of the Convention as they had effect immediately before the coming into force of the Eleventh Protocol.

(4) The references in section 2(1) to a report or decision of the Commission or a decision of the Committee of Ministers include references to a report or decision made as provided by paragraphs 3, 4 and 6 of Article 5 of the Eleventh Protocol (transitional provisions).

(5) Any liability under the Army Act 1955, the Air Force Act 1955 or the Naval Discipline Act 1957 to suffer death for an offence is replaced by a liability to imprisonment for life or any less punishment authorised by those Acts; and those Acts shall accordingly have effect with the necessary modifications.

Short title, commencement, application and extent

22(1) This Act may be cited as the Human Rights Act 1998.

(2) Sections 18, 20 and 21(5) and this section come into force on the passing of this Act.

(3) The other provisions of this Act come into force on such day as the Secretary of State may by order appoint; and different days may be appointed for different purposes.

(4) Paragraph (b) of subsection (1) of section 7 applies to proceedings brought by or at the instigation of a public authority whenever the act in question took place; but otherwise that subsection does not apply to an act taking place before the coming into force of that section.

(5) This Act binds the Crown.

(6) This Act extends to Northern Ireland.

(7) Section 21(5), so far as it relates to any provision contained in the Army Act 1955, the Air Force Act 1955 or the Naval Discipline Act 1957, extends to any place to which that provision extends.

SCHEDULE 1: THE ARTICLES

PART I: THE CONVENTION: RIGHTS AND FREEDOMS

Article 2: Right to life

1   Everyone's right to life shall be protected by law. No one shall be deprived of his life intentionally save in the execution of a sentence of a court following his conviction of a crime for which this penalty is provided by law.

2   Deprivation of life shall not be regarded as inflicted in contravention of this Article when it results from the use of force which is no more than absolutely necessary:

(a) in defence of any person from unlawful violence;

(b) in order to effect a lawful arrest or to prevent the escape of a person lawfully detained;

(c) in action lawfully taken for the purpose of quelling a riot or insurrection.

Article 3: Prohibition of torture

No one shall be subjected to torture or to inhuman or degrading treatment or punishment.

Article 4: Prohibition of slavery and forced labour

1   No one shall be held in slavery or servitude.

2   No one shall be required to perform forced or compulsory labour.

3   For the purpose of this Article the term 'forced or compulsory labour' shall not include:

(a) any work required to be done in the ordinary course of detention imposed according to the provisions of Article 5 of this Convention or during conditional release from such detention;

(b) any service of a military character or, in case of conscientious objectors in countries where they are recognised, service exacted instead of compulsory military service;

(c) any service exacted in case of an emergency or calamity threatening the life or well-being of the community;

(d) any work or service which forms part of normal civic obligations.

Article 5: Right to liberty and security

1   Everyone has the right to liberty and security of person. No one shall be deprived of his liberty save in the following cases and in accordance with a procedure prescribed by law:

(a) the lawful detention of a person after conviction by a competent court;

(b) the lawful arrest or detention of a person for non-compliance with the lawful order of a court or in order to secure the fulfilment of any obligation prescribed by law;

(c) the lawful arrest or detention of a person effected for the purpose of bringing him before the competent legal authority on reasonable suspicion of having committed an offence or when it is reasonably considered necessary to prevent his committing an offence or fleeing after having done so;

(d) the detention of a minor by lawful order for the purpose of educational supervision or his lawful detention for the purpose of bringing him before the competent legal authority;

(e) the lawful detention of persons for the prevention of the spreading of infectious diseases, of persons of unsound mind, alcoholics or drug addicts or vagrants;

(f) the lawful arrest or detention of a person to prevent his effecting an unauthorised entry into the country or of a person against whom action is being taken with a view to deportation or extradition.

2   Everyone who is arrested shall be informed promptly, in a language which he understands, of the reasons for his arrest and of any charge against him.

3   Everyone arrested or detained in accordance with the provisions of paragraph 1(c) of this Article shall be brought promptly before a judge or other officer authorised by law to exercise judicial power and shall be entitled to trial within a reasonable time or to release pending trial. Release may be conditioned by guarantees to appear for trial.

4   Everyone who is deprived of his liberty by arrest or detention shall be entitled to take proceedings by which the lawfulness of his detention shall be decided speedily by a court and his release ordered if the detention is not lawful.

5   Everyone who has been the victim of arrest or detention in contravention of the provisions of this Article shall have an enforceable right to compensation.

Article 6: Right to a fair trial

1   In the determination of his civil rights and obligations or of any criminal charge against him, everyone is entitled to a fair and public hearing within a reasonable time by an independent and impartial tribunal established by law. Judgment shall be pronounced publicly but the press and public may be excluded from all or part of the trial in the interest of morals, public order or national security in a democratic society, where the interests of juveniles or the protection of the private life of the parties so require, or to the extent strictly necessary in the opinion of the court in special circumstances where publicity would prejudice the interests of justice.

2   Everyone charged with a criminal offence shall be presumed innocent until proved guilty according to law.

3   Everyone charged with a criminal offence has the following minimum rights:

(a)   to be informed promptly, in a language which he understands and in detail, of the nature and cause of the accusation against him;

(b)   to have adequate time and facilities for the preparation of his defence;

(c)   to defend himself in person or through legal assistance of his own choosing or, if he has not sufficient means to pay for legal assistance, to be given it free when the interests of justice so require;

(d)   to examine or have examined witnesses against him and to obtain the attendance and examination of witnesses on his behalf under the same conditions as witnesses against him;

(e)   to have the free assistance of an interpreter if he cannot understand or speak the language used in court.

Article 7: No punishment without law

1   No one shall be held guilty of any criminal offence on account of any act or omission which did not constitute a criminal offence under national or international law at the time when it was committed. Nor shall a heavier penalty be imposed than the one that was applicable at the time the criminal offence was committed.

2   This Article shall not prejudice the trial and punishment of any person for any act or omission which, at the time when it was committed, was criminal according to the general principles of law recognised by civilised nations.

Article 8: Right to respect for private and family life

1   Everyone has the right to respect for his private and family life, his home and his correspondence.

2   There shall be no interference by a public authority with the exercise of this right except such as is in accordance with the law and is necessary in a democratic society in the interests of national security, public safety or the economic well-being of the country, for the prevention of disorder or crime, for the protection of health or morals, or for the protection of the rights and freedoms of others.

Article 9: Freedom of thought, conscience and religion

1   Everyone has the right to freedom of thought, conscience and religion; this right includes freedom to change his religion or belief and freedom, either alone or in community with others and in public or private, to manifest his religion or belief, in worship, teaching, practice and observance.

2   Freedom to manifest one's religion or beliefs shall be subject only to such limitations as are prescribed by law and are necessary in a democratic society in the interests of public safety, for the protection of public order, health or morals, or for the protection of the rights and freedoms of others.

Article 10: Freedom of expression

1   Everyone has the right to freedom of expression. This right shall include freedom to hold opinions and to receive and impart information and ideas without interference by public authority and regardless of frontiers. This Article shall not prevent States from requiring the licensing of broadcasting, television or cinema enterprises.

2   The exercise of these freedoms, since it carries with it duties and responsibilities, may be subject to such formalities, conditions, restrictions or penalties as are prescribed by law and are necessary in a democratic society, in the interests of national security, territorial integrity or public safety, for the prevention of disorder or crime, for the protection of health or morals, for the protection of the reputation or rights of others, for preventing the disclosure of information received in confidence, or for maintaining the authority and impartiality of the judiciary.

Article 11: Freedom of assembly and association

1 Everyone has the right to freedom of peaceful assembly and to freedom of association with others, including the right to form and to join trade unions for the protection of his interests.

2 No restrictions shall be placed on the exercise of these rights other than such as are prescribed by law and are necessary in a democratic society in the interests of national security or public safety, for the prevention of disorder or crime, for the protection of health or morals or for the protection of the rights and freedoms of others. This Article shall not prevent the imposition of lawful restrictions on the exercise of these rights by members of the armed forces, of the police or of the administration of the State.

Article 12: Right to marry

Men and women of marriageable age have the right to marry and to found a family, according to the national laws governing the exercise of this right.

Article 14: Prohibition of discrimination

The enjoyment of the rights and freedoms set forth in this Convention shall be secured without discrimination on any ground such as sex, race, colour, language, religion, political or other opinion, national or social origin, association with a national minority, property, birth or other status.

Article 16: Restrictions on political activity of aliens

Nothing in Articles 10, 11 and 14 shall be regarded as preventing the High Contracting Parties from imposing restrictions on the political activity of aliens.

Article 17: Prohibition of abuse of rights

Nothing in this Convention may be interpreted as implying for any State, group or person any right to engage in any activity or perform any act aimed at the destruction of any of the rights and freedoms set forth herein or at their limitation to a greater extent than is provided for in the Convention.

Article 18: Limitation on use of restrictions on rights

The restrictions permitted under this Convention to the said rights and freedoms shall not be applied for any purpose other than those for which they have been prescribed.

PART II: THE FIRST PROTOCOL

Article 1: Protection of property

Every natural or legal person is entitled to the peaceful enjoyment of his possessions. No one shall be deprived of his possessions except in the public interest and subject to the conditions provided for by law and by the general principles of international law.

The preceding provisions shall not, however, in any way impair the right of a State to enforce such laws as it deems necessary to control the use of property in accordance with the general interest or to secure the payment of taxes or other contributions or penalties.

Article 2: Right to education

No person shall be denied the right to education. In the exercise of any functions which it assumes in relation to education and to teaching, the State shall respect the right of parents to ensure such education and teaching in conformity with their own religious and philosophical convictions.

Article 3: Right to free elections

The High Contracting Parties undertake to hold free elections at reasonable intervals by secret ballot, under conditions which will ensure the free expression of the opinion of the people in the choice of the legislature.

PART III: THE SIXTH PROTOCOL

Article 1: Abolition of the death penalty

The death penalty shall be abolished. No one shall be condemned to such penalty or executed.

Article 2: Death penalty in time of war

A State may make provision in its law for the death penalty in respect of acts committed in time of war or of imminent threat of war; such penalty shall be applied only in the instances laid down in the law and in accordance with its provisions. The State shall communicate to the Secretary General of the Council of Europe the relevant provisions of that law.

SCHEDULE 2: REMEDIAL ORDERS

Orders

1(1) A remedial order may –
   (a) contain such incidental, supplemental, consequential or transitional provision as the person making it considers appropriate;
   (b) be made so as to have effect from a date earlier than that on which it is made;
   (c) make provision for the delegation of specific functions;
   (d) make different provision for different cases.

(2) The power conferred by sub-paragraph (1)(a) includes –
   (a) power to amend primary legislation (including primary legislation other than that which contains the incompatible provision); and
   (b) power to amend or revoke subordinate legislation (including

subordinate legislation other than that which contains the incompatible provision).

(3)   A remedial order may be made so as to have the same extent as the legislation which it affects.

(4)   No person is to be guilty of an offence solely as a result of the retrospective effect of a remedial order.

Procedure

2   No remedial order may be made unless –

(a) a draft of the order has been approved by a resolution of each House of Parliament made after the end of the period of 60 days beginning with the day on which the draft was laid; or

(b) it is declared in the order that it appears to the person making it that, because of the urgency of the matter, it is necessary to make the order without a draft being so approved.

Orders laid in draft

3(1)   No draft may be laid under paragraph 2(a) unless –

(a) the person proposing to make the order has laid before Parliament a document which contains a draft of the proposed order and the required information; and

(b) the period of 60 days, beginning with the day on which the document required by this sub-paragraph was laid, has ended.

(2)   If representations have been made during that period, the draft laid under paragraph 2(a) must be accompanied by a statement containing –

(a) a summary of the representations; and

(b) if, as a result of the representations, the proposed order has been changed, details of the changes.

Urgent cases

4(1)   If a remedial order ('the original order') is made without being approved in draft, the person making it must lay it before Parliament, accompanied by the required information, after it is made.

(2)   If representations have been made during the period of 60 days beginning with the day on which the original order was made, the person making it must (after the end of that period) lay before Parliament a statement containing –

(a) a summary of the representations; and

(b) if, as a result of the representations, he considers it appropriate to make changes to the original order, details of the changes.

(3)   If sub-paragraph (2)(b) applies, the person making the statement must –

(a) make a further remedial order replacing the original order; and

(b) lay the replacement order before Parliament.

(4)   If, at the end of the period of 120 days beginning with the day on which the original order was made, a resolution has not been passed by each House approving the original or replacement order,

the order ceases to have effect (but without that affecting anything previously done under either order or the power to make a fresh remedial order).

Definitions

5   In this Schedule –

'representations' means representations about a remedial order (or proposed remedial order) made to the person making (or proposing to make) it and includes any relevant Parliamentary report or resolution; and

'required information' means –

(a) an explanation of the incompatibility which the order (or proposed order) seeks to remove, including particulars of the relevant declaration, finding or order; and

(b) a statement of the reasons for proceeding under section 10 and for making an order in those terms.

Calculating periods

6   In calculating any period for the purposes of this Schedule, no account is to be taken of any time during which –

(a) Parliament is dissolved or prorogued; or

(b) both Houses are adjourned for more than four days.

7(1) This paragraph applies in relation to –

(a) any remedial order made, and any draft of such an order proposed to be made –

(i) by the Scottish Ministers; or

(ii) within devolved competence (within the meaning of the Scotland Act 1998) by Her Majesty in Council; and

(b) any document or statement to be laid in connection with such an order (or proposed order).

(2) This Schedule has effect in relation to any such order (or proposed order), document or statement subject to the following modifications.

(3) Any reference to Parliament, each House of Parliament or both Houses of Parliament shall be construed as a reference to the Scottish Parliament.

(4) Paragraph 6 does not apply and instead, in calculating any period for the purposes of this Schedule, no account is to be taken of any time during which the Scottish Parliament is dissolved or is in recess for more than four days.

SCHEDULE 3: RESERVATION

[PART I: DEROGATION repealed by SI 2001 No 1216]

PART II: RESERVATION

At the time of signing the present (First) Protocol, I declare that, in view of certain provisions of the Education Acts in the United

Kingdom, the principle affirmed in the second sentence of Article 2 is accepted by the United Kingdom only so far as it is compatible with the provision of efficient instruction and training, and the avoidance of unreasonable public expenditure.

Dated 20 March 1952. Made by the United Kingdom Permanent Representative to the Council of Europe.

SCHEDULE 4: JUDICIAL PENSIONS

Duty to make orders about pensions

1(1)   The appropriate Minister must by order make provision with respect to pensions payable to or in respect of any holder of a judicial office who serves as an ECHR judge.

(2)   A pensions order must include such provision as the Minister making it considers is necessary to secure that –

(a) an ECHR judge who was, immediately before his appointment as an ECHR judge, a member of a judicial pension scheme is entitled to remain as a member of that scheme;

(b) the terms on which he remains a member of the scheme are those which would have been applicable had he not been appointed as an ECHR judge; and

(c) entitlement to benefits payable in accordance with the scheme continues to be determined as if, while serving as an ECHR judge, his salary was that which would (but for section 18(4)) have been payable to him in respect of his continuing service as the holder of his judicial office.

Contributions

2   A pensions order may, in particular, make provision –

(a) for any contributions which are payable by a person who remains a member of a scheme as a result of the order, and which would otherwise be payable by deduction from his salary, to be made otherwise than by deduction from his salary as an ECHR judge; and

(b) for such contributions to be collected in such manner as may be determined by the administrators of the scheme.

Amendments of other enactments

3   A pensions order may amend any provision of, or made under, a pensions Act in such manner and to such extent as the Minister making the order considers necessary or expedient to ensure the proper administration of any scheme to which it relates.

Definitions

4   In this Schedule –

'appropriate Minister' means –

(a)   in relation to any judicial office whose jurisdiction is exercisable exclusively in relation to Scotland, the Secretary of State; and

(b)   otherwise, the Lord Chancellor;

'ECHR judge' means the holder of a judicial office who is serving as a judge of the Court;

'judicial pension scheme' means a scheme established by and in accordance with a pensions Act;

'pensions Act' means –

(a)   the County Courts Act Northern Ireland) 1959;

(b)   the Sheriffs' Pensions (Scotland) Act 1961;

(c)   the Judicial Pensions Act 1981; or

(d)   the Judicial Pensions and Retirement Act 1993; and

'pensions order' means an order made under paragraph 1.

HOUSING ACT 2004 (EXTRACTS)

ACCOMMODATION NEEDS OF GYPSIES AND TRAVELLERS

Duties of local housing authorities: accommodation needs of Gypsies and Travellers

225(1) Every local housing authority must, when undertaking a review of housing needs in their district under section 8 of the Housing Act 1985, carry out an assessment of the accommodation needs of Gypsies and Travellers residing in or resorting to their district.

(2)   Subsection (3) applies where a local housing authority are required under section 87 of the Local Government Act 2003 to prepare a strategy in respect of the meeting of such accommodation needs.

(3)   The local authority who are that local housing authority must take the strategy into account in exercising their functions.

'Functions' includes functions exercisable otherwise than as a local housing authority.

(4)   A local housing authority must have regard to any guidance issued under section 226 in–

(a)   carrying out such an assessment as mentioned in subsection (1), and

(b)   preparing any strategy that they are required to prepare as mentioned in subsection (2).

(5)   In this section–

(a)   'Gypsies and Travellers' has the meaning given by regulations made by the appropriate national authority;

(b)   'accommodation needs' includes needs with respect to the provision of sites on which caravans can be stationed; and

(c)   'caravan' has the same meaning as in Part 1 of the Caravan Sites and Control of Development Act 1960.

Guidance in relation to section 225

226(1) The appropriate national authority may issue guidance to local housing authorities regarding–

(a)   the carrying out of assessments under section 225(1), and

(b)   the preparation of any strategies that local housing authorities are required to prepare as mentioned in section 225(2).

(2)   Before giving guidance under this section, or revising guidance already given, the Secretary of State must lay a draft of the proposed guidance or alterations before each House of Parliament.

(3)   The Secretary of State must not give or revise the guidance before the end of the period of 40 days beginning with the day on which the draft is laid before each House of Parliament (or, if copies are laid before each House of Parliament on different days, the later of those days).

(4)   The Secretary of State must not proceed with the proposed guidance or alterations if, within the period of 40 days mentioned in subsection

(3), either House resolves that the guidance or alterations be withdrawn.

(5) Subsection (4) is without prejudice to the possibility of laying a further draft of the guidance or alterations before each House of Parliament.

(6) In calculating the period of 40 days mentioned in subsection (3), no account is to be taken of any time during which Parliament is dissolved or prorogued or during which both Houses are adjourned for more than four days.

Circulars

PLANNING FOR GYPSY AND TRAVELLER CARAVAN SITES (ODPM CIRCULAR 1/06)

Introduction

1   This Circular should be seen in the context of the Government's key objective for planning for housing – to ensure that everyone has the opportunity of living in a decent home.

2   The Government is committed to ensuring that members of the gypsy and traveller communities should have the same rights and responsibilities as every other citizen. This Circular replaces Circular 1/94, *Gypsy Sites and Planning* and provides updated guidance on the planning aspects of finding sites for gypsies and travellers and how local authorities and gypsies and travellers can work together to achieve that aim. The policies in this Circular apply throughout England.

3   A new Circular is necessary because evidence shows that the advice set out in Circular 1/94 has failed to deliver adequate sites for gypsies and travellers in many areas of England over the last 10 years. Since the issue of Circular 1/94, and the repeal of local authorities' duty to provide gypsy and traveller sites there have been more applications for private gypsy and traveller sites, but this has not resulted in the necessary increase in provision.

4   Creating and sustaining strong communities, for the benefit of all members of society including the gypsy and traveller community, is at the heart of the Government's Respect agenda. These communities will depend ultimately on a shared commitment to a common set of values, clear rules and a willingness for people to act together to resolve differences. They will also require effective enforcement action to tackle the poor behaviour of some invididuals and families. We recognise the conflict and distress associated with unauthorised encampments, and the anti-social behaviour that sometimes accompanies such sites. This Circular will help to promote good community relations at the local level, and avoid the conflict and controversy associated with unauthorised developments and encampments.

5   Gypsies and Travellers are believed to experience the worst health and education status of any disadvantaged group in England. Research has consistently confirmed the link between the lack of good quality sites for gypsies and travellers and poor health and education. This circular should enhance the health and education outcomes of gypsies and travellers.

6   Major changes to the planning system have been introduced by the Planning and Compulsory Purchase Act 2004 (the Planning Act (2004)). The planning tools which the Planning Act (2004) makes available and the associated move to more positive planning will help deliver communities that are sustainable and work better for people.

7   Regional Spatial Strategies (RSSs) strengthen planning at the regional level. Local Development Frameworks (LDFs) offer more flexibility to

planners at the local level. Requirements for early community involvement will help to ensure plans better reflect community aspirations and can be implemented more effectively.

8   Priority setting in LDFs is the responsibility of local authorities within the framework provided by national policy and the RSS. Communities will determine through their Local planning authorities what are the priorities for local development. Site-based decisions and allocations are made at this local level. The local housing strategy (LHS) will show how the accommodation needs identified by the accommodation assessment will be met, including those of gypsies and travellers. The Development Plan Documents (DPDs) will identify the location of appropriate sites.

9   The new planning system, as set out in the Planning Act (2004), places emphasis on early consultation between local authorities and the communities they serve. The aim is to ensure that plans properly reflect the needs and aspirations of all sectors of the community. In the case of gypsies and travellers, such early engagement should help in the identification of suitably located sites and a reduction in unauthorised encampments and developments.

10   The Housing Act 2004 will require local housing authorities to include gypsies and travellers in their accommodation assessments and to take a strategic approach, including drawing up a strategy demonstrating how the accommodation needs of gypsies and travellers will be met, as part of their wider housing strategies.

11   This Circular applies equally to the development of public sites by local authorities or registered social landlords (RSLs), to applications for planning permission from gypsies and travellers themselves or from others wishing to develop land for use as a gypsy and traveller caravan site. It applies regardless of whether the site is for residential or transit use, and whatever the expected life of the site itself.

12   The Circular comes into effect immediately. Its main intentions are;

   a)   to create and support sustainable, respectful, and inclusive communities where gypsies and travellers have fair access to suitable accommodation, education, health and welfare provision; where there is mutual respect and consideration between all communities for the rights and responsibilities of each community and individual; and where there is respect between individuals and communities towards the environments in which they live and work;

   b)   to reduce the number of unauthorised encampments and developments and the conflict and controversy they cause and to make enforcement more effective where local authorities have complied with the guidance in this Circular;

   c)   to increase significantly the number of gypsy and traveller sites in appropriate locations with planning permission in order to address under-provision over the next 3-5 years;

   d)   to recognise, protect and facilitate the traditional travelling way of life of gypsies and travellers, whilst respecting the interests of the settled community;

e)   to underline the importance of assessing needs at regional and sub-regional level and for local authorities to develop strategies to ensure that needs are dealt with fairly and effectively;

f)   to identify and make provision for the resultant land and accommodation requirements;

g)   to ensure that DPDs include fair, realistic and inclusive policies and to ensure identified need is dealt with fairly and effectively;

h)   to promote more private gypsy and traveller site provision in appropriate locations through the planning system, while recognising that there will always be those who cannot provide their own sites; and

i)   to help to avoid gypsies and travellers becoming homeless through eviction from unauthorised sites without an alternative to move to.

Gypsies and Travellers – a context

13   The Government recognises that many gypsies and travellers wish to find and buy their own sites to develop and manage. An increase in the number of approved private sites may also release pitches on local authority sites for gypsies and travellers most in need of public provision. However, there will remain a requirement for public site provision above the current levels. Such sites are needed for gypsies and travellers who are unable to buy and develop their own sites, or prefer to rent, and to provide transit sites and emergency stopping places where gypsies and travellers may legally stop in the course of travelling.

14   Gypsies and travellers are estimated to make up less than 1% of the population of England, but only a proportion of gypsies and travellers live in caravans. July 2005 Caravan Count figures show that there are around 16,000 gypsy and traveller caravans, with around three quarters of these on authorised sites. The overall need for gypsy and traveller sites is therefore very small. However, this need has often proved difficult to meet.

Definition

15   For the purposes of this Circular 'gypsies and travellers' means

Persons of nomadic habit of life whatever their race or origin, including such persons who on grounds only of their own or their family's or dependants' educational or health needs or old age have ceased to travel temporarily or permanently, but excluding members of an organised group of travelling show people or circus people travelling together as such.

16   Planning advice relating to travelling showpeople is given in DoE Circular 22/91.

17   Some gypsies and travellers have an actively itinerant lifestyle, including groups of long distance travellers, and are generally self-employed people, sometimes occupied in scrap and scrap-metal dealing, laying tarmacadam, seasonal agricultural work, casual labouring, and other employment. These traditional patterns of work are, however, changing and the community has generally become more settled. For example, a reduction of seasonal agricultural and related work has led to more travellers working in trades which require less mobility.

18   There is a need to provide sites, including transit sites, in locations that meet the current working patterns of gypsies and travellers. In view of the changes in their work patterns these may not be the same areas they have located in or frequented in the past. This needs to be balanced with the responsibility of gypsies and travellers to respect the planning system.

19   A more settled existence can prove beneficial to some gypsies and travellers in terms of access to health and education services, and employment, and can contribute to greater integration and social inclusion within local communities. Nevertheless the ability to travel remains an important part of gypsy and traveller culture. Some communities of gypsies and travellers live in extended family groups and often travel as such. This is a key feature of their traditional way of life that has an impact on planning for their accommodation needs.

Planning process

Overview

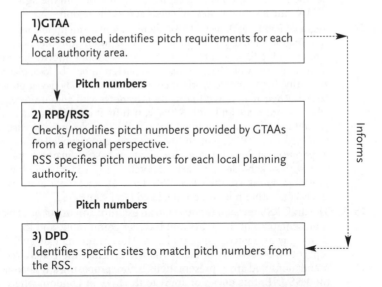

Gypsy and Traveller Accommodation Assessments (GTAAs)

20   The assessment of gypsy and traveller accommodation needs is integral to assessment of general accommodation needs. The new planning process will begin by local authorities assessing gypsy and traveller accommodation needs as part of the gypsy and traveller accommodation assessment (GTAA) process.

21   The data collected through the GTAA process will inform the preparation of Development Plan Documents (DPDs) through the process described below. One of the tests of soundness of a submission DPD at its examination will be whether it is founded on robust and credible

evidence. The need identified by the GTAA could include gypsies and travellers who do not fall within the definition at paragraph 14. This need should still inform the amount of land to be identified by the planning system. This is necessary to ensure local authorities have flexibility to allocate adequate land for their own sites to provide for those they have assessed as in need of caravan accommodation. Further guidance on this can be found in draft guidance document *Gypsy and Traveller Accommodation Assessments.*

Regional Spatial Strategy (RSS)

22   The information from GTAAs on gypsy and traveller need for sites will, as with other housing needs, be a key component in the overall assessment of need which informs the housing policies in the RSS. The regional view of the body responsible for the Regional Housing Strategy (RHS) can help inform the preparation of policies in a draft revision of a Regional Spatial Strategy (RSS).

23   The RSS revision should identify the number of pitches required (but not their location) for each local planning authority in the light of the GTAAs and a strategic view of needs across the region.

24   Regional Planning Bodies (RPBs) should maintain an up-to-date understanding of the likely strategic accommodation requirements of their areas over the lifespan of their RSSs, which should inform the preparation and review of RSSs. In allocating pitch numbers by local planning authority, RPBs should work in concert with the body developing the RHS in their region, with housing providers, with adjoining regions where appropriate and with RPBs' constituent local authorities. This should include county councils who will have relevant expertise due to their historical responsibility for gypsy and traveller issues. It is important that there is a common evidence base, prepared in partnership with stakeholders, in particular with gypsy and traveller housing providers, to inform the RHS, RSS, Local Development Frameworks (LDFs) and other relevant regional and local strategies.

25   The draft RSS revision is subject to an examination in public at which representatives of the gypsy and traveller community, and local residents may be invited to give evidence. The examining Panel will then report to the Secretary of State who will consider the Panel's recommendations and any representations before proposing any changes to the RSS (NB: this does not apply to the SDS in London, where the Mayor will consider the Panel's recommendations).

26   Pitch numbers could be identified by sub-regional area if a joint DPD were produced. A joint DPD could be prepared, with the agreement of the local planning authorities involved, on a county wide or other sub-regional basis.

Community involvement

27   It is expected that at an early stage in the preparation of RSSs and DPDs planning authorities will discuss gypsies and travellers' accommodation needs with gypsies and travellers themselves, their representative bodies and local support groups. A list of some relevant

contacts is given in Annex A, although it should be stressed this is not exhaustive. Gypsies and travellers should also be proactive in ensuring that they engage with local planning authorities to ensure that their views are taken into account.

28 Under the Planning Act (2004) local planning authorities are required to prepare a Statement of Community Involvement (SCI), in which they set out their policy on involving their community in preparing local development documents and on consulting on planning applications.

29 Local planning authorities should put in place arrangements so that communication with gypsies and travellers is direct and accessible, and conflict and tensions are minimised. Identifying and understanding the needs of groups who find it difficult, for a number of reasons, to engage with planning processes is essential. One such difficulty is a lack of resources. As with all other sections of the community, local planning authorities should consider what funding sources are available for such groups. One such potential source of assistance is Planning Aid, contact details for whom can be found in Annex F of this circular. SCIs will be examined during their preparation by Planning Inspectors to ensure that such consultation and involvement will take place, and is sound.

Development Plan Documents (DPDs)

30 The number of pitches set out in the RSS must be translated into specific site allocations in one of the local planning authority's DPDs that form part of the LDF.

31 The core strategy should set out criteria for the location of gypsy and traveller sites which will be used to guide the allocation of sites in the relevant DPD. These criteria will also be used to meet unexpected demand.

32 These criteria based policies must be fair, reasonable, realistic and effective in delivering sites. The adequacy of any criteria will be subject to greater scrutiny under changes to the new planning system introduced by the Planning Act (2004). Planning policies that rule out, or place undue constraints on the development of gypsy and traveller sites should not be included in RSSs or DPDs. The Government has powers to intervene in the plan-making process where it considers that the constraints being proposed by local authorities are too great or have been inadequately justified. This will include where a local planning authority does not adequately address gypsy and traveller site provision in its area.

33 Local authorities must allocate sufficient sites for gypsies and travellers, in terms of the number of pitches required by the RSS, in site allocations DPDs. A requirement of the Planning Act (2004) is that DPDs must be in general conformity with the RSS. Criteria must not be used as an alternative to site allocations in DPDs where there is an identified need for pitches. Local planning authorities will need to demonstrate that sites are suitable, and that there is a realistic likelihood that specific sites allocated in DPDs will be made available for that purpose. DPDs

will need to explain how the land required will be made available for a gypsy and traveller site, and timescales for provision.

34   Identifying and allocating specific plots of land is a more difficult process than using a solely criteria based approach. However it ensures some certainty for local people and gypsies and travellers when planning applications are determined by local planning authorities, or appeals are considered by the Secretary of State.

35   There are a number of ways in which local authorities can identify specific sites and make land available.

a)   Local authorities have discretion to dispose of land for less than best consideration where it will help to secure the promotion or improvement of the economic, social or environmental well-being of the area, as set out in ODPM Circular 06/03.

b)   Authorities should also consider making full use of the registers of unused and under-used land owned by public bodies as an aid to identifying suitable locations. Vacant land or under-used local authority land may be appropriate.

c)   Authorities should also consider whether it might be appropriate to exercise their compulsory purchase powers to acquire an appropriate site.

d)   Cooperation between neighbouring authorities, possibly involving joint DPDs, can provide more flexibility in identifying sites. Such cooperation is particularly important where an authority has strict planning constraints across its area.

36   Local planning authorities should facilitate early involvement in the preparation of DPDs (front-loading) by consulting with the community and all stakeholders. Frontloading is particularly important when the DPD is dealing with site allocations. Local planning authorities should ensure that sites are brought forward early in the process so that the community can be consulted, and they can be subjected to sustainability appraisal. Gypsies and travellers (or other site developers) may also bring forward sites through the DPD process. Those wishing to do so should also ensure sites are brought forward early. National planning policy on front-loading, community involvement, and sustainability appraisal in the LDF revision process can be found in PPS12.

37   All DPDs are subject to independent examination. The conclusions reached by the Inspector appointed to examine a submitted DPD are binding. The local planning authority must incorporate the changes required by the Inspector, and then adopt the DPD. The conclusions which the Inspector may reach include;

a)   that the authority is required to undertake additional work before the DPD can be adopted/examined further;

b)   that part(s) of the DPD should be excluded or changed;

c)   that part of the DPD should be excluded and brought forward as part of a revised or new DPD; and/or

d)   that additional material should be included in the DPD.

A further more serious conclusion could be that a DPD/part of a DPD is unsound. This could lead to a recommendation that the document be withdrawn.

38   Where the local planning authority has not allocated sufficient sites for gypsy and traveller need identified by the accommodation assessment process, the Inspector could recommend that the DPD is altered to include additional sites. However the inspector can only do this where suitable sites have been identified earlier in the plan-making process and it is clear how such sites comply with the tests of soundness set out in PPS12 (paragraph 4.24), and how the procedural and sustainability appraisal processes have been undertaken. It is therefore the responsibility of those promoting the inclusion of such sites to show that correct procedure has been followed.

39   There are also requirements for annual monitoring by both the RPB and the local planning authority. The Planning Act 2004 makes clear that one of the main purposes of annual monitoring reports is to consider whether implementation of the RSS or LDF is being achieved in line with the purposes of the RSS or LDF. If it is not, then regulations require the RPB or local planning authority to set out the reasons why it thinks the policy is not being implemented and what it intends to do about it.

40   Local authorities will also need to have regard to their statutory duties, including those in respect of homelessness under Part VII of the Housing Act 1996 and to their obligations under the Race Relations Act 1976 as amended by the Race Relations (Amendment) Act 2000.

Transitional arrangements

41   In advance of the consideration of new GTAAs at a regional level by the RPB, translated into pitch numbers for DPDs, other means of assessment of need will be necessary. RPBs will need to consider whether there is sufficiently robust information on which to establish district level pitch numbers. They will need to work closely with local authorities who will have access to a range of information on gypsy and traveller families in their area. Where it is not possible to allocate pitch numbers comprehensively in the current round of RSS revisions, RPBs will need to consider interim arrangements. This should include a clear statement as to the regional context including;

a)   priority attached to addressing immediate need and timescale for doing so;

b)   extent of existing provision;

c)   identifying those parts of the region with high numbers of unauthorised sites;

d)   an interim estimate of the additional pitch requirements at regional level;

e)   arrangements for putting in place district level pitch requirements (eg need for further research, engaging local authorities, timetable for any single issue review).

42   This will be important in guiding local planning authorities as they prepare LDDs and ensuring that the RSS is well placed to deliver the regional framework in future. RPBs will need to work closely with local authorities to agree and establish transitional arrangements. A first step is to agree the priority attached to gypsy and traveller provision across the region and how best to address any immediate accommodation needs for gypsies and travellers.

43 Where there is clear and immediate need, for instance evidenced through the presence of significant numbers of unauthorised encampments or developments, local planning authorities should bring forward DPDs containing site allocations in advance of regional consideration of pitch numbers, and completion of the new GTAAs. The early data available from the GTAA will be one of a range of information sources that local authorities should consider when assessing the required level of provision to translate into site allocations in a DPD, and RPBs should consider when allocating pitch numbers to each district. Paragraph 31 above refers to the core strategy setting out criteria in advance of site allocations in a DPD. Where there is an urgent need to make provision, local planning authorities should consider preparing site allocation DPDs in parallel with, or in advance of the core strategy.

44 Other sources of information could include;

a) a continuous assessment of incidents of unauthorised encampments, both short and longer-term;

b) the numbers and outcomes of planning applications and appeals;

c) levels of occupancy, plot turnover and waiting lists for public authorised sites;

d) the status of existing authorised private sites, including those which are unoccupied and those subject to temporary or personal planning permissions; and,

e) the twice-yearly Caravan Count undertaken on behalf of ODPM, which gives a picture of numbers and historic trends.

Local planning authorities will be expected to demonstrate that they have considered this information, where relevant, before any decision to refuse a planning application for a gypsy and traveller site, and to provide it as part of any appeal documentation.

45 Advice on the use of temporary permissions is contained in paragraphs 108–113 of Circular 11/95, *The Use of Conditions in Planning Permission*. Paragraph 110 advises that a temporary permission may be justified where it is expected that the planning circumstances will change in a particular way at the end of the period of the temporary permission. Where there is unmet need but no available alternative gypsy and traveller site provision in an area but there is a reasonable expectation that new sites are likely to become available at the end of that period in the area which will meet that need, local planning authorities should give consideration to granting a temporary permission.

46 Such circumstances may arise, for example, in a case where a local planning authority is preparing its site allocations DPD. In such circumstances, local planning authorities are expected to give substantial weight

to the unmet need in considering whether a temporary planning permission is justified. The fact that temporary permission has been granted on this basis should not be regarded as setting a precedent for the determination of any future applications for full permission for use of the land as a caravan site. In some cases, it may not be reasonable to impose certain conditions on a temporary permission such as those that require significant capital outlay.

Sites in rural areas and the countryside

47   Gypsies and travellers in rural areas often face difficulties in securing an adequate supply of affordable land for their needs. Where there is a lack of affordable land to meet local gypsy and traveller needs (as demonstrated by an up-to-date accommodation assessment) local planning authorities in rural areas should include a 'rural exception site policy' in the relevant DPD.

48   All rural exception sites intended for use as gypsy and traveller caravan sites should be identified as being for this use. Rural exception site policies for gypsies and travellers should operate in the same way as rural exception site policies for housing, as set out in Annex B of PPG3[1] (as updated in January 2005). In applying the rural exception site policy, local planning authorities should consider in particular the needs of households who are either current residents or have an existing family or employment connection.

49   There is a general presumption against inappropriate development within Green Belts. New gypsy and traveller sites in the Green Belt are normally inappropriate development, as defined in Planning Policy Guidance 2: 'Green Belts' (PPG2). National planning policy on Green Belts applies equally to applications for planning permission from gypsies and travellers, and the settled population. Alternatives should be explored before Green Belt locations are considered. Pressure for development of sites on Green Belt land can usually be avoided if the local planning authority allocates sufficient sites elsewhere in its area, in its LDF, to meet identified need. Criteria-based policies in DPDs for the location of gypsy and traveller sites (see paragraphs 31 and 32 above) should not depart from national planning policy as set out in PPG2.

50   The presence of Green Belt will constrain and limit opportunities for identifying gypsy and traveller sites in some areas. The general extent of the Green Belt should be addressed through the RSS in the first instance. PPG2 makes clear that once the general extent of Green Belt has been approved, and once detailed Green Belt boundaries have been established in adopted development plans, they should only be altered exceptionally.

51   Alterations to the Green Belt boundary can be used in exceptional circumstances for housing and other types of development inappropriate for the Green Belt. Such alterations have often been used in cases

1   Also paragraph 33 of consultation on PPS 3, and provisions on rural exception policies in any final PPS 3.

where a local authority's area contains a high proportion of Green Belt land and no other suitable sites outside the Green Belt exist. Such an exceptional limited alteration to the defined Green Belt boundary (which might be to accommodate a site inset within the Green Belt) could be considered to meet a specific, identified need for a gypsy and traveller site in the same way such an alteration could be used for any other type of development. Such a proposal should be brought forward through the plan-making process. Where land is removed from the Green Belt in this way, it should be specifically allocated in a DPD as a gypsy and traveller site only.

52   In areas with nationally recognised designations (Sites of Special Scientific Interest, National Nature Reserves, National Parks, Areas of Outstanding Natural Beauty, Heritage Coasts, Scheduled Monuments, Conservation Areas, Registered Historic Battlefields and Registered Parks and Gardens), as with any other form of development, planning permission for gypsy and traveller sites should only be granted where it can be demonstrated that the objectives of the designation will not be compromised by the development.

53   However, local landscape and local nature conservation designations should not be used in themselves to refuse planning permission for gypsy and traveller sites.

54   Sites on the outskirts of built-up areas may be appropriate. Sites may also be found in rural or semi-rural settings. Rural settings, where not subject to special planning constraints, are acceptable in principle. In assessing the suitability of such sites, local authorities should be realistic about the availability, or likely availability, of alternatives to the car in accessing local services. Sites should respect the scale of, and not dominate the nearest settled community. They should also avoid placing an undue pressure on the local infrastructure.

55   In some cases, perhaps involving previously developed (brownfield), untidy or derelict land, the establishment of a well-planned or soft-landscaped gypsy and traveller site can be seen as positively enhancing the environment and increasing openness.

Mixed planning use

56   Some gypsies and travellers run their businesses from the site on which their caravans are stationed. PPG4 – *Industrial, Commercial Development and Small Firms* sets out guidance on mixed use which is relevant. Local planning authorities should, wherever possible, identify in their DPDs gypsy and traveller sites suitable for mixed residential and business uses, having regard to the safety and amenity of the occupants and their children, and neighbouring residents. If mixed sites are not practicable, authorities should consider the scope for identifying separate sites for residential and for business purposes in close proximity to one another. Some parts of sites unsuitable for residence might be suitable for parking vehicles or storing materials, provided the overall site is suitable for residential use. Mixed uses are not permitted on rural exception sites.

Major development projects

57 A major development or redevelopment project may require the permanent or temporary relocation of a gypsy or traveller site. An onus should be placed on the planning applicant to identify and provide an alternative site, providing the original site has a legal status. The local planning authority should work with the planning applicant and the affected gypsy and traveller community to identify a site (or sites) that would be suitable for relocating this community. In proposing relocation and in seeking a relocation site regard will need to be paid both to the gypsy and traveller community's social, economic and environmental needs and identified social, economic, and environmental benefits that the major development/redevelopment project will bring to the locality and the broader area.

Applications

58 DPDs together with the RSS form part of the 'development plan' and the Planning Act (2004) provides that determinations of applications for planning permission must be in accordance with the development plan unless material considerations indicate otherwise. Local planning authorities should be able to release sites for development sequentially, with sites identified in DPDs being used before windfall sites. Windfall sites are those which have not been specifically identified as available in DPDs. Other considerations for gypsy and traveller site applications are likely to include the likely impact on the surrounding area, the existing level of provision and need for sites in the area, the availability (or lack of) alternative accommodation for the applicants and other personal circumstances.

59 In order to encourage private site provision, local planning authorities should offer advice and practical help with planning procedures to gypsies and travellers who wish to acquire their own land for development. It is strongly recommended that gypsies and travellers consult local planning authorities on planning matters before buying land on which they intend to establish any caravan site, for which planning permission will almost always be required. Further guidance on this is contained in Annexes D and E.

60 Pre-application discussions are particularly important to avoid misunderstanding and subsequent problems over planning permission. Constructive and positive engagement on all sides will promote trust and may help to avoid breaches of planning control. The aim should be as far as possible to help gypsies and travellers to provide for themselves, to allow them to secure the kind of sites they need, but in locations that are appropriate in planning policy terms. This will help to avoid breaches of planning control, and enable firm enforcement against such breaches. In particular, questions of road access, the availability of services, potential conflict with statutory undertakers or agricultural interests, and any significant environmental impacts should be resolved at the earliest opportunity. In line with guidance in PPG25, local planning authorities should consult the Environment Agency about flood risk.

61   Any facts that may be relevant should be established and considered before determining planning applications. Gypsies and travellers should co-operate by responding to requests for information relevant to their applications.

62   Local planning authorities should not refuse private applications solely because the applicant has no local connection. But they are entitled to refuse private applications in locations that do not comply with planning policies, especially where the authority has complied with this guidance and proceeded properly to ensure needs identified by accommodation assessments are being met.

63   Local planning authorities should also have regard to whether the absence of existing provision may prejudice enforcement action, or give rise to grounds for appeal against refusal of an application for a new site.

Sustainability

64   Issues of sustainability are important and should not only be considered in terms of transport mode and distances from services. Such consideration should include;

a)   the promotion of peaceful and integrated co-existence between the site and the local community;

b)   the wider benefits of easier access to GP and other health services;

c)   children attending school on a regular basis;

d)   the provision of a settled base that reduces the need for long-distance travelling and possible environmental damage caused by unauthorised encampment; and,

e)   not locating sites in areas at high risk of flooding, including functional floodplains, given the particular vulnerability of caravans.

65   In deciding where to provide for gypsy and traveller sites, local planning authorities should first consider locations in or near existing settlements with access to local services, eg shops, doctors and schools. All sites considered as options for a site allocations DPD must have their social, environmental and economic impacts assessed in accordance with the requirements of sustainability appraisal.

66   Sites, whether public or private, should be identified having regard to highways considerations. In setting their policies, local planning authorities should have regard to the potential for noise and other disturbance from the movement of vehicles to and from the site, the stationing of vehicles on the site, and on-site business activities. However, projected vehicle movements for gypsy and traveller sites should be assessed on an individual basis for each site. Proposals should not be rejected if they would only give rise to modest additional daily vehicle movements and/or the impact on minor roads would not be significant.

Enforcement

67   The Government's aim is to ensure that planning policies and controls are respected by all sections of the community and that where breaches occur effective enforcement action is taken.

68　In considering enforcement action local authorities should be guided by the advice in PPG 18 Enforcing Planning Control. Further advice on the enforcement powers available to local planning authorities and their use can be found in;

a)　DoE Circular 10/97; *Enforcing Planning Control: Legislative Provisions and Procedural Requirements;*

b)　DoE Circular 18/94; *Gypsy Sites Policy and Unauthorised Camping;*

c)　*Good Practice Guide for Local Planning Authorities on Enforcing Planning Control;* DoE 1997;

d)　*Guidance on Managing Unauthorised Camping;* ODPM, Home Office Feb 2004; and,

e)　ODPM Circular 02/05; *Temporary Stop Notice;* contains information on the new temporary stop notice provisions introduced in the Planning Act (2004).

Appeals

69　There will be occasions when local planning authorities refuse planning permission for gypsy and traveller sites. A Planning Inspector considering any subsequent appeal will have regard to the development plan so far as is relevant, and will take into account all material considerations, which should already have been addressed at the application stage. These will include the existing and planned provision of, and need for, sites in the area, the accuracy of the data used to assess need, the methodology employed in the assessment and how up-to-date it is, information on pitch availability on public and private sites, personal circumstances and alternative accommodation options.

Human rights

70　The provisions of the European Convention on Human Rights should be considered as an integral part of local authorities' decision-making – including its approach to the question of what are material considerations in planning cases. Local planning authorities should consider the consequences of refusing or granting planning permission, or taking enforcement action, on the rights of the individuals concerned, both gypsies and travellers and local residents, and whether the action is necessary and proportionate in the circumstances. If there is any doubt about the application of provisions of the Convention in particular cases, legal advice should be sought. The obligation on public authorities to act compatibly with Convention rights does not give gypsies and travellers a right to establish sites in contravention of planning control.

Race relations

71　Section 19A of the Race Relations Act 1976 (RRA 1976) prohibits racial discrimination by planning authorities in carrying out their planning functions. In addition, the majority of public authorities, including local authorities, have a general duty under the RRA 1976 as amended by the Race Relations (Amendment) Act 2000 to actively seek to

eliminate unlawful discrimination and to promote equality of opportunity and good race relations in all they do. The duty on local authorities to actively seek to eliminate unlawful discrimination, and promote
good race relations does not give gypsies and travellers a right to establish sites in contravention of planning control. In line with their race
equality scheme (legally required under the RRA 1976 (Statutory Duties)
Order 2001) local authorities should assess which of their functions
are relevant to race equality and monitor these functions and policies to
see how they impact on different racial groups. The SCI is particularly
important in this regard.

72 When policies are changed or new ones introduced, authorities should
assess and consult on their likely impact, and where an adverse impact
is identified which cannot be justified, changes should be made. It is particularly important that authorities consider all the racial groups served
by the authority in order to assess the impact of their policies on those
groups. Romany Gypsies and Irish Travellers have been recognised by
the courts as being distinct ethnic groups covered by the RRA 1976.
Under the general duty mentioned above, there is a requirement that
local authorities seek to promote good race relations between Gypsies
and Travellers and the settled community. This is important in the context of gypsy and traveller site planning.

Monitoring

73 Local planning authorities should monitor and critically analyse the
decisions on applications for sites for gypsies and travellers compared
to those of applications for other types of residential development. This
includes all types of housing and other types of caravan site. Authorities
should assess the results of such analysis to inform policy development. In order to ensure that they can identify any adverse impact on
race equality, local planning authorities should monitor applications
from Gypsies and Irish Travellers. The Commission for Racial Equality
recommends that all local authorities include sub-categories for Gypsies
and Irish Travellers within ethnic monitoring forms beneath the 'White
Other' category, as in the school census.

ANNEX A

Select list of organisations representing Gypsies and Travellers
This annex will be updated via the ODPM website as contact details
will change over time.[2]

The Gypsy and Traveller Law Reform Coalition
Banderway House, 156-162 Kilburn High Road
London NW6 4JD
dglg@hotmail.co.uk
www.travellerslaw.org.uk

2   Updated 29 March 2006.

National Travellers Action Group
7 Woodside Park, Hatch Road, Sandy
Bedfordshire SG19 1PT
Telephone: 01767 689736
Codona@aol.com

Advisory Council for the Education of Romany and other Travellers
(ACERT)
Moot House, The Stow, Harlow
Essex CM20 3AG
Telephone: 01279 418 666

National Association of Health Workers with Travellers
Balsall Heath Centre, 43 Edward Road
Birmingham B12 9LB
Telephone: 0117 922 7570/0121 446 2300

National Association of Teachers of Travellers
c/o Cornwall Traveller Education Support Services
16 Carlyon Road, St. Austell
Cornwall PL25 4AJ
Telephone: 01726 77113

Advice and Information Unit Manager
Friends, Families and Travellers
Community Base, 113 Queens Road
Brighton BN1 3XG
Telephone: 01273 234777
Fft@gypsy-traveller.org
www.gypsy-traveller.org

The Gypsy Council for Health, Education and Welfare
8 Hall Road, Aveley, Romford
Essex RM15 4HD
Tel/Fax: 01708 868 986
Enquiries@thegypsycouncil.org
www.thegypsycouncil.org

Irish Travellers Movement in Britain
The Old Library Building
95 High Road, Willesden
London NW10 2ST
Tel: 020 8830 3079
Joe@travellerschaplaincy.org.uk

The Gypsy Council
Springs Lane Caravan Park, Bickerton, Wetherby
North Yorkshire LS22 5ND
Telephone: 01937 842782

Commission for Racial Equality
St Dunstans House, 201-211 Borough High Street
London SE1 1GZ
Telephone 0207 939 0000
Info@cre.gov.uk
www.cre.gov.uk

ANNEX B

Other relevant guidance

This Circular does not affect the advice given generally in other Departmental Circulars,
Planning Policy Guidance Notes (PPGs) and Planning Policy Statements (PPSs). Those which may be of particular relevance are:

PPS1 – Creating Sustainable Communities;
PPG2 – Green Belts;
PPG3 – Housing;
PPG4 – Industrial, Commercial Development and Small Firms;
PPS7 – Sustainable Development in Rural Areas;
PPG9 – Nature Conservation;
PPS11 – Regional Spatial Strategies;
PPS12 – Local Development Frameworks;
PPG13 – Transport;
PPG16 – Archaeology and Planning;
PPG18 – Enforcing Planning Control;
PPG25 – Development and Flood Risk.

DoE Circular 18/94; *Gypsy Sites Policy and Unauthorised Camping and Revision of Advice on 'Toleration'* issued 26 July 2000, and further Guidance on Managing Unauthorised Camping issued in February 2004.

DETR Circular 03/99; *Planning Requirement in respect of the Use of Non-Mains Sewerage incorporating Septic Tanks in New Development.*

ANNEX C

Good practice – criteria

1   The Government believes that gypsies and travellers have the same rights and responsibilities within the planning system as every other cit-

izen. Plan policies and criteria for the establishment of gypsy and traveller caravan sites should be fair, reasonable, realistic and effective, and written in a positive manner that offers some certainty that where the criteria (not necessarily all of them) are met planning permission will be granted.

2   Research has shown that the majority of plan policies state that permission 'may be granted' or that the authority 'will take account of' factors. Ambiguous statements of this nature should be avoided as they increase uncertainty. Alternative wording might include 'Planning permission will be granted provided that the following criteria/requirements are [clearly] satisfied...'.

3   The list of criteria adopted by a local planning authority should not be over-long as the more criteria there are, and the more restrictive they are, the greater the likelihood of authorities refusing planning permission. The Government wishes to see a more positive approach being taken to making adequate provision for gypsies and travellers in appropriate locations – particularly by those local planning authorities whose present policies have failed to meet current needs. The process by which criteria are adopted in DPDs will therefore be subject to close scrutiny by Planning Inspectors.

4   For all kinds of site, consideration must be given to vehicular access from the public highway, as well as provision for parking, turning and servicing on site, and road safety for occupants and visitors. Landscaping and planting with appropriate trees and shrubs can help sites blend into their surroundings, give structure and privacy, and maintain visual amenity. Enclosing a site with too much hard landscaping, high walls or fences can give the impression of deliberately isolating the site and its occupants from the rest of the community, and should be avoided.

5   In general gypsy and traveller sites should not be located on significantly contaminated land, but this does not necessarily rule out all locations near or adjoining motorways, power lines, landfill sites or railways, any more than it does conventional housing. The site needs to have safe and convenient access to the road network.

6   The Government does not consider it appropriate to set a national maximum size for a site, but would suggest that cases should be considered in context, and in relation to the local infrastructure and population size and density.

Criteria which are unacceptable

7   It is not uncommon currently for criteria to be so restrictive and extensive that in practice it is impossible or virtually impossible for an application to comply with them. The following criteria have been taken from local authority plans and represent the sorts of criteria that are considered generally unacceptable.

'Each unit of accommodation on the site shall have been brought onto the site by the occupier(s) for the time being who shall remove the accommodation from the site when ceasing to use it for residential purposes'

This criterion does not accommodate the nomadic and traditional lifestyle whereby many gypsies and travellers have one caravan to live in, and one that is more mobile that they use when travelling.

A requirement that the accommodation is brought onto site by the occupier does not allow provision to be made for other family members who may not themselves, perhaps for reasons of ill-health, physically move their own accommodation onto the site.

'There shall be no more than [x] caravans'

Setting a maximum number as a blanket policy is arbitrary.

Any maximum should be reached through planning conditions but should be related to circumstances of the specific size and location of the site and the surrounding population size and density.

'Applications from gypsies and travellers with no local connection will not normally be allowed'

Gypsies and travellers are by their very nature nomadic and so will not always have local connections. Planning authorities have to determine applications for development from anyone who submits them.

As the businesses which gypsies and travellers have traditionally engaged decline, the new trades and businesses they take up often necessitate new locations.

'The site does not impact on any area with natural/wildlife interest'

All development by its very nature will have some impact on wildlife. The criteria should be more tightly, but reasonably, defined.

'The site shall not encroach into the countryside'

This is unrealistic. Such policies have been used to thwart site provision.

ANNEX D

Guidance to local authorities in dealing with planning Applications from Gypsies and Travellers

1   Gypsies and travellers have the same rights and responsibilities within the planning system as all other applicants for planning permission. In dealing with applications and enquiries from gypsies and travellers, planning officers and planning department staff should act in a professional manner and treat enquiries from gypsies and travellers evenhandedly.

2   It is particularly important if unauthorised development is to be avoided for local planning authorities to establish a level of trust and co-operation with the local gypsy and traveller community. Entrenched positions on both sides are likely to lead to tensions, conflict and delay.

3   Local authorities may wish to consider designating a named person to

deal with all such enquiries/applications or have a named person with whom the applicants can maintain contact, and consider what specific training may be required for staff dealing with gypsy and traveller applications and the associated issues.

4   Local authorities need to provide early, clear pre-application advice and may wish to consider producing leaflets explaining the planning system, and consider using other media – such as video and audio communication – where this would better meet the needs of the gypsy and traveller community. At any pre-application meeting local authorities should give an indication of the chances of getting permission, highlight any possible difficulties and whether these may be overcome and explain the planning process to applicants who are unfamiliar with it.

5   Local authorities need to make gypsies and travellers aware of standards they can expect from the authority, standards expected from them, and their rights to complain, including to the authority's monitoring officer and the Local Government Ombudsmen.

6   Planning departments may need to consult other departments and agencies with an interest, particularly housing, social services and education departments, health and highways authorities. Other important sources of advice are Gypsy Liaison Officers (or their equivalents) usually, but not always, based in County Councils.

ANNEX E

Guidance to Gypsies and Travellers making planning applications

Introduction

1   Members of the gypsy and traveller communities have the same rights and responsibilities within the planning system as members of other communities. Planning permission is normally required for any changes of use of land. As with developments submitted by anyone the only times permission would not be required are;

i)   if the land has already been granted planning permission for a particular type of land use; or,

ii) the use of the land has been established over a period of time without valid planning enforcement action having been taken by the local authority. This time period is 4 years for building or other similar physical works which do not represent a change of land use, or 10 years where the development has represented a change of land use.

Pre-application procedure

2   When looking for a site gypsies and travellers should consider whether;

–   there are any existing sites in the area (with planning permission) available to rent or buy

–   the local authorities know of your need for land and, if so, have they identified any sites that may be available

3   If the answer to the above questions is 'No', and you are looking to buy
         and develop a new site, to ensure that the site you select is suitable to be
         granted planning permission you should;
         –   identify your area of search. Is the reason for your looking for a
             particular location due to family circumstances, work or other
             requirements?
             –   Are there suitable previously developed (ie, brownfield) sites
                 available?
             –   Consider;
             –   means of access
             –   closeness to the main road network
             –   ground conditions and levels of land
             –   accessibility of schools and other facilities
             –   existence of landscaping
             –   capability of being further screened
             –   respect for neighbouring uses
         –   Once you have identified a possible site, find out which local author-
             ity area it is in and contact the local planning authority. Then con-
             sider the local plan policies relevant to gypsy and traveller site use
             – you can get help from the local authority who should explain
             their policies and handle your enquiries fairly and professionally.
         –   You should establish whether the site you are interested in is in
             the Green Belt or other area of special protection. Development
             in such areas is subject to stricter control and the likelihood of get-
             ting planning permission for any development is much lower than
             if the site were on 'ordinary' land. You should consider undertak-
             ing a local search to establish whether there are any restrictions
             (such as injunctions) on the use of the land.
         –   If there are no such restrictions you should consider whether the
             site meets some or all of the criteria set out in the local plan.

Making the planning application

4   You should make your planning application and wait for planning con-
         sent before you go on the site. Entering a site without planning per-
         mission can be a breach of planning control and may be subject to a
         series of enforcement actions. When making your application you
         should provide as much background information (which may include
         the efforts you have made to find a site, why you have selected the par-
         ticular site and details of all the people who plan to live on the site)
         with the application as you can and all the information required on
         the forms. There is often a guide to help you fill out the forms. If you
         need help completing the form the planning department of the local
         authority should help you.

5   Normally gypsy and traveller site development requires a full applica-
         tion. As much detail as possible on the site, including layout, land-
         scaping, access and number of caravans should be provided at the
         outset.

What happens next?

6   Local planning authorities will normally decide applications within eight weeks of them being submitted. If you are refused permission you may appeal to the Secretary of State. You must submit an appeal within six months of the initial application being refused. Details on how to submit an appeal and how the appeal process works is available on the Planning Inspectorate website at www.planning-inspectorate.gov.uk, or from their customer support unit;

The Planning Inspectorate
Customer Support Unit, Room 3/15 Eagle Wing
Temple Quay House, 2 The Square, Temple Quay
Bristol BS1 6PN
Tel: 0117 372 6372
Fax: 0117 372 8128
E-mail: enquiries@planning-inspectorate.gsi.gov.uk

7   Gypsies and travellers should be aware of Planning Aid, a voluntary service run by the Royal Town Planning Institute offering free, independent and professional advice and support on town planning matters to community groups and individuals who cannot afford to employ a planning consultant. For general enquiries about Planning Aid contact the Planning Aid National Unit;

National Planning Aid Unit
Unit 419, The Custard Factory, Gibb Street
Birmingham B9 4AA
Tel: 0121 693 1201
E-mail:info@planningaid.rtpi.org.uk

ANNEX F

Planning conditions and planning obligations

1   The appropriate use of planning conditions or obligations can enable some development proposals to proceed where it might otherwise be necessary to refuse permission.

2   Conditions should be imposed only where they are necessary, relevant to planning and to the development to be permitted, enforceable, precise and reasonable in all other respects. General advice on the use of conditions is given in DoE Circular 11/95.

3   Guidance on the use of planning obligations is given in Circular 05/2005. This guidance sets out the tests for planning obligations, namely that they must be relevant to planning, necessary to make the proposed development acceptable in planning terms, directly related to the proposed development, fairly and reasonably related in scale and kind to the proposed development and reasonable in all other respects.

4   A number of measures may be introduced to overcome planning objections to particular proposals using planning conditions or planning obligations. These might include;

- ensuring adequate landscaping and play areas for children;
- limiting which parts of a site may be used for business operations, in order to minimise the visual impact and limit the effect of noise;
- the number of days the site can be occupied by more than the allowed number of caravans, to permit visitors and allow attendance at family/community events.

In certain circumstances, conditions might also be appropriate to specify the maximum number of days for which gypsy and traveller caravans might be permitted to stay on a transit site.

© Crown copyright 2006

GYPSY SITES POLICY AND UNAUTHORISED CAMPING (DoE CIRCULAR 18/94)

Introduction

1   This Circular offers guidance on the provisions in sections 77 to 80 of the Criminal Justice and Public Order Act 1994 ('the 1994 Act') which affect gypsies and unauthorised campers. The Act received Royal Assent on 3 November 1994, and sections 77 to 80 came into force on the same day.

Definition of 'gipsies'

2   Section 24 of the Caravan Sites and Control of Development Act 1960 ('the 1960 Act'), as amended by section 80 of the 1994 Act, provides that 'gipsies':

> 'means persons of nomadic habit of life, whatever their race or origin, but does not include members of an organised group of travelling showmen, or of persons engaged in travelling circuses, travelling together as such'.

3   The courts have recently clarified the definition of the word 'gipsies' in section 16 of the Caravan Sites Act 1968 ('the 1968 Act'), which was repealed by section 80 of the 1994 Act. In *R v South Hams District Council, ex parte Gibb* and two other applications – *The Times*, 8 June 1994; *The Independent*, 15 June 1994 – the Court of Appeal held that 'gipsies' meant persons who wandered or travelled for the purpose of making or seeking their livelihood, and did not include persons who moved from place to place without any connection between their movement and their means of livelihood. All references to 'gypsies' in this Circular are references to 'gipsies' in this sense.

Powers to control unauthorised camping

4   Section 77 of the 1994 Act empowers a local authority[1] to direct persons residing unlawfully in vehicles within the area of that local authority on highway land, other unoccupied land or occupied land without the consent of the occupier to leave the land and remove their vehicles and any other property they have with them on the land. It is an offence for a person, knowing that such a direction has been given to him, to fail to comply with it as soon as practicable. It is also an offence for a person so directed to re-enter the land concerned with a vehicle within three months of the date of the direction. In any proceedings brought for an offence, it is a defence for an accused person to show that his failure to comply with a direction or his re-entry of land was due to mechanical breakdown,

---

1   In England, a county council, a district council, a London borough council, the Common Council of the City of London and the Council of the Isles of Scilly; and in Wales, a county council or district council until 1 April 1996 (and a county council or county borough council thereafter).

illness or other immediate emergency. If a person who has been directed to leave does so as soon as practicable, and does not re-enter the land within three months of the date of the direction, no offence is committed.

5   Section 78 of the 1994 Act provides that a magistrates' court may, on a complaint by a local authority, make an order requiring the removal from land of any vehicle and property and any person residing in it, and authorising an authority to enter the land and remove the vehicle and property. It is an offence for a person wilfully to obstruct any person authorised to carry out the order. This power is modelled closely on the power that was available to authorities for areas designated under the 1968 Act, although it should be noted that sections 77 and 78 apply to any unauthorised camper, not just to gypsies.

Policy towards unauthorised encampments of gypsies

6   Whilst it is a matter for local discretion to decide whether it is appropriate to evict an unauthorised Gypsy encampment, the Secretary of State believes that local authorities should consider using their powers to do so wherever the Gypsies concerned are causing a level of nuisance which cannot be effectively controlled. They also consider that it would usually be legitimate for a local authority to exercise these powers wherever Gypsies who are camped unlawfully refuse to move onto an authorised local authority site. Where there are no such sites, and the authority reaches the view than an unauthorised Gypsy encampment is not causing a level of nuisance which cannot be effectively controlled, it should consider providing basic services, such as toilets, a refuse skip and a supply of drinking water at the site.

7   Local authorities should also try to identify possible emergency stopping places, as close as possible to the transit routes used by Gypsies, where Gypsy families would be allowed to camp for short periods. Authorities should   consider providing basic services on these temporary sites.

8   Where Gypsies are unlawfully camped on Government-owned land, it is for the local authority, with the agreement of the land-owning Department, to take any necessary steps to ensure that the encampment does not constitute a hazard to public health. It will continue to be the policy of the Secretary of State that Government Department should act in conformity with the advice that unauthorised encampments should not normally be allowed to continue where they are causing a level of nuisance which cannot be effectively controlled. The National Assembly for Wales will act in the same way.

9   The Secretary of State continues to consider that local authorities should not use their powers to evict Gypsies needlessly. He considers that local should use their powers in a humane and compassionate way, taking account of the rights and needs of the Gypsies concerned,

the owners of land in question, and the wider community whose lives may be affected by the situation.[2]

Local authorities' obligations under other legislation

10   Social services departments and local housing authorities are reminded of their obligations under Part III of the Children Act 1989 (Local Authority Support for Children and Families); and Part III of the Housing Act 1985 (Housing the Homeless). The Secretaries of State expect authorities to take careful account of these obligations when taking decisions about the future maintenance of authorised gypsy caravan sites and the eviction of persons from unauthorised sites.

11   Local education authorities should bear in mind their statutory duty to make appropriate educational provision available for all school-age children in their area, whether resident temporarily or permanently. As noted in paragraph 33 of Circular 11/88 and paragraph 9 of Circular 11/92 from the Department for Education (formerly the Department of Education and Science) and paragraph 6 of the annex (revised annually) to Welsh Office Circular 52/90, this duty embraces traveller children. Local education authorities should take careful account of the effects of an eviction on the education of children already enrolled, or in the process of being enrolled, at a school. Where an authority decides to proceed with an eviction, and any families concerned move elsewhere in the same area, alternative educational arrangements must be made in accordance with the requirements of the law appropriate to the children's ages, abilities and aptitudes.

12   The Secretaries of State also expect local authorities who decide to proceed with evictions to liaise with other local authorities who may have statutory responsibilities to discharge in respect of those persons who are being evicted.

13   Local authorities should also bear in mind that families camped unlawfully on land may need or may be receiving assistance from local health or welfare services. When they have decided to proceed with an eviction, they should liaise with the relevant statutory agencies, particularly where pregnant women or newly-born children are involved, to ensure that those agencies are not prevented from fulfilling their obligations towards these persons.

Repeal of Part II of the Caravan Sites Act 1968

14   Section 80(1) of the 1994 Act repeals:
    (a) the duty of local authorities to provide and manage sites (sections 6 and 7 of the 1968 Act);
    (b) the requirement for a county council to consult the relevant district council before adopting a proposal to acquire or appropriate land for such a site (section 8);

2   Paras 6–9 above were inserted by an unnumbered DETR circular dated 26 June 2000.

(c) the Secretary of State's powers to direct a local authority to provide a site (section 9) and to designate the area of a local authority (section 12); and

(d) the powers for a designated authority to deal with unauthorised camping (sections 10 and 11).

15 Section 80(2) of the 1994 Act amends section 24 of the 1960 Act so as to allow a local authority to provide working space on gypsy caravan sites. Section 80(4) of the 1994 Act ensures that the repeal of the definition of the word 'gipsies' in section 16 of the 1968 Act does not affect the interpretation of that word in the definition of a 'protected site' in section 5(1) of the Mobile Homes Act 1983, or in any document embodying planning permission granted under the Town and Country Planning Act 1990 before 3 November 1994.

16 Section 80(3) of the 1994 Act makes transitional arrangements for those cases where the Secretary of State has issued a direction under section 8(3)(a) of the 1968 Act to a local authority to abandon a proposal for a gypsy caravan site, or under section 8(3)(c) of the 1968 Act to make an application to him for planning permission.

17 Directions under section 8(3)(a) of the 1968 Act will remain valid; directions under section 8(3)(b) and (c) of the 1968 Act will cease to have effect. However, where a local authority has made an application for planning permission to the Secretary of State before 3 November 1994, they may elect either to withdraw that application or to request the Secretary of State to determine it. In the latter case, the application would be treated as having been referred to the Secretary of State under section 77 of the Town and Country Planning Act 1990. Local authorities with outstanding directions under section 8(3)(c) of the 1968 Act, may, therefore, wish to notify their decision to the relevant Government Office for their region, or to the Welsh Office.

18 Section 80(5) of the 1994 Act repeals the power of the Secretaries of State for the Environment and for Wales to pay grant to local authorities in respect of capital expenditure for gypsy caravan sites under section 70 of the Local Government, Planning and Land Act 1980, except for the purposes of applications for grant received by the Secretaries of State before 3 November 1994. The repeal of section 70 does not apply to Scotland.

Future management of local authority gypsy caravan sites

19 Section 7 of the 1968 Act made provision for a sharing of functions between county councils and non-metropolitan district councils: county councils were required to acquire or appropriate land, set charges for the use of sites and contribute towards the costs incurred by district councils in managing the sites. District councils were required to provide and manage the site. The majority of public sites in non-metropolitan districts are owned by county councils and managed by district councils.

20 The Secretaries of State consider that the repeal of section 7 of the 1968 Act removes from district councils the delegation to manage sites on land owned by county councils. County councils become responsible for managing these sites by virtue of section 24 of the 1960 Act. Nonetheless, the Secretaries of State consider that authorities have adequate powers to make suitable arrangements for the maintenance and management of sites depending on local circumstances. In particular, section 101 of the Local Government Act 1972 empowers a local authority to arrange for the discharge of its functions by another local authority. Such an arrangement would enable a district council to continue to manage a site and the county council to contribute towards their expenses.

21   The Secretaries of State consider it important that authorities should maintain their existing gypsy caravan sites, or should make suitable arrangements for their maintenance by leasing them to other persons who are willing and able to maintain them.

22   The Secretaries of State also expect authorities to continue to consider whether it is appropriate to provide further permanent caravan sites for gypsies in their areas. Section 24 of the 1960 Act enables county councils, district councils and London borough councils to establish and manage sites or to lease them to another person and, as amended by section 80(2) of the 1994 Act, to provide working space on gypsy caravan sites.

'Gypsy sites and planning'

23   Local authorities are reminded of the advice in Department of the Environment (DoE) Circular 1/94 (Welsh Office (WO) Circular 2/94), 'Gypsy Sites and Planning', dealing with the planning aspects of sites for gypsy caravans.

Bi-annual counts of gypsy caravans

24   The Department of the Environment and the Welsh Office intend to continue to ask local authorities to provide data for the compilation of the biannual counts of gypsy caravans in England and Wales on the same basis as at present.

Cancellations

25   DoE Circular 28/77 (WO Circular 51/77), DoE Circular 57/78 (WO Circular 97/78), and paragraphs 19 to 23 and Annex 2 of DoE Circular 8/81 (WO Circular 13/81) are now cancelled. DoE Circular 11/79 (WO Circular 11/79) is also cancelled, apart from Annex A which lists the capital costs of gypsy caravan site provision which are eligible for grant.

Financial and manpower implications

26   This Circular advises local authorities of the repeal of their duty to provide gypsy caravan sites and of the introduction of new discretionary powers to control unauthorised camping. Its contents are considered unlikely to have any net manpower or resource implications for local authorities.

Contact points

27   Any enquiries on the contents of this Circular may be referred to the following contact points:

in England
R J Netto
Homelessness Policy Division
Department of the Environment, Room N13/08
2 Marsham Street, London SW1P 3EB.
Telephone: 0171 276 4708; or

Ms L Patrick
Homelessness Policy Division
Department of the Environment
Room N13/10, 2 Marsham Street
London SW1P 3EB.
Telephone: 0171 276 3244.

in Wales
Mrs R Douglas
Planning Division, Welsh Office
Room GO40, Cathays Park
Cardiff CF1 3NQ.
Telephone: 0222 823476.

The Chief Executive
County Councils in England and Wales
District Councils in England and Wales
London Borough Councils
Council of the Isles of Scilly
The Town Clerk, City of London

Guidance

GUIDANCE ON MANAGING UNAUTHORISED CAMPING (ODPM/HOME OFFICE 2004)

1. Introduction

Background to the Guidance

1.1 *Managing Unauthorised Camping: A Good Practice Guide* was first issued by DETR and the Home Office in 1998 and has influenced the approaches adopted by local authorities, police and others. There have been a number of developments since 1998, which together have led to a need to re-examine and revise this guidance.

1.2 Relevant developments since the issue of the previous guidance in 1998 include:

- Amendments to DETR Circular 18/94 and to Chapter 5 of the *Good Practice Guide* were issued in July 2000. The amendments dealt with advice about 'toleration' of encampments and made clear that there will always be some circumstances where an unauthorised encampment cannot to be allowed to remain and where prompt action is required.

- The Association of Chief Police Officers (ACPO) issued guidance to its members on Collective Trespass or Nuisance on Land (including unauthorised camping) in 1996, 1999 and again in August 2000 in parallel with the DETR/Home Office *Guide*.

- In 2001 the results of research monitoring the impact of the DETR/Home Office *Good Practice Guide* were published. The report, by Edinburgh College of Art/Heriot-Watt University in conjunction with the Universities of Bristol and Cardiff, concludes that the *Guide* has been fairly influential in how local authorities and police forces tackle unauthorised camping. The research also highlights some perceived inadequacies and gaps in the guidance which this new Guidance aims to address. (See Annex C for a summary of the main findings.)

- The Human Rights Act 1998 (HRA) came into force in October 2000, incorporating the European Convention on Human Rights into British law.

- The Act means that all eviction and enforcement decisions made by public authorities must be 'proportionate'. Potential challenge under the HRA means that all decision-making must be fully recorded and evidenced to withstand scrutiny (see 5.7-5.9 and Annex D).

- The Race Relations (Amendment) Act 2000 has extended responsibilities given by the Race Relations Act 1976. Public authorities - including local authorities and the police - have a general duty to eliminate unlawful discrimination, promote equality of opportunity and good race relations in carrying out their functions. The 2000 Act also gives public bodies specific duties. Both Gypsies and Irish Travellers are now recognised as ethnic minorities against whom discrimination is unlawful. (See Annex D for more details.) In October 2003, the Commission for Racial Equality published a consultation draft entitled *Gypsies and Traveller - A Strategy 2003-2006* which sets out the Commissions own proposed role. It will be finalised during early 2004.

- A new £17 million Gypsy Sites Refurbishment Grant (GSRG) challenge fund was established with funding made available for three years from 2001/2. GSRG meets 75% of approved refurbishment costs for local authority Gypsy sites, with the aim of raising standards and helping to keep existing sites available for use - in part to help reduce the disruption of unauthorised camping. In its third year (2002/3) GSRG was extended to provide 100% funding for provision of transit and stopping place sites on a pilot basis. A further sum of £16 million has been announced for two further years of GSRG support (2004-6) for both site refurbishment and transit site and stopping place provision.

- The *National Policing Plan 2003-2006* identifies that the primary objective for the police service for the Plan's three-year duration is to deliver improved police performance and greater public reassurance with particular regard to four priorities including tackling anti-social behaviour and disorder.

Guidance on Managing Unauthorised Camping

■ In March 2003, the Government published a White Paper *Respect and Responsibility*, which sets out the stand to be taken against anti-social behaviour. Communities, public services and authorities will be empowered to tackle anti-social behaviour. In return everyone is expected to play their part in setting and enforcing proper standards of behaviour. This guidance should be read in the context of that agenda.

■ The Anti-social Behaviour Act 2003 includes measures to tackle anti-social behaviour, littering and fly-tipping. Part 7 introduces a new police power to evict unauthorised campers (see 6.12-6.13).

1.3 The Guidance has been produced against this developing background:

■ In July 2002, the Office of the Deputy Prime Minister (ODPM) and the Home Office issued a joint press release outlining the Government's new approach to tackling unauthorised camping and signalling its intention to introduce stronger police powers to move on unauthorised encampments provided there was adequate site provision; these enhanced powers have now been provided in Part 7 of the Anti-social Behaviour Act 2003.

■ In December 2002, the Government set out, and consulted upon, its broad policy towards unauthorised camping in a *Draft Framework Guide on Managing Unauthorised Gypsy/Traveller Encampments*. Central to the approach is the view that the use of stronger enforcement powers and adequate site provision must be linked.

■ *Managing Unauthorised Camping Operational Guidance* was issued as a consultation paper by ODPM and the Home Office in April 2003 (closing date 23 May 2003). The consultation paper was sent to 1,500 organisations and a total of 87 responses were received from a wide range of organisations and individuals.

■ Following consultation on the *Draft Framework Guide* and the *Operational Guidance*, it was decided that it would be clearer and less confusing to combine the two documents. The current Guidance therefore reflects the Government's broad policy towards unauthorised camping and incorporates comments received through consultation on both documents.

■ As noted above, Part 7 of the Anti-social Behaviour Act 2003 introduces a new police power to evict unauthorised campers. ODPM and the Home Office will consult on guidance on the operation of these new powers in early 2004. Once finalised, it is intended that this will be incorporated into Chapter 6 of the current *Guidance on Managing Unauthorised Encampments* in the section on 'Powers Available to the Police'.

Aims of this Guidance

1.4 This Guidance takes account of all the changes outlined above. Its overall objective is to assist local authorities, police and others to tackle unauthorised camping to minimise the disruption it can cause. In doing this, it aims:

■ To help strike an appropriate balance between the needs and legitimate expectations of members of the settled community, local businesses and other landowners, and Gypsies and Travellers.

■ To set out recommended courses of action which all local authorities and police forces should follow to provide an effective response to unauthorised camping in their areas.

■ To encourage a more consistent approach across the country, building on current good practice and sharing experience.

■ To be practical yet creative in the face of a difficult reality.

■ To show how to engage the settled and Gypsy/Traveller communities in order to achieve 'buy in' to the strategy, which is vital to ensure effective delivery.

Guidance on Managing Unauthorised Camping

1.5 The Guidance is primarily aimed at local authorities and police who share responsibility for managing unauthorised camping, but will also be relevant to all bodies likely to be involved in partnership approaches. While the Guidance is advisory, local authorities and police are strongly advised to bear it mind when devising and implementing their approaches, and are reminded that the courts may consider it as a material consideration in eviction or other enforcement decisions.

Use of Terms

1.6 Certain terms, conventions and abbreviations are used throughout the Guidance, and these are summarised in Box 1. A distinction is made between 'unauthorised camping' (a form of trespass) and 'unauthorised development' (a form of development of land without planning consent). This distinction is important because it affects the enforcement powers, which can be used. While paragraphs 6.20 to 6.24 refer specifically to planning enforcement powers available for dealing with 'unauthorised developments'; most of this Guidance deals with managing 'unauthorised encampments'.

Guidance on Managing Unauthorised Camping

Box 1 : Terms and abbreviations used in the Guidance

Gypsies and Travellers: used as a generic term to denote the whole population of those groups, families and individuals who subscribe to Gypsy/Traveller culture and/or lifestyle. The term encompasses ethnic Gypsies and Travellers and those who fall within the legal definition of a 'Gypsy' (s24 of the Caravan Sites and Control of Development Act 1960 as amended by s80 of the Criminal Justice and Public order Act 1994).

Unauthorised campers: people living on unauthorised encampments.

Unauthorised encampments: term restricted to encampments of caravans and/or other vehicles on land without the landowner or occupier's consent and constituting trespass.

Unauthorised development: Gypsy sites are among the types of development, which require planning permission. This term is used where such development is carried out on land with the agreement of the landowner, but without the appropriate planning permission.

Unauthorised sites: term used in Chapter 2 when describing findings from the Gypsy caravan count which include both unauthorised encampments and unauthorised development.

Sites or Gypsy/Traveller sites: term generally restricted to authorised sites with relevant planning consents (includes sites owned by local authorities and private owners).

Occupier of land: term used in its legal sense as 'the person entitled to possession of the land by virtue of an estate or interest held by him'. This might include a landowner, tenant or licensee but **not** unauthorised campers temporarily in 'occupation' of the land without any legal estate or interest.

ABCs : Acceptable Behaviour Contracts

ACPO : Association of Chief Police Officers

ASB : anti-social behaviour

ASBOs : Anti-Social Behaviour Orders

CJPOA : Criminal Justice and Public Order Act 1994

GSRG : Gypsy Sites Refurbishment Grant

HRA : Human Rights Act 1998

LPA : Local Planning Authority

ODPM : Office of the Deputy Prime Minister

PPG : Planning Policy Guidance Note

RSL : registered social landlord

TCPA : Town and Country Planning Act 1990

1.7 In the course of consultation on this Guidance a number of policy documents and leaflets were submitted as examples of current practice. Some of these are referred to in boxes at various points throughout the Guidance. Rather than reproducing submitted items in full or in part, the titles and author organisations are referred to and can be contacted by those who are interested. No more than five examples have been included under any heading. Chapter 9 provides useful references to other material referred to in this Guidance together with details of how they might be accessed.

Guidance on Managing Unauthorised Camping

2. Context

2.1 Gypsies and Travellers are a part of British life, and have been so for many centuries. They make up a very small minority within the wider population. Some Gypsies and Travellers live in caravans or other vehicles and follow a lifestyle, which is nomadic or semi-nomadic, in that it involves travel during at least part of the year.

2.2 At present there are more Gypsy/Traveller caravans in circulation than there are 'authorised' legal places for them to stop. At any one time there are around 3,500 Gypsy/Traveller caravans on unauthorised sites in England. Hardly any of these could be accommodated on existing authorised sites specifically provided for Gypsies and Travellers.

2.3 Unauthorised encampments vary enormously

- in size : from a couple of vehicles to groups with over 100 caravans

- in location : from the hidden away and unobtrusive to neighbours, to the highly visible and intrusive

- in behaviour of unauthorised campers : from those where no-one on the encampment causes any nuisance to others, to those where many cause nuisance

- in impact on the land : from groups who leave a camping area tidier than they found it, to those who leave the land damaged and with mountains of fly-tipped trade waste and domestic refuse

Numbers and Scale

2.4 Local authorities carry out the twice-yearly Gypsy caravan count for ODPM. It gives an indication of the numbers of Gypsy caravans on authorised (public and private) and unauthorised sites on set dates in January and July. While the counts may not be completely accurate - not least because of the technical problems of counting all Gypsy caravans over a large area - they provide local authorities with useful information about the accommodation needs of Gypsies who reside in or resort to their areas on the count dates. They also provide authorities; the Planning Inspectorate and the Secretary of State with some of the background information required when planning matters (development plans, planning applications, appeals and enforcement actions) are being considered.

2.5 The count has been carried out for over twenty years. Over this period the total number of Gypsy caravans has increased by some 70% while the number on unauthorised sites has decreased by between 500 to 1,000 from 4,600 (as counted in July 1979) thanks to the growth of private and public authorised site provision as well as movement of Gypsies and Travellers into housing.

2.6 In July 2003, about 14,700 Gypsy caravans were counted, of which 3,979 were on unauthorised sites. This latter figure can be split between 2,315 caravans on unauthorised encampments and 1,664 on Gypsy-owned land, which are likely to represent unauthorised developments. July counts consistently reveal higher numbers of Gypsy caravans on unauthorised sites. Over the past few years, on average, there have been about 800 more Gypsy caravans on unauthorised sites across England in July than in January, reflecting a seasonal element in travelling patterns.

2.7 Geographically, the counts consistently show highest numbers of Gypsy caravans on unauthorised sites in Eastern, Southeast and Southwest regions. Some local authorities, for example South Gloucestershire and some districts in Cambridgeshire and Norfolk, consistently have large numbers on unauthorised sites. Very generally, the patterns reflect traditional areas of resort for Gypsies and Travellers and - importantly - work opportunities for Gypsies and Travellers involved in various contracting (eg aspects of the building trade, garden and tree work), trading (eg carpets and furniture) and seasonal agricultural work.

2.8 There are three main Gypsy/Traveller groupings in England: traditional English (Romany) Gypsies, traditional Irish Travellers, and New Travellers. The first two groupings are accepted as

Guidance on Managing Unauthorised Camping

ethnic minorities for the purposes of race relations legislation. There are smaller numbers of Welsh Gypsies and Scottish Travellers. The different groupings have different economic, social, cultural and lifestyle characteristics. While there are many examples of peaceful co-existence of Gypsy/Traveller groups, mixing can sometimes lead to friction.

Recent Research

2.9 Research for ODPM on the provision and condition of local authority Gypsy/Traveller sites in England was carried out by the Centre for Urban and Regional Studies at the University of Birmingham. A summary report was published in October 2002, and the full report in July 2003. The research made the following points.

- There is some evidence of a trend towards greater 'settlement' among some Gypsy/Traveller groups. However, other individuals and families have no desire to 'settle' and will continue to travel actively. Other more 'settled' Gypsies and Travellers - or their children - may take up active travelling when personal or family circumstances allow it. Some Gypsies and Travellers will continue to travel for the foreseeable future.

- In order to accommodate the desire for nomadism, between 2,000 and 2,500 additional authorised transit/mobility pitches were estimated to be needed before 2007. At present there are only about 500 transit pitches provided on authorised local authority and private sites.

- The research also estimated a requirement for up to 2,500 further pitches on residential sites for Gypsies and Travellers, which could be provided either by local authorities or Gypsies and Travellers themselves.

- Gypsies and Travellers, police and local authority personnel acknowledged to the researchers the existence of a minority of 'problem families' among the Travelling community who - whether on sites or on the roadside - are associated with criminal and anti-social behaviour, damage to property and fly-tipping. 'Problem families' cause problems for the majority law-abiding Gypsies and Travellers who also fear that this very visible minority disproportionately affects settled community images and stereotypes of the Travelling community as a whole.

2.10 The general context and recent research suggest:

- While unauthorised camping is much more significant in some areas, almost any local authority is at risk of encampment and should be prepared to deal with encampment.

- Unauthorised encampments vary widely. Local authorities, police and others dealing with unauthorised camping therefore need to be prepared to react to individual circumstances.

- Getting to know local travelling patterns and groups is critical to building a sound strategy. Getting to know individuals and building trust at a personal level with regular Gypsy and Traveller visitors can prevent problems developing.

- The nature of travelling and unauthorised encampment means it cannot be sensibly seen as a purely local phenomenon. An eviction in one area may have the effect of merely pushing the encampment over a local boundary for another authority to deal with. Local authorities and police forces should work together across boundaries to assess needs and determine strategies in response to unauthorised camping over the wider area. At a minimum, authorities should work together at county level, ideally at regional or sub-regional level.

- Good preparation and planning can minimise the disruption of unauthorised encampments. For this, sound intelligence and good networking is essential between local authorities and police forces in an area to keep everyone informed of Gypsy/Traveller groups and their movements. At the least, neighbouring authorities and other agencies that offer services for Gypsies and Travellers should always be informed when a large encampment is to be evicted.

3. Developing a Strategy for Unauthorised Camping

3.1 It is often impossible to predict just where and when an unauthorised encampment will occur. However, a purely reactive response to encampments as they arise is likely to be both inefficient and ineffective. Local authorities, police forces and other bodies need to be clear how they will respond to an encampment, who will take the lead, who else will be involved and under what circumstances.

3.2 To be effective this information should be clearly set out in an unauthorised encampments strategy and protocol. The strategy must be developed through consultation with all key stakeholders if it is to be effective; and it must seek to balance the rights and responsibilities of the travelling and settled communities.

Objectives of an Unauthorised Camping Strategy

3.3 The key objectives in a strategy for unauthorised encampments should include:

- Being able to plan ahead to minimise problems and to avoid the need to deal with everything on a crisis basis.

- Ensuring that the needs and legitimate expectations of all parties - Gypsies and Travellers, landowners and the settled community - are considered.

- Setting a framework within which clear, consistent and appropriate decisions can be made on unauthorised encampments to minimise disruption.

- Linking the approach to unauthorised camping firmly to other strategies and policies affecting Gypsies and Travellers (site provision, planning, health, education, housing etc).

- Directly involving all those with an interest in the process of developing the strategy so as to achieve maximum 'buy-in' and ownership.

- Reaching - as far as is possible - agreement so that all relevant parties will sign up to the strategy and its implementation.

- Clarifying roles and responsibilities so all parties to the strategy know who will do what in different circumstances, within the realistic limits of what is possible and allowing some flexibility for individual stakeholders.

- Ensuring that policies and approaches reflect the human rights of both the settled and travelling communities, and are compliant with race relations legislation including new requirements actively to promote equality of opportunity and good race relations.

- Ensuring the prevention of anti-social behaviour and effective enforcement against perpetrators.

3.4 Each local strategy will have its own objectives. Possible objectives are illustrated in Box 2.

Guidance on Managing Unauthorised Camping

Box 2 : Objectives of a Local Policy on Gypsy and Traveller Issues

The objectives of the policy are:

- To balance the rights and needs of resident communities with those of Gypsies and Travellers.

- To manage unauthorised encampments in an efficient and effective way taking account of the potential level of nuisance for local residents and the rights and responsibilities of Gypsies and Travellers.

- To work with partners in other authorities, the voluntary sector and the Police to address issues of social exclusion amongst Gypsy and Traveller communities.

Formulating the Strategy

Taking the Lead

3.5 It is appropriate that local authorities take the lead in formulating the strategy, and have responsibility for overseeing and monitoring its implementation, and for ensuring that the process is driven forward and does not become bogged down in inter-organisational wrangles and unacceptable delays. In areas of two-tier local government there should be clear agreement whether the county or district council will take the lead; both are clearly key players. Greater consistency and a wider perspective may be achieved where county councils take the lead.

3.6 The process of producing a strategy involves a number of key stages (see Box 3), which must be planned out and timetabled at the start. A named officer of the local authority should undertake this essential task, with the task fully recognised in his/her job description. It would be appropriate for the lead officer to be familiar with Gypsy and Traveller communities and their needs, and able to call on other experienced officers with skills suited to each stage of strategy development.

Guidance on Managing Unauthorised Camping

Box 3 : Key Stages in Developing a Strategy

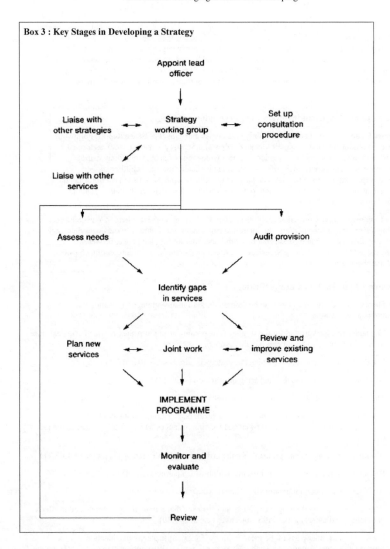

Who Should be Involved?

3.7 While local authorities take the lead, it is essential that many others are involved in the process and are willing to sign up to the strategy when it is agreed and published. Generating commitment among participants is an important part of the strategy building process.

Guidance on Managing Unauthorised Camping

3.8 Annex E shows the stakeholders - including Gypsies and Travellers - who might be involved in the strategy process and the ways in which they might be engaged. Key players should be closely involved, perhaps within a working party or steering group charged with moving the strategy process forward. Focus groups or consultative meetings could be used to engage other stakeholders. A designated local authority officer should be given overall responsibility for seeing the process through; he or she must have sufficient seniority to negotiate commitment from partners.

Box 4 : Consultation and Involvement in Developing a Strategy

Dorset County Council consulted widely on a Gypsy and Traveller Issues Report. Following this consultation a County Council Member Policy and Scrutiny Review Panel was formed which met nine times and heard evidence from a wide range of people including district council officers, county council officers concerned with education and children, police, groups representing Traveller views and a solicitor. One meeting was a site visit to residential site, an unauthorised encampment and to meet a farmer and residents neighbouring another unauthorised encampment.

West Sussex County Council adopted its strategy for Gypsies and Travellers in West Sussex following extensive consultation with interested parties and stakeholders. Bodies consulted included: district, town and parish councils, other local authorities, the police, business interests, landowners and farmers, residents' associations, organisations representing Gypsies, and members of the public.

Elements to be Included in the Strategy

3.9 There are ten essential elements to be thought through in any strategy for dealing with unauthorised camping:

- The legislative background for the strategy (this is summarised in Annex D which also deals more fully with human rights and race equality issues).

- Local information and data on which the strategy is based (see 3.10 and 3.11).

- Arrangements and protocols for sharing information (see 3.12).

- The approach to be taken on site provision (see Chapter 4).

- The policy to be followed when unauthorised encampments arise, setting out clearly the alternative courses of action to be taken and the circumstances which determine that action (see Chapter 5).

- Working arrangements and protocols for the involvement of different agencies (see 3.13-3.21).

- Resources for the strategy and constraints within which partners operate (see 3.22-3.24).

- Arrangements for communicating the strategy widely (see 3.25-3.28).

- Arrangements for monitoring the strategy and ensuring that it remains appropriate and is effective in practice, and meets race equality objectives (see 3.29-3.30).

- Involvement of other parts of the local authority, for example planning, education and social services, to ensure that there is a coherent authority-wide holistic approach to Gypsies/Travellers. In two-tier authorities this will involve both county and district councils (see 3.31).

Local Information for the Strategy

3.10 The starting point for a local strategy must be sound information on the characteristics and cultures of Gypsies and Travellers who reside in and resort to the area. Such information might include numbers, family structures, economic activity, travelling patterns, accommodation needs,

Guidance on Managing Unauthorised Camping

health and education needs. Information on Gypsy/Traveller culture is relevant in helping to develop an effective strategy, which will actually work.

3.11 Gypsy caravan counts provide a starting point. Other potential sources of information include monitoring of unauthorised encampments, planning applications and education records. Box 5 provides examples of Gypsy/Traveller needs assessments, which have used information from a range of sources.

Box 5 : Examples of assessments of Gypsy/Traveller accommodation needs

Assessments of accommodation needs have been made by:

LB Southwark

Derbyshire (through the Derbyshire Gypsy Liaison Group)

Wychavon

Sevenoaks District Council (through the PPG 3 housing needs assessment process)

In addition to information from the caravan count and other secondary sources, these also drew on experience of local professionals and research with local Gypsies and Travellers through interviews and discussions. Detailed references are in Chapter 9.

Fenland District Council has undertaken a one-year information gathering exercise, which has involved Gypsies and Travellers on all local authority and private sites and on the roadside. This identified travelling routes and reasons for coming to the District and highlighted Gypsy/Traveller expectations on health and welfare and led to wider understanding of needs.

Sharing Information

3.12 Sharing information at county and sub-regional level can help particularly when looking at travelling patterns and considering site provision. Where information is shared between partner agencies working together, protocols may be developed to deal with issues of professional confidentiality and data protection. Arrangements will already have been made for sharing information in relation to crime and disorder matters between partners in Crime and Disorder Partnerships.

Working Arrangements and Protocols - Towards Implementation

3.13 A strategy needs to spell out working arrangements. The local authority should be the lead agency in managing unauthorised camping in its area, and the strategic working arrangements should reflect this. The lead authority might, by agreement, be either the county or the district council in two-tier areas. There will be circumstances - which should be spelled out clearly - when other agencies will take the lead, for example the police may lead in the use of Criminal Justice and Public Order Act (CJPOA) s61 where urgent action is needed.

3.14 Named officers should be identified in each local authority and police basic command unit with clear responsibility for dealing with unauthorised camping. These officers need to be at a level, which enables them to take on the ground operational and enforcement decisions. It is important that all key stakeholders - including Gypsies and Travellers, elected members, members of the public and other local authority/police officers - know who these officers are. The information could be made available through the local authority web pages and in leaflets provided to the settled and travelling communities.

3.15 The responsible officer in a local authority should establish procedures for reporting to and informing elected members about encampments. It is particularly important that local members (and parish councils in areas where they exist) are kept closely in touch with action affecting encampments in their wards. They can provide a valuable channel for communication between local authority officers and members of the public as a supplement to direct contacts. It is important that elected members are fully aware of the legislative background, local strategies and policies on managing unauthorised encampments including, for example, their race relations responsibilities.

3.16 Other organisations, departments and sections likely to be involved in dealing with unauthorised encampments and in providing services to Gypsies and Travellers should be identified. These are likely to include Traveller Education Services, social services, environmental health, housing and health services. It may be appropriate to include the RSPCA where unauthorised campers are known to have horses, dogs or other animals. Where trading activities are a cause for concern, trading standards officers, Inland Revenue and Customs and Excise officers might also be included. Lists should be compiled of named contact officers in each stakeholder body with full contact details including telephone, fax and e-mail addresses; these lists must be kept up-to-date as people change jobs or responsibilities.

3.17 Responsibilities within the strategy for dealing with unauthorised camping must be recognised within the job descriptions and workloads of all these officers. While calls on their time will be variable and responsive to the number and nature of encampments arising, it is important to think through cover arrangements for their release from other duties when needed. Over time it should be possible to build up an estimate of the likely demands on their time.

3.18 Regular liaison meetings involving officers in all stakeholder organisations encourage good personal and working relationships to develop. People respond more easily to requests from people they know and trust. Liaison meetings provide an opportunity to discuss current issues and concerns and to review on-the-ground working arrangements in the light of experience.

Box 6 : Examples of Liaison Groups

Bedfordshire County Council set up a multi-agency forum in January 2002, which has commissioned independent research on Traveller community needs.

Kent Unauthorised Encampments Monitoring and Liaison Groups, between them, include representatives of all three tiers of local government, the police, health and Gypsy organisations.

Wiltshire County Council has set up a Gypsy and Traveller Officers' Liaison Group comprising officers from all departments actively involved in managing unauthorised camping; The Group's membership may be widened in the future to include police, health services, district council housing officers and certain voluntary agencies. The County Council has also established a Residents' Consultation Group for residents of its semi-permanent Gypsy sites in the county.

3.19 In some areas working relationships have been further cemented by joint training events where officers from different organisations, with different perspectives and professional interests learn together. Training should be balanced in coverage and include human rights, equalities and race relations. In some places Gypsies and Travellers have been directly involved in providing training to local authority and police personnel.

Guidance on Managing Unauthorised Camping

Box 7 : Examples of Joint Training

Derbyshire Gypsy Liaison Group has been extensively involved in training with the police. In conjunction with **Derbyshire Constabulary** they have produced inter-agency interactive training exercises and facilitation notes on unauthorised encampments.

Fenland District Council runs training for all members of their local strategic partnership, Primary Care Trust, police, fire and rescue and voluntary organisations. This aims to explain the culture and traditions of Gypsy people. A freelance Gypsy journalist is central to the training and explains how public bodies can better work with the media over Gypsy issues.

West Sussex County Council has reached agreement at county level with **Sussex Police** on the way training should be approached. The County Council is encouraging relevant local authority staff in each district to get together with district police commanders to agree local implementation plans.

3.20 In many areas across the country working arrangements between relevant bodies have been formalised into protocols or service level agreements. These set out the respective responsibilities of signatories, lines of command and communication, and may include performance targets.

- Protocols commonly involve local authorities (county and district councils in two-tier local government areas) and police.

- Protocols or service level agreements may also be relevant between lead local authority departments and education, health and welfare departments involved in making welfare enquiries at encampments. Such agreements set out the means of communication to be followed and provide targets for response times.

Box 8 : Examples of Protocols between Local Authorities and Police

Derbyshire: Good practice guide for unauthorised encampments: Joint protocol between Derbyshire County Council, Derbyshire Gypsy Liaison Group, Derbyshire Constabulary and the NHS.

Devon: Joint Policy and Practice Guidelines relating to people of nomadic lifestyle residing in or resorting to Devon: Devon County Council and Devon & Cornwall Constabulary.

Essex: A joint protocol for managing unauthorised encampments in Harlow: Essex County Council, Harlow District Council and Essex Police.

Kent: Kent protocol on the management of unauthorised encampments: Kent County Council, district and unitary councils, Kent County Constabulary.

Leicestershire: The Code of Practice for Travellers in Leicestershire, Leicester and Rutland: county council, district and unitary councils and Leicestershire Constabulary.

Wiltshire: Wiltshire County Council and Wiltshire Constabulary are currently developing a protocol for managing unauthorised camping incidents. This builds upon a successful Inter-Departmental protocol already in place within the County Council, which includes, amongst other sensitive issues, a Disclosure Statement, which addresses data protection and information sharing constraints.

3.21 In a few areas (for example Milton Keynes) arrangements for joint working between the local authority and police are still closer in a jointly staffed 'unit'. Advocates refer to the consistency of approach possible through true joint working; it avoids unnecessary duplication of effort; it means that there is less possibility of people being referred backwards and forwards between organisations. In such a structure it is important that reporting lines and accountability arrangements are carefully thought through.

Guidance on Managing Unauthorised Camping

Box 9 : Joint Working

Northamptonshire: A Countywide Traveller Unit has been established jointly funded by district councils, the county council, police and primary care trust, with a contribution from the Northamptonshire Chamber. Police and health workers are seconded to the Unit.

Resources

3.22 The Government believes that spending to achieve the pro-active approach towards site provision and managing unauthorised camping as set out here represents better value for money than the current position. Spending now on site provision should reduce the costs of dealing with unauthorised camping.

3.23 Local authorities and police should seek to apply Best Value principles to their strategy for dealing with unauthorised camping. Box 10 sets out some of the actions, which might be helpful in an area with extensive and/or frequent unauthorised encampments.

Box 10 : An Application of Best Value Principle to Dealing with Unauthorised Camping

Best Value principles suggest that local authorities and the police should:

- Identify what they are spending at present on dealing with unauthorised camping. Few organisations keep accurate records, which accurately identify all the costs involved in unauthorised camping, for example responding to complaints from the public.

- Estimate the costs borne by others, including local businesses and landowners. It may not be possible always to arrive at a monetary value, but attempting it ensures that wider implications of actions are clearer.

- Consider the indirect costs of unauthorised encampments in terms of, for example, additional costs to health and education services and others involved in fostering the greater social inclusion of Gypsies and Travellers.

- Compare these with the possible costs and benefits of taking a more pro-active approach to site provision and managing unauthorised camping on a partnership basis.

3.24 At present not all authorities have a budget for dealing with unauthorised camping, and staffing responsibilities are sometimes vague. Good practice suggests that all authorities should have a formal budget, based on past experience and best intelligence on future needs.

Communicating the Strategy

3.25 The strategy for unauthorised camping should be published and widely disseminated to local businesses, landowners, local residents, and Gypsies and Travellers. Objectives in publishing and publicising the strategy include:

- Making clear what can be achieved and over what time scales so as to mould realistic expectations among both the settled and Gypsy/Traveller communities.

- Making clear who is responsible for what elements of the strategy and its implementation. For example, it is appropriate that all members of the public should contact the police directly over matters involving crime associated with unauthorised encampments and that Gypsies and Travellers are encouraged to do so. The local authority might be the appropriate point of contact for other issues. This means listing names, telephone numbers and addresses.

Guidance on Managing Unauthorised Camping

3.26 A number of local authorities already provide information leaflets and/or have material on their web-sites dealing with unauthorised camping. Use of web-sites to provide information on local policy accords well with the Government's local e-government strategy.

Box 11 : Example of Information Leaflet on Unauthorised Camping

In **Bedfordshire**, the county council, district councils, Bedfordshire Police and the Bedford & Luton Community NHS Trust have jointly produced a leaflet *Travellers and the Law*.

Kent Unauthorised Encampments Working Group has produced a leaflet *Unauthorised Encampment : a document to answer your frequently asked questions*.

Suffolk County Council has produced a leaflet Unlawful Traveller Encampments in Suffolk, which is largely based on questions and answers.

Telford Borough Council has leaflets primarily intended to provide information to members of the public and landowners; these are also available on its web-site.

3.27 A 'communications strategy' is itself an important element in the strategy towards unauthorised encampments. A positive and co-ordinated approach to managing communication is an important element of a comprehensive strategy. Many bodies are likely to be involved in dealing with unauthorised encampments and other Gypsy/Traveller matters. A key aim of this strategy is to assure the travelling and settled community that effective action is being taken where necessary.

3.28 Deciding a co-ordinated approach to media briefings will reduce confusion and the possibility of conflicting accounts. The Commission for Racial Equality has issued Guidance to journalists on *Travellers, Gypsies and the media* which local authorities may find useful in encouraging a positive, or at least neutral, local press coverage for local encampments and other Gypsy/Traveller issues.

Monitoring the Strategy

3.29 It is important to monitor the strategy as it is implemented and review the need for change in the light of that monitoring.

- Monitoring arrangements need to be planned and resourced from the beginning. It would be appropriate for the local authority, as lead agency, to take responsibility, perhaps reporting back to a steering group including representatives of other key agencies.

- Obviously monitoring should identify progress towards meeting the objectives of the strategy. Protocols and other arrangements for partnership working are other obvious areas to be monitored and reviewed. In all cases, monitoring should identify areas, which have worked well and less well in order to learn from the process in recasting the strategy and/or its implementation.

- Above all, monitoring is required to ensure that the strategy leads to action on the ground. The strategy should not be merely a paper exercise.

3.30 Sound information is essential to monitoring. The Government sees great merit in encouraging local authorities, along with their police partners, to develop improved standard records of unauthorised encampments. As a minimum, information should be collected and monitored on the location of encampments, the number of caravans/vehicles involved and the duration of each encampment. Standardisation of information would allow aggregated data to be assembled across a county or region and would facilitate the exchange of data about unauthorised encampments between different areas. A review of the national Gypsy counts system has been undertaken and an amended system is to be introduced shortly.

Guidance on Managing Unauthorised Camping

A Holistic Approach

3.31 Unauthorised camping does not exist in a vacuum. Developing a strategic approach towards managing unauthorised camping provides an opportunity for local authorities and others to consider policies towards Gypsies and Travellers in a holistic manner, if they have not already done so. Relevant policy areas are land use planning (including development planning, planning control and enforcement), housing and homelessness, environmental health, health and education. Many general strategic approaches to dealing with local issues, crime and social exclusion are also very relevant and might refer to Gypsies and Travellers. Under-pinning all such work is policy on diversity, equality and human rights - not just towards Gypsies and Travellers, but towards the whole population of a local authority area.

Box 12 : Example of Contents of a Policy on Gypsy and Traveller Issues

The Dorset County Council Gypsy and Traveller Policy 2003 is comprehensive in coverage. Its sections are:

1. Introduction

2. Objectives

3. Travelling patterns in Dorset

4. Policies on site Provision and the management of unauthorised encampments

5. Site protection

6. Land use planning

7. Housing

8. Education, health and welfare

9. Making decisions on unauthorised encampments

10. Provision of services for encampments

11. Keeping people informed

12. Strategic background and joint working arrangements

13. Staff and other resource issues

Guidance on Managing Unauthorised Camping

Box 13 : Strategies and Partnerships Relevant to Gypsies and Travellers

- Local strategic partnerships and community strategies

- Community Cohesion Policies

- Supporting People

- Homelessness Strategies

- Children and Young People's Partnerships

- Sure Start and Early Years

- Connexions

- Primary Care Group Trust commissioning plans

- Crime and Disorder Reduction Strategies

- Race Equality Schemes

- Anti-poverty strategies

- Local Agenda 21 strategies

In **Devon** there are examples of holistic working:

- *Travellers Making Connexions : A good practice guide for multi-agency work*, Connexions Cornwall & Devon and Devon County Council

- The Health Forum Social Inclusion Task Group has identified Travellers in Devon as a group where inequalities in health exist alongside other service provision issues. A Traveller Forum has been formed with a wide membership including Travellers. A report is being finalised addressing *Travellers Wellbeing*.

---

4. Site Provision and Unauthorised Camping

4.1 Local authorities do not have a duty to provide sites for Gypsies. They do, however, have the power to do so (under s24 of the Caravan Sites and Control of Development Act 1960). Circulars 1/94 and 18/94 both encourage authorities to consider the need for site provision. Local Planning Authorities essentially control the creation of new public and private authorised sites through development plan policies and development control.

A Range of Accommodation

4.2 Site provision is an essential element in any strategy. In a context where the number of Gypsy caravans exceeds the number of authorised places where they can stop - which is the case in England - provision of suitable accommodation for Gypsies and Travellers must be seen as a vital part of an approach to dealing with unauthorised camping. Population increase and family growth among Gypsies and Travellers must also be considered.

4.3 All local authorities should review the provision of sites for Gypsies and Travellers. Site provision can be provided publicly or privately and take a variety of forms:

- Residential sites provide long-term settled accommodation. Most current local authority site provision is residential. Many private sites also provide long-term accommodation for individual families on an owner-occupier basis or commercially.

- Transit sites are also provided both by local authorities and private owners, though much less frequently. Transit sites, with varying levels of amenities, provide for Gypsies and Travellers who want to stay for a period of up to about three months in an area.

- Less formal stopping places are also rare. These would be identified areas of land to which Gypsies and Travellers could be directed when they come to an area, and where they could stop for a short time - perhaps up to a month.

- Emergency stopping places would be locations where families have stopped which are judged suitable for a short stay. Facilities might be temporarily provided at such locations.

4.4 All local authorities experiencing unauthorised encampments should provide either transit sites or stopping places to cater for Gypsies and Travellers moving within or passing through their area. This might be done on a collaborative basis between neighbouring authorities. Some provision could be made by private individuals at no cost to the local authority.

4.5 Gypsies and Travellers should be involved in site planning and design to ensure that sites are well used and are safe and appropriate to the cultures and lifestyles of Gypsy and Traveller families, including children.

Site Provision and Land Use Planning

4.6 The Government's policy on Gypsy sites and planning is set out in DoE Circular 1/94 and it provides for a flexible approach. The Circular puts Gypsies on the same footing in planning law as everyone else whilst recognising their special circumstances. It is designed to ensure that applications for Gypsy caravan sites are treated in the same way as any other form of development. It places emphasis on assessing the need for Gypsy site provision (also stressed in *Planning Policy Guidance (PPG) 3: Housing*, para 13). Local authorities should identify suitable locations for Gypsy sites in their development plans wherever possible (re-iterated in *PPG 12: Development Plans*, para 4.14). Failing this they should identify clear and realistic criteria for suitable locations as a basis for their site provision policies. Local authorities should encourage Gypsies to consult with them on planning matters before buying land on which they intend to camp and for which planning permission would be required.

Guidance on Managing Unauthorised Camping

4.7 Instances of unauthorised camping may be reduced if local planning authorities follow the advice in DoE Circular 1/94 which encourages them to identify suitable sites in their local plans wherever possible for Gypsies to buy and to settle (see 4.6).

■ Sites on traditional routes are likely to be well used and sustainable. It may be easier to gain acceptance for sites in areas where Gypsies and Travellers traditionally stop and are a known part of the local community.

■ Sites, which are screened from view, may be deemed suitable by Gypsies and Travellers as well as by the settled community.

■ Granting temporary planning permissions for sites in a planned sequence might make provision more acceptable to the settled community. This is particularly appropriate for stopping places where little fixed infrastructure may be involved. Temporary sites could be provided in advance of longer-term development proposals.

Authorised Sites and Managing Unauthorised Camping

4.8 If authorised sites are to contribute effectively to reducing the disruption caused by some unauthorised camping, site management and management of unauthorised camping must be integrated. At the least:

■ Local authority and police officers dealing with unauthorised encampments should have information about vacancies on local authority sites within their area, and ideally in neighbouring areas. Ideally, local authority officers should also be prepared to assist unauthorised campers without local accommodation to find places on privately-owned sites and in permanent housing if this is requested.

■ There must be close working between site managers and local authority and police officers dealing with unauthorised camping over allocations of pitches on sites. Site managers may be aware of issues around Gypsy/Traveller group and family compatibility, which must be taken into account when allocating pitches on residential sites.

■ More specifically, where police are seeking to use the new powers under s62A of the Criminal Justice and Public Order Act 1994 (inserted by the Anti-social Behaviour Act 2003), a police officer must consult the local authorities in whose area the encamped land lies about the availability of suitable pitches on relevant sites. ODPM and the Home Office will be consulting in detailed guidance on the use of these powers, which will then be incorporated into a revised version of this Guidance.

■ Transit sites and stopping places must be managed to prevent Gypsies and Travellers staying longer than the maximum permitted stay. Site turnover must be maintained if such sites are to continue to cater for Gypsies and Travellers with a nomadic lifestyle. Reluctance to move from transit sites and stopping places may indicate a need for further residential site provision.

Site Protection

4.9 Protection of land, which is vulnerable to unauthorised encampment, is a valid part of a strategy, but should not be the sole strategy. Some authorities have undertaken protection works on their own land and/or have advised private landowners how best to secure their land.

■ Site protection work is not cheap. A risk assessment should be carried out before investing, including consideration of risks of encampment, nuisance arising from encampment on that land, and cost of effectively protecting the site.

Guidance on Managing Unauthorised Camping

■ Site protection and continuing development of open land can have the effect of forcing Gypsies and Travellers to camp in prominent and still more unsuitable places including farmland and other private land, prompting complaints from the landowner. Site protection must only be considered alongside the creation of permanent sites, transit sites and stopping places to ensure that there are places for Gypsies and Travellers to stop without causing disruption.

5. Making Decisions on Unauthorised Encampments

5.1 This chapter deals with some of the considerations to be borne in mind by local authorities, police and others when making decisions about how to deal with unauthorised encampments as they occur. Its aim is to help:

■   To make clear, consistent and appropriate decisions on unauthorised encampments.

■   To ensure that a balance is struck between the needs of all parties.

■   To ensure that decisions taken will withstand challenge.

5.2 Sections below cover the policy statement; carrying out welfare enquiries; and reaching decisions.

A Policy Statement

5.3 It is important that the local authority produces a policy statement, which includes:

■   A statement of which travelling people the policy relates to. Many policies relate to **all** travelling groups including non-traditional Travellers since the issues raised by encampments are similar and the education, welfare and homelessness duties owed are identical.

■   Identification of the action to be considered in respect of land not owned by the local authority (see 6.17).

■   The responsibilities of different authorities and agencies. The statement should set out which authority will act in specified circumstances where county and district councils, and sometimes other agencies including national ones, share responsibilities (for example on highways), and the circumstances in which the police might take the lead.

■   The alternative courses of action to be taken. This should set out clearly the circumstances in which eviction processes would be instigated and the circumstances in which an encampment might remain for a period under regular review.

■   The characteristics of encampment sites, which would normally trigger rapid eviction proceedings (see 5.4-5.6).

■   The standards of behaviour expected from unauthorised campers on encampments (see 7.3).

■   The circumstances in which an authority might provide rubbish storage and collection services, water supply or toilets to an encampment (see 7.15).

Box 14 : Examples of Policy Statements and Procedures Guides
Adur District Council: Policy and guidance: Travellers and unauthorised encampments.
Dorset County Council: Dealing with unauthorised camping: procedure.
Leicestershire County Council : Policy and Administration Procedure statement in relation to unauthorised encampments by Gypsies and Travellers
Suffolk County Council : Unlawful Traveller encampments in Suffolk : a strategy
Wiltshire County Council: Policy statement in relation to unauthorised Gypsy and Traveller encampments.

Unacceptable Encampment Locations

5.4 Unauthorised encampments are almost always, by definition, unlawful. However, while there are insufficient authorised sites, it is recognised that some unauthorised camping will continue. There are locations, however, where encampment will not be acceptable under any circumstances. Each encampment location must be considered on its merits against criteria such as health and safety considerations for the unauthorised campers, traffic hazard, public health risks, serious environmental damage, genuine nuisance to neighbours and proximity to other sensitive land-uses. The list in Box 15 of sites where an unauthorised encampment would not normally be acceptable is illustrative only and is not intended to be exhaustive.

Box 15 : Some Examples of Types of Site where Unauthorised Camping would Normally be Unacceptable

■   A Site of Special Scientific Interest (SSSI) where an encampment endangers a sensitive environment or wildlife

■   School car park or playing fields (especially in term time)

■   An urban park

■   Car parks, including hospital, supermarket or leisure facility car parks

■   An industrial estate

■   Recreation ground and public playing fields

■   A site where pollution from vehicles or dumping could damage ground water or water courses

■   A derelict area with toxic waste or other serious ground pollution

■   A village green or other open area within a residential area

■   The verge of a busy road where fast traffic is a danger to unauthorised campers' children

---

5.5 Wherever possible, local authorities and/or police should seek to prevent Gypsies and Travellers from establishing an encampment in an unacceptable location. Where this proves impossible, they should attempt to encourage the unauthorised campers to move to an authorised site where available. Identification of possible 'acceptable' sites could assist local authorities and the police in the management of unauthorised encampments in circumstances where there are no available pitches on authorised sites. If the unauthorised campers refuse to move from an unacceptable location, eviction processes (including appropriate welfare enquiries) should be commenced.

5.6 To be effective, such an approach requires a very swift response from the local authority and/or police. Ideally, initial contact should be made within 24 hours of the encampment being established.

Welfare Enquiries

Requirements to Make Welfare Enquiries

5.7 Local authorities may have obligations towards unauthorised campers under other legislation (mainly regarding children, homelessness and education). Authorities should liaise with other local authorities; health and welfare services who might have responsibilities towards the families of unauthorised campers. Some form of effective welfare enquiry is necessary to identify whether needs exist which might trigger these duties or necessitate the involvement of other sectors, including the voluntary sector, to help resolve issues. The police and other public bodies who might be involved in dealing with unauthorised encampments do not have comparable duties but must still, as public servants, show common humanity to those they meet.

5.8 The Human Rights Act (HRA) applies to all public authorities including local authorities (including town and parish councils), police, public bodies and the courts. With regard to eviction, the issue that must be determined is whether the interference with Gypsy/Traveller family life and home is justified and proportionate. Any particular welfare needs experienced by unauthorised campers are material in reaching a balanced and proportionate decision. The human rights of members of the settled community are also material if an authority fails to act to curb nuisance from an encampment.

5.9 Case law is still developing with regard to the sorts of welfare enquiries, which the courts consider necessary to properly taken decisions in relation to actions against unauthorised encampments. Cases are testing the requirements under different powers, and the requirements placed on different agencies (authorities, police, and other public landowners). Very generally, court decisions to date suggest:

■ All public authorities need to be able to demonstrate that they have taken into consideration any welfare needs of unauthorised campers prior to making a decision to evict.

■ The courts recognise that the police and other public bodies have different resources and welfare duties from local authorities. Generally the extent and detail of appropriate enquiries is less for police and non-local authority 'public authorities'.

■ In the case of local authorities, the onus of making welfare enquiries appears to be greater when using Criminal Justice and Public Order Act 1994 s77, where the use of the section can result in criminal sanctions, than when using landowners' civil powers against trespass. Local authorities should, however, make thorough welfare enquiries whatever powers they intend to use.

5.10 Because local authorities have appropriate skills and resources to enable them to make (or to co-ordinate) welfare enquiries, it is considered good practice for local authorities to respond positively to requests for assistance in making enquiries from the police or other public bodies.

Procedures for Making Enquiries

5.11 Speed of response is key to managing unauthorised encampments so as to minimise disruption. There should be a recognised system, which ensures that all reports of new encampments reach the lead officer as quickly as possible. Passing on information rapidly should be part of protocols and joint working arrangements between agencies/departments (see 3.20). Staff on local authority switchboards and at call centres should know how to handle calls from the public and to whom they should be referred. Police call handlers require similar briefing and information that might take the form of frequently asked questions (FAQs) based on mutually agreed policies.

5.12 Ideally, an initial visit should be made to a new encampment within 24 hours of the authority becoming aware of it unless the location is very unobtrusive or remote. An encampment should always be visited very rapidly if initial reports indicate exceptional problems. The initial visit is the first step in making decisions about, and effectively managing, unauthorised encampments. It has several functions:

■ To check the accuracy of initial reports/complaints of an encampment, and to gather basic information on its location and size. This information enables issues such as land ownership to be checked.

■ Where an encampment location is likely to prove unacceptable (see 5.4-5.5), officers at the initial visit might try to encourage the unauthorised campers to move to an authorised site where a place is available, or to a less immediately unacceptable location chosen by the unauthorised campers themselves.

■ To collect basic information from the unauthorised campers about the families and vehicles involved, and about past and intended future movement, anticipated length of stay and reasons for stay.

Guidance on Managing Unauthorised Camping

- To collect initial information from unauthorised campers on any perceived welfare, health or educational needs. Such information is the starting point for liaison with other relevant departments. Where school-age children are present, the Traveller Education Service should be notified. Similarly social services or health authorities should be notified where there seem to be social, welfare or health needs to be further assessed and met.

- The initial visit should note the state of the encampment - how well it is kept, any damage, rubbish accumulation and so on. This will provide baseline information from which subsequent changes can be monitored. Photographs can provide a useful record of potential health and safety issues; people should not be photographed without their express consent.

- Officers at an initial visit can also note any features of the encampment or its location that is likely to be particularly problematic or which might affect future decisions.

- The initial visit is also an opportunity for giving information to unauthorised campers about:

  □ the standard of behaviour expected of them. Where a Code of Expected Behaviour has been developed (see 7.3 et seq), copies should be provided and, where necessary in the event of any reading difficulties, be clearly explained to avoid misunderstanding;

  □ what is going to happen next, what procedures the authority or police are likely to follow and what this means for the unauthorised campers; and

  □ names and addresses of local services and sources of advice likely to be useful to the unauthorised campers. Information ideally should include locations of housing providers, health, education and social services, and waste disposal facilities.

Box 16 : Examples of Information Leaflets Provided to Gypsies and Travellers

Information leaflets for Gypsies and Travellers normally set out the main policy approach adopted by the local authority, a code of expected behaviour and useful contact addresses for services and advice.

Devon County Council: On the Road - Guidelines for people of a nomadic lifestyle

Dorset County Council: Notice to Travellers

Essex County Council: Guidance notes for Gypsy/Travellers in Essex

Suffolk County Council: Notice to Travellers on unauthorised camp sites

---

5.13 Welfare enquiries should always be carried out as swiftly as possible where the initial visit indicates that the unauthorised campers may have serious unmet health or welfare needs or where it seems likely that the encampment will lead to serious disruption or nuisance.

5.14 It is vital that all information given and received during visits and enquiries is clearly recorded. This is helpful to the local authority, especially if different officers are involved at a later date. It will also form the basis of an audit trail for subsequent decisions in case of challenge. Pro formas have been developed by many authorities (see Box 17) to collect and record this initial information. Some authorities and police forces have developed scoring matrices as an aid to assessing risk and decision making.

Guidance on Managing Unauthorised Camping

Box 17 : Example of a Pro-Forma used to Record Data on Encampments

Adur District Council: Welfare checks for Travellers

Coventry City Council: Traveller enquiry form, and Form for guidance of authorising officer

Devon County Council: Unauthorised occupation notification, and Personal circumstances questionnaire

Devon & Cornwall Constabulary: Checklist and record of action taken by officers attending alleged trespass on land

Leicestershire County Council: Unauthorised occupation Social Assessment Report

---

5.15 Information gathered in the course of visits and enquiries is subject to data protection legislation. Authorities should make clear the purposes for which information is being collected and give assurances about how it will be used and to whom it might be passed. Chapter 9 provides reference to the web-site of the Information Commissioner for guidance on data protection issues.

5.16 Local authorities have no powers to insist that information be given. Some information may be confidential and require the unauthorised camper to give consent to follow up, for example, medical records. A sensitive approach is necessary, and authorities should always bear in mind issues of confidentiality and data protection. Where information is refused, the fact that questions were asked and not answered should be clearly recorded to avoid any subsequent claim for failure to take some relevant consideration into account. If unauthorised campers give reasons for not responding, these should also be noted. Unauthorised campers should be informed of any possible consequences of not providing information when requested. If they want to provide information through another person they trust, they should be able to do so provided that arrangements can be made quickly.

5.17 Reasonable attempts should be made to get information from unauthorised campers not present at the time of a visit. Other members of the group may sometimes be able to provide information. A letter or self-completion form may be left with clear instructions for its return (at no cost to the unauthorised camper). All such actions should be clearly recorded, and if there is still no response, this should be noted.

5.18 When visiting and managing unauthorised encampments, local authorities and police should adopt the same legal and careful health and safety procedures and practices as they apply to any other activity they are engaged in.

Reaching Decisions

5.19 Decisions about what action to take in connection with an unauthorised encampment must be made in the light of information gathered. Decisions must always be:

- 'Lawful' - that is in line with local policy and procedures, taking into account relevant considerations and not taking into account the irrelevant.

- 'Reasonable' in the legal sense of not being perverse or irrational in the light of the evidence available.

- 'Balanced' in that they take account of the rights and needs of both the settled community and Gypsies and Travellers.

- 'Proportionate' - what is proportionate will vary according to the precise circumstances of each encampment, including the nature of the location and the behaviour and needs of the unauthorised campers.

Guidance on Managing Unauthorised Camping

Making Decisions

5.20 Any welfare needs of unauthorised campers are a material consideration for local authorities when deciding whether to start eviction proceedings or to allow the encampment to remain longer. Welfare needs do not give an open-ended 'right' for unauthorised campers to stay as long as they want in an area. For example, the presence of a pregnant woman or school age children does not, per se, mean that an encampment must remain indefinitely. To defer an eviction which is justified on other grounds, the need must be more immediate and/or of a fixed term. Box 18 gives some examples of welfare needs to be considered by local authorities, although the list is not intended to be exhaustive and all cases must be judged on their individual merits. Good practice suggests that eviction should be delayed while such acute welfare needs exist and are being met; during this period the encampment should be pro-actively managed (see Chapter 7).

Box 18 : Some Examples of Welfare Needs to be Considered in Eviction Decisions

Advanced pregnancy: a period shortly before and after birth in normal circumstances; longer on medical advice if there are complications.

Ill health: indicators might include a hospital appointment booked; in-patient treatment of a close family member; period during which a condition can be diagnosed, stabilised and a course of treatment started.

Educational needs: children in school if within 4 weeks of the end of term or if access to special education has been gained.

5.21 In some circumstances it may be appropriate to exclude a single person or family with welfare need from eviction action taken against the larger group. However, this must always be sensitively handled to ensure that an individual is not isolated and unsupported, leading to still greater need. In practice, groups may prefer to move on together. It is important that the appropriate authority follows up identified welfare needs whether or not the encampment is moved on.

Arrangements for Making Decisions

5.22 Responsibility for taking decisions must be clearly identified within the authority's (and/or police) policies and procedures, whether delegated to officers or retained by elected members.

5.23 Some authorities have established special procedures for reaching decisions, for example:

- Structures which ensure that decisions are taken by officers who have not been directly involved in site visits or contact with unauthorised campers. It is argued that this increases the consistency, logic and objectivity of decisions. Since all evidence is presented to the 'authorising officer' in writing such a procedure ensures that there is a clear record of the decision and the issues considered.

- Some authorities have arrangements for joint site visits and/or case conferences for reaching decisions on 'difficult' cases. Such procedures ensure that all parties are represented and have the opportunity to influence the decision. Case conferences could include representatives of the unauthorised campers and the local settled community, although there would need to be clear 'rules' for making decisions in the absence of consensus.

5.24 It is important that decisions to pro-actively manage encampments for a period are kept under review. Circumstances can change quickly, for example if newcomers join the encampment and swell its size unacceptably or if behaviour deteriorates.

Recording Decisions

5.25 All decisions (including any decision to allow an encampment to remain for a period) must be fully recorded and documented. Any damage and nuisance should be charted in writing; a

Guidance on Managing Unauthorised Camping

photographic or video record might also be taken in support. Records should also be kept of all complaints received about the encampment, with comments as to their validity. Information passed to unauthorised campers should be recorded, along with offers of assistance made - for example help with a housing application, offer of a pitch on an authorised site - and the response. Similarly it would be good practice to record the fact that an encampment was unproblematic and did **not** cause nuisance or damage. Any complaints received, including any from Gypsy/Traveller unauthorised campers, should be recorded.

5.26 Records can provide valuable information on the number and nature of unauthorised encampments in an area and which sites are particularly prone to encampment. This information is useful in assessing the need for further site provision, site protection priorities and in setting budgets and appropriate staffing levels. It provides material on which a risk-based response to encampments could be developed drawing on past experience relating to the site or the group/family involved. Standard minimum information, to be collected in all areas, as suggested in paragraph 3.30, would facilitate information sharing and better planning.

6. Resorting to Eviction

6.1 This chapter covers the eviction process itself. Once a decision to evict an unauthorised encampment has been properly taken, the aims should be:

■ To act quickly and efficiently.

■ To use powers most appropriate to the circumstances.

■ To reduce scope for challenge through the courts by ensuring that policies and procedures are properly followed so as to reduce cost and delay.

6.2 The first three sections relate to eviction powers available to local authorities, police and other landowners. The final section in the chapter (6.20-6.24) deals with local planning authority powers to enforce against unauthorised development (ie Gypsies and Travellers 'developing' land as a caravan site without planning consent).

Powers Available to Local Authorities

6.3 Many encampments are dealt with through negotiation. Where this fails, local authorities have two main sets of powers to tackle unauthorised encampments:

■ A landowner (including a local authority) can obtain a possession order in the civil courts requiring the removal of trespassers from property, including land. Under the Civil Procedures Rules Part 55 the claim must be issued in the County Court in whose jurisdiction the property or land is situated. Exceptionally the claim may be issued in the High Court if there is substantial risk of public disturbance or of serious harm to persons or property which properly require immediate determination.

■ The Criminal Justice and Public Order Act 1994 (CJPOA) gives local authorities in England and Wales powers to make directions to leave land being used by itinerant groups (s77). It is an offence to fail to comply with such a direction. In proceedings for an offence under this section, it is a defence for the accused to show that his failure to leave or to remove the vehicle or other property as soon as practicable, or his re-entry with a vehicle, was due to illness, mechanical breakdown or other immediate emergency. If the direction to leave is not complied with, the local authority can apply to magistrates' court for an order requiring the removal of vehicles and any occupants from the land (s78).

6.4 Box 19 summarises some of the main features of the two sets of powers, highlighting differences and similarities.

Box 19 : Some Features of Civil and Criminal Justice and Public Order Act Powers for Local Authorities

Civil Powers	CJPOA ss77 and 78
Only on land in LA ownership	On private as well as LA land where encampment is without the consent of the occupier of the land
Possession orders are effective against anyone on the land, not necessarily those resident when the notice was first served	Only effective against people directed to leave. All newcomers must be served with directions to leave

Guidance on Managing Unauthorised Camping

Civil orders can cover wide geographical areas where a real threat of further encampment can be demonstrated	It is an offence for unauthorised campers to return within three months to land they have been directed to leave; only applies to the same individuals
There is no defence to an action for trespass (other than showing non-trespass)	It is a defence for the accused to show that his failure to leave or to remove the vehicle or other property as soon as practicable, or his re-entry with a vehicle, was due to illness, mechanical breakdown or other immediate emergency
No criminalising effect	Can have the effect of criminalising Gypsy/Traveller unauthorised campers who fail to move when directed to leave, a factor taken seriously by the courts. In practice, authorities normally proceed against the unauthorised campers by way of complaint for an order requiring them to remove their vehicles from the land, and not for the criminal offence of contravening a direction to leave the land.
County court bailiffs can be used; their services must be paid for and may lead to delay in enforcement. . It is recommended that the police attend such evictions in order to prevent a breach of the peace	Responsibility for eviction lies with the local authority. Officers or agents of the local authority may use reasonable force to evict. It is recommended that the police attend such evictions in order to prevent a breach of the peace
Often seen as safe and relatively straightforward	Potentially quicker than civil powers, but greater risk of being effectively contested

Local authorities have responsibilities to make welfare enquiries when reaching eviction decisions, to take into account considerations of common humanity, and to honour the other statutory duties they may have towards the unauthorised campers
Unauthorised campers can attend and be represented at the court hearing
Decisions can be similarly challenged by means of judicial review on the grounds that they have been reached improperly

6.5 Other legal measures may be available to local authorities:

■   The Government believes that local authorities should always follow a route which requires a court order. As local authorities and public bodies, authorities must have regard to considerations of common humanity or other statutory duties, and must ensure that the human rights of unauthorised campers are safeguarded.

■   Local highways authorities have powers to evict unauthorised campers from highway land in certain circumstances under the Highways Acts. Section 143 of the Highways Act 1980 requires unauthorised campers to be given 28 days notice to leave, and its use may be unsuitable where rapid eviction is called for.

■   Local bylaws may have provisions for evicting unauthorised campers from car parks, parks or other public areas.

Guidance on Managing Unauthorised Camping

Powers Available to the Police

6.6 Powers are available to the police under the Criminal Justice and Public Order Act 1994 ss61-62E.

Criminal Justice and Public Order Act 1994 Section 61

6.7 Under s61 of the CJPOA, the police have discretionary powers to direct trespassers to leave land. The senior police officer present can direct trespassers to leave if reasonable steps have been taken by or on behalf of the landowner/occupier to ask them to leave and there are two or more people intending to reside on the land. Any one of three further conditions must be met:

- if any of those persons has caused damage to the land or to property on the land; or

- used threatening, abusive or insulting words or behaviour towards the occupier, a member of his family or an employee or agent of his; or

- those persons have between them six or more vehicles on the land.

Section 61 cannot be used on land on the highway (with limited specific exclusions listed by s61 (9)(b)). It is an offence to fail to leave the land as soon as reasonably practicable or to enter the land again as a trespasser within three months of the date the direction was given.

6.8 The current ACPO guidance notes that there can be no blanket policies, but refers to some of the circumstances in which it might be appropriate to use s61 against an encampment.

- The statutory conditions must obviously be met (see 6.7). Case law (*Fuller*) has determined that any notice period given to unauthorised campers must have expired before s61 can be used. In other words, the unauthorised campers must clearly have failed to respond to requests from or on behalf of the legal occupier of the land to leave before the police can act. Some police forces have streamlined this process by drawing up standard documents which, when signed by the owner/occupier of the land, give the police authority to act as their agents in dealing with the encampment.

- The fact that a landowner initially allows an encampment to remain does not preclude subsequent police action so long as it is clear that reasonable steps have since been taken by the landowner/occupier to get the unauthorised campers to move, and that they have failed to do so.

- The fact that a local authority has started to make welfare enquiries cannot be taken as an indication that the encampment is being allowed to remain since this is an essential precondition for eviction action.

- The decision to use s61 is an operational one. Its early use should always be considered where it is likely to be a proportionate response, and especially where there is evidence of:

  □ unacceptable behaviour by unauthorised campers at the encampment, including individual criminal activity, which cannot be controlled by means other than eviction;

  □ significant disruption to the life of the surrounding community;

  □ serious breaches of the peace or disorder caused by the encampment.

- Where triggers such as the above are experienced, good practice suggests that police should be prepared to act as long as the statutory conditions are met. Police forces/commands should not adopt blanket policies or presumptions either for or against the use of s61.

6.9 Home Office Circular 45/1994 says 'The decision whether or not to issue a direction to leave is an operational one for the police alone to take in the light of all of the circumstances of the particular case. But in making his decision the senior officer at the scene may wish to take account of the personal circumstances of the trespassers; for example, the presence of elderly persons, invalids, pregnant women, children and other persons whose well-being may be jeopardised by a precipitate move.' Case law (*Small*) has established that, while police officers do not have to undertake welfare

Guidance on Managing Unauthorised Camping

enquiries as such, they must be aware of humanitarian considerations in reaching their decisions and must ensure that all decisions are proportionate. A decision may be taken to explicitly exclude individuals or families with serious welfare needs from a s61 direction to leave.

6.10 Above all, s61 should be used within the framework of a jointly agreed strategy for managing unauthorised camping (see Chapter 3). Local authorities, police and other stakeholders should agree the sorts of circumstances in which s61 might be considered appropriate. It is also important that s61 should be used consistently within a local area.

Box 20 : Example of a Local Agreement for the Use of Section 61

The joint protocol on unauthorised encampments within the Borough of Northampton between **Northampton Borough Council** and **Northamptonshire Police** includes a local agreement for the use of s61. It specifies exceptional circumstances in which the police may be requested by the Council or choose themselves to consider using their powers under s61.

6.11 Regular exchange of monitoring information on unauthorised encampments between police and local authority personnel is important. In particular, each party should keep the other informed about decisions taken and progress.

Criminal Justice and Public Order Act 1994 Section 62A to 62E

6.12 Sections 67 to 71 of the Anti-social Behaviour Act 2003 insert sections 62A to 62E into the Criminal Justice and Public Order Act 1994 (CJPOA). The legislation provides the police with a power to direct trespassers to leave land and to remove any vehicles and other property from the land, where there is a suitable pitch available on a caravan site elsewhere in the local authority area. Where a direction has been given to a person, it is an offence for that person to enter any land in the local authority as a trespasser within three months of the direction being given.

6.13 This power will be enacted on 27 February 2004 and ODPM and the Home Office are consulting separately on draft guidance for its implementation in practice. Once guidance on the use of s62 is finalised, it will be incorporated into this Guidance.

Powers Available to Other Landowners

6.14 Several government bodies are major landowners and their land may be subject to unauthorised encampment - examples include the Forestry Commission and the Highways Agency. Public bodies should ask local authorities to assist with welfare enquires and local authorities should be prepared to help with these.

6.15 Private landowners may obtain a possession order through the civil courts requiring the removal of trespassers from their land, using Civil Procedures Rules Part 55 in the county court. Private landowners have no welfare responsibilities towards Gypsies and Travellers and would not be expected to take unauthorised campers' needs into account when deciding to evict.

6.16 Some private landowners seek to avoid the expense and costs of going to court by using common law rights to recover land from trespassers using 'reasonable force' as necessary. Such action is lawful, and some firms of bailiffs have carried out many evictions effectively and without trouble. Good practice guidelines for common law evictions would seek to ensure that no more than necessary 'reasonable force' is used and might include:

- Police should always be notified of an eviction and called in to stand by to prevent a breach of the peace.

- If police advise that it is inappropriate to carry out an eviction, it should always be delayed until an agreed time.

Guidance on Managing Unauthorised Camping

6.17 There is a role for local authorities and police in managing unauthorised camping on private land.

■ As a minimum, local authorities should inform private landowners about their rights to recover land from trespassers, through the courts or using common law powers; authorities should not offer legal advice to landowners but rather refer them to Citizens' Advice Bureaux or solicitors. Authorities should remind landowners about the importance of using reputable bailiffs and only 'reasonable force'.

■ Within the overall strategy for managing unauthorised camping, the local authority might consider acting more directly against encampments when requested by a private landowner, particularly if the police are not prepared to use s61 to evict the encampment.

■ Police should take action if any criminal offences are perpetrated during eviction action by bailiffs or private firms.

Some Procedural Points

6.18 This guidance is not concerned with detailed procedures involved in court actions for eviction. Some pointers to good practice for local authorities were noted in *Managing Unauthorised Camping: A Good Practice Guide* issued in 1998 and are still valid:

■ Both main sets of powers for taking eviction action involve their own detailed procedures for serving notices, entering cases into court, providing statements (civil powers) or witnesses (CJPOA) for evidence and so on. There is advantage in drawing up a detailed procedures guide as a checklist that everything is done properly and no necessary action missed. Losing an eviction action through an avoidable mistake is a waste of resources, and threatens the credibility of the authority.

■ In drawing up detailed procedures, the close involvement of a legal officer is essential. Day-to-day liaison for legal advice while dealing with a specific encampment is also desirable to avoid omissions and to ensure the most effective case for eviction is built.

■ Most authorities will probably use in-house legal expertise for preparation and court work. In some circumstances it may be desirable to use an external solicitor, which can be cost-effective where a local solicitor has special expertise.

■ Good relations should be built with court officials to ensure a speedy service and to ensure that particularly urgent cases can be given priority when needed. The leaflet *Getting the best out of the court system: Claims for possession* issued by DTLR, the Court Service and the Welsh Assembly stresses the importance of establishing links with local courts. It is, of course, essential to establish what paperwork the courts will require and to ensure that it is always provided. It is also desirable to develop fast-track in-house processes to fit around court workings.

■ It is important to be able to show that directions have been properly served if cases are to succeed at court. This normally means either personal service on the occupiers of each vehicle and/or attaching a copy of the direction to each caravan as well as posting the direction on the site. A verbal explanation of the direction should be given wherever possible as a supplement to the written documents to cater for possible reading difficulties.

■ It is usual to proceed against unnamed persons occupying the land. This is specifically allowed in the CJPOA and may be the only practical course where unauthorised campers are unwilling to give their names. Getting comprehensive information on vehicles is important for identification purposes.

■ Most authorities will probably think it appropriate to use council personnel to serve notices and so on. Where external bailiffs or other agents are employed, the authority must be satisfied that their behaviour is at all times lawful and in accord with human rights and race relations requirements.

Guidance on Managing Unauthorised Camping

- Serving directions, and site visits in general, can raise issues of personal safety for officers involved. Sensible precautions should be taken to avoid confrontation and personal danger. In certain circumstances, a police presence may be appropriate while notices are served.

- Local authorities have discretion to set notice periods beyond the legal minimum. For example, the direction to leave served under the CJPOA can require unauthorised campers to leave in 24 hours, 48 hours or a longer period. Decisions about the length of notice given should be taken in the light of the circumstances of each encampment, with a view to being more generous where problems are not extreme.

Preparing for Eviction

6.19 Eviction proceedings should not be commenced unless the authority is able to go the whole way to forced eviction if necessary.

- Every effort should be made to avoid forced eviction.

- Many encampments include children, who will find forced eviction especially stressful and frightening. All authority and other personnel involved in an eviction should remember this and seek to ensure that their actions have the least possible harmful effect on children.

- Authorities should think, in general terms at least, about options for forced eviction. Plans should be formulated on such matters as which personnel would be involved and which towing contractors would be used. An in-principle agreement should be reached with the police about where towed vehicles would be put.

- Other services should be alerted prior to a forced eviction. This should include warning social services (who may need to provide temporary care for children in the rare cases where parents are arrested and held in custody), Traveller Education Services and homelessness officers, and could also involve finding accommodation for horses and dogs.

- Many authorities do not employ council staff in forced evictions. Where bailiffs or other agencies and contractors are employed, a code of expected behaviour should be drawn up. This code must recognise that private bodies have a local authority's human rights and race relations responsibilities while acting as their agent.

- A senior local authority officer should always attend forced evictions to ensure that all agents follow codes of behaviour. The officer should attempt to encourage the unauthorised campers to move voluntarily wherever possible.

- Police should be involved at a very early stage in planning a forced eviction. They will be able to advise on personal safety issues. In addition, forced evictions could have implications for traffic management and the like.

- Elected members and other local stakeholders should be notified in advance of forced eviction. It is also appropriate routinely to inform neighbouring local authorities and police areas since the displaced unauthorised campers may look for other encampment sites locally.

- The respective roles of the local authority, police and other agencies in forced eviction should be clearly established in the local strategy for managing unauthorised camping. Since this is an area where good practice is hard to establish, it is particularly important that all agencies should monitor and evaluate local instances of eviction and learn from that experience.

Enforcing against Unauthorised Development

6.20 Where Gypsies and Travellers (or anyone else) buy land and develop it as a caravan site without planning consent, any enforcement must be through the planning system; the powers described above against trespass cannot be used.

Guidance on Managing Unauthorised Camping

6.21 A breach of planning control is not in itself an offence; enforcement is a matter for the discretion of the local planning authority. Decisions to enforce must be made on planning grounds. Some key factors may include whether the breach of control unacceptably affects public amenity, highway safety, the Green Belt, public landscape, or the existing use of land or buildings meriting protection in the public interest. The action taken should be proportionate to the breach.

6.22 The current enforcement regime provides a mix of powers with which to deal with breaches of planning control in a controlled but flexible manner. The main powers are summarised in Box 21.

Box 21 : Main Planning Enforcement Powers to be used against Unauthorised Development

The discretionary powers available to local planning authorities (LPAs) were set out in the Planning and Compensation Act 1991 which amended the Town and Country Planning Act 1990 (TCPA 1990). Section references below refer to the TCPA 1990 as amended.

Planning contravention notice (s171C): This may be used where it appears that there may have been a breach of planning control and the LPA requires information about the activities on the land or to find out more about the nature of the recipient's interest in the land.

Enforcement notice (s172): This requires steps to be taken to remedy the specified breach within a given period. There is a right of appeal to the Secretary of State against an enforcement notice. If the notice is upheld, failure to comply is an offence with a maximum penalty on conviction of £20,000 (unlimited in the Crown Court).

Stop notice (ss183-184): This has the effect of immediately stopping any activity which contravenes planning control; an enforcement notice must also be served. There is no right of appeal to a stop notice, but compensation may be payable if an appeal against the associated enforcement notice is allowed on legal grounds. If a stop notice is contravened the resulting offence can be prosecuted in the Magistrates' Court with a maximum penalty on conviction of £20,000 (unlimited in the Crown Court).

Breach of condition notice (s187A): Where there is a failure to comply with any condition or limitation imposed on a grant of planning permission this procedure provides a fast-track enforcement option to secure compliance with no statutory right of appeal to the Secretary of State.

Injunctions (s187b): The LPA is able to seek an injunction in the High Court or County Court to restrain any actual or expected breach of planning control. It is not necessary to serve an enforcement notice prior to applying for an injunction.

Direct action (s178): Where any steps required by an enforcement notice are not taken within the compliance period, the LPA may enter the land and take the required steps and recover reasonable costs incurred in doing so. The whole enforcement process must have been completed before direct action is possible.

Compulsory purchase (s226 (1)(b)): With the authorisation of the Secretary of State, an LPA may compulsorily acquire any land in their area 'for a purpose which it is necessary to achieve in the interests of the proper planning of an area in which the land is situated'. There is scope for objection and a public local inquiry. This has been successfully used against unauthorised development in order to restore land to its lawful use for agriculture.

6.23 Case law has determined that all enforcement measures must be proportionate in the context of the Human Rights Act, and in particular the Gypsy/Traveller's rights under Article 8. Guidance on using planning enforcement powers is available in Circular 10/97, Planning Policy Guidance 18: *Enforcing Planning Control* and *Enforcing Planning Control: Good Practice Guide for Local Planning Authorities*.

Guidance on Managing Unauthorised Camping

6.24 The planning enforcement system in England is currently being reviewed. One of the issues being considered is whether local authority enforcement powers are effective or whether more are needed to tackle breaches of planning control. Revised guidance to local authorities is also being considered. An announcement about the review is expected in 2004.

7. Managing Unauthorised Encampments

7.1 Although unauthorised camping is unlawful, it is likely to continue while there are insufficient spaces to accommodate Gypsies and Travellers on authorised sites. While more places are being provided it is vital that local authorities, with their police and other partners, pro-actively manage encampments to minimise the disruption caused. The principles involved are:

■ To enforce the same standards of behaviour by unauthorised campers as are expected of the settled community.

■ To respond rapidly to any deterioration of behaviour and growing disruption from an encampment.

■ To facilitate access to services for Gypsy/Travellers on encampments.

■ To keep all parties informed of decisions and actions.

7.2 The chapter also covers the special issue of dealing with mass gatherings by Gypsies and Travellers (7.30-7.37).

Behaviour at Encampments

7.3 Many local authorities (see Box 22) have drawn up Codes for Gypsy/Traveller unauthorised campers, detailing both locational and behaviour expectations. 'Acceptable behaviour' codes might include some or all of the following items:

■ Small scale encampments, which can be accommodated with less disruption.

■ No aggressive and threatening behaviour towards local authority and/or police officers or members of the public.

■ Dogs and other animals to be kept under control.

■ No persistent noise which disturbs others, especially at night, for example from work on the camp, vehicles, generators, dogs or music.

■ Keeping the encampment site clean and tidy, avoiding littering and/or fly tipping on or near the site.

■ No damage either to the site encamped or the surrounding area or nearby property.

■ No criminal activity on the part of unauthorised campers.

Box 22 : Examples of Codes of Expected Behaviour
The code for Travellers in **Essex**
Guidance notes for Travellers in **Leicestershire, Leicester City *and* Rutland**

7.4 In drawing up a Code of Expected Behaviour, local authorities should consult Gypsies and Travellers, local businesses and other landowners and other members of the settled community. The objective should be to reach consensus on behaviour standards which it is appropriate to require, and which are sensitive to cultural differences between the Travelling and settled communities.

7.5 As noted above, a basic principle in establishing a Code of Expected Behaviour is applying the same standards as would be applied to members of the settled community. In this context it is important to consider 'individual' and 'group' behaviour and responsibilities. In the settled community, a whole street or estate would not be evicted because of the criminal or anti-social behaviour of one

Guidance on Managing Unauthorised Camping

person or household. Wherever possible, police and local authorities should seek to enforce appropriately against a troublemaker rather than automatically evicting an encampment as a whole.

7.6 It is also important to identify and take action against unacceptable behaviour towards encampments by members of the settled community. Harassment of, and violence against, Gypsy/Traveller unauthorised campers are quite unacceptable. Local authorities and police, as public bodies, have responsibilities under the Race Relations (Amendment) Act 2000 to promote good race relations.

7.7 Tackling unacceptable behaviour of whatever sort requires - as outlined in Chapter 5 - rapid response, regular monitoring and determination to take appropriate enforcement action as necessary.

Dealing with Crime and Anti-Social Behaviour

7.8 Some encampments are associated with criminal and anti-social behaviour. The Government is clear that criminal and anti-social behaviour is not acceptable from unauthorised campers, just as it is not acceptable from members of the settled community. The White Paper *Respect and Responsibility* sets out the stand to be taken against anti-social behaviour. Measures provided (see 7.11-7.12 and Box 23) empower communities, public services and authorities to tackle anti-social behaviour. In return the Government expects everyone to play their part in setting and enforcing proper standards of behaviour. This Guidance should be read in the context of that agenda.

7.9 Dealing with any criminal behaviour on the part of unauthorised campers is properly the responsibility of the police. Other enforcement agencies may be involved depending on the nature of the crime, including Trading Standards Officers, Inland Revenue and Customs and Excise enforcement officers where there are indications of fraudulent trading, tax or excise evasion. A co-ordinated approach to enforcement is the key.

7.10 No group should be above the law. Where action is justified, there should be no blanket presumption against enforcing against members of the Travelling community on grounds of expediency. Where law enforcement agencies demonstrate a commitment to taking action where appropriate and are clearly determined to tackle crime, it is probable that some Gypsy/Traveller unauthorised campers will avoid that locality and some may amend their behaviour. A pro-active approach taken in one area may increase unauthorised camping in an adjoining area where a less active approach is taken. Consistency of approach is desirable.

7.11 Anti-social behaviour (see Box 23) can also arise at some unauthorised encampments. Both police and local authorities have a role here. Under the Police Reform Act 2002, the Government introduced improved measures for tackling anti-social behaviour including allowing Anti-Social Behaviour Orders (ASBOs) to be made following conviction for a criminal offence as well as on application to the civil magistrate's court, and allowing ASBOs to prohibit specified acts of anti-social behaviour across any geographical area up to and including the whole of England and Wales. This should help counter displacement of anti-social behaviour. Orders can also be made in the county court where the defendant is the principal party in related proceedings such as possession proceedings or eviction notices where the persons to be evicted from the area are named individuals. These changes were accompanied by Home Office guidance published in November. The white paper *Respect and Responsibility* strengthens the changes described above and outlines new measures which are to be introduced. The Anti-Social Behaviour Act 2003 will introduce further relevant changes to ASBOs, allowing Housing Action Trusts and county councils to apply for ASBOs, enabling persons to be joined to county court proceedings to seek an order against them and empowering local authorities to prosecute ASBO breaches.

7.12 It is important that local authorities and police seriously consider the possibility of using ASBOs against unauthorised campers and/or negotiating Acceptable Behaviour Contracts (see Box 23). The use of either measure would represent an opportunity to discuss behaviour with unauthorised campers, defining with and for them what is and is not acceptable.

Box 23 : Tackling Anti-Social Behaviour

The Crime and Disorder Act 1998 introduced Anti-Social Behaviour Orders (ASBOs) to tackle persistent anti-social behaviour (ASB). The scope of the orders was extended by the Police Reform Act 2002, which was accompanied by Home Office guidance on ASBOs and ABCs. Further improvements to the functioning of ASBOs were made in the Anti-Social Behaviour Act 2003.

ASB: is defined in the Crime and Disorder Act 1998 s1 as behaving in *'a manner that caused or was likely to cause harassment, alarm or distress to one or more persons not of the same household'*

ASBOs: are available to local authorities, police (including the British Transport Police) and Registered Social Landlords (RSLs') by application at a magistrates' court or on conviction in criminal proceedings. Orders are available in the county court where the person is the Defendant in related proceedings. Interim orders can also be obtained. From early 2004 Housing Action Trusts and county councils will also be able to apply for ASBOs, and persons will be able to be joined to county court proceedings where their anti-social behaviour is relevant to the principal proceedings for the purpose of seeking an order against them. To obtain an ASBO it is necessary to show that the person(s) concerned have acted in an anti-social manner and an order is necessary to protect others from further anti-social acts by the individual(s). The rules of evidence are civil but a standard of proof equivalent to the criminal standard (beyond reasonable doubt) should be applied. The order must be negative, prohibiting the individual(s) from specified actions (which can include a general prohibition of acting in an anti-social manner) in specified areas which can be any defined part of or the whole of England and Wales. Breach of an ASBO is a criminal offence and has to be proved to the criminal standard of evidence beyond reasonable doubt. Conviction for breach carries the normal maximum sentence in the Magistrates' Court (6 months in prison, a fine or both) and five years and/or a fine in the Crown Court.

Acceptable Behaviour Contracts: have been developed, initially by Islington Council, as an informal way of dealing with low-level ASB and nipping it in the bud. They can be used with adults and young people and are tenure-neutral although they have been used mainly against teenagers in social rented housing. The perpetrator is interviewed by a council officer in the presence of parents and police, and is asked to sign a 'contract' agreeing not to engage in specified anti-social acts. The ABC principles might be adapted for use in relation to Gypsies/Travellers and unauthorised encampments. An ABC is not legally binding but it can be cited in proceedings such as for an ASBO at a later date.

Other measures: are available which can be used against specific forms of ASB, including:

- Environmental Protection Act 1990 where a problem is judged prejudicial to health or a statutory nuisance - normally enforced by the local authority environmental health department

- Noise Act 1996 - normally enforced by the local authority environmental health department

- Protection from Harassment Act 1997 - if ASB or unauthorised camper behaviour constitutes harassment, police could prosecute under this Act, or the person to whom harassment has occurred may claim damages and an injunction

- Public Order Act 1986

- Criminal Damage Act 1971

Guidance on Managing Unauthorised Camping

7.13 Measures to tackle crime and ASB must be set within a strategic framework. Dealing with any criminal and anti-social behaviour associated with unauthorised encampments should be considered by local Crime and Disorder Reduction Partnerships as part of their mandatory strategies (see Box 24).

Box 24 : Crime and Disorder Prevention Partnerships

The Crime and Disorder Act 1998 requires the police and local authorities - together with police authorities, health authorities and probation committees - to work together, in partnership with other agencies, to develop and implement a strategy for reducing crime and disorder in each district and unitary local authority area. County councils are to be involved in all strategies within their area. The Act also requires local authorities to have regard to crime and disorder when considering all other matters.

Police and local authorities (and other partners) must follow a three year cycle:

- Conduct and publish an audit of local crime and disorder problems, taking into account the views of those who live and work in the area

- Determine priorities for action

- Devise and publish a strategy which tackles these priority problems, including objectives and targets

- Monitor progress, fine tuning the strategy as required

Dealing with Waste and Fly-tipping

7.14 Accumulations of rubbish and waste - including human waste, domestic and trade refuse - represent one of the most common problems associated with unauthorised encampments. Accumulations can be visually unpleasant, smelly, hazardous and costly to clear up. Preventing a build up of waste and/or removing it is a central element in a policy of pro-active management of encampments.

Preventing Waste

7.15 Local authorities have an important role in preventing accumulation of waste by ensuring that unauthorised campers keep encampments clean and tidy:

- Many authorities provide supplies of plastic sacks and arrange regular collection of bagged refuse. This can work well with unauthorised campers who want to conform to a Code of Expected Behaviour, and will reduce the costs of cleaning up after the encampment has left. Regular removal of domestic refuse should deter tipping by members of the settled community.

- Some groups of Gypsies and Travellers are willing to use skips for domestic waste. Again, provision and removal may be cost-effective if the alternative is a build-up of refuse acting as a magnet for other fly tipping by members of the settled community. Local authorities should check that skips would be used before providing them. It is good practice to seek to recover costs from the unauthorised campers.

- One of the common complaints about unauthorised encampments is of people urinating and defecating in public. Public defecation is a difficult and sensitive issue. The practice is a nuisance and a health hazard. However, Gypsies and Travellers have strict cultural codes about hygiene and consider it unclean to use toilet facilities in a caravan or to share facilities. When managing encampments local authorities should liaise with unauthorised campers. They should make plain that public defecation is not acceptable behaviour, and discuss what form of toilet provision the local authority can assist with to prevent it and any arrangements for payment for the service.

Guidance on Managing Unauthorised Camping

7.16 Regular monitoring visits to encampments should reinforce messages about keeping the site clean and tidy. Unauthorised campers need to realise that, under a pro-active approach to managing unauthorised encampments, failure to keep the site clean and tidy in breach of a Code of Expected Behaviour is likely to lead to rapid eviction. Some local authorities, which have adopted such an approach and shown a determination to encourage acceptable behaviour, have found that behaviour of unauthorised campers has improved; in some instances groups which previously left encampment sites in very poor condition are now much tidier. This is extremely cost-effective in reducing the need to spend large sums on cleaning up.

Enforcement Action

7.17 Dealing with illicit waste disposal and fly tipping is difficult - whether the culprits are Gypsy/Traveller unauthorised campers or members of the settled community. Local authorities, police and the Environment Agency all have roles to play and co-ordinated action is necessary. Gypsy/Traveller unauthorised campers should be clearly informed that everyone who produces, treats, carries or disposes of controlled waste has a 'duty of care' under s34 of the Environment Protection Act 1990. Licensed carriers should take trade waste to appropriately licensed facilities in accordance with this duty of care. Information leaflets provided to unauthorised campers should identify nearby licensed waste facilities.

7.18 Enforcement measures are available (see Box 25). Collecting sufficient evidence for successful prosecution requires - as with the measures for countering crime and ASB outlined above - determination and partnership working from the agencies involved. The case study in Box 26 shows that action can succeed.

Box 25 : Measures for Enforcing against Pollution, Littering and Fly-tipping

Water Resources Act 1991 (as amended by the Environment Act 1995) gives the Environment Agency powers to prosecute those found illegally depositing waste into controlled waters and causing a pollution offence.

Environmental Protection Act 1990 makes fly-tipping a criminal offence with a maximum penalty of a £20,000 fine and/or imprisonment up to 6 months (unlimited fine or imprisonment of up to 5 years if convicted at a Crown Court). The Government has asked the Environment Agency to vigorously prosecute any person found to be illegally disposing of waste, where they have evidence. The waste collection authority and the Environment Agency may remove fly-tipped waste and recover costs from those responsible for causing the offence. The Environment Agency has set up an emergency telephone hotline (0800 807060) for members of the public to notify them of fly tipping (and water pollution incidents). The National Fly-Tipping Prevention Group includes a number of national organisations.

Environment Protection Act 1990 (Part III) gives local authorities powers to act against statutory nuisances (prejudicial to health or a nuisance). Local authorities can serve an abatement notice, which can be appealed. Failure to comply with an abatement notice is an offence.

Anti-social Behaviour Act 2003 extends the range of powers available to local authorities for dealing with fly tipping, for instance, by giving them powers to stop, search and seize vehicles suspected of being used for fly tipping and to investigate incidents.

Guidance on Managing Unauthorised Camping

Box 26 : A Case Study of Action against Fly-tipping

Officers from the Environment Agency met officers of Leicestershire Constabulary in December 2002 to discuss a strategy for dealing with illegal tipping by Travellers near the M50/M1 interchange. On 13 January 2003, the police contacted the Environment Agency to confirm that their officers had witnessed the deposit of around 3 tonnes of soil amongst other waste on the site. The offender was unable to satisfactorily respond to accusations of illegal tipping lodged by the police and they were able to arrest him under Police and Criminal Evidence Act 1984 powers. An Agency officer assisted the police in the interview process and provided the police with specimen charges.

The offender was subsequently bailed to appear at a later date to answer the charges lodged against him. He appeared at Loughborough Magistrates' Court and pleaded guilty to one charge of depositing waste without the benefit of a waste management licence, contrary to s33 (1)(a) of the Environmental Protection Act 1990. He was fined £250 and ordered to pay £65 costs.

7.19 Regular site monitoring is essential if evidence is to be gathered for successful enforcement. Environmental health authorities, police and the Environment Agency need to work closely together. Surveillance to identify individuals responsible for fly tipping is likely to be resource-intensive. Covert surveillance is now governed by the Regulation of Investigatory Powers Act 2000; the Home Office has issued guidance on the use of CCTV in relation to both the Human Rights and Data Protection Acts.

Rapid Clear-up

7.20 Whilst the measures outlined above may help reduce the accumulation of rubbish, cleaning up will still be needed after some encampments.

- Sites should be cleared as soon as possible after they are vacated.

- Where appropriate, responsibilities must be agreed between county and district councils for site clearance so that there is no delay due to uncertainty or dispute. Joint arrangements - including some apportionment of costs - must be set out in a joint agreement or protocol specifying speed of response.

- Some refuse left may need special care in collection and disposal, including hazardous industrial waste, excreta and drug-related waste. Contractors should be warned accordingly.

Recording Information

7.21 The state of the site on departure and the clean-up cost are relevant factors to record in the encampment log. A group's previous behaviour may well inform the approach adopted if they visit the area again. If the sharing of standard information becomes more common, poor behaviour in one area may in future also inform the approach adopted in another area.

Facilitating Access to Services

7.22 It is an important objective of a pro-active approach to managing encampments that Gypsy/Traveller unauthorised campers are enabled to access health, welfare and education services during the period of their stay. It is in everyone's interests that Gypsy/Traveller children are encouraged and enabled to complete their education. Arranging access to services will be easier when unauthorised campers conform to a Code of Expected Behaviour and may be permitted to stay longer. Local authorities should facilitate access to services and act as main contact point for specialist service providers. Information from the welfare enquiries will indicate what services are required.

Guidance on Managing Unauthorised Camping

A Robust Approach to Eviction

7.23 A pro-active approach to managing unauthorised camping involves keeping encampments under review. Police and local authorities should be prepared to review eviction decisions as circumstances change since the balance of interests will change as well. While a decision to evict might not have been 'proportionate' initially, experience of disruption to the settled community, crime or anti-social behaviour may justify eviction at a later date. The fact that an encampment has been permitted to remain for a period does not preclude eviction proceedings - whether by the local authority or police using s61 - being started at a later date provided proper procedures are followed.

Keeping People Informed

7.24 As noted in Chapter 3, communications and publicity arrangements are an important element in any strategy for managing unauthorised camping. It is important that other agencies/departments, Gypsies and Travellers, elected members and members of the settled community are kept informed about what is happening and what can be expected to happen with encampments.

7.25 An agreed communications strategy between partner organisations in an area should determine which agency will lead on providing information. Normally this should be the local authority in its role as lead agency in dealing with unauthorised camping. Communications with the press and members of the public should be co-ordinated and consistent to avoid confusion. One aim of a communications strategy should be to increase understanding and tolerance between the settled and travelling communities in line with duties to promote good race relations placed on local authorities and police by the Race Relations (Amendment) Act 2000.

7.26 Gypsy/Traveller unauthorised campers should always be clearly informed about what is expected of them and what is going to happen. Information should normally be by word of mouth as well as written to avoid communication problems because of any reading difficulties. Contact and communication should be at least weekly.

7.27 Any encampment is likely to be of concern to local residents and businesses. Elected members should be regularly briefed on encampments in their wards; they can pass information on to their constituents. In addition, the local authority should provide information to local residents, and especially to complainants, using resources of the internet and e-mail where appropriate.

7.28 Special arrangements may be appropriate for large and/or high profile encampments. In addition to the measures described above, these might include:

■ Regular press briefings.

■ Well-publicised advice lines for Gypsies and Travellers and other members of the public to ring for information.

■ A special leaflet or newsletter to be distributed locally explaining background, events and plans for dealing with the encampment.

■ Links to regularly updated information through the council's web-site. Police and other agencies likely to be approached for information should include hyperlink connections to information on local authority web pages.

7.29 Such measures will obviously be costly in staff time. However, in the case of a major encampment local authorities and police will have to deal with complaints and queries anyway, and planning will make this easier. Being pro-active in this way should reduce scope for rumour and misinformation, and confusion. It could provide opportunities to manage the message to avoid unnecessarily negative coverage and reduce inter-community tension. It could also be helpful in gathering evidence for fly-tipping or other ASB which could be used in enforcement action.

Guidance on Managing Unauthorised Camping

Dealing with Mass Gatherings

7.30 Gatherings, which bring families together for a short period of time for weddings, funerals or traditional fairs and other events, are an important element of Gypsy/Traveller culture. These traditional gatherings must always be handled sensitively and with respect.

7.31 In the past few years a number of other mass gatherings of Gypsies and Travellers have occurred, when several hundred vehicles and people have met up and camped for a period, as at Great Yarmouth (December 1999) and Bournemouth (December 2001).

7.32 Mass gatherings are not spontaneous events but are to some extent planned by those taking part. The Government believes that it is not acceptable for large numbers of Gypsies and Travellers (or anyone else) to turn up in an area and cause severe disruption. The Government also recognises that there are large gatherings which are part of the Gypsy and Traveller tradition such as Appleby Fair in Cumbria.

7.33 The responsibility for managing lawful gathering should lie with the Gypsies and Travellers themselves. Gypsies and Travellers, ideally, should provide advance notice of a mass gathering, and should themselves make arrangements for water, refuse and hygiene services. At the very least, Gypsy/Traveller 'leaders' at a gathering should be prepared to negotiate with local authority and police officers and to act in a co-operative manner so as to minimise disruption.

7.34 Local authorities and police can make advance plans for dealing with such mass gatherings (including those where 'leaders' do not co-operate fully):

- It would be appropriate to include handling a major gathering and encampment of Gypsies and Travellers within the local emergency plan and local Crime and Disorder Plans.

- In emergency plans, local authorities should think ahead about how they might prepare emergency accommodation, negotiate with farmers for the use of their fields, identify supplies of portable toilets, water supply, waste disposal etc. The authority's Chief Emergency Planning Officer might become involved in preparing and co-ordinating plans.

- Close joint working between local authority personnel and police is key to managing mass gatherings. Dealing with hundreds of people and vehicles is likely to be beyond the resources of a single authority or police area. Local authorities and police have come together for joint planning at regional level in some parts of the country following recent experiences in order to be able to rapidly mobilise resources on a sufficient scale.

- Joint planning should extend to sharing information and intelligence aimed at anticipating the size and location of gatherings.

7.35 Section 14A of the Public Order Act 1986 provides for the prevention of 'trespassory assemblies', and s14 provides for the imposition of conditions on all assemblies. Section 14C of the Public Order Act 1986 creates a power for police to turn people away from trespassory assemblies when a banning order is in force. Box 27 gives more details. Acting to ban a mass gathering under these powers clearly requires close co-operation and agreement between the local police and local authority. This can only be contemplated when advance intelligence of the gathering is available sufficiently long in advance to allow the various procedures to be followed and approvals to be sought. Enforcing such a ban - if agreed by the Secretary of State - will obviously have major staffing implications.

Guidance on Managing Unauthorised Camping

Box 27 : Preventing Trespassory Assemblies

Public Order Act 1986 s14A

A public assembly is a gathering of 20 or more people on land in the open air. A Chief Police Officer may take steps to prohibit such an assembly, provided that:

- The assembly must be on land to which the public has no right of access or limited right of access **AND**

- The assembly is likely to be held without the permission of the owner/occupier of the land or to conduct itself in a way as to exceed the limits of any permission or limits the public's right of access **AND**

- May result in serious disruption to life of the community.

If these conditions are fulfilled the Chief Officer may apply to the District Council for an order preventing trespassory assemblies for a specific period. This order may only be granted with the permission of the Secretary of State for the Home Department. The order may ban assemblies for up to 4 days within a radius of 5 miles. The order may be renewed.

It is an offence to organise such an assembly knowing that it as been prohibited, or to take part knowing it has been prohibited.

Public Order Act 1986 s14C

Creates a power for police to turn people away who are travelling towards trespassory assemblies. It is operative within the area covered by the banning order. A person who fails to comply is liable to arrest.

Public Order Act 1986 s14

A senior police officer is able to impose conditions on public assemblies. The officer may impose conditions if s/he reasonably believe that the assembly may result in:

- Serious public disorder **OR**

- Serious damage to property **OR**

- Serious disruption to the life of the community.

These conditions, which must be in writing, may be in regard to location, duration and maximum numbers attending. It is an offence to knowingly organise a public assembly in breach of the conditions, or to take part knowingly. These offences carry a statutory power of arrest.

7.36 When an illegal mass gathering is anticipated and likely to go ahead, emergency plans may need to be implemented. All relevant bodies, especially local authorities and police, should be on alert. Security (24 hour) may be appropriate to protect especially vulnerable and sensitive pieces of land.

7.37 Should a mass gathering take place, enforcement action as detailed in Chapter 6 should be considered.

Box 28 : An Aide Memoire on Mass Incursions

Drawing on recent experiences of mass gatherings, the National Crime and Operations Faculty, Uniform Operational Support at Bramshill put together:

Mass Incursions : An Aide Memoire

Guidance on Managing Unauthorised Camping

8. Evaluation of the Guidance

8.1 The Office of the Deputy Prime Minister and the Home Office are committed to evaluating the impact of this Operational Guidance to check:

- the extent to which local authorities and the police have adopted the Guidance; and

- its effectiveness in bringing about improvements on the ground.

8.2 In the light of evaluation - and changing circumstances - further Guidance may be issued in future as appropriate. ODPM and the Home Office will be pleased to receive comments on the Operational Guidance and suggestions for ways in which it might be improved.

Guidance on Managing Unauthorised Camping

9. Useful References and Contacts

Various pieces of guidance have been referred to in this Operational Guidance. These are listed below, together with other useful references ordered in the relevant Chapters of the Guidance. Useful contacts are listed at the end. ALL INTERNET ADDRESSES ARE VALID AT DECEMBER 2003.

Chapter 1

Department of Environment, Transport and the Regions/Home Office (1998) Managing *Unauthorised Camping: A Good Practice Guide*, DETR; Revised Chapter 5 issued July 2000

Cowan, D, Donson, F, Higate, P, Lomax, D & Third, H (2001) *The Management of Unauthorised Camping: Monitoring the Good Practice Guide*, Research Paper 77, Edinburgh College of Art/Heriot-Watt University

Commission for Racial Equality (2003) *Gypsies and Travellers - A Strategy 2003-2006 Consultation Draft*, CRE (http://www.cre.gov.uk/downloads/docs/GandT_strat.doc)

Gypsy Sites Refurbishment Grant (GSRG) 2004/05: Bidding Guidance
(http://www.odpm.gov.uk/stellent/groups/odpm_housing/documents/page/odpm_house_025116.hcsp)

Home Office (2002) *National Policing Plan 2003-2006 (http://www.policereform.gov.uk/natpoliceplan/)*

Home Office (2003) *Respect and Responsibility (http://www.official-documents.co.uk/document/cm57/5778/5778.pdf)*

Chapter 2

Counts of Gypsy caravans are published on the ODPM website at
(http://www.odpm.gov.uk/stellent/groups/odpm_housing/documents/page/odpm_house_6025
29.xls)

Niner, P (2002) *The Provision and Condition of Local Authority Gypsy/Traveller Sites in England*, ODPM
(http://www.odpm.gov.uk/stellent/groups/odpm_housing/documents/page/odpm_house_602542.hcsp)

Niner, P (2003) *Local Authority Gypsy/Traveller Sites in England*, ODPM
(http://www.odpm.gov.uk/stellent/groups/odpm_housing/documents/page/odpm_house_023012.pdf)

Chapter 3

Derbyshire Gypsy Liaison Group (1998) *Moving Base*, DGLG

Hopkinson, G, Ingram, M & Wishart, B (undated) *Where's the Real Choice? What are the accommodation needs of Travellers in Wychavon?* Evesham & Pershore Housing Association

Southwark Housing (2000) *Needs of the Traveller Community in Southwark*, LB Southwark

Morris, R & Clements, L (2002) *At what cost? The economics of Gypsy and Traveller encampments*, The Policy Press

Local e-Government Strategy (http://www.localegov.gov.uk/Nimoi/sites/ODMP/resources/20021127 Final NS with cover.pdf)

Commission for Racial Equality (2000) *Guidance for Journalists: Travellers, Gypsies and the Media*, CRE (http://www.cre.gov.uk/media/guidetj.html)

DETR (2001) *Local strategic partnerships - Government guidance*
(http://www.neighbourhood.gov.uk/formatteddoc.asp?id=95)

Guidance on Managing Unauthorised Camping

LGA (2002) *Guidance on Community Cohesion*
(http://www.homeoffice.gov.uk/docs/cc_guidance.pdf)

DETR (2001) *Supporting People: policy into practice,* see http://www.spkweb.org.uk

Children and Young People's Strategic Partnerships (within Local Strategic Partnerships)

Sure Start, see http://www.surestart.gov.uk

Connexions, see http://www.connexions.gov.uk

Home Office (1999) Guidance on Statutory Crime and Disorder Partnerships, see
http://www.homeoffice.gov.uk/docs/partcont.html

Race Equality Schemes, see http://www.cre.gov.uk/duty/duty_schemes.html

Department of Transport, Local Government and the Regions (2002) *Homelessness Strategies: A
Good Practice Handbook*, DTLR
(http://www.odpm.gov.uk/stellent/groups/odpm_homelessness/documents/pdf/odpm_home_pdf_6015
17.pdf)

Chapter 4

DoE Circular 1/94: *Gypsy Sites and Planning*, January 1994 (see Annex B)

Planning Policy Guidance 3 *Housing*, ODPM
(http://www.odpm.gov.uk/stellent/groups/odpm_planning/documents/pdf/odpm_plan_pdf_606933.pd
f)

Planning Policy Guidance 12 Development *Plans*, ODPM
(http://www.odpm.gov.uk/stellent/groups/odpm_planning/documents/pdf/odpm_plan_pdf_606929.pd
f)

Chapter 5

Web-site of the Information Commissioner's - http://www.informationcommissioner.gov.uk

Chapter 6

Fuller v Chief Constable of Dorset, [2001] EWHC Admin 1057

Home Office Circular 45/1994

R v The Commissioner of the Metropolis ex parte Small (not reported)

Department of Environment, Transport and the Regions/Home Office (1998) *Managing
Unauthorised Camping: A Good Practice Guide*, DETR; Revised Chapter 5 issued July 2000

DTLR, the Court Service and the Welsh Assembly: *Getting the best out of the court system: Claims
for possession (http://www.courtservice.gov.uk/cms/media/best_court_system.pdf)*

Planning Policy Guidance 18 *Enforcing Planning Control* 1991
(http://www.odpm.gov.uk/stellent/groups/odpm_planning/documents/page/odpm_plan_606903.pdf)

DoE Circular 10/97 *Enforcing Planning Control: Legislative provisions and Procedural
Requirements
(http://www.odpm.gov.uk/stellent/groups/odpm_planning/documents/pdf/odpm_plan_pdf_606834.pdf)*

DoE *Enforcing Planning Control: Good Practice for Local Planning Authorities*, 1997

Chapter 7

Guidance on Managing Unauthorised Camping

Home Office (2003) *Respect and Responsibility (http://www.official-documents.co.uk/document/cm57/5778/5778.pdf)*

Home Office (2002) *A Guide to Anti-Social Behaviour Orders and Acceptable Behaviour Contracts (http://www.crimereduction.gov.uk/asbos9.pdf)*

Environment Protection Act 1990 s34, *Waste Management: The Duty of Care: A Code of Practice (http://www.defra.gov.uk/environment/waste/management/doc/pdf/waste_man_duty_code.pdf)*

Fly Tipping Stakeholders Forum, *Fly Tipping Guidance (http://www.environment-agency.gov.uk/commondata/105385/flytip.PDF)*

Home Office (2001) CCTV: *Implications for Public Space Surveillance in the Light of the Data Protection Act 1998* see http:// www.crimereduction.gov.uk/cctv7.htm

Home Office (2001) *CCTV and the Human Rights Act*, see http:// www.crimereduction.gov.uk/cctv13.htm

Mass Incursions: An Aide Memoire Contact: National Crime and Operations Faculty, Uniformed Operational Support, Bramshill (01256 602777)

Useful Contacts

Gypsy/Traveller bodies and support groups

Advisory Council for the Education of Romany and Other Travellers (ACERT)

Moot House, The Stow, Harlow, Essex CM20 3AG

01279 418666

Gypsy Council

(President: Hughie Smith) Spring Lanes Caravan Park, Bickerton, Nr Wetherby, North Yorks LS22 5ND

01937 842782

Gypsy Council for Education, Culture, Welfare and Civil Rights

(Chairman: Charles Smith)

8 Hall Road, Aveley, Romford, Essex RM15 4HD

01708 868986

Irish Traveller Movement in Britain

The Old Library Building, Willesden Green Library Centre, 95 High Road, Willesden, London NW10 2ST

020 8459 7638

London Gypsy and Traveller Unit

6 Westgate Street, London E8 3RN

020 8533 2002

Derbyshire Gypsy Liaison Group

Ernest Bailey Community Centre, New Street, Matlock, Derbyshire DE4 3FE

01629 583300

Guidance on Managing Unauthorised Camping

Friends, Families and Travellers

Community Base, 113 Queens Road, Brighton, East Sussex BN1 3XG

01273 234777

Community Law Partnership

Ruskin Chambers, 191 Corporation Street, Birmingham, West Midlands B4 6RP

0121 685 8595

Travellers' Times

The Rural Media Company, Sullivan House, 72080 Widemarsh Street, Hereford HR4 9HG

01432 344039

Central Government

ODPM

Gypsy and Traveller Branch , Eland House, Bressenden Place, London SW1E 5DU

020 7944 4400

Home Office

Crime Reduction and Community Safety Group, 50 Queen Annes Gate, London SW1H 9AT

0800 000 1585

Department for Education and Skills

Ethnic Minority Achievement Unit, Sanctuary Building, Great Smith Street, London SW1P 3BT

0870 000 2288

Department of Health

Primary Care Access, Quarry House, Quarry Hill, Leeds LS2 7UE

020 7210 4850

Other bodies

Commission for Racial Equality

St Dunstan's House, 201-211 Borough High Street, London SE1 1GZ

020 7939 0000

Local Government Association

Local Government House, Smith Square, London SW1P 3HZ

020 7644 3000

National Association of Gypsy and Traveller Officers

c/o George Summers, Estates Practice Department, Hampshire County Council, The Castle, Winchester, Hampshire SO23 9DS

01962 847315

National Association of Health Workers with Travellers

Guidance on Managing Unauthorised Camping

(Chair : Sarah Rhodes) Travellers Health Project, Central Health Clinic, Tower Hill, Bristol BS2 0JD

0117 922 7570

National Association of Teachers of Travellers

c/o Lucy Beckett, Advisory Service for the Education of Travellers, Room L25, Cricket Road Centre, Cricket Road, Oxford OX4 3DW

01865 428089

Annex A: DoE Circular 18/94

A: DoE Circular 18/94: Gypsy Sites Policy and Unauthorised Camping + Revision of Advice on 'Toleration' issued 26 July 2000

Annex B: DoE Circular 1/94

B: DoE Circular 1/94: Gypsy Sites and Planning

Annex C: Summary Points from Research Monitoring the Good Practice Guide on Managing Unauthorised Camping

In 2001 the results of research monitoring the impact of the DETR/Home Office Good Practice Guide were published[1]. The research was carried out by Edinburgh College of Art/Heriot-Watt University in conjunction with the Universities of Bristol and Cardiff. It involved a telephone survey of 263 local authorities which explored the pattern of unauthorised camping. Some of the main findings relating to unauthorised camping are:

Unauthorised camping is a widespread phenomenon - 92% of responding local authorities had experience of it in the twelve months before the survey.

The average number of reported incidents of unauthorised camping in the past year was 22, although this varied widely and almost half of authorities reported ten incidents or fewer. A separate incident could be the same Gypsy/Traveller group moving onto different sites in the area. The speed with which an encampment is moved on is one factor in the number of separate incidents experienced.

The average number of different locations in an authority area subject to unauthorised camping in the last year was 13, again with wide variation.

Unauthorised camps involving 20 caravans and more were far less common than camps involving a dozen caravans or fewer. Only 8% of responding local authorities had experienced an encampment of 50 or more caravans in the past year.

Local authority respondents said that most encampments were small scale and relatively unproblematic while a minority were extremely high profile and associated with crime, damage, dumping and other anti-social behaviour.

Irish Travellers were most often reported as having camped on unauthorised sites in the past year (70% of authorities), followed by Gypsy Travellers (58%) and New Travellers (23%).

The most common sites for unauthorised encampments were vacant or derelict land, industrial estates, car parks and roadsides or verges. Other types of sites, for example, parks and recreation areas, green lanes and bye-ways, farm land and wooded areas were used less often.

The three main factors influencing unauthorised camping were seasonal travelling, work opportunities and visiting other Gypsies and Travellers in the area.

Local authorities' experiences of changes over the past five years were mixed, with no clear trends emerging in terms of frequency of unauthorised camping, number of locations used, use of authorised sites or number of caravans in the groups.

---

[1] Cowan, D, Donson, F, Higate, P, Lomax, D & Third, H (2001) *The Management of Unauthorised Camping: Monitoring the Good Practice Guide,* Research Paper 77, Edinburgh College of Art/Heriot-Watt University

Annex D: A Summary of the Legislative Framework

This annex summarises the main legislative framework relevant to a strategy for managing unauthorised camping. Most of the provisions are described in greater detail in the text of the Guidance. Exceptionally, human rights and race relations responsibilities which are referred at various points in the text are set out in more detail below.

Site Provision

- The Caravan Sites and Control of Development Act 1960 s24 gives local authorities discretionary powers to provide caravan sites.

- While there is no duty on local authorities to provide Gypsy sites, DoE Circular 18/94 makes clear that authorities should maintain their existing Gypsy caravan sites, and should continue to consider whether it is appropriate to provide further permanent caravan sites for Gypsies in their areas.

- Government is currently reviewing policy on Gypsy site provision. Gypsy Sites Refurbishment Grant makes limited funding available for provision of transit and emergency stopping places.

- Private site provision is governed by planning legislation. DoE Circular 1/94 sets out the Government's policy on Gypsy site provision and urges local planning authorities to consider, and to look favourably, at applications for Gypsy sites in development planning and development control.

Dealing with Unauthorised Encampments

- There is no specific legislative duty placed on local authorities to deal with unauthorised encampments by Gypsies and Travellers.

- Local authorities can take action as landowners through civil actions against trespass using Civil Procedure Rules Part 55, heard in a County Court.

- Local authorities have powers given by the Criminal Justice and Public Order 1994 ss77 and 78 (see Chapter 6). These require cases to be brought in the Magistrates' Court.

- Common law rights to recover land from trespassers are also available to local authorities over land they occupy. Authorities are, however, advised not to use such powers unless there is exceptional justification for doing so and, for example, the police are unable to use their powers under s61 of the CJPOA (see 6.5 above).

- DoE Circular 18/94 provides guidance to local authorities on the exercise of s77 powers, and reminds them of their other duties towards Travellers in terms of education, children and homelessness legislation.

- Case law (starting with the judgement of Sedley J in *R v Wealden District Council ex parte Wales*) has developed and clarified the courts' expectations of the welfare enquiries and decision-making processes local authorities should adopt in making evictions under 1994 Act and other powers.

- Where Travellers camp on land which they own or on other private land with the consent of the landowner, district councils may take planning enforcement action, or prosecute for running a caravan site without a site licence.

- The Police have parallel powers granted by s61 of the CJPOA (see Chapter 6). Action under s61 is normally much quicker than under s77, and the welfare considerations less onerous although there are certain conditions in the legislation which have to be fulfilled before eviction can take place.

Guidance on Managing Unauthorised Camping

- The Anti-social Behaviour Act 2003 added new ss61A and 62A into the CJPOA which give police enhanced eviction powers in circumstances where there are suitable pitches on relevant Gypsy sites to accommodate the caravans affected. These sections come into force on 27 February 2004 and guidance as to their operation will be issued.

Other Enforcement Measures

- District authorities have powers to deal with statutory nuisance (which could include, for example, rubbish accumulation at unauthorised encampments) and noise (see Chapter 7 of this Guide).

- The Crime and Disorder Act 1998 places a duty on chief police officers and local authorities to work together to develop and implement a strategy for reducing crime and disorder. Section 17 imposes a duty on all local authorities (and others) to *'without prejudice to any other obligation imposed upon it . . . exercise its functions with due regard to . . . the need to do all it reasonably can to prevent crime and disorder in its area'.*

Service Provision for Gypsies and Travellers

- Gypsies and Travellers are entitled to access health, housing, education and welfare services as citizens in the same way as members of the settled community.

- There is specific recognition of the needs of Traveller children in accessing education, with a Traveller Grant payable under s488 of the Education Act 1996.

Human Rights

The Human Rights Act 1998 incorporates the European Convention on Human Rights into British law. Several Convention rights are relevant in dealing with unauthorised camping. The main relevant rights are:

Article 8: Right to respect for private and family life

1. Everyone has the right to respect for his private and family life, his home and his correspondence.

2. There shall be no interference by a public authority with the exercise of this right except such as is in accordance with the law and is necessary in a democratic society in the interests of national security, public safety or the economic well-being of the country, for the prevention of disorder or crime, for the protection of health or morals, or for the protection of the rights and freedoms of others.

Case law has established that, while neither eviction action against trespassers nor planning enforcement is incompatible with HRA, either could potentially breach Article 8 rights if not properly used. Authorities, and other public bodies covered by the HRA, must be able to demonstrate that all eviction and enforcement decisions are 'proportionate' in weighing individual harm (in the loss of 'home' for the Gypsy or Traveller) against the wider public interest. Potential challenge under the HRA means that all decision-making must be fully recorded and evidenced to withstand scrutiny.

First Protocol, Article 1: Protection of property

Every natural and legal person is entitled to the peaceful enjoyment of his possessions. No-one shall be deprived of his possessions except in the public interest and subject to the conditions provided for by law and by the general principles of international law.

The preceding provisions shall not, however, in any way impair the right of a State to enforce such laws as it deems necessary to control the use of property in accordance with the general interest or to secure the payment of taxes or other contributions or penalties.

Guidance on Managing Unauthorised Camping

This Article might be seen as protecting the settled community's right to quiet enjoyment of their possessions, which might be threatened by nuisance, noise or anti-social behaviour from a problematic unauthorised encampment. This should be one of the considerations to be borne in mind by local authorities and police when considering eviction action. To date there is no relevant case law.

First Protocol, Article 2: Right to education

> No person shall be denied the right to education. In the exercise of any functions which it assumes in relation to education and to teaching, the State shall respect the right of parents to ensure such education and teaching in conformity with their own religious and philosophical convictions.

Education of Gypsy/Traveller children is frequently raised in cases dealing with eviction proceedings, and particularly with planning enforcement actions against unauthorised development. In such cases the question resolves itself to one of the balance between the individual harm to Gypsy/Traveller childrens' educational needs and the public interest harm in allowing unauthorised development to persist. To date there is no specific case law on arguments relying on this Article in this context.

Article 14: Prohibition of discrimination

> The enjoyment of the rights and freedoms set forth in this Convention shall be secured without discrimination on any ground such as sex, race, colour, language, religion, political or other opinion, national or social origin, association with a national minority, property birth or other status.

While Article 14 rights are potentially engaged in any action concerning Gypsies and Travellers (as ethnic groups and national minorities), the Article can only be successfully argued if another Article is found to be breached. Where a claim under any Article is rejected, it follows that any claim under Article 14 also falls.

Race Relations and Equalities

The Race Relations Act 1976 as amended by the Race Relations (Amendment) Act 2000 gives public authorities - including ODPM, the Home Office, local authorities and the police - a general duty to eliminate unlawful discrimination, and to promote equality of opportunity and good race relations in carrying out their functions. It also gives listed public bodies specific duties including one to create and publish a Race Equality Scheme which details how they will meet the general duty. In developing new policies or strategies public authorities must assess their impact on different racial groups, and they must consult. If the impact is negative and disproportionate to the aim of the policy, it must be changed. Once implemented, policies must be monitored for their effect on different racial groups. Authorities must publish the results of monitoring and consultation.

Both Gypsies and Irish Travellers are recognised as ethnic minorities. Policies for managing unauthorised camping are likely to affect Gypsies and Travellers significantly. The RRA means that local authorities and police must assess the impact of proposed policies on Gypsies and Irish Travellers and must consult on them. If the policies are likely to have a disproportionately negative impact on Gypsies and Irish Travellers, authorities must ensure that this impact is not disproportionate to the aims and importance of the policies. If it is, it is important to take measures to reduce this adverse impact or consider other ways to achieve the aims, which would mitigate its negative effect.

Since eviction of unauthorised campers and enforcement against unauthorised development are likely to have a large effect on the public, and in particular on the Gypsy/Traveller population, they are functions highly relevant to the RRA general duty and should be prioritised in Race Equality Schemes. When evicting and enforcing, authorities need to ensure that they act in a way which meets the three elements of the general duty and so as to have the minimum negative impact on the Gypsies and Travellers involved.

Guidance on Managing Unauthorised Camping

Local authorities and police must always be able to show that they have properly considered the race and equalities implications of their policies and actions in relation to unauthorised encampments and unauthorised development by Gypsies and Irish Travellers. They must be able to demonstrate that their polices and actions are proportionate bearing in mind all the circumstances of the case.

Guidance on Managing Unauthorised Camping

Annex E: Interests to be involved in the Development of a Strategy for Unauthorised Camping

Organisation/party	Main topics of interest	Possible means of involvement
Local authorities **NB** In two-tier areas both county and district councils will be involved	Planning and information; race relations; site provision and land use planning; site protection; housing and homelessness; Traveller education; social services; refuse collection; unauthorised camping; communication and public relations	Lead development of Strategy development; key personnel involved in working groups or committees; others in ad hoc groupings and/or written consultation
Local politicians, councillors and MPs	All aspects including unauthorised encampment	Leadership and engendering support for the Strategy
Local Health Authority	Gypsy/Traveller health in all forms of accommodation and on unauthorised encampments; welfare assessments	Nominated officer to be consulted as Strategy develops; continuing involvement in implementation
Neighbouring local authorities	All aspects to inform own Strategies	Joint planning and shared working could be efficient and lead to a sub-regional approach
Police	Planning and information; race equality; dealing with crime, anti-social behaviour and threats to public order from unauthorised encampments; communication and public relations	Key player in developing the Strategy; continuing role in its implementation
Gypsies and Travellers	All aspects including needs assessment; service delivery; advice on site provision and unauthorised camping	Through national, regional or local representative bodies; consultation with local Gypsies and Travellers on their needs and aspirations. Written material, conferences and individual personal contact
Gypsy/Traveller support groups and advisors	Potentially all aspects including unauthorised encampment	Local contact, conferences, consultation through written media

Guidance on Managing Unauthorised Camping

Parish and town councils	Site provision and land use planning; site protection; unauthorised camping; and communications and public relations	Consultation on perceived issues, priorities and ideas; consultation on draft and final Strategy. Written material and conferences
Settled community	Especially site planning and land use planning; site protection; and unauthorised camping	Consultation on perceived issues, priorities and ideas; consultation on draft and final Strategy. Written material and feedback arrangements. Citizen jury?
Private landowners	Unauthorised camping	Consult on perceived problems and constraints and to agree respective roles in acting on unauthorised encampments
Crime & Disorder Reduction Partnership, Local Strategic Partnerships	Dependent on nature of partnership	Exchange information and consultation to ensure consistency and shared priorities
Highways Agency	Unauthorised camping	Consult to agree respective roles in acting on unauthorised encampments
Environment Agency	Fly tipping and pollution associated with unauthorised encampments	Consult to agree respective roles in acting on unauthorised encampments
Forestry Commission	Major land owner in some areas which may be affected by unauthorised camping	Consult to agree respective roles in acting on unauthorised encampments
English Nature	Unauthorised camping as it affects Sites of Special Scientific Interest	Consult to identify key areas and agree respective roles in acting on unauthorised encampments
National Trust	Major land owner in some areas which may be affected by unauthorised camping	Consult to agree respective roles in acting on unauthorised encampments
Ministry of Defence	Major land owner in some areas which may be affected by unauthorised camping	Consult to agree respective roles in acting on unauthorised encampments
Local press and other media	All aspects of the Strategy; especially site provision and unauthorised camping	Regular media briefings and invitations to all public events to ensure full appreciation of the issues and to encourage balanced coverage

SUPPLEMENT TO 'MANAGING UNAUTHORISED CAMPING: A GOOD PRACTICE GUIDE' (ODPM/HOME OFFICE 2005)

Introduction

The Unauthorised Camping Guidance was originally published on the ODPM and Home Office websites in February 2004. It was intended to be updated when consultation on the new provisions introduced in the Anti-social Behaviour Act 2003 (amending the Criminal Justice and Public Order Act 1994) was complete. This consultation has now ended, and guidance on those provisions appears below.

Guidance will also be issued on the management of unauthorised developments, including the use of planning enforcement powers by local authorities. As there are many common issues relating to the management of unauthorised developments and unauthorised encampments, guidance on both types of unauthorised sites will be incorporated into a single document, which will be published in hard copy when complete.

S62A to S62E of the Criminal Justice and Public Order Act 1994

Sections 60 to 64 of the Anti-social Behaviour Act 2003 insert sections 62A to 62E into the Criminal Justice and Public Order Act 1994 (CJPOA).

The legislation provides the police with a power to direct trespassers to leave land and to remove any vehicles and other property from the land, where there is a *suitable pitch* available on a *relevant caravan site* elsewhere in the local authority area. Where a direction has been given to a person it is an offence for that person to fail to leave the land as soon as reasonably practicable or to enter any land in the local authority area as a trespasser within 3 months of the direction being given.

Power to remove trespassers where an alternative site is available

Under Section 62A, the senior police officer present may direct trespassers to remove themselves and their vehicles and property from land where a *suitable pitch* on a caravan site is available within the same local authority area.

The power may be used where:

• at least two persons are trespassing;
• the trespassers have between them at least one vehicle;
• the trespassers are present on the land with the common purpose of residing there for any period;
• it appears to the officer that the person has one or more caravans in his possession or under his control on the land, and that there is a *suitable pitch* on a *relevant caravan site* for that caravan or each of those caravans;
• the occupier of the land (ie the freehold owner or lessee), or a person acting on the occupier's behalf has asked the police to remove the trespassers from the land.

A *relevant caravan site* is one which is situated in the same local authority area as the land on which the trespass has occurred, and which is managed by a local authority, registered social landlord, or other person or body as specified by order by the Secretary of State. In two tier authority areas, where a district council is situated within a wider county council area, the *relevant caravan site* may be anywhere within the county council area.

The meaning of *suitable pitch* is not defined in the legislation. Of course, it is for the courts to interpret legislation, but the Secretary of State considers that a *suitable pitch* is one that provides basic amenities including water, toilets and waste disposal facilities. Other factors include the potential for community tension and issues of public order/anti-social behaviour need to be considered especially where the Trespasser intends to remain on the site for the 3 month period. This could include an authorised transit site or stopping place. There should be a reasonable expectation that the pitch will be available for peaceful occupation for at least three months, except where the trespasser is expecting to move on before that time.

In determining whether a *suitable pitch* is available, the police officer must consult the local authority within whose area the land is situated. In two tier authority areas, where a district council is situated within a wider county council area, the *suitable pitch* may be anywhere within the county council area. A suitable pitch will only be available if there are currently no waiting lists for that site.

Local authorities and the police are both public authorities bound by the Human Rights Act 1998, and it is unlawful for a public authority to act in a way which is incompatible with a Convention right. In advising on whether a *suitable pitch* is available, the local authority should take account of the results of welfare enquiries undertaken at the encampment, which may give rise to human rights issues. In particular, efforts should be made to find *suitable pitches* that would enable the unauthorised campers to remain together. If the size of the encampment is such that this is not possible, then efforts should be made to ensure that any dependent members of the encampment are not separated from necessary support. For example, every effort should be made to keep together parents and dependant children, or adults supporting elderly or infirm relatives.

Where the senior police officer present at the scene reasonably believes that these conditions are satisfied in relation to a person and land then he may direct the person:

- to leave the land (including roads or the roadside);
- to remove any vehicle and other property he has with him on the land.

The direction may be communicated to the person to whom it applies by any constable at the scene.

Failure to comply with a direction: offences

Under Section 62B, a person commits an offence if he knows a direction has been given which applies to him and:

- he fails to leave the land as soon as reasonably practicable; or
- he enters any land in the area of a *relevant local authority*, as a trespasser, within 3 months of the direction being given with the intention of residing there.

Where the land in respect of which the direction was given is situated in the area of more than one local authority, that is, which is situated within the area of a district council, but which is also within the area of a county council, then an offence is only committed if further trespass occurs in the area of the district council (which is the *relevant local authority*) where the original trespass occurred.

A person guilty of an offence is liable to imprisonment for up to 3 months or a fine not exceeding level 4 on the standard scale (currently £2,500) or both.

A constable in uniform who reasonably suspects that a person is committing this offence may arrest him without a warrant.

In proceedings relating to such an offence, it is a defence to show:

(1) that the person was not trespassing on the land; or
(2) that the person had a reasonable excuse:
   - for failing to leave the land as soon as reasonably practicable; or
   - for entering land in the *relevant local authority* area as a trespasser with the intention of residing there; or
(3) that, at the time the direction was given, the person was under the age of 18 years and was residing with his parent or guardian.

'Reasonable excuse' may mean illness/injury to a member of the group or vehicle failure etc which prevents them moving off but it would be a decision for the officer at the scene to establish whether this was indeed a 'reasonable excuse' in the circumstances.

Failure to comply with direction: seizure

Under Section 62C, a constable may seize and remove a vehicle from the land.

This power may be exercised where a direction under section 62A has been given and the constable reasonably suspects that a person to whom the direction applies has, without reasonable excuse:

- failed to remove the vehicle on the land which appears to the constable to belong to him or to be in his possession or under his control; or
- entered any land in the area of the *relevant local authority* as a trespasser with a vehicle within 3 months of the direction being given, with the intention of residing there.

(Where the land lies in more than one local authority, that is, in a district council within a county council's area, then the power of seizure only relates to the area of the district council (the *relevant local authority*) where the original trespass occurred.

Under these new powers the term 'vehicle' means the same that is applied to section 61 of the Criminal Justice and Public Order Act 1994, to cover:

(a) any vehicle, whether or not it is in a fit state for use on roads, and includes any chassis or body, with or without wheels, appearing to have formed part of such a vehicle, and any load carried by, and anything attached to, such a vehicle, and

(b) a caravan as defined in section 29(1) of the Caravan Sites and Control Development Act 1960;

S62A to S62E – practical implementation

Role of the occupier

Before the police can act, the occupier of the land, or person acting on his behalf, must ask the police to remove the trespassers from the land.

Before contacting the police, occupiers or their agents are advised to check that the following conditions apply:

- there are two or more persons trespassing on the land;
- they have between them at least one vehicle on the land;
- and they are intending to reside on the land for any period.

It is often the case that talking to the unauthorised campers can lead to an agreement that they will leave shortly and no further action may be necessary.

Where the occupier or person acting on his behalf considers that the above conditions apply, and believes the unauthorised campers intend to remain, he may ask the police to remove them from the land.

Where the occupier is a public body

Where the occupier of the land is a public body (such as a local authority or the Highway Agency), then every effort should be made to avert forced eviction.

In cases where the trespassers are members of an ethnic minority, such as Romany Gypsies or Irish Travellers, public bodies are required under the Race Relations Acts to have due regard to the need (among other matters) to promote good race relations in their dealings, including managing an unauthorised encampment.

Those on an encampment should be treated with the same courtesy and respect as would be extended to members of the settled community, and officials should be sensitive to different cultural perspectives.

Before police are asked to give a direction under S62A, local authorities and other public bodies should have undertaken the welfare enquiries set out in Chapter 5 of the Guidance on Managing Unauthorised Encampments.

Where eviction is considered to be the only option, and the public body believes the conditions required for S62A to S62E of the CJOPA are satisfied, and the local authority has confirmed that a *suitable pitch* is available, then the public body may ask the police to remove the unauthorised campers from the land.

GUIDE TO EFFECTIVE USE OF ENFORCEMENT POWERS

PART 1: UNAUTHORISED ENCAMPMENTS (ODPM, 2006)

Introduction

1   Some parts of the country experience regular unauthorised encampments, which can cause disruption and conflict locally, and can be expensive and time-consuming to clear. The Government's policies on Gypsy and Traveller accommodation and enforcement are set within a framework of rights and responsibilities in which everyone's rights must be equally respected but where, at the same time, equal standards of behaviour are expected from all. Creating and sustaining strong communities is at the heart of the Government's Respect agenda and will have benefits for the settled and Gypsy and Traveller communities alike.

2   Unauthorised camping is a problem which requires a range of solutions. The Government has already introduced new housing and planning policies to ensure that in the future the accommodation needs of Gypsies and Travellers will be properly understood and properly addressed, part of which is a new obligation on local authorities to identify suitable locations in their areas that can be used for the establishment of new public and private Gypsy and Traveller sites. In the meantime the Government is working with the Gypsy and Traveller community to find pragmatic local solutions to accommodation shortages while the longer-term policies take effect.

3   But part of the solution also lies in swift and effective enforcement. Where problematic encampments are allowed to remain, or repeatedly return, community hostility and conflict will be inflamed, and a sustainable long-term solution will become much harder to achieve. Effective enforcement will promote confidence in the ability of local agencies to manage Gypsy and Traveller issues properly, and forms an essential backdrop to the provision of more authorised sites. Local people need to know that they and their local environment can be and will be protected.

4   Strong powers are available to the police, local authorities and other landowners to deal with unauthorised encampments. This document provides a detailed step-by-step practical guide to the use of these powers.

5   It also sets out advice on:
   • Choosing the most appropriate power.
   • Speeding up the process.
   • Keeping costs down.
   • The eviction process.
   • Preventing further unauthorised camping.

6   This document is intended for elected officials and others in the community who have an interest in how unauthorised camping by Gypsies and Travellers is managed in their area, and provides information to local authority officers and other landowners on options for dealing with such incidents.

7   This guidance explains the ways in which enforcement action can be made quicker, cheaper and more effective. Local authorities should also be aware that the wider policy they adopt towards Gypsy and Traveller issues will also make a great deal of difference. Enforcement action can be taken more swiftly, and can be more effective, where appropriate authorised provision for Gypsies and Travellers is in place within a local authority's area.

8   The use of joint protocols between the local authority, the police and any other relevant agencies is also highly effective in establishing how individual cases will be dealt with, and making sure that all parties are clear about their responsibilities and how they will work together.

9   Local authorities have an obligation to carry out welfare assessments on unauthorised campers to identify any welfare issues that need to be addressed, before taking enforcement action against them. Where police are taking enforcement action, it is good practice for them to liaise with the local authority over any welfare issues. It is also good practice for local authority officers to be present at any eviction from public land, to ensure that any welfare issues that arise at that time can be dealt with appropriately.

10   The Government is also establishing a new Task Group which draws together central and local Government, the police and other agencies to address the wide variations in the use of enforcement powers and to champion best practice. The group will act as expert advisers to the Office of the Deputy Prime Minister (ODPM) and the Home Office, who are working together to consider potential new measures to further strengthen enforcement, alongside the provision of more authorised sites.

11   Information on the Government's wider policies concerning Gypsies and Travellers, *Local authorities and Gypsies and Travellers – guide to responsibilities and powers*, can be found on the ODPM website at the following address: www.odpm.gov.uk/gypsysites

12   The information contained in this document should be read in conjunction with the joint ODPM/Home Office document, *Guidance on Managing Unauthorised Camping* and its supplementary document on Section 62A-E police powers. This gives more detailed advice on a range of matters, including toleration, joint working protocols and obligations on local authorities and other public agencies in respect of welfare enquiries.

13   Further documents will follow in this series which will provide guidance on dealing with unauthorised developments of land without planning permission, and anti-social behaviour, including fly-tipping.

Unauthorised encampment – the powers in summary
Common law powers
- can only be used by the landowner;
- are used to regain possession of land;
- does not require the involvement of the courts;
- enforced by the landowner and/or private bailiffs where necessary;
- does not provide any sanctions offence for the return of trespassers onto land.

Part 55 Civil Procedure Rules
- can only be used by the landowner;
- are used to regain possession of land;
- require civil court procedure;
- possession is enforced by county court bailiffs, where necessary;
- do not provide any sanctions for the return of trespassers onto land.

Sections 77-78 of the Criminal Justice and Public Order Act 1994
- can only be used by a local authority;
- can be used on any land within the local authority's area, irrespective of ownership;
- are used to remove identified individuals from land;
- only require the involvement of the courts when unauthorised campers do not leave when directed to do so;
- possession is enforced by local authority officers or private bailiffs employed by the local authority;
- the return of unauthorised campers and/or their vehicles to the location within three months carries criminal sanctions.

Sections 61-62 of the Criminal Justice and Public Order Act 1994
- can only be used by the police;
- can be used on any land except the highway;
- are used to remove identified individuals and/or their vehicles from land;
- there must be two or more persons trespassing on the land before the power can be used;
- do not require the involvement of the courts;
- possession is enforced by the police;
- the return of unauthorised campers to the location within three months carries criminal sanctions.

Section 62A-E of the Criminal Justice and Public Order Act 1994
- can only be used where an alternative site is available;
- can only be used by the police;
- can be used on any land;
- is used to remove identified individuals and/or their vehicles from the land;

- does not require the involvement of the courts;
- possession is enforced by the police;
- the return of unauthorised campers to the local authority area within three months carries criminal sanctions.

Unauthorised encampment – the powers in detail

Common law powers

14 All landowners can use their common law rights to recover land (ie, the tort of trespass against property). This allows the person in possession of land to evict an individual from their land, seek damages for their trespass on their land, and/or seek an injunction to prevent the trespass from occurring again.

15 Case law has established that a trespasser who enters land peaceably is entitled to a request to leave the land before being forcibly removed, while a trespasser who has entered land with force and violence may be removed without a previous request to depart.

16 If the trespasser does not leave the land the possessor of the land may use no more force than is reasonably necessary to evict him or her. Private bailiffs may be used to carry out the eviction. The issue of what is 'reasonable force' is a question of fact to be decided in beach individual case, however it must be an honestly held belief that in the particular circumstances the force that is used is reasonable, rather than excessive. Use of excessive force could give rise to a claim against the landowner by the trespassers.

17 Whenever a landowner is considering the use of common law rights he/she should notify the police of his/her intentions so that police officers can be present to prevent any breach of the peace.

18 If the police advise that, in the particular circumstances, it is inappropriate to attempt an eviction, action should always be delayed until such time as the police believe that it is safe to continue.

19 Parliament provides strong statutory powers to local authorities to enable them to deal with incidents of unauthorised camping under Section 77 of the Criminal Justice and Public Order Act 1994. The civil courts also offer an avenue to deal with unauthorised camping under Civil Procedures Rules Part 55.

Part 55 Civil Procedure Rules

20 Part 55 of Civil Procedure Rules allow any landowner to regain possession of his/her land. Where the land is leased, the terms of the lease will determine who has this power – longlessees and many short-lessees will be responsible for evictions, where they are 'person entitled to occupation of the land'. Someone with only the right, or permission, to use the land (ie, who does not have a controlling interest in it, for instance someone with the right to graze livestock) would not generally be able to recover possession of the land in this way if it is trespassed upon.

21 The first step is for the landowner to ask the trespassers to leave the land. If they refuse to do so, or ask to be allowed to remain for what the landowner considers to be an unacceptable time period, the landowner can then begin action against the unauthorised campers through the County Court.

22   If the objective is to achieve eviction as rapidly as possible, the landowner should alert the County Court to the need for expediting the case as soon as they are aware of the encampment's arrival.

23   The landowner completes the relevant documentation, including any evidence in relation to the encampment (photographs, witness statements and so on) and presents this to the court manager in the County Court. A date for a hearing is then agreed.

24   The Court then provides the landowner with the claim form to serve on the defendants (the papers can be issued to 'persons unknown' if it is not possible to ascertain the identities of the unauthorised campers). Service of the claim form can then be made by the landowner or his appointed representative (process servers can be employed to carry this out) either by handing the claim to the unauthorised campers directly, or by posting the claim in a prominent position on the land if this is not possible.

25   At the hearing, the facts of the case are set out before the judge. The landowner should provide documentation which satisfies the judge that the landowner has a legitimate interest in the land. The judge will be concerned to establish that the unauthorised campers have been dealt with appropriately before granting an eviction order but, thus satisfied, may grant the order immediately. In some cases, for instance, where the defendants have attended the hearing to defend the claim, the hearing may be adjourned to allow more time for more evidence to be gathered.

26   If the defendant fails to leave the land by the date of the hearing and the judge has agreed to grant possession to the landowner, a warrant will be issued immediately. Bailiffs (who will be court-appointed in most circumstances) will then visit the encampment and notify the defendant(s) of the eviction date and time and provide them with the eviction notice. Once again, this may be handed directly to the unauthorised campers or posted prominently on the land.

27   On the date of the eviction (which must be at least twenty four hours from the time at which the notice of eviction was served) the landowner or his appointed representative will accompany the bailiff to witness the eviction. The police should be alerted so that they can provide appropriate advice and be on hand to ensure that there are no breaches of the peace. After the eviction has taken place the land owner will then sign the warrant of possession to acknowledge that he has regained possession of the land (if court bailiffs are not available to carry out the eviction, private bailiffs may be employed in this capacity).

28   It should be noted that, where the landowner is a local authority or other public body, the necessary welfare assessments should be carried out alongside the court procedures and should be completed before any eviction is carried out.

29   Further details of the court procedures and forms can be found on line at: http://www.dca.gov.uk/civil/procedures_fin/index.htm

Sections 77-78 of the Criminal Justice and Public Order Act 1994

30   Section 77 of the CJPOA gives local authorities the power to direct individuals to remove their vehicles and belongings and to leave highway land, or any land occupied without the consent of the landowner, whether owned by the local authority itself or by any other public or private landowner.

31   Before commencing any action to evict an unauthorised encampment, local authorities have an obligation to carry out welfare assessments of the unauthorised campers. This may necessitate the involvement of local NHS bodies, where health issues are apparent.

32   Local authorities may then draw up a Direction which instructs the unauthorised campers to leave on a particular date and time. This document is approved and signed by an authorised signatory of the local authority (usually a solicitor or legal executive employed by the authority). It also identifies either individuals or vehicles on the unauthorised encampment.

33   The Direction is then served on the unauthorised campers by a local authority officer (the document must be given directly to one of the named unauthorised campers or affixed prominently to one of the vehicles).

34   If the campers have failed to move and/or remove any vehicles and other property by the date specified in the Direction, or return to the same location within three months of the date of the Direction, they are then committing a criminal offence and may be arrested by the police. If a prosecution is successful they may then be given a custodial sentence of up to three months, or be liable to a fine of up to £1,000.

35   In practice however, it can be more effective for local authorities to pursue unauthorised campers who have contravened a direction under Section 77 by using their powers under Section 78 of the CJPOA. This allows local authorities to advise the Magistrates' Court of the contravention and, if the court is satisfied, then they may grant an Order for Removal of Persons and Vehicles.

36   In the first instance, the Listing Clerk at the Magistrates' Court should be contacted in order to obtain a date for a court hearing, which is required before the Order can be issued. Depending on the location of the encampment, the local authority may ask the court to expedite the process so that the unauthorised campers can be moved quickly.

37   The appropriate local authority officer then attends the Application Court to make an application for a summons, which can be issued immediately. This summons requires the person(s) in charge of the caravan(s) to appear before a court hearing to answer the complaint.

38   The summons is then served on the unauthorised campers by the appropriate local authority officer or by a process server contracted to perform this service for the local authority.

39   A hearing in the Magistrates' Court is set for later in the day on which the summons is served, or on the following working day. A solicitor

must appear at the hearing on behalf of the local authority. Good practice indicates that, where possible, the same solicitor should be used in all court proceedings relating to unauthorised camping by Gypsies and Travellers so that they have a good working knowledge of the legislation. The solicitor should be provided with all of the necessary court documents as well as any relevant background information (the findings of welfare enquiries for example). The solicitor will request that the magistrate grants an Order for Removal of Vehicles and Persons.

40   If the unauthorised campers attend the hearing and contest the eviction, the case may be adjourned in order to allow time to hear all the evidence. However, if the magistrate is satisfied that the correct procedures have been followed, the Order will be granted immediately in normal circumstances.

41   Once granted, the Order should be served on the unauthorised campers as soon as possible by a local authority officer or process server, as above.

42   Twenty-four hours must be allowed to elapse between serving the Order and any action to remove the unauthorised campers. At any point thereafter, the local authority (or private bailiffs employed on their behalf) may remove the unauthorised campers and their vehicles from the land. As with any eviction, police should be present to ensure that no breach of the peace takes place.

Sections 61-62 of the Criminal Justice and Public Order Act 1994

43   If the landowner or his agent has asked the unauthorised cam pers to leave the land by a particular date and time, and they have failed to do so, and any of the three following conditions have also been met:

- the unauthorised campers have caused damage to the land or property on the land;
- they have used threatening, abusive or insulting words or behaviour to the occupier, a member of his family or his employee or agent;
- there are six or more vehicles on the land.

44   The police can use Section 61 of the CJPOA to direct unauthorised campers to leave the site. They can do this without reference to the courts.

45   The initial step is for the landowner to make a formal request to the police that they use their powers under the CJPOA.

46   A senior police officer then considers whether it is appropriate to use the power, based on various factors:

- whether there are there other activities on the encampment, such as serious breaches of the peace, disorder, criminal activity or anti-social behaviour which would necessitate police involvement under their wider powers;
- given the impact of the unauthorised encampment on the environment and the local settled community, is it reasonable and proportionate to use police powers;
- is action by the police legally sustainable;
- are sufficient resources available.

47   Although case law (*R v The Commissioner of the Metropolitan Police ex p Small*) has established that police officers are not under any obligation to undertake welfare enquiries with unauthorised campers, they must be aware of humanitarian considerations when considering action to remove an encampment. The joint ODPM/Home Office document 'Guidance on managing unauthorised camping' recommends that local authorities should be involved in the process.

48   Once a decision to use police powers is made, a uniformed police officer visits the encampment and advises the occupiers that they are required to leave by a certain date and time, and provides them with a copy of the legislation. The police may determine the period of notice to the unauthorised campers to leave, and this may be hours or days. The police may also videotape their visit to the encampment in case of later challenge or dispute.

49   If the unauthorised campers fail to leave by the date and time specified by the police officer, or return to that location within three months of the direction, they are then committing an offence and liable on summary conviction to imprisonment for a term not exceeding three months or a fine not exceeding £2,500. Further, if a direction issued under Section 61 is contravened, a police officer may then seize and remove the vehicles under Section 62 of the CJPOA. Vehicles would be impounded in an appropriate police facility with a fee payable for their return.

Section 62A-E of the Criminal Justice and Public Order Act 1994

50   Section 62A of the CJPOA allows the police to direct trespassers to remove themselves and their vehicles and property from land where a suitable pitch on a relevant caravan site is available within the same local authority area (or within the county in two-tier local authority areas).

51   A suitable pitch on a relevant caravan site is one which is situated in the same local authority area as the land on which the trespass has occurred, and which is managed by a local authority, registered social landlord, or other person or body as specified by order by the Secretary of State. In two tier authority areas, where a district council is situated within a wider county council area, the relevant caravan site may be anywhere within the county council area.

52   The power may be used where the following conditions are met:
- at least two persons are trespassing;
- the trespassers have between them at least one vehicle on the land;
- the trespassers are present on the land with the common purpose of residing there for any period;
- it appears to the officer that the person has one or more caravans in his possession or under his control on the land, and that there is a suitable pitch on a relevant caravan site for that caravan or each of those caravans;
- the occupier of the land (ie, the freehold owner or lessee), or a person acting on the occupier's behalf has asked the police to remove the trespassers from the land.

53   If the unauthorised campers do not leave when directed to do so under **Section 62A**, or if they return to the district within three months after being directed, they are committing an offence, and the police may then use their powers under **Section 62B** of the CJPOA to arrest and detain them. If the campers are subsequently convicted of an offence under the Act, they may then be subject to a custodial sentence of not more than three months, or a fine not exceeding level 4 on the standard scale (currently, a maximum of £2,500).

54   The police may also use their powers under **Section 62C** of the CJPOA to seize and remove the vehicles and property from the land. Vehicles would be impounded in an appropriate police facility with a fee payable for their return.

55   Local authorities will need to confirm that appropriate alternative pitches are available in the area before the police use their powers (note the duty to consult local authorities within the area under Section 62A (5)) and, as with Section 61 of the CJPOA, it is good practice for local authorities to be involved in the process to ensure that any welfare needs are identified.

56   Specific guidance on the use of ss.62A-E powers was issued in March 2005, and is available on the ODPM website at:www.odpm.gov.uk/gypsysites.

Choosing the most appropriate power

57   The powers set out above all have different characteristics, and accordingly will be appropriate for different circumstances. The questions set out below will help agencies to determine the most appropriate power to use in different circumstances. In addition to the information that is provided here on relevant powers, it is important for the relevant enforcement provisions to be considered carefully in each situation to ensure that all requirements can be met. Local authorities and police forces should also agree protocols so that an overall policy and clear lines of responsibility are in place before the need for action arises.

58   The questions set out below will help agencies to determine the most appropriate power to use in different circumstances.

How important is speed?

59   It is unlawful for Gypsies and Travellers to camp on land they do not own without the landowner's permission. There are locations where immediate action to remove them should be taken because the presence of the encampment is seriously disrupting the ability of the settled community to make use of facilities or to conduct their business, for instance:

• on school grounds during term time;
• on urban parks;
• on business or retail parks.

60   Similarly, swift action should be taken where the encampment is located on contaminated land or where the encampment is very close to a busy highway, potentially endangering the health and safety of the campers and others, or on land of a particularly sensitive nature, a Site of Special

Scientific Interest (SSSI) for example.

61   In the above circumstances, Section 61 of the CJPOA is likely to be the most appropriate power, provided that the conditions for its use are met. The police can act immediately without reference to the courts, and can direct travellers to leave the site within a matter of hours. Clearly, this course of action will be more effective if there is an alternative site to which Gypsies and Travellers can be directed, either pitches on an authorised transit site, or a location which is deemed to be a more 'acceptable' unauthorised site.

Are there problems on the encampment such as anti-social behaviour, public disorder and so on?

62   In these circumstances it will be appropriate for the police to deal with these issues directly using their wider powers, and for them to disperse the encampment using s61 or s62A.

Is it desirable to evict some but not all the trespassers?

63   If the anti-social behaviour is focused amongst particular individuals in the group, or if a member of the group is ill, it may be appropriate to take action to evict some people but not others. In this case it may be most effective to use the powers under ss77-78 CJPOA, which focus on named individuals or vehicles, or to use the police powers.

Is the group of unauthorised campers stable, or are different vehicles arriving and departing?

64   Where the occupants of an unauthorised encampment change frequently, it may be more effective to use Civil Procedures Rules Part 55, which relate to the land itself, rather than the powers under the CJPOA, which require the individuals or vehicles on the encampment to be identified. Where these change, a new direction will have to be drawn up.

Do the unauthorised campers present welfare issues?

65   Local authority officers should conduct thorough welfare enquiries when a new encampment of Gypsies and Travellers arrives in the area. Where pressing needs for particular services are identified as part of the local authority's enquires, relevant departments or external agencies should be contacted in order to meet these needs as appropriate (health services, social services, housing departments and so on).

66   If necessary, removal of the encampment could be delayed while urgent welfare needs are addressed (unless, as above, the site on which the unauthorised campers are using is particularly sensitive or hazardous, in which case the unauthorised campers should be asked to relocate to a more appropriate location in the vicinity). Further, it may be possible to negotiate a date for the encampment to leave if, for instance, the Gypsies and Travellers have camped in the vicinity for a specific purpose; in order to attend an outpatient's appointment at the local hospital for example.

Is enforcement necessary?

67   If the Gypsies and Travellers are cooperative, only wish to stay for a short time and the encampment is not in a sensitive location, it may only be necessary to monitor the situation pending their departure. It may also be appropriate to provide the unauthorised campers with some means of disposing of rubbish and waste in order to minimise clear-up costs when they have left.

Is the decision to evict likely to be challenged?

68   In this case it may be appropriate to use Part 55 Civil Procedure Rules so that a judge can affirm the decision to evict based on the available evidence.

Are there suitable pitches available on relevant sites in the local authority area to which the unauthorised campers might go?

69   If this is the case, s62A of the CJPOA can be used.

Do particular groups repeatedly return to the area?

70   In this case it may be appropriate for the police to use their powers under section 62A, where there are suitable pitches available in the area. Section 62A can prevent campers returning to anywhere in the local authority area for a period of three months.

71   Where groups return to a specific location, ss61-62 and 77-78 can be used to prevent them returning to that location for a period of three months. It may also be appropriate to explore further options such as injunctions or Anti-Social Behaviour Orders.

Speeding up the process

Making authorised provision

72   Enforcement action will be quicker and more effective, and a wider range of powers can be used, where appropriate authorised provision is made for Gypsies and Travellers within the area. The Housing Act 2004 requires local authorities to undertake accommodation needs assessment for Gypsies and Travellers who reside in or resort to their areas, and then to set out a strategy to meet those needs. Adequate provision will have wide benefits in the management of unauthorised camping as:

- there will be less unauthorised camping in the first place;
- the police will not be restricted in the use of ss62A-E CJPOA if suitable pitches are available;
- legal challenges are less likely to occur or succeed;
- the courts are more likely to grant possession orders to local authorities who show they are acting responsibly in carrying out their wider duties and who deal with each incident of unauthorised camping on its merits.

Being prepared

73   Arrangements should be reached in advance, both within local authorities and the police themselves, but also between the parties, about how cases of unauthorised camping will be dealt with.

74   Local authorities should ensure that reports of unauthorised camping can be acted upon swiftly. They should nominate a named officer who has the appropriate level of authority to make operational decisions on the ground, and cover arrangements should be put in place for those instances where this officer is unavailable.

75   Procedures should be agreed with each agency that will be involved in the eviction process (including the police and those departments and agencies that may be called upon for assistance as a consequence of welfare enquiries). Good working relations, and clear lines of responsibility, particularly between the local authority and the police, can do a great deal to speed the processes up. Some areas that use police powers effectively have units staffed by both local authority employees and police officers.

Avoiding legal challenge

76   Considerable delays can occur if the unauthorised campers mount a legal challenge to the eviction. In some cases, this may be as part of a court process. However, a challenge can also be mounted to any public body via judicial review on the grounds that its decision-making was flawed. However, this risk can be minimised.

77   Local authorities should ensure that, in accordance with their wider obligations, and to ensure that they comply with Human Rights legislation, proper welfare enquiries are carried out to determine whether there are pressing needs presented by the unauthorised campers and that, where necessary, the appropriate agencies are involved as soon as possible.

78   Local authorities should also ensure that they follow proper procedures in dealing with an unauthorised encampment, and that their actions are fully documented. Comprehensive advice is set out in, *Managing Unauthorised Camping*, jointly issued by ODPM and Home Office, and available on the ODPM website at: www.odpm.gov.uk/gypsysites.

79   Local authorities should also prepare carefully for court appearances, making sure that evidence/court papers etc are in order, and that all legal requirements (such as serving notices) have been met.

Working with the courts

80   Local authorities should maintain regular contact with their local court service and discuss with them in advance any issues that are expected to arise. It may also be helpful for local authority officers to join the Court User Group, which is a forum for discussing new legislation, and provides opportunities to raise issues such as court practice.

81   When unauthorised camping takes place and it is deemed that court action is appropriate, the court should be advised of any intention to file an application immediately (without waiting until all the paperwork is complete), so that the date for a hearing can be expedited.

Keeping costs down

82   Speeding up the enforcement process will in itself help to keep costs down, so the points set out in the previous section will be relevant here as well. In addition, the following points should be considered.

Avoiding unnecessary enforcement action

83   Before taking action, landowners should consider whether enforcement is absolutely necessary. It may be that in certain circumstances, alternatives to eviction action are appropriate, for example:

- where unauthorised campers have chosen an unobtrusive location in which to camp it may be preferable to agree a departure date with them;

- where unauthorised campers have chosen to stop in an unacceptable location, but where the local authority has also identified a location in the vicinity which would be much less damaging or obtrusive, unauthorised campers could be encouraged to move to this location.

84   If eviction is deemed necessary, in many cases the trespassers will leave after being served with an initial notice under Part 55 or a direction under the CJPOA powers, and no further enforcement action will be needed.

Avoiding unnecessary clean-up costs

85   Waste clearance from sites that have been used as unauthorised encampments should be undertaken rapidly in order to minimise the amount of fly-tipping that may take place after the encampment has gone. Where they can be identified, fly-tippers can also be fined for depositing waste illegally.

Avoiding unnecessary legal costs

86   Expertise and legal advice relating to unauthorised camping may be available from the district or county council, and landowners, parish councils and so on are advised to ensure that they have consulted with these bodies before taking further action. Good practice guidance and general advice on the management of unauthorised camping is also available from the ODPM, although the Department is not able to offer definitive legal advice on specific cases.

87   Local authorities should consider which parts of the enforcement process may be appropriately carried out by their own staff, as this is likely to be cheaper than contracting the work out to others. However, the local authority will wish to satisfy itself that their staff has the necessary expertise, and that their safety can be assured.

The eviction process

88   Where an eviction is being carried out by a local authority, its appointed representatives or the police, a local authority officer should always attend, as the local authority may have obligations to offer assistance to those who have been evicted, due to their wider social responsibilities. This may include temporarily caring for children where parents or guardians have been arrested and held in custody, or offering alternative accommodation to those Gypsies and Travellers who are identified as being homeless and in priority need.

89   Local authorities should also ensure that the appropriate departments, such as housing, social services, education and NHS bodies are made

aware of the eviction and are in a position to be able to respond swiftly to any requests for assistance. If unauthorised campers have pets or livestock it may also be appropriate to involve the relevant bodies, the RSPCA for instance, in finding appropriate accommodation for them.

90   If an eviction is being carried out by a local authority or bailiffs, the police should be advised at an early stage so that they can advise and assist in relation to the issue of personal safety in order to minimise the possibility of physical harm. Police should also be on hand when an eviction is taking place in order to ensure that breaches of the peace do not occur. If the police recommend that the eviction should not proceed for any reason, action should be delayed until an agreed time.

91   If private bailiffs are to be used to evict unauthorised campers, stringent vetting should take place to ensure that those employed in this capacity are appropriately qualified to do so. The bailiffs should also indemnify the landowner against any potential liability (in terms of further costs incurred due to possible legal action) in respect of their activities to evict the unauthorised campers.

92   Wherever possible, the forthcoming eviction should be discussed with those on the encampment, and they should be notified of the date and time for the eviction. This will give those on the encampment time to prepare to leave, and will help to ensure that the eviction runs as safely and smoothly as possible.

93   However, there may be circumstances in which this is not appropriate – for example where those on the encampment have announced their intention of violently resisting the eviction. In this case it will be essential that the eviction is thoroughly planned, with the full involvement of the police at an early stage, and that every care is taken to ensure the safety of everyone involved.

Preventing further unauthorised camping

Following up on enforcement action

94   Where a particular group of Gypsies and Travellers repeatedly camp in a specific location, and the police or the local authority have used their powers under the CJPOA to remove them, it is important that the criminal sanctions set out in the legislation are pursued if the unauthorised campers return within three months of being directed to leave.

Other legal action

95   Other legal remedies such as injunctions and Anti-Social Behaviour Orders (ASBOs) may be used to prevent Gypsies and Travellers from returning to an area where they have caused problems in the past. Local authorities may be able to obtain these remedies at the same time as taking court action for possession or eviction. Guidance on their use can be found at: www.together.gov.uk.

96   If injunctions or ASBOs are obtained to prevent unauthorised camping by particular groups, it is important that breaches are followed up with the appropriate legal sanctions, such as fines or imprisonment.

Provision of appropriate sites

97 The most effective method of combating unauthorised camping is to provide sites in accessible locations for those Gypsies and Travellers who pass through the area. This may not be limited to official residential and transit sites; it might also include particular locations which have been identified in the district where Gypsies and Travellers can stop for limited and agreed short periods of time, without having any adverse impact on the settled community.

Site protection measures

98 Site protection measures could also be considered in locations which are particularly vulnerable to unauthorised camping, for instance by creating earth bunds, or embankments, around the site, or by introducing height restrictions to entrances.

Additional sources of information

Part 55 Possession Claims – Department for Constitutional Affairs guidance, available on the internet at: ww.dca.gov.uk/civil/procrules_fin/contents/parts/part55.htm#4223902

Guidance on Managing Unauthorised Camping – ODPM/Home Office joint guidance, available on the internet at: ww.odpm.gov.uk/stellent/groups/odpm_housing/documents/page/odpm_house_027535.hcsp

Additional Guidance on Sections 62A-E CJPOA:

www.odpm.gov.uk/stellent/groups/odpm_housing/documents/page/odpm_house_035805.hcsp

Information on the Government's Policies relating to Gypsies and Travellers:

www.odpm.gov.uk/gypsysites

Information on HM Courts Service: www.hmcourts-service.gov.uk/cms/aboutus.htm

Information on tackling anti-social behaviour in the community: www.together.gov.uk

Information on fly-tipping: www.defra.gov.uk/environment/localenv/flytipping/index.htm

Glossary of terms

Breach of the Peace – a disturbance of public peace or order. Traditionally, one of the roles of the police is to 'keep the peace'. Breach of the peace is a common law offence.

Common Law – law determined as a result of decisions made by the courts as distinct from law laid down by statute.

Civil Offence – civil law governs the relationships and transactions between citizens set out in statute and common law. The majority of civil actions are heard in the 218 county courts, where cases are presided over by a district judge.

Criminal Offence – criminal law mostly involves the rules laid down by the state concerning the conduct of citizens. Most minor criminal cases, called summary offences, are heard in local Magistrates' Courts either by a panel of lay magistrates assisted by a legally-trained clerk, or by a legally-trained district judge sitting alone. The most serious offences, called indictable-only offences, are passed on by the Magistrates' Courts to the Crown Court to be heard, usually by a judge and jury. Only Crown Court judges have the power to pass sentences above a certain level of severity, and so some cases may be transferred from Magistrates' Courts for sentencing once a verdict has been reached. There are 78 Crown Court centres throughout England and Wales.

County Court – the court which deals with the majority of civil actions. Cases are presided over by a district judge.

County Court bailiff – they are employees of the County Court, and enforce County Court Judgements, such as warrants of execution for debts. They also have a role in evictions of unauthorised campers under Civil Procedures Rules Part 55.

Fly-Tipping – the illegal and unauthorised dumping of waste.

Human Rights Act – an Act passed in 1998, and brought into force in October 2000, which requires all public authorities making decisions that affect individuals to consider whether those decisions are reasonable and proportionate, bearing in mind all the circumstances.

Injunction – an order made by a Civil Court (County or High Court) which usually prohibits a somebody from doing something, based on the fact they have done it before, usually seriously and/or often. If an injunction is breached, the person can be fined or imprisoned for a contempt of the court by not according with the terms of the injunction.

Magistrates' Court – the lowest kind of criminal court in England and Wales and other common law jurisdictions. A Magistrate's Court is presided over by two or more Justices of the Peace (magistrates), or by a stipendiary magistrate, and dispenses summary justice, under powers usually limited by statute. The court will also determine committals to the Crown Court.

Private Bailiff (or Enforcement Agent) – someone who is responsible for the enforcement of court orders. Private landowners can also use them where there is no court order. Employed in the private sector. Private bailiffs can also be used to evict unauthorised campers following court proceedings under Civil Procedures Rules Part 55 where court bailiffs are not available.

Process Server – a privately employed individual who personally delivers a process (a writ compelling attendance in court) or court papers to a defendant (process servers are normally employees of private investigation companies).

Protocol – an agreement of an approach, usually between various different public bodies.

Site of Special Scientific Interest – this is a planning policy definition, and it is the name given to specific pieces of land which should not be disturbed or developed. They may be the home of, or an area resorted to by, a rare or protected animal or bird, the site may include a rare type of vegetation, or the land may contain a special geological feature or something else unique. By definition, they must not have houses, caravan sites or other development on them.

Statutory Powers – powers given by an Act of Parliament, as distinct from powers under common law.

Title (to land) – the evidence of someone's ownership of a piece of land, based on tracing the history of it, and showing legal transfer of ownership to them.

Tort – a civil wrong committed by one person against another (eg, trespassing on their land).

Unauthorised development – development of a site on land owned by Gypsies and Travellers, but for which they do not have planning permission.

Unauthorised encampment – trespassing by Gypsies and Travellers on land which they do not own (eg, playing fields, farmers' fields or other private land).

Welfare Assessments – action carried out by local authority officers with unauthorised campers to identify and address any issues that require the involvement of other local authority departments and agencies in terms of immediate health, education etc needs.

APPENDIX – PRIMARY LEGISLATION

Criminal Justice and Public Order Act 1994 Part V

[Not reproduced. See above in appendix B for relevant sections of CJPOA 1994.]

Useful organisations

National organisations and government departments

Administrative Court Office
Royal Courts of Justice
Strand
London WC2A 2LL

Administrative Court (Wales)
Law Courts
Cathays Park
Cardiff CF10 3PG

Advisory Council for the Education of Romany and other Travellers
c/o Moot House
The Stow
Harlow
Essex CM20 3AG

Advisory Service for Squatters
Angel Alley
84b Whitechapel High Street
London E1 7QX
Tel: 020 3216 0099 / 0845 644 5814
Fax: 020 3216 0098
E-mail: advice@squatter.org.uk
Website: www.squatter.org.uk

Commission for Equality and Human Rights
(from October 2007)
Website: www.cehr.org.uk

Communities and Local Government
Gypsy and Traveller Unit
1/F8 Eland House
Bressenden Place
London SW1E 5DU
Tel: 020 7944 4933
E-mail: gypsies@communities.gsi.gov.uk
Website: www.communities.gov.uk

Department for Children, Schools and Families
Sanctuary Buildings
Great Smith Street
London SW1P 3BT
Tel: 0870 000 2288
Fax: 01928 794248
E-mail: info@dfes.gsi.gov.uk
Website: www.dfes.gov.uk

Department of Health
Richmond House
79 Whitehall
London SW1A 2NS
Tel: 020 7210 4850
Website: www.dh.gov.uk

Educational Advice for Travellers
PO Box 36
Grantham
Lincolnshire NG31 6EW

Friends, Families and Travellers
Community Base
113 Queens Road
Brighton BN1 3XG
Tel: 01273 234777
Fax: 01273 234778
E-mail: fft@gypsy-traveller.org
Website: www.gypsy/traveller.org

Groundswell
Elmfield House
5 Stockwell Mews
London SW9 9GX
Tel: 020 7737 5500
Fax: 020 7733 1305
E-mail: info@groundswell.org.uk
Website: www.groundswell.org.uk

Gypsy Council
Springs Lane Caravan Park
Bickerton
Nr Wetherby
North Yorkshire LS22 5ND
Tel/fax: 01937 842782

Gypsy Council, The
8 Hall Road
Aveley
Essex RM15 4HD
Tel/fax: 01708 868986
E-mail: thegypsycouncil@btinternet.com
Website: www.thegypsycouncil.org.uk

Independent Police Complaints Commission
Website: www.ipcc.gov.uk

International Gypsy & Traveller Affairs
Moate Farm
Stodmarsh Road
Canterbury
Kent CT3 4AP
Tel: 01227 789652

International Romani Union
c/o East Anglian Gypsy Council (see below under 'local organisations')

Irish Traveller Movement in Britain
The Resource Centre
356 Holloway Road
London N7 6PA
Tel: 020 7607 2002
Fax: 020 7607 2005
E-mail: info@irishtraveller.org.uk
Website: www.irishtraveller.org.uk

Labour Campaign for Travellers' Rights
Prof Thomas Acton
E-mail: thomasacton@hotmail.com

National Assembly for Wales
Cardiff Bay
Cardiff CF99 1NA
Tel: 02920 825111
Website: www.wales.gov.uk

National Association of Gypsy and Traveller Officers
Website: www.nagto.org.uk

National Association of Health Workers with Travellers
Janine Adkins
CHD Travellers
Clwydian House
University of Wales
College of Medicine
Technology Park
Wrexham
Tel: 01978 352880

National Association of Teachers of Travellers
Website: www.natt.org.uk

National Federation of Gypsy Liaison Groups
Mr P Mercer
Office 4
Ernest Bailey Community Centre
New Street
Matlock
Derbyshire DE4 3FE
Tel/fax: 01629 760435
E-mail: info@nationalgypsytravellerfederation.org
Website: www.nationalgypsytravellerfederation.org

National Romani Rights Association
c/o Basil Burton
10 Dugdell Close
Ferndown
Dorset BH22 8BH
Tel: 01202 893228
E-mail: basilburton@hotmail.co.uk

National Romani Gypsy Traveller Alliance
E-mail: nrgta@uk49.fsnet.co.uk

National Traveller Action Group
3a Hope Lane
St Johns Fen End
Kings Lynn
Norfolk PE14 8JD
Tel: 01945 430995
Mob: 07890 596718
E-mail: codona9@aol.com

Ofsted
Royal Exchange Buildings
St Ann's Square
Manchester M2 7LA
Tel: 08456 404045
E-mail: enquiries@ofsted.gov.uk
Website: www.ofsted.gov.uk

Press Complaints Commission
Halton House
20/23 Holborn
London EC1N 2JD
Tel: 0845 600 2757
Fax: 020 7831 0025
E-mail: complaints@pcc.org.uk
Website: www.pcc.org.uk

Pride not Prejudice
c/o Derbyshire Gypsy Liaison Group (see below under 'local
organisations')

Shelterline
(24hour national housing help)
Tel: (Freephone) 0808 800 4444
Website: England – england.shelter.org.uk; Wales –
www.sheltercymru.org.uk

The Land is Ours
Chapter 7
The Potato Store
Flax Drayton Farm
South Petherton
Somerset TA13
Tel: 01460 249204
E-mail: chapter7@tlio.org.uk
Website: www.tlio.org.uk

The Showmen's Guild of Great Britain
Tel: 01642 230638
Website: www.showmensguild.com

Travellers Advice Team
Community Law Partnership
4th Floor, Ruskin Chambers
191 Corporation Street
Birmingham B4 6RP
Tel: 0121 685 8595
CLS Direct funded advice line: 0845 120 2980
Out of hours emergency number: 07768 316755
Fax: 0121 236 5121
E-mail: office@communitylawpartnership.co.uk

Travellers Aid Trust
PO Box 16
Llangyndeyrn
Kidwelly
Carmarthenshire SA17 5BN
Tel/fax: 01269 870621
E-mail: info@travellersaidtrust.org
Website: www.travellersaidtrust.org

Traveller Law Reform Project
6 Westgate Street
London E8 3RN
Tel: 07956 450916
Fax: 020 8533 7110
E-mail: info@travellerslaw.org.uk
Website: www.travellerslaw.org.uk

Travellers' School Charity
PO Box 2
Goodwick
Pembrokeshire SA64 0ZQ
Tel: 01239 810759
Website: www.travellersschool.plus.com

Travellers' Times
The Rural Media Company, Sullivan House
72–80 Widemarsh Street
Hereford HR4 9HG
Tel: 01432 344039
Fax: 01432 270539
E-mail: travellerstimes@ruralmedia.co.uk
Website: www.travellerstimes.org.uk

Treasury Solicitor
One Kemble Street
London WC2B 4TS

UK Association of Gypsy Women
12A Pease House
Horsemarket
Darlington DL1 5PW
Tel: 01325 357859
Mob: 07748 670200
Fax: 01325 487334
E-mail: ukassociationofgypsywomen@yahoo.co.uk

Local organisations

There is a vast array of local organisations dealing with Gypsy and Traveller issues. Full details of local organisations can be obtained from one of the national organisations mentioned above. We list below some of the most active and prominent of these local organisations.

Avon Traveller Support Group
65 Hawthorn Grove
Combe Down
Bath BA2 5QF
Tel/fax: 01225 835130

Brent Irish Advisory Service
95 Willesden High Rd
Willesden Green
London NW10 2SF
Tel: 020 8459 6655
Fax: 020 8459 6699
E-mail: bias.brent@btconnect.com
Website: www.biasbrent.co.uk

Bromley Gypsy Traveller Project
230 Sandway Rd.
St. Mary Cray
Orpington
Kent BR5 3TF
Tel: 01689 839052
Emergency no: 07903 474124
Fax: 01629 820645
E-mail: travs@tiscali.co.uk

Cambridgeshire Travellers' Advocacy Service;
Cambridgeshire Travellers Initiative
7e High Street
Fenstanton
Cambridgeshire PE28 9LQ
Tel: 01480 496577
Fax: 01480 496566
Website: www.ormiston.org/community/opus24.html

Canterbury Gypsy & Traveller Support Group
Moate Farm
Stodmarsh Road
Canterbury
Kent CT3 4AP
Tel: 01227 453441 / 07765 174141
Emergency no: 0845 644 8879

Cardiff Gypsy and Traveller Project
114 Clifton Street
Roath
Cardiff CF24 1LW
Tel/fax: 029 2021 4411
E-mail: timcgtp@btconnect.com

Children's Society Traveller Children's Project
Unit 5 Westway Garage
Marksbury
Bath BA2 9HN
Tel: 01761 479368
Mob: 07774 838309
Fax: 01761 479820
E-mail: dxh@childrenssociety.org.uk

Derbyshire Gypsy Liaison Group
Ernest Bailey Community Centre
Office 3, New Street
Matlock
Derbyshire DE4 3FE
Tel: 01629 583300
Fax: 01629 57851
E-mail: info@dglg.org
Website: www.dglg.org
BSL signers available and minicom

East Anglian Gypsy Council
Plot 3, Oxney Road Caravan Site
Peterborough PE1 5NX
Tel/fax: 01733 347112
E-mail: P.Mercer@hotmail.co.uk

East Midlands Gypsy and Traveller Forum
c/o Derbyshire Gypsy Liaison Group (see above)

Herefordshire Travellers Support Group
Trefoil, Brinsop Common
Hereford HR4 7AS
Tel: 01432 760350
E-mail: paebkam@aol.com

Hull Gypsy and Traveller Exchange
E-mail: john_mercer_hull@yahoo.co.uk

Irish Traveller Movement 2006 (UK)
(covers Kent)
Moate Farm
Stodmarsh Road
Canterbury
Kent CT3 4AP
Tel: 01227 453441 / 07765 174141
Emergency no: 0845 644 8879

Leeds Gypsy and Traveller Exchange
Ground Floor
Crown Point House
169 Cross Green Lane
Leeds LS9 OBD
Tel: 0113 240 2444
Mob: 07974 574889
E-mail: info@leedsgate.co.uk

Leeds Justice for Travellers
9 Mowbray Court
Seacroft
Leeds LS14 6UN
Tel: 0113 264 8658

Leicester Gypsy Council Liaison Group
Rosevale House
Hinkley Road
Sapcote LE9 4LH
E-mail: LGCLGROUP@aol.com

Lincolnshire Gypsy Liaison Group
The Stables
Padmoor Lane
Upton
Gainsborough
Lincolnshire DN21 5NJ
Tel: 07761 816233

London Gypsy and Traveller Unit
6 Westgate Street
Hackney
London E8 3RN
Tel: 020 8533 2002
Fax: 020 8533 7110
E-mail: info@lgtu.org.uk
Website: www.lgtu.org.uk

Ormiston Norfolk Travellers Initiative
Breckland Business Centre
St Withburga Road
Dereham
Norfolk NR19 1ED
Tel: 01362 854264

South West Alliance of Nomads
Tel: 01202 537523
E-mail: welcome@gypsytravellerhelp.org
Website: www.gypsytravellerhelp.org

Southwark Traveller Action Group
The Peckham Settlement
Goldsmith Road
Peckham
London SE15 5TF
Tel: 020 7639 1823
Fax: 020 7635 9830
Website: www.peckhamsettlement.org.uk

West Midlands Education Service for Travelling Children
The Graiseley Centre
Pool Street
Wolverhampton WV2 4NE
Tel: 01902 714646
Fax: 01902 714202

York Travellers Trust
20 Falsgrave
Clifton
York YO30 7AZ
Tel: 01904 630526
Fax: 01904 675444
E-mail: travellerstrustyork@yahoo.co.uk

European organisations

Council of Europe
Website: www.coe.int

European Roma Rights Center
Website: www.errc.org

Bibliography

BOOKS ON GYPSY AND TRAVELLER ISSUES

Acton, *Gypsy politics and social change*, Routledge, Kegan Paul, 1974

Clark and Greenfields, *Here to stay: the Gypsies and Travellers of Britain*, University of Hertfordshire Press, 2006

Coxhead, *The last bastion of racism? Gypsies, Travellers and policing*, Trentham, 2007

Evans, *Stopping places: a Gypsy history of South London and Kent*, University of Hertfordshire Press, 2004

Fraser, *The Gypsies*, Blackwell, 1995

Hawes, *Gypsies, Travellers and the Health Service*, Policy Press, 1997

Hawes and Perez, *The Gypsy and the state: the ethnic cleansing of British society*, The Polity Press, 1996

Hyman, *Sites for Travellers: a study in five London boroughs*, London Race and Housing Research Unit, 1989

Kenrick, *Gypsies: from the Ganges to the Thames*, University of Hertfordshire Press, 2004

Kenrick and Bakewell, *On the verge: the Gypsies of England*, University of Hertfordshire Press, 1990

Kenrick and Clark, *Moving on: the Gypsies and Travellers of Britain*, University of Hertfordshire Press, 1996

Kenrick and Puxon, *The destiny of Europe's Gypsies*, Chatto-Heinemann, 1972

Leigeois, *Gypsies and Travellers: socio-cultural data, socio-political data*, Council of Europe, 1987

MacLaughlin, *Travellers and Ireland: whose country, whose history?*, Cork University Press, 1995

Morris and Clements, *Gaining ground: law reform for Gypsies and Travellers*, University of Hertfordshire Press, 1999

Morris and Clements, *At what cost? The economics of Gypsy and Traveller encampments*, The Policy Press, 2002

Okely, *The Traveller-Gypsies*, Cambridge University Press, 1983

Ò Riain, *Solidarity with Travellers*, Roadside Books, Dublin, 2000

Sandford, *Rokkering to the Gorjios*, University of Hertfordshire Press, 1973

Sheehan, ed, *Travellers: citizens of Ireland*, Parish of the Travelling People, Dublin, 2000

Smith, *Romany Nevi-Wesh*, Nova Foresta Publishing, 2004

Stewart, *The puzzle of Roma persistence*, University of Hertfordshire Press, 1997

Vesey-Fitzgerald, *Gypsies of Britain*, Readers Union, 1973

Worthington, ed, *The battle of the Beanfield*, Enabler Publications, 2005

LEGAL TEXTBOOKS

Arden, Hunter and Johnson, *Homelessness and allocations*, 7th edn, Legal Action Group, 2006

Arden et al, *Encyclopedia of housing law and practice*, Sweet & Maxwell, 2007

Baker, Carter and Hunter, *Housing and human rights law*, Legal Action Group, 2001

Butterworths Encyclopaedia of planning law and practice, Butterworths, 2007

Carr, Cottle, Baldwin and King, *The Housing Act 2004: a practical guide*, New Law Series, 2004

Child Poverty Action Group, *Welfare benefits and tax credits handbook*, CPAG, 2007/08

Clements and Thompson, *Community care and the law*, 4th edn, Legal Action Group, 2007

Jourdan, *Adverse possession*, Butterworths, 2003

Jowell and Cooper, eds, *Understanding Human Rights Act principles*, Hart Publishing, 2001

Luba and Davies, *Housing allocations and homelessness: law and practice*, Jordans, 2006

Manning, *Judicial review proceedings: a practitioner's guide*, 2nd edn, Legal Action Group, 2004

Palmer et al, *Discrimination law handbook*, 2nd edn, Legal Action Group, 2007

OTHER BOOKS

Baumann, *Modernity and the Holocaust*, Polity Press, 1989

Lentin and McVeigh, *Racism and anti-racism in Ireland,* Beyond the Pale, 2002

Muller-Hill, *Murderous science*, Methuesen, New York, 1988

Walvin, *There ain't no black in the Union Jack*, Routledge, 1973

REPORTS

General reports

Commission for Racial Equality, *Common Ground Equality, good race relations and sites for Gypsies and Irish Travellers*, CRE, 2006

Commission for Racial Equality, *Gypsies and Travellers: a strategy for the CRE, 2004–2007*, 2004

Equality of Opportunity Committee, National Assembly for Wales, *Review of service provision for Gypsies and Travellers*, 2003

Institute for Public Policy Research, *Moving forward: the provision of accommodation for Travellers and Gypsies*, 2004

Minority Rights Group, *Roma/Gypsies: a European minority*, 1995

Niner, *Preparing regional spatial strategy reviews on Gypsies and Travellers by regional planning bodies*, CLG, 2007

Niner, *Accommodation needs of Gypsy-Travellers in Wales*, Welsh Assembly Government, 2006

Niner, *Counting Gypsies and Travellers: a review of the Gypsy caravan count system*, ODPM, 2004

Niner, *Local authority Gypsy/Traveller sites in England*, ODPM, 2003

Niner, *The provision and condition of local authority Gypsy/Traveller sites in England*, ODPM, 2002

Power, *Room to roam: England's Irish Travellers*, The Community Fund, 2004

Stonewall, *Profiles of prejudice*, 2003

Reports on education

Committee of Inquiry into the Education of Children from Ethnic Minority Groups, *Education for all*, 1985

DfES, *Aiming high: raising the achievement of Gypsy and Traveller pupils*, 2003

Ofsted, *Managing support for the attainment of pupils from minority ethnic groups*, 2001

Ofsted, *Raising the attainment of minority ethnic pupils*, 1999

Ofsted, *The education of Travelling children: a survey of educational provision for Travelling children*, 1996

Reports on health

Chartered Institute of Environmental Health, *Travellers and Gypsies: an alternative strategy*, 1995

Council of Europe, *Breaking the barriers: Romani women and access to public health*, 2003

Derbyshire Gypsy Liaison Group, *A better road*, 2003

Van Cleemput et al, *The health status of Gypsies and Travellers in England*, University of Sheffield, 2004

Index

Abandonment of nomadism, 4.71, 4.72
Abatement notices, 7.106
ACAS, 8.57
Accommodation, 1.34–1.78. *See also* Accommodation available for occupation; Bed and breakfast; Homelessness; Local authority rented sites
Accommodation available for occupation
  meaning, 6.7
Admission to schools. *See* Schools
Advertisements
  race discrimination, and, 8.28–8.30, 8.71
Agriculture, 4.19
Allocation of pitches, 3.29–3.32
  matters to be considered by local authorities, 3.30
  priority, 3.32
  waiting list system, 3.31
  written policies, 3.31
Animals
  facilities for, 3.41
  highway, on, 5.89
  horses, keeping, 3.41
Antisocial behaviour, 5.169
AONB (Areas of Outstanding Natural Beauty), 4.47, 4.48
Appeals
  enforcement notices, 4.15–4.161
  homelessness, 6.43–6.49
  refusal of planning permission, against. *See* Planning permission
Applications for planning permission. *See* Planning permission

Armed forces
  homelessness, and, 6.13
Article 8 decision making, 2.13–2.63
  application of *Daly* approach in cases involving Gypsies and Travellers, 2.51–2.53
    compulsory purchase, 2.53
    direct action, 2.52
    statutory review of planning appeals, 2.51
  domestic decisions post–Human Rights Act 1998, 2.43–2.63
    Daly approach, 2.44–2.50
    margin of discretion, 2.45
    proportionality, 2.44–2.50
    two–stage approach, 2.48–2.50
  exercise of domestic court's original jurisdiction to grant planning enforcement injunctions, 2.54–2.62
    factors to be weighed in balance, 2.56–2.59
    submissive approach to decisions of local planning authorities, 2.54, 2.55
  justification for interference, 2.22–2.43
    interference in accordance with law, 2.23, 2.24
    legitimate aim, 2.25–2.57
    necessary in democratic society, 2.28, 2.29
    planning enforcement powers, 2.25–2.27
  limitations, 2.60
  nature and extent of interference with Article 8 rights, 2.20, 2.21
  nature of rights in issue, 2.15–2.19
  Porter approach, 2.54–2.62

Article 8 decision-making *continued*
proportionality, approach of
European Court of Human
Rights, 2.30–2.42
evidence, 2.41
factors affecting width of
margin of appreciation, 2.34,
2.35
national authorities, 2.42
positive obligation, recognition
of, 2.39
procedural safeguards,
importance of, 2.36–2.38
relevant factual matters,
2.40–2.42
wide margin of appreciation,
2.31–2.33
reasons given by domestic courts
for decisions on proportionality,
2.63
stationing of caravans, 2.17
Travelling Showpeople, 2.60–2.61
Article 14, 2.64–2.91
access to public services, and, 2.78
assessment by domestic courts,
2.73–2.77
questions to be posed by judge,
2.73
conventional housing, relevance of
offers of, 2.90, 2.91
European Court of Human Rights'
approach, 2.67–2.72
burden of proof, 2.69
margin of appreciation, 2.68
standard of proof, 2.70–2.72
evictions from rented local
authority sites, 2.79–2.85
nature of obligation, 2.64–2.66
planning enforcement, and,
2.86–2.89
planning permission for Gypsy
and Traveller sites, 2.90, 2.91
relevant discrimination cases post
– Human Rights Act 1998,
2.78–2.91
stop notices, and, 2.86–2.89

Banishment, 1.12
Battle of the Beanfield, 1.44

Bed and breakfast
suitability, 6.87–6.89
Bibliography, App D
Breach of statutory duty, 1.34
Buildings
meaning, 5.40
Business use of sites
restrictions on, 3.40
Bullying
schools, 7.53–7.54
Bye–laws, 5.94–5.108
certainty, 5.101
copy of, 5.97, 5.104
enforcement, 5.105
Forestry Commission, 5.106
general law, and, 5.100
intra vires, 5.99
local authorities, 5.94–5.108
meaning, 5.94
public authorities, 5.94–5.108
reasonableness, 5.102
validity, 5.98
waiver, 5.103

Caravan Sites Act 1968, s6, 4.1
repeal of, 4.2
Caravans, 4.26, 4.27
meaning, 4.27, 4.28, 5.46, 5.57
stationing on land
development, and, 4.26
Charges
local authority sites, and, 3.3
Children
disabled, 3.51
grants, 3.51
social services, 3.51
Civil Procedure Rules Part 55,
5.20–5.31
hearing, 5.22–5.24
postponement of order,
5.22–5.24
suspension of order, 5.22–5.24
High Court, matter commenced
in, 5.17
notice, 5.18–5.21
service properly effected, whether,
5.18–5.21
time limits for notice, 5.19–5.21
title, proof of, 5.16

Civil Procedure Rules Part 55
continued
trespassers, 5.11–5.15
warrant of possession, 5.25–5.31
warrant of restitution, 5.25–5.31
who can use, 5.10–5.15
Class, 1.10, 1.32
CLG Gypsy Count, 3.1, 3.2
Colour, 1.10
**Commission for Equality and
Human Rights**, 2.96–2.98, 8.3,
8.4
duty, 8.4
injunctions, 8.77
inquiries, 8.78
investigations, 8.72–8.75
power to institute or intervene in
legal proceedings, 8.79
power to issue compliance notice,
8.105–8.108
powers, 8.3, 8.72–8.79
unlawful act notices, 8.76
Common humanity
planning law, and, 4.144, 4.145
Common law powers of eviction,
5.109–5.117
Criminal Law Act 1977 s6, 5.117
persons entitled to possession,
5.109–5.111
reasonable force, 5.112–5.114
Community care services, 7.87–7.89
Compulsory purchase orders
redevelopment of sites, and,
3.53–3.55
Conditional fees, 3.47
Conditions of occupancy
implied terms, 3.35
local authorities, 3.35, 3.36
written agreement, 3.36
Conventional housing, offers of
human rights, and, 4.119–4.124
Crime, fear of
planning law, and, 4.91
**Criminal Justice and Public Order
Act 1994, s61**
additional three criteria, 5.43–5.46
buildings, 5.40
damage to land or property on
land, 5.44

**Criminal Justice and Public Order
Act 1994, s61** *continued*
direction to leave, 5.32–5.37
notice by occupier, 5.41, 5.42
obtaining court order, 5.50, 5.51
police, and, 5.32–5.37
'reasonable steps by or on behalf
of the occupier to ask them to
leave', 5.41, 5.42
six or more vehicles, 5.46
statutory defence, 5.47–5.49
threatening, abusive or insulting
words or behaviour, 5.45
'the senior police officer present',
5.36, 5.37
trespassing on land, 5.39, 5.40
'two or more persons with the
common purpose of residing',
5.38
**Criminal Justice and Public Order
Act 1964, s62A**, 5.52–5.72
caravans, 5.57
'common purpose of residing
there', 5.56
'communicated to the person',
5.66
'consult every local authority',
5.67
occupier, 5.65
offences, 5.68, 5.69
police, 5.52
statutory defence, 5.70–5.72
suitable pitch, 5.58–5.64
'the senior police officer present',
5.54
'trespassers', 5.55
**Criminal Justice and Public Order
Act 1994, s77**, 5.73–5.82
'again enters the land within
the period of three months',
5.79
'as soon as practicable', 5.78
consent of occupier, 5.75
local authorities, 5.73
obtaining court order, 5.81, 5.82
offence, 5.73
statutory defence, 5.80
vehicle or vehicles, 5.76
'written notice', 5.77

Criminal offences
 homelessness, 6.50

Damage to land, 5.44
 fly–tipping, 5.44
Damages, 3.35
Dampness, 3.46, 3.48
Data Protection Act 1998
 medical records, and, 7.92–7.98
Death penalty, 1.12
Dedicating landowner
 highway, and, 5.92
Definition of gypsy. *See* **Gypsies**
Definition of New Travellers. *See*
 New Age Travellers
Development, 4.18–4.19
 agriculture, 4.19
 forestry, 4.19
 meaning, 4.18, 4.19
 stationing of caravans on land,
  and, 4.26
Development plan, 4.9–4.16
 new system, 4.11
 objection to absence of
  appropriate policies, 4.16
 old system, 4.10
 planning applications determined
  in accordance with, 4.14
 planning applications for gypsy
  and traveller sites, and,
  4.59–4.63
 regional spatial strategies, 4.11, 4.12
Direct action
 planning law, and, 4.165–4.168
Disability discrimination
 education, and, 7.56
Disability Discrimination Act 1995
 security of tenure, and, 3.33, 3.34
  disability, meaning, 3.33
  permission, meaning, 3.33
Disabled facilities grants, 3.50
Discrimination
 Article 14, ECHR. *See* **Article 14**

Education, 7.2–7.66
 Article 2 of Protocol 1, 2.94, 2.95
 aims of government, 7.5
 children under school age, 7.61,
  7.62

Education *continued*
 disability discrimination, and, 7.56
 ECHR Protocol 1 Article 2, 7.6
 enforced mobility, and, 7.3
 home, 7.57–7.60
 otherwise than at school,
  7.57–7.60
 poor level of attendance, 7.4
 race discrimination, and,
  7.47–7.52, 8.36
 raising achievement of Gypsy and
  Traveller pupils, 7.63–7.66
 unauthorized sites, and, 7.65,
  7.66
 right to, 7.6–7.13
  duties of LEAs, 7.9–7.11
  NATT annual booklet, 7.13
  parental preference, 7.11
 schools. *See* **Schools**
 special educational needs,
  7.31–7.33
 statistics, 7.2
Education supervision order, 7.29
**Egyptian, Gypsy as adaptation of
 word**, 1.9
Emergency
 homelessness, and, 6.72
Employment
 race discrimination, 8.35
Enforcement notices, 4.146, 4.147
 appeals, 4.155–4.161
 prosecution for breach,
  4.162–4.164
Entertainers, 1.14
Environment
 local authorities, 3.46–3.48
 nuisance, 3.46
Environmental health, 7.101–7.107
 abatement notices, 7.106
 fresh water, 7.102–7.104
 permanent sites, 7.105
 site prejudicial to health, 7.107
 statutory nuisance, 7.106
Environmental Protection Act 1990,
 3.46–3.48
 rodent infestation, 3.48
 statutory nuisance, 3.46–3.48
Ethnic groups, 8.44–8.51
Ethnic monitoring, 8.99–8.100

Ethnicity, 1.32
Europe, repressive legislation in, 1.14
European Convention on Human
    Rights
    Article, 8. *See* **Article 8 decision
    making**
    Article 14. *See* **Article 14**
    Protocol 1 Article, 2. *See* **Education**
European organisations, App C
European Union Race Directive,
    8.119–8.122
Evictions from rented local authority
    sites
    Article 14, and, 2.79–2.85
Evictions from unauthorised
    encampments, 5.1–5.174
    antisocial behaviour, and, 5.169
    article 8, and, 5.4–5.8
    bodies involved in, 5.2
    bye–laws, 5.94–5.108. *See also*
    Bye–laws
    Civil Procedure Rules Part, 55,
    5.10–5.31. *See also* **Civil
    Procedure Rules Part**, 55
    common law powers,
    5.109–5.117
    Criminal Justice and Public Order
    Act 1994 s61, 5.32–5.51. *See also*
    **Criminal Justice and Public
    Order Act 1994 s61**
    Criminal Justice and Public Order
    Act 1994 s62A, 5.52–5.72. *See
    also* **Criminal Justice and Public
    Order Act 1994 s62A**
    Criminal Justice and Public Order
    Act 1994 s77, 5.73–5.82. *See also*
    **Criminal Justice and Public
    Order Act 1994 s77**
    Highways Act 1980, 5.83–5.93. *See
    also* **Highways Act 1980**
    individuals involved in, 5.2
    injunctions. *See* **Injunctions**
    judicial review, 5.1
    methods, 5.3
    planning enforcement *See*
    Planning enforcement
    possession orders, width of,
    5.160–5.164. *See also* **Possession
    orders**

Evictions from unauthorised
    encampments *continued*
    public law challenges, 5.3,
    5.119–5.159. *See also* **Public law
    challenges to eviction**
    substantive defences, 5.3
    trespassers, 5.4
Extended families
    homelessness, and, 6.68

Facilities, 3.40, 3.41
    business use, 3.40
Fairs, 1.15, 1.16
Family associations
    meaning, 6.83
Festivals, 1.44
Fire precautions, 3.42–3.45
    failure to provide/maintain
    fire–fighting equipment, 3.45
    fire authority, 3.42
    fire safety, 3.44
    model standards, 3.43
    recommendations, 3.44
Firle bonfire incident, 1.1–1.3
Fly–tipping, 5.44
Forestry, 4.19
Forestry Commission
    bye–laws, 5.106
    public law challenges to eviction,
    and, 5.156–5.159
Framework Convention for the
    Protection of National
    Minorities, 8.123–8.128
    goals, 8.125
    periodic reports, 8.127
    principles, 8.125
    significance of, 8.126
Function of travelling, 1.16

Gates, walls and fences
    below specified heights, 4.21
Genocide, 1.19
'Genuine' Gypsies, 1.18
Government departments
    public law challenges to eviction,
    and, 5.153–5.159
Grants, 3.49–3.51
Great Famine, 1.22, 1.23, 1.25
Green Belt, 4.47–4.58

Green Belt *continued*
  inappropriate development,
    4.50–4.53
  personal circumstances, and,
    4.93–4.100
  planning applications for Gypsy
    and Traveller sites, and,
    4.47–4.58
Government departments,
    Appendix C
Gypsies
  accommodation for, 1.34–1.38
  anti–vagrant ideology, and, 1.13
  cultural values, 1.46
  dark skin colour, 1.10
  defining, 1.32, 1.33
  early discrimination, 1.10
  economic dimensions of
    nomadism, 1.16
  European persecution, 1.14
  fairs, and, 1.15
  Henry VIII's Proclamation of
    1530, 1.11
  historical context, 1.8–1.16
  Nazi holocaust, and, 1.19, 1.20
  origins, 1.8
  punishment, 1.12
  racialising, 1.17–1.21
  'real Romani', and, 1.18
  meaning, for the purposes of Race
    Relations legislation, 8.52, 8.53
Gypsy and Traveller Site Grant, 3.49
Gypsy sites and planning, 4.2

Harassment, 3.11, 8.23–8.27
  race discrimination, and,
    8.23–8.27
Harvest fairs, 1.15
Havel, Vaclav
  gypsies, on, 4.193
Hawkers, 1.15, 1.33
Healthcare, 7.67–7.106
  access to, 7.79–7.86
  casualty departments, 7.85
  community care services,
    7.87–7.89
  discrimination, and, 7.82–7.84
  ECHR, and, 7.90, 7.91
  evictions, and, 7.80

Healthcare *continued*
  gypsy and traveller health
    research, 7.77, 7.78
    concerns, 7.77
    problems, 7.77, 7.78
  medical records, 7.92–7.100
  mental, 7.87–7.89
  NHS bureaucracy, and, 7.81
  NHS structure. *See* **NHS structure**
  NHS Walk–In centres, 7.85
  privacy, and, 7.92–7.100
  registration with GP, 7.86
  right to, 7.67
Henry VIII's Proclamation 1530, 1.11
High Court
  application in respect of refusal of
    planning permission,
    4.136–4.140
Highways
  Circular 1/06, and, 4.45
  meaning, 5.83
  obstructing, 5.83–5.93
Highways Act 1980, 5.83–5.93
  animals on highway, 5.89
  damages to road users, 5.88
  dedicating landowner, 5.92
  impoundment of vehicles, 5.90
  local authorities, 5.83–5.93
  ownership of highway, 5.92
  police, 5.83–5.93
  'thing unlawfully deposited', 5.90,
    5.91
  trespassory assemblies, and, 5.86,
    5.87
  verges, 5.87
Hippies, 1.39
Historical context, 1.8 –, 1.16
Home, family and private life, right
    to respect for. *See* **Article 8**
    decision making
Homelessness, 6.1–6.103
  accommodation available for
    occupation, 6.7
  appeals, 6.43–6.49
  code of guidance, 6.42
  criminal offences, 6.50
  effect of legislation on Gypsies and
    Travellers, 6.51–6.102
  chain of causation, 6.74–6.79

Homelessness *continued*
    deliberate act or omission, 6.80
    emergency, 6.72
    extended family groups, 6.68
    Gypsy way of life, and,
    6.53–6.55
    houseboat dwellers, 6.57
    information to be submitted,
    6.65
    intentional homelessness, 6.62,
    6.74–6.82
    interviews, 6.66, 6.67
    investigation, 6.64
    leaving conventional housing,
    6.82
    literacy skills, and, 6.65
    local connection, 6.83–6.85
    making application, 6.63–6.68
    no place where entitled or
    permitted to place caravan or
    vehicle, 6.58–6.62
    'permission', 6.60
    'permitted' encampment, 6.81
    priority need, 6.69–6.72
    'settled accommodation', 6.76
    suitable interim
    accommodation, 6.86–6.95. *See
    also* **Suitable interim
    accommodation**
    'tolerated' period, 6.61
    Travelling Showpeople, 6.59
    vulnerability, 6.69, 6.70
  full duties, 6.26–6.30
    discharge of, 6.27
    ending, 6.30
    'suitable' accommodation, 6.28
  full duty to accommodate,
    6.96–6.102
    compatibility of groups or
    families, 6.99
    cultural aversion to
    conventional housing, and, 6.97
    expert reports, 6.102
    National Land Use Database,
    6.98
    New Travellers, 6.100
  ineligible persons, 6.4
  intentional, 6.12
  legislation, 6.1–6.50

Homelessness *continued*
  limited duties, 6.21–6.25
    advice and assistance, 6.21, 6.23
    allocation provisions, 6.22
  local connection, 6.13, 6.14, 6.31,
    6.32, 6.83–6.85
    armed forces, 6.14
    detainees, 6.14
    employment, 6.83
    exceptions, 6.84
    'family associations', 6.83, 6.85
    'normal residence', 6.83, 6.85
  meaning, 6.5
  preliminary duties, 6.15–6.19
    local connection, 6.17
    notification, 6.16, 6.18
    occupation pending decision,
    6.19
  principal duties, 6.20–6.30
  priority need, 6.9–6.11
    Wales, 6.10
  protection of property, 6.33–6.36
  'reasonable to continue to occupy',
    6.8
  review, 6.37–6.39, 6.43–6.49
    purposes, 6.39
  statutory provisions, 6.2, 6.3
  strategies, 6.37–6.41
Homelessness reviews and appeals
  procedure, App A
Horse fairs
  Articles 11 and 14, 2.92, 2.93
Horses, keeping, 3.41
Housing
  race discrimination, 8.40
Housing benefit, 3.37, 3.38
Human rights
  offers of conventional housing,
    and, 4.119–4.124
  planning law, and, 4.103–4.118
Human Rights Act 1998, 2.1–2.99
  Article 2 of Protocol 1: education,
    2.94, 29.5
  Article 8 decision making,
    2.13–2.63. *See also* **Article 8
    decision-making**
  Articles 11 and 14
    culture, 2.92, 2.93
    horse fairs, 2.92, 29.3

Human Rights Act 1998 *continued*
Article 14. *See* **Article 14**
most relevant Convention rights,
2.7–2.12
public authorities, and, 2.1–2.6
discretionary powers, 2.5
security of tenure, and. *See*
Security of tenure
Hunts, Gypsy, 1.17

Impoundment of vehicles, 5.90
Incitement to racial hatred, 8.43
Injunctions, 51.56–5.166
CEHR, and, 8.76
judicial review, and, 5.166
planning law, and. *See* **Planning**
injunctions
Intentional homelessness
meaning, 6.12
Irish Travellers, 1.22–1.28
colonial experience in Ireland,
and, 1.24
Irish emigration, and, 1.27
Irish nationalism, and, 1.26
origins, 1.22
prejudice, and, 1.23, 1.28
racial group, as, 1.4, 1.6
'respect', 1.25
Italy
racialising gypsy people in, 1.17

Judicial review
eviction, and, 5.1
injunctions, and, 5.166
procedure, App A

Lack of sites
dire effect of, 5.168
Land
meaning, 5.39
Language, 1.23
Learning difficulty
meaning, 7.31
Literacy skills, 3.36
homelessness applications, and,
6.65
Local authorities
allocation of pitches. *See*
Allocation of pitches

Local authorities *continued*
obstructing highways, and,
5.83–5.93
planning enforcement, 5.118
provision of sites, 3.4–3.9
public law challenges to eviction,
and, 5.119–5.144
race equality duty, 8.80–8.116
use of bye–laws, 5.94–5.108
Local authority related sites,
3.11–3.55
security of tenure, 3.11–3.28. *See*
also **Security of tenure**
Local authority rented sites – legal
regime, 3.11–3.55
Local connection
meaning, 6.31, 6.32
Local organisations, App C
Local planning policy. *See*
Development plan

Maintenance of sites, 3.7, 3.35, 3.49
Mass trespass
police, and, 5.152
Medical records, 7.92–7.100
Access to Medical Reports Act
1988, 7.92
Data Protection Act 1998, 7.92–7.98
ECHR Article 8, 7.99, 7.100
Mental healthcare, 7.87–7.89
Migrant workers, 1.29, 1.30
Migration, 1.8, 1.22, 1.24, 1.27
Minorities, special needs of
planning law, and, 4.114
Mobile Homes Act 1983
security of tenure, and, 3.12, 3.13
Modernisation Agency, 7.70
Murder
racially motivated, 1.28

National Land Use Database, 6.98
National organisations, App C
National Parks, 4.47
National planning policy, 4.8
Nazi holocaust, 1.19, 1.20
Netherlands
racialising Gypsy people in, 1.17
'New Age' Travellers, 1.7, 1.39–1.45
'hippies', 1.39

'New Age' Travellers *continued*
'nomadic', 1.40
'Peace Convoy', 1.44
'The Mutants', 1.45
NHS structure, 7.68–7.76
Department of Health
responsibilities, 7.69
Modernisation Agency, 7.70
primary care, 7.75
primary care trusts, 7.73–7.75
SpHAs, 7.72
strategic health authorities, 7.71
No Traveller signs, 8.71
race discrimination, and, 8.20
Nomadic
meaning, 1.40
Nomadism, 1.29–1.31
abandonment of, 4.71, 4.72
ending of, 1.29–1.31
planning law, and, 4.69–4.84
Non–local authority sites, 3.56–3.61
protected site, 3.56–3.61
Nuisance, 3.46
statutory, 3.46–3.48, 7.106

Obstructing highway, 5.83–5.93
Occupancy conditions for local
authority sites, 3.35–3.36
Occupier
meaning, 5.65
Official sites. *See* Local authority
rented sites; Rented
Gypsy/Traveller sites

Peddlers, 1.14
Permitted development, 4.21
gates, walls and fences, 4.21
Pikey
use of term, 1.1
Planning
race discrimination, 8.37
Planning applications
refusal, 4.3
Planning applications for Gypsy and
Traveller sites, 4.29–4.124
alternative sites, availability of,
4.90
Circular 1/06, 4.31–4.46
aims, 4.34

Planning applications for Gypsy and
Traveller sites *continued*
functions of LPAs, 4.39–4.43
highway considerations, 4.45
reason for, 4.32
rural settings, 4.43
sustainable development, 4.44
unmet need, and, 4.42
crime, fear of, 4.91
designated areas, 4.47–4.58
development plan policies,
4.59–4.63
ethnic Gypsies and Travellers,
4.67–4.84
Green Belt, 4.47–4.58. *See also*
Green Belt
Gypsies and Travellers, meaning,
4.82
Gypsies, meaning, 4.69
Gypsy status, 4.67–4.84
Gypsy status and Circular 1/06,
4.79–4.84
Gypsy status and pre–2006 case
law, 4.69–4.78
human rights as material
consideration4.103–4.118
article 8, 4.105–4.118
margin of appreciation, 4.111
minorities, special needs of,
4.114
right to respect for private and
family life, 4.107–4.116
human rights and offers of
conventional housing,
4.119–4.124
loss of Gypsy status, 4.77–4.78
material considerations, 4.64–4.66
matters to be taken into account,
4.29–4.124
natural screening, and, 4.58
need for sites, 4.85–5.89
needs, approach based on, 4.58
nomadism, and, 4.69–4.84
personal circumstances,
4.92–4.102
Green Belt, and, 4.93–4.100
very special circumstances,
4.94–4.102
policy considerations, 4.30

relevant government policy and
    advice, 4.30
retention of nomadic status, 4.80
sieve map process, 4.57
site location, 4.47–4.58
undesignated rural land, 4.55
Planning authorities, 4.17
Planning enforcement, 5.118
Article 14, and, 2.86–2.89
local authorities, 5.118
***Planning for Gypsy and Traveller
    caravan sites***, 4.5
Planning injunctions, 4.169–4.189
applications to vary, 4.189
committal to prison, and, 4.171,
    4.178
contempt, 4.189
countervailing considerations,
    4.172
discretion of court, 4.174–4.176
'just and convenient', 4.183
personal circumstances, and,
    4.177
public interest, and, 4.181
suspension, 4.187, 4.188
Planning inquiries
funding for, 4.191
Planning law, 4.1–4.195
direct action, 4.165–4.168
enforcement 41.41–4.192
common humanity,
    considerations of, 4.144, 4.145
government guidance, 4.142,
    4.143
enforcement notices, 4.146,
    4.147
immunity from enforcement,
    4.22–4.25
limitation periods, 4.22–4.25
injunctions, 4.169–4.189. *See also*
    Planning injunctions
legislation, 4.6, 4.7
option to take no action, 4.190
stop notices, 2.86, 2.89, 4.148,
    4.149
temporary stop notices, 4.150
Town and Country Planning Act
    1990, 4.6, 4.7
Wales, 4.192

Planning permission, 4.20,
    4.125–4.140
appeal against refusal, 4.132–4.135
matters to be considered, 4.134,
    4.135
procedures, 4.133
application for, 4.125–4.131
information to be submitted,
    4.125, 4.126
application to High Court,
    4.136–4.140
conditions, 4.127–4.131
occupancy limited to Gypsies,
    4.130
six tests for, 4.129
Gypsy and Traveller sites, for
Article 14, and, 2.90, 2.91
Planning system
structure of, 4.6–4.124
Police
direction to leave, 5.32–5.37
obstructing highway, and,
    5.83–5.93
power to remove trespassers:
    alternative site available, 5.52,
    5.53
public law challenges to eviction,
    and, 5.145–5.152
race equality duty, 8.91–8.93
Possession orders, 5.160–5.164
identification of land, 5.164
scope of, 5.160–5.164
suspension of, 3.18
width of, 5.160–5.164
Poverty, 1.36, 1.37
Primary care
meaning, 7.75
Procedures, Appendix A
Property
meaning, 5.44
Protected site
meaning, 3.56–3.61
Provision of sites, 3.3–3.10
approach of government, 3.9
grants, 3.49–3.51. *See also* **Grants**
local authorities, 3.4–3.9
Public authorities
Article 8 decision making. *See*
    Article 8 decision making

Public Authorities *continued*
  Human Rights Act 1998, and,
    2.1–2.6
  meaning, 5.153
  public law challenges to eviction,
    and, 5.153–5.159
  race discrimination, 8.38
  use of bye–laws, 5.94–5.108
Public interest
  planning injunction, and, 4.181
Public law challenges to eviction,
    5.119–5.159
  alternative locations, need for,
    5.136
  Forestry Commission, 5.156–5.159
  government departments,
    5.153–5.159
  duties, 5.154, 5.155
  humanitarian considerations,
    5.121., 5.122, 5.131
  inquiry process, 5.133, 5.134
  local authorities, 5.119–5.144
  location of encampments, 5.132
  management of unauthorised
    camping, 5.137
  nuisance, 5.121
  police, and, 5.145–5.152
    case–law position, 5.147
    factors prompting action, 5.149
    guidance, 5.150
    humanitarian considerations,
      5.151
    'mass trespass', 5.152
    welfare considerations, 5.146
  public authorities, and,
    5.153–5.159
  records of inquiry process, 5.133
  responsibility for decisions,
    5.135
  site provision, and, 5.128–5.131
  strategies, and, 5.127
  toleration of encampment, and,
    5.135–5.140
  unacceptable behaviour, and, 5.135
  Wales, 5.129
  welfare inquiries, 5.142, 5.143
  welfare issues, 5.123–5.126
  welfare of children, and, 5.123,
    5.124

Race, 1.32
Race discrimination, 8.1–8.129
  ACAS, 8.57
  advertisements, 8.28–8.30, 8.71
  advice and assistance, 8.55
  aiding unlawful act, 8.33
  burden of proof, 8.63–8.67
  challenging discriminatory
    legislation, 8.117, 8.118
  county courts, 8.56, 8.60
  current position, 8.1, 8.2
  direct, 8.7–8.12
    comparator, 8.9, 8.10
    example, 8.11, 8.12
  education, and, 7.47–7.52, 8.36
  employers' associations, 8.41
  employment, 8.35
  employment tribunals, 8.56–8.59
  enforcing act of 1976, 8.54–8.71
  equality duty, 8.80–8.116. *See also*
    Race equality duty
  ethnic groups, 8.44–8.51
    Gypsies and Travellers,
      8.45–8.51
    Rastafarians, 8.51
    Scottish Gypsy Travellers, 8.49
    Travellers, 8.50
    Welsh Gypsy Travellers, 8.49
  ethnicity, 8.52, 8.53
  European Union Race Directive,
    8.119–8.122
  forms, 8.6
  Framework Convention for the
    Protection of National
    Minorities. *See* **Framework
    Convention for the Protection
    of National Minorities**
  goods, facilities or services, 8.39
  harassment, 8.23–8.27
  housing, 8.40, 8.58
  impact of legislation, 8.129
  incitement to racial hatred, 8.43
  indirect, 8.13–8.20
    colour and nationality, 8.14
    condition or requirement,
      8.14
    exclusions, 8.19
    'No Traveller' sign, 8.20
    'practice', 8.17

Race discrimination *continued*
proportionate means of
achieving legitimate aim, 8.15
provision, criterion or practice,
8.15–8.20
race or ethnic or national
origins, 8.15–8.20
instructions to discriminate, 8.31
inferences, 8.63–8.67
grounds of colour or nationality,
8.67
grounds of race or ethnic or
national origin, 8.66
legal framework, 8.5, 8.6
levers for change, 8.123–8.128
membership clubs, 8.42
No Traveller signs, 8.71
nomadism, 8.52, 8.53
opportunities, 8.117–8.122
planning, 8.37
pressure, 8.32
professional and trade
associations, 8.41
public functions, 8.38
pursuing complaint, 8.55–8.60
questionnaire procedure, 8.61,
8.62
evasive and equivocal replies,
8.62
failure to reply, 8.62
racial groups, 8.44–8.51
recommendations for future,
8.117–8.122
scope of Race Relations Act 1976,
8.34–8.43
segregation, 8.21
statistics, 8.2
time limit for making complaint,
8.68–8.70
trade unions, 8.41
victimisation, 8.22
Race equality duty, 8.80–8.116
central government, 8.97, 8.98
Common Ground, 8.109–8.116
CRE inquiry, 8.109–8.116
community tension, 8.113,
8.114
identification of areas of good
practice, 8.111

Race equality duty *continued*
organisational problems, 8.115
recommendations, 8.116
devolved administrations, 8.97,
8.98
ethnic monitoring, 8.99–8.100
health bodies, 8.96
judicial review, 8.101–8.104
local authorities, 8.89, 8.90
police, 8.91–8.93
potential benefits, 8.87
proactivity, 8.86
sanctions for non–compliance,
8.101–8.108
schools, 8.83, 8.94, 8.95
specific duties of public
authorities, 8.82
Statutory Code of Practice, 8.85
use in practice, 8.86–8.98
Race meetings, 1.15
Racial groups, 8.44–8.51
meaning, 8.44
Racial hygiene
pseudo–science, 1.18, 1.19
Redevelopment of sites, 3.52–3.55
compulsory purchase orders,
3.53–3.55
Regional planning policy. *See*
Development plan
Relevant caravan site
meaning, 5.62
Relevant site manager
meaning, 5.62
Rent/site fee, 3.37–3.39
housing benefit, 3.37, 3.38
Supporting People, 3.39
Rented gypsy/traveller sites, 3.1–3.62
meaning, 3.1
provision of, 3.3–3.10
statistics, 3.1
Repairs, 3.35, 3.36
Rodent infestation, 3.48
Romani Gypsies
racial group, as, 1.4, 1.6
Romani language, 1.23

School attendance order, 7.20
Schools
admission to, 7.14–7.16

Schools *continued*
attendance at, 7.17–7.29
bullying, 7.53–7.54
'dual registration', 7.28
exclusion, 7.34–7.46
balance of probabilities, 7.38
challenge to hearings, 7.39
duties, 7.37
ECHR Article 6, 7.40
ECHR Protocol 1 article 2,
7.43
powers, 7.35
reinstatement, 7.41, 7.42
specialist legal advice, 7.44
suitable education, 7.45
prosecution of parent, 7.21–7.24
defences, 7.25–7.27
race equality duty, 7.31, 8.94,
8.95
suitable education, 7.18
transport to school, 7.30
unauthorised absences, 7.19
Seasonal employment, 1.16
Security of tenure, 3.11–3.28
Disability Discrimination Act
1995, 3.33, 3.34
'factual issues', 3.25, 3.26
harassment, and, 3.11
Human Rights Act 1998, and,
3.15–3.28
article 8, ECHR, 3.15–3.17,
3.21–3.28
suspension of possession orders,
3.18
lack of, 3.11, 3.12
Mobile Homes Act 1983, and,
3.12, 3.13
need to change law, 3.18–3.20
non-local authority sites, 3.56–3.61
policy/administrative issues, 3.25,
3.26
Segregation
race discrimination, and, 8.21
Shelta language, 1.23
Sieve map process, 4.57
Site fees, 3.37–3.39
Sites, lack of, 9.2–9.6
Sites, need for
planning law, and, 4.85–4.89

Sites of Special Scientific Interest
(SSSI), 4.47, 4.48
Six or more vehicles, 5.46
Special educational needs, 7.31–7.33
learning difficulty, 7.31
Statutory nuisance, 3.46–3.48, 7.106
Stop notices 4,148, 4.149
Article 14, and, 2.86–2.89
temporary, 4.150–4.154
Strategic health authorities, 7.71
Suitable interim accommodation,
6.86–6.95
accommodation outside local
authority's area, 6.94
article 8, and, 6.93
bed and breakfast, 6.87–6.89
cultural aversion to conventional
housing, 6.89
identification of temporary sites,
6.95
last resort, 6.92
minimum line of suitability,
6.91
relevant considerations, 6.90
suitable, 6.87
urgency, 6.92
Wales, 6.88
Suitable pitch, 5.58–5.64
compatibility of groups or
families, 5.61
meaning, 5.58
relevant caravan site, 5.62
relevant site manager, 5.62
Sustainable development
holistic approach, 4.44

Temporary stop notices, 4.150–4.154
Thing unlawfully deposited
highway, on, 5.90, 5.91
Threatening, abusive or insulting
words or behaviour, 5.45
'Tinkers', 1.14
Town and Country Planning Act 1990
s288
applications procedure,
App A
Town and Country Planning Act 1990
s289
appeals procedure, App A

Travellers
accommodation for, 1.34–1.38
cultural values, 1.46
meaning, 8.53
Travelling Showpeople, 2.60–2.61,
6.59
Trespassers, 5.4–5.8
Trespassory assemblies, 5.86, 5.87
Unitary development plans, 4.10
Useful organisations, App C

Vagabonds, 1.13
Vehicles
impoundment, 5.90
meaning, 5.46
Verges of highways, 5.87
Victimisation
race discrimination, and, 8.22

Wales
planning law, 4.192
priority need, 6.10
sites, provision of, 5.129
suitable interim accommodation,
6.88
Warrant of possession, 5.25–5.31
Warrant of restitution, 5.25–5.31
Water
supply of, 7.102–7.140
Writ of restitution, 5.25–5.31